COGNITION AND THE SYMBOLIC PROCESSES

Applied and Ecological Pe

COGNITION AND THE SYMBOLIC PROCESSES:

Applied and Ecological Perspectives

Edited by

Robert R. Hoffman
Adelphi University

David S. Palermo
The Pennsylvania State University

LEA LAWRENCE ERLBAUM ASSOCIATES, PUBLISHERS
1991 Hillsdale, New Jersey   Hove and London

Lawrence Erlbaum Associates, Inc., Publishers
365 Broadway
Hillsdale, New Jersey 07642

Library of Congress Cataloging-in-Publication Data

Cognition and the symbolic processes : applied and ecological
  perspectives / edited by Robert R. Hoffman, David S. Palermo.
      p.   cm.
  Includes papers presented at the conference "Speaking, Reading,
Thinking, and Development" held at the University of South Florida,
Jan. 16–17, 1987.
  Includes bibliographical references and index.
  ISBN 0-8058-0903-1. — ISBN 0-8058-0904-X (pbk.)
  1. Cognition. 2. Psycholinguistics. 3. Perception. I. Hoffman,
Robert R.   II. Palermo, David Stuart.
  BF311.C54865   1991
  153 — dc20   90-22617
                                                                    CIP

Printed in the United States of America
10 9 8 7 6 5 4 3 2 1

Contents

VIII. APPLICATIONS OF COGNITIVE PSYCHOLOGY

Preface

The purpose of this preface is to describe the conference from which this volume stemmed, and to acknowledge the support and assistance of the organizations and individuals who made the conference and volume possible.

COGNITION AND THE SYMBOLIC PROCESSES

The first volume in the series "Cognition and the Symbolic Processes" (Weimer & Palermo, 1974) had as its starting point the "current revolution in psycholinguistics and cognitive psychology" (p. xi; see chapters by Brewer, Dulany, Bransford, Franks, Miller, and Weimer). The second volume (Weimer & Palermo, 1982) seems, in retrospect, to reflect the goal of a somewhat more comfortably established science: "the construction of a psychology of the higher mental processes" (Weimer & Palermo, 1982, p. ix). This constructive effort began in the wake of the immediately prior decade, which had witnessed the rejection of older associationistic and behavioristic approaches (and even some of the early information-processing theories). In that wake, Volume 2 seems, among other things, to herald the "arrival" of ecological psychology (see chapters by Fowler, Pattee, Shaw, Profitt, and Pribram).

The present volume perhaps represents a further step in the maturation of cognitive psychology. Views that were once hotly debated, such as the Gibsonian approach, are now thoroughly engaged in both laboratory research and numerous interesting applications. If anything, this volume represents the arrival of "applied cognitive psychology." Certainly, other recent publications and events reflect the trends and influences that are manifested here. For example, a new journal, *Ecological Psychology*, has begun publication. There is also a new journal titled *Applied Cognitive Psychology*. In addition, we could point to the rise of neofunctionalist and contextualist viewpoints, which dovetail with ecological psychology in their emphasis on ecological validity and applied research (for reviews, see Hoffman & Deffenbacher, in press; Hoffman & Nead, 1983).

Like the previous "Cognition and the Symbolic Process" volumes, this book is "directed toward those who are engrossed in the problems of cognition and the symbolic processes" (Weimer & Palermo, 1974, p. xi), with the goal of laying out current theoretical and methodological issues, and new directions for research and applications. In addition, this volume is also intended to capture the overall "state of the art" by describing recent research methods and results in many of the areas of experimental psychology, including language, learning, memory, speech perception, semantics, motor skills, visual perception, problem solving, and individual differences.

THE CONFERENCE

Previous volumes in this series stemmed from conferences held at Pennsylvania State University. This volume stems from a conference held at the University of South Florida, January 16–17, 1987. The conference title was "Speaking, Reading, Thinking, and Development: The Accomplishments and Goals of Modern Research." While perhaps a bit wordy, the title was intended to embrace the three major themes of the conference: (1) To provide a forum for debate on current theoretical issues, (2) To capture the state of the art in reviews of research methods and results, and (3) To generate ideas for new research directions and methodologies.

The chapters by Brooks and Van Hanneghan, Brewer and Samarapungavan; Diehl, Kluender, Walsh, and Parker; Franks, Bransford, Brailey, and Purdon; and those by Becker, Gough, Johnson, Clifton, Dember, and Neisser, all reflect their presentations at the conference. Other participants—Liberman, Pick, Pittenger, Shaw, Studdert-Kennedy, and Turvey—contributed chapters that differed from their original conference presentations, but which nonetheless directly reflect the goals of the conference and the spirit of this volume. The chapters by Foss and Speer; Hoffman, Waggoner, and Palermo; Mark, Dainoff, Moritz, and Vogele; and those by Greeno, Horton, Kraft, Premack, Ross, and Warren, were all prepared subsequent to the conference, but were also stimulated by its themes and goals. The chapter by Jenkins was originally presented as the keynote address at the 1984 Adelphi University Conference on Applied Experimental Psychology.

ACKNOWLEDGMENTS

The editors thank Charles Cofer, John Flavell, Eleanor Gibson, Terry Halwes, Leah Larkey, William Mace, Anne Pick, Eliot Saltzman, Winifred Strange,

Robert Verbrugge, and Walter Weimer for contributing to the conference, either in the open debates, as chairs of sessions, as discussants of papers, or as presenters. For a variety of reasons, these participants were unable to contribute to this volume. We can only hope that the spirit of their contributions, if not the letter, is preserved in this record.

The South Florida conference was made possible by grants from the Office of Naval Research and the National Institute of Child Health and Human Development. The activities involved in conference management received additional support from the Office of Academic Affairs and the Office of the Dean of the College of Social and Behavioral Sciences of the University of South Florida. The editors would like to thank James Kavanagh of the National Institute of Child Health and Human Development for nurturing the conference. Dean Wallace Russell of the University of South Florida was also extremely supportive and helpful as we went through the grant proposal process.

Louis Penner and the staff of the Department of Psychology at the University of South Florida were of immeasurable help when it came to the details of conference management. Judith Becker, Doug Nelson, Linda Polka, and Terrel Tuten of the Department of Psychology, and also Psi Chi members Ron Parker, Sharon Royal, and Peggy Stoner, rendered assistance by working at the reception desk, by helping with audiovisual aids, and by helping shuttle people around. Without their help in the minutiae of conference management, the conference would not have been possible, let alone operate smoothly.

At Adelphi, Dean Sean Cashman of the College of Arts and Sciences and David Gorfein of the Department of Psychology lent both financial and spiritual assistance to the project, especially during the preparation of this volume. Finally, thanks to Angela Mavarro for typing the Author Index.

REFERENCES

Hoffman, R. R., & Deffenbacher, K. (in press). A brief history of applied cognitive psychology. *Applied Cognitive Psychology.*

Hoffman, R. R., & Nead, J. M. (1983). General contextualism, ecological science, and cognitive research. *Journal of Mind and Behavior, 4,* 507–560.

Weimer, W. B., & Palermo, D. S. (Eds.). (1974). *Cognition and the symbolic processes.* Hillsdale, NJ: Lawrence Erlbaum Associates.

Weimer, W. B., & Palermo, D. S. (Eds.). (1982). *Cognition and the symbolic processes, (Vol. 2).* Hillsdale, NJ: Lawrence Erlbaum Associates.

Dedication

The South Florida conference was a celebration of the accomplishments of James J. Jenkins. Looking across his work, one cannot see any strict division of basic and applied psychology. Jim always makes it clear to students that applied research is not secondary to "pure science," but of equal value. He emphasizes the belief that applied concerns keep pure research from going off into fruitless involutions—the idea that research should possess some degree of ecological validity. Hence, it is appropriate that a conference focusing, in part, on ecological psychology and the applications of experimental psychology should serve as the occasion to celebrate Jim's accomplishments.

Following his service in World War II, Jenkins "got hooked on the notion of combining my social-service drive with psychology, and getting psychology to work for the common man."[1] The only place that he had heard of where work along such lines was being conducted was the University of Minnesota, so he applied there, and eventually received a PhD in industrial psychology in 1950, under the guidance of Donald G. Paterson. Jenkins taught and trained research psychologists at Minnesota from 1950 to 1984, when he accepted an appointment as chairman of the Department of Psychology at the University of South Florida.

With colleagues, he has conducted research in language, speech perception, learning, memory, cognitive psychology, and many topics in applied experimental psychology, especially the study of individual differences. He has published more than 130 experimental reports, books, and chapters. He is perhaps best known for his early work on associative–mediational theories of learning, and on aphasia, his subsequent role in the "psycholinguistic revolution," and his continuing program of research on speech perception.

---

[1]Baars, B. (1986). *The cognitive revolution in psychology*. New York: Guilford Press.

Jim was a central figure in the establishment of the Center for Research in Human Learning at the University of Minnesota. He was twice a fellow of the Center for Advanced Study in the Behavioral Sciences and has been guest investigator at the Haskins Laboratories. He has served as president of the Midwestern Psychological Association, chairman of the Division of Experimental Psychology of the American Psychological Association, chairman of the Society of Experimental Psychologists, and chairman of the Board of Governors of the Psychonomic Society.

Many of Jenkins's former students can be counted as prominent psychologists. (Indeed, Jim has served on scores of dissertation committees.) Hints about Jim's impact on students can be gleaned from the many letters sent on the occasion of the conference. Some brief quotes: "He is devoted to his students." "He is the best teacher I've ever seen." "He encourages students to think broadly, and to play with and develop whatever they come up with." "He shapes the way students think, but never imposes himself on their ideas." "He leaves the student feeling competent, creative, and excited." Perhaps most telling is the frequent expression of love and respect his students feel for him.

In his historiographical treatise, *The Cognitive Revolution in Psychology,* Baars (1986) discusses Jenkins's impact on psychology:

> Jenkins' work is remarkable in its flexibility and in Jenkins' willingness to depart from hallowed traditions to solve the puzzles of language. Jenkins was willing to abandon experimental methods that did not seem to work, for others that seemed more promising. This was professionally risky at a time when the "proper method" was taken to distinguish scientific from unscientific psychology. But in retrospect it seems clear that adherence to very limited experimental designs and techniques hindered more than helped progress. Jenkins was able to overcome such "methodolatry" over a period of time, but this was by no means easy. (p. 238)

Baars's interview with Jenkins includes a great deal of interesting autobiographical and historical information, including Jenkins's recounting of the early days of "verbal behavior" research, the psycholinguistic revolution, the rise of cognitive psychology, and the recent focus on contextualist, neofunctionalist, and ecological viewpoints.

Here are some of the comments on Jim's abilities and accomplishments as a scientist, taken from the conference letters: "He is one of the century's foremost researchers and theorists." "He has an uncanny knack for recognizing, elaborating, and assimilating an interesting idea." "He imparts to students and colleagues a sense of exictement, he makes ideas and issues come alive." "He has the flexibility to move ahead when a paradigm has run its course." "He has had the most profound effect on my own scientific development." (Even people who were not his former students said that!) Perhaps most telling is the comment, a common one, which went something like this: "I can recall no occasion over my decades in academia when I have taken as much pleasure in writing a letter of support."

The editors and contributors affectionately dedicate this volume to James J. Jenkins.

A Letter to James J. Jenkins

January 8, 1987

Dr. James J. Jenkins
Department of Psychology
University of South Florida

Dear Jim:

It is always a delight when a colleague one personally admires receives formal recognition and honor. We are all very pleased by the wonderful *Festschrift* your students and colleagues have organized, and you must be very proud indeed.

On every dimension, your contribution to the field of psychology has been outstanding. Your record for training students is one of the most remarkable in the history of our department—and, indeed, in psychology as a field. In your years at the University of Minnesota, you mentored 46 PhDs, more than any other member of the experimental psychology faculty and nearly as many as our all-time champion, *your* mentor, D. G. Paterson. (And that's not counting the great number of students who were formally the advisees of others, but upon whom, as a teacher, you had an everlasting intellectual impact.) Moreover, your intellectual progeny have done you (and us) proud, standing out as the finest examples of Minnesota-trained psychologists. They have achieved success and great distinction. In addition, their work continues to reflect your deep concern for charting the relationship between specific phenomena and broader issues of the discipline. Much of the high regard our department enjoys derives from the distinction you and your students have achieved, and we owe you a great deal for this.

Your effect on your fellow faculty members at Minnesota was nurturant, profound, and enduring. You created an atmosphere of intellectual life and vitality in our department which has been very difficult to sustain since you left. Your unique ability to see (and help others see!) connections among diverse topics and the value of different perspectives brought a very positive and appealing unity to the field. Your ability to build intellectual bridges promoted interactions among scholars that might not otherwise have taken place. That Jenkins warmth, cheer, encouragement, provocativeness, and perennial sense of optimism about psychology and its wholeness, are all much missed up here in the north.

Through your contributions to the field of individual differences, then to the study of learning and memory, and later to psycholinguistics, you were an important actor, together with Paul Meehl and certain others, in establishing the precedents at Minnesota which continue to make it OK for faculty to move from one area of interest to another. This kind of openness is not found everywhere, and it has, no doubt, played an important role in preventing, at Minnesota, the separation between applied and theoretical areas that characterizes so many other departments. We place great value on this tradition, and thank you for helping form this important quality of our departmental character.

Your contributions as a researcher, teacher, mentor, colleague, and college citizen have been matched line by line by your extensive professional participation at the national level, and your national eminence brought further distinction to our Department. We hope you realize, Jim, how much the service you have rendered on all those committees and councils has been appreciated by the profession at large.

In sum, dear friend, you have been and continue to be a role model for students, faculty, and colleagues at all levels of the academy. Your career at Minnesota will stand forever as one to be emulated, and your continuing contributions at Florida will extend your impact on psychology even further for many years into the future. We are honored and proud to be associated with you and to be able to call you our friend.

Sincerely,

The Faculty
Department of Psychology
University of Minnesota

Bruce Overmier	Bill Fox	Gail B. Peterson
Ellen S. Berscheid	Norman Garmezy	Warren W. Roberts
Thomas J. Bouchard	Gordon Legge	Mark Snyder
Dwight A. Burkhardt	Gloria R. Leon	Auke Tellegen
Jim Butcher	Lloyd H. Lofquist	Neal Viemeister
John P. Campbell	Paul E. Meehl	David J. Weiss
Marvin Dunnette	Mary Jo Nissen	

JAMES J. JENKINS

PERSPECTIVES

1 Introduction

Robert R. Hoffman
Adelphi University

David S. Palermo
Pennsylvania State University

In this introductory chapter we briefly summarize the contributions in this volume. Our purpose is to highlight the topic or key ideas in each chapter, and also to look at the chapters as a set to illuminate the unifying themes, which are those of the conference from which they stemmed. Those themes were: (1) To provide a forum for debate on current theoretical issues, (2) To capture the state of the art in reviews of research methods and results, and (3) To generate ideas for new research directions and methods. The contributors were encouraged to ponder questions that are fundamental to cognitive psychology, such as: How do people learn to read? What happens during the processes of speech perception? How do people acquire problem-solving skills? How do cognitive and motor skills develop and integrate with one another?

A great deal of research has been conducted on such important questions in the last decade, during which cognitive psychology has enjoyed its recognition as a specialty area. Recently, there has been increasing interest in applied topics, such as the nature of cognitive processes in instructional settings, the problem-solving skills of experts, and memory in real-world contexts. An additional goal of the conference was to embrace discussions of recent applications of cognitive psychology.

The two main chapters in this Perspectives section provide some context for the rest of the volume. Horton reflects on the recent history of cognitive psychology, and Neisser offers some speculations on the shape of an ecological cognitive psychology.

Part II focuses on speech perception. Liberman and Mattingly discuss the "modularity" thesis of brain organization in the context of recent research on phonetics. Studdert–Kennedy discusses the hypothesis that language has an innate basis, also in light of recent research evidence. Diehl, Kleunder, Walsh,

3

and Parker describe their recent experiments on the perception of phonological contrasts and the link between acoustics and speech production.

Part III treats language comprehension at a number of levels, going from Johnson's research and theorizing on word recognition, to Clifton's research and theorizing on syntactic effects in sentence comprehension, to Foss and Speer's studies of context effects in sentence comprehension, and finally to Gough's integrative theory of reading.

Part IV has motivation as its unifying theme. Dember reminds us forcefully about the basis of cognition in motivation and emotion. Hoffman, Waggoner, and Palermo present an analysis of metaphors for emotion that appear in both natural language and in scientific theories of emotion. Finally, Ross presents an analysis of the structure of poems. This chapter focuses on the relations of phonetic and semantic levels of poetry, but has as its underlying theme what could only be called "the effort after meaning" and the inherently motivational nature of language comprehension. Appropriate to its topic, the chapter itself is written in a refreshingly poetic style.

Part V focuses on the development of knowledge and problem-solving skills. In their chapters, Brewer and Samarapungavan, and Pittenger, review research on children's acquisition of knowledge about physical events and laws. Both chapters compare alternative hypotheses about reasoning and about mental representation, and both point to the role of experience in cognitive development. Furthermore, Brewer and Samarapungavan consider implications for theories and philosophies of science. In his chapter, Greeno discusses recent research on mathematical reasoning and problem solving, with an eye toward applications in instructional design. The final chapter in this section, that by Franks, Bransford, Brailey, and Purdon, discusses recent research on the problem-solving skills of college-age students. This research uses learning/transfer designs to reveal instances in which people fail to access and utilize relevant information. Franks et al. also consider educational implications and applications.

Part VI follows up on the previous section by focusing on pedagogy. Premack's chapter starts off the section with a bold essay on the meaning of "pedagogy" in light of observations of primate behavior. Becker reports her recent studies on the ways in which parents teach pragmatic skills to their children. Jenkins expresses his views about applied psychology, and the question of how to prepare students for applied research work.

Part VII covers perceiving and acting, and some interesting applications in particular. Kraft reviews research, including his own innovative experiments, on people's perceptual understanding of the structure of motion pictures and the techniques used in cinematography to depict events, emotions, and social relations. Carello and Turvey present a fascinating ecological analysis of the "illusions" of baseball (e.g., the curve ball). Kugler, Shaw, Vicente, and Kinsella–Shaw present an ecological—if not biophysical—analysis of intentional behavior, with examples ranging from the mound-building of termites to humans' perception of affordances while driving automobiles. The perceptual and functional guidance of action is illustrated in the chapter by Pick and Rosengren, in which they review recent research, including their own new studies on the mental representation of spatial relations and childrens' development of mobility skills, such as choosing paths and taking perspectives.

Part VIII includes three chapters that focus on the application of cognitive psychology and ecological notions to selected problem areas. Brooks and Van Haneghan review research on the cognitive deficits in mental retardation, and discuss retardation from an ecological perspective, which emphasizes the perception of events and affordances in contrast to the traditional information-processing approach. In their chapter, Mark, Dainoff, Moritz, and Vogele adopt an ecological approach in their research on a classic problem in ergonomics: How to design a good chair. This chapter illustrates the affinity of ecological views with applied research, and culminates in an outline of a general ecological approach to ergonomic design. Finally, Warren discusses the difficulties that arose when traditional research methods from the perception and learning laboratories were applied to problems in aviation psychology. He also discusses the ways in which the practical problems necessitated the creation of new research methods and new approaches, such as those suggested by ecological psychology.

Looking across the chapters, a unifying theme appears in addition to the obvious focus on ecological psychology and on applications: There is an apparently relaxed attitude toward what were once hot theoretical or philosophical issues, such as whether ecological psychology has anything to say about cognition. Those who are aligned with ecological psychology seem to be busy pursuing the implications of their views in research and applications, some very close to cognition. Those who are aligned with cognitive psychology seem to be comfortable with the simultaneous consideration of both cognitivistic and ecological notions, taking what is needed from each in service of their research interests.

Surely, there is still concern with basic issues, as illustrated by Dember's chapter on motivation, Liberman and Mattingly's chapter on the "modularity" thesis, Premack's chapter on pedagogy, Studdert–Kennedy's chapter on linguistic nativism, and Hoffman and Palermo's chapter on the use of metaphors in psychological theories of emotion. There is also a drive to push basic theory as far as it will go, as illustrated in Neisser's chapter on ecological cognitive psychology and Kugler et al.'s chapter on intentional systems. Of course, there is a tacit understanding that the support for all the theoretical questions comes only from controlled experimentation; hence, a majority of the chapters include reviews of basic research.

But nowhere in this volume will one find any sharp distinction between basic and applied science. Indeed, those chapters that present research on traditional topics using traditional methods nonetheless have clear ties to applications. For example, the chapters by Diehl, Kleunder, Walsh, and Parker; Foss and Speer; and those by Johnson, Clifton, Gough, and Ross, all focus on the comprehension of written language—from the phonetic level to the syntactic level—and are therefore inherently related to the practical questions of communication and reading.

As one looks across the volume, there are cases in which basic theory is applied, and cases in which applications force revisions in basic theory; cases where traditional methodologies are used in service of practical research, and cases where new domains of application drive the invention of new methods.

Our collective legacy to those who read this volume is the spirit of fearless creative adventure.

2 Retrospections on the Study of Memory and Cognition

David L. Horton
University of Maryland

Over the course of my career there have been a number of developments that have influenced my thinking concerning the study of human memory and cognition. In this chapter I will briefly discuss some of the more significant of those developments. The approach will be historical in nature and highly selective in that it will focus only on those ideas and conceptualizations that have had the greatest impact on my own thinking.

I begin with the status of memory research in the early 1950s since I took my first psychology course in 1952 and entered the graduate program at the University of Minnesota in 1955. I then discuss developments over the subsequent decades.

LEARNING AND MEMORY

Around 1950, human memory was generally seen as a unitary system and the primary focus in research was to discover the reasons why the memory system failed (cf. McGeoch & Irion, 1952). This orientation stemmed from the view that whenever there was sufficient stimulus intensity to detect a stimulus or sufficient change in stimulus energy to detect a change, perception was more or less veridical and automatic. The next step was to learn the appropriate response to make in the presence of the stimulus being presented, thus forming a stimulus–response association. The details of forming such associations were often rather complex (cf. Hull, 1943) but once they were formed (i.e., learned) the associations were thought to be maintained unless they were subjected to experimental extinction, counterconditioning, or some other unlearning process.

The dominant theory of memory, or more appropriately of forgetting, that had evolved by that time was interference theory, and it focused quite explicitly on why memory failures occurred. Interference theory emphasized retroactive and proactive sources of forgetting. Retroactive interference was said to occur when memory for previously formed associations was interfered with because of more recently acquired associations. Proactive interference occurred when previously formed associations interfered with memory for more recently formed associations. The particular details of proactive and retroactive interference were quite complex (see Keppel, 1968) but they generally followed the stimulus–response, associationistic approach that characterized theories of learning at that time.

During the 1950s a shift began to occur in the focus of memory research, from an emphasis on memory failures to an emphasis on successes of memory. This orientation began with the work of researchers such as Cofer and Foley (1942), Bousfield (1953), and others, but it was most clearly elucidated by the work of James J. Jenkins and his students at the University of Minnesota (cf. Jenkins, 1963; Horton & Kjeldergaard, 1961), The emphasis in this work was on the role of mediational processes in explaining the memory successes that occurred in the absence of explicit learning, thus to hint at aspects of what came to be referred to as the creativity found in human language and cognition. The approach, admittedly, was based on associationistic theory as was interference theory, but the topic of interest was memory successes rather than memory failures.

INFORMATION PROCESSING
AND COGNITIVE PSYCHOLOGY

In the late 1950s and early 1960s, the study of short-term memory (STM, as opposed to long-term memory, of LTM) challenged the notion that memory was a unitary system governed by a single, specifically prescribed set of principles (cf. Peterson & Peterson, 1959). The basic argument was that forgetting from STM resulted from spontaneous decay of the memory trace, whereas forgetting from LTM obeyed the principles of interference theory. However, a classic paper by Melton (1963) appeared to put this challenge to rest by showing that the basic phenomena of both STM and LTM could be explained according to the principles of interference theory. The impact of Melton's paper was so great that the proceedings of one of the more influential conferences of this decade (Dixon & Horton, 1968) did not contain any papers which explicitly challenged the unitary view of the memory system.

By the mid-1960s a number of developments were beginning to produce significant changes in the conception of human memory, in effect what was to become the field of cognitive psychology. One of the most important was the work of the eminent linguist, Noam Chomsky (1957), which was brought to the attention of most psychologists by George Miller (1962). Chomsky's work focused on the creativity found in human language, that is, upon our ability to produce and understand an indefinite number of sentences. The explanation for this creativity was presumed to be found in "cognitive" generative processes, which were not accessible to introspection and therefore constituted tacit or implicit knowledge. Such knowledge is not taught to us explicitly, as, for example, are the rules of arithmetic. However, just as the rules of arithmetic allow us to solve problems we have never seen before, the implicit knowledge that governs language allows us to understand sentences we have never heard or seen before. The implications of Chomsky's early work for experimental psychology, particularly with respect to stimulus—response accounts of language and cognition, were probably best articulated in the proceedings of the Kentucky conference (Dixon & Horton, 1968).

A second major development derived from the publication of Waugh and Norman's (1965) paper dealing with primary and secondary memory. Primary memory was seen as having limited capacity and forgetting was due to displacement, while secondary memory was seen as having unlimited capacity with forgetting being due to the classic mechanisms of interference theory. In additon, incoming information had to pass through primary memory in order to enter secondary memory. This paper not only revived the distinction between STM and LTM as potentially separable memory systems, but it also served as a renewed impetus for the information-processing view of human memory, which can be traced to the work of Broadbent (1957, 1958).

One of the most comprehensive presentations of the information-processing approach can be found in a series of papers by Atkinson and Shiffrin (cf. Atkinson & Shiffrin, 1968; Shiffrin & Atkinson, 1969). Information was seen as flowing from a sensory register to a short-term memory store and then to a long-term memory store. While this characterization of information processing had certain parallels with the associationistic view of stimulus information going from sensation to perception to learning and then memory, it involved a much more "cognitive" approach. In the general model proposed by Atkinson and Shiffrin, the flow of information was governed by a series of "control processes" rather than by a relatively automatic associative mechanism. For example, these "control processes" were seen as regulating such activities as rehearsal, memory search, and response output in addition to transferring information from one memory store to another.

The information-processing approach has had a profound influence on research and theory in human experimental psychology, and that influence continues at the present time. However, I believe that other developments, which I will discuss later on, have greatly weakened the popularity of the information-processing approach.

A third major influence in the mid 1960s was Ulric Neisser's text *Cognitive Psychology* (1967). This book not only introduced the term cognitive psychology to the field that now goes by that name, but it served to integrate a variety of important research and theoretical contributions that had appeared during the previous decade. Neisser's book brought together work on attention reported by Cherry (1953), Broadbent (1958) and others, the work on sensory memory by Sperling (1960) and Averbach and Coriell (1961). There was also the fascinating research on speech perception by Liberman and others at Haskins Laboratories, which had not appeared prominently in the psychological literature until Cofer published a major paper by Liberman, Cooper, Shankweiler, and Studdert–Kennedy in the 1967 *Psychological Review*. Thus, Neisser's text served to change the way many experimental psychologists looked at their field.

CONTEXTUALISM AND COGNITIVE PSYCHOLOGY

Some very exciting developments have recently taken place in cognitive psychology. Although many of these developments are independent of one another, together they serve to focus on a point of view that plays a central role in contemporary conceptions of memory and cognition.

One such development centers around the work of James J. Jenkins (1974) and his students. In Jenkins's discussion of contextualist philosophy he states:

> What is remembered in a given situation depends on the physical and psychological context in which the event was experienced, the knowledge and skills that the subject brings to the context, the situation in which we ask for evidence of remembering, and the relation of what the subject remembers to what the experimenter demands. (p. 793)

Jenkins (1974) cites numerous experimental demonstrations of the contextualist point of view. For instance, Hyde and Jenkins (1969) showed that the ability of subjects to recall and cluster word pairs, such as salt and pepper, king and queen, or table and chair, after they have been presented in a random order, depends on the meaning of the words being comprehended and it is not simply an automatic consequence of associative strength. During initial presentation, if participants rate the meaning of these words as pleasant or unpleasant, without any memory instructions, they recall and cluster the words as well as intentional learners that are given explicit memory instructions prior to list presentation. However, if participants are focused on the form, but not the meaning of the words, by asking them if the word would be spelled with the letter "e," recall and clustering are substantially reduced. This is one example, but the literature since then is a testimony to the relevance of contextualist thinking. As Horton and Mills (1984) pointed out in their *Annual Review* chapter on human learning and memory, the contextualist thesis is alive and well at both the empirical and theoretical levels in cognitive psychology.

A second major development was provided by the work of Craik and Lockhart (1972) in their "levels" or "depth of processing" framework for memory research. The levels-of-processing account challenged the then-popular view of multiple memory stores. Instead, Craik and Lockhart emphasized the notion that deeper encodings (semantic) are more meaningful than shallow encodings (nonsemantic) and that deeper encodings are more durable. In fact, they cite the work of Hyde and Jenkins (1969) noted earlier, as one example of depth of processing. While the depth-of-processing approach continues to be plagued by the lack of an independent definition of depth and by continued demonstrations of contextual dependencies showing that depth usually, but not always, leads to better retention (cf. Horton & Mills, 1984), most everyone would agree that Craik and Lockhart accomplished their objective of providing a framework for memory research.

A third development centers around the work of Endel Tulving and his associates, which led to the encoding specificity hypothesis (Tulving & Thomson, 1973) and to the distinction between episodic and semantic memory (Tulving, 1972). Tulving and Thompson state the encoding specificity principle as follows: "Specific encoding operations performed on what is perceived determine what is stored, and what is stored determines what retrieval cues are effective in providing access to what is stored" (p. 369). For example, suppose you are shown a list of word pairs. One member of each pair is capitalized and it is the to-be-remembered word. The other member of the pair appears in lowercase letters and you are told that it is not important to remember this word but looking at it may help you remember the capitalized word. The list includes pairs such as ground/COLD, train/BLACK, and so on. After the list is presented you are asked to identify the capitalized words just presented in a recognition test. Following this, you are given a list of the lowercase words and you are asked to recall the capitalized word that was presented with each lowercase word. The surprising finding is that memory performance in cued recall with the lowercase words as cues is better than it is in recognition with the capitalized words actually being presented (Tulving, 1983).

The encoding specificity hypothesis firmly established the distinction between encoding processes and retrieval processes in the study of human memory. This distinction, in turn, provided a basis for talking about separable memory systems in terms of different encoding processes and different retrieval operations. The distinction also fitted nicely with Jenkins's (1974) statement on contextualism because of the emphasis on contextual factors during both encoding and retrieval.

MULTIPLE MEMORY SYSTEMS

When Tulving introduced the distinction between episodic and semantic memory, he viewed it as a potentially useful way of classifying our knowledge about human memory. Episodic memory was seen as being autobiographical in nature and events stored in episodic memory were supposedly encoded in terms of the time and place of occurrence. Semantic memory, on the other hand, stores more general information about our language and our knowledge of the world where the time and place of original encoding is less important.

Episodic and semantic memory were not seen as being completely distinct, but as partly overlapping. When learning a list of words, for example, the list is stored in episodic memory, but during list learning the meaning of the individual words is drawn from semantic memory. The episodic and semantic memory distinction has been useful to many scholars, although in recent years considerable research has been directed to the issue of whether episodic and semantic memory represent functionally distinct memory systems. That is, in contrast to the traditional view that memory is a unitary system, the episodic–semantic distinction has led some to raise the issue of how many memory systems might be possible.

A number of psychologists have discussed the possibility of multiple memory systems in recent years. One of the more explicit statements is provided by Tulving (1983, 1985). He distinguishes between procedural and propositional memories. The category of procedural memory consists of a large number of perceptual-motor and cognitive skills. Procedural memory is demonstrated by performing a task requiring one or more of these skills. Propositional memory consists of a large body of knowledge that can be expressed symbolically. Propositional memory can be expressed in a variety of ways, including recognition and recall. Tulving also suggests that propositional memory can be further divided into episodic and semantic memory.

The empirical evidence concerning multiple memory systems, particularly the episodic–semantic distinction, is decidedly mixed (cf. Horton & Mills, 1984; Johnson & Hasher, 1987). Because of the interplay between episodic and semantic memory, a basic difficulty that arises in attempting to evaluate this evidence is whether or not a particular task involves episodic memory or semantic memory, or both (cf. Hannigan, Shelton, Franks, & Bransford, 1980).

Memory Without Awareness

One line of evidence which is consistent with the episodic–semantic distinction derives from the study of densely amnesic individuals. In contrast to normal individuals, these amnesic patients typically perform very poorly on conventional recognition tests that presumably require episodic memory. However, amnesic individuals perform as well as normals on tasks that appear to draw on semantic memory and do not require awareness of remembering. For example, the word fragment completion task in which a stimulus such as T_B_E is responded to as the word TABLE does not require the individual to remember consciously having seen the word TABLE in a previously studied list, and yet priming effects from prior study are just as strong for amnesics as normals in this task (cf. Warrington & Weiskrantz, 1974). That is, word fragments are more likely to be completed correctly when they are chosen from previously studied words as opposed to equally familiar words that have not been studied previously. In addition, the effect of prior study is just as strong in amnesics as it is in normals.

A second example can be found in the work of Jacoby and Witherspoon (1982). They presented to their participants (both amnesics and normals) a series of homophones, each with a question designed to bias the less-frequent spelling of each homophone. For example, "reed" (read) was biased by asking a question such as "can you name a musical instrument that employs a reed?" The participants were then given a spelling test or a conventional recognition memory test involving words previously presented as well as new words. Again, amnesics performed quite poorly in recognition memory, but they performed as well as normals on the spelling test. That is, both normals and amnesics spelled the words in the way that was biased by the previous questions even though the amnesics do not appear to remember participating in that stage of the investigation. Of course, these observations of memory failures in recognition memory for amnesics and memory successes in tasks that do not explicitly require an awareness of remembering do not assure the validity of the episodic–semantic distinction. However, these findings do raise questions concerning the possibility of different encoding and storage systems irrespective of what names they go by.

SOME SPECULATIONS

No doubt, my thinking about the study of human memory and cognition has been influenced considerably by developments and conceptualizations other than those I have discussed here. Articles and books I have read, and discussions with others also were important factors. For the present, however, these constitute my memory failures—it is the memory successes that I have shared with the Reader.

I have said elsewhere (Horton, 1987) that I consider the study of human memory to be the most central aspect of experimental cognitive psychology. I believe the study of human memory and cognition has come a long way since 1950. One aspect of this progress involved the consideration of memory successes as well as memory failures in our data base. The study of human memory can no longer be considered as only the study of forgetting. I also consider human memory to be governed by tacit or implicit knowledge akin to the generative processes Chomsky has introduced for language, as well as by something akin to the "control processes" introduced by psychologists following the information-processing appoach.

It is difficult to pinpoint theoretical developments that will be of major importance in the coming years. However, the conceptualization of human memory provided by Tulving (1983) will probably be quite influential. In

Elements of Episodic Memory, Tulving proposes a general model of memory that incorporates the main features of the contextualist position as stated by Jenkins (1974). The model deals with the encoding and retrieval of events in a dynamic fashion that emphasizes process considerations. The model also comes squarely to grips with the issue of consciousness in remembering.

On the subject of theoretical issues, I suspect that the recent focus on multiple memory systems is likely to draw attention to some very interesting questions. For example, Tulving (1983) cites a number of scholars who suggest that childhood amnesia may be due to the later development of a system akin to episodic memory as opposed to semantic memory. The study of memory and aging also raises questions pertinent to multiple memory systems. Memory failures in the elderly appear generally to be episodic, as opposed to semantic.

Memory failures in the elderly may have other implications for the kind of encoding processes we employ. For example, much of the research on memory failures in the elderly involves rote learning tasks. While rote learning may be a very effective encoding strategy in college students, it may not be very effective, and hence not used often, in the elderly. In any case, it appears that the study of memory failures as well as memory successes in the elderly may pose some interesting and researchable questions concerning the issue of multiple memory systems.

While the study of human memory and cognition has come a long way since 1950, I believe the future will see even greater advances. The contextualist position (cf. Jenkins, 1974) appears to be well in place in terms of both encoding and retrieval operations. The depth-of-processing general viewpoint seems likely to be maintained, particularly if the dimension of depth can be better articulated. I suspect that differences in encoding and retrieval operations will receive considerable study as will multiple memory systems. Perhaps we will progress to the point of being able to say something interesting about individual differences in cognitive abilities. In any event, the future of the study of memory and cognition looks exciting, and I look forward to participating in it.

REFERENCES

Atkinson, R. C., & Shiffrin, R. M. (1968). Human memory: A proposed system and its control processes. In K. W. Spence & J. T. Spence (Eds), *The psychology of learning and motivation* (Vol. 2.) New York: Academic Press

Averbach, E., & Coriell, A. S. (1961). Short-term memory in vision. *Bell System Technical Journal, 40,* 309–328 (Monograph 3756).

Bousfield, W. A. (1953). The occurrence of clustering in the recall of randomly arranged associates. *Journal of General Psychology, 49,* 229–240.

Broadbent, D. E. (1957). A mechanical model for human attention and immediate memory. *Psychological Review, 64,* 205–215.

Broadbent, D. E. (1958). *Perception and communication.* Lodon: Pergamon Press.

Cherry, E. C. (1953). Some experiments on the recognition of speech with one and with two ears. *Journal of the Acoustical Society of America, 25,* 975–979.

Chomsky, N. (1957). *Syntactic structures.* The Hague: Mouton.

Cofer, C. N., & Foley, J. P. (1942). Mediated generalization and the interpretation of verbval behavior: I. Prolegomena. *Psychological Review, 49,* 513–540.

Craik, F.I.M., & Lockhart, R. S. (1972). Levels of processing: A framework for memory research. *Journal of Verbal Learning and Verbal Behavior, 11,* 671–684.

Dixon, T. R., & Horton, D. L. (Eds.). (1968). *Verbal behavior and general behavior theory.* Englewood Cliffs, NJ: Prentice–Hall.

Hannigan, M. L., Shelton, T. S., Franks, J. J., & Bransford, J. D. (1980). The effect of episodic and semantic memory on the identification of sentences masked by white noise. *Memory and Cognition, 8,* 278–284.

Horton, D. L. (1987). Memory and Cognition. In R. H. Price, M. Glickstein, D. L. Horton, S. J. Sherman, & R. H. Fasio, (Eds.), *Principles of Psychology* (2nd ed.). Glenview, IL: Scott Foresman.

Horton, D. L., & Kjeldergaard, P. M. (1961). An experimental analysis of associative factors in mediated generalization. *Psychological Monographs, 75,* II (Whole No. 515).

Horton, D. L., & Mills, C. B. (1984). Human learning and memory. *Annual Review of Psychology, 35,* 361–394.

Hull, C. L. (1943). *Principles of behavior.* Englewood Cliffs, NJ: Prentice–Hall.

Hyde, T. S., & Jenkins, J. J. (1969). Differential effects of incidental tasks on the organization of recall in a list of highly associated words. *Journal of Experimental Psychology, 82,* 472–481.

Jacoby, L. L., & Witherspoon, D. (1982). Remembering without awareness. *Canadian Journal of Psychology, 36,* 300–324.

Jenkins, J. J. (1963). Mediated associations: Paradigms and situations. In C. N. Cofer & B. S. Musgrave (Eds.), *Verbal behavior and learning: Problems and processes* (pp. 210–245). New York: McGraw–Hill.

Jenkins, J. J. (1974). Remember that old theory of memory? Well, forget it! *American Psychologist, 29,* 785–795.

Johnson, M. K., & Hasher, L. (1987). Human learning and memory. *Annual Review of Psychology, 38,* 631–668.

Keppel, G. (1968). Retroactive and proactive inhibition. In T. R. Dixon & D. L. Horton (Eds.), *Verbal behavior and general behavior theory.* Englewood Cliffs, NJ: Prentice–Hall.

Liberman, A. M., Cooper, F. S., Shankweiler, D., & Studdert–Kennedy, M. (1967). Perception of the speech code. *Psychological Review, 74,* 431–461.

McGeoch, J. A., & Irion, A. L. (1952). *The psychology of human learning* (2nd ed.). New York: Longmanns.

Melton, A. W. (1963). Implications of short-term memory for a general theory of memory. *Journal of Verbal Learning and Verbal Behavior, 2,* 1–21.

Miller, G. A. (1962). Some psychological studies of grammar. *American Psychologist, 17,* 748–762.

Neisser, U. (1987). *Cognitive Psychology.* Englewood Cliffs, NJ: Prentice–Hall.

Peterson, L. R., & Peterson, M. J. (1959). Short-term retention of individual verbal items. *Journal of Experimental Psychology, 58,* 193–198.

Shiffrin, R. M., & Atkinson, R. C. (1969). Storage and retrieval processes in long-term memory. *Psychological Review, 76,* 179–193.

Sperling, G. A. (1960). The information available in brief visual presentations. *Psychological Monographs, 74* (Whole No. 498).

Tulving, E. (1972). Episodic and semantic memory. In E. Tulving & W. Donaldson (Eds.), *Organization of memory* (pp. 382–403). New York: Academic Press.

Tulving, E. (1983). *Elements of episodic memory.* New York: Oxford University Press.

Tulving, E. (1985). How many memory systems are there? *American Psychologist, 40,* 385–398.

Tulving, E., & Thomson, D. M. (1973). Encoding specificity and retrieval processes in episodic memory. *Psychological Review, 80,* 352–373.

Warrington, E. K., & Weiskrantz, L. (1974). The effect of prior learning on subsequent retention in amnesic patients. *Neuropsychologia, 12,* 419–428.

Waugh, N. C., & Norman, D. A. (1965). Primary memory. *Psychological Review, 72,* 89–104.

3 Direct Perception and Other Forms of Knowing

Ulric Neisser
Emory University

I will start with perceiving; if there is any other place to start, I've never found it. But this chapter, which begins with direct perception, is concerned with several other kinds of knowing as well: interpersonal perception, language, and categories. I will also consider how perceptually given knowledge and linguistic knowledge may be initially related; specifically, how a language learner discovers that spoken words stand for particular objects in the immediate environment. Questions like these have to be faced sooner or later; the study of cognition must not remain indefinitely divided into independent subdisciplines. In particular, it seems important to show that the ecological approach to perception, which specifically denies that perceiving depends on inferential or symbolic processes, can be combined with a more conventionally cognitive approach to language and thought. For this reason, the range of topics to be considered here is unusually broad, and the argument on most of them is correspondingly sketchy. My aim is not to offer definitive analyses of all these kinds of knowledge, but to illustrate how they might—indeed, how I believe they do—fit together.

The opening section, which presents an account of what J. J. Gibson (1979) called "direct perception," will be rather specific. To establish a firm basis for what follows, I will review several different kinds of motion-produced information and what they enable us to see. Subsequent sections of the chapter will deal with interpersonal perception (a somewhat different process), with the acquisition of language (for which both kinds of perception are prerequisite), with basic-level categories (which also have a primarily perceptual basis), and with what George Lakoff (1987) calls "idealized cognitive models."

COHERENT STIMULUS INFORMATION
AND DIRECT PERCEPTION

To perceive is to find out about one's immediate ecological situation by picking up stimulus information. Gibson (1979) was the first to insist that a proper understanding of that activity requires three distinct levels of analysis. The first of these levels is concerned with the real environment itself, the second with the stimulus information that specifies the environment to a perceiver, and the third with the activity of the perceiver in picking up that information. In the most central form of perception, which Gibson called "direct," the three levels can be further characterized as follows:

1. *What* we perceive directly is the "immediate ecological situation." This includes the layout of the ground and of nearby objects, together with their shapes, sizes, movements, and physical affordances. It also includes our own position and our own actions. As Gibson rightly insisted (1979, p. 126), all direct perception is coperception of the environment and the self.

2. In general, the study of the stimulus information for vision is called "ecological optics." Direct perception depends primarily on motion-produced information: looming (Schiff, Caviness, & Gibson, 1962); occlusion (Gibson, Kaplan, Reynolds, & Wheeler, 1969); kinetic depth (Wallach & O'Connell, 1953), and so on. Looming, the explosive magnification of a sector of the optical array, is a particularly good example. It is produced whenever an object moves toward the eye. The sector of the array corresponding to the object gets larger and larger as it approaches, while background objects are progressively occluded. Under natural conditions, looming always specifies the approach of an object. That is not all it specifies. Given uniform velocity, the (inverse of the) rate of optical magnification actually gives the time remaining until the object collides with the perceiver (Lee, 1980). There is every reason to believe that human perceivers (and those of other species) make good use of this information in coordinating their behavior.

3. The "activity of the observer" includes not only ocular adjustments and exploratory behavior but also the neural activity of the visual system itself. This crucial point has often been misunderstood. To claim that perception is direct is to deny that it depends on inference from "sensations," but not that it depends on neural activity. The brain is just as real as the environment, and there is every reason to be interested in it. Nevertheless, it is easy to see why Gibson rejected the neuropsychological speculation of his time: Unless we know what the visual brain must accomplish, we cannot expect to discover how it works.[1] William Mace's famous maxim, "Ask not what's inside your head but what your head's

---

[1]Although David Marr's (1982) computational analysis of vision is superficially quite different from Gibson's, Marr's insistence on beginning that analysis at the level of "computational theory" (rather than going immediately to algorithms or mechanisms) reflects essentially the same insight.

inside of" (1977, p. 43), is sound methodological advice for early theory development in vision.

These forms of movement-produced information have a number of noteworthy properties.

1. Except at a few singular points, they have a spatially continuous structure. *Tau,* for example, changes smoothly rather than abruptly across most of the array.

2. They also have a temporally continuous structure; changes occur smoothly over time except at occasional singular moments.

3. These structures are *dense,* in Nelson Goodman's (1968) sense; there are no empty gaps in them.

4. The information is consistent across scales of measurement, having the same sort of structure at several levels of detail. *Tau* does not appear only in the microstructure of a given sector of the array (corresponding to an approaching surface), but also in the expanding contour of the surface as a whole.

5. These structures are highly *redundant*. Information of different kinds, from different sectors of the array, (often even in different modalities!) specifies the same characteristic properties of objects and events.

6. Motion-produced information does not merely specify the surface features of an object; it can also specify structural properties such as rigidity, mass, and center of motion. We can *see* these characteristics of objects as they move (Runeson & Frykholm, 1983, Walker, Owsley, Megaw–Nyce, Gibson, & Bahrick, 1980).

7. Under normal conditions (i.e., the physical and optical conditions that prevailed during the evolution of the visual system), these forms of information are invariably veridical. There are no optical illusions where the layout of the nearby environment is concerned. Occlusion, explosive magnification, and similar optical structures are produced only by the corresponding real states of affairs; they cannot come into existence in any other way. (Nowadays things are different; we can produce them with electronic and optical devices, so their veridicality is no longer guaranteed.)

8. Conversely, those real states of affairs *inevitably* give rise to the information structures in question. The laws of optics guarantee it. In any world where light travels in straight lines and is reflected from surfaces, the layout and movement of objects will be just as perceptible as they are here.

9. Finally, the ability to pick these forms of information appears early in life. Recent studies have shown, for example, that very young infants are sensitive to occlusion (Baillergeon, Spelke, & Wasserman, 1985), looming (Carroll & Gibson, 1981) and the kinetic depth effect (Kellman, 1984). Infants probably perceive the general layout of the environment much as adults do, though perhaps with less resolution and detail.

How does the visual system pick up information of this kind? What parts of the brain are involved? What do they do? We do not yet know the answers to these questions, but a bit of speculation may not be out of place. Direct perception probably depends, at least in part, on what neuropsychologists call the "where" system. This system is based both in the superior colliculus (Ingle, 1967) and the posterior parietal cortex (Ungergleider & Mishkin, 1982). Monkeys with a damaged "where" system cannot easily reach for or localize objects, though they have no difficulty in recognizing them. This system somehow resonates to the structure of movement-produced information, perhaps adopting a dynamic configuration that is itself functionally continuous and dense. The resulting perception is "direct" in the sense that (a) The structure of the information necessarily specifies the characteristics of the ecological situation; and (b) Aspects of that structure, still specifying those characteristics, are adopted by the visual system.

In my view, not every form of perception is "direct" in this sense. The identification and categorization of objects, for example, is rarely based on motion-produced information. Sometimes recognition depends entirely on the presence of a single localized feature; on other occasions, it is based solely on inference from context. All such inferences are fallible, and instances of misrecognition are common enough. I may believe the person across the room is X when it is really Y, or take that animal to be a dog when it is actually a fox. Recognition depends on systems and principles quite different from those which underlie direct perception of the layout of the environment.

To understand perception, then, we must first discover the stimulus information on which it depends. But doing this is much harder than it looks; indeed, the discovery cannot be made just by looking. Although we pick up optical structure whenever we see anything at all, we do not see that structure itself. Instead, we see what it specifies. This means that the underlying basis of direct perception is not available in phenomenal experience or to systematic introspection. That is why it is so difficult to study. We can see the real world around us—directly— but we cannot see the information structures in the light which make that very achievement possible. The discovery and description of those structures is a difficult scientific task, and one that we have only begun.

The fact that the basis of vision is itself invisible has had important intellectual consequences. Perhaps the most striking is that almost everyone—*except* philosophers and psychologists—has always taken it for granted that perception is somehow direct. After all, we can see that nothing intervenes between the object and the perceiver! That is perhaps why we often use "I see" for the best and most immediate form of understanding: It means "I know directly, without intermediate steps." In this way, perception serves as one form of *idealized cognitive model* (Lakoff, 1987) for knowing in general.

The information in the light is still out there, waiting to be understood. One of the most exciting things about the ecological approach to perception is just this objective formulation of the problem. Ecological psychologists do not construe their task in terms of formulating the right mental model, as other cognitive scientists do, but of finding out about something that really exists and is presently unknown. Our hero is not Descartes but Columbus. Most of what the psychology of perception needs to know at this point is not in the mind but in the world: The problem is to discover it.

We have made some progress. Modern studies of occlusion, looming, and kinetic depth have produced significant new knowledge about the information on which perception depends. Nevertheless, there is still a great deal to be done. We have only begun to explore the information that specifies simple motor afford-ances, for example, although Warren's (1984) studies of stair climbing are a step in the right direction. We have not carefully studied the way that successive vistas are linked together as perceivers move about: a critical aspect of orienta-tion to the extended environment. We know a good deal about the development of perception in early infancy, but little about how that development is coupled to other aspects of maturation and experience; in general, we do not understand perceptual learning very well yet. We also need to know much more about less direct forms of perception, of which recognition (discussed earlier) is the most obvious case. A second important case—one that seems more or less on the boundary between direct perception and recognition—occurs when we perceive the actions and reactions of other human beings. This problem deserves discus-sion in its own right.

INTERPERSONAL PERCEPTION

By "interpersonal perception" I mean our ability to perceive the communicative gestures and actions of other individuals, and especially the relation of their gestures to our own. I look at you as you look at me; we take appropriate turns in our actions and verbalizations; each of us can *see* (and hear, and perhaps feel) that we are participating in an ongoing interaction. And we are not mistaken in this: While the underlying meaning of the interaction may well be different for you than it is for me, there can be no dispute about the fact that it is taking place.

All of us are familiar with such experiences as adults, but in fact they begin very early in life—just as early as direct perception itself. Everyone has watched young infants and their mothers taking pleasure in each other's company, each of them highly responsive to the other. Recent studies by Murray and Trevarthen (1985) have expanded these observations, and shown how finely tuned that coordination is. In these studies, 2-month-old infants and their mothers com-municate via closed-circuit television. In the baseline condition each of them sees the other full-face, in real time, and hears the other's vocalizations. Eye contact is easily maintained; communication is immediate and satisfactory, and both parties seem to enjoy it. Their reciprocal activity and mutual attention create a state of affairs that Trevarthen and Hubley (1978) call *primary intersubjectivity*. During this part of the experiment, the mother's actions are also recorded on videotape. After a few minutes, a change is introduced. Now the infant no longer sees the mother in real time; instead, he or she is shown the videotape that was recorded earlier. The screen shows mother smiling and vocalizing just as before, but her eye movements, gestures, and vocalizations are no longer coordinated with those of the watching infant. The result is a dramatic alteration in behavior. The infant's demeanor changes almost immediately; within a few seconds he or she typically turns way, begins to fidget, and generally exhibits signs of distress.[2]

What is perceived in interpersonal perception is more than just the gestures and actions of the other individual. Those gestures are real enough, but their coordination with what *we* are doing is equally real and often even more important. That coordination can itself be perceived. The existence of primary intersubjectivity is both visible and audible; often it is tangible as well. This kind of perceiving has a great deal in common with direct perception:

- Both appear very early in life, and are evidently based on genetically established mechanisms.
- Both pick up information about the perceiver's ongoing relationship with something external: in one case with the local physical environment, in the other with another human being.
- In both cases perception is veridical; no illusions occur under natural conditions. We are often mistaken when we try to infer another person's thoughts and feelings, but we make no mistake when we perceive that they are looking at us, speaking to us, and reciprocally engaged with us.

Although these similarities are suggestive, we still know very little about the stimulus information on which interpersonal perceiving depends. Is it primarily motion-produced? Is it continuously and redundantly present at many levels in the optical array, like the information that specifies the layout of the local environment? Perhaps it is, but at present we cannot rule out certain other possibilities. For all we know, everything may depend on one or two specific cues instead: eye contact and vocal turn taking are obvious possibilities. The universal facial expressions studied by Paul Ekman (1973) and others may also be relevant, though they have rarely been studied in situations involving social interaction. More research is urgently needed here. From an ecological point of view, we cannot begin to understand any form of perception until we have discovered the information on which it depends.

---

[2]If the experiment is run the other way, so that the *mother* sees her baby on videotape rather than (as she believes) in real time, she, too, will exhibit distress. She may conclude, for example, that something is the matter with the baby.

If that task still remains before us, so does another that may prove even more difficult. At about 9 to 12 months of age, human infants begin to display a more sophisticated form of interpersonal coordination, which Trevarthen and Hubley (1978) have christened *secondary intersubjectivity*. At this point the child's interest is no longer limited to its immediate interactional partner and the dyadic relation between partner and self; it also extends to nearby objects that are, or might become, the focus of that partner's attention. The child begins to look in the direction in which the partner is pointing; soon thereafter, in the direction in which the partner is merely looking (Butterworth & Grover, 1988). At this age children can apparently perceive a triadic state of affairs: *My partner* is interested in *it,* and so am *I.* The child also initiates such interactions, trying to get the adult to look at something, bring something, or fix something. Here the two kinds of perceiving we have considered begin to come together. The direct perception of an object and the interpersonal perception of another individual's gestures are being purposefully and effectively coordinated. It is only at this point, I believe, that acquisition of language becomes possible.

LANGUAGE AND REFERENCE

To see how language initially depends on perception, it is useful to begin with the case of simple nouns. (Other parts of speech pose different problems, as does syntax in general, but I will not consider them here.) Consider a hypothetical occasion on which a 12- or 18-month-old child might learn the word "cup." What is probably going on?

- A cup is physically present; some of its properties and affordances are specified by optical information.
- The child is actively and directly perceiving (some of) those properties, that is, *attending* to the cup.
- The mother is also attending to the cup; she may be holding it, for example, or handing it to the child.
- The child, who is capable of secondary intersubjectivity, perceives that the mother is attending-to/interested-in/ doing-something-with the cup.
- The mother says "cup." (Actually she may say something more complex, such as "Here's the cup!" or "Do you want this cup?" or "Be careful with the cup!") Even if the child does not yet understand these sentence frames, the crucial noun will probably be in an acoustically emphasized position that makes it easy to notice.
- The child perceives that the mother is making a definite vocal gesture (i.e., saying 'cup") as part of the act of attending to the cup.

The upshot of all this is that the child accepts the mother's vocal gesture as a marker of her interest in the cup itself. What this amounts to is, in effect, the realization that the mother has used the word as a *symbol* for the object.[3]

On this analysis, the acquisition of language must proceed primarily at moments of what Jerome Bruner (e.g., Ninio & Bruner, 1978) has called "joint attention." My colleague Michael Tomasello (e.g., Tomasello & Farrar, 1986) has recently demonstrated this point in an elegant series of studies. Indeed, he has not only shown that joint attention is essential for the learning of new words, but that some kinds of joint attention are better than others. The kind that works best is initiated by the child, with the adult joining in later. Episodes initiated by the adult, in contrast, seem to be less effective.

Tomasello and Farrar (1986) demonstrated these points in two kinds of experiments. First, they videotaped the interactions of mothers with their 15- and 21-month-old children as the children examined and handled various ordinary objects. The tapes were then coded for gaze direction and other visible indicators of attention, so that each interchange could be divided into periods when joint attention was present and other periods when it was absent. This coding was done without sound, but it turned out that most of the vocalizations of both parties did occur during periods of joint attention. More important, it was possible to count the number of episodes of joint attention (for each mother–child dyad) in the session as a whole. The frequency of these episodes, recorded for each child at 15 months, was significantly correlated with the size of the same child's vocabulary half a year later.

A second study compared two different ways in which adults (mothers or experimenters) can bring episodes of joint attention into existence. On the one hand, they can note what the child is attending to and proceed to focus on the same object themselves; on the other, they can first select an object and then call the child's attention to it. In the experiment, 18-month-old children were taught the names of various new objects ("clip," "wrench," etc.) in these two different ways. In one condition the infant was allowed to play with the object for a while before the experimenter followed in by saying its name. In the other condition, the experimenter waited until the child was doing nothing in particular, then drew attention to the object and named it. The results of subsequent comprehension tests (i.e., of opportunities for the child to respond to requests such as "Give me the clip") showed that the first method was by far more effective.

It appears, then, that the acquisition of a first vocabulary depends on the child's (and the parent's) ability to coordinate interpersonal perception and object perception effectively. It is in episodes of joint attention that the child comes to distinguish spoken words from other human noises—to treat them, correctly, as

---

[3]The situation is actually more ambiguous than this, because the mother is also interested in the ongoing *action*, for example, in successfully handing the cup to the child. As a result, the child may initially assume that "cup" refers to the action rather than to the object. This often happens in fact.

signifying intentional states. The parent is using the word as a symbol for the object, and the child knows it. There is a striking difference here between *homo sapiens* and other species. Human children jump naturally and easily to that symbolic conclusion; indeed, they can hardly be prevented from doing so. The young of other primate species, in contrast, can barely be brought to it even with laborious and protracted training procedures. I do not know why this should be the case, but the facts are no longer in doubt. (Recent research suggests that pygmy chimpanzees may be a partial exception: see Savage-Rumbaugh, McDonald, Seucik, Hopkins, & Ruberts, 1986.) The most we can say, at present, is that the difference must have some evolutionary genetic basis.

On this view, the acquisition of language is not so much a matter of learning responses as of developing a special sort of perceptual skill. To become aware of the symbolic function of a spoken word is to perceive, simultaneously, both the object itself and the speaker's referential intent. What is involved is not just direct perception in Gibson's sense, but it is perception all the same. No theory of language development that leaves perception out of account can do justice to the facts.

CATEGORIES

What does the child know when he or she mastered a simple noun? "Cup" is not the proper name of a particular object; it refers to a whole taxonomic category. What defines that category, from the young child's point of view? Indeed, what defines it for adult speakers of the language? This issue has recently been the subject of considerable discussion (for a partial summary, see Neisser, 1987). It has gradually become clear that the so-called "classical theory," which treats a category simply as a set of objects defined by the presence of certain distinctive features, is deeply flawed. It does not do justice to either the perceptual or the intellectual aspects of categorization. On the perceptual side, categories such as *cup* are indicated more by an object's overall appearance and its affordances for action than by any set of specific features. For this reason, some members of a given category are invariably more central and "prototypical" than others. On the intellectual side, assigning an object to a category—especially to a natural kind (such as *tree* or *dog*—implies much more than just the presence of a few defining attributes; it typically invokes a rich web of belief about an extended domain of experience.

Children's first categories—the ones that correspond to simple nouns such as *cup*—are similar in structure to the class of adult categories that Eleanor Rosch (1978) christened the "basic level." That is, all the plausible members of a given category look a good deal alike, and they are used or handled in a roughly similar way. This is what distinguishes basic-level categories such as *cup, plate, bowl, bed, chair,* or *table* from "superordinate" categories such as *crockery* or *furni-*

ture, which do not all look alike and have widely varying affordances. Young children speak freely of beds and chairs long before they use superordinates such as "furniture." In short, their categories are perceptually based.

In recent research, Carolyn Mervis (1987) has shown that there is some room for intergenerational disagreement even at the basic level. Children's first categories may not be the same as adults, even when both are based on perception, because they may not notice the same characteristics or give them the same importance. This insight has enabled Mervis to resolve the old controversy about whether early categories are "overextended" or "underextended." Both can occur. When children generalize too widely, perhaps by using "ball" for round candles and Christmas tree ornaments as well as balls, it is because they have disregarded certain features that adults find important; in this case, the presence of a wick or the function of decorating a tree. When they undergeneralize, refusing to use "duckie" for a stylized picture, it is because the picture lacks too many of the features that they take as relevant to the basic-level category *duck.*

It seems clear that naming begins at the basic level, where language and perception are most closely coordinated. Children learn concrete nouns by perceiving the object, the spoken word, and the speaker's intention all at once, in episodes of joint attention. To be sure, this is only one aspect of the acquisition of language. Speakers do not just name objects, they use sentences; they do not speak only about objects at hand, but of many other matters as well. I do not wish to gloss over the difficulty of explaining these achievements. Nevertheless it seems certain that they, too, depend on forms of joint attention. To understand language is to understand not only what is meant but also who means it.

COGNITIVE MODELS

Language begins in coordination with perception, but soon becomes an independent source of knowledge in its own right. As Vygotsky (1962) saw very clearly, the acquisition of language leads to a striking change in mental life. Children now know not only what they have seen, but also what they have been told. In the long run, this may be the best definition of language that we have. The claim that only human beings have language, in spite of many serious efforts to teach it to other primate species, does not depend so much on the apes' failure to reach some technically defined criterion of linguistic behavior as on an ultimate failure of communication. The point is not just that chimpanzees have some difficulty with symbols, or that they don't engage in appropriate conversational turn taking, or that they cannot formulate sentences. All this is true enough (Terrace, Petitto, Sanders, & Bever, 1979), but the most impressive fact—in my view—is that you can't *tell* them very much. For example, you can't say "The experiment is over now, and you have to go back to the holding cage. Sorry!" (For more discussion of this issue, see A. Neisser, 1983, pp. 202–234.)

Without language we would have nothing to think about except what we ourselves had perceived, perhaps modestly supplemented by derivatives of perception such as mental imagery. Having language—and other symbol systems as well—we can set that restriction aside. We can consider other people's experience as well as our own, reflect on the remote past and distant future, manipulate indefinitely many abstract concepts and map them back on to what we perceive. In doing so, we develop a wide range of conceptual structures—structures that often direct what we say and do, and contribute to the selection of what we perceive. Following Lakoff (1987), I will call these structures "idealized cognitive models." The meanings of most everyday words depend on such models; they are based not only on what we have seen but on interpretations of what we have heard, read, and believed.

Often, the same word draws on more than one idealized cognitive model for its meaning. Lakoff's (1987) analysis of the concept *mother* provides a striking example. According to what we might call the "birth model," the mother is the person who gave birth to the child. But there is also a genetic model (in which she is one of two contributors to its genetic makeup), a marriage model (in which she is married to the child's father), and a very familiar nurturant model (in which she is the one who protects and nourishes the child). In the prototypical case, all these mothers are the same person; in the real world, they may not be. Our everyday language itself reflects the complexity of this concept. When we say "necessity is the mother of invention," our metaphor draws on the birth model; in "He wants his girl friend to mother him," on the very different nurturant model. Here as elsewhere, the meanings of words depend on the cognitive structures in which they are embedded.

The dependence of meanings on cognitive structures is just as characteristic of scientific concepts as of ordinary language. The word *force*, for example, no longer means what it once did in pre-Newtonian science. It is now defined as the product of mass times acceleration, and both of these are Newtonian concepts in their own right. In earlier days, the idea of force was not clearly differentiated from such notions as momentum, energy, or vigor. The same principle applies to *light wave*, a concept originally defined in terms of an all-pervading ethereal substance. If the cognitive structures that support such concepts do not fit the world properly—that is, if the scientific theories in question turn out to be wrong—then the concepts themselves must be altered or abandoned. This happens fairly often. The knowledge that we gain through direct perception is necesssrily valid (at least under ecologically natural conditions), but cognitive models carry no equivalent guarantee. They can be wrong in very significant ways. If one can be a birth mother without being the genetic mother—as is possible nowadays—then this concept of *mother* requires re-examination; if there is no ether, *light wave* cannot mean what it did before. All we can do in such cases is try to find out more about the world, take what we have discovered into account, and do our best to formulate a new model that fits better than the one we had before.

CONCLUSION

For centuries, philosophers and psychologists have had a particular cognitive model of knowing itself. In that traditional account, knowledge can only be based on inductive inference from fallible sensory input. Like pre-Newtonian physics, that model may have outlived its usefulness. Perception is not necessarily fallible; in many cases, it is direct. Direct perception is based on the nervous system's evolved ability to tune itself to objectively existing coherent information structures—structures that necessarily specify real characteristics of the environment. Moreover, interpersonal perception provides us with clear and unambiguous knowledge of our immediate relations with other people—people who have knowledge of their own to share with us. What we learn from them, in language, enables us to develop rich networks of knowledge that goes far beyond what we can perceive. The beliefs based on those networks are indeed fallible—each of us surely believes a great many things that will turn out not to be true—but in principle they are also corrigible. Even where we are wrong today, we may be right tomorrow. The different kinds of knowing available to us can supplement and correct one another. Veridical perception of the immediate environment is everyone's inalienable birthright; other forms of understanding, though less direct, can also bring us closer to the truth.

ACKNOWLEDGMENT

So many people have contributed to the development of these ideas that it is impossible to acknowledge them all. Nevertheless, two individuals deserve special mention here. The first is James J. Gibson, whose unswerving adherence to the principle that we must begin with the objectively existing information has changed my professional life. The second is the "other J. J.," James J. Jenkins: His constructive contextualism, breadth of vision, and cheerful openness to new and radical ideas sets an example to us all.

REFERENCES

Baillargeon, R., Spelke, E. S., & Wasserman, S. (1985). Object permanenance in five-month-olds. *Cognition, 20,* 191–208.
Butterworth, G., & Grover, L. (1988). The origins of referential communication in human infancy. In L. Weiskrantz (Ed.), *Thought without language.* Oxford, England: Oxford University Press.

Ekman, P. (1973). Cross-cultural studies of facial expression. In P. Ekman (Ed.), *Darwin and facial expression*. New York: Academic Press.

Carroll, J. J., & Gibson, E. J. (1981). *Differentiation of an aperture from an obstacle under conditions of motion by three-month-old infants*. Paper presented at the Society for Research in Child Development, Boston.

Gibson, J. J. (1979). *The ecological approach to visual perception*. Boston: Houghton Mifflin.

Gibson, J. J., Kaplan, G. A., Reynolds, H. N., & Wheeler, K. (1969). The change from visible to invisible: A study of optical transitions. *Perception and Psychophysics, 5*, 113–116.

Goodman, N. (1968). *Languages of art*. New York: Bobbs–Merrill.

Ingle, D. (1967). Two visual mechanisms underlying the behavior of fish. *Psychologische Forschung, 31*, 44–51.

Kellman, P. J. (1984). Perception of three-dimensional form by human infants. *Perception and Psychophysics, 36*, 353–358.

Lakoff, G. (1987). Cognitive models and prototype theory. In U. Neisser (Ed.), *Concepts and conceptual development*. New York: Cambridge University Press.

Lee, D. N. (1980). The optic flow field: The foundation of vision. *Philosophical Transactions of the Royal Society of London*, B290, 169–179.

Mace, W. M. (1977). James J. Gibson's strategy for perceiving: Ask not what's inside your head, but what your head's inside of. In R. Shaw & J. Bransford (Eds.), *Perceiving, acting, and knowing: Toward an ecological psychology*. Hillsdale, NJ: Lawrence Erlbaum Associates.

Marr, D. (1982). *Vision*. New York: W. H. Freeman.

Mervis, C. B. (1987). Child-basic object categories and early lexical development. In U. Neisser (Ed.), *Concepts and conceptual development*. New York: Cambridge University Press.

Murray, L., & Trevarthen, C. (1985). Emotional regulation of interactions between two-month-olds and their mothers. In T. M. Field & N. A. Fox (Eds.), *Social perception in infants*. Norwood, NJ: Ablex.

Neisser, A. (1983). *The other side of silence*. New York: Knopf.

Neisser, U. (Ed.). (1987). *Concepts and conceptual development: Ecological and intellectual factors in categorization*. New York: Cambridge University Press.

Ninio, A., & Bruner, J. (1978). The achievement and antecedents of labelling. *Journal of Child Language, 5*, 1–16.

Rosch, E. (1978). Principles of categorization. In E. Rosch & B. B. Lloyd (Eds.), *Cognition and categorization*. Hillsdale, NJ: Lawrence Erlbaum Associates.

Runeson, S., & Frykholm, G. (1983). Kinematic specification of dynamics as an informational basis for person-and-action information: Expectation, gender recognition, and deceptive intention. *Journal of Experimental Psychology: General, 112*, 585–615.

Savage–Rumbaugh, S., McDonald, K., Sevcik, R. A., Hopkins, W. D., & Rubert, E. (1986). Spontaneous symbol acquisition and communicative use by pygmy chimpanzees *(pan paniscus)*. *Journal of Experimental Psychology: General, 115*, 211–235.

Schiff, W., Caviness, J. A., & Gibson, J. J. (1962). Persistent fear responses in rhesus monkeys to the optical stimulus of "looming." *Science, 136*, 982–983.

Terrace, H. S., Petitto, L. A., Sanders, R. J., & Bever, T. G. (1979). Can an ape create a sentence? *Science, 206*, 891–902.

Tomasello, M., & Farrar, M. J. (1986). Joint attention and early language. *Child Development, 57*, 1454–1463.

Trevarthen, C., & Hubley, P. (1978). Secondary intersubjectivity: Confidence, confiding, and acts of meaning in the first year. In A. Lock (Ed.), *Action, gesture and symbol*. London: Academic Press.

Ungergleider, L. G., & Mishkin, M. (1982). Two cortical visual systems. In D. J. Ingle, M. A. Goodale, & R. J. W. Mansfield (Eds.), *Analysis of visual behavior*. Cambridge, MA: MIT Press.

Vgotsky, L. S. (1962). *Thought and language*. Cambridge: MIT Press.

Walker, A. S., Owsley, C. J., Megaw–Nyce, J. S., Gibson, E. J., & Bahrick, L. E. (1980). Detection of elasticity as an invariant property of objects by young infants. *Perception, 9,* 713–718.

Wallach, H., & O'Connell, D. N. (1953). The kinetic depth effect. *Journal of Experimental Psychology, 45,* 205–217.

Warren, W. H. (1984). Perceiving affordances: Visual guidance of stair climbing. *Journal of Experimental Psychology: Human Perception and Performance, 10,* 683–703.

II SPEECH PERCEPTION

4 Modularity and the Effects of Experience

Alvin M. Liberman
Haskins Laboratories

Ignatius G. Mattingly
Haskins Laboratories and University of Connecticut

Experience is essential to the development of speech in the child, so we should ask of any psychological theory of speech how the effects of experience are to be accommodated. What does the theory have to say about how the child learns which phonetic distinctions are relevant in his native language and about how he adjusts to the phonetic capabilities of his own particular vocal tract as it changes in size and shape? As we show in this chapter, the more and less conventional views of speech account for such effects of experience in categorically different ways. Our aim is not to weigh these different accounts against the evidence, but only to use them to illuminate an important difference between the theories from which they follow.

SOUND LOCALIZATION AND EXPERIENCE

Before taking up the theories about speech, we should be as explicit as we can about two different ways in which experience might affect percepts and their relations to everything else. For that purpose, we begin with the example of sound localization. We do this not because sound localization is simple, for it is, in fact, marvelously complex, but because it is well understood and lends itself readily to displaying the theoretical choices with which we are concerned. Consider, then, two conceivable accounts of sound localization, together with their different implications for the ways in which experience might affect development.

By any account, the information for localization takes the form of interaural disparities of time of arrival and intensity (Hafter, 1984). Complicating the processes by which such information is used is the fact that the disparities vary, not only as a function of source location, but also of frequency, aural acuity, distance between the ears, and orientation of the head. Further complications arise, of course, when several sources are present at once.

On one theory, the currently prevailing one, sound localization is managed by a neural mechanism narrowly and exclusively adapted to cope with the attendant complications and derive location of a source of sound from the information about disparity. We will refer to this mechanism as a module, using the term in the sense of Fodor (1983). That such a sound-localizing module exists has been shown most plainly in experiments on the barn owl (Knudsen, 1984; Konishi, Takahashi, Wagner, Sullivan, & Carr, 1988). In these experiments, investigators have found cells in the inferior colliculus that respond selectively to sounds according to their location in space, and thus form a map. Moreover, it has been possible to observe some of the processes by which this map is derived. But what is of particular importance for our purposes is that, though the information critical for location takes the form of disparities of time and intensity, with appropriate corrections for frequency, source coherence, and phase ambiguities, the positions of the neural responses are fixed by coordinates that are purely spatial; the proximal stimulus dimension of disparity is not represented. Information about this dimension is therefore not available outside the localization module, and the owl presumably does not perceive it. All this being so, we assume that the spatially organized neural responses correspond to the perceptual primitives.

But it is conceivable that, contrary to the neurobiological data and the most obvious facts about the perception of sound location by human beings, someone might nevertheless maintain that the disparities *were* perceived, and that the organism's knowledge of sound-source location was the result of a higher-level or cognitive computation based on these perceived disparities. Certain disparities would be associated with certain locations, or perhaps there might be some heuristic computation for getting locations from disparities. Let us now consider how experience might be expected to have an effect, depending on whether the modular or cognitive account is the more nearly correct one.

The experience of interest is the change in the relation between the location of the source and the disparity cues as a consequence of changes, either natural or deliberately produced, in the acuity of the ears or the distance between them. The young barn owl's ear may be plugged by the curious experimenter; the child's ears get farther apart as his head grows. In either case, there is a change in the amount of disparity for a given deviation in source location from the midline or a given amount of head rotation. Yet the owl somehow makes the appropriate adjustments in its sound-localizing behavior, and the child continues to localize sounds correctly as he grows (Knudsen, 1988).

On the first and generally accepted view of sound localization, the effects of experience must take place within the module. Indeed, exactly this has been found to be the case in the asymmetrically deafened barn owl, for Knudsen

(1988) has shown that the neural map is itself recalibrated so as to maintain the veridical relation, obtained before the owl was deafened. Thus, it is the perceptual representation itself that is "corrected," not the cognitive connection between this representation and others. Apparently, the module adapts to the new environment at a precognitive level. In the case of the child, one can plausibly suppose that something of the same sort occurs when the disparities change as the head grows bigger.

On the other view of sound localization, the organism would have first to learn—by trial and error, logical inference, or instruction—that a certain seemingly arbitrary range of perceived disparities was, in fact, relevant to sound localization, and then, more specifically, how each disparity was to be interpreted as location. Such learning would, of course, have to take into account the complication that, for a fixed location, the disparities are different as a function of frequency and, even worse, that at each frequency, the disparities change as the head gets bigger. Altogether, a formidable cognitive task. Of course, the task is no less formidable as it is done by the sound-localizing module. The difference is simply that the module is specifically and superbly adapted to its complex task, and carries it out without taxing in the least such cognitive capacities as the child might have.

Thus, the effects of experience that are cognitive contrast with the precognitive kind most obviously in the locus of the effects. In the precognitive kind, the effects are, as we saw, on the internal workings of the relevant module and thus on the perceptual representations themselves; in the cognitive variety, on the other hand, they would have to be in the connection between those representations and others. A further difference is that, while the precognitive calibrations of the module are highly selective in regard to the environmental conditions they respond to, cognitive learning is obviously quite promiscuous, being capable of forming connections to a wide variety of representations. Thus, an animal can be taught to make any of an indefinitely large number of responses whenever it perceives sound at a particular location. But this would in no way affect the localization module or the perceptual representations it produces; those would have changed only in response to environmental conditions that alter the relation between interaural disparities and the location of the sound source.

SPEECH AND EXPERIENCE

Turning now to speech, we see that the conventional view is analogous to the view of sound localization that is incorrect. For it is most commonly supposed about speech that underlying its perception are processes and primitives no different from those of nonspeech (Crowder & Morton, 1969; Kuhl, 1981; Miller, 1977; Oden & Massaro, 1978; Stevens, 1975). All sounds, whether they convey phonetic information or not, are supposed to excite the same specializations of the auditory system and evoke such standard auditory primitives as pitch, loudness, and timbre. The perceived difference between a stop consonant and a Morse code signal are only in the particular values that are assigned to each component of a common set of perceptual primitives. There are no specifically phonetic primitives.

Since, on this view, phonetic structures are not marked as a distinct class, the child must learn, obviously by some cognitive process, which of the indefinitely many percepts that belong to a common auditory mode are relevant to phonetic communication and which are not, and then, more specifically, which percepts are to be assigned to which phonetic categories. In this respect, learning to perceive speech would be, in principle, something like learning Morse code. In practice, it would be very much harder, of course, because, unlike the dots and dashes of Morse code, the sounds of speech bear a peculiarly complex relation to the phonetic structures they convey. One might suppose that, in trying to come to grips with this relation, the child would be aided by the results of experimenting with the acoustic consequences of his own articulatory gestures. But here again the conventional view imposes a considerable cognitive burden, for it assumes that the primitives of the speech production system are not specific to speech, but are rather common to a general action mode. Therefore, the child would have to discover about the phonetically unmarked movements of his articulators, just as he would about the unmarked auditory percepts, which ones were relevant to phonetic communication and what the more specific nature of their relevance might be. And, since the motor primitives would have nothing in common with the perceptual primitives, they would have to be linked, and establishing those links would necessarily be a highly cognitive process, depending, for the most part, on unrestrained trial and error.

So, on the conventional view of speech perception, development would have to take place at a stage beyond the primitives that any module produces. Also, of course, it would be relatively unconstrained in regard to the nature of the signals, processes, or events, that become connected; so, in this respect, too, learning to communicate with speech would be like learning Morse code.

But there is another view of speech, one that has implications more in accord with the most obvious facts of language development (Liberman & Mattingly, 1985, 1989). On this view, there is a phonetic module, a biologically coherent system specialized for the production and perception of phonetic structures. The primitives of this module, common to production and perception, are the articulatory gestures that serve as the building blocks of the phonological system. Thus, the phonetic module produces primitive representations that are specifically phonetic, hence categorically set apart from all others. There is, then, no need for a cognitive process that enables the child to learn to attribute communicative significance to some arbitrarily defined class of otherwise undistinguished representations. Moreover, as in the case of the sound localization module, experience calibrates and recalibrates the perceptual representations by processes that are entirely internal to the module. It is by means of this calibration that the child adjusts to the subset of phonetic gestures appropriate to his own language and to the changing anatomy of his vocal tract. Such precognitive calibration acts on specifically phonetic primitives; the effect of experience is to guide that calibration, not to teach the child how to translate nonphonetic primitives into phonetic categories. A consequence is that the only experiences that count for the module are those that are relevant to the phonetic environment.

It is particularly appropriate that we consider this matter in a book that honors James Jenkins, because there is an experiment by Jenkins and his colleagues that provides relevant data (Miyawaki, Strange, Verbrugge, Liberman, & Jenkins, 1975). This experiment was designed to assess the effects of linguistic experience on phonetic perception, and to find the locus of the effect. Using synthetic approximations to the syllables [ra] and [la] that differed only in the extent and direction of the third-formant transition, Jenkins and his colleagues found, first, that native speakers of English reliably sorted the syllables properly and showed a pronounced peak in discrimination at a point on the acoustic continuum of third formant transitions that corresponded to the English phonetic boundary. Speakers of Japanese, on the other hand, discriminated the syllables very poorly, and their discrimination functions showed no signs of a peak at the point that corresponded to the English boundary. It is important that the two groups differed, not just in their ability to attach phonetic labels appropriately, but in the functions that were generated when they tried simply to discriminate one stimulus from another on any basis whatsoever. This indicates that the American listeners did not perceive these stimuli as the Japanese did, and then, by some cognitive process, apply the phonetic labels their language had taught them. Rather, the difference was in the precognitive, purely perceptual aspects of the process. And, obviously, the difference was a result of the differing linguistic experience of the groups, for, as is well known, the [r]–[l] distinction is not functional in Japanese. But Jenkins and his colleagues also undertook to find out just what it was that linguistic experience had affected. For that purpose they tested the ability of the American and Japanese listeners to discriminate the critical third-formant transition cue when, in isolation from the rest of the syllable, it did not sound like speech, but rather like a nonspeech 'bleat'. The result was that the two language groups discriminated the critical acoustic cue equally well. Thus, effect of linguistic experience was specifically on the phonetic system, not more generally on auditory perception.

The results of the experiment by Jenkins and his colleagues accord well with the view advanced in this chapter. Relevant linguistic experience acts on the internal workings of a phonetic module, with the result that the effect is on the representation itself, not on the way it becomes cognitively attached to phonetic labels or prototypes that exist at some further stage.

REFERENCES

Crowder, R. G. & Morton, J. (1969). Pre-categorical acoustic storage (PAS). *Perception & Psychophysics, 5,* 365–373.

Fodor, J. (1983). *The modularity of mind.* Cambridge, MA: MIT Press.

Hafter, E. R. (1984). Spatial hearing and the duplex theory: How viable is the model? In G. M. Edelman, W. E. Gall, & W. M. Cowan (Eds.), *Dynamic aspects of neocortical function* (pp. 425–448). New York: Wiley.

Knudsen, E. I. (1984). Synthesis of a neural map of auditory space in the owl. In G. M. Edelman, W. E. Gall, & W. M. Cowan (Eds.), *Dynamic aspects of neocortical function* (pp. 375–396). New York: Wiley.

Konishi, M., Takahashi, T. T., Wagner, H., Sullivan, W. E., & Carr, C. E. (1988). Neurophysiological and anatomical substrates of sound localization in the owl. In G. M. Edelman, W. E. Gall, & M. W. Cowan (Eds.), *Auditory function: Neurobiological Bases of Hearing,* (pp. 137–149). New York: Wiley.

Kuhl, P. K. (1981). Discrimination of speech by nonhuman animals: Basic auditory sensitivities conducive to the perception of speech-sound categories. *J. Acoust. Soc. Am., 70,* 340–349.

Liberman, A. M., & Mattingly, I. G. (1985). The motor theory of speech perception revised. *Cognition, 21,* 1–36.

Liberman, A. M., & Mattingly, I. G. (1989). A specialization for speech perception. *Science, 243,* 489–494.

Miller, J. D. (1977). Perception of speech sounds in animals: Evidence for speech processing by mammalian auditory mechanisms. In T. H. Bullock (ed.), *Recognition of complex acoustic signals* (Life Sciences Research Report 5, pp. 49–58). Berlin, Dahlem Konferenzen.

Miyawaki, K., Strange, W., Verbrugge, R., Liberman, A. M., & J. J. Jenkins. (1975). An effect of linguistic experience: The discrimination of [r] and [l] by native speakers of Japanese and English. *Perception & Psychophysics, 18*(5), 331–340.

Oden, G. C., & Massaro, D. W. (1978). Integration of featural information in speech perception. *Psychological Review, 85,* 172–191.

Stevens, K. N. (1975). The potential role of property detectors in the perception of consonants. In G. Fant & M. A. Tatham, (Eds.), *Auditory analysis and perception of speech,* New York: Academic Press.

5 A Note on Linguistic Nativism

Michael Studdert-Kennedy*
Haskins Laboratories

INTRODUCTION

Current discussions of language development seldom avoid distinguishing nature from nurture. Lip service may be paid to "epigenetic experience" or to "interaction between genes and environment," but the belief that we can divide the causes of development into two discrete, additive classes remains largely untouched. Even a casual scan of two fairly recent collections of essays on language acquisition (MacWhinney, 1986; Wanner & Gleitman, 1982) reveals recurrent words and phrases assuring us that the issue is not yet dead: "innate," "natural," "prepared to learn," "initial state," "genetic endowment," and so on.

These nativist concerns are a relic, at least in part, of the confrontation between behaviorism and generative linguistic theory that precipitated modern psycholinguistics. Not surprisingly then, the most concise and influential statements of the nativist position come from Chomsky himself. For example:

> Knowledge of language . . . should be regarded as a system of principles that develops in the mind by the fixing of values for certain parameters on the basis of experience. . . . the system of knowledge attained is largely preformed, as much a part of our biological endowment as is the organization of our body. (Chomsky, 1986, p. 272)

Knowledge of a particular language, or language competence, is thus said to be formed by interaction between an innate schema ("universal grammar") and the grammer of the language being learned. Universal grammar is defined as "a

---

*Also at the University of Connecticut and Yale University.

theory of the 'initial state' of the language faculty, prior to any linguistic experience" (Chomsky, 1986, pp. 3–4). "Innate" is evidently to be taken in its root meaning, "inborn, present at birth," or, putting a modern gloss on it, "determined solely by genes." Language performance (function) is then the product of a partly innate competence (form).

In my view, this position is untenable for at least two reasons: First, it is incompatible with what we know of the mechanisms of gene action. Second, it reverses the true course of development by running counter to the Darwinian principle that form grows from function, not function from form (e.g., Mayr, 1982, chapters 8–10). Universal grammar is not a prescription, or genetic program, for development, but is at most a partial and *a posteriori* description of the phenotypical product of the developmental system. (For a deeply argued critique of the concept of a genetic program and many other issues in the nature–nurture debate, see Oyama, 1985.) In other words, universal grammar, if isolable at all, is a consequence of development, not its cause.

In what follows I will attempt to justify this view by arguing that: (1) Development of the neural substrate supporting any complex behavior is induced, in part, by the behavior itself; (2) The invariant course of development observed in complex, species-specific behaviors is determined, in part, by invariants in the environment to which all members of a species are exposed; (3) The proper study of language development is a description and, where possible, functional analysis of its sequence—a postnatal "embryology" that makes no appeal to supposed genetic determinants. I will conclude by illustrating the approach with a brief, speculative account of the emergence of phonological segments through successive cycles of differentiation and integration. The account is offered as an alternative to the prevailing assumption that consonants and vowels, or at least their featural descriptors, are innately given axioms of a "universal phonetics" (Chomsky & Halle, 1968; for a fuller discussion, see Lindblom, MacNeilage, & Studdert–Kennedy, in preparation; Studdert–Kennedy, in press).

THE CONTROL OF DEVELOPMENT BY GENES AND BEHAVIOR

The Role of Regulatory Genes

The role of genes in development posed a seemingly insoluble puzzle to embryologists in the early 20th century (Raff & Kaufman, 1983). The puzzle was that an animal's entire complement of genes (its genome) was present in every cell of the embryo, yet the embryo differentiated into cells as diverse in structure and function as those of the eye, skin, liver. "Those who desire to make genetics the basis of the physiology of development will have to explain how an unchanging complex (of genes) can direct the course of an ordered developmental stream" (Lillie, 1927, p. 367).

The first steps toward an explanation were actually being taken at the time Lillie wrote by Ford and Huxley (1927). These researchers discovered genes that control the *rate* at which certain developmental processes occur. For example, eye color in the brackish-water shrimp, *Gammarus chevreuxi,* is determined by the balanced action of genes controlling the rate at which red and black coloring matter is deposited. Genetic variants also control the *time of onset* of eye pigment deposition. In a general discussion of timing effects, Ford and Huxley (1927) noted the human secondary sexual characteristic of greater sitting (relative to standing) height in females than in males; the difference arises because, although juvenile leg and arm growth proceed at the same rate in both sexes, limb growth is switched off earlier in the female. Mutations in genes that control the timing and ratios of growth rates in various parts of the skull are now believed to account for transformations of skull shape and size across evolutionarily related species, including chimpanzee and man, first described by D'Arcy Thompson (1917/1961, chapter 9; see also de Beer, 1951; Gould, 1977; Huxley, 1932).

Timing and rate genes were the first step toward the more general concept of regulatory genes (Goldschmidt, 1940; Raff & Kaufman, 1983; Waddington, 1966). Regulatory genes control the pattern and integration of structural gene expression over various parts of the developing organism, as well as its timing. In other words, they solve Lillie's problem. At apt times in the developmental sequence, regulatory genes select from the "unchanging complex" of genes, present in every cell, those that will be active for a certain period in particular regions of the embryo; they switch on and off the hemoglobin gene in a blood cell, the insulin gene in the pancreas, light-sensitive pigment genes in the eye, and so on. (The reason that every gene is present in every cell now becomes obvious. If they were not, the different genes appropriate for a given cell would have to be differentiated at the same time as their cell. Development would then require, it seems, a "master gene complex" to control the process throughout the embryo. But what would control the master gene complex? No end to this.)

Induction of Growth by the Spatio-temporal Context of Cells in the Embryo

In their role as switch mechanisms, regulatory genes contribute to embryonic induction. This is the process by which one part of an embryo influences a neighboring part, setting it on a course of development that it would not otherwise have followed (Waddington, 1966). For example, in amphibian embryos, the front tip of the brain induces formation of the nose organs; outgrowths a little farther back, later to be eyes, induce the overlying skin to form lenses; still farther back, parts of the brain induce ears, and so on (Waddington, 1966). That the process is indeed one of induction is demonstrated by experiments in which, for example, skin from another part of the embryo, grafted over the eyebud, comes to form a lens (Raff & Kaufman, 1983, chapter 5).

The interest of embryonic induction, for the present discussion, is threefold: First is its mechanism. Though far from fully understood, the process (like all embryological processes) entails a complex, cyclical sequence of interactions between genes and their surrounding nuclear sap and cytoplasm. If we enter the cause–effect cycle at the point of cell action, we find some genotropic (gene-controlling) substance in the cytoplasm switching on a regulator gene. Thus, "it is the 'state of the cytoplasm' that decides which particular gene locus will be active" (Waddington, 1966, p. 63). The gene then releases a "regulator substance" that interacts with the cytoplasm to set an operator gene into action; the operator gene controls the release of enzymes by a set of structural genes, and these control, by messenger RNAs, the production of proteins and the formation of tissues. In due course, the tissue gives rise to new genotropic substances, and the cycle of mutual selectivity between gene and cytoplasm begins again.

The important point here is that we cannot isolate any single component of the process as the key determinant. We may certainly say that genes control a certain process, and that is a convenient way to talk. We may no less conveniently say that the cytoplasm, or the gene's spatiotemporal context, controls the process, although that may be rather more difficult to pin down. But, in point of fact, neither statement is correct. Each component, without the other, is inert; both are essential to the emergence of form.

The second interest of embryonic induction lies in the interlocking processes of its temporal sequence. In the development of the amphibian eye, as already noted, cells first differentiate over a limited area at the front of the brain; they are then integrated into a cup, the eventual site of the retina; once sufficiently integrated, cells of the eye cup induce neighboring skin cells to differentiate into cells characteristic of a lens. An analogous process can be traced in the development of a limb: first a bud, then repeated cycles of differentiation and integration of cells to form bones, muscles and nerves; finally, differentiation by cell death and other processes of the digits. Such successive cycles of differentiation and integration may offer an instructive model for the development of the neural structures and processes that underlie language behavior, and indeed for the development of the behavior itself.

Particularly important for the present argument is that gene action and the consequent processes of cell differentiation, growth, and integration may be induced by postnatal behavior. The third interest of induction then is that the process does not stop at birth, nor are its determinants confined to the internal physicochemical processes sketched here.

Postnatal Induction of Neural Growth by Behavior

An extensive literature attests to the effect of early sensory and sensorimotor experience on the fine structure of the visual system, and to the sensitive phases during which experience is most likely to have effects (e.g., Blakemore &

Cooper, 1970; Held, 1985; Spinelli & Jensen, 1979). Induction processes, set in motion by the organism's own postnatal activity, also stimulate development in neural structures necessary for motor control. For example, certain motor areas of the adult opossum brain are organized into neural columns, or barrels, corresponding to the digits of its forelimbs. The columns are absent at birth, when the infant (essentially an extrauterine embryo) enters its mother's pouch. If one limb is cut off at birth, neural columns for the digits on that limb do not develop (Johnson, Hamilton, Hsung, & Ulinski, 1972). Evidently, differentiation of the columns is normally induced by the activity of the digits that they will ultimately control. Analogous effects occur in the cortical representation of mouse vibrissae (Durham & Wolsey, 1985).

We may extend the inductive process, by inference, to the structures underlying certain communicative behaviors in birds. For example, the mallard duckling responds to its mother's call immediately after hatching. However, the response depends on the duckling having emitted its own (dissimilar) sounds during its last days in the egg, when it had already begun to breath air. For if the egg is opened early by an experimenter and the duckling is prevented from making these sounds (either by fitting a rubber band around its bill or by blocking its syrinx with a plastic substance that is later absorbed), the duckling, though otherwise normal, no longer responds to its mother's call upon hatching (Gottlieb, 1976). Evidently, differentiation of the neural structures underlying response to the maternal call is normally induced by the duckling's own bill clapping. If behavioral induction is engaged to guide vocal communication in a precocial species, with a primitive call system essential to predator avoidance in the first days of life, we should not be surprised if it is also engaged for an altricial species with many years of infant and juvenile dependency and the most complex system of vocal communication known.

In fact, a variety of evidence for postnatal behavioral induction of the neural substrate for language is already on hand. Here we should bear in mind that the human infant, like the infant opossum, is little more than an extrauterine embryo during its early postnatal months, and that infancy is followed by a long period of childhood during which the brain continues to grow. Lenneberg collated evidence for a rapid drop in cortical cell density during the first 2 years of life, and for a concomitant increase in dendritic arborization, with a notably rapid increase in the neuropil around Broca's area between 6 and 24 months (1967, Fig. 4.6, pp. 160–161). Density of the neuropil continues to increase through puberty, and Huttenlocker (1979) has shown that, in human frontal cortex, the increase is accompanied by an increase in synaptic density over the same period (see also Changeux, 1985). Presumably, all this growth is under both genetic and environmental control: we should not expect the same pattern of growth in a species with a different life-cycle.

Postnatal development of cortical structure, more directly related to language, can also be inferred from event-related potentials (ERPs), recorded from electrodes on the scalp. Several studies by Neville and her associates (Neville, 1985, in press) have compared ERPs in children and adults with radically different language backgrounds: English and American Sign Language (ASL). In one study, flashes of light were presented either foveally or at eight degrees of visual angle into the periphery, while ERPs were recorded from frontal, anterior temporal, and temporal electrodes. The subjects were either normal, English-speaking adults or congenitally deaf, but otherwise neurologically normal, adults whose first language was ASL. ERPs to peripheral (but not foveal) light flashes were strikingly and significantly different over the *auditory* anterior temporal and temporal regions for hearing and deaf subjects. The results suggest that auditory cortex, deprived of auditory input, may be coopted to process visual information. That the differences between normal and deaf subjects were confined to the visual periphery is consistent with the fact that the deaf must rely on vision to detect important events in the periphery, including patterns of hand shape and movement in ASL (Siple, 1978). Other studies have shown significant ERP differences between English-speaking and ASL adults while reading English; between native and nonnative ASL signers while viewing signs; and in a nonlanguage task (matching line drawings to photographs) between normal and deaf children, and between deaf children who were and were not learning ASL.

These studies warn us to be wary of the modish metaphors of "hard wiring" and "software programs." They recall a dictum of the great English neurophysi-ologist, Henry Maudsley: "The nervous system of man and animals is moulded structurally according to the modes of its functional exercise" (Maudsley, 1876, p. 41). In other words, neural structure emerges with neural function. Accord-ingly, the invariant course of development, typical of a particular species, may be guided as much by invariants of behavior, in response to an invariant environment, as by the species' characteristic genome.

THE INHERITANCE OF INVARIANT ENVIRONMENTS

None of the foregoing should be interpreted as denying the occurrence of genetically determined characters, many of them traceable to a single gene. In fact, McCusick (1983) tabulates 1,637 single-gene disorders in humans, includ-ing Huntington's disease, phenylketonuria and color-blindness. However, the invariant phenotypical expression of these genes depends as much on their invariant biochemical context as on the genes themselves.

For example, phenylketonuria is a biochemical disorder in which certain amino acids, due to metabolic failure, build up in the body and lead to mental retardation. The defect can be corrected by restricting a child's diet to foods that do not contain the amino acids. The defect would never have occurred, its gene silent, had the diet not contained the offending amino acids in the first place. Of course, the cure merely relieves the symptoms, not the underlying metabolic defect. However, nothing in principle, though no doubt much in practice, prevents us from possibly discovering other biochemical properties in the child's cells that might be altered, so that the metabolic disorder never occurred. Similarly, nothing in principle prevents us from discovering and adjusting properties of the cytoplasmic regulatory substances involved in genetic control of the deposition of light-sensitive pigments in the eye, and so preventing color-blindness. In short, although genetic engineering may focus on the gene or the chromosome, that is because these components are more readily isolated than the equally important biochemical components of the cell, or of the tissues that the cells compose.

My general point here then is that reliance on environmental constancies as a means of ensuring normal development is a commonplace of ontogeny and evolution. An obvious behavioral example comes from the extensive work on song learning in passerine birds (e.g., Marler, 1970; Kroodsma, 1971; Petrinovich & Baptista, 1987). If a male white-crowned sparrow is hatched and reared in isolation, it will sing, as an adult, a crude "insect-like" pattern, only roughly similar in structure to the song of its normal peers. However, if the isolate is exposed to full song, during a sensitive phase from about 10 to 100 days after hatching, it will then sing as an adult (some 2–8 months later) the full dialect to which it has been exposed. Thus, normal song development depends on an invariance in the growing bird's normal environment—exposure to full song during a brief period as a nestling and fledgling. (Anyone inclined to view the unexposed isolate's crude song as embodying the "universal grammar" of white-crowned sparrow song might reflect on the likely content of a human universal grammar, as revealed by a similarly isolated human infant.)

As a further example of the role of environmental invariance in development, consider the phenomena of filial and sexual imprinting in precocial birds. A mallard duckling, even if deprived of sensitivity to its mother's call by an experimenter, will follow it by visual cues to the water. Following is essential not only for immediate survival, but also for species identification and later sexual behavior (though the two functions may have different sensitive phases; Bateson, 1982). As is well known, ducklings, goslings, and chicks will readily follow almost any slow-moving object, not only their mothers, during a limited sensitive phase. Errors in imprinting may then have disastrous effects on later behavior. For example, Vidal (1976) has shown that a domestic cock, imprinted on a slow-moving red plastic cube attached to a rotary motor, will later, when sexually mature, attempt to mount and copulate with the cube. Surely, if anything were coded solely in the genes, we would expect it to be the mating behavior on which the reproductive fitness of an animal depends. Yet, even in the lowly chicken, evolution has entrusted normal development of this behavior to the environment no less than to the genes. Perhaps I should add that imprinting errors are not confined to domestic animals, "all out of shape from toc-to-top," due to a history of inbreeding, but may be induced in wild species, such as zebra and Bengali finches (Immelmann & Suomi, 1981).

These bizarre ontogenetic diversions can occur because evolution relies for its effects not only on genes, but on normally invariant environments. This is an important point because it breaks the habit of thought by which we see the invariant characters of a species as genetic ("universal grammar"), its variable characteristics as environmental (different languages). In fact, genes are highly variable and environments are often effectively constant. During periods of environmental stasis, genetic variation in a population will not be picked up, and the phenotype will remain relatively stable. During periods of environmental change, genetic variation will be exploited, leading to rapid diversification of the species' gene pool and, perhaps, to speciation. Hence, the "punctuated equilibria" of evolution, posited by Eldredge and Gould (1972; Eldredge, 1986).

In short, an animal inherits both its genome and the environment in which the genome can take effect. Each is tailored to the other. (In this respect, as Oyama [1985, p. 131] has remarked, the analogy of biological to social inheritance is rather exact: Children typically inherit not only their parents' wealth, but the social position from which to exploit it, or be exploited.) Initially, the biological environment is that of the embryo, later that of the world in which the animal moves. Of course, the internal environment of the embryo is narrowly physicochemical; but so, too, in its ultimate mode of action on the organism, is the external. Just how an animal's activity induces changes in its neural structure, we do not know. But we know that it does, and that physicochemical changes inside the animal must mediate those changes.

Finally, I should re-emphasize two obvious but important facts. First, gene action does not cease at birth. Genes, present at conception, contribute to every stage of development, from the first division of the fertilized egg to death. That is evident from the simple fact that each species has its characteristic life-cycle. Second, gene expression is *contingent:* it depends on the current maturational state of the organism, including the effects of its present and past environments. The expression of genetic susceptibility to certain diseases—lung cancer, emphysema, heart disease, and so on—is normally delayed to a relatively late age, and depends on the extent of an individual's exposure to a particular environment. Lung cancer is rare among nonindustrial, nonsmoking peoples. But the genes that contribute to its development are presumably available in the gene pool. Another example is the increasingly early age of puberty in developed societies. Among the hunter-gatherer Dobe !Kung, girls reach menarche between 16 and 17 (Howell, 1979); in modern societies, menarche now occurs at about 12.5 years (Lancaster & Lancaster, 1983). Onset of puberty is certainly under genetic control, but it is also sensitive to environmental contingencies. Among the environmental factors contributing to the change is diet. An enriched diet evidently assures earlier achievement of the level of physical resources necessary to sustain pregnancy, childbirth, and lactation, and so induces earlier onset of the menstrual cycle.

If we extend the notion of delayed contingent gene expression to language, our enchantment with the "initial state" begins to fade. Presumably, the genes that will ultimately contribute to language development are present at birth, as they have been since conception. But their expression depends on the child's exposure to a language. If the child is profoundly deaf, or otherwise drastically deprived of language input (e.g., Curtiss, 1977), spoken language will not develop at all, or only with much difficulty. More than this, when language does begin to develop, it necessarily does so through a particular language, and each new stage is contingent on prior stages: Babbled syllables precede words, words precede sentences, simple sentences precede complex, and so on. Thus, whatever is universal in languages is neither prior to nor separable from, but integral to and simultaneous with, the development of a particular language. Function and form emerge hand in hand. In this respect, language resembles any other species-specific behavior, of which the development is determined by ecological and genetic universals of the species.

LANGUAGE AS SPECIES-SPECIFIC, BUT NOT INNATE

The argument of the preceding pages is entirely compatible with Chomsky's view of language as being "as much a part of our biological endowment as is the organization of our body" (Chomsky, 1986, p. 272), a view with which I agree. However, the argument is also compatible with the view that language is innate only in the sense that it is species-specific—that is, developmentally fixed in the species, and determined by genetic and ecological conditions normally common to all its members. This is a view that Chomsky explicitly rejects:

> Obviously the questions of innateness and species-specificity are distinct. It has been alleged that I and others have taken "innate" and "species-specific" to be "synonyms". . . . I am unaware of any examples of such confusion, although there are a number of articles refuting it. (Chomsky, 1986, p. 48, fn. 13)

By "innate," as we have already seen (p. 2), Chomsky means "preformed, present at birth, determined solely by genes." His views are therefore fundamentally at odds not only with the simple fact that *nothing* is determined solely by genes, but also with standard embryological theory from which preformationism was banished even before Darwin wrote (Gould, 1977). His views are also inimical to research that seeks to establish the observable conditions of language development. For, as Bateson (1982) has remarked, discussing the relation between behavioral development and evolution: "The introduction of 'innate behavior' or 'innate rules' into the vocabulary simply compounds the difficulties of doing decent empirical research" (p. 140). This is because, by labeling a character "innate," we discourage further study of its nature and origin.

Heuristically, the wisest course to follow, when we are tempted to invoke the term, is to ask how the character might have become "innate" in the first place. How did it get into the genes? What conditions might have picked up a particular genetic variant, or suite of variants, and fostered its radiation through the population? Speculative though this enterprise may be, we are not entirely without recourse, for several reasons.

First, every evolutionary change is a change in development, so that the complex, polygenic forms we now observe are necessarily the product of successive ontogenies. A partial record of their evolution may then be preserved in their ontogeny (Darwin, 1859/1964, chapter 13; Garstang, 1922; Gould, 1977; Raff & Kaufman, 1983). Second, language does not develop by maturation alone (cf. Borer & Wexler, 1987). Its development will not go forward without specifically linguistic input. Third, language develops postnatally, so that its course is open to systematic observation. Finally, language behavior is a complex, hierarchic structure, of which the development is rich in sequential dependencies: syllables and formulaic phrases before phonemes and features (see following), words before simple sentences, simple sentences before lexical categories, lexical categories before complex sentences, and so on. The sequence may lend itself to description in terms of recurrent, overlapping cycles of differentiation and integration.

The proper study of language development then is a sort of postnatal embryology of behavior, a description of the sequence of conditions, both inside and outside the organism, both linguistic and extralinguistic, that induce language growth. Just how language-specific genes and the environment that controls their expression contribute to this development is so far beyond the scope of present knowledge that we have little to gain from substituting "innate" for a frank admission of ignorance. Rather, it is precisely by rejecting the fiats of nativist dogma that we may be led into a deeper understanding of the nature and function of linguistic form.

AN ILLUSTRATION: EARLY DEVELOPMENT
OF PHONOLOGICAL FORM

The Nativist Approach and an Alternative

The main reason for studying the early development of phonology is to understand the nature and function of its forms by discovering their origin. What prelinguistic perceptual capacities of the infant are harnessed for linguistic use? What properties of the vocal apparatus (or the hand) both force and permit language to take on its characteristic formational structure by which an unlimited lexicon is built from a finite set of phonetic elements? How is the link forged between an auditory (or visual) pattern and the articulatory patterns from which it arose? We cannot make headway in answering these questions by positing innate feature detectors, specialized for speech perception (e.g., Eimas, 1982), or an "innately specified" perceptuomotor link (Liberman & Mattingly, 1985, p. 3). The effect of such proposals is to discourage, if not proscribe, empirical study of the questions.

The main basis for the claim of innate, speech-specific mechanisms of perceptual analysis was the large body of work initiated by the studies of Eimas and his colleagues (Eimas, Siqueland, Jusczyk, & Vigorito, 1971; see also Eimas, 1974, 1975). This work showed that, during the first 6 months of life, infants could discriminate virtually any speech sound contrast on which they were tested, in a fashion predictable from studies of adult categorical perception (see Aslin, Pisoni, & Jusczyk, 1983, for review). However, the theoretical import of this work was undermined by demonstrations of (1) categorical perception of nonspeech sounds (e.g. Pastore et al., 1977), and (2) categorical perception of speech sounds by chinchillas and macaques (Kuhl, 1987).

Other considerations also cast doubt on the claim. First are two curious facts: (1) None of the studies of infant discriminative capacity shows any evidence for developmental change over the first 8 months of life; (2) Older children, even up to the age of 5 or 6, make substantial numbers of perceptual errors on consonant contrasts (voicing, nasality, place of articulation) that cause no difficulty for infants (Barton, 1980; cf. Studdert–Kennedy, 1986). Taken with the findings from the animal studies just mentioned, these two facts invite the inference that studies of infant speech discrimination are simply assessing the psychoacoustic capacities, shared with many other animals, on which speech perception is based. Notice, moreover, that we have no grounds for believing that the infant applies these capacities to the segmental analysis of speech, outside the constraints of the laboratory, until syllables and segments begin to take on their communicative function in the second half of the first year of life.

A second consideration that casts doubt on the claim of innate segmental analysis is that it reverses the normal course of development by proposing that speech perception develops from the specific to the general, rather than from the general to the specific. The child is said, in effect, to build perceptual syllables by integrating segments or features without having first derived these components by differentiation of the syllable. Exactly the same objection may be raised to the claim for "an internal, innately specified vocal-tract synthesizer" (Liberman & Mattingly, 1985, p. 26) that automatically analyzes the speech signal into its gestural components.

The latter proposal has the further difficulty that it leaves unexplained the gap between a child's capacity to perceive and to produce speech. The gap is attested by the diverse articulatory strategies that children adopt in their early attempts at "difficult" words. These strategies include substitution of gestures (e.g., stops for fricatives), assimilation to a single place of articulation of consonants within a word that have different places of articulation (consonant harmony), and outright avoidance of lexical items containing segments that fall outside the current repertoire of articulatory routines (Menn, 1983; Schwartz, 1988).

An alternative to these nativist proposals might trace the gradual development of linguistic function, as the child discovers the structure of speech, through the interplay of perception and production. In this process the roles of production and perception are not equal. To speak correctly, a child must perceive correctly, but the reverse does not hold. For example, certain victims of cerebral palsy never speak, but still learn to understand speech, and even to read and write (Fourcin, 1975). The development of perception precedes and presumably guides the development of production, and from the process there normally emerges the perceptuomotor link.

Early Perceptual Development

We have two anchor points for the early development of phonetic perception, one at the beginning and one toward the end of the first year. For the path between these points we must largely rely, at present, on inferences from the development of production. At birth, an infant prefers its mother's voice to a stranger's (DeCasper & Fifer, 1980), provided she speaks with normal prosody (Mehler, Bertoncini, Barrière, & Jassik–Gerschenfeld, 1978). The preference seems to be induced by intrauterine exposure to the low frequencies of the mother's voice (DeCasper & Spence, 1986; Spence & DeCasper, 1987). Four-day-old infants distinguish between utterances spoken in their native language and utterances spoken in a language they have not previously heard, even when the speech is low-pass filtered at 400 Hz (Mehler et al., 1988). Apparently, then, infants' earliest sensitivity, induced by exposure to the sounds of the surrounding language, is to the rhythm and melody of speech.

By the middle of the first year, infants become sensitive to the boundaries between clauses in their native language (Hirsh–Pasek et al., 1987; Jusczyk, 1989), and by the 11th month to the boundaries between words (Kemler Nelson, 1989). By this time they have also begun to lose their earlier sensitivity to segmental phonetic contrasts in an alien language (Werker & Tees, 1984), provided these contrasts can be assimilated to native phonological contrasts (Best, McRoberts, & Sithole, 1988). This shift in attentional focus toward phonetic contrasts that serve a linguistic function in the surrounding language seems to require that the year-old infant already possess at least a modest receptive lexicon (cf. Benedict, 1979), analyzed into recurrent segmental components. Thus, perceptual development over the first year entails differentiation of the rhythmic prosodic structure of speech into syllables, the units of speech rhythm, followed by differentiation of the syllable into subsyllabic components. For insight into the nature of these components and into the later integrative processes by which phonological segments (consonants and vowels) ultimately emerge, we must turn to the development of speech production.

Early Development of Production

A detailed account of the development of speech production is well beyond the scope of this chapter. Here, I offer no more than a few highlights to illustrate the proposed sequence from prelinguistic cries and mouthings to the emergence of phonological segments as the child's lexicon grows. I assume that each overt step in the development of production is grounded in an earlier, corresponding, covert step in the development of perception.

We can discern six broad stages (Table 5.1). Stark (1986) divides the period before the onset of babbling into three stages: reflexive crying and vegetative sounds, cooing and laughter, and vocal play. Reflexive crying has, of course, a communicative, but nonlinguistic function. Cries, executed with a relatively unconstricted vocal tract, typically have the formant structure of low to mid-front vowels. Vegetative sounds, the grunts, sighs, clicks, pops, and lip smacks associated with breathing and feeding are formed with either an open, vowel-like or a constricted, consonant-like configuration of the vocal tract. The cooing, or comfort, sounds of Stark's second stage, have the form of a nasal consonant or a nasalized vowel. Thus, around the end of the fifth month, the infant already has a modest repertoire of protoconsonantal and protovocalic elements that can be marshaled for linguistic use.

During the following stage of vocal play, three important changes lay the ground for the onset of babbling. First, sounds begin to shift their function (a typical evolutionary and ontogenetic process): they become "divorced from their

TABLE 5.1
Stages[a] of development in vocal sound production

Stage	Description	Approximate age of onset (month)
1	Reflexive crying and vegetative sounds	At birth
2	Cooing and laughter	2–5
3	Vocal play	3–7
4	Reduplicated, canonical babbling (integration of prelinguistic patterns of movement into syllables[b])	6–10
5	Variegated babbling and first words (differentiation of syllables into component gestures[b])	11–15
6	Integration of recurrent sound–gesture patterns into consonants and vowels[b]	18–30

Compiled and adapted from Oller (1980, 1986) and Stark (1986).
[a]The sequence of stages is consistent across children, but the age of onset varies, and within a child the stages may overlap extensively.
[b]For an explanation of these hypothesized processes, see text.

previous cry, vegetative or comfort sound contexts, and are used in a variety of communicative situations" (Stark, 1986, p. 159). Second, sounds begin to form longer and more complex sequences: strings of consonant-like clicks, trills and friction noises, or of vowel-like resonances with increasingly varied pitch and quality. Third (an important combinatorial change), the infant begins to superimpose movements of tongue, jaw, and lips on the laryngeal actions associated with cry (Koopmans–van Beinum & Van der Stelt, 1986), so that the proportion of supraglottal to glottal articulations gradually increases (Holmgren, Lindblom, Aurelius, Jalling, & Zetterstrom, 1986).

The integration of laryngeal and upper articulator action leads into the fourth stage, canonical babbling, which typically begins, often quite abruptly, in the seventh or eighth month. Oller (1980, 1986) describes several acoustic properties that distinguish the canonical consonant–vowel, or consonant–vowel–consonant, syllable from earlier vocalizations. The most characteristic property is that the relative timing of the closing and opening phases of a syllable resembles that of adult syllables. Perhaps this is not surprising, since we now know that infant babbling is entrained by adult speech; babbling does not emerge at the normal age in deaf infants (Oller & Eilers, 1988; Oller, Eilers, Bull, & Carney, 1985; Stoel–Gammon & Otomo, 1986). (However, "babbling" with the fingers may emerge on schedule in deaf infants exposed to ASL [Newport & Meier, 1985; Petitto & Marentette, 1989].)

The adult-like properties of canonical babble invite phonetic transcription and, indeed, the reliability of transcription increases with the onset of babble. However, we should not be misled into supposing that the infant has independent control of the consonant-like and vowel-like parts of a syllable. Strings of babbled syllables tend to be reduplicative, using the same points of closure and the same open configurations: [bababa], [nenene], [dIdIdI]. Thus, the rhythmic lowering and raising of the jaw occurs with little or no independent movement of the tongue (Davis & MacNeilage, 1990).

In fact, it is precisely when the child begins to differentiate the closing and opening gestures of successive syllables that it enters the fifth stage of "variegated" (Oller, 1980) syllable strings, giving the impression of variations in consonant and/or vowel ([nenI], [mænə], [dɛdi]). About this time the child (already sensitive to word boundaries, as we have noted) makes its first recognizable attempts at adult words and phrases, usually (in English children) consisting of one or two syllables. Typically, a child selects for imitation words that match the "vocal motor schemes" (McCune & Vihman, 1987) of its current babble, and avoids words that do not (Menn, 1983). The two modes of output, words and babble, proceed concurrently, often for many months, with words gradually coming to predominate.

Each word or phrase seems to be a "prosodic unit" (Macken, 1979), its production planned as a whole. Evidence for this comes, for example, from "consonant harmony," or "assimilation at a distance" (Menn, 1983), by which a child fails to execute different places and/or manners of articulation within the same word: *dog* [gɔg]; *lady* [jeiji], *duck* [tʌt]. The data of Davis and MacNeilage (1990), collected on a single child from 14 to 20 months of age, are replete with instances of both "consonant" and "vowel" assimilation. At the same time, these authors report an inverse relation between the two processes: When the child succeeded in combating assimilation in the open phases of the syllable, she often failed to do so in the closing phases and vice versa. This demonstrates an incipient segregation of the opening and closing phases of a syllable. Thus, the principal achievement of the fifth stage is internal modification of the integrated syllable by differentiation of its phases into their component gestures. These gestures are the developing forms of the patterns of vocal tract constriction that will constitute the units of an adult phonology (Browman & Goldstein, 1986, 1989).

The sixth and final stage of the hypothesized path from mouth sounds to segments entails the integration of gestural patterns of syllabic constriction and opening into the cohesive perceptuomotor structures we know as consonants and vowels (Studdert–Kennedy, 1987). There seem to be two aspects of this process. First is the grouping of all instances of a sound–gesture pattern into a single class, presumably on the basis of their perceptuomotor, or phonetic, similarity. Second is the distributional analysis and grouping of these sound–gesture patterns into higher-order classes (consonants and vowels) on the basis of their functions as onsets, nuclei, and codas, in the structure of syllables (cf. Lindblom, 1989; Lindblom, MacNeilage, & Studdert–Kennedy, 1984). Thus, the effect of this final integrative step is the formation of discrete articulatory control structures, the phonemic elements of lexical representations. The function of these structures, insulated from mutual interference during the planning of an utterance, may be to facilitate the summoning and rapid, successive activation of recurrent articulatory routines (Menn, 1983) in multiword utterances.

On this account, then, neither consonants and vowels, nor their featural descriptors, are innately given axioms of universal phonetics. Rather, they are the products of a species-specific developmental system, from which endogenous and exogenous factors cannot be disentangled. We have no reason to believe that the development of syntactic competence, or indeed of any cognitive capacity, is less subject to interlocking genetic and environmental contingencies.

CONCLUSION

I have argued that appeals to "innate" determinants of language development are little more than verbal devices to cover our ignorance. Moreover, standard nativist accounts of language development are incompatible with what we know of gene action, and they fly in the face of the evolutionary and ontogenetic principle by which form grows from function rather than function from form.

I have proposed instead that we view language universals as the product of a species-specific developmental system that relies on environmental no less than genetic invariants. I have attempted to illustrate the approach with a speculative sketch of the process by which phonological segments might emerge from prelinguistic perceptual and motor capacities, through successive cycles of differentiation and integration.

Implicit in this account is the notion that the extent of gestural overlap within and between syllables ("coarticulation") should be greater in children whose consonants and vowels have not yet, or have only recently, emerged as encapsulated units of motor control than in older children or adults. Also, if we take adult segmental speech errors as evidence for the functional status of consonants and vowels in the planning of speech production (e.g., Shattuck–Hufnagel, 1983, 1987), we might expect that nonsystematic segmental errors would not occur in very early child speech, but would gradually increase as consonants and vowels crystallize and as adult-like planning processes come into play. Tests of these hypotheses will require systematic study of the gestural organization of early child speech (e.g., Nittrouer, Studdert–Kennedy, & McGowan, 1989) and of the development of adult-like patterns of speech error (e.g., Stemberger, 1989).

REFERENCES

Aslin, R. N., Pisoni, D. B., & Jusczyk, P. W. (1983). Auditory development and speech perception in infancy. In M. Haith & J. Campos (Eds.), *Carmichael's handbook of child psychology: Infancy and developmental psychology* (pp. 573–687). New York: Wiley.

Barton, D. (1980). Phonemic perception in children. In G. H. Yeni–Komshian, J. F. Kavanagh, & C. A. Ferguson (Eds.), *Child phonology* (Vol. 2, pp. 97–116). New York: Academic Press.

Bateson, P. P. G. (1982). Behavioral development and evolutionary processes. In King's College Sociobiology Group, Cambridge (Eds.), *Current Problems in sociobiology* (pp. 133–151). New York: Cambridge University Press.

Benedict, H. (1979). Early lexical development: Comprehension and production. *Journal of Child Language, 6,* 183–200.

Best, C. T., McRoberts, G. W., & Sithole, N. W. (1988). Examination of perceptual reorganization for nonnative speech contrasts: Zulu click discrimination by English-speaking adults and infants. *Journal of Experimental Psychology: Human Perception and Performance, 14,* 345–360.

Blakemore, C., & Cooper, G. F. (1970). Development of the brain depends on the visual environment. *Nature, 228,* 477–480.

Borer, H., & Wexler, K. (1987). The maturation of syntax. In T. Roeper & E. Williams (Eds.), *Parameter setting* (pp. 123–172). Dordrecht, Holland: D. Reidel.

Browman, C., & Goldstein, L. (1986). Towards an articulatory phonology. *Phonological Yearbook, 3,* 219–252.

Browman, C., & Goldstein, L. (1989). Articulatory gestures as phonological units. *Phonology, 6* 201–251.

Changeux, J. P. (1985). *Neuronal man.* New York: Pantheon,

Chomsky, N. (1986). *Knowledge of language.* New York: Praeger Special Studies.

Chomsky, N., & Halle, M. (1968). *The sound pattern of English.* New York: Harper & Row.

Curtiss, S. (1977). *Genie: A psycholinguistic study of a modern-day "wild child."* New York: Academic Press.

Darwin, C. (1859/1964). *On the origin of species* (Facsimile edition). Cambridge, MA: Harvard University Press.

Davis, B. L., & MacNeilage, P. F. (1990). Acquisition of correct vowel production: A quantitative case study. *Journal of Speech and Hearing Research, 33,* 16–27.

de Beer, G. R. (1951). *Embryos and ancestors.* Oxford, England: Clarendon Press.

DeCasper, A. J., & Fifer, W. P. (1980). Of human bonding: Newborns prefer their mothers' voices. *Science, 208,* 1174–1176.

DeCasper, A. J., & Spence, M. J. (1986). Prenatal maternal speech influences newborns' perception of speech sounds. *Infant Behavior and Development, 8,* 133–150.

Durham, D., & Wolsey, T. A. (1985). Functional organization in cortical barrels of normal and vibrissae-damaged mice. *Journal of Comparative Neurology, 235,* 97–110.

Eimas, P. D. (1974). Auditory and linguistic processing of cues for place of articulation in infants. *Perception and Psychophysics, 16,* 513–521.

Eimas, P. D. (1975). Auditory and phonetic coding of the cues for speech: Discrimination of the /r-l/ distinction by young infants. *Perception and Psychophysics, 18,* 341–347.

Eimas, P. D. (1982). Speech perception: A view of the initial state and perceptual mechanisms. In J. Mehler, E. C. T. Walker, & M. Garrett (Eds.), *Perspectives on mental representations.* Hillsdale, NJ: Lawrence Erlbaum Associates.

Eimas, P. D., Siqueland, E. R., Jusczyk, P., & Vigorito, J. (1971). Speech perception in infants. *Science, 171,* 303–306.

Eldredge, N. (1986). *Time frames.* New York: Simon & Schuster.

Eldredge, N., & Gould, S. J. (1972). Punctuated equilibria: An alternative to phyletic gradualism. In T. J. M. Schopf (Ed.), *Models in paleobiology* (pp. 82–115). San Francisco: Freeman, Cooper.

Ford, E. B., & Huxley, J. S. (1927). Mendelian genes and rates of development in *Gammarus chevreuxi. British Journal of Experimental Biology, 5,* 112–121.

Fourcin, A. J. (1975). Language development in the absence of expressive speech. In E. H. Lenneberg & E. Lenneberg (Eds.), *Foundations of language development* (Vol. 2, pp. 263–268). New York: Academic Press.

Garstang, W. (1922). The theory of recapitulation: A critical restatement of the biogenetic law. *Journal of the Linnaean Society, 35,* 81–101.

Goldschmidt, R. (1940). *The material basis of evolution.* New Haven: Yale University Press.

Gottlieb, G. (1976). Early development of species-specific auditory perception in birds. In G. Gottlieb (Ed.), *Neural and behavioral specificity* (pp. 237–280). New York: Macmillan.

Gould, S. J. (1977). *Ontogeny and phylogeny.* Cambridge, MA: Belknap Press.

Held, R. (1985) Binocular vision—behavioral and neuronal development. In J. Mehler & R. Fox (Eds.), *Neonate cognition* (pp. 37–44). Hillsdale, NJ: Lawrence Erlbaum Associates.

Hirsh-Pasek, K., Kemler, Nelson, D. G., Jusczyk, P. W., Cassidy, K. W., Druss, B., & Kennedy, L. (1987). Clauses are perceptual units for young infants. *Cognition, 26,* 269–286.

Holmgren, K., Lindblom, B., Aurelius, G., Jalling, B., & Zetterstrom, R. (1986). On the phonetics of infant vocalization. In B. Lindblom & R. Zetterstrom (Eds.), *Precursors of early speech* (pp. 51–63). Basingstoke, England: Macmillan.

Howell, N. (1979). *Demography of the Dobe !Kung.* New York: Academic Press.

Huttenlocher, P. R. (1979). Synaptic density in human frontal cortex—developmental changes and effects of aging. *Brain Research, 163,* 195–205.

Huxley, J. S. (1932). *Problems in relative growth.* New York: Dial Press.

Immelmann, K., & Suomi, S. F. (1981). Sensitive phases in development. In K. Immelmann, G. W. Barlow, L. Petrinovich, & M. Main (Eds.), *Behavioral development* (pp. 295–431). New York: Cambridge University Press.

Johnson, J. I., Hamilton, T. C., Hsung, J. C., & Ulinski, P. S. (1972). Gracile nucleus absent in adult opossums after leg removal in infancy. *Brain Research, 38,* 421–424.

Jusczyk, P. W. (1989, April). *Perception of cues to clausal units in native and non-native languages.* Paper presented at meeting of the Society for Research in Child Development, Kansas City, MO.

Kemler, Nelson, D. G. (1989, April). *Developmental trends in infants' sensitivity to prosodic cues correlated with linguistic units.* Paper presented at a meeting of the Society for Research in Child Development, Kansas City, MO.

Koopmans–van Beinum, F. J., & Van der Stelt, J. M. (1986). Early stages in the development of speech movements. In B. Lindlbom & R. Zetterstrom (Eds.), *Precursors of early speech* (pp. 37–50). Basingstoke, England: Macmillan.

Kroodsma, D. (1981). Ontogeny of bird song. In K. Immelmann, G. W. Barlow, L. Petrinovich & M. Main (Eds.), *Behavioral development* (pp. 518–532). New York: Cambridge University Press.

Kuhl, P. K. (1987). Perception of speech and sound in early infancy. In P. Salapatek & L. Cohen (Eds.), *Handbook of infant perception* (Vol. 2, pp. 275–382). New York: Academic Press.

Lancaster, J. B., & Lancaster, C. S. (1983). Parental investment: The hominid adaptation. In D. J. Ortner (Ed.), *How humans adapt: A biocultural odyssey* (pp. 33–56). Washington, DC: Smithsonian Institution Press.

Lenneberg, E. H. (1967). *Biological foundations of language.* New York: Wiley.

Liberman, A. M., & Mattingly, I. G. (1985). The motor theory of speech perception revised. *Cognition, 21,* 1–36.

Lindblom, B. (1989). Some remarks on the origin of the "phonetic code." In C. von Euler, I. Lundberg, & G. Lennerstrand (Eds.), *Brain and reading* (pp. 27–44). Basingstoke, England: Macmillan.

Lindblom, B., MacNeilage, P., & Studdert–Kennedy, M. (1984). Self-organizing processes and the explanation of language universals. In B. Butterworth, B. Comrie, & O. Dahl (Eds.), *Explanations for language universals* (pp. 181–203). The Hague: Mouton.

Lindblom, B., MacNeilage, P. F., & Studdert–Kennedy, M. (in preparation). *Evolution of spoken language.*

Lillie, F. R. (1927). The gene and the ontogenetic process. *Science, 66,* 361–368.

Macken, M. A. (1979). Developmental reorganization of phonology: A hierarchy of basic units of organization. *Lingua, 49,* 11–49.

McCusick, V. A. (1983). *Mendelian inheritance in man* (7th ed.). Baltimore: Johns Hopkins University Press.

MacWhinney, B. (Ed.). (1986). *Mechanisms of language acquisition.* Hillsdale, NJ: Lawrence Erlbaum Associates.

Marler, P. (1970). A comparative approach to vocal learning: Song development in white-crowned sparrows. *Journal of Comparative and Physiological Psychology, Monograph 71*(2), 1–25.

Maudsley, H. (1867/1977). *The physiology and pathology of the mind.* New York: Appleton. (Reprinted in *Significant contributions to the history of psychology, Series C: Medical psychology,* Vol. 4. Washington, DC: University Publications of America)

Mayr, E. (1982). *The growth of biological thought.* Cambridge, MA: Belknap Press.

McCune, L., Vihman, M. (1987). Vocal motor schemes. *Papers and Reports on Child Language Development, 26,* 72–79.

Mehler, J., Bertoncini, J., Barrière, M., & Jassik–Gerschenfeld, D. (1978). Infant perception of mother's voice. *Perception, 7,* 491–497.

Mehler, J., Jusczyk, P., Lambertz, G., Halsted, N., Bertoncini, J., & Amiel–Tison, C. (1988). A precursor of language acquisition in young infants. *Cognition, 29,* 143–178.

Menn, L. (1983). Development of articulatory, phonetic and phonological capabilities. In B. Butterworth (Ed.), *Language production,* (Vol. 2, pp. 3–50). London: Academic Press.

Neville, H. J. (1985). Effects of early sensory and language experience on the development of the human brain. In J. Mehler & R. Fox (Eds.), *Neonate cognition* (pp. 349–363). Hillsdale, NJ: Lawrence Erlbaum Associates.

Neville, H. J. (in press). Whence the specialization of the language hemisphere? In I. G. Mattingly & M. Studdert–Kennedy (Eds.), *Modularity and the motor theory of speech perception.* Hillsdale, NJ: Lawrence Erlbaum Associates.

Newport, E. L., & Meier, R. P. (1985). The acquisition of American Sign Language. In D. I. Slobin (Ed.), *The cross-linguistic study of language acquisition, Vol. I: The data* (pp. 881–938). Hillsdale, NJ: Lawrence Erlbaum Associates.

Nittrouer, S., Studdert–Kennedy, M., & McGowan, R. S. (1989). The emergence of phonetic segments: evidence from the spectral structure of fricative-vowel syllables spoken by children and adults. *Journal of Speech and Hearing Research, 32,* 120–132.

Oller, D. K. (1980). The emergence of the sounds of speech in infancy. In G. Yeni–Komshian, J. F. Kavanagh, & C. A. Ferguson (Eds.), *Child phonology, Vol. 1: Production* (pp. 93–112). New York: Academic Press.

Oller, D. K. (1986). Metaphonology and infant vocalizations. In B. Lindblom & R. Zetterstrom (Eds.), *Precursors of early speech* (pp. 21–35). Basingstone, England: Macmillan.

Oller, D. K., & Eilers, R. E. (1988). The role of audition in infant babbling. *Child Development, 59,* 441–449.

Oller, D. K., Eilers, R. E., Bull, D. H., & Carney, A. E. (1985). Prespeech vocalizations of deaf infant: A comparison with normal metaphonological development. *Journal of Speech and Hearing Research, 28,* 47–63.

Oyama, S. (1985). *The ontogeny of information.* New York: Cambridge University Press.

Pastore, R. E., Ahroon, W A., Buffuto, K. J., Friedman, C. J., Puleo, J. S., & Fink, E. A. (1977). Common factor model of categorical perception. *Journal of Experimental Psychology: Human Perception and Performance, 4,* 686–696.

Petitto, L. A., & Marentette, P. (1989, April). *The equipotentiality of speech and gesture for language: Evidence from deaf children's babbling in sign.* Paper presented at a meeting of the Society for Research in Child Development, Kansas City, MO.

Petrinovich, L., & Baptista, L. (1987). Song development in the white-crowned sparrow: Modification of learned song. *Animal Behavior, 35,* 961–974.

Raff, R. A., & Kaufman, J. C. (1983). *Embryos, genes, and evolution.* New York: Macmillan.

Shattuck–Hufnagel, S. (1983). Sublexical units and suprasegmental structure in speech production. In P. F. MacNeilage (Ed.), *The production of speech* (pp. 109–136). New York: Springer–Verlag.

Shattuck–Hufnagel, S. (1987). The role of word-onset consonants in speech production planning: New evidence from speech error patterns. In E. Keller & M. Gopnik (Eds.), *Motor and sensory processes of language* (pp. 17–51). Hillsdale, NJ: Lawrence Erlbaum Associates.

Schwartz, R. G. (1988). Phonological factors in early lexical acquisition. In M. D. Smith & J. L. Locke (Eds.), *The emergent lexicon* (pp. 185–222). New York: Academic Press.

Siple, P. (1978). Linguistic and psychological properties of American sign language: An overview. In P. Siple (Ed.), *Understanding language through sign language research* (pp. 3–23). New York: Academic Press.

Spence, M. J., & DeCasper, A. J. (1987). Prenatal experience with low-frequency maternal-voice sounds influence neonatal perception of maternal voice samples. *Infant Behavior and Development, 10,* 133–142.

Spinelli, D. N., & Jensen, F. E. (1979). Plasticity: The mirror of experience. *Science, 203,* 75–78.

Stark, R. E. (1986). Prespeech segmental feature development. In P. Fletcher & M. Garman (Eds.), *Language acquisition* (2nd ed., pp. 149–173). New York: Cambridge University Press.

Stemberger, J. P. (1989). Speech errors in early child language production. *Journal of Memory and Language, 28,* 164–188.

Stoel–Gammon, C., & Otomo, K. (1986). Babbling development of hearing-impaired and normally hearing subjects. *Journal of Speech and Hearing Disorders, 51,* 33–41.

Studdert–Kennedy, M. (1986). Sources of variability in early speech development. In J. S. Perkell & D. H. Klatt (Eds.), *Invariance and variability of speech processes* (pp. 58–76). Hillsdale, NJ: Lawrence Erlbaum Associates.

Studdert–Kennedy, M. (1987). The phoneme as a perceptuomotor structure. In A. Allport, D.

MacKay, W. Prinz, & E. Scheerer (Eds.), *Language perception and production* (pp. 67–84). London: Academic Press.

Studdert–Kennedy, M. (in press). Language development from an evolutionary perspective. In N. Krasnegor, D. Rumbaugh, R. Schiefelbusch, & M. Studdert–Kennedy (Eds.), *Behavioral foundations of language development*. Hillsdale, NJ: Lawrence Erlbaum Associates.

Thompson, D. W. (1917/1961). *On growth and form*. New York: Cambridge University Press (abridged edition).

Vidal, J. P. (1976). *Empreinte filiale et sexuelle—réflexions sur le processus d'attachment d'aprés une ètude expérimentale sur le coq domestique*. Docteur des Sciences Thèse, University of Rennes, France.

Waddington, C. H. (1966). *Principles of development and differentiation*. New York: Macmillan.

Wanner, R., & Gleitman, L. R. (Eds.). (1982). *Language acquisition*. New York: Cambridge University Press.

Werker, J. F., & Tees, R. C. (1984). Cross-language speech perception: Evidence for perceptual reorganization during the first year of life. *Infant Behavior and Development, 7,* 49–63.

6 Auditory Enhancement in Speech Perception and Phonology

Randy L. Diehl
Keith R. Kluender
Margaret A. Walsh
Ellen M. Parker
University of Texas at Austin

Without exception, phonological contrasts (e.g., the voicing distinction in medial stop consonants) are realized by a multiplicity of acoustic correlates, and these correlates tend to be rather uniform across languages, often approximating phonetic universals. This universality has typically prompted phoneticians to seek explanations based on physical or physiological constraints on speech production. Correspondingly, some theorists have argued that phonetic trading relations (where the perception of one acoustic-phonetic dimension is affected by the setting of another acoustic parameter) result primarily from the listener's tacit knowledge of the regularities of speech production and their acoustic consequences. We offer the alternative hypothesis that many cue-covariation universals and phonetic trading relations are based on properties of the human auditory system. We suggest that acoustic correlates of a phonological contrast covary as they do because speech communities tend to select cues that have mutually reinforcing auditory effects. To evaluate this auditory hypothesis, our strategy has been to demonstrate a given trading relation between acoustic dimensions that signal a phonological contrast and then to determine whether the same type of trading relation occurs for analogous acoustic dimensions when they signal perceptual distinctions among nonspeech stimuli.

INTRODUCTION

It is worth reminding ourselves from time to time just how many natural obstacles there are to successful speech communication. Environments tend to be noisy and reverberant, many of us suffer from partial hearing loss, and wide variation in vocal-tract characteristics and dialect make the listener's task all the

59

more difficult. One can assume that, in the face of these obstacles, phonologies or sound systems of languages have evolved to be fairly robust signaling devices.

An obvious way that a phonological system achieves such robustness is by arranging its inventory of phonetic segments or phonemes so as to optimize auditory distinctiveness. For example, Liljencrants and Lindblom (1972) showed that for languages with six or fewer vowels, the vowel inventories are well predicted by a simple principle of maximal acoustic (auditory) distance (see also Disner, 1984). It is no surprise that the point vowels, /i/ (as in *seed*), /a/ (as in *sod*), and /u/ (as in *sued*), which represent acoustic extrema, are shared by a large majority of languages (Maddieson, 1984).

Redundancy is, of course, another means of enhancing intelligibility. This takes a variety of phonological forms, including phonotactic constraints governing the order and position of phonetic segments (e.g., in English, word-initial /d/ cannot be followed by /1/) and so-called redundancy rules regulating which phonetic features can go together to make up a segment (e.g., English nasal consonants are normally voiced).

This chapter focuses on a rather different kind of redundancy. We present evidence that phonological contrasts (i.e., contrasts among functional sound units of language) are signaled by ensembles of articulatory/acoustic variables that have mutually enhancing auditory effects. Where previously the covariation of certain acoustic cues has been explained in terms of physical or physiological constraints on speech production, we offer the alternative hypothesis that many such instances of cue covariation result from a general strategy of language communities to preserve intelligibility.

THE AUDITORY ENHANCEMENT HYPOTHESIS

Decades of research on the production and perception of speech have yielded convincing support for the following conclusions: (a) any phonological contrast in any utterance position is realized by a covarying set of articulatory/acoustic events; (b) to the extent that an acoustic event is correlated with a given phonological contrast, it has cue value with respect to that contrast (Diehl & Kluender, 1987). Consider, for example, the distinction between voiced and voiceless stop consonants. Lisker (1977) cataloged no fewer than 16 articulatory/acoustic variables that are associated with the contrast between voiced /b/ and voiceless /p/ in utterance-medial position alone. Of these variables, four are especially significant: /b/ is produced with a shorter lip-closure duration than /p/; the /b/ closure is preceded by a longer vowel; the /b/ closure interval contains low-frequency periodic energy corresponding to laryngeal vibration; and the /b/ closure interval is followed by a lower fundamental frequency. All four of these variables are capable of signaling the voiced-voiceless contrast in English (Haggard, Ambler, & Callow, 1970; Lisker, 1957, 1978; Raphael, 1972).

Phoneticians have usually tried to explain covariations of articulatory/acoustic events in terms of physical or physiological constraints on speech production. This has been especially true when a covariation occurs widely among languages, approximating a phonetic universal. For example, a variety of explanations have been proposed for the finding that, in most languages, vowels are longer in front of voiced than in front of voiceless medial and final consonants, and almost all of these explanations have been based on putative constraints on speech production (Chen, 1970; Lisker, 1974).

Within the field of speech perception, there has been a corresponding tendency to explain the perceptual effects of covarying cues in terms of the listener's tacit knowlege of underlying articulatory processes and their acoustic consequences. For example, Repp (1982, 1983) has taken this approach in discussing phonetic "trading relations," which are said to exist when a change in the value of one acoustic cue can be offset by a change in another cue so that overall phonetic quality is preserved. Equivalently, a trading relation is demonstrated when the location of a phonetic category boundary along one acoustic dimension is affected by the setting of another acoustic parameter. Notice that trading relations are a direct consequence of phonetic redundancy: If there are multiple acoustic correlates of a phonological contrast, and if these correlates have cue value with respect to the contrast, then they can, in principle, be "traded" to preserve phonetic or phonological category membership.

Repp argued that the diverse phonetic trading relations that have been observed are not readily explained in terms of general auditory principles; he suggested that they instead derive from the listener's specialized knowledge of the acoustic regularities of speech—regularities that are rooted in production constraints. By this view, the multiplicity of cues for a phonological contrast are simply unavoidable consequences of the way that phonetic segments are produced. (See Liberman & Mattingly, 1985, also this volume, for a related production-oriented account of trading relations and other phenomena of speech perception.)

Over the past several years, we have been exploring an alternative hypothesis about the origin of trading relations and, more generally, of phonetic universals involving covariation of cues. Our hypothesis is that many of these universals derive in part from human auditory capabilities rather than from purely physical or physiological constraints on speech production. To illustrate, let us consider again the ensemble of cues that are associated with medial voicing contrasts in English and most other languages. We propose that, within certain broad limits imposed by physics and physiology, talkers can, in principle, exert independent control over laryngeal vibration during closure, closure duration, preceding vowel duration, and fundamental frequency following closure (Kluender, Diehl, & Wright, 1988). These voicing correlates covary as they do across languages because speech communities tend to select acoustic cues that have mutually reinforcing auditory effects. Talkers signal phonological contrasts using a "conspiracy" of cues that enhances the perceptual distinctiveness of phonemes. Notice that we are not merely claiming that more cues are better than fewer (although this may well be true). Rather, we are saying that certain cues can have optimal perceptual effect only in the context of other cues. (A similar account of cue covariation has recently been elaborated by Stevens, Keyser, & Kawasaki, 1986.)

There are several reasons why we were drawn to a general auditory hypothesis concerning cue covariation. First, despite a long history of attempts to explain particular cases of cue covariation in terms of production constraints, many of these attempts have been unsuccessful. For example, Lisker (1974) has argued convincingly that none of the major production-based accounts of the vowel-length differences associated with medial and final voicing distinctions survives careful analysis (see also Javkin, 1976, and Kluender, Diehl, & Wright, 1988).

Second, for the purposes of modeling human speech perception, our auditory hypothesis offers several advantages. Such a model will include a specification of the general auditory contribution to speech perception and also a list of all speech-specific facts, tacitly known by the listener, that are relevant to phonetic categorization. To the extent that the perceptual effects of cue covariation (i.e., trading relations) can be directly explained by general auditory processes and constraints, they need not be assigned to the listener's store of speech-specific knowledge, and the overall model is thereby simplified. This is, of course, no more than a restatement of C. Lloyd Morgan's famous canon: Never opt for higher-level psychological explanations when lower-level ones will do. An auditory account also achieves greater explanatory generality than a corresponding tacit-knowledge account, because it applies across both speech and non-speech domains. Additionally, we know a good deal more about the functioning of the general auditory system than we do about the storage and deployment of tacit knowledge, speech-specific or otherwise. Thus, an auditory account of cue covariation effects will in most cases be easier to derive from known principles. In sum, although we do not deny the perceptual role of speech-specific knowledge, we think that an appeal to such knowledge should always be an explanation of last resort.[1]

A final virtue of our general auditory hypothesis it that is makes reasonably strong and testable predictions. If two or more acoustic variables have mutually enhancing auditory effects in signaling a phonological contrast, then they should have similar effects in cuing a distinction between nonspeech categories. Our strategy has been to demonstrate trading relations (or cue enhancement effects)

---

[1] These arguments also apply *mutatis mutandis* against accounts that invoke a biologically organized speech-processing *module* (Liberman & Mattingly, 1985, also this volume) rather than speech-specific tacit knowledge acquired via general learning mechanisms (Repp, 1982, 1983).

for speech stimuli and then to test whether parallel effects occur for analogous nonspeech stimuli. To the extent that the auditory hypothesis is correct, one would expect to see agreement between the speech and nonspeech results.

MEDIAL VOICING CONTRASTS: CLOSURE DURATION AND PRECEDING VOWEL DURATION

In one series of studies, we focused on medial voicing contrasts, exemplified by the distinction between the words *rabid* and *rapid*. Recall that this distinction is signaled *inter alia* by lip closure duration, preceding vowel duration, presence or absence of laryngeal pulsing during closure, and fundamental frequency after the closure interval. Kluender, Diehl, and Wright (1988) examined, in particular, closure duration and preceding vowel duration. Two speech stimulus series, both ranging perceptually from /aba/ to /apa/, were created by varying the closure interval of the medial consonant. The two series differed only with respect to the duration of the initial vowel segment. Both stimulus series were generated by digitally editing a naturally produced token of /apa/, and thus there was no laryngeal pulsing during the closure interval.

We also prepared nonspeech analog stimuli that mimicked the temporal properties and peak amplitudes of the two series of /aba/-/apa/ stimuli. Each analog stimulus consisted of two square-wave segments separated by a silent interval. The square-wave segment durations were equal to the corresponding syllable durations, and the speech closure intervals were precisely duplicated as the silent gaps in the square-wave stimuli.

In a given stimulus condition, participants were first trained with feedback to press one of two buttons corresponding to each of the series-end-point stimuli. Then during the experimental session, they listened to the entire series and were asked to label each item by pressing the button corresponding to the series-end-point stimulus judged to be more similar to that item. Figure 6.1 shows the two-category labeling results for the /aba/-/apa/ stimuli and for the corresponding square-wave stimuli. Plotted as a function of medial silent interval is the percentage of times each item was labeled as more like the series-end-point stimulus with the shortest silent interval. (We refer to such labeling as *short-gap* responses.) In the speech case, this corresponds to the percentage of /b/ responses, as opposed to /p/. As expected from earlier work (e.g., Port & Dalby, 1982), the presence of a long initial vowel shifted the labeling boundary toward longer closure durations. That is, a long initial vowel made a given stimulus sound more /b/-like.

Interestingly, we found a similar pattern of results for the square-wave stimuli, which were identified by a different group of participants. A long initial segment caused the labeling boundary to move toward greater medial-gap dura-

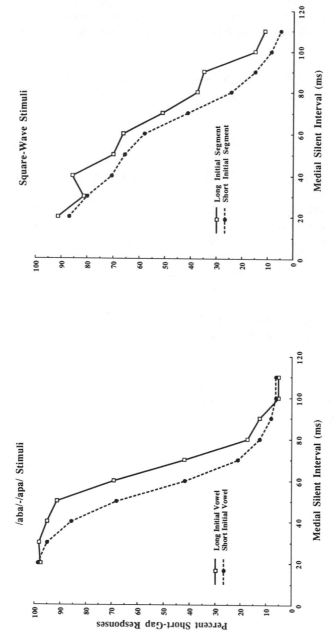

FIG. 6.1. Mean percentage of short-gap responses for /aba/-/apa/ stimuli and square-wave stimuli (Adapted from Kluender, Diehl, & Wright, 1988).

tions, and the magnitude of the shift was comparable with that for the speech stimuli. It is true that there was somewhat greater variance in the labeling functions for nonspeech, but this is not surprising, given the relative novelty of the square-wave patterns. We emphasize that these stimulus patterns were highly nonspeech-like, and when asked to describe them, none of the participants applied phonetic labels of any kind. This is important because it apparently rules out an explanation of the results based on the premise that listeners were in fact hearing or trying to hear the square-wave stimuli as speech.

How does one explain the influence of initial vowel length on the perception of medial voicing? We think a reasonable auditory hypothesis is that medial-gap duration is judged relative to initial segment duration in both speech and non-speech. A long initial segment makes a given medial gap seem shorter by contrast and hence, in the case of speech, more like a voiced segment. A short initial segment, on the other hand, makes a medial gap appear longer (i.e., in speech, more voiceless). Thus, vowel-length differences are a means of enhancing the auditory distinctiveness of the closure-duration cue for consonant voicing.

The auditory principle of durational contrast that we have just invoked may, in fact, apply to a wider range of phonological patterns. Where segment duration is used contrastively in a language, one may expect to observe a general tendency for the length of adjacent segments to vary inversely. For example, to enhance a consonant-length distinction, a language community may tend to lengthen vowels in front of phonemically short consonants and to shorten them before phonemically long consonants. It turns out that just this pattern is found in a fairly wide variety of languages. In Icelandic, Norwegian, and Swedish, and also in Tamil, a South Indian language, the pattern is phonologically formalized: In stressed syllables, phonemically long vowels are always followed by phonemically short consonants, and phonemically long consonants are always preceded by phonemically short vowels (Elert, 1964; Fintoft, 1961; Lisker, 1958). Also, in French and Italian, where vowel length is not phonemic, long consonants and geminates tend to be preceded by shorter vowels (Jones, 1967).

MEDIAL VOICING CONTRASTS: CLOSURE DURATION, LARYNGEAL PULSING, AND FUNDAMENTAL-FREQUENCY CONTOUR

Parker, Diehl, and Kluender (1986) conducted a study similar to that of Kluender et al. (1988), except that the variables of interest were closure duration and presence or absence of laryngeal pulsing during closure. Earlier perceptual studies of medial voicing demonstrated a robust trading relation between closure duration and laryngeal pulsing: The presence of pulsing during closure shifted the perceived voiced–voiceless boundary toward longer closure durations (Lisker, 1978).

We sought to replicate this trading relation and then to test whether similar perceptual effects could be obtained with nonspeech analog stimuli that were not phonetically categorizable. As in the previous study, two speech stimulus series, both ranging from /aba/ to /apa/, were created by varying the closure interval of a natural token of /apa/. The two series differed only with respect to the presence or absence of laryngeal pulsing during closure. We also synthesized several sets of nonspeech analog stimuli that replicated the temporal and peak amplitude properties of the speech stimuli. These nonspeech stimulus sets had differing fundamental-frequency (F0) contours in the vicinity of the medial gap.

For the /aba/-/apa/ stimuli, the presence of a short segment of laryngeal pulsing during closure produced a shift in the labeling boundary toward more *short-gap* or /b/ responses (similar to the effect of a longer initial vowel segment in the study by Kluender et al., 1988). For the square-wave stimuli, laryngeal pulsing during the medial gap also produced a shift toward more short-gap responses. However, this nonspeech effect was reliable only when the F0 contour following the medial gap was similar to what occurs after voiced consonants (i.e., rising from an initially low value).

On the basis of these results, we draw two conclusions. First, the enhancement effect of closure pulsing on perceived closure duration is of a general auditory nature and is not specific to speech. In particular, we suggest that a medial gap partially or completely filled with laryngeal pulsing appears shorter (hence, in the case of speech, more voiced). Second, the F0 correlate of voicing perceptually enhances the closure-pulsing correlate. This is probably because they both contribute to a sustained interval of low-frequency periodic energy in the vicinity of the consonant (see Stevens & Blumstein, 1981, for a similar view). Also, the perceived shortening of the closure interval may depend on a certain degree of pitch continuity between closure pulsing and the following vowel. Perceptual integration of temporally adjacent signals is known to be enhanced by spectral continuity (e.g., Bregman & Dannenbring, 1973).

Our claims about the enhancing effect of F0 contour on the perception of other voicing cues are consistent with some recent work of Kingston (1986), who showed that F0 variation is not simply an unavoidable physical by-product of the voiced–voiceless contrast. Instead, he argued that F0 is specifically regulated for its cue value in languages where voicing is a distinctive, rather than allophonic, correlate of speech sounds.

INITIAL VOICING CONTRASTS: VOICE-ONSET TIME AND FIRST-FORMANT ONSET FREQUENCY

Parker (1988) investigated a well-known trading relation in the perception of voicing contrasts among word-initial stop consonants (e.g., *do* vs. *to*). A major cue signaling such contrasts is voice-onset time (VOT), the interval between the release burst and the onset of periodicity associated with laryngeal vibration (Lisker & Abramson, 1970). The location of the voiced-voiceless perceptual boundary along the VOT dimension has been shown to depend on the onset frequency of the first formant (F1), with lower F1-onset frequencies shifting the boundary toward greater VOT values (Lisker, 1975; Summerfield & Haggard, 1977).

Following Pisoni (1977) and Summerfield (1982), Parker synthesized non-speech analogs of VOT stimuli. Each consisted of two co-terminous sine-wave segments, with the onset of the lower-frequency tone delayed relative to that of the higher-frequency tone by varying durations. Two stimulus series were created, one with a lower-tone frequency of 250 Hz, and the other with a lower-tone frequency of 750 Hz. The frequency of the higher tone in both series was fixed at 1250 Hz.

In these stimuli, the two tones are assumed to be analogous to the first and second formants of speech stimuli, and the tone-onset time (TOT) variation is taken to correspond to voicing delays in VOT stimuli. Pisoni (1977) found that listeners discriminate and identify TOT stimuli in a manner comparable to VOT stimuli, and he suggested that performance in both cases is determined by an auditory limit on temporal resolution of onset differences.

Participants in Parker's study were asked to judge whether or not the onsets of the two tones were simultaneous. The results of one experiment are shown in Figure 6.2, which plots the percentage of judgments of simultaneous tone onset as a function of the actual delay of the lower tone. Notice that when the lower-tone frequency was 250 Hz (rather than 750 Hz), significantly longer onset delays were required in order for subjects to detect the nonsimultancity. This pattern of results essentially duplicates the speech trading relation between VOT and F1-onset frequency.

The magnitude of the nonspeech version of the trading relation was rather surprising because in a similar experiment Summerfield (1982) found only a small and unreliable effect of lower-tone frequency on judgments of onset simultaneity. Accordingly, Parker repeated the experiment with a variety of stimulus and procedural modifications. In each of six additional experiments, the original results were replicated. The nonspeech trading relation appears, therefore, to be quite reliable.

Parker's findings suggest that the trading relation between VOT and F1-onset frequency arises at least in part from general auditory factors that are not specific to speech. Converging support for this conclusion derives from cross-species comparisons. Both chinchillas and English-speaking humans show the same systematic variation in the VOT labeling boundary as a function of consonant place-of-articulation: The voiced-voiceless category boundary occurs at a higher VOT value for velar stops than for labial or alveolar stops (Kuhl & Miller, 1978; Lisker & Abramson, 1970). This parallel behavior is puzzling indeed if the human labeling performance is solely attributed to tacit knowledge of the physics

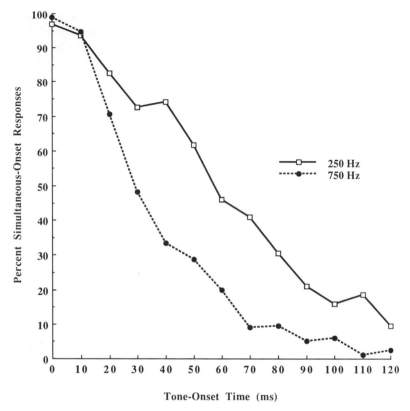

FIG. 6.2.   Mean percentage of stimuli judged as having simultaneous tone onset as a function of actual tone-onset time (Adapted from Parker, 1988).

and physiology of speech production (e.g.. Summerfield, 1975). However, a general auditory account based on Parker's results would predict just such variation in the VOT boundary. For any given VOT value, velar stops, with their longer F1 transitions, tend to have lower F1-onset frequencies than alveolar or labial stops. An auditory account would also explain why listeners require longer VOT values to perceive a stop as voiceless in front of high vowels, which have low F1 frequencies, than in front of low vowels (e.g.. Diehl, Lang, & Parker, 1980).

STOP-GLIDE CONTRASTS: TRANSITION DURATION, FOLLOWING VOWEL DURATION, AND RISE TIME

Like other phonological contrasts, the stop-glide distinction is signaled by a variety of covarying cues. Among these, formant transition duration and amplitude rise time are perhaps most prominent (Liberman, Delattre, Gerstman, &

Cooper, 1956; Mack & Blumstein, 1983; Shinn & Blumstein, 1984). In general, stops (such as /b/) are produced with shorter transitions and a more abrupt amplitude rise than glides (such as /w/). Miller and Liberman (1979) demonstrated another factor affecting the perception of stops and glides. When the following vowel is lengthened, the location of the /ba/-/wa/ boundary is shifted toward longer transition durations. Miller and Liberman interpreted this effect as an appropriate perceptual normalization for variation in speaking rate. By this view, a longer vowel suggests a slower rate of articulation, and to compensate perceptually for this, listeners adjust their stop-glide boundaries to longer transition values.

It is possible, however, that the effect is simply another instance of the durational-contrast principle at work. Perhaps a longer vowel makes the formant transition interval seem shorter and thus more stop-like. If so, the effect should be obtained with nonspeech analog stimuli that mimic the temporal characteristics of the /ba/-/wa/ stimuli.

To test the durational-contrast hypothesis, Diehl and Walsh (1989) conducted a series of experiments using single sine-wave analogs of stops and glides. These stimuli consisted of an upwardly ramped tone of varying duration followed by either a short or a long steady-state sinusoid. (Amplitude envelope was held constant for all stimuli.) The sine-wave patterns approximately modeled the first-formant trajectories of the /ba/ and /wa/ stimuli used by Miller and Liberman. However, they were not at all speechlike in quality.

Participants were first trained to categorize the endpoints of the two stimulus series as having either an abrupt or gradual onset. After training, they heard all stimuli from both series and were instructed to identify them on the basis of the training categories.

The results are shown in Figure 6.3. Transition or ramp duration is indicated on the abscissa, and on the ordinate is the percentage of times each stimulus was judged as more like the short-transition endpoint. (We call these *abrupt-onset* responses.) The category boundary shift was significant and in the direction predicted by the durational-contrast hypothesis. That is, a longer total stimulus duration shifted the boundary toward longer transition duration. This, of course, parallels the speech result of Miller and Liberman.

Although the sine-wave stimuli used in this experiment were very nonspeech-like, the frequency contours were schematically similar to actual first-formant trajectories of /ba/ and /wa/. One might argue that this schematic similarity was somehow sufficient to engage a "speech mode" of perception on the part of the listeners (see, e.g., Best, Morrongiello, & Robson, 1981). As a somewhat more stringent test of the durational-contrast hypothesis, Diehl and Walsh (1989) conducted a similar experiment, using sine-wave patterns in which the initial frequency transition was falling rather than rising. These stimuli modeled first-formant contours that simply cannot occur in naturally produced stops and glides. Again, there was a significant boundary shift in the direction predicted by

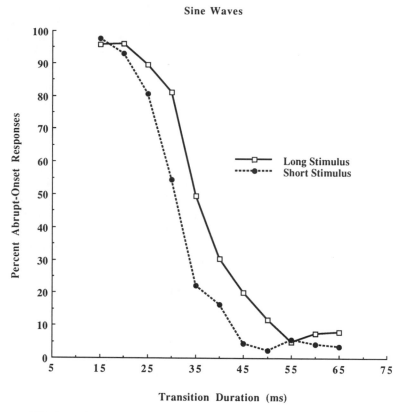

FIG. 6.3. Mean percentage of abrupt-onset responses for sine-wave stimuli with rising frequency transitions (Adapted from Diehl & Walsh, 1989).

the durational-contrast hypothesis. If anything, the effect was greater than that
found for the more speechlike rising-transition stimuli.

Thus, we obtained clear evidence that the vowel-length effect found for stops
and glides can be duplicated with nonspeech analog stimuli that are not phonetically categorizable. (See Pisoni, Carrell, & Gans, 1983, for a related set of
findings.) As with the findings of Kluender et al. (1988) that were reviewed
earlier, the general auditory principle of durational contrast seems to provide a
simple, unified account of both the speech and nonspeech effects.

Recall that the stop-glide contrast is signaled by amplitude rise time as well as
transition duration. Recently, Walsh and Diehl (in prep.) found evidence that
these variables also have mutually enhancing effects on the perception of nonspeech analogs of stops and glides. When listeners were asked to judge single
sine-wave stimuli varying in transition duration as having either an abrupt or a
gradual onset, a short rise time produced more "abrupt" responses than a long

rise time. A likely auditory basis of this trading relation is that rapid frequency transitions and short rise times both contribute to a higher degree of spectral "splatter" (i.e., dispersion of energy across a wide frequency band), which may be a principal cue for abrupt onsets in general.

In most of the instances of cue enhancement we have reviewed, the separate cues result from gestures or gestural components that are, in principle, independently controllable by talkers (see, e.g., Kluender et al., 1988). In such instances, the cue covariation may be viewed as a strategy of language communities to enhance the perceptual distinctiveness of segments. It seems obvious, however, that the assumption of independent gestural control does not apply to the case of rise time and transition duration, both of which are largely, if not completely, a reflection of vocal-tract opening time. Is it a mere coincidence that cues linked by articulatory constraints also turn out to have mutually reinforcing auditory effects? If so, it is puzzling that such "coincidences" appear to be rather common in the speech domain. For example, the auditory enhancement effect that Parker (1988) found for the variables VOT and F1-onset frequency corresponds rather neatly to an aerodynamic/mechanical constraint on the covariation of these variables (Diehl & Kluender, 1987; Summerfield, 1975).

Following Lindblom, MacNeilage, and Studdert-Kennedy (in preparation), we suggest that these seemingly fortuitous correspondences actually reflect the processes of linguistic natural selection. Out of the large set of possible vocal signals that language communities might use to carry phonological information, they tend to select those signals that are highly valued on both articulatory grounds (e.g., minimal energy expenditure) and auditory grounds (e.g., maximal contrast). If a certain pattern of cue covariation is physically or physiologically "natural" and at the same time leads to the enhanced auditory distinctiveness of segments and features, one would expect that pattern to occur widely among languages.

VOWEL SYSTEMS

Earlier we noted that vowel inventories of languages tend to satisfy a principle of maximal auditory contrast (Disner, 1984; Liljencrants & Lindblom, 1972).[2] The most obvious manifestation of this tendency is the high incidence of the acousti-

---

[2]Although the contrast principle is a good predictor of vowel inventories, it should be noted that under normal speaking (and listening) conditions, vowels are often produced in a manner that is not maximally contrastive. Rapidly articulated or unstressed vowels in consonantal context typically exhibit formant trajectories that "undershoot" the more extreme frequency values of sustained, isolated vowels (Lindblom, 1963; Stevens & House, 1963). However, in general, there is sufficient vowel information distributed over the entire syllable to compensate for the somewhat reduced distinctiveness of the peak formant values (Jenkins, Strange, & Edman, 1983; Parker & Diehl, 1984; Strange, Jenkins, & Johnson, 1983).

cally extreme "point" vowels among the world's languages. Of the 317 representative languages sampled in UPSID (the UCLA Phonological Segment Inventory Database described by Maddieson, 1984), /i/, /a/, and /u/ occur in 290, 279, and 266 languages, respectively. By comparison, the next most common vowels, /o/ and /e/, occur in 139 and 118 UPSID languages. It is very unlikely that the point vowels are favored on articulatory grounds, since their production requires *greater* muscular force than more central vowels (MacNeilage & Sholes, 1964).

Some distinctive acoustic characteristics of the point vowels may be summarized as follows:

1. /i/ has a low-frequency first formant (F1) and a high-frequency second formant (F2), whose proximity to higher formants (F3 and F4) creates a relatively intense band of high-frequency energy (2000 Hz-4000 Hz).
2. /u/ has low-frequency values for both F1 and F2, resulting in a relatively intense low-frequency energy band (200 Hz-800 Hz).
3. /a/ has a high frequency F1 in the vicinity of a low-frequency F2, creating an energy concentration in the mid-frequency range (700 Hz-1200 Hz).

As Stevens, Keyser, and Kawasaki (1986) have suggested, the point vowels provide an excellent example of how talkers use a multiplicity of gestures or gestural components in order to enhance phonological contrasts. Traditionally, phoneticians have described vowels in terms of three articulatory parameters: tongue height, tongue frontness (or backness), and degree of lip rounding. To a reasonable approximation, raising the tongue body lowers F1, fronting the tongue body raises F2, and lip rounding lowers F2. Thus, in the production of /i/ a fronted tongue and unrounded lips jointly yield a high F2, whereas in the production of /u/, a retracted tongue and rounded lips have the opposite result. These enhancement effects undoubtedly explain why about 94% of front vowels in the UPSID sample are unrounded, while about the same percentage of back vowels are rounded (Maddieson, 1984).

The /u/ rounding gesture may itself be analyzed into two components: Lip protrusion (which lengthens the oral cavity) and constriction of the labial aperture. Both of these components independently contribute to a lower F2 frequency and hence a more distinctive vowel (Stevens et al., 1986). Further F2 lowering can be had by actively lowering the larynx, which, like lip protrusion, lengthens the vocal tract. Riordan (1977) showed that when lip rounding is physically prevented, talkers resort to larynx lowering in order to produce acoustically acceptable tokens of /u/. But even under normal speaking conditions, talkers apparently tend to lower the larynx for back vowels and raise it for front vowels, enhancing the acoustic effects of the tongue and lip gestures (MacNeilage, 1969).

In the production of /i/, the frequency elevation of the higher formants is reinforced by raising the tongue blade (above and beyond the normal tongue body elevation) to form a narrower palatal constriction (Stevens et al., 1986). In addition, the lips are not merely unrounded (as in /a/), they are actively spread, resulting in a further upward shift in the frequencies of the higher formants (Ohala, 1980).

The low-frequency F1 characteristic of both /i/ and /u/ results from a high tongue-body position. In contrast, the distinctively high F1 frequency associated with /a/ is produced by jointly lowering the tongue body and jaw. We suggest that nasalization is an additional means by which language communities enhance the auditory distinction between high and low vowels. Across languages, low vowels tend to be more nasalized than high vowels (Ohala, 1974). Purely mechanical explanations of this effect (e.g., based on some indirect coupling of the tongue and velum) appear to be ruled out, since there is clear electromyographic evidence (Lubker, 1968) of *active* velar raising (which reduces nasalization) during high vowels. An early modeling study by House and Stevens (1956) may provide the key to understanding the effect. They found that the result of nasal coupling is, among other things, to raise F1 frequency for all vowels, but especially for the high vowels /i/ and /u/. Since a low F1 is a distinctive acoustic attribute of high vowels, nasalization would have the effect of making them less distinctive. On the other hand, since /a/ has a distinctively high F1, nasalization can only make the vowel more distinctive. Thus, nasalization appears to be used in vowel production to enhance the high-low contrast just as lip rounding is used to enhance the front-back contrast.

This survey of articulatory and acoustic correlates of the point vowels offers clear support for our basic thesis. Perceptual distinctiveness of phonemes is achieved by the use of multiple gestures and cues that have mutually enhancing auditory effects.

CONCLUDING REMARKS

There are a good many natural obstacles to successful speech communication. In the face of these obstacles, phonological systems tend to follow two design strategies: One is to maximize the acoustic (and hence auditory) distance among phonemes; the other is to use a high level of phonetic redundancy. Both of these strategies are evident in the general class of phenomena we have discussed here. Our claim is that language communities mark phonological contrasts by selecting an ensemble of gestures or gestural components that have mutually reinforcing auditory effects, resulting in phonemes that are less confusable. From this perspective, many speech trading relations and phonetic universals involving covariation of cues are seen as being at least partly rooted in general auditory capabilities. In the studies reviewed here, it has been shown how auditory factors such as durational contrast can account for a variety of speech perception effects that have previously been explained in terms of the listener's specialized knowledge of speech production. Further exploration of general auditory constraints may help to make the problem of speech perception theoretically tractable and may also yield explanations for a broad range of heretofore puzzling phonetic and phonological universals.

ACKNOWLEDGMENTS

This work was supported by National Institutes of Health Grant HD 18060.

K. R. Kluender is now at the Department of Psychology, University of Wisconsin at Madison. E. M. Parker is now at AFHRL/MOMJ, Brooks Air Force Base, Texas.

REFERENCES

Best, C. T., Morrongiello, B., & Robson, R. (1981). Perceptual equivalence of acoustic cues in speech and nonspeech perception. *Perception & Psychophysics, 29,* 191–211.

Bregman, A. S., & Dannenbring, G. L. (1973). The effect of continuity on auditory stream segregation. *Perception & Psychophysics, 13,* 308–312.

Chen, M. (1970). Vowel length variation as a function of the voicing of the consonant environment. *Phonetics, 22,* 129–159.

Diehl, R. L., & Kluender, K. R. (1987). On the categorization of speech sounds. In S. Harnad (Ed.), *Categorical perception* (pp. 226–253). Cambridge: Cambridge University Press.

Diehl, R. L., Lang, M., & Parker, E. M. (1980). A further parallel between selective adaptation and contrast. *Journal of Experimental Psychology: Human Perception and Performance, 6,* 24–44.

Diehl, R. L., & Walsh, M. A. (1989). An auditory basis for the stimulus-length effect in the perception of stops and glides. *Journal of the Acoustical Society of America, 85,* 2154–2164.

Disner, S. F. (1984). Insights on vowel spacing. In I. Maddieson, *Patterns of sounds* (pp. 136–155). Cambridge: Cambridge University Press.

Elert, C.-C. (1964). *Phonological studies of quantity in Swedish.* Stockholm: Almquist & Wiksell.

Fintoft, K. (1961). The duration of some Norwegian speech sounds. *Phonetica, 7,* 19–39.

Haggard, M., Ambler, S., & Callow, M. (1970). Pitch as a voicing cue. *Journal of the Acoustical Society of America, 47,* 613–617.

House, A. S., & Stevens, K. N. (1956). Analog studies of the nasalization of vowels. *Journal of Speech and Hearing Disorders, 21,* 218–232.

Javkin, H. R. (1976). The perceptual basis of vowel duration differences associated with the voiced/voiceless distinction. Report of the Phonology Laboratory, No. 1, 78–92, University of California at Berkeley.

Jenkins, J. J., Strange, W., & Edman, T. R. (1983). Identification of vowels in "vowelless" syllables. *Perception & Psychophysics, 34,* 441–450.

Jones, D. (1967). *The phoneme: Its nature and use.* Cambridge: Cambridge University Press.

Kingston, J. (1986). Are F0 differences after stops accidental or deliberate? *Journal of the Acoustical Society of America, 79,* S27 (Abstract).

Kluender, K. R., Diehl, R. L., & Wright B. A. (1988). Vowel-length differences before voiced and voiceless consonants: An auditory explanation. *Journal of Phonetics, 16,* 153–169.

Kuhl, P. K., & Miller, J. D. (1978). Speech perception by the chinchilla: Identification functions for synthetic VOT stimuli. *Journal of the Acoustical Society of America, 63,* 905–917.

Liberman, A. M., Delattre, P. C., Gerstman, L. J., & Cooper, F. S. (1956). Tempo of frequency change as a cue for distinguishing classes of speech sounds. *Journal of Experimental Psychology, 52*, 127–137.

Liberman, A. M., & Mattingly, I. G. (1985). The motor theory of speech perception revised. *Cognition, 21*, 1–36.

Liljencrants, J., & Lindblom, B. (1972). Numerical simulation of vowel quality systems: The role of perceptual contrast. *Language, 48*, 839–862.

Lindblom, B. (1963). Spectrographic study of vowel reduction. *Journal of the Acoustical Society of America, 35*, 1773–1781.

Lindblom, B., MacNeilage, P. F., & Studdert-Kennedy, M. (in preparation). *Evolution of spoken language.* New York: Academic Press.

Lisker, L. (1957). Closure duration and the intervocalic voiced-voiceless distinction in English. *Language, 33*, 42–49.

Lisker, L. (1958). The Tamil occlusives: Short vs. long or voiced vs. voiceless? *Indian Linguistics, 19*, Turner Jubilee I, 294–301.

Lisker, L. (1974). On 'explaining' vowel duration variation. *Glossa, 8*, 223–246.

Lisker, L. (1975). Is it VOT or a first-formant transition detector? *Journal of the Acoustical Society of America, 57*, 1547–1551.

Lisker, L. (1977). Rapid versus rabid: A catalogue of acoustic features that may cue the distinction. *Journal of the Acoustical Society of America, 62*, S77 (Abstract).

Lisker, L. (1978). On buzzing the English /b/. *Journal of the Acoustical Society of America, 63*, S20 (Abstract).

Lisker, L., & Abramson, A. S. (1970). The voicing dimension: Some experiments on comparative phonetics. In *Proceedings of the 6th International Congress of Phonetic Sciences, Prague, 1967* (pp. 563–567). Prague, Czechoslovakia: Academia.

Lubker, J. F. (1968). An electromyographic-cinefluorographic investigation of velar function during normal speech production. *Cleft Palate Journal, 5*, 1–18.

Mack, M., & Blumstein, S. E. (1983). Further evidence of acoustic invariance in speech production: The stop-glide contrast. *Journal of the Acoustical Society of America, 73*, 1739–1750.

MacNeilage, P. R. (1969). *A note on the relation between tongue elevation and glottal elevation in vowels* (Monthly Internal Memorandum, January, pp. 9–26). University of California, Berkeley.

MacNeilage, P. F., & Sholes, G. N. (1964). An electromyographic study of the tongue during vowel production. *Journal of Speech and Hearing Research, 7*, 209–232.

Maddieson, I. (1984). *Patterns of sounds.* Cambridge: Cambridge University Press.

Miller, J. L., & Liberman, A. M. (1979). Some effects of later-occurring information on the perception of stop consonant and semivowel. *Perception & Psychophysics, 25*, 457–465.

Ohala, J. J. (1974). Experimental historical phonology. In J. M. Anderson & C. Jones (Eds.), *Historical linguistics II: Theory and description in phonology* (pp. 353–389). Amsterdam: North Holland Publishing Company.

Ohala, J. J. (1980). The acoustic origin of the smile. *Journal of the Acoustical Society of America, 68*, S33 (Abstract).

Parker, E. M. (1988). Auditory constraints on the perception of stop voicing: The influence of lower-tone frequency on judgments of tone-onset simultaneity. *Journal of the Acoustical Society of America, 83*, 1597–1607.

Parker, E. M., & Diehl, R. L. (1984). Identifying vowels in CVC syllables: Effects of inserting silence and noise. *Perception & Psychophysics, 36*, 369–380.

Parker, E. M., Diehl, R. L., & Kluender, K. R. (1986). Trading relations in speech and nonspeech. *Perception & Psychophysics, 39*, 129–142.

Pisoni, D. B. (1977). Identification and discrimination of the relative onset time of two component tones: Implications for voicing perception in stops. *Journal of the Acoustical Society of America, 61*, 1352–1361.

Pisoni, D. B., Carrell, T. D., & Gans, S. J. (1983). Perception of the duration of rapid spectrum changes in speech and nonspeech signals. *Perception & Psychophysics, 34,* 314–322.

Port, R. F., & Dalby, J. (1982). Consonant/vowel ratio as a cue for voicing in English. *Perception & Psychophysics, 32,* 141–152.

Raphael, L. F. (1972). Preceding vowel duration as a cue to the perception of the voicing characteristics of word-final consonants in English. *Journal of the Acoustical Society of America, 51,* 1296–1303.

Repp, B. H. (1982). Phonetic trading relations and context effects: New experimental evidence for a speech mode of perception. *Psychological Bulletin, 92,* 81–110.

Repp, B. H. (1983). Trading relations among cues in speech perception: Speech-specific but not special. Paper presented at the 10th International Congress of Phonetic Sciences, Utrecht, Netherlands, August 1983. Reprinted in Haskins Laboratories: Status Report on Speech Research, 1983, SR-76, 129–132.

Riordan, C. J. (1977). Control of vocal-tract length in speech. *Journal of the Acoustical Society of America. 62,* 998–1002.

Shinn, P., & Blumstein, S. E. (1984). On the role of the amplitude envelope for the perception of [b] and [w]. *Journal of the Acoustical Society of America, 75,* 1243–1252.

Stevens, K. N., & Blumstein, S. E. (1981). The search for invariant acoustic correlates of phonetic features. In P.D. Eimas & J. L. Miller (Eds.), *Perspectives on the study of speech* (pp. 1–38). Hillsdale, NJ: Lawrence Erlbaum Associates.

Stevens, K. N., & House, A. S. (1963). Perturbation of vowel articulations by consonantal context: An acoustical study. *Journal of Speech and Hearing Research, 6,* 111–128.

Stevens, K. N., Keyser, S. J., & Kawasaki, H. (1986). Toward a phonetic and phonological theory of redundant features. In J. S. Perkell & D. H. Klatt (Eds.), *Invariance and variability in speech processes* (pp. 426–449). Hillsdale, NJ: Lawrence Erlbaum Associates.

Strange, W., Jenkins, J. J., & Johnson, T. L. (1983). Dynamic specification of coarticulated vowels. *Journal of the Acoustical Society of America, 74,* 695–705.

Summerfield, A. Q. (1975). How a full account of segmental perception depends on prosody and vice versa. In A. Cohen & S. G. Nooteboom (Eds.), *Structure and process in speech perception* (pp. 51–66). New York Springer-Verlag.

Summerfield, A. Q. (1982). Differences between spectral dependencies in auditory and phonetic temporal processing: Relevance to the perception of voicing in initial stops. *Journal of the Acoustical Society of America, 72,* 51–61.

Summerfield, A. Q., & Haggard, M. (1977). On the dissociation of spectral and temporal cues to the voicing distinction in initial stop consonants. *Journal of the Acoustical Society of America, 62,* 435–448.

Walsh, M. A., & Diehl, R. L. (in prep.). Formant transition duration and amplitude rise time as cues to the stop/glide distinction. Submitted for publication.

III LANGUAGE COMPREHENSION

7 Holistic Models of Word Recognition

Neal F. Johnson
Ohio State University

One of the interesting trends in cognitive psychology over the past 15 or 20 years has been the growing interest in reading, both as an experimental task and an object of study. The beginning of this interest was marked, and to a degree instigated, by the now-classic papers by Reicher (1967) and Wheeler (1970) on the word-superiority effect. However, coincident with the appearance of these two papers was the republication in 1968 of Edmund Burke Huey's classic volume *The Psychology and Pedagogy of Reading* (1908), and that event, possibly more than any other, may be the real basis for the current interest in reading.

The significance of the reappearance of the Huey book is that it reintroduced experimental psychology to the topic of reading, and a careful reading of the book shows it to be surprisingly current in terms of both the theoretical and the empirical issues it covers. In fact, it almost appears as if the field became frozen in 1908, and then reappeared in an unaltered form 60 years later, with not only the same issues and concerns at the forefront, but even the methods and techniques used by the new investigators were the same or similar to those used in the past.

Part of the explanation for the dry period in reading research has to be the impact of the behaviorist revolution, and the way thinking within experimental psychology was influenced by radical behaviorism. Most particularly, it is difficult to construe any interesting issue within the domain of reading research in terms of the type of two-place interitem relationship required by the models common to the type of behavioristic associationism that was characteristic of the time between 1920 and 1960. In addition, given the dominant role of that perspective during those years, issues not readily handled within that framework were simply disregarded (Dixon & Horton, 1968).

In any event, the impressive reality is that when one reads Edmund Burke Huey's book in the late 1980s it seems to be substantially more contemporary than do many other books and major monographs in cognitive psychology that were written at the time of the republication of Huey's volume. In fact, with regard to the specific issue to be considered in this paper (i.e., holistic processes in word recognition), Huey's views, and the bases for those views, represent a fairly complete characterization of the issue both as it stood in 1908 and as it stands circa 1988. We now have a little more data to provide, and we probably use some words not common to the experimental psychology of 1908, but it does seem that the conclusions that we can draw could be stated by using direct quotes from Huey. That is, the bottom line in terms of what we have discovered so far regarding holistic processing is that Huey's conclusions were correct, and they were correct for the reasons he gave.

THE ISSUE OF HOLISTIC PROCESSING

The focus of this chapter is on the nature of holistic processing in word recognition. However, by stating the issue in that manner it should be noted clearly that it presupposes the reality of holistic processing, and the issue to be considered is not that of documenting the phenomenon, but rather of defining its nature.

An Initial Definition

The preliminary basis for the presupposition, as well as the initial definition, is evidence with which Huey probably would be much more comfortable than would contemporary cognitive psychologists. Specifically, it is the case that when I look at a word I have a rush of immediate experience that can only be defined as being the word, and if I am asked about the letters that go into making up the word I can do that only with subsequent efforts, and at best, those efforts seem to be secondary to those involved in the initial experience.

Furthermore, these secondary efforts seem to entail processing events and psychological representations that occur only if I am asked about component information. If my task does not demand that level of information, not only does the letter information seem to be unavailable, but those effortful processing events required to obtain the component information also seem not to have occurred.

To illustrate this point in a different way, and with data only slightly more in accord with today's accepted standards, we once asked participants who came to the lab for another experiment to describe their immediate experience when we showed them something that was printed on a card. It was a between-groups design with 12 participants in each of three conditions, and for one condition the participants were shown the word TABLE, while for a second condition the printed item was the nonsense word GLURK, and for the third condition it was the consonant sequence SBJFQ.

The interesting data are that when the display was a word all the responses to the initial question (i.e., what did you see?) involved using the term *word* as the basis for the description, and no participant used the word *letter*. When probed further with the question "Is there any other way to describe what you saw?", only two participants used the word *letter* in their response, and in both cases it was highly qualified such as "I suppose you could describe it as some letters."

The same basic result was obtained when the display was GLURK. It did take some prompting to get some participants to go beyond just the term *nonsense* in their description (e.g., "What is it that is nonsense?"), but eventually every participant used either the term *word* or *syllable,* and no participant used the term *letter* in their description. To the second question (i.e., "Is there another way to describe it?"), 4 of the 12 participants finally used the word *letter,* but even in this case there was a surprising resistance to describing their experience using terms that referred to the display's components, as opposed to terms that referred to the visual pattern as a whole. (The modal response to the second question was "No.").

Finally, just to illustrate the fact that participants are able to use the term *letter* in descriptions of immediate experience, when the display was a consonant sequence every participant used the term *letter* and no participant used a term that referred to the pattern as a whole in response to the first question. That also was true in response to the second question, except for a single participant who chose to say "Well, it isn't a word."

The point here is that in terms of immediate conscious experience, if we are dealing with a display for which perceivers have a prelearned encoding that can be used to represent the pattern as a whole, or they know a rule system that can be used to generate such an encoding, the perceiver's immediate experience does not seem to include any usable representation of component information. Even when participants are encouraged to manipulate or analyze the experience by trying to construe it in alternative forms, they still seem to be locked into global characterizations of the stimulus event.

It is this phenomenon, then, that can be used as an definition of holistic encoding, and *holistic processing* can be defined broadly in terms of those psychological events that transpire prior to, and result in, the availability of such a holistic representation. In what follows I would like to document the phenomenon further, and in somewhat less introspective ways, and then try to provide at least a preliminary characterization of the nature of the processing that results in this phenomenal event that I am describing as holistic.

Evidence for Holistic Encoding

Some of the earliest experiments that have been used to document the phenomenon of holistic processing were those reported by Cattell (1886), and they
represent a basic paradigm that has been used in many contemporary demonstrations. Specifically, Cattell demonstrated that the time needed to recognize a letter and the time needed to recognize a word were about the same, and
that the time needed for word recognition was not influenced by the number of
letters within the words.

However, even more direct evidence was provided by the work of Erdmann
and Dodge (described by Huey, 1908/1968). Their participants seemed able to
identify words under conditions in which they were not able to identify the
individual letters that formed the words. Huey described studies by these investigators in which participants could not resolve the features of letters, either
because the distance between the point of fixation and spatial location of the
target letter was too great (i.e., it was out too far in the visual periphery), or
because the distance between the eye and the point of fixation was too great,
given the size of the letter. In both situations, however, even though the visual
features of the letters that made up the words could not be resolved, participants
were able to identify words formed from those letters.

Contemporary models that assume interacting levels of representation (e.g.,
Rumelhart, 1977; McClelland & Rumelhart, 1981) probably can handle these
types of data, in that they can account for the possibility of a relatively certain
identification of a word before a comparably certain identification of the letters
from within the word. However, the fact that letter-level processing within such
models is dependent on the prior availability of word-level representations
suggests a rather casual or loose connection between letter-level knowledge and
word-level knowledge with regard to any dependency relationship. Given that is
the case, the Erdmann and Dodge data can be taken to indicate at least a degree
of independence between the two levels of representation, in that in their task
there probably was no clear letter-level knowledge that was based only on
data-driven processing.

More recently there have been other experiments that also have demonstrated
that word or pattern-level representations have a certain priority over letter or
component-level representations when words are displayed for recognition. For
example, the work of Reicher (1967) and Wheeler (1970) has demonstrated that
participants are better able to detect and identify a letter under degraded conditions if the letter appears as part of a word, than if the letter appears as part of a
nonsense item, or even if it appears in isolation. As shall be noted in what
follows, we now have a fairly good understanding of this word-superiority
effect, including a rather clear definition of the conditions under which it appears
(e.g., see Johnston & McClelland, 1980; Johnston, 1981), and although these
data suggest it is a product of the type of bottom–up processing of the component

information that precedes the availability of the word-level representation, their account also requires the presupposition of a priority of word-level representations over any lingering letter-level codes.

Another line of recent work on this issue has been that of Healy and Drewnowski (for a representative sample of this work see Healy, 1976; Drewnowski & Healy, 1977, Drewnowski, 1978; Healy & Drewnowski, 1983; Proctor & Healy, 1985). The overall result they have obtained is that familiar words (e.g., *the* and *and*) tend to conceal their letters, as evidenced by detection errors in a proofreading type of detection task, and the magnitude of the concealment is positively correlated with both the familiarity of the word and the reading skill of the perceiver. These data, then, also suggest that word processing is holistic to the extent that the word-level code takes priority, and in turn, that code seems to interfere with the availability of the letter-level codes.

The last line of work I would like to describe is an effect we have demonstrated in my lab at Ohio State (Johnson, 1975; Johnson, Turner–Lyga, & Pettegrew, 1986). Sloboda (1976, 1977) has labeled the phenomenon the word-priority effect, and quite simply it is a demonstration that if participants are asked to detect whether an upcoming display is a particular word (e.g., TABLE) they are faster than if their task is to determine whether the word display contains a particular letter (e.g., T).

This effect is quite robust, and does not depend on incomplete processing of the words. For example, it is obtained when the target letter is always the first letter of the word (Johnson, 1975; Johnson & Marmurek, 1978); when target words and foils (i.e., the display for a NO item) always differ by only a single letter (e.g., MAKE and TAKE) (Sloboda, 1976, 1977; Johnson et al., 1986); and when the word-level task involves a semantic decision rather than simple word detection (e.g., they respond YES if it is an animal name as opposed to responding YES to *lion*) (Johnson, 1979).

A GENERAL MODEL OF HOLISTIC PROCESSING

The pattern-unit model (Johnson, 1975, 1977) was proposed to account for these data, and although it is quite similar to the unitization model of Healy and Drewnowski (1983), there are some important differences. The core assumption within the model is that precognitive representations of small visual patterns are always processed by first attempting to assign a single pattern-level cognitive representation to the array, and that step always succeeds if participants know a rule system or have a prelearned code that can be used for the assignment (e.g., the code for a single letter). If such a rule system or code is not available, then the initial attempts at pattern-level encoding would fail, and only through such failure would the participant be able to know the pattern was not unitizable.

However, if those initial attempts to encode the pattern as a whole do fail, then it would be necessary to encode it on a component-by-component basis.

Regarding this part of the model, there are three points to note. The first is that integratable patterns are always treated as wholes. Second, the only way nonintegratable patterns can be identified as being nonintegratable is by people failing in their attempt to encode the pattern as a whole. Third, the initial successful encoding of nonintegratable patterns is at the component level. Finally, if participants would need to identify a component of an array, they always would be delayed in doing so by the initial attempts to encode the pattern as a whole, regardless of whether those attempts were successful.

The second part of the model involves assumptions regarding the way in which the preliminary precognitive representation is established. Just as with the Healy–Drewnowski unitization model (1983), the pattern-unit model assumes preliminary precognitive encoding of the display, which provides the raw material used by the cognitive encoding mechanisms. It assumes that there are three pieces of data necessary in order to have a viable visual representation of the display, and that these are independently encoded. The first is simple-feature information, (such as representations of straight lines, diagonals, and curves); the second is juncture information, which would include particularly the intersections of simple features; and the third type of information is positional, which represents the spatial location of the assemblages of simple features that are integrated by the juncture features.

The model supposes that initial visual information processing involves the extraction or encoding of these three types of information. In addition, it is assumed that the role of the juncture features is to position the simple features relative to one another, and in a sense they are assumed to weld the simple features into tightly integrated feature assemblages that correspond to the visual information of letters.

As stated, the model would seem to imply a sequential encoding process for these three types of features, but such an assumption is not necessary, (even though in fact that may be the real situation). However, with respect to the model, the important issue is that the encoding of these differing types of information be *relatively* independent.

Once the component-level processing provides an adequate visual representation, with both the level and criterion for adequacy left unspecified within the model, cognitive processing then provides an encoding for the display as a whole using either prelearned codes or the knowledge of rule systems that can be used to generate such codes. The rules of this process are the following: (1) The initial attempts are always to assign an encoding to the pattern as a whole, and not to provide encodings for the component information; (2) After an encoding has been assigned it is tested for adequacy, and if it is adequate it is passed on and registered in working memory; (3) If the initial code assigned is not adequate, the encoder is signaled to try again, and that process would be repeated through some arbitrary number of failures; and (4) If no adequate representation is provided by the coder after the fixed number of attempts, a parsing mechanism is introduced that uses physical information to partition the display into its elements, and the resulting component units are then introduced sequentially to the coding mechanism, with each element being treated in the same manner as has been described.

The major difference between encoding the pattern as a whole, and the encoding of elements following parsing, is not whether holistic processing occurs, but rather the level of unit for which it is successful. In addition, the resulting difference at the end of processing is whether there is a single pattern or word-level code in memory, or there is a code available for each individual component with no pattern-level representation. Overall, however, what is important to note is that the model assumes that holistic processing is always the initial mode of operation, and component-level processing occurs only if that fails.

More Evidence of Component Concealment

The previously described data regarding the word-superiority effect (Reicher, 1967; Wheeler, 1970) and the word-priority effect (Johnson, 1977, 1981; Johnson et al., 1986), as well as the proofreading data reported by Healy and Drewnowski (1983), all suggest that with regard to word perception there is a certain immediacy to the availability of the word or pattern-level information that is lacking for the component information. In addition to that, however, the pattern-unit model has several rather specific expectations regarding what must occur when participants attempt to deal with component information.

For example, if the foregoing considerations are correct, then if the presented display is integratable in the sense that the participants can assign it a unitary code, what should be available after that process is only the unitary pattern-level code. If the participants' task is to identify the first letter of the display, that word-level code would be irrelevant, and if they were to return their attention to the display in an effort to identify the first letter, again they would see only the letter array (i.e., the word). That, by definition, would only result in another holistic encoding of the display. The problem, then, concerns how perceivers ever obtain an encoding of the needed letter information.

Within the context of this view of holistic encoding, if the perceivers would need to deal with component-letter information from within a word, it would appear that the only possibility would be to derive the letter information from the initial holistic encoding by decoding it into letter codes within memory. However, if that were the case, then even though the participants were looking directly at the letter array (i.e., the word) they would not really be engaging in a visual scan of that display, but rather a memory scan of the derived letter codes, and there are two important implications of that construction of the issue.

The first implication is that if the participants' task was to determine whether a word display began with a particular letter (e.g., B), encodings of all the other letters also should be in memory at the time they make their decision. In the event the predesignated target did not appear in the initial position, but did appear elsewhere in the display (i.e., a NO item), there would be the potential for a confusion. On the other hand, if the display was a consonant array that could not be encoded holistically, the participants would have parsed the display, and a memorial encoding for only the initial letter would be available at the time of the decision. In that event, participants should not experience confusion, and the results of a recent experiment support both of these expectations (Johnson, 1986a).

A second implication of the model is that if participants are to detect a letter within a letter array, but the target can appear anywhere such that its position is unknown to the perceiver, then the task would require a search of the array. Given that task, with participants searching the environment for a target that they are holding in memory (i.e., a visual scan), the evidence suggests that the search is self-terminating in that participants stop their scan when they encounter the item they are seeking. That search strategy is demonstrated by the fact that if the size of the item set to be searched is increased, there is a larger effect on search time when the target is absent than when it is present (i.e., the fact that a target is not present can be determined only after a complete scan, but target presence can be detected before the entire display is searched).

If the task is changed slightly, and the item set to be searched is in memory rather than the environment, the task would involve a memory scan. The available evidence (Sternberg, 1966; Krueger & Shapiro, 1980; Johnson, 1986a, Johnson & Carnot, 1987) would suggest that in this situation participants engage in an exhaustive scan to the extent that they appear to always scan all the items before making a decision. That strategy is demonstrated by the fact that if the size of the search set is increased, then the scan time is increased equally for YES and NO items (i.e., in the case of a YES item they do not terminate the scan when they encounter the target, and the set is scanned completely just as occurs necessarily when the target is absent).

In terms of the current issue, the pattern-unit model suggests that when participants are to engage in a visual scan of a displayed word in order to find a predesignated target letter, even though the task is a visual scan, participants should have to turn it into a memory scan, because the only way they could obtain the needed letter information would be to derive it from the initial holistic encoding of the word. On the other hand, that would not be necessary for the scan of a consonant array, because the initial attempts at holistic encoding would fail, and participants would deal with the display on a letter-by-letter basis.

The results of an experiment designed to examine this prediction (Johnson, 1986a) seem quite consistent with these expectations. For consonant arrays, an increase in the size of the search set resulted in a larger increase in search time when the target was absent than when it was present, but that was not the case for word displays. That would suggest that participants did scan their memories when searching for letters within words, but scanned the environment when the display was a consonant array.

Overall, the foregoing considerations and data document the reality of what has been referred to as holistic representations. The data also offer support for the idea that these representations are the product of a processing sequence that is relatively automatic, not dependent on the nature of the display, and one that inhibits the availability of component-level information. Another way of stating this point is that one always attempts to identify small letter patterns holistically, and only if those attempts fail does one attempt to cope at the letter level.

Component-level encoding

Despite this relatively strong conclusion regarding the preceivers' inability to encode letter information from within words in a direct manner, it obviously is the case that there must be letter processing and letter identification in some sense, because, as noted earlier, that is the information that defines the word. In fact, models that are based on the idea of holistic processing (e.g., Healy & Drewnowski, 1983, 1983; Johnson 1975, 1977, 1981) usually do include some clear specifications regarding the nature of such processing.

In terms of the type of component-level processing described by the pattern-unit model, there are now a number of experiments that not only provide evidence supporting the reality of the processing events, but also suggest the sequencing of the processing events that is implied but not stated within the model. For example, the work of Treisman (Treisman & Gelade, 1980; Treisman & Schmidt, 1982) and Prinzmetal (1981) on conjunction errors in perception suggests a point in time when feature information is available, but the features are more or less free floating with regard to their relationship to other features (i.e., the feature sets are not integrated). If participants are to detect a plus sign in a briefly presented but complex display, there is a very high false positive rate (e.g., in excess of 25%) if there is no plus sign in the array, but there is both a vertical and a horizontal line. On the other hand, when there were just two horizontal or two vertical lines, and not one of each, the false positive rate was as low as 5%. Illusory conjunctions of this sort do seem to indicate the availability of the simple feature information, and the fact that such availability is independent of information regarding the conjunction of information (i.e., juncture features).

Next, it is assumed that junctures or feature conjunctions are the basis for integrating feature sets into feature assemblages that correspond to the visual representation of letters. To illustrate this point, we conducted a series of experiments in which participants were asked to detect the presence of a feature in a suprathreshold display. There were two lines of material in each display, and the top line consisted of either a right or left diagonal (i.e., $/$ or $\setminus$) or it was a semicircle open either to the right or left. Immediately under that feature was another feature that was either identical to that on the top line, including orientation, or it was of the other class (i.e., a semicircle under a diagonal or vice versa). In addition, on the bottom line there was always a second feature of the same class as the first, and it was always in the other orientation and either superimposed on or to the right of the feature that was under the top feature.

The participants were to determine whether the feature on the top line and the one immediately under it were the same, and the results indicated that if the features on the bottom line touched (e.g., the pattern was a $\vee$, a $\wedge$, or an X) participants were very slow at detecting a match, but if they were separated by even a slight amount they were quite fast. It would appear that when the features touched they formed a higher-order pattern that concealed the component features.

The next level of component processing considered by the pattern-unit model is the location of the feature assemblages (i.e., the letter representations) in terms of where they are in space and where they are relative to one another. For the model, the critical issue is that the establishment of the assemblage on the one hand, and the locating of the assemblage in space on the other, should result from at least relatively independent processes.

One experimental paradigm (Adams, 1979) that provides illustrative data is a task in which the time between the onset of a briefly presented target word and the onset of a subsequent mask (stimulus onset asynchrony, or SOA) was varied, and the participants were asked to report a displayed target word. The result reported by Adams is that prior to the SOA that yielded the first correct whole-word response, the number of correct letters reported, disregarding whether they are in the correct position, did not vary as a function of SOA. On the other hand, if a letter was scored as correct only if it was also in its correct position, then there was an increase in performance as a function of SOA across these subthreshold levels. That is, there did seem to be a time span over which there was no increase in the amount of available letter information, while over that same time span there did appear to be a change in the amount of letter-position information. That finding does seem to fit quite well with the idea that the integration of letter assemblages on the one hand, and the positioning of those assemblages in space on the other, are processing events that are independent of one another.

Finally, it is clear that at some point the letter information must be properly positioned with respect to the other letters within the display so that it is possible to identify the pattern. The theoretical and empirical issue concerns whether that positioning occurs prior to the type of integrative encoding that is required when the information is moved into working memory, or does it occur as a consequence of such cognitive encoding.

Marmurek (1977) has provided rather specific data on this point. He employed a task in which participants were to either compare a target letter with the first letter of a displayed word, or they were to compare a word target with a displayed word. Both the predesignated target and the display were presented visually, and in two different tasks the target either appeared and then went off before the critical display appeared, or the target and critical display appeared simultaneously with the target immediately above the critical display word (in which case the target was not *pre*designated).

Marmurek's (1977) rationale was similar to that used by Eichelman (1970), Gough and Cosky (1977), and Posner (1969). It was assumed that if the target and critical display were presented successively, then participants would have to encode the target into memory in order to mediate the delay before the critical display appeared. In turn, that should mean that the critical display also would have to be provided with a cognitive encoding such that a comparison could be made to the target. The results, as expected, revealed that participants made word-level decisions faster than decisions regarding component letters, in the successive task.

However, with a simultaneous presentation, the target and critical display are processed together during the entire time of encoding. Under such conditions, a comparison and decision can be based on precognitive representations, provided they were sufficiently complete (Posner, 1969). Marmurek's (1977) results revealed that participants did not make mistakes, indicating the letter information was properly positioned, but there was no evidence that word-level unitization had occurred. That is, in the simultaneous comparison task participants were accurate, but they made component letter level decisions more quickly than they did word-level decisions. That result indicates that letter positioning occurred before word-level unitization, which implies that unitization is not the positioning mechanism. Furthermore, it makes good sense that unitization would be dependent on the prior correct positioning of the letters.

This illustrative summary of the evidence for component-level processing and encoding makes it abundantly clear that whatever the nature of the processing that results in holistic encoding, it cannot be the case that component-level processing is bypassed, and such processing must be included as at least a preliminary step in word identification. The problem, then, is to account for this fact in the context of the additional fact that word processing appears to be holistic.

Attention and Holistic Processing

The resolution I would like to propose for the foregoing problem is not new in the sense that it is exactly the solution proposed by Edmund Burke Huey in 1908, as well as others since that time (e.g., see Johnston & McClelland, 1980). That is, the proposed resolution assumes that holistic encoding does not reflect the way in which we encode information initially, but rather the way in which attention is deployed to those encodings once the encoding process is complete.

Huey (1908/1968) talks about this point in terms of "a hierarchy of recognition habits, the exercise of the higher drafting away consciousness that would otherwise serve for completing the recognition of the particular letters" (p. 112). In addition, similar to the Healy–Drewnowski (1983) model, he suggests that the recognition of word–wholes would inhibit incipient recognition of component information. Huey suggests that evidence supporting component-level processing could be an artifact of the degraded displays that were used. If the visual conditions do not allow the perceiver to encode information in a way that is adequate to establish a word-level representation, then attention will be deployed to the next highest level available, which could be either letters or features depending upon the quality of the display (see Johnson, 1975, for a similar point).

Evidence for this hypothesis regarding the role of attention in demonstrations of holistic processing comes from a study by Johnson and Blum (1988). Prior data (Johnson, 1986b) have demonstrated that participants are faster at detecting a letter when the letter appears in isolation than when it appears as the first letter of a string of letters, even when the string is redundant and consists of multiple instances of the same letter (e.g., BBBBB). This effect does not seem to be simply the result of lateral masking, and it has been attributed to the fact that the initial unsuccessful attempts to encode the letter string holistically delay the point in time when an encoding of the initial letter becomes available.

In the Johnson and Blum (1988) study two different predisplay fixation fields were used. One consisted of five dots, and when the critical display was a five-letter string, one letter replaced each dot. When the critical display was a single letter in isolation it appeared in the position of the first dot, and with that being the case the participants were always to determine whether the pre-designated target letter matched the letter that replaced the first dot. However, given that the dots were quite discrete, the participants were able to identify clearly the place in the predisplay fixation field to which they should attend, and that would allow them to narrowly prefocus their attention to that spatial location.

The other predisplay fixation field consisted of three rows of Xs, and the critical letter always appeared in the position of the fourth X of the middle row. In that the field was much more homogeneous, and therefore more amorphous, the critical location was less clearly defined. Given that, it was expected that with this predisplay fixation field it would be much more difficult for the participants to identify the appropriate anchor on which to prefocus their attention than would be the case for an array of five dots.

The results indicated that with the X-field the standard latency advantage for single-letter displays was obtained. However, when the predisplay fixation field consisted of just five dots, the latency difference between identifying a letter in isolation and identifying the first letter of a five-letter string completely dis-appeared. It would appear, then, that if participants can narrowly prefocus their attention so that its spatial extent includes only a single component of a larger visual pattern, then holistic encoding can be avoided, and that would seem to implicate the manner in which attention is deployed as the mechanism underlying holistic encoding.

Conclusions

Within cognitive functioning, unitization phenomena are some of the most common effects that can be demonstrated. However, while most unitization effects are the product of deliberate recoding efforts on the part of the participant, the holistic encoding of words seems to occur more or less automatically. That is, in a number of the studies just reviewed the critical evidence for holistic encoding came from the fact that its occurrence interfered with performance in tasks that did not require word-level information, but did require component-level information.

These studies also seem to suggest that when these automatic attempts at holistic encoding are successful not only does the interference take the form of delaying component-level decisions, but it also seems to prevent the direct encoding of the component-level information. That is, several of the studies suggested that in such cases it is necessary for participants to derive component-level information from word-level codes rather than by encoding it directly.

From such data as these it is clear that holistic encoding does occur, but from studies that employed degraded displays it also is clear that in addition there is at least some type of component-level encoding occurring in these tasks. When processing was stopped before a holistic encoding could be achieved, varying amounts and types of component information seemed to be available, depending on the amount of processing that had occurred. The problem, then, is to reconcile the strong evidence of holistic encoding with the equally strong evidence that component-level encoding also must be occurring. That is, if component-level encoding is occurring, why is it that only the pattern-level encoding is im-mediately available to cognitive processing mechanisms?

At least part of the answer seems to be that the evidence suggesting that word encoding is holistic may not be a product of the way the information is encoded initially, but rather a result of the way attention is deployed to psychological representations of the information once the initial encoding process is complete. That is, attention is deployed in a top–down manner, with the highest level encoding having priority. If it is further assumed that under normal circum-stances attention is deployed *only* to the highest level encoding, then essentially all the currently available data can be explained with this model. Both Huey

(1908/1968) and Johnston and McClelland (1980) have offered this idea as an account of holistic processing, and Johnson and Blum (1988) provide it with some rather direct support.

In general, then: (1) Holistic processing seems to be quite real; (2) It should not be taken to imply that component-level encoding does not occur; and (3) The basic mechanism seems to be the way attention is deployed. What makes this conclusion interesting is that it is essentially the same point Huey (1908/1968) made when he reviewed the evidence available at the end of the 19th century.

With regard to the broader and more applied issues involved in the study of reading, the foregoing considerations suggest that there may be certain levels of encoding that can occur without attentional control. Furthermore, except for unusual circumstances, it would appear that participants cannot allocate attention to these levels of encoding even when the demands of the task suggest such allocation to be optimal.

On the positive side, it is clear that the absence of attentional demands at the level of letter encoding increases the cognitive resources available for more complex encoding. For example, while encoding at the level of features and letters might be automatic, establishing those linkages between information currently being processed and pre-existing knowledge states which are necessary for comprehension may not be as automatic, and establishing those linkages may place demands on attention. However, there also is a cost to such efficiency, and the most obvious case is the proofreading problem. In particular, with attention focused on the pattern-level representation, it is very easy to miss errors at the letter or component level.

In addition, in terms of costs, when learning to read, if it is important to know the nature of the parts of components of the patterns in order to understand the rules whereby they are combined to form the higher-order patterns, then it is clear that the type of component-level concealment described by the foregoing research is going to be a problem. Specifically, it would appear that there is a need for special instructional programs to overcome the opaqueness of the word-level representations and make the components of letters (features) and words (letters) more obvious to the perceiver-learner. To that extent, then, this work also provides the beginnings of an empirical and theoretical rationale for reading readiness programs, and although the research has been at a rather basic level, with the primary focus being on theoretical issues, this point suggests that there are rather direct and significant practical applications as well.

REFERENCES

Adams, M. J. (1979). Models of word recognition. *Cognitive Psychology, 11*, 133–176.

Cattell, J. M. (1886). The time taken up by cerebral operations. *Mind, 11*, 377–392.

Dixon, T. & Horton, D. L. (1968). *The Kentucky Conference: Verbal behavior theory and its relation to general S–R theory.* New York: Prentice–Hall.

Drewnowski, A. (1978). Detection errors on the word *the:* Evidence for the acquisition of reading levels. *Memory & Cognition, 6,* 405–409.

Drewnowski, A., & Healy, A. F. (1977). Detection errors on *the* and *and:* Evidence for reading units larger than the word. *Memory & Cognition, 5,* 636–647.

Eichelman, W. H. (1970). Familiarity effects in a simultaneous matching task. *Journal of Experimental Psychology, 86,* 275–282.

Forster, K. I. & Chambers, S. M. (1973). Lexical access and naming time. *Journal of Verbal Learning and Verbal Behavior, 12,* 627–635.

Gough, P. B., & Cosky, M. J. (1977). One second of reading again. In N. J. Castellan Jr., D. Pisoni, & G. Potts (Eds.), *Cognitive theory (Vol. 2).* Hillsdale, NJ: Lawrence Erlbaum Associates, pp 271–288.

Healy, A. F. (1976). Detection errors on the word *the:* Evidence for reading units larger than letters. *Journal of Experimental Psychology: Human Perception and Performance, 2,* 235–242.

Healy, A. F., & Drewnowski, A. (1983). Investigating the boundaries of reading units: Letter detection in misspelled words. *Journal of Experimental Psychology: Human perception and Performance, 9,* 413–426.

Huey, E. B. (1908/1968). *The psychology and pedagogy of reading.* Cambridge, MA: MIT Press.

Johnson, N. F. (1975) On the function of letters in word identification: Some data and a preliminary model. *Journal of Verbal Learning and Verbal Behavior, 14,* 17–29.

Johnson, N. F. (1977). A pattern-unit model of word identification. In D. LaBerge & S. J. Samuels (Eds.). *Basic processes in reading: Perception and comprehension.* Hillsdale, NJ: Lawrence Erlbaum Associates, pp. 91–125.

Johnson, N. F. (1979). The role of letters in word identification: A test of the pattern-unit model. *Memory & Cognition, 7,* 496–504.

Johnson, N. F. (1981). Integration processes in word recognition. In O. Tzeng & H. Singer, (Eds.), *Perception of print: Reading research in experimental psychology.* Hillsdale, NJ: Lawrence Erlbaum Associates, pp. 29–63.

Johnson, N. F. (1986a). On looking at letters within words: Do we "see" them in memory? *Journal of Memory and Language, 25,* 558 570.

Johnson, N. F. (1986b). On the detection of letters within redundant arrays. *Perception & Psychophysics, 40,* 93–100.

Johnson, N. F. (1987). On the role of attention in models of word recognition: Do we see words or letters when we read? Presidential address, Midwestern Psychological Association, Chicago.

Johnson, N. F., & Blum, A. J. (1988). When redundancy hurts letter detection: An attempt to define one condition. *Perception & Psychophysics, 43,* 147–155.

Johnson, N. F. & Carnot, M. J. (1990). On time differences in searching for letters in words and nonwords: Do they emerge during the initial encoding or the subsequent scan? *Memory & Cognition, 18,* 31–39.

Johnson, N. F. & Marmurek, H. H. C. (1978). Identification of words and letters within words. *American Journal of Psychology, 91,* 401–415.

Johnson, N. F., Pugh, K. R., & Blum, A. J. (1989). More on the way we "see" letters from words within memory. *Journal of Memory and Language, 28,* 155–163.

Johnson, N. F., Turner–Lyga, M., & Pettegrew, B. S. (1986). Part–whole relationships in the processing of small visual patterns. *Memory & Cognition, 14,* 5–16.

Johnston, J. C. (1981). Understanding word perception: Clues from studying the word-superiority effect. In O. J. L. Tzeng & H. Singer (Eds.), *Perception of print: Reading research in experimental psychology.* Hillsdale NJ: Lawrence Erlbaum Associates, pp. 65–84.

Johnston, J. C., & McClelland, J. L. (1980). Experimental tests of a model of word identification. *Journal of Verbal Learning and Verbal Behavior, 19,* 503–524.

Krueger, L. E., & Shapiro, R. G. (1980). Why search for target absence is so slow (and careful!): The more targets there are the more likely you are to miss one. *Journal of Experimental Psychology: Human Perception and Performance, 6,* 662–685.

Marmurek, H. H. C. 1977). Processing letters in words at different levels. *Memory & Cognition, 5,* 62–72.

Posner, M. I. (1969). Abstraction and the process of recognition. In G. Bower (Ed.), *Advances in Learning and Motivation* (Vol. 3). New York: Academic Press, pp. 44–100.

Prinzmetal, W. (1981). Principles of feature integration in visual perception. *Perception & Psychophysics, 30,* 330–340.

Proctor, J. D., & Healy, A. F. (1985). A secondary-task analysis of a word familiarity effect. *Journal of Experimental Psychology: Human Perception and Performance, 11,* 286–303.

Reicher, G. M. (1967). Perceptual recognition as a function of meaningfulness of stimulus material. *Journal of Experimental Psychology, 81,* 275–280.

Rumelhart, D. E. (1977). Toward an interactive model of reading. In S. Dornic (Ed.), *Attention and performance* (Vol. 6). Hillsdale, NJ: Lawrence Erlbaum Associates, pp. 573–603.

Sloboda, J. A. (1976). Decision times for word and letter search: A wholistic word identification model examined. *Journal of Verbal Learning and Verbal Behavior, 15,* 93–101.

Sloboda, J. A. (1977). The locus of the word-priority effect in a letter detection task. *Memory & Cognition, 5,* 371–376.

Sternberg, S. (1966). High speed scanning in memory. *Science, 153,* 652–654.

Treisman, A. M., & Gelade, G. (1980). A feature integration theory of attention. *Cognitive Psychology, 12,* 97–136.

Treisman, A. M., & Schmidt, H. (1982). Illusory conjunctions in the perception of Objects. *Cognitive Psychology, 14,* 107–141.

Wheeler, D. D. (1970). Processes in word recognition. *Cognitive Psychology, 1,* 59–85.

8 Syntactic Modularity in Sentence Comprehension

Charles Clifton, Jr.
University of Massachusetts

When cognitive psychology was new, one of the best games we could play was to study how people comprehend and produce sentences. I recall talking with Jim Jenkins and some of his other students about how one could possibly do an experiment about "colorless green ideas." It all seemed so important. Chomsky's (1957, 1965) new transformational grammar seemed to show us that people are capable of cognitive accomplishments that were astonishing but not necessarily mysterious. We just had to show, in experimentally clever ways, that people could really do the things that a transformational grammar described; we very badly wanted to show that the Chomskian enterprise was on the right track in developing an account of these accomplishments; and we knew we had to develop some kind of theory about what went on in the mind when a person was doing wondrous things with language.

This early enthusiam resulted in a spate of experiments demonstrating the psychological reality of this or that grammatical structure or relationship. Unfortunately, it seemed to fail in the task of coming up with a theory of how sentences are processed. The best theory going was the much-maligned Derivational Theory of Complexity, which had precious little support and provided negligible insight into mental processes, never mind that it was so tightly wedded to a particular grammatical analysis that tests of it would totally lose their relevance when the analysis changed (cf. Fodor & Garrett, 1967; Gough & Diehl, 1978). We early psycholinguists gave up on the task, contenting ourselves with kitchen-sink theories of sentence comprehension (or "detective model" theories, in the more charitable words of Lyn Frazier, 1979). What passed for theory was nothing more than lists of vaguely stated superficial clues to sentence structure, together with the claim that people use these clues and do everything else needed to make sense out of sentences (see Clark & Clark, 1977, for the

95

prototype of this sort of account). Since this seemed to be the best that could be done, it was necessary to do something else. Psycholinguists should study something they could understand, such as word recognition; or they should study something nobody could ever seriously expect to understand, such as text comprehension.

I want to argue that this retreat was ill advised. The problems of sentence processing are just as important as they seemed in the early 1960s. The best way to attack them is by closely aligning our experimental endeavors with linguistic theory. And a coherent, illuminating, even surprising theory of sentence comprehension is not an impossible will-o'-the-wisp, but a real possibility. Despite our frustrations, we were pointed in a good direction 25 years ago. The difference is that in the last quarter century, linguistic theory has changed and become much more useful as a buttress to psychological theory, and psycholinguists have become much more sophisticated and adventuresome in their theorizing and experimentation.

In this chapter, I will outline some of the research done by my colleagues and myself. I will show how we have attempted to determine whether a syntactic processing system constitutes a module (cf. Fodor, 1983) whose functioning can be described largely without appeal to the action of semantic and pragmatic processing systems, and whether the syntactic processing system itself has a modular internal structure. Before describing this research, I will state the goals and orienting assumptions we have adopted to guide our research on language comprehension.

GOALS OF AN ACCOUNT OF LANGUAGE COMPREHENSION

Ultimately, we want to provide an account of how people combine marks on paper or vibrations of the air together with knowledge in order to create new knowledge. It seems clear that readers and listeners can, eventually, use all the knowledge at their disposal in understanding sentences. They use knowledge of language, knowledge of the topic being discussed, knowledge of the speaker or writer—whatever is relevant. Nonetheless, it is possible that listeners and readers have abilities that are specialized for the perception of language, just as organisms generally seem to have specialized visual, auditory, and other abilities. We want to explore the possibility that these specialized abilities constitute a system that is organized in a modular fashion.

Modularity

Fodor (1983) has provided an extensive analysis of modularity in cognition. A module is a computational subsystem adapted to perform certain relatively simple computations in a quick and efficient manner, working for the most part independently from other modules. Fodor proposes that a module is character-ized by a cluster of several properties, the most important of which (from our viewpoint) is the property of "informational encapsulation." A processing system that has this property is sensitive to only a limited range of information. The computations it performs in processing one kind of information are done without regard to the current value of other kinds of information. A module that is specialized for processing speech might analyze a given acoustic input in the same way, regardless of whether or not the resulting word fits syntactically into the current discourse. Similarly, a module that is specialized for processing syntactic structure might analyze a given string of words in the same way, regardless of whether or not the analysis makes semantic sense or fits in a plausible way into the discourse context.

This modularity position appears to be inconsistent with the observation that all knowledge is potentially used in language comprehension. The inconsistency is only apparent, however. The language-processing modules can be organized into a language processing system. They must have some way of communicating between one another, and with any (presumably nonmodular) general-purpose reasoning system (cf. Forster, 1979). The substantive claim of the modularity position is that the channels of communication between the modules are very narrow, able to carry only limited kinds of information.

The program of constructing a modular theory of language processing faces two primary challenges: to determine what the distinct modules are, and to determine how they interface with one another. The first challenge demands the identification of any interesting and important computations within one modular domain that are carried out in the same way, regardless of the state of apparently relevant information in other domains. The second challenge requires the de-velopment of a theory of how computations made in distinct modules can be integrated with one another, so that the final output of the modular system is appropriately sensitive to all the information that language comprehenders are sensitive to.

Frazier (1985, 1987) proposed one useful way of characterizing a modular system and theorizing about constraints on communication among modules. She suggested that each module has its own vocabulary in terms of which it can construct representations of information. It can process only that information that is represented in the representational vocabulary of the module, which might include the vocabulary of acoustic spectra, spectral transitions, and the like, in the case of a speech perception module, or the vocabulary of syntactic categories and syntactic relations such as "dominate" and "c-command" in the case of a syntactic module. (Any modern linguistics text can be consulted for the defini-tion of terms such as this. Van Riemsdijk & Williams [1986] is an excellent one.) Modules are defined, in part, in terms of the information relevant to them, and thus in terms of their representational vocabularies. Information about letters or speech sounds is relevant to the lexical module (if there is such a thing), but is of no possible value to the syntactic module. Information about c-command is important to the syntactic module, but logically irrelevant to the lexical recognition module or to a semantic processing system. Truth and reference are the essence of semantics, but the syntactic module may be insensitive to them.

However, modules must be able to communicate among themselves, if any integration of different sources of information is to come about. Frazier's proposal claims that modules can communicate with one another solely on the basis of their shared vocabulary. Thus, a lexical recognition module and a syntactic processing module could communicate on the basis of lexical entries, or perhaps syntactic categories, representational vocabulary which they share. A syntactic processing module and a semantic processing system might share the vocabulary of thematic relations (relations such as "agent," "goal," "source," "experiencer," and "theme"; Gruber, 1965; Jackendoff, 1972).

The central claim of a modularity theory, from this perspective, is that communication among distinct processing systems is limited, in principled ways. If this is so, the long-term task is to determine what the modules are, to learn what representational vocabulary they have, to identify the processing principles they follow, and to determine how they communicate with one another. The short-term goal, however, is to gather evidence about whether there is any reason to believe that the language-processing system is organized in a modular fashion. Perhaps world knowledge, discourse pragmatics, and everything else *does* influence the recognition of speech sounds and the initial analysis of grammatical relations between words. If such a situation does obtain, there is no reason to embark upon the quest for an adequate modular theory of language comprehension. I want to argue, on the basis of empirical data, that the language-processing system does not work in such a fashion.

Research Strategies

First, though, a few words about how we go about searching for evidence for modularity. In the early days of psycholinguistics, we would try to infer how a sentence was processed by studying the trace it left in memory (Clifton & Odom, 1966; Mehler, 1983; Miller, 1962) or by measuring how long it took to answer a question about it (Gough, 1966). If I am correct in the view that everything we know can conceivably affect the final comprehension of a sentence, this was just the wrong thing to do. It could only provide us information about the final output of the language-processing system, not about its specialized initial operations. We have to look at the moment-to-moment or "on-line" processing of a sentence if we are to learn anything specific about the function of any linguistically specialized system. We have to see what the system does before the point where everything people know has time to come along and cover up its traces.

Fortunately, this seems to be possible. One thing that has made it possible is the existence, even prevalence, of temporary ambiguities in language. We are not aware of these ambiguities, but they do exist. Consider a sentence fragment such as "The man left. . . ." One can easily write many continuations of this fragment, reflecting different structural analyses: "The man left after dinner," "The man left his briefcase," "The man left home," "The man left at home felt sad." Such ambiguities, temporary or permanent, are what make sentence parsing hard, and interesting. If they did not exist, then it would be trivially easy to do sentence comprehension in a deterministic manner, without any backtracking (Marcus, 1982). But they do exist, and people do have to deal with them.

If people deal with the ambiguities as a normal consequence of sentence comprehension, then by determining how they deal with ambiguities we can learn about the sentence comprehension process. We can ask questions such as: Do people create several representations, or just one representation, or none at all, when they reach a point of temporary ambiguity? If a single representation is constructed, what principles govern its construction? What categories of information are used in constructing this initial representation? If later information proves the initial representation to be in error, how is it revised? By determining what information is used in creating and resolving different types of temporary ambiguities, we can get evidence about the existence of distinct modules in the language-processing system. By determining how the information is used, we can identify the processing principles each module follows.

MODULARITY IN PHRASE STRUCTURE PARSING

Processing Temporary Ambiguities

Frazier and Rayner (1982), and many researchers who followed them, have studied temporary ambiguities to provide clear evidence about the principles a syntactic processor follows. In a typical experiment, people read sentences whose initial segments are grammatically ambiguous, but whose later segments resolve the ambiguity. A string such as *I knew the answer . . .* can be completed as in (1a), in which *the answer* is the direct object of the verb, or as in (1b), in which *the answer* is the subject of a sentence complement to the verb *know.* A string such as *I put the box on the cart. . . ."* can be continued as in (2a), in which *on the cart* modifies the verb *put,* or as in (2b), in which it modifies *the box.* In the most infamous example of all (Bever, 1970), the string *The horse raced past the barn fell. . . .* can be continued as in (3a), a simple sentence in which *the horse* is grammatical subject of *raced,* or as in (3b), in which the string is a complex noun phrase that can be paraphrased as "The horse that was raced past the barn. . . ."

(1a) I knew the answer *very well.*

(1b) I knew the answer *was correct.*

(2a) I put the box on the cart *before my break.*

(2b) I put the box on the cart *into the van.*

(3a) The horse raced past the barn *yesterday.*

(3b) The horse raced past the barn *fell.*

Various researchers (Ferreira & Clifton, 1986; Frazier, 1979; Frazier & Rayner, 1982; Mitchell & Holmes, 1985; Speer, Foss, & Smith, 1986; and Rayner, Carlson, & Frazier, 1983, among others) have measured readers' eye movements while they read sentences like these (or obtained other measures of local sentence-processing difficulty). In general, they found that reading speed slowed, and readers made frequent regressive eye movements, in the disambiguating region (italicized) of the (b) sentences in (1–3), compared with the disambiguating regions of the (a) sentences. Thus, it appears that readers and (listeners; cf. Slowiaczek, 1981; Carroll & Slowiaczek, 1987) construct only a single analysis of the ambiguous string (up to the underlined regions of the examples). If this analysis is consistent with the remainder of the sentence, as it is in the (a) cases, reading goes smoothly. If the analysis is inconsistent with the remainder of the sentence, then the reader is "garden-pathed," and must spend time and effort revising the analysis (see Frazier, 1979, for the most complete presentation of the logic behind this claim).

The Minimal Attachment Strategy

Why do readers construct the analysis that they do construct first? The superficial answer is that they follow the minimal attachment strategy, one of the sentence-parsing strategies identified by Frazier (1979). The ambiguities in (1–3) arise because a given phrase can be related to the other phrases in the left part of the string in different ways, as illustrated in Fig. 8.1. There is a systematic difference between the minimal attachment cases, on the left, and the nonminimal attachment cases, on the right, if one assumes that a phrase structure representation of the sentence is built as it is read from left to right. One or more syntactic nodes that are not needed in the (a) cases must be added in order to attach the ambigious phrase into the existing structure in a way consistent with the (b) cases. Thus, the ambiguous phrases in the (a) cases are attached into a phrase structure by adding the minimal number of new syntactic nodes, so the (a) sentences are referred to as minimal attachment cases, and the strategy of constructing representations of such sentences the minimal attachment strategy. The (b) sentences are the nonminimal attachment cases.

A deeper answer to the question of why readers construct the analyses they do comes from the realization that the minimal attachment strategy is not merely an arbitrary strategy. The strategy follows from some principles that the syntactic module obeys, primarily the principle of acepting the first available analysis (a principle that seems to apply in other realms of sentences parsing; cf. Frazier, 1987).

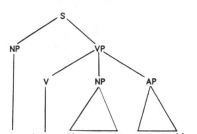

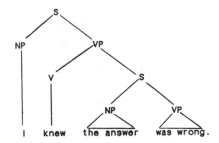

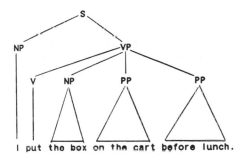

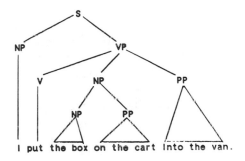

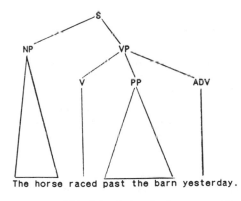

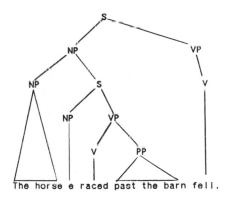

FIG. 8.1   Syntactic structures of illustrative Minimal Attachment and Non-minimal Attachment sentences.

In the initial steps of sentence parsing, a reader uses his or her knowledge of the lexicon, knowledge of the phrase structure rules of the language, and presumably, knowledge of case, to construct a phrase structure representation of a sentence. The reader identifies words, assigns them to syntactic categories (when the assignment is unambiguous; cf. Frazier & Rayner, 1987), and then determines what phase structure rules have these categories as right-hand members. For instance, when the reader receives the word *the* in (1a) he or she identifies it (unconsciously, of course) as a Determiner (D), and notes that D appears on the right-hand side of a rule that rewrites a Noun Phrase (NP) as a Determiner plus some other items. The reader is therefore licensed to add an NP to his or her analysis of the sentence. Phrase structure rules are consulted in a recursive fashion. Therefore, all phrase structure rules with NP as a right-hand member are identified. There are many such rules, including a rule that rewrites a Verb Phrase (VP) as a Verb plus a NP, and a rule that rewrites a Sentence (S) as a NP plus a VP, which in example (1) will trigger a rule rewriting a VP as a V plus an S complement.

Phrase structure rules are assumed to be consulted in parallel, with the goal of attaching the incoming word into the structure that had been built up to that point. The reader follows the very general principle of accepting the first available analysis (Frazier, 1987), presumably minimizing effort and the time that words are held in memory in an unstructured fashion. For example, in (1) the NP posited in the way described can be immediately attached as the daughter of VP, as in (1a), while the rule that rewrites S as NP plus VP must also be accessed to create the structure of (1b). Since one can reasonably assume that it will take longer to apply a greater number of rules, the analysis of (1a) will usually be created before the analysis of (1b). As soon as an attachment is made, the operation of this syntactic structure building module ceases, as far as the word in question is concerned. Thus, if later material requires the analysis in (1b), the reader must spend the time and effort to revise the initial analysis of the sentence.

Meaning and Minimal Attachment

The evidence presented earlier to show that readers are garden-pathed on non-minimal attachment sentences thus indicates that the language-processing system uses phrase structure rules to construct analyses of sentences, and follows the principle of adopting the first available analysis in using these rules. But this evidence does not by itself show that there is a modular syntactic analysis system. To have evidence for modularity, we would have to show that strategies such as the minimal attachment strategy operate unaffected by meaning or pragmatics or the contextual plausibility of the message beging constructed. Many people have doubted that they do (e.g., Crain & Steedman, 1985; McClelland, 1987). And in a sense, they are right, since the output of the strategies must be corrected by meaning and context. We can say "The man hit the girl with the wart" with pretty decent assurance that common sense will override the minimal attachment interpretation of a very peculiar instrument of hitting. But still, it may be that the strategies first yield their normal analysis, regardless of meaning or context, and then some other processes intervene to create a more cognitively acceptable analysis.

The best evidence that the minimal attachment strategy operates the same, regardless of meaning or discourse context, comes from Ferreira and Clifton (1986; cf Clifton & Ferreira, 1989, for a more recent discussion). In one experiment, we measured eye movements during the reading of sentences with a temporary ambiguity, one resolution of which was consistent with the minimal attachment strategy, and the other inconsistent with it. In some cases, the minimal attachment analysis resulted in a semantic anomaly; in other cases it did not.

We used sentences that had the form of (3a) and (3b), discussed earlier. An example of a sentence from the experiment appears in (4). In the presumably preferred minimal attachment reading, the first NP is taken as the subject of the verb *examined*. This analysis is blocked in (4b) and (4d), the syntactically disambiguated versions. The relative pronoun *that* syntactically indicates that the initial phrase of the sentence is a complex NP, containing a passive relative clause. Thus, syntactic information forces the nonminimal attachment analysis in these cases. Examples (4c) and (4d) are *semantically* unambiguous from the start. The verb *examined* requires an animate agent, so *evidence* cannot be its agent. Rather, *evidence* can only be the theme of the verb. Thus, *evidence* and *examine* cannot be in a subject–verb relation to one another, so (4c) and (4d) have semantic information that could in principle force a nonminimal attachment analysis.

(4a) *Syntactic and semantic temporary ambiguity:* The defendant examined *by the lawyer* turned out to be unreliable.

(4b) *Syntactically disambiguated:* The defendant that was examined *by the lawyer* turned out to be unreliable.

(4c) *Semantically disambiguated:* The evidence examined *by the lawyer* turned out to be unreliable.

(4d) *Syntactically and semantically disambiguated:* The evidence that was examined *by the lawyer* turned out to be unreliable.

The underlined region (in all our sentences, the agent *by*-phrase or other type of prepositional phrase; this region was not, of course, underlined for the reader) was intended to provide final disambiguating information, indicating that the correct analysis was the nonminimal attachment analysis. Previous research (cited earlier) indicated that reading would be disrupted in the disambiguating region of (4a), compared to its control, (4b), which was already syntactically unambiguous. Presumably, the reader must revise his or her initial minimal attachment analysis in (4a). This did happen, as can be seen the measures of reading time presented in Table 8.1. The semantically disambiguated sentence (4c) is the interesting one. Semantic information would make the minimal attachment reading anomalous; evidence can't examine. If a reader can use such semantic information to overcome syntactic strategies, then the preference for the minimal attachment analysis should disappear. It did not, as can be seen in Table 8.1.

It is interesting to note that readers did look longer at the verb in (4c) than in the nonanomalous (4a) as if they realized that something was wrong. Still, their sensitivity to anomaly did not guide their parsing, and they seemed to be just as badly garden-pathed as ever when the clearly disambiguating material arrived.

Tom Bever (personal communication) called our attention to the fact that not all of our sentences were as clearly disambiguated by the *by*-phrase (or other prepositional phrase) as we had intended. Instead, the clearly disambiguating material came only after the prepositional phrase in these sentences. Since disambiguation that forces a nonminimal attachment interpretation of a sentence is presumably what slows reading in our experiment, reading should not have been slowed in the prepositional phrase region of these sentences. It should have been slowed only later, when effective disambiguating material was presented.

We reanalyzed our 16 sentences into two groups. One group had nine sentences that Bever judged were adequately disambiguated by the prepositional phrase. The other group contained the seven remaining sentences that were disambiguated only later. Illustrations of the two types of sentences appears (5)

TABLE 8.1
First Pass Reading Times, in msec per Character; Nonminimal Attachment Sentences with and without Semantic Anomalies

Sentence Form	Verb	Region of Sentence Disambiguating Prepositional Phrase	Remainder of Sentence
Temporarily Ambiguous Animate (4a)	33.3	40.4	31.9
Unambiguous, Animate (4b)	31.9	30.7	33.1
Temporarily Ambiguous, Inanimate (4c)	37.7	38.4	32.6
Unambiguous, Inanimate (4d)	30.1	30.3	28.6

and (6); (5) shows sentences whose prepositional phrase presumably disambiguated the sentence, while (6) shows sentences whose clear disambiguation
came only later.

(5a) The visitor (ship) sighted by the lookout probably brought bad news.

(5b) The singer (song) listened to by the spellbound audience was the most . . .

(5c) The man (meal) brought to the high priest could hardly be described . . .

(6a) The tramp (trash) smelled by the dog was laying on the sidewalk.

(6b) The children (stories) told about the incident were a big source of concern.

(6c) The author (book) read by the student was very hard to understand.

The sentences where disambiguation by the prepositional phrase was judged
to be successful (5) showed the pattern of data I have presented so far, as can be
seen in Table 8.2. The syntactically ambiguous versions of these sentences were
read slowly in the region of the prepositional phrase. The remaining sentences
(6) were not read slowly during the prepositional phrase, but instead, were read
slowly in the region right after it, which is in fact the effective disambiguating
region.

This experiment does seem to show that readers do not use semantic information about the animacy requirements of verbs to guide their initial syntactic
analysis of sentences. However, a theorist who believes that sentence processing
does not reflect the operation of a specialized syntactic module, but instead
shows the working of a general problem-solving mechanism, might object that
these animacy requirements constitute a logical subtlety that readers are not very
good at using. Such a theorist might note that language is used in context, and

TABLE 8.2
First Pass Reading Times in msec per Character;
Separated by Region of Effective Disambiguation

Sentence Form	Region of Sentence	
	Prep Phrase Region	Next Region
Sentences disambiguated by prepositional phrase		
Temporarily ambiguous	41.9	27.5
Syntactically unambiguous	29.6	29.7
Sentences disambiguated after prepositional phrase		
Temporarily ambiguous	35.7	40.8
Syntactically unambiguous	32.0	27.4

that readers and listeners would surely use context to guide their analysis of sentences. This theorist might even suggest that findings about how sentences are processed out of context really don't count for much.

Context and Minimal Attachment

Consider how minimal attachment ambiguities could be processed in context. For instance, consider the ambiguity between NP and VP attachment of a prepositional phrase, as in (2a) and (2b) (repeated below; see also Fig. 8.1)

(2a) I put the box on the cart *before my break.*
(2b) I put the box on the cart *into the van.*

Following a suggestion of Crain and Steedman's (1985), the only time it would be appropriate to use the NP-atachment analysis of "put the box on the cart . . ." is when context provides a box on a cart and one or more other boxes not on carts, so that we can use the prepositional phrase to indicate which box we are referring to. I don't happen to accept the analysis; I can refer to the shirt on my back even if it is the only one around. Nonetheless, it might seem that presenting a sentence like this out of context would present a pragmatic bias against the NP attachment analysis. Perhaps, then, the minimal attachment preference is not a syntactic structure preference at all, but a pragmatic preference (see Crain & Steedman for the full argument; see Clifton & Ferreira, 1987, for some counter-arguments).

We tested this claim (Ferreira & Clifton, 1986) by presenting temporarily ambiguous sentences like those in (7) in contexts that should bias one reading or the other. (The phrase whose structural attachment is ambiguous is capitalized in the example; the disambiguating phrase is italicized.)

(7a) *Minimal attachment:* Sam loaded the boxes ON THE CART *before his coffee break.*
(7b) *Nonminimal attachment:* Sam loaded the boxes ON THE CART *into the van.*

We had experimental participants read such sentences in the context of paragraphs like those in (8) that either introduced an indefinite quantity of referents (neutral), as in (8a); introduced just a single set of referents which could not appropriately be described by the ambiguously attached phrase (consistent with minimal attachment, VP modification), as in (8b); or introduced two sets of referents, one of which could be described by the ambiguously attached phrase (consistent with the nonminimal attachment, NP modification reading), as in (8c).

(8a) *Neutral, both readings possible*
Sam worked at a factory warehouse. His job was to make sure that boxes of merchandise were ready to be delivered. Sam wanted to go for his coffee break, but his boss said he had a little more work to do. He wanted Sam to free up a cart for some guys in another department. *Sam loaded the boxes on the cart before his coffee break.* (OR, *Sam loaded the boxes on the cart into the van.*) Then he was free to take a much needed break.

(8b) *Biased, vp attachment reading (minimal attachment)*
Sam worked at a factory warehouse. His job was to make sure that boxes of merchandise were ready to be delivered. Sam wanted to go for his coffee break, but his boss said Sam had to fill up one more cart before he could go. The boss knew some guys from another department needed the cart. *Sam loaded the boxes on the cart before his coffee break.* Then he was free to take a much needed break.

(8c). *Biased, np attachment reading (nonminimal attachment)*
Sam worked at a factory warehouse. His job was to make sure that boxes of merchandise were ready to be delivered. Sam had to fill up a van so it could go out. He had a pile of boxes on a cart and another pile on the floor. *Sam loaded the boxes on the cart onto the van.* Then he was free to take a much needed break.

Crain and Steedman predicted—and frankly, we expected—that the minimal attachment preference would go away in contexts like (8c). It did not, as can be seen in Table 8.3. Readers had just as much trouble when the sentence turned out to have a nonminimal attachment reading that was pragmatically appropriate for the context as when it did not. They seemed to have no trouble with minimal attachment readings, regardless of their pragmatic appropriateness. At least, they showed these patterns of results in their eye movement patterns and in their pattern of self-paced reading times.

Other results, also shown in Table 8.3, showed that the context information was available to readers, and that they did use it eventually. When they were asked questions at the end of each passage, they were more accurate in the conditions where context pragmatically supported the analysis than in the conditions where it did not. As I have been saying, readers will use all the information at their disposal eventually, including context information; but it turns out that they do not use this information, available or not, during initial sentence parsing.

There is much more to say about how phrase structure rules are used in parsing. Many people who hear the arguments I have given suggest that all we need is a stronger context, or sharper anomalies. Perhaps that is so. I suspect that some contexts will overcome the parsing strategies. For instance, if one has just

TABLE 8.3
Minimal and Nonminimal Attachment Sentences in Biasing and Neutral Contexts

Condition	Region of Sentence		Regression	Percentage Correct
	Ambiguous Prep. Phrase	Disambiguating Region		
Minimal attachment				
Neutral context	21 (5)	22 (3)	0.216	74%
Biasing context	25 (2)	26 (2)	0.194	89%
Nonminimal attachment				
vc Neutral context	20 (14)	31 (30)	0.579	71%
Biasing context	19 (7)	33 (19)	0.715	78%

First pass (and second pass) reading times in msec per letter: proportions of regressions, and percentage correct are indicated.

read about some boxes on a cart, referred to by the phrase "the boxes on the cart," and sees this same phrase in the next sentence, he or she is probably less likely to make a minimal attachment analysis (cf. Frazier, Taft, Roeper, Clifton, & Ehrlich, 1984). The enterprise of determining just what information the syntactic parsing module is sensitive to is a legitimate and potentially rewarding one.

Further, as indicated earlier, the task of determining how analyses provided by a syntactic parsing module are integrated with other knowledge must be addressed. Clearly, a successful parse is not the end result of comprehension. An extreme illustration of this is found in the work of Bransford and Johnson (1973), who showed that people essentially fail to comprehend easily parsed sentences when no context is available to specify their interpretation. Several researchers have taken up this task, and have begun to learn how various types of semantic and pragmatic information are used in arriving at a final interpretation of sentences (e.g., Rayner et al., 1983; Mitchell & Holmes, 1985; Speer et al., 1986). However, rather than review this work (which has barely begun) I will turn to a related question: How fine-grained is the modular organization of the sentence comprehension system? It appears that there is a syntactic module that operates independently of semantics and pragmatics. Does this module itself have modular subcomponents that operate independently of one another?

MODULARITY IN PROCESSING LONG-DISTANCE DEPENDENCIES

I have spoken as if phrase structure rules constituted the only grammatical knowledge relevant to the syntactic module. However, not all sentence structures can be successfully parsed by reference to phrase structure rules alone (Clifton & Frazier, 1989; Fodor, 1979; but cf. Crain & Fodor, 1985). Consider cases such as those illustrated in (9). These are sentences which used to be, and in some theories still are, handled by the transformation rules that so fascinated psycholinguists back in the early days of experimental psycholinguistics. In each case, the sentence must be analyzed as if a virtual phrase occurred in a position that no phrase actually occurs in. The position without a phrase is referred to as a "gap" (or an empty element), and is represented in (9) by a '____' or the symbol "PRO"; the phrase that must be interpreted as if it occurred in this position is referred to as a "filler," and is italicized in (9). A gap and its associated filler have the same subscript, which is used to indicate that they are coindexed (and, roughly speaking, referentially identical).

(9a) *Relative clause:* The boy *that*₁ the man saw ____₁ went home.

(9b) *Complement clause: The boy*₁ wanted PRO₁ to go home.

(9c) *Purpose clause: The boy*₁ bought *a book*ⱼ PRO₁ to read ____ⱼ.

(9d) *Rationale clause: The boy*₁ lent some books to Tom Pro₁ to keep Billy from borrowing them.

(9e) *WH-question: Who*₁ did the boy take ____₁ home?

Lyn Frazier and I have spent several years studying how people identify gaps and relate them to fillers in sentences like those in (9) (cf. Clifton & Frazier, 1989). We have obtained some intriguing if preliminary data that suggest that there is modularity *within* the syntactic processing system. Consider the sentences shown as (10–12).

(10a) *What* did John think his friends should win (____) at ____?

(10b) *What* did John think his friends should excel at ____?

(11a) *What* did John think [the girl who always won (*____)] received ____?

(11b) *What* did John think [the girl who always excelled] received ____?

(12a) John thought the girl should win convincingly.

(12b) John thought the girl should excel convincingly.

Sentences (10a) and (10b) differ in that *win* is a verb that is generally used with a direct object, while *excel* is not (Connine, Ferreira, Jones, Clifton, &

Frazier, 1984). We have shown (Clifton, Frazier, & Connine, 1984) that subjects have more difficulty comprehending (10a) than (10b) when they had to read each sentence and then judge its acceptability as a sentence of English. We suggest that this is because readers tend to posit an NP object for *win*, take that NP to be a gap, and to assume that the gap corresponds to the filler "What." This is shown to be wrong by the last word of the sentence, requiring a reanalysis of the sentence and hence slowing reaction time. The verb *excel*, on the other hand, is an intransitive verb, which does not provoke the reader falsely to postulate a gap after it. Thus, the reader is still waiting for a gap when the last word of the sentence (10b) appears, and thus analyzes it correctly. We have replicated this difference in the studies reported here, as can be seen in Table 8.4. Sentences (12a) and (12b), which have no filler or tempting filler-gap assignment, serve as lexical controls for the comparison between (10a) and (10b).

The contrast between Sentences (11a) and (11b) is the interesting one. Here, the tempting gap is after the verb "win" in (11a). But notice that this gap is inside a relative clause. It is ungrammatical to relate a gap inside a relative clause to a filler outside the clause (Ross, 1967). You can't say "Which prize did the girl who won?" If the syntactic processing system is uniform, and all syntactic information is made available for use together, then readers should not be tempted by this false gap inside the relative clause. After all, we have no reason to believe that readers overlook phrase structure information with any substantial frequency, so why should they overlook available information about syntactic constraints upon extraction from a relative clause?

On the other hand, the syntactic processing system might itself be organized in a modular fashion, and information about phrase structure and about how fillers and gaps can be related to one another ("constraints on coindexing") may be processed by separate modules (consistent with Chomsky's [1981] modularization of syntax). If this is so, we might very well expect readers falsely to postulate a gap after the transitive verb in the relative clause. They might first assign a phrase structure analysis to the sentence and assign coreferential indexes

TABLE 8.4
Time and Accuracy of Sentence Judgments to Sentences with Fillers and Gaps

Condition	Judgment Time (msec)	Percentage Errors
Transitive verb, Grammatical gap (10a)	1147	24%
Intransitive verb, Grammatical gap (10b)	1075	21%
Transitive verb, Ungrammatical gap (11a)	1168	24%
Intransitive verb, Ungrammatical gap (11b)	1125	18%
Transitive verb, No-gap control (12a)	1105	7%
Intransitive verb, No-gap control (12b)	1093	8%

using the heuristics and principles I have discussed so far, and only later check for consistency with coindexing constraints.

The data, shown in Table 8.4, indicate that the latter possibility may be correct (see also Frazier, 1985; Clifton & Frazier, 1989). There is a tendency, marginal in statistical significance but consistent across three separate experiments, for people to read the sentences with a preferred transitive verb inside the relative clause (Sentence 11a) more slowly than the sentences with an intransitive verb (Sentence 11b). This indicates to us that readers momentarily assigned the filler "What" to the false gap inside the island, following phrase structure information and gap-finding heuristics (Clifton & Frazier, 1989) but ignoring information about coindexing constraints (see Freedman & Forster, 1985, for a related analysis; see Crain & Fodor, 1985; Fodor, 1985, for some criticisms of these analyses).

CONCLUSIONS

The research strategy advocated here is not one that is designed to give its practitioners a comfortable feeling of insight into the phenomena we all experience when we are trying to understand someone. Neither is it a strategy that results in a flattering picture of language users as very flexible and powerful general-purpose information-processing devices. However, it is a strategy that has, in my opinion, resulted in substantial success in meeting the goals we set for ourselves a quarter-century ago. We now know quite a lot about how people use grammatical rules in the process of comprehending sentences. And even more than that, it is a strategy that has resulted in support for an intriguing view of mind, a view that claims we can obtain a sharp understanding of the parts of mind that are generally relatively simple, special-purpose, computational devices, precisely tuned to the details of one relevant and limited part of the environment.

ACKNOWLEDGMENTS

The research reported here was supported in part by grant MH–18708 to Charles Clifton and Lyn Frazier. I would like to thank Fernanda Ferreira, Lyn Frazier, Keith Rayner, and Robert Hoffman for their comments on an earlier version of this chapter.

REFERENCES

Bever, T. (1970). The cognitive basis for linguistic structures. In R. Hayes (Ed.), *Cognition and language development*. New York: Wiley.

Bransford, J. D., & Johnson, M. K. (1973). Considerations of some problems of comprehension. In W. G. Chase (Ed.), *Visual Information processing*. New York: Academic Press.

Carroll, P., & Slowiaczek, M. (1987). Modes and modules: Multiple pathways to the language processor. In J. L. Garfield (Ed.), *Modularity in sentence comprehension: Knowledge representation and natural language understanding,* Cambridge, MA: MIT Press.

Chomsky, N. (1957). *Syntactic Structures.* The Hague: Mouton.

Chomsky, N. (1965). *Aspects of the theory of syntax.* Cambridge, MA: MIT Press.

Chomsky, N. (1981). *Lectures on government and binding: The Pisa lectures.* Dordrecht, Netherlands: Foris.

Clark, H., & Clark, E. (1977). *Psychology and language.* New York: Harcourt Brace Jovanovich.

Clifton, C., Jr., & Ferreira, F. (1987). In J. L. Garfield (Ed.), *Modularity in knowledge representation and natural language understanding,* Cambridge, MA: MIT Press.

Clifton, C., Jr., & Ferreira, F. (1989). Ambiguity in context. *Language and Cognitive Processes, 4,* SI77-104.

Clifton, C., Jr., & Frazier, L. (1989). Comprehending sentences with long-distance dependencies. In G. M. Carlson & M. K. Tanenhaus (Eds.), *Linguistic structure in language processing.* Dordrecht, Netherlands: Reidel.

Clifton, C. J. Frazier, L., & Connine, C. (1984). Lexical expectations in sentence comprehension. *Journal of Verbal Learning and Verbal Behavior, 23,* 696–708.

Clifton, C., Jr., & Odom, P. B. (1966). Similarity relations among certain English sentence constructions. *Psychological Monographs, 80,* (No. 5, whole No. 613).

Connine, C., Ferreira, F., Jones, C., Clifton, C., Jr., & Frazier, L. (1984). Verb frame preferences: Descriptive norms. *Journal of Psycholinguistic Research, 13,* 307–319.

Crain, S., & Fodor, J. D. (1985). How can grammars help parsers? In D. Dowty, L. Kartunnen, & A. Zwicky (Eds.), *Natural language parsing.* Cambridge, England: Cambridge University Press.

Crain, S., & Steedman, M. (1985). On not being led up the garden path: The use of context by the psychological parser. In D. Dowty, L. Kartunnen, & A. Zwicky (Eds.), *Natural language parsing.* Cambridge, England: Cambridge University Press.

Ferreira, F., & Clifton, C., Jr. (1986). The independence of syntactic processing. *Journal of Memory and Language, 25,* 348–368.

Fodor, J. A. (1983). *Modularity of mind.* Cambridge, MA: MIT Press.

Fodor, J. A., & Garrett, M. (1967). Some syntactic determinants of sentence complexity. *Perception and Psychophysics, 2,* 289–296.

Fodor, J. D. (1979). Superstrategy. In W. E. Cooper & E. C. T. Walker (Eds.), *Sentence processing.* Hillsdale, NJ: Lawrence Erlbaum Associates.

Fodor, J. D. (1985). Deterministic parsing and subjacency. *Language and Cognitive Processes, 1,* 3–42.

Forster, K. (1979). Levels of processing and the structure of the language processor. In W. E. Cooper & E. C. T. Walker (Eds.), *Sentence processing.* Hillsdale, NJ: Lawrence Erlbaum Associates.

Frazier, L. (1979). *On comprehending sentences: Syntactic parsing strategies.* Bloomington: Indiana University Linguistics Club.

Frazier, L. (1985). Modularity and the representational hypothesis. *Proceedings of NELS 12, The Northeastern Linguistics Society.* Amherst, MA: Graduate Linguistics Students Associations.

Frazier, L. (1987). Sentence processing. In M. Coltheart (Ed.), *Attention and Performance X.I.I.* Hillsdale, NJ: Lawrence Erlbaum Association.

Frazier, L., & Rayner, K. (1982). Making and correcting errors during sentence comprehension: Eye movements in the analysis of structurally ambiguous sentences. *Cognitive Psychology, 14,* 178–210.

Frazier, L., & Rayner, K. (1987). Resolution of syntactic category ambiguities: Eye movements in parsing lexically ambiguous sentences. *Journal of Memory and Language, 26,* 505–526.

Frazier, L., Taft, L., Roeper T., Clifton C., & Ehrlich, K. (1984). Parallel structure: A source of facilitation in sentence comprehension. *Memory & Cognition, 12,* 421–430.

Freedman, S. E., & Forster, K. I. (1985). The psychological status of overgenerated sentences. *Cognition, 19,* 101–132.

Gough, P. (1966). The verification of sentences: The effects of delay of evidence and sentence length. *Journal of Verbal Learning and Verbal Behavior, 5,* 492–496.

Gough, P., & Diehl, R. (1978). Experimental psycholinguistics. In W. O. Dingwall (Ed.), *A survey of linguistic science.* Stamford, CT: Greylock.

Gruber, J. (1965). *Studies in lexical relations.* Doctoral dissertation, Massachusetts Institute of Technology, Cambridge.

Jackendoff, R. S. (1972). *Semantic interpretation in generative grammar.* Cambridge, MA: MIT Press.

Marcus, M. (1982). *A theory of syntactic recognition for natural language.* Cambridge, MA: MIT Press.

McClelland, J. (1987). How we use what we know in reading: An interactive-activation approach. In M. Coltheart (Ed.), *Attention and Performance* (Vol. 12). Hillsdale, NJ: Lawrence Erlbaum Associates.

Mehler, J. (1963). Some effects of grammatical transformations on the recall of English sentences. *Journal of Verbal Learning and Verbal Behavior, 4,* 346–351.

Miller, G. (1962). Some psychological studies of grammar. *American Psychologist, 17,* 748–762.

Mitchell, D., & Holmes, V. (1985). The role of specific information about the verb in parsing sentences with local structural ambiguity. *Journal of Memory and Language, 24,* 542–559.

Rayner, K., Carlson, M., & Frazier, L. (1983). The interaction of syntax and semantics during sentence processing: Eye movements in the analysis of semantically biased sentences. *Journal of Verbal Learning and Verbal Behavior, 22,* 358–374.

Ross, J. (1967). *Constraints on variables in syntax.* Unpublished doctoral Dissertation, Massachusetts Institute of Technology, Cambridge.

Slowiaczek, M. L. (1981). *Prosodic units as language processing units.* Unpublished doctoral dissertation, University of Massachusetts, Amherst.

Speer, S. R., Foss, D. J., & Smith, C. (1986, November). *Syntactic and thematic contributions to sentence complexity.* Paper presented at the meetings of the Psychonomic Society, New Orleans.

Van Riemsdijk, J., & Williams, E. (1986). *Introduction to the theory of grammar.* Cambridge, MA: MIT Press.

9 Global and Local Context Effects in Sentence Processing

Donald J. Foss
Shari R. Speer
The University of Texas at Austin

The psychologist who chooses to investigate
verbal behavior cannot long avoid becoming entangled
in problems of verbal context. (Jenkins, Mink, & Russell, 1958, p. 127)

As your eye darts across this page, the material in successive fixations is integrated, yielding the (veridical) impression that the world of the page is relatively stable and predictable. Analogously, during (most) normal language comprehension the information in a single proposition or clause is integrated with prior material, giving comprehenders the impression that the content of the material has a certain stability and coherence—that it is about something. Readers and listeners assume that writers and speakers intend their messages to cohere; consequently, they interpret unclear cases as clearly as they can, seeking relevance and stability even when the message does not do a good job of displaying it. Comprehenders construct a model consistent with the input and with the bedrock facts of the world as they assume them to be (Quine, 1953). In addition, they may form expectations about what is to come, and the processing of later material may be influenced by those expectations. Speakers, too, rely upon context as they structure what they say. The use of anaphoric devices, ellipses, audience-appropriate jargon, and so on, are among the many indications of that fact. As the introductory quote from Jenkins et al. illustrates, the problem of context in understanding verbal behavior has long been recognized. Indeed, the number and complexity of the variables that determine what gets said is so great that it is unreasonable to have as one's goal to predict what an individual will say in a given set of circumstances. A more realistic goal is to discover the manner and mechanisms by which context produces its effects.

Consider a thought experiment involving eye movements. Suppose we devise a study in which the information in the visual display changes from one eye fixation to the next so that odd-numbered fixations tell one story and even-numbered fixations tell a different one. One can perhaps get a feel for such an experiment by trying to keep track of the following two passages (in each case the initial sentence of an essay) while reading them strictly left to right; italicized material comes from one source (Snow, 1967), while material in regular print from another (Hardy, 1940/1967). We find that even such a short passage gives us great difficulty:

> *It was* It is *a perfectly* a melancholy *ordinary night* experience *at Christ's* for a *high table*, professional *except that* mathematician *Hardy* to find *was dining* himself *as a* writing about *guest.* mathematics.

Any reader of this chapter will be able to construct various theoretical accounts for the difficulty of such a passage. For present purposes, we wish to focus on one source, the impact of prior material on the way that incoming information is processed. Two possible effects are of interest to us here. First, lexical processing may be slowed when two sources are interleaved in this fashion, since contextual influences on lexical processing would surely be attenuated. Second, integrating information across odd-numbered fixations and, separately, across even-numbered ones, would almost certainly influence how (and, indeed, whether) that integration takes place.

The psycholinguistic literature has dealt often with these two issues: the role of context on word recognition, and the problem of integrating new material into an ongoing discourse representation (see Foss, 1988, for a selective review). The latter is also a variant of the very general topic of establishing and maintaining coherence during discourse and story comprehension. In this chapter, we wish to revisit these topics, summarizing new data that bear on them, and relating them to theories and other facts that we believe are relevant to these issues. Our main thesis is that context affects the processing of linguistic information in ways not wholly consistent with "classic" accounts based on the mechanisms of semantic priming. On the other hand, the data are consistent with a newer view of priming that we will review here, and with theories that emphasize the importance of semantic integration. To accomplish these goals we will first describe some work concerned with context effects on lexical processing, and will review the explanations that have been offered for those effects. We will then report on work carried out in our laboratory, including new work on the comprehension of auditorily presented materials, and discuss our interpretation of it. That interpretation makes contact with the literature on "semantic flexibility"; we then use these ideas to make predictions about the outcomes of future studies.

CONTEXT AND LEXICAL PROCESSING

Many studies have examined the effects of context on the processing of words that occur late in a sentence (e.g., Stanovich & West, 1983; Schwanenflugel & LaCount, 1988). Of course, one can define "context" in a variety of ways; Schwanenflugel and Shoben (1985) describe three: (1), the degree of constraint (how likely it is that the context suggests a single next word); (2), the experiment-wide predictability of the word—a variable in which the likelihood of a high-constraint item is manipulated across sentences (i.e., in some experiments the highly constrained sentences continue as expected on most trials, in other experiments those sentences actually continue in an unexpected fashion on most trials); and (3), the congruity of context and test item. Fischler and Bloom (1985) describe the latter as the "proportion of sentence contexts [that] are followed by words that are plausible, or congruous [but not necessarily highly predictable], in that context." Contexts promoting both facilitation and inhibition have been examined (for reviews, see Stanovich & West, 1983; Seidenberg, Waters, Sanders, & Langer, 1984). Although there clearly are effects of these various forms of context on the processing of individual items in both lists (e.g., Neely, 1977) and sentences (e.g., Blank & Foss, 1978), many investigators would agree with the conclusion expressed by Fischler and Bloom about lexical access, to wit, that "during the normal reading . . . it would seem that none of the three main processes of contextual effects [the three summarized above] . . . have much of a role to play in reading for meaning" (1985, p. 138). Thus, a lot of energy has been spent investigating a seemingly small effect.

Why are the effects of context on lexical access so small? Two reasons have been adduced. One is that sentence comprehension itself requires processing resources that are needed to form expectancies about upcoming words (Stanovich & West, 1983). That is, when one is struggling to understand what has already been presented, it is difficult to speculate about what is coming. Thus, some of the effects that one may observe in studies using lists of words may not appear in sentence processing experiments. A second reason is that the speed of lexical access is generally so fast for skilled readers and listeners that context can rarely demonstrate its effectiveness. Our colleague Phil Gough is fond of pointing out how quickly one understands a word like "elephant" when it appears out the blue; improving on that speed is difficult.

Of course, an empirically small effect is consistent with a large theoretical commitment. Those who believe that context guides retrieval from the mental lexicon thereby rule out a substantial class of theories about sentence processing—those claiming that lexical access is an autonomous, informationally encapsulated process. In other words, the view that retrieval is guided by (supralexical) context is incompatible with the assumptions of modularity (e.g., Fodor, 1983; Marslen–Wilson & Tyler, 1987). Thus, a significant metatheoretical issue about the proper class of theories for language processing may turn on a few milliseconds of difference in measures of lexical processing—and how they are interpreted.

Explanations for Context Effects: Priming vs. Integration

Let us review briefly the most influential explanation for how context effects on lexical processing are said to operate: semantic priming. Descriptively, priming is said to occur when the processing of one word leads to speeded processing of another. Generally the explanations for priming emphasize spreading activation within the system of lexical representation. Numerous models of priming have been forwarded, perhaps the most popular ones being variants of Posner and Snyder's (1975) two-factor theory (see Stanovich & West, 1983, for a recent version; for a critical review of these models and their predictions, see Lorch, 1982). The first factor is a fast-acting spread of activation within the "mental lexicon"; activation spreads from a word to its semantic relatives. Its operation is automatic in the sense that it does not require attention nor does its operation hinder any other mental activity. Also, it occurs within the lexicon, so it is compatible with the modularity thesis. The second factor is a slower-acting, attention-requiring component. Its operation can interfere with other activities that require processing resources. To the extent that priming relies upon the second factor, its operation will be attenuated by other attention-demanding activities associated with comprehension. The work of Neely (1977), using word lists, is often cited as providing evidence compatible with the two-factor theory.

Another explanation for context effects in natural language processing does not rely upon priming but instead upon speeded integration of semantically related materials (Foss & Ross, 1983, discuss such an account). An integration perspective suggest that the locus of semantic priming is not the lexicon; at least that is not the sole locus. Instead, semantic facilitation effects occur at the level of the comprehension process where the meanings of individual words are amalgamated to form the meanings of phrases and sentences. As the listener attempts to understand what he or she hears, a semantic representation is constructed. Processing is speeded when new input is readily "consistent" with the representation that has already been formed from the preceding input. In yet other models, the semantic representation produced by integration constrains the spread of activation to associates in the lexicon so that only words related to the current representation are activated (Carpenter & Daneman, 1981). "High-level" discourse information, such as topic-related material and core propositions, may remain active in the representation (van Djik & Kintsch, 1983). In this view, the amount of time and the number of words separating two related items makes little difference as long as the main focus of the discourse does not change (e.g., Foss, 1982; Sharkey & Mitchell, 1985).

Investigators studying context effects have examined cases in which there is no associative relation between the target word and any one word in the prior context. Instead, there is a relation between the "topic" and the target. For example, the context *The old man sat with his head down and did not hear a word of the sermon during mass* might be followed by a test word *sleep* (as it was in a study by Till, Mross, & Kintsch, 1988). Such "topical inference words . . . show no priming at stimulus onset asynchronies (SOAs) [the time between the presentation of "mass" and the presentation of "sleep"] up to 500 msec" (p. 292). Facilitation does exist at an SOA of 1000 msec, but Till et al. argue that such facilitation is due to a deferred inference, or as we might say, to an integration effect.

A few theorists attempt to stay within the bounds of activation theory, but deny that it is strictly an intralexical phenomenon. For example, Kleiman (1980) suggested that "schemas" as well as lexical items, automatically activate a set of associates. A related suggestion was made by Auble and Franks (1983). The latter examined the ease of identification for masked target words preceded by priming sentences. The sentences were either easy to understand or difficult. Target words were recognized more readily when they followed an easy-to-understand priming sentence. Furthermore, there was no such facilitation for targets when they were related to individual words within the priming sentence but not related to the overall meaning of the priming sentence. Thus, this form of "priming" is not based on lexical relations. It does not actually fit the description of priming we gave earlier, to wit, that "priming is said to occur when the processing of one word leads to speeded processing of another." To the extent that the theoretical explanation for the effect turns on prior activation of particular items, the appellation priming may be appropriate. We assume that the theoretical connection is that the locus of the effect depends on connections between material stored in long-term memory—in this case between topics, schemata, and so on, and individual lexical items, connections that lead to passive activation of the lexical items independent of whether or not they occur in the input. We might dub this "topical priming," just to have a separate name for it. In contrast, an integration explanation requires that the material actually occur in the input and that the locus of the effect is tied up with the dynamics of comprehension beyond the level of lexical activation.

To review, explanations for the descriptive facts of priming and facilitation phenomena can be conveniently divided along two dimensions, lexical versus nonlexical, and priming versus integration. By far most attention has been directed toward automatic intralexical priming explanations, and our critique will focus upon them as well. In what follows, we will generally assume that priming refers to lexical priming. Foss and Ross (1983) dubbed such explanations LLA models (lexical–lexical activation). According to these models, "When a stimulus occurs, certain subsets of words in the mental lexicon . . . —those semantically related to the stimulus word(s)—become active . . . [they] are 'indirectly accessible' from the stimulus" (pp. 172–173). However, Foss and Ross argued that "it is neither necessary nor sufficient that semantically related words occur near to each other for semantic facilitation to occur during sentence processing" (p. 189). In other words, they suggested that the correct model of facilitation is not a member of the class of LLA models.

Most investigators would probably agree that it is not necessary for two semantically related items to occur near to each other in order to observe faster processing of the second. A word late in a sentence may be integrated into its semantic representation more readily if a related word has occurred earlier. However, such a result should not be credited to LLA priming and so does not bear directly upon that phenomenon, except for the necessity to show that the phenomenon is not in fact due to LLA priming. This has been done by Foss (1982) and by O'Seaghdha (1989). The latter used a lexical decision task, finding that subjects responded to *book* more rapidly than to *floor* in the context, *The author of this_*. However, there was no advantage for book in the context, *The author this from_*. O'Seaghdha's work is consistent with the slogan, "No semantic facilitation without syntactic coherence," which seems quite appropriate for an explanation founded on integration.

In contrast, and very important for our main point, we doubt that most theorists would agree with the other side of the claim, namely that the occurrence of two related words in adjacent positions is not sufficient for LLA priming. There is a very large number of studies in the literature demonstrating the effectiveness of such a manipulation; indeed, it is the paradigm case. However, Foss and Ross (1983) presented some evidence in support of the view that adjacency in a sentence need not lead to facilitation of the second of two related items. Their study was not definitive, though, and their discussion ignored some apparent counterexamples.

We intend to look again at the argument that speeded processing is not the inevitable result when two semantically related words occur next to each other in sentences. A fresh look seems warranted since, as we will show, the results of this work may bear on issues of processing, organization of linguistic information, and the modularity thesis.

FACILITATION FROM DISCOURSE SEMANTICS

Consider what should occur if, say, the word *nurse* is immediately preceded by the word *doctor's* in a sentence (e.g., *The doctor's nurse handed him a scalpel*). According to the most prevalent view of priming, when *doctor's* has been accessed, activation will spread from it to related items, in particular to *nurse*. The latter will then be more rapidly recognized than had *doctor's* not occurred. Note that the explanation for such facilitation is based on the first of the mechanisms of priming—the fast-acting, nonattention-demanding, automatic mechanism. Alternatively, if we consider the integration interpretation of facilitation, it should still be easier to integrate the phrase *doctor's nurse* than, say, *man's nurse*. Admittedly the latter is a prediction derived from intuition rather than from an actual theory of semantic integration, but the intuition seems a secure one.

Foss and Ross (1983) introduced a somewhat different way of conceptualizing this situation. Recall that one of the major functions of a semantic representation is to help "pick out" the appropriate referents in the world (or, more accurately, in one's model of the world). The referents picked out by a phrase (its semantic values, if you will) can be very different from the referents of the individual words that compose the phrase. Thus, "leather" picks out one set of elements, "genuine leather" picks out the same set, but "simulated leather" picks out quite a different set, one that shares no elements with the others. Foss and Ross noted the obvious, namely that a semantic representation of each phrase is developed as comprehension proceeds. They went on to suggest that:

> Once the semantic interpretation of a phrase has been computed, the comprehender examines memory to see whether a representation of that interpretation exists there and, if so, the set of concepts and words semantically or pragmatically related to it are then indirectly accessible. Thus, the items that are accessible are those related to the high-level interpretation of the phrase (or higher constituent). . . . [T]he set of words that is indirectly accessible from a phrase may be different from the set that is indirectly accessible from its constituent words. (p. 173)

The semantic interpretation of the head of a phrase and the interpretation of the phrase itself seem typically to overlap in terms of the referents or situations to which they refer. A broken wrist is still a wrist, and even a broken promise is still a promise. (As noted, this is not always the case; a broken date is no longer a date.) Consequently, if a later-occurring word is related to the head of a phrase it may typically be related to the phrase itself. In that case, it will appear that the occurrence of the head has made the later word indirectly accessible. But, according to Foss and Ross, that is an illusion. It is really the occurrence of the phrase that has done the work. Foss and Ross considered what would happen if a word (w_j) is related to its immediate predecessor (w_{j-1}), but not to the semantic interpretation of the sentence up to and including w_{j-1}. According to their hypothesis, w_j will not be indirectly accessible; its processing will not be speeded. Thus, we should find cases where the processing of *nurse* in *doctor's nurse,* or the processing of *camera* in *photographer's camera* is no faster than its processing in *man's nurse,* or *executive's camera.* Foss and Ross presented some evidence in support of this hypothesis. Since our work builds upon the paradigm that they introduced, we will review their study in some detail.

Global vs. Local Facilitation

Each experimental trial in the Foss and Ross study contained a critical word of interest (e g., *camera* in the following examples) that was preceded by contexts of two different types. One context we will call "local" (local context refers to the word immediately preceding the critical word). The local context was either semantically (and associatively) related to the critical word (e.g., *photographer's camera*) or not (e.g., *man's camera*). The other context we will call "global," which refers loosely to the topic or setting of the discourse up to the critical word. The global context, too, was either semantically related to the critical word or not. Now consider the situation in which the semantic interpretation of the global context is not (directly) related to the critical word. In that case we expect neither faster lexical access nor faster semantic integration—even when the local context word is directly related to the critical word. This prediction is contrary to a standard spreading activation theory of semantic priming. Concrete examples may clarify the materials and the prediction.

Subjects in Foss and Ross's first experiment listened to a group of two or three sentences comprising a very short narrative or vignette. They were asked to comprehend the items and, in addition, to perform the phoneme-monitoring task, pushing a button when one of the words in the narrative began with a phoneme that was specified in advance of the trial. Foss and Ross were interested in the relative amount of time needed to process a critical word (e.g., *camera*) in the vignette. The word carrying the target phoneme occurred immediately following the critical word; reaction time (RT) to the target phoneme served as an indicator of the relative amount of processing required for the critical word.

As noted, the experiment involved two independent variables: local and global context. To manipulate local context, the critical word was immediately preceded by a semantically related possessive (e.g., *photographer's*) on half of the trials, and by a relatively neutral possessive (e.g., *man's*) on the remaining half of the trials. To manipulate global context, they placed a "setting" word early in the first sentence of each trial. These settings were chosen so that they could significantly influence the semantic interpretation of the material that followed. Half of the trials contained a neutral setting word (e.g., *workroom*), while the other half contained a word that we considered semantically unrelated to the critical word (e.g., *bakery*).

Global context words in the neutral condition were chosen so that the listener could reasonably continue to focus upon a typical characteristic of the actor (e.g., photographer in a workroom encourages the interpretation that photographic equipment is involved). Unrelated words were chosen so that the listener would compute an interpretation of the sentence that was not closely related to the typical characteristics of the actor. For example, in (4), which follows, the listener is essentially told that the photographer is in a bakery. The rest of the vignette, up to the word *camera*, permits the listener to construe the input as being about aspects of the setting (i.e., it is bakery-related) and not about stereotypical aspects of a photographer. (The target phoneme for these sentences is /g/.)

Global context: Neutral; Local context: Neutral
(1) Mornings spent looking over things in the workroom were always pleasurable for the man. The sights and smells filled him with anticipation. It was clear that the man's camera gave him an ideal means of capturing his favorite moments.

Global context: Neutral; Local context: Related
(2) Mornings spent looking over things in the workroom were always pleasurable for the photographer. The sights and smells filled him with anticipation. It was clear that the photographer's camera gave him an ideal means of capturing his favorite moments.

Global context: Unrelated; Local context: Neutral
(3) Mornings spent looking over things in the bakery were always pleasurable for the man. The sights and smells filled him with anticipation. It was clear that the man's camera gave him an ideal means of capturing his favorite moments.

Global context: Unrelated; Local context: Related
(4) Mornings spent looking over things in the bakery were always pleasurable for the photographer. The sights and smells filled him with anticipation. It was clear that the photographer's camera gave him an ideal means of capturing his favorite moments.

According to our hypothesis, the time to respond to the target phoneme should be faster in (2) than in (1). Indeed, as far as we know, every theory of priming or semantic integration would make this prediction. More interestingly, the present hypothesis leads to the prediction that there will be no difference in the time to respond to (3) and (4), even though the critical word in (4) is immediately preceded by a semantically and associatively related word. The global context in (4) will determine the ease of processing *camera;* the local context will have little or no effect. Thus, the present view predicts that an interaction will be observed between the two types of context. Standard theories of semantic priming predict that *camera* will be processed more rapidly in (4) than in (3). In other words, such theories predict a main effect for local context and no interaction between global and local context.

The results of Foss and Ross's first experiment are shown in Table 9.1. The most important point to note about these data is the significant interaction. When the global context was neutral, then RTs were faster when the critical word was immediately preceded by a semantically related item than when it was im-

TABLE 9.1
Mean reaction times (msec) for Experiment I.

Global Context	Local Context	
	Neutral (man's)	Related (photographer's)
Neutral (workroom)	561	534
Unrelated (bakery)	558	572

Context words are shown for the critical word *camera*. Data from Foss & Ross (1983).

mediately preceded by a more neutral one. On the other hand, the reverse was true when the global context was unrelated. In that case, RTs were not faster (indeed, they were somewhat slower) when the local context was biased than when it was not.

There are a number of reasons for revisiting this issue. One of the most important is that the results of Foss and Ross's work seem to be inconsistent with others in the literature. For example, it is a commonly (though not universally) accepted thesis that multiple interpretations of ambiguous words are accessed when the ambiguity first appears—even when context is consistent with just one of the interpretations (e.g., Swinney, Onifer, Prather, & Hirshkowitz, 1979; Kintsch & Mross, 1985; but see Duffy, Morris, & Rayner, 1988, for some contradictory evidence). If context does not limit access to just the appropriate interpretation of an ambiguous word, how can it preclude activation of a word's close associates? In fact, Foss and Ross did not obtain evidence that such associates are always activated. We will address these issues in some detail. First, however, we will summarize some of the additional research we conducted.

GLOBAL VS. LOCAL FACILITATION: ADDITIONAL STUDIES

We carried out a small extension of Foss and Ross's study in order to see whether it would replicate, taking that opportunity to improve upon the materials that they used. We wanted to be sure that the global context words (e.g., the setting words) actually do lead listeners to interpret the following material as related to it—in other words, that the global context items actually influence the semantic interpretation of the following material and the listeners' expectations about what is likely to follow.

In order to select the sentence groups for our study, we carried out a pretest involving a written completion task. Two versions of each of 45 items (including those from Foss and Ross's experiment) were presented, complete up to but not including the critical word, for example:

(5) Mornings spent looking over things in the {bakery/workroom} were always pleasurable for the photographer. The sights and smells filled him with anticipation. It was clear that the photographer's . . .

Forty University of Texas undergraduate students served as subjects for the pretest. Sentence groups to be pretested were split into two materials sets such that no subject completed two versions of the same item. For a sentence to be judged acceptable for use in the experiment, at least 17 subjects had to complete it in a manner consistent with the intended meaning of the global context (the setting word).

Of the 24 sentence groups used, eight were identical to those used in the prior study; eight were slightly altered (compare sentences 6–9 with 1–4); and eight were completely different from those used previously.

A notable difference between the materials used in this experiment and those used by Foss and Ross involved the neutral version of the possessive (the local context item) that immediately preceded the critical word. In their study, the neutral word was either *"man's"* or *"woman's."* In the present experiment, we used a variety of words, neutral with respect to the setting and critical words (see examples 6 and 8). These were more nearly balanced with the biased words in terms of frequency and length.

Global context: Neutral; Local context: Neutral
(6) Mornings spent looking over things in the workroom were always pleasurable for the executive. The sights and smells filled him with anticipation. It was clear that the executive's camera gave him an ideal means of recording his favorite moments.

Global context: Neutral; Local context: Related
(7) Mornings spent looking over things in the workroom were always pleasurable for the photographer. The sight and smells filled him with anticipation. It was clear that the photographer's camera gave him an ideal means of recording his favorite moments.

Global context: Unrelated; Local context: Neutral
(8) Mornings spent looking over things in the bakery were always pleasurable for the executive. The sights and smells filled him with anticipation. It was clear that the executive's camera gave him an ideal means of recording his favorite moments.

Global context: Unrelated; Local context: Related
(9) Mornings spent looking over things in the bakery were always pleasurable
for the photographer. The sights and smells filled him with anticipation. It
was clear that the photographer's camera gave him an ideal means of recording his favorite moments.

We constructed 24 sets of narratives modeled after (6) through (9). Four lists
were developed; each contained all 24 stories, equally divided among the four
types that have been shown. Across the lists, each narrative occurred in all four
versions. Twenty-eight filler trials, similar in style to the experimental items,
were also included in each set of materials; some of them did not contain the
specified target phoneme, while others varied the target position, sometimes
putting it in the first or second sentence of the narrative. Eighty undergraduates
from the University of Texas at Austin participated in the experiment. We
instructed our subjects to comprehend the stories and to carry out the phoneme-
monitoring task.[1] The target phoneme was specified just prior to each trial
(narrative). We used a paraphrase task, with trials sprinkled throughout the
study, to check whether subjects were comprehending the materials.

The overall results of our experiment are shown in Table 9.2. Although there
is a significant effect due to the local context (related local contexts yield faster
RTs than do unrelated ones), the most important effect to examine is once again
the interaction. As can be seen, the effect of local context is relatively large when
the global context is neutral (549 msec when local context is related versus 594
msec when it is neutral), but when the global context is unrelated, then the effect
of local context is minuscule (569 msec versus 575 msec). Statistically, this
interaction was only marginally significant ($F(1, 78) = 7.15, p < .10$). However,
a planned comparison between the local contexts showed that related local
contexts were processed significantly faster ($p<.01$) than neutral local contexts
when the global context was neutral; they were not different when global context
was unrelated.

This experiment, along with that of Foss and Ross, confirms our predictions.
Facilitation of the second of two semantically related words is not necessarily
automatic. In particular, facilitation appears to require that the semantic interpretation of the larger context be directly related to the interpretation of the
critical word. These results are not consistent with typical LLA models, for
example, those that posit automatic spread of activation from a lexical node
whenever that node is accessed.

---

[1]We used the phoneme-monitoring task for three reasons. First, it was used by Foss and Ross,
and we wanted to extend their work. Second, and more importantly, that task has been shown to be
sensitive to semantic context effects on lexical processing (e.g., Blank & Foss, 1978; Foss, Cirilo, &
Blank, 1979). Third, and even more importantly, since almost all of the work on sentence context
effects has been done using either the lexical decision task or the naming task, we thought it desirable
to examine the issue using another paradigm.

TABLE 9.2
Mean reaction times (msec) for Experiment I

	Local Context	
Global Context	Neutral (executive's)	Related (photographer's)
Neutral (workroom)	594	549
Unrelated (bakery)	575	569

Context words are shown for the critical word *camera*.

We must note that there are others who have challenged the claim that spreading activation is automatic, including a few investigators who work with word pairs, the traditional materials for studying priming. In one such experiment, Smith, Theodor, and Franklin (1983) found that semantic priming was attenuated if subjects made a nonsemantic decision about the prime word. Thus, priming was diminished when subjects had to decide if the first word had one syllable versus more than one, and no priming was observed when subjects had to decide if the prime word contained a specified letter. In these cases, it appears that subjects did not process the prime word in an effective manner, focusing on surface aspects of the word rather than on its interpretation. If the semantic interpretation of the word was not actively processed, then activation could not spread to associatively related words. Similarly, Parkin (1979) showed that the amount of interference for color naming obtained in a modified Stroop task depended on the manner in which the priming word was processed, with superficial processing leading to no interference. Finally, Snow and Neely (1987) manipulated the relationships between prime and target words by having some items semantically related (CAT/dog), some items physically different but nominally the same (DOG/dog), and some physically identical items (dog/dog). They varied the proportion of items in each of these relationships in a between-subject design. Snow and Neely reasoned that subjects could process the stimuli at a relatively low level when a large proportion of the trials were physically identical (the subjects could then make the lexical decision on the basis of physical similarity). And, indeed, they found that priming was diminished when a large proportion of items in the test list were physically identical; furthermore, this happened even when the time between onset of the prime and target stimuli was very short (80 msec), just the circumstances in which one would expect the automatic processes to be operating. (Snow and Neely suggest that a postlexical check of the relation between prime and target can override automatic semantic priming.)

Thus, while the results from studies of word pairs generally support the thesis that spreading activation is an automatic process, there is at least some work that calls into question the generality of the automatic component. It is not clear, though, that normal sentence processing is analogous to the circumstances under which attenuated (or nonexistent) priming has been observed in studies of word pairs. Indeed, it would seem otherwise; listeners must deeply process each word in order to develop a semantic interpretation of the entire sentence.

ADDITIONAL MODELS AND NEW DATA

To this point we have emphasized the priming explanation for the speedier processing of words. Foss and Ross, Auble and Franks (1983), and Kleiman (1980) also emphasized a priming explanation, suggesting that words related to the semantic interpretation of the discourse were primed (topical priming), not those related to individual words. In the remainder of this chapter we will explore two alternative explanatory routes. As has been alluded, one of them is based on the possibility that semantically related words are more easily and quickly integrated into the ongoing discourse representation than are more neutral words. In order to give content to this idea we must eventually specify a mechanism that will permit differences in integration speeds to occur. Clearly, such a mechanism will involve the levels of semantic or pragmatic processing; we need a theory of how the discourse entities are entered into a discourse model and how their relations are specified. Although a detailed model is not forthcoming here, what we will do is to make additional predictions that should follow from models of this class, and then see whether those predictions hold. In addition, we will examine yet another modified model of priming, one that is quite different from those we have dubbed LLA models.

In the experiment manipulating global and local context, we observed faster processing of the critical word (e.g., *camera*) when it was preceded by the local priming word (e.g., *photographer's*) just in case the global context was consistent with the typical (perhaps the stereotypical) activities of a photographer. We claim that this result is inconsistent with the typical LLA model of spreading activation, which predicts that priming is automatic and therefore ubiquitous. An integration model can, we presume, be built to account for the facilitation we observed. Consider, though, the likely predictions of such a model when the critical word *(camera)* is not readily incorporated into the discourse representation provided by the unrelated global context *(bakery)*. Since the global context is "about" something other than photography, integrating the critical word into the ongoing discourse representation should, perhaps, take more time than when the global context can be construed to be about photography-related activities *(workroom)*. The camera isn't immediately relevant to bakery activities. (Of course, one quickly can construct a scenario for why a camera might be relevant. But it does seem as though such a construction takes extra processing.) Although there was a slight difference in that direction observed in our work, the effect was very small and not significant (549 msec versus 569 msec). The global contexts in that study were dubbed "related" or "neutral," seemingly appropriate labels. It is possible to strengthen the contrast between those conditions, and we set out to do so.

Strong Global Context

We determined that a more direct test of the effects of global context was required. Accordingly, we constructed a set of materials in which the contrast was increased between the levels of the two independent variables, local and global context. Instead of using neutral versus related contexts, we used un-related and related contexts in both cases. Local context was again manipulated by preceding the critical word (e.g., *surfboard* in the following examples) with a semantically related possessive (e.g., *surfer's*) on half the trials, and with an unrelated possessive (e.g., *pilot's*) on the other half of the trials. Global context was manipulated by presenting a related setting word (e.g., *beach*) on half the trials, and on the other half a setting word (e.g., *runway*) that was pragmatically unrelated to the meaning of the critical word. The global-context words in the latter condition were chosen so that the interpretation of the sentence was not readily compatible with the typical setting for the critical words (e.g., surfboards are not stereotypically on runways nor in the possession of pilots). In addition, unrelated global-context words were chosen such that they were semantically consistent with the unrelated local-context words (e.g., pilots are often found near runways). Examples of the materials are shown in (10) through (13).

Global context, related; Local context, related
(10) On the beach, the surfer enjoyed the feel of the wind on his face. The surfer's surfboard cost a lot of money, but now he was glad he had purchased it.

Global context, related; Local context, unrelated
(11) On the beach, the pilot enjoyed the feel of the wind on his face. The pilot's surfboard cost a lot of money, but now he was glad he had purchased it.

Global context, unrelated; Local context, related
(12) On the runway, the surfer enjoyed the feel of the wind on his face. The surfer's surfboard cost a lot of money, and he hoped it would successfully survive the baggage area of the small jet.

Global context, unrelated; Local context, unrelated
(13) On the runway, the pilot enjoyed the feel of the wind on his face. The pilot's surfboard cost a lot of money, so he planned to entrust it to his favorite flight attendant.

Examples (10) through (13) represent only one-half of the materials. Another parallel set was constructed in which *airplane* was the critical word, so that *runway* and *pilot's* were the related global and local context words, while *beach* and *surfer's* were the unrelated context words. In this way we controlled for a number of additional extraneous variables.

We conducted this experiment twice, each time with 60 subjects. Subjects listened to 20 experimental sentences (five of each type) and 20 fillers, carrying out the phoneme-monitoring task. The target phoneme occurred immediately after the critical word in the experimental sentences (its the /k/ in *cost* in the examples given). Subjects were asked to give a written paraphrase after some of the sentences.

If facilitation of the critical word is due to automatic spreading activation (a model of the LLA type), then there should be an effect of local context (conditions 10 and 12 should be faster than 11 and 13). If facilitation of the critical word is due to ease of integration with the ongoing discourse representation, then conditions 10 and 11 should be faster than 12 and 13. (We will momentarily present a set of predictions derived from another priming-based model, albeit one based on a different principle than LLA models.)

The results from the two experiments are presented in Tables 9.3 and 9.4.

TABLE 9.3
Mean reaction times (msec) for Experiment II

Global Context	Local Context	
	Related (surfer's)	Unrelated (pilot's)
Related (*beach*)	610	629
Unrelated (*runway*)	665	653

Context words are shown for the critical word *surfboard*.

TABLE 9.4
Mean reaction times (msec) for Experiment III

Global Context	Local Context	
	Related (surfer's)	Unrelated (pilot's)
Related (*beach*)	650	678
Unrelated (*runway*)	730	726

Context words are shown for the critical word *surfboard*.

They show a consistent pattern. Overall, reaction times are significantly faster when the global context is related to the critical word than when it is unrelated ($F = 7.23$, $p < .01$ for the data in Table 9.3, and $F = 23.74$, $p < .01$ for the data shown in Table 9.4). In neither case is there an overall effect due to local context, nor is there an interaction between these variables.

To summarize, data from a series of experiments have shown that processing a critical word is not necessarily facilitated if it is immediately preceded by a semantically related prime word. On the other hand, processing is facilitated if the semantic interpretation of the prior material in toto is related to the critical word. Thus, facilitation appears to occur when one can say that the critical word can be readily integrated into the discourse representation. These results again call into question LLA models of priming.

We would like to highlight another result from the last experiment. Note that we did not observe an RT difference in examples (10) and (11). Thus, a phrase such as *pilot's surfboard* appears to be processed just as rapidly as a phrase such as *surfer's surfboard* if both the pilot and the surfer have been located on the beach by the prior global context. (There is in both Tables 9.3 and 9.4 a slight tendency for the latter to yield shorter response times, but the effect is less than 4% of the absolute values of the RTs and is not statistically reliable.) From at least one perspective this lack of an effect is a remarkable finding. The literature on priming provides ample evidence that unrelated prime words yield slower processing of target words. Indeed, there are many circumstances in which the inhibition effect due to unrelated words is larger than the facilitation effect. It clearly seems sensible to view *pilot* as an item that would inhibit the processing of *surfboard;* but no such inhibition is in evidence here.

Our attempt to deal with this issue, as well to deal more thoroughly with the apparent discrepancy of our results with those of Swinney et al. (1979), Kintsch and Mross (1985), and others, led us to consider the relation between the present work and that of a related topic, one dubbed "semantic flexibility" in the literature.

SEMANTIC FLEXIBILITY AND ACCESS OF LEXICAL ITEMS

Semantic flexibility refers to the claim that the encoding of an unambiguous word is determined by the context within which it occurs. Barclay, Bransford, Franks, McCarrell, and Nitsch (1974) found that the final noun of a sentence such as, *The man lifted the piano* is better recalled when subjects are provided with the cue *something heavy* than when they are given the cue *something with a nice sound;* the opposite is true for the sentence, *The man played the piano*. Barclay et al. suggested that the relevance of each of a word's semantic properties is contextually determined and stored in the encoded representation of the word. To say it somewhat differently, semantic flexibility "proposed that the comprehension of a noun in a sentence involves the selective activation (or instantiation) of only those semantic features or meaning postulates that are relevant to the specific linguistic context" (Greenspan, 1986, pp. 539–540).

The initial studies investigating this phenomenon, such as those conducted by Barclay et al., utilized recall paradigms and focused on memory representations. As one might expect, there is a controversy in the literature about the extent to which semantic flexibility involves selective activation at the time a word is initially processed. Barsalou (1982) and Greenspan (1986) suggest that some properties of a concept always come to mind, independent of context; these are dubbed context-independent (CI) properties. "CI properties form the core meanings of words" (Barsalou, 1982, p. 82). They have high diagnosticity and they are "properties" relevant to how people normally interact with instances of the concept. In contrast, context-dependent (CD) properties come to mind only in relevant contexts. To borrow Barsalou's example, the roundness of a basketball is a CI property, while its buoyancy is a CD property. Buoyancy might be highlighted in a context such as, *The child remained afloat by clutching the basketball*.

Greenspan (1986) investigated selective activation in unambiguous nouns by using a cross-modal task in which subjects were presented with an auditory sentence and, after a 1-second delay, a visual test item. They were asked to make a lexical decision about the latter. When the test word was *wood,* subjects responded rapidly to it after either context sentence: *Henry chopped up the tree;* or, *The children played in the tree*. Wood is a CI property of tree and so *wood* is activated whenever *tree* is, leading to the rapid decision in each case. However, the test item *climb* was only responded to rapidly after the latter context sentence, not after the former one. Barsalou found a conceptually similar result using a different paradigm.[2]

Recall that we are concerned to explain why we did not observe inhibition of *surfboard* when it occurred immediately after *pilot's* in sentences such as (11), which we repeat here for convenience. As noted earlier, there is evidence in the priming literature that an unrelated word—one that calls to mind a topic distinct from the target word—will slow the processing of the target. Why didn't this happen in our work? We can use the results from the work on semantic flexibility to construct an explanation for this fact. Consider what happens when *pilot* is first processed in (11):

---

[2]But see Whitney, McKay, Kellas, and Emerson, 1985; and Tabossi, 1988, for other results. Whitney et al. claim that both CI and CD properties are activated momentarily, that the CI properties have a longer term effect independent of context, and that the CD properties only have a longer-term effect when they are consistent with a context that biases the interpretation in the CD direction. In contrast, Tabossi claims that the materials in Whitney et al. are flawed, and she presents some evidence that the CI properties are not so independent after all. We will not resolve this issue here, nor need we do so. We will simply make use of the CI construct.

(11) On the beach, the pilot enjoyed the feel of the wind on his face. The pilot's surfboard cost a lot of money, but now he was glad he had purchased it.

To the extent that there is CI information that will be activated upon first hearing *pilot,* that information will no doubt include some indication that the typical pilot guides an airplane. In addition, there will be context-independent knowledge that a pilot is an adult human, usually wears a uniform, is typically a well-compensated male, that some pilots guide other craft such as ships and so on. From this we could deduce that a pilot can engage in most human activities, including appreciating fine wines, writing mystery stories in his or her spare time, or enjoying vacations on beaches. In the context of (11), the latter is particularly apropos.

Consider what may happen during the processing of the first sentence in (11). We are given a setting (the beach) and an experiencer (the pilot). When *pilot* first occurs, its CI information is recovered from the mental lexicon. In that setting, however, the unique aspects of the typical referent of *pilot* are not as important to the understanding of the sentence as are the general ones, especially the fact that a pilot is an adult human. From this, the comprehender will construct in the discourse model a representation of an adult (not in uniform) on holiday at the beach. That encoding will be the one utilized during the next stages of the comprehension episode; for example, it will be the one recovered when the anaphoric pronoun *his* is encountered later in the same sentence. (The encoding may be modified at that point as well, just in case the gender of the experiencer had not previously been stored in the discourse model.) Importantly, we propose that the modified representation is the one recovered when the possessive, *The pilot's,* occurs at the beginning of the next sentence. At that point the stereotypical CI information that one has about pilots is not most salient; rather, the salient information is that which has been recently encoded with the pilot in the discourse representation.[3] In the case under discussion, the CD information is related to the beach. And that is one possible reason why as much facilitation is observed between *pilot's* and *surfboard* as between *surfer's* and *surfboard.*

IMPLICATIONS

The present line of reasoning leads in at least two directions. On the one hand, we could try to extend it in an effort to resuscitate a (now substantially modified) priming explanation for our results. On the other hand, we could examine the

---

[3]We suspect that the reference must be to "the pilot" rather than to "a pilot"; the definite article is a cue (not a completely reliable one, of course) that the discourse representation contains the relevant information.

relation between the idea of modified encodings and an explanation based on semantic integration. We will very briefly do both.

First, consider explanations based on spreading activation accounts of priming. Earlier we noted that numerous investigators have found evidence for the automatic activation of both interpretations of ambiguous words (e.g., Swinney et al., 1979; Kintsch & Mross, 1985; Seidenberg, Tanenhaus, Leiman, & Bienkowski, 1982), and we noted that failures to find such activation have typically occurred when subjects did not process the words semantically (e.g., Snow & Neely, 1987). In contrast, there is no evidence for automatic activation in the work reported here, in Foss and Ross (1983), nor in a few other studies such as those conducted by Auble and Franks (1983), nor—in some conditions— by Duffy et al. (1988). We suggest that information about a lexical item comes from distinct sources, depending on whether or not the item has occurred previously in a discourse unit. When a lexical item first occurs, comprehenders recover information about it from the mental lexicon—the repository of knowledge about that item. However, when the item recurs in the same discourse unit, comprehenders (also) recover information associated with the entity that has been set up in the ongoing discourse model. That information will be context-dependent. In addition, other items related to the entity in the model may also be made available at that time—whether this would be an automatic consequence or not remains to be seen. Together, these effects will yield priming that is sensitive to the context; this can be construed to be a version of what we earlier dubbed topical priming. It predicts a result that is quite different from that predicted by LLA models. The latter rely on associations from "within the lexicon," which is generally interpreted to mean that they are context-insensitive.

Second, the results that we observed might be due to a combination of factors, including greater ease of integrating certain new material into the discourse model. For some time after the initial occurrence of *pilot* the CD (beach-related) information will be immediately available when *pilot* recurs. Semantic integration will take place more readily if new information is related to the information already in the mental model. It will be easier to carry out the process of semantic composition, wherein the semantics of a phrase are built from the semantics of its constituents, if the appropriate raw materials for the composition process are recovered immediately upon encountering those constituents. One thing that a model of integration should do is to describe the process by which the ongoing construction of the discourse representation functions to determine the relevance of the set of semantic properties associated with individual words. Perhaps part of what integration means is the successive selection of the subset of properties when words are encoded as part of the discourse representation. That will have taken place already by the second occurrence of the world. As noted earlier, this suggestion is a somewhat vague one, absent a particular model for how semantic integration takes place, and we have not proposed such a model here. For now this merely has the status (to us, at least) of a plausible route to follow. It seems possible to use it to explicate the notion of coherence, an important construct in understanding comprehension.

Predictions

The foregoing two views lead to a similar prediction. We observed rapid processing when the global context is related to the critical word. Note that the priming word occurs twice in these sentences. After its first presentation, CD information is made salient and, by hypothesis, is quickly recovered when the priming word recurs. Our priming-based explanation for the various aspects of the foregoing results depends largely on this hypothesis. Consider, then, what would happen if the global setting word was followed by the first occurrence of the priming word and, immediately after that, by the critical word: for example, *While at the beach, the pilot's surfboard gave him a hard time.* Time to process *surfboard* should now be longer than in a sentence such as, *While at the beach, the surfer's surfboard gave him a hard time.* That should be the case if the CI aspects of *pilot* are recovered the first time it occurs. Both the modified priming and the integration views predict this result. (Of course, LLA models also predict it. But they cannot account for our results.) Variations on this theme that discriminate among the views may also be possible, and we are exploring them.

The foregoing approach can also reconcile our results with those observed by such investigators as Swinney et al. (1979), Kintsch and Mross (1985) and others; to wit, that all interpretations of a lexical ambiguity are activated briefly when an ambiguous word occurs. In these studies the test of the ambiguity takes place immediately after its first presentation, typically using the cross-modal priming paradigm. Note what will happen according to the view presented here: If context is used to influence the representation in the discourse model, then that (contextually modified) representation would be the one activated on the *next* presentation of the ambiguity. Thus, even immediate presentation of the test item in the cross-modal paradigm would find evidence for only one interpretation of the ambiguity when it appeared in the discourse for the second time. (In contrast, if the other interpretation were not necessary to the proper understanding of the sentence, a substantial interference effect should be observed.) To our knowledge the experiments needed to test these ideas do not yet exist in the literature.

By introducing a modified priming interpretation of our results and others we do not want to suggest that priming plays a large role in normal sentence comprehension. That issue is still open. We certainly think that more detailed versions of both priming and integration can and will be constructed in an effort to account for the results. Such models are needed if we are to understand coherence. We began this chapter by noting that comprehenders interpret unclear cases as clearly as they can in an effort to build a coherent representation of the input. And we noted that understanding the problems of: (a) integrating new material into the ongoing discourse representation, and (b) context effects on word recognition, were keys to dealing with the problem of coherence. If the representation of items in the discourse model is context-dependent, and if it is those items that are first recovered when words recur, then the two problems can be addressed from within the same theoretical framework.

Finally, we would like to point out one implication of the present approach for the debate about modularity. Many investigators (e.g., Marslen–Wilson & Tyler, 1987) have supposed that discourse-level influences on lexical processing are incompatible with a modular view of language. However, if we take the view that initial access occurs from an encapsulated lexicon and yields CI information, and subsequent access occurs from the discourse model and yields the CD information, then such a case against modularity is not so clear.

In summary, our experiments demonstrate that processing the second of two highly related items is not always speeded—not even when they occur adjacently and when we can be certain that the first word is semantically processed. Facilitation of the second word occurs when the topic or setting is related to it. Our discussion of these results has made three points. First, models of priming that belong to what we call the LLA class cannot account for the data. Second, an integration account probably can account for the data. Third, a modified model of priming may also be able to do the job. The modifications are based on the construct of semantic flexibility and on the view that the recovery of information associated with lexical items is different when the item first occurs in a discourse and when it occurs later. The source of information on the second occurrence is a discourse model being constructed and carried along in memory. This view leads to testable predictions, including predictions about the processing of lexical ambiguity.

Somewhat remarkably, the effort to understand the contributions of lexical information to the ongoing comphrehension process has doubled back on itself. It may be necessary to unpack the role of discourse on the individual word as much as the reverse. Thus, "The psychologist who chooses to investigate verbal behavior cannot long avoid becoming entangled in problems of verbal context."

POSTSCRIPT: A PERSONAL NOTE

Donald J. Foss

One evening at dinner not long ago Jim Jenkins described his mentor, Donald G. Paterson, one of the founders of applied psychology in the United States, and (like Jim himself) a prolific producer of research articles and PhDs. Apparently, Paterson was something of an autocrat; but this is not the place to convey anecdotes about him. However, much as he admired Paterson, it seems clear that Jim did not pattern himself after him in style. In contrast, I have no doubt that Jim's students want to pattern themselves after him; we'd like to emulate his treatment of budding scholars, his infectious enthusiasm, and his commitment to truth rather than to tradition. What a challenge! I wonder if he knows the degree of guilt he has inspired in most of us who can't pull it off like the master.

There can be few in the annals of the profession who took such pains to nurture people, both in the service of helping them develop as individuals and in helping develop the ideas they might have. With great effort, I'll limit myself to a single anecdote. I remember feeling free to call Jim up at home one Saturday during winter quarter of my first year in graduate school. I'd had some notion or other about an experiment that could be run in a group on Monday, just before the end of term. He was more than encouraging, he was effusive out of all proportion to the idea; but what an ego boost. I then had to get it done, even though—as usual in research—the materials took longer than expected to construct so I had to stay up all night to get the damn thing ready. If he would have told me I *had* to get it ready, I suppose I would have done it, but I might then have ducked around the corner the next time I saw him coming and suspected that he had some work for me. Instead, I got to brag to him and to myself about how these data were in hand to be mused over during the break. How did he do that?

I had the privilege of being around Minnesota during the era of the Great Paradigm Shift, when Jim and some of his students discovered the importance of rule-governed behavior in general and its relevance for language in particular. Few men have been leaders in two distinct research traditions, but Jim pulled off that feat. With the hindsight bred by years, I've come to believe that the man and his science came into harmony during that era. The cognitive revolution, which Jim Jenkins helped to lead, gave more credit to internal mechanisms than did the paradigm it replaced. Jim had to be more comfortable with such a self-starting perspective, for that is what he values and inspires. During the same time period, he was instrumental in founding the Center for Research on Human Learning, a hotbed of freedom for arguing ideas and trying to test them with data. At the end of my time there I conducted a dissertation whose aim was, in part, to show that Jenkins and Palermo's (1964) mediational view of language learning was wrong. Jim supported me in that venture and guided the work throughout, even though it was critical of a major theoretical paper that he had coauthored only a short time earlier. That atypical approach to science is typical for him. As he has said, "For me, it's all about having a goal."

The world has turned a goodly number of times since the day I drove east to what was then *The* Center for Cognitive Studies, but I never go for long without thinking how lucky I was to have been at that place at that time with that leader. Guilt and all, it's a wonderful experience to be one of J-cubed's students.

ACKNOWLEDGMENT

Work reported here was supported in part by the Texas Advanced Research Program, No. 4378, to Donald J. Foss and Carlota S. Smith, and by Army Research Institute Contract, No. MDA903–82–C––0123, to DJF. The authors thank Patrick Carroll for helpful comments on an earlier version of this chapter. We didn't take all his suggestions; the remaining unclarities and infelicities are our own.

Shari R. Speer is now at Northeastern University.

REFERENCES

Auble, P., & Franks, J. J. (1983). Sentence comprehension processes. *Journal of Verbal Learning and Verbal Behavior, 22,* 395–404.

Balota, D. A., & Lorch, R. F. (1986). Depth of automatic spreading activation: Mediated priming effects in pronunciation but not in lexical decision. *Journal of Experimental Psychology: Learning, Memory, and Cognition, 12,* 336–345.

Barclay, J. R., Bransford, J. D., Franks, J. J., McCarrell, N. S., & Nitsch, K. (1974). Comprehension and semantic flexibility. *Journal of Verbal Learning and Verbal Behavior, 13,* 471–481.

Barsalou, L. W. (1982). Context-independent and context-dependent information in concepts. *Memory & Cognition, 10,* 82–93.

Blank, M., & Foss, D. J. (1978). Semantic facilitation and lexical access during sentence processing. *Memory & Cognition, 6,* 644–652.

Carpenter, P., & Daneman, M. (1981). Lexical retrieval and error recovery in reading: A model based on eye fixations. *Journal of Verbal Learning and Verbal Behavior, 20,* 137–160.

Duffy, S. A., Morris, R., & Rayner, K. (1988). Lexical ambiguity and fixation times in reading. *Journal of Memory and Language, 27,* 429–446.

Fischler, I. S., & Bloom, P. A. (1985). Effects of constraint and validity of sentence contexts on lexical decisions. *Memory & Cognition, 13,* 128–139.

Fodor, J. (1983). *The modularity of mind: An essay on faculty psychology.* Cambridge, MA: Bradford.

Foss, D. J. (1982). A discourse on semantic priming. *Cognitive Psychology, 14,* 590–607.

Foss, D. J. (1988). Experimental psycholinguistics. *Annual Review of Psychology, 39,* 301–348.

Foss, D. J., Cirilo, R. K., & Blank, M. A. (1979). Semantic facilitation and lexical access during sentence processing: An investigation of individual differences. *Memory & Cognition, 7,* 346–353.

Foss, D. J., & Ross, J. R. (1983). Great expectations: Context effects during sentence processing. In G. Flores D'Arcais & R. J. Jarvella (Eds.), *The process of language understanding* (pp. 169–191). Chichester, England: Wiley.

Greenspan, S. L. (1986). Semantic flexibility and referential specificity of concrete nouns. *Journal of Memory and Language, 25,* 539–557.

Hardy, G. H. (1940/1967). *A mathematician's apology.* Cambridge, England: Cambridge University Press.

Jenkins, J. J., Mink, W. D., & Russell, W. A. (1958). Associative clustering as a function of verbal association strength. *Psychological Reports, 4,* 127–136.

Jenkins, J. J., & Palermo, D. S. (1964). Mediational processes and the acquisition of linguistic structure. In U. Bellugi & R. Brown (Eds.), *The acquisition of language. Monographs of the Society for Research in Child Development, 29*(1, Serial No. 92), pp. 141–169.

Kintsch, W., & Mross, E. F. (1985). Context effects in word recognition. *Journal of Memory and Language, 24,* 336–349.

Kleiman, G. M. (1980). Sentence frame contexts and lexical decisions: Sentence–acceptability and word–relatedness effects. *Memory & Cognition, 8,* 336–344.

Lorch, R. F., Jr. (1982). Priming and search processes in semantic memory: A test of three models of spreading activation. *Journal of Verbal Learning and Verbal Behavior, 21,* 468–492.

Marslen–Wilson, W., & Tyler, L. K. (1987). Against modularity. In J. L. Garfield (Ed.), *Modularity in knowledge representation and natural language understanding.* Cambridge, MA: MIT Press.

Neely, J. H. (1977). Semantic priming and retrieval from lexical memory: Roles of inhibitionless spreading activation and limited-capacity attention. *Journal of Experimental Psychology: General, 106,* 226–254.

O'Seaghdha, P. (1989). The dependence of lexical relatedness effects on syntactic connectedness. *Journal of Experimental Psychology: Learning, Memory, and Cognition, 15,* 73–87.

Parkin, A. J. (1979). Specifying levels of processing. *Quarterly Journal of Experimental Psychology, 31,* 179–195.

Posner, M. I., & Snyder, C. R. R. (1975). Attention and cognitive control. In R. L. Solso (Ed.), *Information processing and cognition: The Loyola Symposium.* Hillsdale, NJ: Lawrence Erlbaum Associates.

Quine, W. V. O. (1953). *From a logical point of view.* Cambridge, MA: Harvard University Press.

Schwanenflugel, P., & LaCount, K. L. (1988). Semantic relatedness and the scope of facilitation for upcoming words in sentences. *Journal of Experimental Psychology: Learning, Memory, and Cognition, 14,* 344–354.

Schwanenflugel, P. J., & Shoben, E. J. (1985). The influence of sentence constraint on the scope of facilitation for upcoming words. *Journal of Memory and Language, 24,* 232–252.

Seidenberg, M. S., Tanenhaus, M. K., Leiman, J. M., & Bienkowski, M. (1982). Automatic access of the meanings of ambiguous words in context: Some limitations of knowledge-based processing. *Cognitive Psychology, 14,* 489–537.

Seidenberg, M. S., Waters, G. S., Sanders, M., & Langer, P. (1984). Pre- and postlexical loci of contextual effects on word recognition. *Memory & Cognition, 12,* 315–328.

Sharkey, N. E., & Mitchell, D. C. (1985). Word recognition in a functional context: The use of scripts in reading. *Journal of Memory and Language, 24,* 253–270.

Smith, M. C., Theodor, L., & Franklin, P. E. (1983). The relationship between contextual facilitation and depth of processing. *Journal of Experimental Psychology: Learning, Memory, and Cognition, 9,* 697–712.

Snow, C. P. (1967). Foreward to G. H. Hardy, *A mathematician's apology.* Cambridge, England: Cambridge University Press.

Snow, N., & Neely, J. H. (1987, November). *Reduction of semantic priming from inclusion of physically or nominally related prime-target pairs.* Paper presented at the annual meeting of the Psychonomic Society, Seattle.

Stanovich, K. E., & West, R. F. (1983). On priming by a sentence context. *Journal of Experimental Psychology: General, 112,* 1–36.

Swinney, D. A., Onifer, W., Prather, P. & Hirschkowitz, M. (1979). Semantic facilitation across sensory modalities in the precessing of individual words and sentences. *Memory & Cognition, 7,* 159–165.

Tabossi, P. (1988). Effects of context on the immediate interpretation of unambiguous nouns. *Journal of Experimental Psychology: Learning, Memory, and Cognition, 14,* 153–162.

Till, R. E., Mross, E. F., & Kintsch, W. (1988). Time course of priming for associate and inference words in a discourse context. *Memory & Cognition, 16,* 283–298.

van Djik, T., & Kintsch, W. (1983). *Strategies of discourse comprehension.* New York: Academic Press.

Whitney, P., McKay, T., Kellas, G., & Emerson, W. A., Jr. (1985). Semantic activation of noun concepts in context. *Journal of Experimental Psychology: Learning, Memory, and Cognition, 11,* 126–135.

10 The Complexity of Reading

Philip B. Gough
University of Texas

At least since Huey (1908), students of reading have agreed that reading is complex. Nearly two decades ago, at the instigation of Jim Jenkins, I attempted to portray this complexity in a model of reading (Gough, 1972). The model was precise enough to be falsified, and it was; it proved heuristic.

But the model served another function. In the years since it was proposed, it has often been taken (e.g., Rumelhart, 1977) to represent a more general thesis, that is, that reading proceeds from print to meaning, from the bottom up. This was contrasted to its antithesis, the view that reading begins, not with print, but instead with the reader's hypotheses or expectations. Reading works its way from there to print; it proceeds from the top down. Most students of reading have decided that the truth lies between these extremes. The resulting synthesis, that reading is an interactive process, has come to be the accepted view. The aim of the present chapter is to reflect on the model, and to ask whether its main thesis, the bottom–up view, might still be worth considering.

ONE SECOND OF READING

Gough (1972) presented a model intended to describe what happens in the first second after print is reflected onto the retina. The model consisted of a series of seven stages, beginning with an iconic representation of the printed word, proceeding through recognition of its letters and their phonological recoding to its meaning. Word meanings were placed in primary memory, where they were integrated into sentences. To read aloud, the resulting sentence was then edited into a script, which was then delivered by the vocal system.

The model was wrong in at least two of its specific claims. For one thing, the

141

model claimed that we recognize words letter by letter, from left to right. Research on the word superiority effect (Reicher, 1969; Wheeler, 1970) has made it very clear that the letters in a word (or a pseudoword) are recognized in parallel, not serially. The model was probably right in assuming that word recognition is mediated by letter detection (McClelland & Rumelhart, 1981; Rumelhart & McClelland, 1982; though see Seidenberg & McClelland, 1989), but the letter recognition may not be complete, and it is certainly not accomplished one letter at a time, from left to right.

A second claim was that the recognition of every word is mediated by phonological form, the so-called "phonological recoding hypothesis." A substantial body of research has argued against this hypothesis (Gough, 1984; McCusker, Bias, & Hillinger, 1981). Most students of word recognition now agree that the recognition of familiar words is "direct," that is, unmediated by phonological form.

That the model was wrong with respect to these specifics was, I think, a virtue. This is not to say that it wouldn't have been better to be right. But I have always believed that it is better to be specifically wrong than vaguely right; we learn more from the clear falsification of a clear (and plausible) hypothesis than we do from a demonstration of a general idea. In this instance, I would argue that we learned much more about word recognition from the attempt to refute these hypotheses than we did from their rivals.

Take, for example, the idea that we recognize words letter by letter. Since Cattell (1886), the major alternative to the idea that the letter is the perceptual unit in word recognition has been the idea that the unit is the whole word (e.g., Samuels, LaBerge, & Bremer, 1978). But this hypothesis, by itself, predicts nothing at all about word recognition. Its predictive power derives from the letter-by-letter hypothesis, or, more exactly, the negation of it. Its advocates took the letter-by-letter hypothesis, derived a prediction from it (e.g., that semantic decision latency should increase with word length; Samuels et al., 1978), and then showed that this prediction was disconfirmed. The letter-by-letter model is proved wrong, but it did the heuristic work.

Or take the phonological recoding hypothesis. This hypothesis yielded a number of predictions about word recognition, several of which have been proven wrong (Gough, 1984). The alternative to this hypothesis is the idea that we recognize words by "direct visual access" (e.g., Coltheart, 1978). But note that the direct access hypothesis has no content save that of denying that word recognition is mediated by phonological form. It is nothing but the negation of the phonological recoding hypothesis, and all it predicts is that the predictions of the phonological recoding hypothesis will be false. Like the serial letter hypothesis, the phonological recoding hypothesis did the work.

The model was wrong in (at least) these two details. It was also incomplete. For one thing, while it attested to the complexities involved in assigning syntactic structure to sentences, it completely ignored what must happen beyond the sentence level. Research has amply demonstrated that there is more to the comprehension of discourse than the comprehension of its sentences (Sanford & Garrod, 1981).

But the larger issue is whether the model was on the right track. The model has often been taken, by Rumelhart (1977) and others, as illustrative of the idea that reading proceeds from the bottom up, that is, proceeding from print to the meaning of words independent of what was happening at higher levels. On this view, word recognition takes place before the word is entered into the developing sentence structure; neither that structure, nor the higher-order processes that determine it, should influence lexical access.

Numerous studies have shown that this is wrong, that context does have powerful effects on word recognition. These results have led most scholars of reading to argue for what they call an "interactive view" of reading, that the recognition of a word is jointly determined by information arising from the form of the word (up from the bottom) and the higher-order structures and processes into which the word is entering (down from the top).

But there is good reason to believe that the effects of context are not as strong, or at least as extensive, as the research might lead us to believe. I have pointed out (Gough, 1983) that virtually every published study of the effects of context has used carefully selected contexts: their targets are always nouns, always sentence final, always highly predictable. Given that function words account for nearly half of the words in running text, nouns constitute a minority of the words in print. Given that printed sentences average more than 21 words in length (Kucera & Francis, 1967), the final nouns of sentences account for only a small fraction of that minority. And given that the mean predictability of content words in text is about .10 (the mode is 0; Gough, Alford, & Holley–Wilcox, 1981), words as predictable as those usually studied in experiments are only rarely encountered in text. It seems possible to me that the recognition of many, if not most, words may not be influenced by their context at all.

Equally important, the effect of context has been shown to vary with reader ability. A number of studies have shown that poor readers show larger effects of context than good readers (Stanovich, 1980). The reason seems clear: Good readers get little benefit from context, because they recognize words so well in isolation. What this suggests is that skilled reading may be, in large measure, bottom–up.

THE DISSOCIATION OF DECODING AND COMPREHENSION

Reading may well begin with word recognition, but it does not end there; word recognition (i.e., finding the meaning of each word on the printed page) is clearly not the only process involved in reading. After a text's words are recognized, there is much for the mind to do. The right meaning must be assigned to each word (Foss, 1988), and it must be fitted into a syntactic structure to arrive at a meaning for the sentence (Frazier, 1987). That meaning must be integrated with the meaning of prior sentences to arrive at a discourse structure (van Dijk & Kintsch, 1983). And the whole must be assimilated to the apperceptive mass, the mind, of the reader. In short, after decoding, there must be comprehension.

It may well be that these two major processes interact, that in the skilled reader the processes are woven together into an intricate tapestry. Indeed, there can be no doubt that the two processes, decoding and comprehension, are intercorrelated, and that the correlation is positive: The reader skilled at decoding tends to be skilled at comprehension, and the child with decoding problems will probably also have comprehension difficulties.

But there is clear evidence that the two processes can be dissociated (Gough & Tunmer, 1986). The average kindergartner can understand English, and comprehend a story, with no ability to decode at all. And there is evidence for this dissociation (comprehension without decoding) even after years of reading instruction. Whatever the roots of the specific reading disability often called dyslexia (Snowling, 1987; Vellutino, 1979), the dyslexic is defined by having normal, or even superior, ability to understand the spoken language, yet has difficulty reading. Finding a hidden denominator to dyslexia has proved difficult. But what every dyslexic exhibits on the surface is a disability in decoding.

The opposite form of dissociation, decoding in the absence of comprehension, also exists. After he went blind, Milton taught his daughters to decode Greek (without understanding the language) so that he might reread the classics through them. Many of us can at least approximate the decoding of a language such as Spanish, while totally lacking the ability to understand its spoken form. And this dissociation can be found even within our own language. There are evidently reading-disabled children who have normal or even superior decoding skill, yet listen (and read) very poorly (Healy, 1982).

THE COMBINATION OF DECODING AND COMPREHENSION

The two skills, decoding and comprehension, can be dissociated. But to achieve skilled reading, the two skills must be combined. It could reasonably be argued that reading (R) should be considered the sum of decoding (D) and comprehension (C), or $R = D + C$.

There is certainly evidence which would support a generalization like this. Reading ability does, in general, increase with decoding ability. Good readers, defined by reading comprehension tests, name words faster and more accurately than poor readers (Perfetti & Hogaboam, 1975). And reading ability must, in general, vary with listening ability, for good readers are, on the average, brighter than poor readers.

But while it is a good first approximation, describing reading as the sum of decoding and comprehension is not quite accurate. If we think of each variable (R, D, & C) as ranging from 0 (nullity) to 1 (perfection), it seems clear that literacy of any kind can result only when both components are present to some degree. A complete absence of decoding skill (D = 0), for example, results in illiteracy, whatever the individual's level of comprehension. Similarly, an inability to comprehend, no matter what the level of decoding, must result in an inability to read. Instead of the sum of decoding and comprehension, reading is better described as their product: R = D × C. Let us call this the Simple View of Reading.

TESTING THE SIMPLE VIEW

The Simple View can be directly tested. If we had measures of decoding, listening, and reading ability, then we could ask whether the product of the first two correlates significantly with the latter.

The problem with this test is that it is too easy. We already know that decoding ability correlates with reading ability (e.g., Perfetti & Hogaboam, 1975), and we also know that listening comprehension correlates with reading ability (e.g., Curtis, 1980). Given this, their product will almost certainly correlate with reading ability. The only interesting question we can ask is its size: given the strongest form of the Simple View (i.e., that only decoding and comprehension determine reading ability), then if we have good measures of the two variables, their correlation should approach unity.

A more demanding test of the hypothesis would be to see whether the product of decoding and comprehension predicts reading better than their sum. This test is, in fact, very demanding, for the two competitors, sum and product, make almost the same predictions about reading ability: The poor decoder and listener will make a poor reader, an average decoder and listener will make an average reader, and a good decoder and listener will make the best reader. On a three-dimensional surface defined by the three variables, the only place the two models differ is along the edges: the multiplicative model says that if you cannot decode (or listen) then you cannot read, no matter how well you listen (or decode), while the additive model says that superior decoding can compensate for a lack of listening comprehension, and vice versa. Thus the multiplicative model could be shown to be better than the additive model only if you have individuals with adequate ability on one variable but none on the other. Given the assumption that the two abilities are positively correlated, they must be scarce.

SOME DATA

It occurred to us that we might find them in a bilingual population. Hoover and Gough (1990) were able to obtain all three measures on a set of 210 bilingual children in Texas who took part in a study conducted by the Southwest Educational Development Laboratory. Each child was given the Interactive Reading Assessment Test (Calfee & Calfee, 1979, 1981) at the end of the first grade, and each child who remained in the study was given the same test at the end of the second, third, and fourth grades.

The IRAS contains three subtests important to us, a reading comprehension test, a listening comprehension test, and a decoding test. The reading subtest consists of a set of nine passages of increasing difficulty. Comprehension is assessed with free recall and a probe question; the child's score is the number of passages read successfully (i.e., with adequate recall and comprehension; see Calfee & Calfee, 1979, 1981, for the scoring procedure). Listening comprehension is assessed by a parallel set of passages read to the child, and scored in exactly the same way.

Decoding was measured with the synthetic word decoding subtest. This test consists of nine short lists of pseudowords of increasing difficulty, ranging from simple consonant-vowel-consonant settings (CVCs) such as *hin* and *pame* in the easiest list to polysyllables such as *rhosmic* and *conspartable* in the most difficult. The child's score is, approximately, the number of lists decoded correctly.

The study thus gave us reading, decoding, and listening comprehension scores on 210 children in the first grade, 206 of the same children in the second, 86 in the third, and 55 in the fourth. We used these data to test three implications of the Simple View.

The first was the prediction that the product of decoding and comprehension would predict reading better than their sum. Using hierarchical multiple regression, we first entered decoding and (listening) comprehension (as an unordered pair of variables). This yielded a very impressive multiple correlation at each grade level (.85, .85, .88, .92, successively). But at each grade level, adding the product of decoding and comprehension significantly increased the multiple r (to .86, .87, .92, .95). Given that the reliabilities of the reading, decoding, and comprehension measures are less than one, these correlations could hardly be higher. The product of decoding and comprehension clearly predicts reading, and it does so better than their sum.

We next examined the relation between reading and listening. Anyone would expect that these two variables should be correlated, and they are. We observed that the correlation between reading and listening increased from .46 in the first grade to .71, .80, and .87 in the second, third, and fourth, respectively. But, on the Simple View, the relation between the two variables must depend on decoding. When decoding is perfect (i.e., when D = 1), then reading is just listening (R = C). But without decoding there is no reading; when D = O, R = O, whatever the value of C. So we expect to see that the dependence of reading on listening must vary directly with decoding: the slope of the regression of R on C must increase with D, while the intercept should remain the same. (It is worth noting that the additive hypothesis, that R = D + C, makes the opposite prediction.)

The increase we observed across grade levels is presumably an instance of this. Assuming that decoding increases from grade to grade, we would expect that the correlation of reading and listening should also increase, as it does. (We think this explains the oft-observed change in the relation between reading achievement and intelligence. In their review of this relationship, Stanovich, Cunningham, & Feeman [1984] report that the median correlation observed in the first grade is .45, while in the later grades it rises to .65.)

Not only is there an increase in the correlation between reading and listening across grade levels, we found it within grades as well. Within each grade level, the slope of the regression of reading on listening increased monotically with decoding. Hence it is not simply a developmental change: Whatever the source of variability in decoding ability, as that ability increases, so does the dependence of reading ability on listening ability.

A third implication of the Simple View might be the most interesting. Anyone would, we think, expect that the two component skills, decoding and comprehension, are positively correlated. In fact, the Texas study provides clear evidence of this fact: At each grade level, the bilingual children exhibited a significant positive correlation between decoding and listening (.42, .59, .54, .72, in grades one through four, successively). But this fact is independent of the Simple View, for this view makes no claim whatsoever about the intrinsic relation between decoding and comprehension. It states only that, whatever the values of D and C, their product should equal R.

But the constraint that the product must equal R makes an interesting suggestion with respect to disabled readers. Consider, for example, readers with R = .10 (on a scale ranging from 0 to 1). On the multiplicative hypothesis, a reader could achieve this reading level with D = 1.0 and C = 0.1, or with D = 0.1 and C = 1.0, or an infinite set of other possibilities. But a high D must be associated with a low C, and vice versa. Among the reading disabled, the better the decoder, the worse the comprehender, and the better the comprehender, the worse the decoder. The multiplicative model suggests, then, that among the reading disabled, the correlation between decoding and comprehension should be negative, rather than positive.

We examined this hypothesis by asking what happens to the correlation between D and C when we look only at children who cannot read the simplest of the IRAS passages. In the first grade, there were 144 such children. In this group, the correlation between D and C was −.12. In the second grade, there were still 45; they showed a correlation of D and C of −.09. The most striking results were observed in the third grade. As noted among the 86 third graders, the correlation of D and C was .54. But among the 13 most disabled readers in that grade, we found a correlation of −.55: the better the disabled third grader can listen, the more serious his or her problem with decoding.

THE BOTTOM–UP VIEW RECONSIDERED

The results of the study are thus entirely consistent with the Simple View. The product of decoding and listening comprehension correlates almost perfectly with reading ability. The correlation of reading and listening comprehension varies directly with decoding ability. And the relation between decoding and listening comprehension, positive in the general population, becomes negative among the reading disabled in elementary school. Taken together with their double dissociation in older clinical populations, the evidence clearly supports the commonsensical notion that reading has two major components: decoding and comprehension.

Those two components may well interact. But they can be separated, and they can be separately measured. And those separate measurements account for individual differences in reading ability remarkably well. There is little variance left for their interaction to explain.

An interactive view may well be the correct view of the reading process. But the parts, not the interaction, constitute reading ability.

REFERENCES

Calfee, R., & Calfee, K. (1979). *Interactive reading assessment system*. Department of Psychology, Stanford University, Stanford, CA.

Calfee, R., & Calfee, K. (1981). *Interactive reading assessment system*. Stanford University, Stanford, CA.

Cattell, J. M. (1886). The time it takes to see and name objects. *Mind, 11,* 63–65.

Coltheart, M. (1978). Lexical access in simple reading tasks. In G. Underwood (Ed.), *Strategies of information processing*. London: Academic Press.

Curtis, M. E. (1980). Development of components of reading skill. *Journal of Educational Psychology, 72,* 656–669.

Foss, D. J. (1988). Experimental psycholinguistics. *Annual Review of Psychology, 39,* 301–348.

Frazier, L. (1987). Sentence processing: A tutorial review. In M. Coltheart (Ed.), *Attention and performance* (Vol. 12). Hillsdale, NJ: Lawrence Erlbaum Associates.

Gough, P. B. (1972). One second of reading. In J. F. Kavanagh & I. G. Mattingly (Eds.), *Language by ear and by eye*. Cambridge, MA: MIT Press.

Gough, P. B. (1983). Context, form, and interaction. In K. Rayner (Ed.), *Eye movements in reading*. New York: Academic Press.

Gough, P. B. (1984). Word recognition. In P. D. Pearson (Ed.), *Handbook of reading research*. New York: Longman.

Gough, P. B., Alford, J. A., & Holley–Wilcox, P. (1981). Words and contexts. In O. L. Tzeng & H.

Singer (Eds.), *Perception of print: Reading research in experimental psychology.* Hillsdale, NJ: Lawrence Erlbaum Associates.

Gough, P. B., & Tunmer, W. E. (1986). Decoding, reading, and reading disability. *Remedial and Special Education, 7,* 6–10.

Healy, J. (1982). The enigma of hyperlexia. *Reading Research Quarterly, 17,* 319–338.

Hoover, W. A., & Gough, P. B. (1990). The simple view of reading. *Reading and Writing, 2,* 127–160.

Huey, E. B. (1908). *The psychology and pedagogy of reading.* New York: Macmillan.

Kucera, H., & Frances, N. (1967). *A computational analysis of everyday English.* Providence: Brown University Press.

McClelland, J. L., & Rumelhart, D. E. (1981). An interactive activation model of context effects in letter preception: Part 1. An account of basic findings. *Psychological Review, 88,* 375–407.

McCusker, L. X., Bias, R. G., & Hillinger, M. L. (1981). Phonological recoding and reading. *Psychological Bulletin, 89,* 217–245.

Perfetti, C. A., & Hogaboam, T. W. (1975). The relationship between single word decoding and reading comprehension skill. *Journal of Educational Psychology, 67,* 461–469.

Reicher, G. M. (1969). Perceptual recognition as a function of meaningfulness of stimulus material. *Journal of Experimental Psychology, 81,* 275–280.

Rumelhart, D. E. (1977). Toward an interactive model of reading. In S. Dornic (Ed.), *Attention and performance* (Vol. 6). Hillsdale, NJ: Lawrence Erlbaum Associates.

Rumelhart, D. E., & McClelland, J. L. (1982). An interactive activation model of context effects in letter perception (P. 2). *Psychological Review, 89,* 60–94.

Samuels, S. J., LaBerge, D., & Bremer, C. D. (1978). Units of word recognition: Evidence of developmental change. *Journal of Verbal Learning and Verbal Behavior, 17,* 715–720.

Sanford, A. J., & Garrod, S. C. (1981). *Understanding written language: Explorations in comprehension beyond the sentence.* New York: Wiley.

Seidenburg, M. S., & McClelland, J. L. (1989). A distributed developmental model of word recognition and naming. *Psychological Review, 96,* 523–568.

Snowling, M. (1987). *Dyslexia.* New York: Basil Blackwell.

Stanovich, K. E. (1980). Toward an interactive-compensatory model of individual diferences in the development of reading fluency. *Reading Research Quarterly, 16,* 32–71.

Stanovich, K. E., Cunningham, A. E., & Feeman, D. J. (1984). Intelligence, cognitive skills, and early reading progress. *Reading Research Quarterly, 19,* 278–303.

van Dijk, T. A., & Kintsch, W. (1983). *Strategies of discourse comprehension.* New York: Academic Press.

Vellutino, F. R. (1979). *Dyslexia: Theory and research.* Cambridge, MA: MIT Press.

Wheeler, D. D. (1970). Processes in word recognition. *Cognitive Psychology, 1,* 59–85.

IV COGNITION AND MOTIVATION

11 Cognition, Motivation, and Emotion: Ideology Revisited

William N. Dember
University of Cincinnati

I am going to pick up in this chapter where I left off more than a dozen years ago when I first addressed the issue of ideology in an article entitled "Motivation and the Cognitive Revolution" (Dember, 1974). My main intent then was to get motivational theorists thinking about a phenomenon that they seem to have ignored totally, and to get them to try to find a way of incorporating it into their theories: the motivational potency of ideation in general and of ideology in particular. I did receive some interesting letters in reaction to the article but, as far as I can tell, the major lasting impact came from the title itself. The phrase, "cognitive revolution," has become a familiar one in the literature in personality and clinical psychology (e.g., Lazarus, Coyne, & Folkman, 1982) and has been picked up recently by Baars (1986) for a volume of interviews with leading figures in behavioral and cognitive psychology, including Jim Jenkins; however, I am not aware of any significant reformulations in motivational theory in response to my invitation.

My intent here is to raise the consciousness of leaders or protoleaders in cognitive theory, in hopes of challenging them to broaden their concerns so as to include in their conceptions the motivational and emotional aspects of cognition. What I know of cognitive theories suggests that they address people's in-formation-processing capabilities and limitations, their use of language, rules, and schemata in the service of motive-satisfaction, problem solving, and adapta-tion. In that sense, cognition is the servant of motivation, a means to an end. My present concern is for those instances, which I believe to be many, when cognitions themselves provide the driving force; when ideas, if you will, become motives, and when instrumental acts are performed in *their* service.

To make it clearer what I have in mind, and for those who may not be familiar with the kinds of instances I cited in my 1974 article, I will first briefly review

153

some of them here, and add a few more contemporary examples. Following that, I want to reinforce my argument with some quotes from the late Arthur Koestler. Next, I will cite interview data collected by Stanley Kaplan, a psychiatrist, revealing the considerable stress suffered by jurors who had handed down a guilty verdict in the case of a young man accused of murder, for whom they had developed a strong sense of sympathy over the course of the trial. Then I will turn to the historian James Billington, who has written cogently on the origins of revolutionary ideology, and finally the Renaissance scholar, and baseball commissioner at the time of his death, A. Bartlett Giamatti, whom I will quote at length toward the end of this chapter. It was reading Billington that helped me realize how closely my present concern connects with my earlier contribution to motivational theory, the Dember and Earl (1957) theory of choice, an insight which I will briefly elaborate toward the end of the chapter. Giamatti, in the language of a humanist, captures the essence of ideology and also tells us something important about context.

Woven throughout the fabric of this chapter is a simple thesis: Cognition, motivation, and emotion, though properly separable for the sake of pedagogical and scientific convenience, do not, in real people, come in fully isolated modules. In that sense, motivation and emotion are topics inherent in cognitive science.

MOTIVATIONAL POTENCY OF IDEATION

The "data" for my 1974 article consisted of newspaper or magazine clippings about incidents that seemed to reflect a common theme: the occurrence of actions, typically harmful to oneself or to others, and performed not in the heat of passion or for some base motive (e.g., robbery to obtain money for a fix), but rather under the mandate of an idea or a system of beliefs. For example, a young boy drank a lethal solvent, taken from a school laboratory, because some friends had dared him to; his death was slow and painful. Similarly, a "24-year old truck driver won a $500 bet from two of his friends by jumping off the George Washington Bridge—a 212-foot plunge into the Hudson River. He did not live to collect the bet" (Dember, 1974, p. 166).

In both of those examples the central idea motivating the self-destructive act was implanted through verbal interchange involving a dare or a bet. I acknowledge the possibility of other sources of motivation in such examples, perhaps an unconscious death wish, or the need to appear brave in front of one's friends, and thereby gain their respect and admiration.

Nevertheless, I cite these incidents, not being able to know what motives were in fact operative, in part because I believe they are pertinent in their own right and mostly because they are suggestive of a primitive form of ideational motivation that manifests itself more clearly and fully in other instances.

Here is an incident which I paraphrased from an item in the April 23, 1973, issue of *Newsweek:*

An assistant pastor and a layman of the Holiness Church of God in Jesus Name, of Carson Springs, Tennessee, died in agony after drinking a mixture of strychnine and water—testing their faith in the Bible, where in Mark 16; 16–18 it is asserted that "if they drink any deadly thing, it shall not hurt them." (Dember, 1974, p. 166)

Now, in this instance, the motivations are also undoubtedly complex, but I think we get closer to what I am looking for—that is, people acting under the demands of a system of ideas or beliefs. The pastor and the layperson not only receive permission from the Bible to drink the strychnine cocktail, they are in a sense encouraged to do so, since if their faith is firm, they will be protected from the harm that would otherwise accrue to such an action, and thereby also publicly affirm their faith. Unfortunately for them, they failed the test. Instances similar to this one are common, so much so that they have lost their dramatic appeal, except when large numbers are involved, as in the Jonestown tragedy, where adherents to a mixture of political and religious ideology, prodded by the charismatic Reverend James Jones, committed mass suicide and murder.

The week I began preparing this chapter, the media were saturated with violent events that by now may well have been forgotten. To remind you of just four of them: (1) Shiite Muslims hijacked a TWA flight from Athens to Rome, and held 39 male passengers and three crewmen hostage, after having shot and killed one of the passengers in cold blood; (2) An Air India flight went down off the coast of Ireland, with all passengers aboard killed, presumably the result of a bomb planted on the plane by Sikh extremists; (3) An explosion in the luggage-handling section of the Tokyo airport killed three employees, again apparently the work of Sikh extremists; (4) Nine civilians and four off-duty U.S. Marines were machine-gunned to death at an outdoor cafe in El Salvador by revolutionaries dressed in the uniform of government soldiers. There were other incidents I have not mentioned, and I have no doubt that the same week saw the occurrence of many other such events that failed to come to public attention for lack of dramatic appeal. More recently were the September, 1986, multiple bombings in Paris, the plane hijacking in Karachi, and the brutal murders in an Instanbul synagogue.

Now, my interest here is not with violence or terrorism per se. I focus on terrorist acts for what they may reveal about the motivational potency of the ideologies that I presume those acts to be serving. And, of course, not every act of terrorism exemplifies the operation of ideological motivation. But it is sufficient for my purpose that there be some such instances.

Aside from good theory, we are in great need here of data that go beyond anecdote and journalistic reports. If we could bring ideologues into the laboratory to study their cognitions, what questions should we ask that might inform us about the issue I am raising? For example, is there some marker to look for that would set apart those cognitions that have motivational potency from those that serve ordinary information-processing functions? I will return to such questions at the end of this chapter, but want first to touch bases with Koestler, Kaplan, Billington, and Giamatti. We can learn a lot from colleagues in other disciplines.

INSIGHTS FROM OTHER DISCIPLINES

Arthur Koestler, whom you may know as the author of the novel, *Darkness at Noon* (1941) studied psychology, worked as a journalist, and has written cogently on such topics as science, creativity, and the comic. In his final years, he made rather foolish forays into parapsychology, but that should not detract from the credibility of his earlier insights. He certainly knew the revolutionary mentality from the inside as well as from a more objective perspective. A few quotes from one of his lesser known works, *Janus,* published in 1978, provide a summing up of his earlier psychobiological ideas.

Citing Paul MacLean's notion of the human triune brain—that we have inherited both a reptilian and a lower mammalian brain onto which has been superimposed the neocortex—Koestler writes:

> If neurophysiological evidence had not taught us the contrary, we would have expected it to reveal an evolutionary process which gradually transformed the primitive old brain into a more sophisticated instrument—as it transformed gill to lung, or the forelimb of the reptilian ancestor into the bird's wing, the flipper of the whale, the hand of man. But instead of transforming old brain into new, evolution *superimposed* a new superior structure on an old one with partly overlapping functions, and without providing the new brain with a clearcut power of control over the old. To put it crudely: evolution has left a few screws loose between the neocortex and the hypothalamus. MacLean has coined the term schizophysiology for this endemic shortcoming in the human nervous system. The hypothesis that this type of schizophysiology is part of our genetic inheritance, built into the species as it were, could go a long way towards explaining some of the pathological symptoms listed before. The chronic conflict between rational thought and irrational beliefs, the resulting paranoid streak in our history, the contrast between the growth-curves of science and ethics, would at least become comprehensible and could be expressed in physiological terms. And any condition which can be expressed in physiological terms should ultimately be accessible to remedies. . . .
> For the moment let us note that the origin of the evolutionary blunder which gave rise to man's schizophysiological disposition appears to have been the rapid, quasi-brutal *superimposition* (instead of *transformation*) of the neocortex on the ancestral structures and the resulting *insufficient coordination* between the new brain and the old, and *inadequate control* of the former over the latter. (1978, pp. 10–11)

Though I find Koestler's argument generally compelling, I must take exception with the last clause in the last sentence: that our problems stem from lack of adequate control of the old brain by the new brain, that is, lack of control over emotion by cognition. All of Koestler's other arguments, as I will illustrate with this next quote from *Janus,* point to a relationship that goes in the other direction:

> We are thus driven to the unfashionable conclusion that the trouble with our species is not an excess of *aggression,* but an excess capacity for fanatical *devotion.* Even a cursory glance at history should convince one that individual crimes committed for selfish motives play a quite insignificant part in the human tragedy, compared to the numbers massacred in unselfish loyalty to one's tribe, nation, dynasty, church, or political ideology. . . . The emphasis is on unselfish. Excepting a small minority of mercenary or sadistic disposition, wars are not fought for personal gain, but out of loyalty and devotion to king, country or cause. Homicide committed for personal reasons is a statistical rarity in all cultures, including our own. Homicide for unselfish reasons, at the risk of one's own life, is the dominant phenomenon in history. (1978, p. 14)

Devotion, commitment, loyalty, ideology—those are terms I would be inclined to associate with the neocortex, rather than with the amygdala or hypothalamus. I tried to argue for the point that Koestler makes (Dember, 1974) in connection with another of the examples I cited, this one the case of Diana Oughton, who was killed along with two members of the Weather Underground when bombs they were constructing in a Greenwich Village apartment exploded. Diana came from a well-to-do Midwestern family and has been described as very caring, sensitive, and warm-hearted. In an article about her biography, which appeared in the *Saturday Review,* the author, with proper caution, writes "At some risk of oversimplification, it is nevertheless safe to say that in Diana Oughton, as in others, emotions came to rule the brain" (Cook, 1971, p. 35). With equal caution I commented, "The reviewer may be right in that particular instance, but I would like to suggest the plausibility of just the opposite interpretation: Diana's ideology came to rule her emotions" (Dember, 1974, p. 167).

As I read Koestler, he points the finger for the world's major ills not at unbridled emotion, but at ideology unrestrained and unmodulated by compassion. In Diana's case, I would speculate that her commitment to the Weatherman agenda was sufficiently strong to override and perhaps even nullify any apprehension she must have felt about the harm that could come to people (as it turned out, to herself and her collaborators) who happened to be around when those bombs she was making went off.

Of course, emotion totally free of cognitive controls is not so healthy either. But as I said:

[T]he dominance of behavior by rational, cognitive processes will [not] necessarily assure personally and socially desirable outcomes. On the contrary, there may be as much to fear from unbridled ideation (especially in its extreme form, ideology) as there is from unconscious fantasies or unrestrained emotions. (Dember, 1974, p. 168)

I have recently been made aware of a common situation in which the dictates of cognition and the moderating pressure of emotion come into stark conflict. My colleague, Stanley Kaplan of the University of Cincinnati Psychiatry Department, published a very nice piece in the July, 1985, issue of *Psychology Today* on the dilemma facing jurors in a recent murder trial in Cincinnati. The defendant, who had been severely abused as a child, and badly mistreated by schoolmates and others, succeeded in enlisting the sympathy of the jurors. At the same time, the latter had accepted their responsibilities as jurors, and the evidence of guilt was quite convincing. Despite their strong empathic feelings for the defendant, they were compelled by the evidence and by the rules of jurisprudence, which they had sworn to uphold, to find him guilty and recommend the death penalty.

The article by Kaplan (1985) focused on the emotional sequelae for the jurors of the conflict between acting responsibly and acting compassionately. Service on that jury proved for most of them a very trying experience, and many exhibited the symptoms associated with posttraumatic stress syndrome. For my purposes, the interesting point is the way in which a commitment to the rules of proper jury behavior—a kind of short-term, mini-ideology—enabled those nice people in effect to put to death a man for whom they had come to care. Perhaps the jury room would be a fruitful setting for research on the motivational potency of ideation. If it were, and were accessible, and we knew what questions to ask, their would surely be no shortage of subjects to provide the data now so sorely lacking.

It is interesting that I illustrate the paradigm shift (Kuhn, 1962) which I dubbed the "cognitive revolution" by reference to the violent actions of terrorists and revolutionaries, since all revolutions are at their heart cognitive. Revolutionaries gain their credence and enlist their supporters through the potency of their ideas. As Koestler put it: "Wars are not fought for territory, but for words" (1978, p. 15).

The historian James Billington, in a book with the beautiful title *Fire in the Minds of Men* (1984), writes about the 18th-century roots of contemporary revolutionary ideology. In particular, he characterizes the early formulators and spokespersons of the French revolution, which was extremely violent, as not themselves violent people. On the contrary he writes:

[M]ost of the important early revolutionaries seem surprisingly free of unusual personal characteristics. . . . Like most other French children of their time, they were fond of their mothers, of their native regions, and of mildly sentimental, apolitical literature.

Revolutionaries in the subsequent romantic era were rarely as idiosyncratic and antisocial as artists and poets, and less committed to violence than is generally realized. The schools of thought that played the most important roles in developing a revolutionary tradition all saw themselves as providing the rationality that would end violence.

The fascinating fact is that most revolutionaries sought the simple, almost banal aims of modern secular man generally. What was unique was their intensity and commitment to realizing them. (Billington, 1980, p. 13)

Billington's description of 18th-century French revolutionaries is confirmed in a recent study of left-wing Italian terrorists, based on journalistic accounts as well as pre-trial interviews: "what has been most striking . . . is the 'normalcy' of their personalities" (Pasquino & Della Porta, 1986, p. 173). While some form of psychopathology (for example, a fascination with weapons and violence) may indeed characterize many members of terrorist organizations (see Merkl, 1986), it apparently is not an essential feature on the terrorist mentality.

Reading further in Billington and surveying the present world scene calls up an image of people struggling to cope with social, political, economic, and personal circumstances that verge on the chaotic. One sees inequity and injustice everywhere; poverty coexisting with great wealth, political leaders saying one thing and doing another, and, above all, instability and uncertainty. In Lebanon, for example, the Druze and Shiites cooperated on June 30, 1985, in the safe transport of American hostages from Beirut to Damascus. On July 1, the next day, they were shooting at one another in the streets. Much of the chaos is, of course, intentionally provoked for presumed political gain, or at least for attention, by various revolutionary groups. But the point is that even without these deliberately set "fires," the world for people living in such circumstances is chaotic and confusing; in the language of the Dember and Earl (1957) theory, their world is excessively complex.

Excessive complexity is aversive. Given the freedom and the resources, one would retreat from it, seeking circumstances closer to one's ideal level of complexity. But the people we are talking about have little freedom and few resources. What response do you have when you are stuck in circumstances that are beyond your ability to comprehend and with which you lack the resources to cope? The solution, it seems to me, lies not in literally changing the circumstances, which seems impossible, but in symbolically transforming them, such that the incomprehensible can be understood and the unmanageable can be handled. To turn chaos into order, one needs some kind of simplifying conceptual system.

It is my contention that ideology provides the requisite system; that ideology serves the same function in this context that theory provides for science. To pursue that analogy further, it is obvious that not every scientist or consumer of science needs to be a profound theorist; we can get by with, indeed put up with, only a few theories at a time, and their creation can be left to a few powerful intellects. The rest of us can gain comfort by adopting the most appealing of the competing theories. Similarly, people suffering from the kinds of political, social, economic, and personal cognitive overload that I alluded to earlier can take great solace in ready-made ideological systems that help render an otherwise intolerably confusing world comprehensible, if not bearable. It is through ideology that excessive complexity can be reduced to manageable simplicity. A good ideological system provides answers to all questions, and moreover sets rigid guidelines for action, thus enabling the confused both to understand the world and to live in it.

In May 1982, I attended the commencement ceremony at Yale and was treated to a moving baccalaureate address by then-President Giamatti. His notions seemed quite consonant with mine, though presented in a poetic style that I greatly admire but would not even try to emulate. In the absence of anything resembling hard empirical data, I take his comments as a kind of validation of my own analysis. Giamatti also provides, in his use of the term, "circumstances," borrowed from Edmund Burke, an interesting version of the concept of contextualism that is central to the thinking of many of the participants in this conference.

President Giamatti was speaking to the graduates about an experience he had had earlier that spring in Jerusalem at Yad Vashem, a memorial to the Holocaust:

Yad Vashem is a monument to the heroes and martyrs of the Holocaust and a memorial to the six million Jews systematically murdered by the Nazis. To descend beneath the stark, concrete plaza to the underground museum is to descend into Hell at one remove. It is to go into mass moral chaos and yet it is only a representation, in photograph, artifact and text, of the horror of the camps and monstrosity of the events and the minds that made them. . . . Coming up from underground, I was forced to face the consequences of ideology. I had seen close up, even if at a remove, what can result when human beings ignore circumstances; that is, ignore our common moorings in our accumulated, common humanity. . . . Why does any ideology tend to be authoritarian? Because any system of ideas that consciously purifies itself of previous condition or prior context . . . and claims to contain all value must logically also wish to exert complete control. Any scheme for regulating life that systematically asserts it is internally and systematically complete, a law and a morality and a context of value and a machine for living unto itself, must logically will to exercise its power completely, or its claims for itself are invalid. The self-righteousness of all ideologies is a function of their self-perceived completeness; each element reflects the alleged correctness of every other. These closed systems are attractive because they are simple and are simple because they are such masterly evasions of contradictory, gray complex reality. . . .
(Giamatti, 1982, pp. 14–15)

I do not know whether all the following items are necessary, or sufficient, to capture the entire process, but I assert that being fully committed to an ideology is tantamount to having become an ideological convert, following a sequence characterized by the terms, chaos, confusion, complexity, commitment,[1] and conversion. What is the price of conversion to an ideology? Clearly, a virtually complete loss of control over one's choices. Conscience and compassion might have to be set aside, and indeed one's own survival can become a secondary consideration. But those are mainly personal and moral concerns. What is there here for cognitive science?

A CHALLENGE TO COGNITIVE SCIENTISTS

It's hard to know where to start, and here is where I am appealing to cognitive scientists for assistance. I think it would be interesting, for example, to determine whether there are differences between the cognitive structures of ideological converts and of people who share that ideology, but who have acquired it through a gradual and subtle process of acculturation. Do ideological converts suffer pangs of conscience when, under the dictates of ideology, they must perform violent and destructive acts? Can the Dianas of the world remain caring, sensitive, and warm-hearted while setting off their bombs? I once believed not, but thinking of the jurors in the murder trial, who suffered great emotional turmoil as a result of performing their duty as jurors, makes me wonder. Is there an abrupt moment of conversion, like Saul's on the road to Tarsus, best modeled by a form of mathematics like catastrophe theory, or is the process of conversion continuous, following the smooth curves of calculus. More generally, how might the issues I have raised here be both enlightened by and enrich cognitive science? Most generally, how can we construct our broad psychological theories so as to incorporate cognition, motivation, and emotion into a single, unified system without losing sight of their separate, special functions?

REFERENCES

Baars, B. J. (1986). *The cognitive revolution in psychology*. New York: Guilford Press.
Billington, J. H. (1984). *Fire in the minds of men: Origins of the revolutionary faith*. New York: Basic Books.
Brickman, P. (1987). *Commitment, conflict, and caring*. Englewood Cliffs, NJ: Prentice–Hall.
Cook, F. J. (1971). A review of *Diana: The making of a terrorist* by Thomas Powers. *Saturday Review*, May 1, p. 35.

---

[1]A brilliant analysis of the concept of commitment is offered by the late Philip Brickman (1987) and his collaborators in a book published shortly after the manuscript for the present chapter was completed.

Dember, W. N. (1974). Motivation and the cognitive revolution. *American Psychologist, 29,* 161–168.

Dember, W. N., & Earl, R. W. (1957). Analysis of exploration, manipulation, and curiosity behaviors. *Psychological Review, 64,* 91–96.

Giamatti, A. B. (1982). In the middle distance: The baccalaureate address. *Yale Alumni Magazine,* June, 14–16.

Kaplan, S. M. (1985). Death, so say we all. *Psychology Today, 19,* (7), 48–53.

Koestler, A. (1941). *Darkness at noon.* New York: Macmillan.

Koestler, A. (1978). *Janus.* New York: Random House.

Kuhn, T. S. (1962). *The structure of scientific revolutions.* Chicago: University of Chicago Press.

Lazarus, R. S., Coyne, J. C., & Folkman, S. (1982). Cognition, emotion and emotion. The doctoring of Humpty–Dumpty. In R. W. J. Neufeld (Ed.), *Psychological stress and psychopathology* (pp. 218–239). New York: McGraw-Hill.

Merkl, P. H. (1986). Conclusion: Collective purposes and individual motives. In P. M. Merkl (Ed.), *Political violence and terror* (pp. 335–374). Berkeley: University of California Press.

Pasquino, G., & Della Porta, D. (1986). Interpretation of Italian left-wing terrorism. In P. M. Merkl (Ed.), *Political violence and terror* (pp. 169–189). Berkeley: University of California Press.

12

Metaphor and Context in the Language of Emotion

Robert R. Hoffman
Adelphi University

John E. Waggoner
Bloomsburg University

David S. Palermo
Pennsylvania State University

INTRODUCTION

In this chapter we explore the language of emotion, especially the role of metaphor. Metaphor pervades the everyday language people use to talk about emotions. It also pervades the language that scientists use in their theories and research on emotion. It is known that metaphor is an important tool in the analysis of scientific theories and research (see, for instance, Gentner & Grudin, 1985; Hesse, 1966; Hoffman, Cochran, & Nead, 1990; Turbayne, 1971). Analysis of the metaphors reveals underlying assumptions and mental models which can be refined or refuted. It is possible that analysis of metaphors for emotion may reveal the assumptions of theories of emotion, and might also suggest new directions for research.

We begin this chapter with a brief statement of the problem of defining emotion. Next, we survey the major theories of emotion, pointing out their metaphorical nature, and some of the assumptions of the metaphors. Following that is an analysis of some of the research on emotion language and the perception of emotional gestures. Much of the available research treats emotions "out of context." The chapter culminates in a discussion of recent research that has used methods and materials incorporating context. We conclude by stressing the importance of ecological validity for theories of emotion.

EMOTION AND LANGUAGE

Young wrote in 1927 that the psychology of emotion was a field "full of confusion and contradiction" (1927, p. 186). Claparède echoed this in his 1928 monograph on emotion. In more recent times, the subjective, personal nature of emotion has led some to question its legitimacy as a topic for scientific inquiry (e.g., Bindra, 1969; Kantor, 1966). Although emotions may be phenomena that are "central" to our view of human nature (Candland, 1977, p. 4), problems arise when an attempt is made to describe and characterize emotions.

The Definition Problem

The issue of what qualifies as an emotion, especially in reference to empirical studies of emotion language, is very complex (see Clore, Ortony, & Foss, 1987; Ortony, Clore, & Foss, 1987).[1] One thing that does seem clear is that the language of emotion is laden with metaphors. Many emotion words are obviously metaphorical, and many others are invariably metaphorical in terms of their etymology. Obvious metaphors are feeling "empty," "burdened," "depressed," "bitter," "insecure," "trapped," "tense," "upset," "stressed," "bubbly," "on guard," and "picked on." One can "burn with anger," "fall in love," or be "under pressure." An example of a hidden metaphor is the word "hedonic," which is often relied on in definitions of emotion. Etymologically, it comes from the Greek word denoting the pleasure of sweets. A bit less hidden is the word "feeling," which stems from the Greek and Latin words for touch, and the terms "emotion," "motivation," and "affect," which stem from Latin words for the causes of action or "mental agitation."

The study of emotion, today as in the past, relies on definitions of emotion that reduce to either: (1) Abstract terms that are etymologically themselves metaphors (such as "hedonic" and "arousal"), (2) Feeling states that are used to exemplify emotions, and that are generally clear-case metaphors (such as "depression"), or (3) Ad hoc descriptions of situations that are likely to evoke or involve a given emotion. Our knowledge of emotions such as vanity, bitterness, pride, optimism, or indignation seems to depend heavily on our ability to talk about situations in which the emotions occur. When asked to imagine experiencing various emotions, research participants invariably do so by thinking of situations in which the emotions and accompanying sensations would be likely to occur (Pennebaker, 1979).

A number of theorists find this state of affairs problematic (e.g., Brady &

---

[1]Emotions can be distinguished from affects, from moods, and from personality traits (Mees, 1985). The word "affect" involves reference to the value that emotional experiences have for the organism. "Emotion" involves some kind of behavioral or gestural expressiveness (or something that could be expressed) as well as a particular kind of experience or subjective feeling state. Words that denote this feeling are descriptive of a state of consciousness but are not necessarily "acted out" or expressed (Young, 1973), and are not descriptive of a state of affairs in the world. Words like "proud," "aggressive," "submisive," and "optimistic" are used to describe both transient emotional reactions and personality traits. Moods and personality traits are long-term or repetitively occurring emotional reactions (Ortony, Clore, & Foss, 1987; Plutchik, 1980). Moods have been characterized as being shifting, yet pervasive, feeling states of varying duration, usually not intense nor clearly tied to specific provoking events, as is the case with emotions (Wessman, 1979).

Emurian, 1978; Mandler, 1975a). They eschew semantic analyses in research on emotion language, since language, it is believed, is plagued by vagaries, ambiguities, and irrelevant cultural or social meanings. Our view is that an analysis of the language of emotion will be an important component in any comprehensive explanation of emotion phenomena, even though language cannot be assumed to provide a unique, univocal, or even direct representation of emotional experience.

METAPHOR AND THEORIES OF EMOTION

The history of the psychology of emotion is essentially a history of theoretical debate about metaphors. There have been theories that define emotion as dependent on "feedback" from physiological reactions (e.g., Cannon, 1932; James, 1884; Mandler, 1976; Pribram, 1970; Schachter, 1972). There have been theories that define emotion as being dependent on instinctual "energies" (e.g., Bowlby, 1969; Freud, 1915; McDougall, 1908). For example, Lacey and Lacey (1970) stated that "autonomic responses can be viewed as meter readings of . . . arousal or activation" (p. 205). Over the course of history of psychology, however, three sets of metaphors stand out: (1) mechanistic metaphors, which are manifested today as information-processing and computer metaphors, (2) the metaphor that basic emotions are like "primary" colors, and (3) a statistical metaphor that focuses on the hypothetical dimensions of emotion.

Computer Metaphors

In the years since about 1965 there have appeared many information-processing theories that refer to emotion. In these theories, emotions are regarded as being the manifestation of cognitive "structures," "affect maps," "meaning networks," and "neural programs" (see Iran–Nejad, Clore, & Vondruska, 1981), or processing events, such as "overload" (Leventhal, 1974; Siminov, 1970) and processing "loops" (Candland, 1977).

Information-processing metaphors have been used to express a number of emotion phenomena. For example, the evaluation of emotional or physiological states can go on at a nonconscious level, and only the products of the evaluation may be available to consciousness. In this case, one can speak of the analysis of states as taking place "automatically." The notion of "parallel processing" can be used to account for the phenomenon that thoughts and feelings sometimes occur simultaneously (Lazarus, 1982; Zajonc, 1980).[2]

---

[2]A fundamental problem for the computer metaphors is that it is not clear that emotion (or any other psychological phenomenon, for that matter) can be fully reduced to computations. The claim that they can is the very heart of cognitive science and artificial intelligence (for a recent discussion of this and related issues, see Dreyfus & Dreyfus, 1986, or Haugeland, 1985).

Regardless of the parallel processing assumption, the computer metaphor assumes a causal sequencing model in which the cognitive, perceptual, and physiological components are linked, one presumably causing another. For example, cognitive and perceptual evaluation of physiological processes may determine the quality and intensity of the emotion a person experiences in a given situation. In fact, several researchers have demonstrated such relationships between perceptions or cognition and bodily changes (e.g., Andrasik & Holroyd, 1980; Schachter, 1964; Sirota, Schwartz, & Shapiro, 1976; Valins, 1970). There appears to be no reason why such relations cannot be captured in a model based on the computer metaphor. Most theorists, however, seem wedded to a single cause–effect relationship, leaving other possible relations or sequences out of their models. Compare, for example, the causal sequences described by Lazarus (1984), Plutchik (1980), Solomon (1980), and Zajonc (1980).

There are situations in which particular sequences do indeed seem to take place. For example, many people have reported experiences in which a sight led to escape followed by fear, such as running after seeing a bear, only to experience fear fully after getting away. However, the long-held implicit assumption of "one sequence" has no direct research evidence to support it, and furthermore, the assumption is not supported by experience. For example, there are situations where a number of emotions of varying intensities overlap in experience. This may be the experiential origin of the idea that an emotion can be a "mixture."

Color Mixture Metaphors

A great deal of research has been conducted on those emotions which cause severe maladaptive problems, such as depression and anxiety. However, most current theories of emotion focus on a set of so-called "basic" emotions. A small set of emotions (surprise, disgust, pain or distress, anger, sadness, fear, and joy) develops according to a regular sequence in the neonatal and infancy stages (Izard, 1972). The social emotions of shame, guilt, and contempt appear shortly thereafter. Each of these basic emotions can be related to evolution in terms of survival functions (Darwin, 1872; Plutchik, 1980). Each appears to be related to a unique pattern of movement of facial muscles, fairly common across various cultures (Ekman, Levenson, & Friesen, 1983; Izard, 1971; Redican, 1975). There is also convincing evidence that neonates can imitate the facial gestures that accompany basic emotions (Meltzoff, 1983), and that infants' behavior is influenced by the facial gesturing of basic emotions by parents and other adults (Field, 1982; Klinnert, Einde, Butterfield, & Campos, 1986). Furthermore, each basic emotion is related to a fairly unique pattern of autonomic arousal (Ekman et al., 1983). In other words, it is possible to differentiate roughly some basic emotions in terms of autonomic reaction patterns (e.g., heart rate, galvanic skin response, pupil diameter, and the like) (Averill, 1969; Ekman et al., 1983; Grings & Dawson, 1978). For instance, heart rate increases for anger and fear, but not for sadness and disgust.

Since the number of emotions and feelings that have been listed by various researchers ranges from about 50 to more than 400, it is not surprising that it is difficult to get a consensus on what the primary ingredients of emotions are. Table 12.1 illustrates this.

Many theorists use a "color mixture" metaphor to explain how the variety of emotions stems from a hypothetical combinatorial process. It is assumed that the basic emotions are "primary" and that they somehow "mix" together in a

TABLE 12.1
Some Postulated Emotion Primaries and Dimensions

Primaries	Dimensions
Borgatta (1961) Lonely, tired, warmhearted, thoughtful, startled, defiant.	*Abelson and Sermat (1962); Schlosberg (1954)* Pleasant–unpleasant, Attention–rejection, Sleep–tension
Ekman et al. (1983) Fear, anger, happiness, disgust, surprise, sadness	*Bush (1973); Russell and Mehrabian (1977)* Pleasure–displeasure, Arousal–nonarousal, Dominance–submissiveness
Izard (1972) Joy, surprise, distress, anger, disgust, shame, fear, interest, excitement	*Davitz (1969)* Hedonic tone, Activation Relatedness, Competence
Nowlis (1965) Aggression, anxiety, urgency, elation, concentration, fatigue, vigor, social affection, sadness, skepticism, egotism, nonchalance	*Frijda (1970)* Pleasant–unpleasant, Derision–mildness, Simple–complicated, Intensity–attention, Self-assured–insecure, Natural–artificial, Surprised–not surprised
Osgood (1966) Anger, amazement, surprise, joy, pleasure, disgust, interest, complacency, fear	*Gladstones (1962)* Pleasant–unpleasant, Sleep–tension, Expressionless–mobile
Plutchik (1980) Acceptance, trust, fear, terror, surprise, astonishment, rage, sadness, disgust, loathing, expectancy, joy, ecstasy	*McNair and Lorr (1964)* Tension, anger, vigor, depression, fatigue, friendliness, confusion
Tomkins (1980) Interest, excitement, joy, enjoyment, surprise, startled, distress, anguish, fear, terror, shame, humiliation, contempt, disgust, anger, rage	
Wenger, Jones, and Jones (1956) Terror, fear, pain, rage, anger, grief, sorrow, sexual excitement, disgust, embarrassment, startled	

Dimensions indicated by a single word are degradations (such as level of tension or level of activation) whereas dimensions indicated by two words are polar (such as pleasant versus unpleasant).

formulaic fashion, thereby generating the "secondary" or "more complex" emotions (Izard, 1977; Millenson, 1967; Tomkins, 1980; Watson, 1930). Plutchik (1980), for example, used the laws of color mixture explicitly, to try to derive an "emotion solid." First, a group of research participants rated the basic emotions (the "primaries") for intensity (e.g., anger is high intensity, sadness is low) and for their similarity (e.g., sadness and grief are similar, ecstasy and disgust are dissimilar). Other participants saw a list of emotion words, and for each one they had to indicate which two or three "primaries" were its components. The data from this phase allowed Plutchik to arrange the primaries in an "emotion circle." In the second phase of the research, another group of participants examined pairs of the primaries with the task of generating emotions that would represent their mixture. Examples of high-frequency responses were "fear + surprise = alarm," and "surprise + sadness = disappointment."

In general, there was some agreement for emotion words that were adjacent on the emotion circle, but not for the mixtures of primaries that were two or three times removed. The variance in the data effectively dashed the hope of generating an emotion "solid," but Plutchik sallied forth nonetheless. His ruminations on "emotionimerty" included such hypothetical formulas as this: "If a mixture of acceptance and fear produces submission, then acceptance and anger should produce dominance" (1980, p. 164).

Theorists who have adopted the "primaries" metaphor have (apparently) made little attempt to reveal the underlying "mixture" process by experimental demonstration. What are the states or processes (other than word judgments) that can combine to produce the mixtures? Autonomic reaction patterns do not reliably discriminate among most emotions (Candland, 1977; Mandler, 1979; Patkai, 1971). Indeed, most emotions have never been empirically studied in terms of the acompanying physiological changes. In any event, a combinatorial process, if it does exist, is almost certainly not based solely on those physiological reaction parameters which are easily measured using current technology (Davitz, 1969; Frijda, 1970; Leshner, 1977; Strongman, 1978; Tarpy, 1977).

Statistical Dimension Metaphors

A number of investigators have attempted to identify the essential attributes of emotions by searching for the "dimensions" that are necessary and sufficient to define all emotional states. The mathematical metaphor that is involved here comes from the statistical method widely used in emotion research: Factor analysis of people's judgments about emotion words (e.g., Abelson & Sermat, 1962; Borgatta, 1961; Ekman, 1965; Engen, Levy, & Schlosberg, 1958; Gladstones, 1962; Nowlis, 1965; Russell & Mehrabian, 1977).[3]

---

[3]The issue of the difference between mathematical description and mathematics-as-metaphor is an interesting and important issue, surveyed by Jones (1980), and deserving further analysis.

In the research associated with this metaphor, participants judge the degree to which an emotion denotes "activity versus passivity," for example. The mathematical technique derives an abstract "space" in which the various emotions are represented by points, each point (emotion name) having a projection onto (some degree of) each dimension of judgment. Classes or types of emotions can be identified by the clustering of emotion words within the space (Osgood, 1966).

The commonly held assumption underlying this metaphor is that the scaling space represents a mental space: Experiencing or comprehending an emotion is regarded as a process of mental metrication, the computation of spatial coordinates.[4] Here, the researchers are reifying their statistical method, a fallacy of representations that often occurs in mentalistic psychology (Hoffman & Nead, 1983).

Theorists disagree on what dimensions are needed to define emotions. Most do agree that all emotions are to some extent either pleasant or unpleasant, and that all emotions entail some degree of arousal or activation. Several researchers also agree that emotions have some degree of deliberation versus impulsiveness. Osgood (1966) has named this the Control dimension. According to his analysis, an emotion such as loathing would be marked as very unpleasant, highly active, and involving a great deal of control.

Theorists disagree that three dimensions are sufficient to characterize all emotions. A listing of the various dimensions that have been proposed appears in Table 12.1. As the two columns in Table 12.1 are intended to suggest, the attempt to define essential dimensions often results in such an extensive list that there remains little apparent difference between a typological (How many primaries?) and a dimensional analysis (Strongman, 1978).

The definition problem for theories of emotion seems to hinge upon the overreliance on particular metaphors, and also upon the contextual complexities of emotional experience. Yet, much research on emotion language takes emotions entirely out of context.

TAKING EMOTIONS OUT OF CONTEXT

Traditionally, research on emotion takes emotions out of context either by presenting photographs of faces or by presenting emotion terms as isolated words.

Frozen Faces

A great deal of research has been conducted in which people are asked to judge the emotions depicted in photographic views of faces. This is perhaps the most commonly used method in the study of the perception of faces and facial

---

[4]This is a mixed metaphor, combining dimensions with computations. This particular mixture is natural enough, given the predominance of computer metaphors and the fact that most factor analyses are carried out using computers.

emotional gestures. Research has shown that people can reliably discern happiness and disgust in photographs of faces, even if the photographs are of people of widely different races (Ekman, Friesen, & Ellsworth, 1972). However, other emotions, even some "basic" ones, such as fear, sadness and anger, are not always easily discernable or discriminable in photographs (Rosenthal, Hall, Archer, DiMatteo, & Rogers, 1979), especially if people have to judge photographs of faces of people from a different culture or racial group (Ekman, 1973; Ekman, Sorenson, & Friesen, 1969).

The dynamics of facial gestures are highly complex and subtle. This is evidenced by the effort required of the researchers who have to code data on facial expressions from videotapes (see Ekman, 1985; Ekman & Friesen, 1974; Ekman & Oster, 1979; Meltzoff, 1983; Meltzoff & Moore, 1977; Rosenthal et al., 1979). Despite the complexity (or more likely because of it), the dynamics of facial gestures are highly informative to perceivers (infants included) (Bassili, 1978; Klinnert, Einde, Butterfield, & Campos, 1986). People can be remarkably accurate in their perception of bodily motion in dynamic displays (Cutting, 1978; Runeson & Frykholm, 1983), and judments of facial expression are more accurate and easier to make if body motion and posture are also observable (Burns & Beier, 1973; DePaulo, Rosenthal, Eisenstat, Finkelstein, & Rogers, 1978).

Isolated Words

In the typical experiment on emotion language, participants are given tasks in which they have to make rating scale judgments about emotion terms, presented as isolated words. Various factor-analytical techniques show the ever-present Pleasant–unpleasant dimension and the Activation dimension, but no overall coherent interpretation seems possible (see the attempt to generate a circular geometry, by Russell, 1980). Participants assign different rating scale values and assign different words to label various expressive patterns, and they pick out different expressive patterns when asked to describe a given emotion (Bush, 1973). Discrepancies between group averages and individuals' data are generally larger for emotion words than for color names or pronouns.

About all one can conclude from this emotion research is that there is some orderliness in the way people judge emotions words. But the problem of identifying the basis for the orderliness remains. Should we conclude, with Mandler (1975b) and others, that the reason for the lack of orderliness is that language is inherently vague and ambiguous? We think not. The reason that there is some orderliness in the ratings data is the same as why there isn't more: Orderliness is in experience, and real experiences involve much more than isolated words and rating scales. To say that "The child behaved in a way that expressed unpleasantness, high activation, and lack of control" fails to give nearly the same impression as stating that the child is horrified of the dark. In other words, problems are encountered when there is no event or experience to serve as a referent for emotion words. Some linguists concerned with this problem in semantics do not even attempt to account for the meaning of sentences in which emotion words occur, because of the independent (or, contextually dependent) meanings of emotion words (e.g., Kempson, 1977).

Participants in the "isolated words" research no doubt spend at least some of their time envisioning scenarios or contexts, to add flesh to the word stimuli. On a broader scale, it becomes apparent when one contemplates the vast array of feeling and emotion words that it is possible to identify situations or contexts in which each one of them might be experienced or expressed. Caplan and Hanes (1985) explored this by analyzing and cross-classifying 250 emotion words and 250 feeling words in terms of their etymology, their dictionary definitions, and their synonymic relations to each other. Using published ratings data as well, Caplan and Hanes were able to form groupings or clusters of words. For instance, "rage," "love," "lust," and "desire" are semantically clustered under "passion." The cluster for "upset" included "confused," "fearful," "angry" and "pained." Words within clusters are conceptually similar, according to the dictionaries and the available ratings data. The important finding, however, is that words within clusters would generally never be acceptable substitutes or synonyms for one another in specific contexts.

Traditional emotion research focuses on the components of emotions, to the neglect of the question of when and why emotions occur. The importance of "situational cues" and "goal expectations" in the experience of different emotions has been recognized by a number of investigators (e.g., Ekman et al., 1972; Frijda, 1969; Izard, 1972; Mees, 1985; Schachter, 1970). However, most researchers and theorists do not analyze the antecedent contexts and events that are likely to invoke or involve different emotions. Emotions are not easily-labeled things "in" organisms, nor are they simple reactions triggered by "cues." Rather, they are complex events, often difficult to describe verbally, that transpire in organism–environment interactions. Many emotion theorists and researchers, however, seem to regard the "language" of emotions as consisting of isolated words whose meaning may be established by calculating the "mean similarity rating" (cf. Plutchik, 1980, pp. 167–172).

To summarize, much of the research and theorizing on emotion does not analyze the antecedent contexts and events that induce different emotions, although the importance of situational factors to the identification and experiencing of emotion has been stressed by a number of investigators (e.g., Ekman et al., 1972; Frijda, 1969; Izard, 1972; Schachter, 1970). If we are interested in an analysis of what emotions consist of and how they can be distinguished and defined, it will be necessary to analyze the complex array of emotional experiences at a contextual level.

PUTTING EMOTION BACK INTO CONTEXT

We now discuss several examples of empirical and experimental studies which either directly implicate context as a powerful factor in emotion, or which deliberately employ context-setting tasks or stimulus materials. Our first example is the recent work by Ortony and his colleagues on a functional classification scheme for emotion words (Iran–Nejad et al., 1984; Ortony et al., 1987; see also Mees, 1985) and an experimental test of the scheme (Clore et al., 1987).

Ortony et al. began by questioning the assumption that ratings of meaning similarity could be analyzed in terms of a small set of "universal" dimensions. They argued that the dimensions that have been traditionally used to describe emotion are so general as to be essentially uninformative. For example, published word ratings on the dimensions of Evaluation, Potency, and Activity are more similar for *sympathy* and *food* (which is decidedly not an emotion) than for *sympathy* and *love*. Their own theoretical approach began when they "noted that many distinctly poor examples of emotions seem quite emotional when considered in the context of feeling something as opposed to being something" (Clore et al., 1987, p. 761). They developed a functional classification scheme that distinguishes internal and external conditions, and within the internal conditions category, further distinguishes nonmental bodily states from mental states (i.e., affect states, behavioral states, and cognitive states). Based on their functional classification, Ortony et al. predicted that some words would be regarded as an emotion in the sense of "feeling" (e.g., feeling ignored), but would be regarded as references to environmental conditions in the sense of "being" (e.g., being ignored).

Ortony and his colleagues asked participants to rate their confidence that particular words referred to an emotion, as either a feeling (e.g., feeling angry) or a state (e.g., being angry). Thus, the stimulus materials were "not quite isolated" words, that is, they were presented in either a "feeling _____" or a "being _____" context. Hence, this study serves as a stepping stone to our discussion of other research where context is more elaborate. Ortony et al. used a corpus of more than 475 words, composed from the published lists of emotion words used in previous research. Discriminant and cluster analyses of the ratings confirmed some of the predictions of the functional classification scheme. For example, the clearest cases of emotions were terms classified as Affective States. This set included the "basic" emotions we referred to earlier (e.g., anger, fear, happiness, etc.) and more than 200 others, including concern, ecstasy, irritation, jealousy, and sorrow. Words that were regarded as Cognitive Conditions, and hence less likely to be regarded as emotion words, included baffled, defiant, patient, and startled, among some 60 others. Also distinguished were External Conditions: words such as abused, deprived, lucky, and oppressed, among some 55 others.

To be sure, some words were classified differently by the scheme versus the empirical data. For instance, impatience was classified a priori as an Affective Condition, but was regarded as a Physical or Bodily State by the participants. Overall, however, a majority of the terms fell into the predicted categories. Hence, a hierarchical layout of the cluster results conformed in many ways with the a priori scheme. Ortony et al. (1987) concluded that:

> The best examples of emotions are ones that possess the following components: (a) they are internal, *mental* as opposed to physical or external conditions, (b) they are good examples of *states,* and their predominant *referential focus* is on *affect,* as opposed to behavior, cognition, or some combination of these. (p. 358)

The more of these contextual or referential components a term possesses, the more likely it is to be regarded as a good example of an emotion (see also Mees, 1985; Shields, 1984). The authors emphasized the implications for research methodology:

> The linguistic context in which subjects implicitly consider the terms is usually uncontrolled and unknown. We suspect that poor examples may find their way into published lists of emotion terms because they are considered, at least implicitly, in the context of feeling rather than being. (Clore et al., 1987, p. 761).

Empirical Studies of Natural Language Emotion Metaphors

Unlike previous studies of "the affective lexicon," Ortony et al. did not take it for granted that each of the hundreds of available candidate emotion words is actually regarded by people as denoting an emotion (see also Mees, 1985). Other work which takes an empirical approach includes anthropological investigations of natural language by Lutz (1988) and by Lakoff and his colleagues (e.g., Lakoff & Kovecses, 1987).

Lutz's recent investigation of the emotion language and experience of the Ifaluk islanders in the South Pacific clearly shows the cultural relativity of emotion language and concepts. Emotion language involves a rich, learned, cultural matrix of values, concepts, situations, and subjective judgments, all of which are used "to negotiate and create social reality" (p. 10). This view, in concert with the theorizing of Ortony et al., suggests that emotions provide the support for acting in social situations and for acting out social scenarios (see also Averill, 1980; Eibl–Eibesfeldt, 1980; Gergen, 1985). If this is true, much of the metaphorical-conceptual baggage of Western civilization should not be assumed in a theory of emotion which is intended to be comprehensive.

One first step in generating a non-Eurocentric theory of emotion would be to spell out the complexities of our own emotion language, that is, that of American English speakers. Linguist George Lakoff and his colleagues (Kovecses, 1988; Lakoff, 1987a, 1987b; Lakoff & Johnson, 1980; Lakoff & Kovecses, 1987;

Lakoff & Turner, 1989) have collected hundreds of instances of natural language sentential metaphors, and used their own knowledge of contextual and cultural factors to derive the underlying metaphor "themes." This work has revealed a great deal of systematicity in the scores of common metaphors that are used to talk about emotions (see also Nafe, 1924; Stern, 1931). This systematicity of metaphorical language occurs at both general and particular levels.

At the general level are metaphors that describe all emotional experience. One such theme defines rational thought as "up" and emotions as "down" (e.g., He couldn't "rise above" his emotions, The discussion "fell" to an emotional level). Two other basic themes are of the body as a "container" for emotions, and of emotions as "fluids." These themes give rise to such phrases as: She couldn't "contain" her joy, and, Pride "welled up" in her. According to another theme, many common utterances define happiness as "up" and sadness as "down" (e.g., I felt "down in the dumps," My spirits "rose"). There is also a general metonymic principle underlying the language of emotion: The physiological and behavioral effects of emotions can substitute for the emotion (Kovecses, 1988). One can "shake with anger," since one of the effects of anger (at least in our folk theory of anger) is bodily agitation. Another example is to say that one is "tearing one's hair out" to indicate extreme anger.

Specific emotions also have particular themes. Kovecses analyzed the themes found in language about anger, pride, and love. The most common theme for anger is "heat," which may be applied in different ways, depending on whether one focuses on solid objects—in which case the basic relationship is instantiated in such phrases as "burn" with anger—or liquids as in "You make my blood boil." The basic themes can be elaborated: An increase in intensity of anger can be likened to the rising of a fluid ("welled up") or to an increase in pressure ("bursting"). Other themes include anger as an opponent ("subdue" one's anger, "fight back" one's anger), and anger as a burden (get it "off your chest").

The concept of heat is also used in a theme for love (e.g., She "set my heart on fire," She "carries a torch" for him), and changes in intensity are reflected in degree of heat—the affectionate "warm glow" versus the "heat" of passion. Additional themes for love include the idea that love is a form of insanity (e.g., He was "crazy" about her, She was "madly" in love), a kind of magic (e.g., to say a person was "bewitched," "in a trance," "charmed," "hypnotized," or "spellbound"), and that love is a unity of complementary parts (to be someone's "better half").

Pride shares some of the themes of anger (e.g., to be "filled" with pride) and also has its own particular themes, such as the animation of pride (Her pride was "injured"), and pride as an object (It "tore her pride to shreds"). The specific metaphor themes for conceit include an up/down dimension (to "be on a high horse") and a size dimension ("too big for his britches"). A theme specific to vanity is of a sensual person (e.g., to "tickle" one's vanity).

Looking across all the general and particular themes for a given emotion, Lakoff and his colleagues have discerned the underlying systematicities—those features of the events or situations that form the common threads or "event schemata." For example, in the case of the themes for anger, the prototypical scenario involves: (1) some offending event, (2) anger, (3) an attempt at control, (4) a loss of control, and (5) an act of retribution. The prototypical love scenario involves: (1) a person searching for love, (2) finding it, (3) trying to keep control of emotions, but (4) falling into a state of lack of control, (5) experiencing physiological effects and behavioral reactions, and (6) fulfilling love in the state of marriage.

While the research of Lakoff et al. is not experimental, it is ambitiously empirical. Furthermore, the work is ecologically valid relative to the "isolated words" research. Finally, the work of Lakoff et al. is a rich source of testable hypotheses (Honeck, 1989). For example, one would expect considerable overlap between the event schemata derived by Lakoff et al. and the functional-contextual classifications entailed by the theory of Ortony et al. (and a similar theory by Mees, 1985).

The research we have described so far implicates the role of context and includes contextual factors in the theorizing. Our next examples are of experiments that deliberately include context as a variable, either in the stimulus materials or in the interpretation task presented to the participants.

Metaphor Production in the Description of Emotion

Davitz and Mattis (1964) were interested in the use of metaphors to communicate emotional meanings. In the first phase of their study, they presented a set of Rorschach inkblots to participants who were asked to report for each inkblot any percepts that involved either anger, anxiety, joy, love, or sadness. Some example reports were "A kind of insect which annoys me" and "Two reindeer having a war" for anger; "A monster coming after me" for anxiety; "A laughing person sitting in a chair" for joy, "Two bears hugging each other" for love; and "Looks like dirty tears" for sadness. Many of the inkblots were described as animate things (e.g., hissing cats, fighting dogs, charging bulls). The participants relied heavily on metaphors to describe feelings (e.g., "hollow," "fragmented"). In general, the responses focused in situations in which the various emotions would be invoked. Beyond this, subtle situational factors often supported fine discriminations among emotions, such as disambiguating imminent hostility (i.e., anxiety) from impending hostility (i.e., anger).

In the next phase of their research, the statements were presented to another group, which had to judge which of the emotions was involved for each statement. They were able to do so reliably (about 80% agreement, overall). This result was validated by using additional groups of participants. The research culminated in a test for ability to express emotional meanings metaphorically. Scores on this test proved to be highly correlated with other measures of sensitivity to emotion.

Fainsilber and Ortony (1987) also examined the production of metaphors that describe emotions. Participants in their study were asked to think of situations in which they had experienced a certain emotion, and to describe their feelings in the situation. Situations pertaining to eight emotions (happiness, pride, gratitude, relief, sorrow, fear, resentment, and shame) were examined. The participants' descriptions were analyzed to determine the frequency of metaphor use; results indicated that metaphors were used about 15% of the time. They produced such phrases as "a storm brewing up inside" for resentment, and "pressure just went away" to describe relief. Fainsilber and Ortony concluded that metaphorical language is used because some of the subjective qualities of emotions cannot be described with literal language. Given that emotion language is highly frequent in natural language (Hoffman & Kemper, 1987; Lakoff & Johnson, 1980), this could explain why many of the metaphors their participants produced were idiomatic, that is, common or frozen metaphors (i.e., having a conventional literal meaning), much like the double-function terms studied by Asch (1958).

The studies by Davis and Mattis and that by Fainsilber and Ortony are clearly ecologically valid relative to the "isolated word" studies. They examined the language that people use (somewhat) spontaneously to describe emotions. They made reference to the naturally occurring situations and contexts in which emotions are experienced. Fainsilber and Ortony instructed participants to generate situations, and both they and Davis and Mattis discovered that metaphoric descriptions of emotions often make reference to situations and contexts in which emotions occur. While these studies represent a step toward a fuller understanding of the relations between metaphor, emotions, and context, researchers have yet to focus on the reasons why particular metaphors (or idioms) are used to describe one emotion rather than another. To use an example that Fainsilber and Ortony provide, they made no effort to explain why "a storm brewing inside" was used to describe resentment rather than happiness. Presumably, the event schema approach of Lakoff et al. could be of assistance in this matter.

Comprehension of Emotion Metaphors

Another line of recent research focuses on the comprehension of metaphors that describe emotional reactions and their situational contexts. For example, Kozlowski (1975) embedded emotion words in meaningful sentence contexts. The participants were presented with metaphors such as "A young bachelor is an eager engine," and "A panicked crowd is a wild wave charging." One group of participants rated the topics and vehicles on Osgood's dimensions of Activity, Potency, and Evaluation. Another group of participants rated the metaphors for their aesthetic "goodness". The results showed that topic-vehicle similarity was related to positive Evaluation. In other words, Kozlowski was able to demonstrate experimentally that the emotional component of the sentence metaphor was related to judgments of the metaphor's meaning. Kozlowski argued that further research along these lines needs to be even more responsive to context (p. 790), in order to explain the reason why particular metaphors are used to describe particular emotions or their contexts.

Such research is illustrated by the work of Waggoner (1989), who investigated an hypothesis from Lakoff's cognitive model of emotion—that a metaphorical temperature dimension might form the link between some emotions and their contexts. The materials were sentential descriptions of emotions which used physical object terms as the metaphoric descriptors (e.g., "Betty was ice," "Joe was a volcano"). Participants were presented with a number of metaphors along with the names for some emotional states as candidate interpretations for each metaphor. The task was to decide which of the states fit each metaphor, and to explain their decisions. The materials were designed to investigate the role of two types of information in the comprehension process: (1) information provided by the traditional three dimensions of the Semantic Differential, and (2) information provided by the correspondence between the emotions and the physical objects on the temperature dimension, a major component of Lakoff's model of emotion.

In concert with other research, the explanations that the participants gave of their choices often made reference to situational contexts (involving the metaphor vehicle), suggesting that knowledge of emotion includes context as an integral component. In concert with the "isolated words" research, the results reflected the dimensions of Evaluation, Activity, and Potency. However, the mappings between the psychological domain and the domain of objects that serve as metaphor vehicles also reflected the temperature dimension (e.g., "lava" as a metaphor vehicle is taken as an example of the "anger is a hot fluid" metaphor).

The studies we have cited to this point involve emotion words presented in context, either by giving instructions to relate words to appropriate contexts or situations (in the production studies) or by using sentence contexts (the comprehension studies). However, metaphor sentences, like all sentences, rarely appear outside of a broader context. The influence of broader context on a number of measures of metaphor comprehension, appreciation, and so on has been amply documented (e.g., Gibbs & Gerrig, 1989; McCabe, 1983; Ortony, Schallert, Reynolds, & Antos, 1978). An example of how one might take broader context into account is a study of children's ability to comprehend emotion metaphors, conducted by Waggoner and Palermo (1989). Children 5, 7, and 9 years old, and a group of college students were asked to interpret metaphors that concluded one-paragraph prose passages. The situation described in each passage was intended to be ambiguous with regard to one of two possible contrasting emotions that could be involved. The specific emotion was indicated by the metaphor. Here is an abbreviated example:

> Betty went to the fair with her father. She wanted a stuffed animal, and begged him to knock over the bottles with three baseballs. After he had thrown the third ball, Betty was a:
>> bouncing bubble
>> sinking boat.

Following the presentation of each paragraph, the participants had to choose an emotion as an interpretation for the concluding metaphor, and then provide an explanation for their interpretation.

A pilot study had shown that both the emotions and the contexts are all well known to children, and yet the young children had difficulty in explaining their interpretations. This finding is in concert with some previous research on the development of metaphor comprehension (cf. Keil, 1986; Winner, Rosenteil, & Gardner, 1976). In contrast to previous research, however, the youngest children *were* able to interpret many of the metaphors, and there was no great difference in performance as a function of metaphor novelty. The method of presenting metaphors in broader contexts thus made it possible for children to comprehend "psychological metaphors" at an age when some previous research would suggest that they should have considerable difficulty. Thus, some of the principles underlying the language of emotion are grasped at a relatively early point in development. Current research is investigating the role of different types of context (i.e., passages that are either congruent or incongruent with the metaphors) in order to determine the degree to which children grasp these principles.

Summary of the Research

To summarize, the research we have described involved context in addition to or instead of isolated emotion words. Situational context may be used to stimulate the recall of emotional experiences, it may be used as the surround for embedded metaphors, or, in the anthropological investigations and the metaphor production studies, context appears as a salient property of the language that people use spontaneously to describe emotions.[5]

CONCLUSIONS

Historically speaking, the studies of the relation of physiology to emotion have not yielded the simple answers once hoped for. Each emotion is not tied to a particular and readily distinguishable pattern of physiological changes. The

---

[5]One should not conclude from our emphasis on metaphor that the *only* ecologically valid research on emotion language involves metaphor. Much of the research on children's comprehension of emotion language involves context in the description of situational information. For example, Gnepp (1983), Reichenbach and Masters (1983), Hoffner and Badzinski (1989), and others have investigated children's ability to use a variety of cues, including contextual information and information provided by facial expressions, to determine emotional experiences. In this research, children are presented with contextual information and then with stimuli (usually drawings of faces), and are asked to describe which emotion is involved. This basic paradigm is similar to that used by Waggoner and Palermo (1989).

"isolated words" studies of emotion language also yielded no firm conclusions. While the research that used photographic depictions of static facial gestures confirmed the developmental/functional notion of "basic" emotions, it did little to reveal the complexities that underlie the majority of emotional experiences. Furthermore, theorizing about emotion involves tough definition problems with metaphors underlying the theorizing. Recent anthropological work suggests that theorists may have been overly constrained by their Eurocentric point of view and the assumption that a single simple explanation will hold for all emotional experience.

Recent theorizing has taken a functionalist tack in generating schemes for classifying emotion words (e.g., Mees, 1985; Ortony et al., 1987). That is, the emphasis is on when and why emotions occur, their goal situations and contexts. Context-sensitive research such as that we have described appears to offer some hope for a resolution of a number of theoretical issues and definitional problems. Research stimuli can include contextual information, through the use of sentence contexts for emotion words or through the use of prose scenarios. Research can permit the participants to reveal their full knowledge of emotional experience, without forcing them to conform their knowledge to rating scale response measures, for example.

The following factors will need to be incorporated in any theory of emotion that is intended to be comprehensive: (1) The social and cultural context, (2) The experiencer's perception of the situation, (3) The experiencer's appraisal and interpretation of the situation, (4) The social and cultural norms used in the comprehension of experience, (5) The experiencer's physiological reactions, (6) The experiencer's perceptual evaluation and interpretation of those physiological reactions, (7) The experiencer's behavioral reactions, and (8) The experiencer's hedonic impression. Finally, the theory must account for the dynamic interactions of the components.

A comprehensive theory of emotion will reflect a sensitivity to ecological validity in a broad functionalist sense. That is, it will implicate the evolutionary, and adaptive significance of emotions (as in Chance, 1980; Clore, et al. 1987; Iran–Nejad et al., 1981; Plutchik, 1980, 1984; Scott, 1980; Weinrich, 1980). Although emotional experience is rich and varied, new emotions do not appear every day; the range of emotional experience is constrained (but not strictly limited) by the environment and our evolution in it, and hence by our physiological and psychological characteristics.

ACKNOWLEDGMENT

The authors would like to thank Marjorie Caplan for her comments on an earlier draft of this chapter. They also express their gratitude to James J. Jenkins, for all that he has done by way of contributions to experimental psychology, and for his support and friendship. Along with the other contributors to this volume, we thank him for instilling in us the freedom to be creative, the joy of research, the intrigue of theory, and the recognition that experimental psychology can contribute to the betterment of humankind. We respect the characteristics that have made him a distinguished scientist, we admire the characteristics that make him a distinguished human being, and we love the man.

REFERENCES

Abelson, R. P., & Sermat, V. (1962). Multidimensional scaling of facial expression. *Journal of Experimental Psychology, 63,* 546–554.

Andrasik, F., & Holroyd, K. A. (1980). A test of specific and nonspecific effects in the biofeedback treatment of tension headache. *Journal of Consulting and Clinical Psychology, 48,* 575–586.

Asch, S. (1958). The metaphor: A psychological inquiry. In R. Tagiuri & L. Petrullo (Eds.), *Person, perception, and interpersonal behavior,* (pp. 86–94). Stanford, CA: Stanford University Press.

Averill, J. R. (1969). Autonomic response patterns during sadness and mirth. *Psychophysiology, 5,* 399–414.

Averill, J. R. (1980). A constructivist view of emotion. In R. Plutchik & H. Kellerman (Eds.), *Emotion: Theory, research, and experience* (Vol. 1, pp. 305–339). New York: Academic Press.

Bassili, J. N. (1978). Facial motion in the perception of faces and emotional expressions. *Journal of Experimental Psychology: Human Perception and Performance, 4,* 373–379.

Bindra, D. A. (1969). A unified interpretation of emotion and motivation. *Annals of the New York Academy of Science, 159,* 1071–1083.

Borgatta, E. F. (1961). Mood, personality and interaction. *Journal of General Psychology, 64,* 105–137.

Bowlby, J. (1969). Psychopathology of anxiety: The role of affectional bonds. In M. H. Lader (Ed.), *Studies of anxiety* (pp. 80–92). Ashford, MA: Headley.

Brady, J. V., & Emurian, H. H. (1978). Behavior analysis of motivational and emotional interactions in a programmed environment. *Nebraska symposium on motivation* (Vol. 26, 81–122). Lincoln, NE: University of Nebraska Press.

Burns, K. L., & Beier, E. G. (1973). Significance of vocal and visual channels in the decoding of emotional meaning. *Journal of Communication, 23,* 118–130.

Bush, L. E. (1973). Individual differences in multidimensional scaling of adjectives denoting feelings. *Journal of Personality and Social Psychology, 25,* 50–57.

Candland, D. K. (1977). The persistent problems of emotion. In D. K. Candland, J. P. Fell, E. Keen, A. K. Leshner, R. M. Tarpy, & R. Plutchik (Eds.), *Emotion* (pp. 1–84) Monterey, CA: Brooks/Cole.

Cannon, W. B. (1932). *The wisdom of the body.* (2nd ed.) New York: Norton.

Caplan, M., & Hanes, D. (1985). *Shades of meaning: The languages and contexts of emotions.* Unpublished manuscript, Adelphi University, Garden City, NY.

Chance, R. A. (1980). An ethological assessment of emotion. In R. Plutchik & H. Kellerman (Eds.), *Emotion: Theory, research, and experience,* (Vol. 1, pp. 81–111). New York: Academic Press.

Claparède, E. (1928). Feelings and emotions. In *Feelings and Emotions: The Wittenberg Symposium.* Worcester, MA: International University Press.

Clore, G. L., Ortony, A., & Foss, M. A. (1987). The psychological foundations of the affective lexicon. *Journals of Personality and Social Psychology, 53,* 751–766.

Cutting, J. (1978). Generation of synthetic male and female walkers through manipulation of a biomechanical invariant. *Perception, 7,* 393–405.

Darwin, C. W. (1872/1965). *The expression of emotions in man and animals*. Chicago, IL: University of Chicago Press.

Davitz, J. R. (1969). *The language of emotion*. New York: Academic Press.

Davitz, J. R., & Mattis, S. (1964). The communication of emotional meaning by metaphor. In J. R. Davitz (Ed.), *The communication of emotional meaning* (pp. 157–176) New York: McGraw–Hill.

DePaulo, B. M., Rosenthal, R., Eisenstat, R. A., Finkelstein, S., & Rogers, D. L. (1978). Decoding discrepant nonverbal cues. *Journal of Personality and Social Psychology, 36*, 313–323.

Dreyfus, H., & Dreyfus, S. (1986, summer). Why expert systems do not exhibit expertise. *IEEE Expert*, pp. 86 90.

Eibl–Eibesfeldt, I. (1980). Strategies of social interaction. In R. Plutchik & H. Kellerman (Eds.), *Emotion: Theory, research, and experience*, (Vol. 1, pp. 59–79). New York: Academic Press.

Ekman, P. (1965). *Emotion in the human face*. New York: Pergamon Press.

Ekman, P. (1973). Cross-cultural studies of facial expression. In P. Ekman (Ed.), *Darwin and facial expression* (pp. 169–222). New York: Academic Press.

Ekman, P. (1985). *Telling lies*. New York: Norton.

Ekman, P., & Friesen, W. V. (1974). Detecting deception from the body or face. *Journal of Personality and Social Psychology, 29*, 288–298.

Ekman, P., Friesen, W. V., & Ellsworth, P. (1972). *Emotion in the human face*. New York: Pergamon Press.

Ekman, P., Levenson, R. W., & Friesen, W. V. (1983). Autonomic nervous system activity distinguishes among emotions. *Science, 221*, 1208–1210.

Ekman, P., & Oster, H. (1979). Facial expressions of emotion. *Annual Review of Psychology, 30*, 527–554.

Ekman, P., Sorenson, E. R., & Friesen, W. V. (1969). Pan-cultural elements in facial displays of emotion. *Science, 164*, 86–88.

Engen, T., Levy, N., & Schlosberg, H. (1958). The dimensional analysis of a new series of facial expressions. *Journal of Experimental Psychology, 55*, 454–458.

Fainsilber, L., & Ortony, A. (1987). Theoretical issues in natural language processing: The role of metaphors in the description of emotion. *Technical Report, Center for the Study of Reading*. University of Illinois, Urbana–Champaign, IL.

Field, T. M. (1982). Social perception and responsivity in early infancy In T. M. Field, A. Huston, H. Quay, L. Troll, & G. Finley (Eds.), *Review of human development* (pp. 20–31). New York: Wiley.

Freud, S., (1915/1957). Instincts and their vicissitudes. *Standard Edition* (Vol. 14, pp. 109–141). London: Hogarth Press.

Frijda, N. H. (1969). Recognition of emotion. In L. Berkowitz (Ed.), *Advances in Experimental Social Psychology* (Vol. 4, pp. 167–223). New York: Academic Press.

Frijda, N. H. (1970). Emotion and recognition of emotion. In M. B. Arnold (Ed.), *Feelings and emotions* (pp. 241–250). New York: Academic Press.

Gentner, D., & Grudin, J. (1985). The evolution of mental metaphors in psychology: A 90-year retrospective. *American Psychologist, 40*, 181–192.

Gergen, K. J. (1985). The social constructionist movement in modern psychology. *American Psychologist, 40*, 309–320.

Gibbs, R. W., & Gerrig, R. J. (1989). A special issue: Context and metaphor comprehension. *Metaphor and Symbolic Activity, 4*, 123–124.

Gladstones, W. H. (1962). A multidimensional study of facial expression of emotion. *Australian Journal of Psychology, 14*, 95–100.

Gnepp, J. (1983). Children's social sensitivity: Inferring emotions from conflicting cues. *Developmental Psychology, 19*, 805–814.

Grings, W. W., & Dawson, M. E. (1978). *Emotions and bodily responses*. New York: Academic Press.

Haugeland, J. (1985). *AI: The very idea*. Cambridge, MA: MIT Press.

Hesse, M. (1966). *Models and analogies in science*. Notre Dame, IN: University of Notre Dame Press.

Hoffman, R. R., Cochran, E. L., & Nead, J. M. (1990). Cognitive metaphors in experimental psychology. In D. Leary (Ed.), *Metaphors in the history of psychology*. (pp. 173–229). Cambridge, England: Cambridge University Press.

Hoffman, R. R., & Kemper, S. (1987). What could reation-time studies be telling us about metaphor comprehension? *Metaphor and Symbolic Activity, 2*, 149–186.

Hoffman, R. R., & Nead, J. M. (1983). General contextualism, ecological science, and cognitive research. *Journal of Mind and Behavior, 4*, 507–560.

Hoffner, C., & Badzinski, D. M. (1989). Children's integration of facial and situational cues to emotion. *Child Development, 60*, 411–422.

Honeck, R. P. (1989). Review of *Women, fire and dangerous things* by George Lakoff. *Metaphors and Symbolic Activity, 4*, 279–284.

Iran-Nejad, A., Clore, G. L., & Vondruska, R. J. (1984). Affect: A functional perspective. *Journal of Mind and Behavior, 5*, 279–310.

Izard, C. E. (1971). *The face of emotion*. New York: Appleton Century Crofts.

Izard, C. E. (1972). *Patterns of emotions: A new analysis of anxiety and depression*. New York: Academic Press.

Izard, C. E. (1977). *Human emotions*. New York: Plenum Press.

James, W. (1884). What is an emotion? *Mind, 9*, 188–205.

Jones, R. (1980). *Physics as metaphor*. Minneapolis: University of Minnesota Press.

Kantor, J. R. (1966). Feeling and emotions as scientific events. *Psychological Record, 16*, 377–404.

Keil, F. (1986). Conceptual domains and the acquisition of metaphor. *Cognitive Development, 1*, 73–96.

Kempson, R. M. (1977). *Semantic theory*, New York: Cambridge University Press.

Klinnert, M. D., Einde, R. N., Butterfield, P., & Campos, J. J. (1986). Social referencing: The infant's use of emotional signals from a friendly adult with mother present. *Developmental Psychology, 22*, 427–432.

Kovecses, Z. (1988). *The language of love: The semantics of passion in conversational English*. Lewisburg, PA: Bucknell University Press.

Kozlowski, L. T. (1975). Similarity of affective meaning and the evaluation of metaphor. *Perceptual and Motor Skills, 41*, 787–790.

Lacey, J. I., & Lacey, B. C. (1970). Some autonomic-central nervous system interrelationships. In P. Black (Ed.). *Physiological correlates of emotion* (pp. 205–227). New York: Academic Press.

Lakoff, G. (1987a). The metaphorical language of rape. *Metaphor and Symbolic Activity, 2*, 73–79.

Lakoff, G. (1987b). *Women, fire, and other dangerous things: What categories reveal about the mind*. Chicago: University of Chicago Press.

Lakoff, G., & Johnson, M. (1980). *Metaphors we live by*, Chicago: University of Chicago Press.

Lakoff, G., & Kovecses, Z. (1987). The cognitive model of anger inherent in American English. In D. Holland & N. Quinn (Eds.), *Cultural models in language and thought* (pp. 195–221). Cambridge, England: Cambridge University Press.

Lakoff, G., & Turner, M. (1989). *More than cool reason: A field guide to poetic metaphor*. Chicago: University of Chicago Press.

Lazarus, R. S. (1982). Thoughts on the relations between emotion and cognition. *American Psychologist, 37*, 1019–1024.

Lazarus, R. S. (1984). On the primacy of cognition. *American Psychologist, 39*, 124–129.

Leshner, A. I. (1977). Hormones and emotion. In D. Candland, J. Fell, E. Keen, A. Leshner, R. Tarpy, & R. Plutchik (Eds.), *Emotion*. (pp. 85–148). Monterey, CA: Brooks Cole.

Leventhal, H. (1974). Emotions: A basic problem for social psychology. In C. Nemeth (Ed.), *Social psychology: Classic and contemporary interactions* (pp. 1–51). Chicago: Rand McNally.

Lutz, C. A. (1988). *Unnatural emotions: Everyday sentiments on a Micronesian atoll and their challenge to Western theory*. Chicago: University of Chicago Press.

Mandler, G. (1975a). The search for emotion. In L. Levi (Ed.), *Emotions: Their parameters and measurement* (pp. 1–15). New York: Raven Press.

Mandler, G. A. (1975b). *Mind and emotions*. New York: Wiley.

Mandler, G. A. (1976). *Mind and emotion*. New York: Wiley.

Mandler, G. A. (1979). Emotion. In E. Hearst (Ed.), *The first century of experimental psychology*. Hillsdale, NJ: Lawrence Erlbaum Associates.

McCabe, A. (1983). Contextual similarity and the quality of metaphor in isolated versus extended contexts. *Journal of Psycholinguistic Research, 12*, 41–68.

McDougall, W. (1908). On the nature of instinct. Excerpts reprinted in D. Bindra & J. Stewart (Eds.), *Motivations* (pp. 6, 8, 52, 57). Baltimore: Penguin Books.

McNair, D. M., & Lorr, M. (1964). An analysis of mood in neurotics. *Journal of Abnormal and Social Psychology, 68*, 620–627.

Mees, U. (1985). What do we mean when we speak of feelings?: On the psychological texture of words denoting emotions. *Sprache und Kognition, 1*, 2–20.

Meltzoff, A. N. (1983). Newborn infants imitate adult facial gestures. *Child Development, 54*, 708–709.

Meltzoff, A. N., & Moore, M. K. (1977). Imitation of facial and manual gestures by human neonates. *Science, 198*, 75–78.

Millenson, J. R. (1967). *Principles of behavioral analysis*. New York: Macmillan.

Nafe, J. P. (1924). An experimental study of the affective qualities. *American Journal of Psychology, 35*, 507–544.

Nowlis, V. (1965). Research with the mood adjective checklist. In S. S. Tomkins & C. E. Izard (Eds.), *Affect, cognition, and personality* (pp. 352–389). New York: Springer.

Ortony, A., Clore, G. A., & Foss, M. A. (187). The referential structure of the affective lexicon. *Cognitive Science, 11*, 361–384.

Ortony, A., Schallert, D. L., Reynolds, R. E., & Antos, S. J. (1978). Interpreting metaphors and idioms: Some effects of context on comprehension. *Journal of Verbal Learning and Verbal Behavior, 17*, 465–477.

Osgood, C. E. (1966). Dimensionality of the semantic space for communication via facial expression. *Scandinavian Journal of Psychology, 7*, 1–30.

Patkai, P. (1971). Catecholamine excretion in pleasant and unpleasant situations. *Acta Psychologica, 35*, 351–363.

Pennebaker, J. W. (1979, August). *Self-perception of emotion and specificity of physiological sensations*. Paper presented at the annual convention of the American Psychological Association, New York.

Plutchik, R. (1980). A general psychoevolutionary theory of emotion. In R. Plutchik & H. Kellerman (Eds.), *Emotion: Theory, research, and experience* (Vol. 1, pp. 3–32). New York: Academic Press.

Plutchik, R. (1984). Emotions: A general psychoevolutionary theory. In K. Scherer & P. Ekman (Eds.), *Approaches to emotion*. Hillsdale, NJ: Lawrence Erlbaum Associates.

Pribram, K. (1970). Feelings as monitors. In M. B. Arnold (Ed.), *Feelings and emotions*. New York: Academic Press.

Redican, W. K. (1975). Facial expression in nonhuman primates. In L. A. Rosenblum (Ed.), *Primate behavior* (Vol. 4, pp. 103–195). New York: Academic Press.

Reichenbach, L., & Masters, J. C. (1983). Children's use of expressive and contextual cues in judgement of emotion. *Child Development, 54*, 993–1004.

Rosenthal, R., Hall, J. A., Archer, D., DiMatteo, M. R., & Rogers, D. L. (1979). The PONS test: Measuring sensitivity to nonverbal cues. In S. Weitz (Ed.), *Nonverbal communication* (2nd ed.). New York: Oxford University Press.

Runeson, S., & Frykholm, G. (1983). Kinematic specification of dynamics as an informational basis for person-and-action perception: Expectation, gender recognition, and deceptive intention. *Journal of Experimental Psychology: General, 112,* 585–615.

Russell, J. A. (1980). A circumplex model of affect. *Journal of Personality and Social Psychology, 39,* 1161–1178.

Russell, J. A., & Mehrabian, A. (1977). Evidence for a 3-factor theory of emotions. *Journal of Research in Personality, 11,* 273–294.

Schachter, S. (1964). The interaction of cognitive and physiological determinants of emotional state. In L. Berkowitz (Ed.), *Advances in experimental social psychology* (Vol. 1, pp. 49–80). New York: Academic Press.

Schachter, S. (1970). The assumption of identity and peripheralist-centralist controversies in motivation and emotion. In M. Arnold (Ed.), *Feelings and emotions* (pp. 111–121). New York: Academic Press.

Schachter, S. (1972). *Emotion, obesity and crime.* New York: Academic Press.

Schlosberg, H. (1954). Three dimensions of emotion. *Psychological Review, 61,* 81–99.

Scott, J. P. (1980). The function of emotions in behavioral systems: A systems theory analysis. In R. Plutchik & H. Kellerman (Eds.), *Emotion: Theory, research and experience* (Vol. 2, pp. 35–56). New York: Academic Press.

Shields, S. A. (1984). Distinguishing between emotion and nonemotion: Judgements about experience. *Motivation and Emotion, 8,* 355–369.

Siminov, P. V. (1970). The information theory of emotion. In M. B. Arnold (Ed.), *Feelings and emotions* (pp. 145–149). New York: Academic Press.

Sirota, A. D., Schwartz, G. E., & Shapiro, D. (1976). Voluntary control of human heart rate: Effect on reaction to aversive stimulation. A replication and extension. *Journal of Abnormal Psychology, 85,* 473–477.

Solomon, R. L. (1980). The opponent-process theory of acquired motivation: The costs of pleasure and the benefits of pain. *American Psychologist, 35,* 691–712.

Stern, G. (1931). *Meaning and change of meaning with special reference to the English language.* Bloomington: Indiana University Press.

Strongman, K. T. (1978). *The psychology of emotion* (2nd ed.). New York: Wiley.

Tarpy, R. M. (1977). The nervous system and emotion. In D. Candland, J. Fell, E. Keen, A. Leshner, R. Tarpy, & R. Plutchik (Eds.), *Emotion* (pp. 149–187). Monterey, CA: Brooks Cole.

Tomkins, S. S. (1980). Affect as amplification: Some modifications in theory. In R. Plutchik & H. Kellerman (Eds.), *Emotion: Theory, research, and experience* (Vol. 1, pp. 141–164). New York: Academic Press.

Turbayne, C. (1971). *The myth of metaphor.* Columbia: University of South Carolina Press.

Valins, S. (1970). The perception and labelling of bodily changes as determinants of emotional behavior. In P. Black (Ed.), *Physiological correlates of emotion* (pp. 229–243). New York: Academic Press.

Waggoner, J. E. (1989, April). *Affective and denotative determinants of the meaning of psychological metaphors.* Presented at the 60th annual meeting of the Eastern Psychological Association, Boston.

Waggoner, J. E., & Palermo, D. S. (1989). Betty is a bouncing bubble:: Children's comprehension of emotion-descriptive metaphors. *Developmental Psychology, 25,* 152–163.

Watson, J. B. (1930). *Behaviorism.* Chicago: University of Chicago Press.

Weinrich, J. D. (1980). Toward a sociobiological theory of the emotions. In R. Plutchik & H. Kellerman (Eds.), *Emotion: Theory, research and experience* (Vol. 1, pp. 113–137). New York: Academic Press.

Wenger, M. A., Jones, F. N., & Jones, M. H. (1956). *Physiological psychology.* New York: Holt, Rinehart, & Winston.

Wessman, A. E. (1979). Moods: Their personal dynamics and significance. In C. E. Fozard (Ed.), *Emotions, personality, and psychopathology* (pp. 73–102). New York: Plenum Press.

Winner, E., Rosenteil, A. K., & Gardner, H. (1976). The development of metaphoric understanding. *Developmental Psychology, 12,* 289–297.

Young, P. T. (1927). Studies in affective psychology. *American Journal of Psychology, 38,* 157–193.

Young, P. T. (1973). *Emotions in man and animals.* Huntington, NY: Kreger.

Zajonc, R. B. (1980). Feeling and thinking: Preferences need no inferences. *American Psychologist, 35,* 151–175.

13 FOG CAT FOG

Háj Ross
Universidade Federal de Minas Gerais, Brazil

I know no better way to place a frame around the things I would like to say in this chapter than to quote the opening words of a beautiful article by Roman Jakobson and Stephen Rudy (1981): "Yeats' 'Sorrow of Love' Through the Years":

> Paul Valéry, both a poet and an inquisitive theoretician of poetry as an "art of language," recalls the story of the painter Dégas, who loved to write poems, yet once complained to Mallarmé that he felt unable to achieve what he wanted in poetry despite being "full of ideas." Mallarmé's apt reply was: "Ce n'est point avec des idées, mon cher Dégas, que l'on fait des vers. C'est avec des mots."
>
> IT IS NOT AT ALL WITH IDEAS, MY DEAR DÉGAS,
THAT ONE WRITES LINES OF POETRY.
IT IS WITH WORDS.
>
> In Valéry's view Mallarmé was right, for the essence of poetry lies precisely in the poetic transformation of verbal material and in the coupling of its phonetic and semantic aspects.

What follows will be an exploration of the notion of "poetic transformation," by a person struck by the contrast that Mallarmé was able to put so beautifully pithily. What exactly does it mean to *write with words?*

To give you some idea of what this perhaps curious phrase might mean, I would like to examine the structure of Carl Sandburg's beautiful, short poem *Fog,* viewing the poem as growing organically out of the particular kind of gesture we make with our throat and mouth when we say the title word. My aim will be to demonstrate that this gesture, or dance for our vocal tract, is a kind of verbal music, a one-syllable melody, which runs through the poem and provides coherences for it in just the same way that the famous **da da da DOMMM** of Beethoven's Fifth runs through that great symphony. I would also like to help you see why it can be valuable to work toward such a microscopic understanding of the music of a poem, for this music is not a background against which we are to contemplate the ideas of the poem. Rather, this musical structure, this phonetic architecture, is part of the idea. The idea and the patterns it makes on the page and in our minds are each other.

I hope that as the drama of this poem, this writing with the word fog, unfolds, it will become increasingly clear why poems in other languages, which might seem to be "about" fog, must necessarily link us to radically different experiences. Or to put it a bit more precisely, they must link us in such different ways that we can only wonder whether the same experiences are being evoked. For instance, any poems whose central words were brume, Nebel, neblina, or kiri, which are the words for "fog" in French, German, Portuguese, and Japanese, respectively, would be radically different, precisely because these other words offer such different melodic possibilities. To write a poem **with** any one of the five words for fog that I have mentioned, a great poet must be able to sense the musicalities of each word and link these to aspects of the image, concept, or experience of fog. When all of these aspects interconnect, harmonize, merge— when they *rhyme*, in the deepest sense of that word—then a poem with the brilliance of Sandburg's arises. Let us look at the resonances that Carl Sandburg set in motion with his 22 words.

FOG

The fog comes
on little cat feet.
It sits looking
over harbor and city
on silent haunches
and then moves on.

—Carl Sandburg (from Wolfe, 1965).

Before we start with the detailed process of what my poet–friend Jack DeWitt calls "ripping a poem to pieces," which may call up emotions in the reader ranging from puzzlement through boredom to outrage against such literary sacrilege, let me state at the outset that I love this poem very much, despite having already ripped it into as many pieces as I have been able to, and being bent on continuing the rippage. I want to share with the reader the joy that this verbal song evokes in me, and also the thrill of following a very elusive intellectual spoor. For we are at the same time confronted with the cameo beauty of Sandburg's words and with a puzzling fact.

I think that probably very many of us who went to school in the United States read this poem at one time or another in our schooling. We had to. This poem, like hundreds of others, was assigned; it is one of the famous American poems. Many of us dutifully plodded through our homework, and read at least some of the assigned poems, possibly this one among them. (After all, it was a short one).

Now let me ask the reader to perform an experiment with me. Whether or not you have ever read the poem before, don't read it again just now. Cover it up with something, or look away from it. I have a question for you: Are there any lines in the poem that you remember?

Moreover, if today was not the first time that you read this poem, did you, by any chance, happen to remember any of its lines even before rereading the poem? Are you one of the many people who, *without any effort or intention at all*, have etched into your memory, out of all the thousands of lines that you dutifully looked at while plodding through your high school assignments, this line "on little cat feet"?

My experience has been that of the scores of people who I have told that I am working on Sandburg's poem about fog, many, many have said something like, "Oh yes, 'The fog comes(in)/on little cat feet.' That one." The first line they don't always get letter perfect, but the second line, *they have gotten down cold*.

I submit that the existence of so many of those unwitting memorizers, in the face of a generally deadening encounter with poetry at school, poses us a real riddle. Namely, what did Sandburg do that was (and is) so right?

There is some magic in these four words, and I want to know where it comes from. I know that probably many of you will want to say something like, "Well, it is the rightness of the image, the aptness of the comparison. After all, cats and fog are alike in being able to move quietly and fluidly, and also in being shrouded in mystery. Sandburg just *saw* well." And I don't want to take issue with you here, for I agree entirely. Poets, like all artists, need great eyes—they have to be able to perceive similarities that others may have been asleep to. But that is not enough. For let me ask you how many of you misremembered the second line? How many thought it was either one of these?

> on little cat paws
> on small cat feet

I bet that it was very few indeed. These are, if you will pardon my bluntness, crummy poetry. And yet their crumminess cannot be said to derive from their poor imagery, for the image, and the comparison, the perception of hidden similarity, that give on little cat feet its memorability, are the same. Rather, what distinguishes Sandburg's indelible four words from my two lousy four-word "translations" of them is only the differences between their musics. For Sandburg not only had great eyes, he had great ears. And the secret of poetry is to be found somewhere in a country where sight and sound fuse. I would like to invite you to join me in a safari to that country.

α

To start with, I would like to ask you to make an assumption about poetry that may initially strike you as very unlikely:

In the musical fabric of a poem, every sound has its importance, its very own part in the melody of the poem as a whole.

That is, I suggest that we see the individual sounds in the poem as being a bit like the individual instruments in a symphony orchestra. And just as the strings have different kinds of music to make than do the brasses, and the brasses than the drums, so also the vowels in a poem will have different functions than will the fricatives (the sounds that make friction in the air—that hiss or hush or buzz—such as f, v, s, z, sh, th), and the fricatives than the stops, such as p, b, t, d, k, and g. The poet's job is to take the words that are involved in the experience that the poem evokes, and to listen to the kinds of sound colors that are provided in the little melodies that are made by the particular phonetic "instruments" that these important words contain. And then to paint with just these colors.

To give a very quick example, let us look at the English word fog. This word starts with the fricative [f], which is then followed by the long vowel that phoneticians write as [c:] (the colon indicates that a vowel is long), with the syllable being closed by the stop [g]. If we compare the acoustic event of this word—a sequence of fricative–long vowel–stop—with the event suggested by the Japanese word for fog, kiri[kiDi] (which sounds more like what we would write as keedy than about anything else we could suggest in the English writing system), we see that the Japanese melody is very different from the English one. The Japanese one consists of two very short open syllables, which *rhyme*. By contrast, the English melody consists of one much slower, closed, syllable, with a "large" vowel (note how we have to open our mouths wide to say fog, while our mouths are nearly closed when we say kiri). The English syllable is brought to an abrupt finish by the closing stop [g].

Armed with these initial, quite obvious observations about the music of the **word** fog, let us return for a look at the conceptual structure of Sandburg's poem. We see first that it has three clause-like sections, A, B, and C, one for each of the poem's tensed verbs.

A. The fog comes
   on little cat feet.

B. It sits looking
   over harbor and city
   on silent haunches
C. and then moves on.

We can see that there are many ways in which these three sections resemble each other. Each has just one "finite," or tensed, verb in its first line, and each of these verbs is a monosyllable. The subject of each of these three verbs is the fog. In C, this is not true visually, for the subject of moves has been elided, but it is true notionally nonetheless. Furthermore, each of the three sections also *ends* the same way—with an on-phrase. The first two on-phrases are even more similar to one another, for each has, as the object of on, a plural noun phrase referring to a body part of the cat. The last on is followed by nothing—no cat body part. Why? The cat has left! That is also why the subject of the last verb has been deleted; when the fog/cat moves on, no part of it is left in the sentence.

This ABC sectioning is of course a structural analogy to one way of perceiving an *experience* of fog, as consisting of the fog's approach, then the state of being fogged in, and finally the fog's departure. The number of lines that Sandburg allots to each of these three parts of the fog experience is congruent with the following kind of subjective time for each.

Arrival of fog	State of being fogged in	Departure of fog
Medium duration	Longest duration	Shortest duration
(2 lines)	(3 lines)	(1 line)

Most readers seem to agree on this ordering of the lengths of each of the three sections of an experience of fog—that the state of being fogged in is clearly the longest, since we never know when it is going to end, and that the arrival of the fog is typically slower than its departure. After all, we can say, "the fog lifted," while I have never heard anyone say, "the fog dropped."

What is relevant for our present concerns—namely, the way the music of a word interpenetrates with and *creates* the structure of any poem that it appears in—is evident when we ask how we perceive the durations of the three-part phonetic sequence in fog: fricative–long vowel–stop. Clearly, the vowel is the longest, with the fricative being longer than is the stop. So A–B–C "rhymes" with the three-part music of fog, as we can see if we map the phonetics of fog onto the foregoing analysis of the subjective time of a fog experience.

Arrival of fog	State of being fogged in	Departure of fog
Medium duration	Longest duration	Shortest duration
(2 lines)	(3 lines)	(1 line)
[f]	[o:]	[g]

The poet slows down the middle (stative) section, B, not only by allotting more lines to it than to any other section, but also by putting most of the poem's long words in B. The poem begins and ends in the same way—with words of one syllable. And in the last line of the first section, we find just one bisyllable, <u>little</u>, which serves as a transition to the slow section, B.

Every line of B has a bisyllable at the end of it—and it is only this section that has long words at the ends of lines. Section B has <u>all</u> of the long words except the one in section A, which by chance (?) is <u>little</u>. And in B, there is just one line with more than two long words in it: line 4. This line is a special one conceptually, too: the two words <u>harbor</u> and <u>city</u> are the only ones in the poem that allude to the world of human beings.

An interesting question to ask ourselves is this: What would line 4 have been like if these two human-linked nouns had appeared in the reverse order? I think that we can agree that if Sandburg had written <u>over city and harbor</u>, we would have concluded that the fog was moving in the opposite direction—that it had originated inland, and was moving off out to sea. But in our poem, this is not the case. This fog comes in from the vastest thing on the surface of the planet—from the ocean, from the depths. It may arrive on "little" feet, but it grows tall. It rises high enough to cover the harbor, that human institution whose function is to serve as a haven for the brave boats that dare to traverse the Vastness. It continues to rise until it completely covers, and holds in its grip, humanity's proudest construction: the City. The city is where the illusion is strongest that there is safety in numbers, where we humans like to think that we have mastered the environment completely.

At the very end of line 4, the poem's longest line, whose seven syllables (and three bisyllables) have brought time to its slowest pace, the fog comes to us, who are held prisoners in our "magnificent" city. Our insignificance and powerlessness are emphasized by the smallness and quickness of <u>city</u>'s two vowels. Line 4 is the only line that ends with a vowel, and since the next line begins with a vowel, the tiny last vowel of <u>city</u> can ease gradually into the next line's opening vowel, possibly suggesting a small, fading, unanswered cry. . . .

We are, at the end of line 4, in the grip of the fog, a presence that has been made increasingly animate, and even personified, by the sequence of words <u>comes</u>, <u>feet</u>, <u>sits</u>, and <u>looking</u>, a being who moves as fluidly and quietly as a cat, a being just as unpredictable and mysterious as a cat, a being with all the mythic power (and even menace?) of the Feline . . . and time stops. . . .

*

In the next line, the mention of the adjective <u>silent</u> opens the possibility of the opposite of silence—could this vast being perhaps speak and judge us? We do not know. We are frozen into immobility. All we can do is to surrender into the waiting.

And then suddenly, its departure as rapid as its arrival was gradual, the fog lifts, is gone, is on its way to look over others, and hold them, too, in its thrall. The rapidity of the fog's departure is signaled by the shortness of the words in the last line, by the fact that <u>moves</u> has no audible subject, and by the shortness of the last <u>on</u>-phrase.

Experientially, fog can be seen to have a sonata structure: ABA. Our poem starts and ends with motion verbs (<u>comes</u> and <u>moves</u>), which sandwich a durative verb, a verb of stillness; <u>sits</u>, even though the word <u>looking</u>, which follows <u>sits</u>, tells us that there is no break in the activity of the fog. Paradoxically, this activity of looking, followed by the act of refraining from speaking, makes the center of the ABA structure the peak of agency, of animacy, of the visitor to our city. And as John Sinclair has pointed out, our own experiences of fog tell us that there is a tradeoff of agency here: It is just where the fog can look that we cannot. Thus where the fog is at the peak of its power, we are at our very weakest. What is relevant for my concerns here is the fact that the phonetic structures of <u>fog</u> and of <u>cat</u> can also be seen as being of the form ABA—two consonants that sandwich a vowel. So the verbal melodies of <u>fog</u> and <u>cat</u> "rhyme" in yet another way with the structure of the experience of fog.

Now let us return briefly to the poem's six bisyllables. We find that they always come in pairs: the first two begin with [l], then we find a line with one beginning in [h] and one beginning in (phonetic) [s], followed by a line whose two bisyllables come in the reverse order; the one beginning in [s] preceding the one in [h]. These three bisyllable pairs always appear on consecutive lines, so arranged that if the first member of the pair appears early in the line, its "echo" in the next line will end the line, or vice versa. Thus there is a deeply *chiastic*, or crossing (literally, "x-like"), pattern that Sandburg sets up with his placing of the poem's long words, as we can see diagrammed in Fig. 13.1.

There are no more bisyllables to link up, but our ears hear more similarities: the last two monosyllables of line 2 have the front vowels [æ] and [i:] followed by [t]'s, and the first two words of line 3 are monosyllables whose front vowel [I] is also followed by [t]. Furthermore, the [t f] sequence between <u>cat</u> and <u>feet</u> is

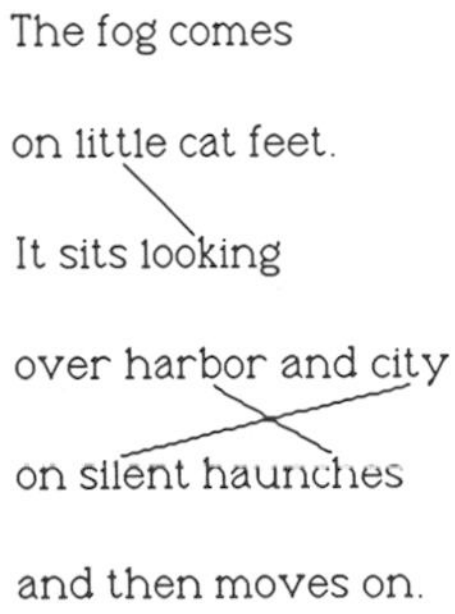

The fog comes

on little cat feet.

It sits looking

over harbor and city

on silent haunches

and then moves on.

FIG. 13.1. Bisyllabic chiastic pairs in Carl Sandburg's "Fog."

highly similar to the [t s] sequence between <u>It</u> and <u>sits</u>. This if we also link these pairs of consecutive [t]-final monosyllables up, we are left with the following, more symmetrical structure of Fig. 13.2.

But there are still more chiastic relationships to indicate, the clearest being the relationship between <u>it sits</u> and <u>city</u>, which I see as a sort of echo of the <u>cat feet</u>/<u>It sits</u> linkage between lines two and three. I think, however, that the first place that we hear phonetic crossing is between the last two syllables of the first line and the last two of the second line. <u>Fog</u> and <u>feet</u> contain the only two [f]'s of the poem, and <u>comes</u> and <u>cat</u> are the only two words that begin with [k].

"Hey! Waidaminit!" I can almost hear some readers saying. "Why should we care about all these formal patterns? What do they have to do with what the poem <u>means</u> to us? I can sympathize with such objectors, and while I would not insist that such structures always must be linkable to meaning, I feel that in this poem, such a connection is possible. One interpretation of such crossing patterns, which make equivalent, in a certain sense, the orders of elements AB and BA, is interpenetration—the commingling of A and B—in our case, of fog and cat. While an essayist could simply *say* that fog and cats move like each other, a poet *enacts* this kind of perception, choosing crossing structures, which dissolve boundaries between entities previously felt to be distinct. Structures like this chiastic one come from a kind of universal symbolic alphabet, which I believe to be used not only in poetry, but also in other forms of art and in ritual.

If I am right in seeing these crossing structures as being used to enact a kind of poetic fusion, then it is significant that the two lines between which there is the least evidence of this kind of crossing are lines 5 and 6—just the place where the fog-cat leaves. So the fog is functioning as the *agent* of the chiastic structure, which we could show in its fullest form as in Fig. 13.3.

I believe, too, that Sandburg uses nasality as an index of motion. Note that each of the first four lines has just one nasal, and that these nasals are in syllables of steadily decreasing phonetic prominence. The first word to contain a nasal, <u>comes</u>, is highly salient. It is the first verb, and a verb of motion at that. It has full word stress, even more stress in the first line than does its subject, <u>fog</u>. This

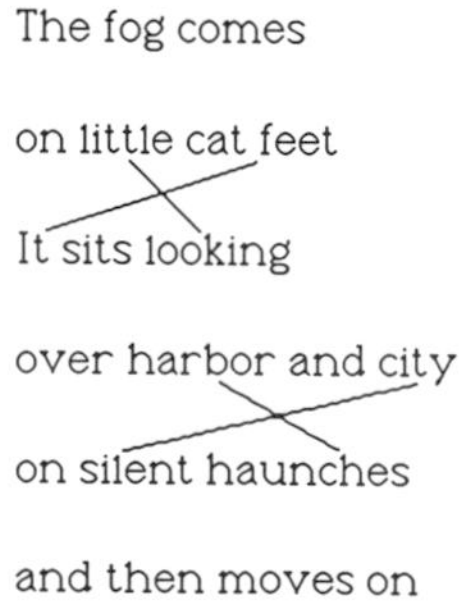

The fog comes

on little cat feet

It sits looking

over harbor and city

on silent haunches

and then moves on

FIG. 13.2.   Bi- and mono-syllabic chiastic pairs in "Fog."

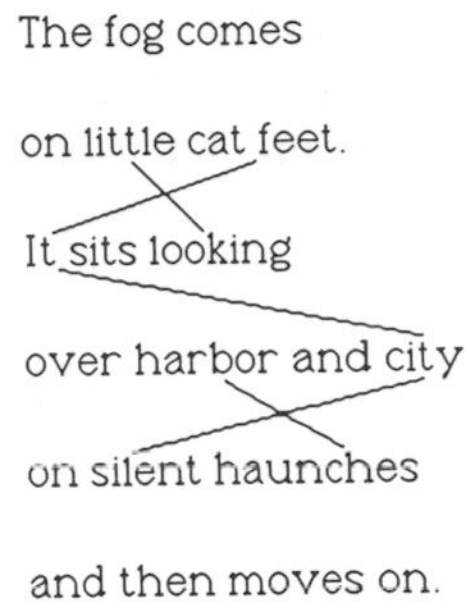

The fog comes

on little cat feet.

It sits looking

over harbor and city

on silent haunches

FIG. 13.3. The complete chiastic structure of "Fog."

and then moves on.

is a way of saying, in the language of poetry, that one thing that will be important in the poem is the activity, the motion, of the poem's topic. And what distinguishes this type of motion from other possible monosyllabic verbs of motion that the poet could have used (slides, creeps, moves, walks, etc.) is its direction: This fog comes to **us**.

There is a very tight patterning in the poem's first line which makes the first nasal [m] stand out even more visibly. For notice that the word fog has a labial [f] before its back vowel, and following the vowel, a stop consonant, the velar[g], made in the back of the mouth. By contrast, comes has the positions of velar and labial reversed: the velar[k] precedes its back vowel, while the labial [m] follows it. What makes this reverse particularly noticeable is the tongue-stopping phonetic sequence [g k], two velars, differing only in their voicing, coming between the first two content words. Thus line 1 gives a phonetic preview of the being stopped, and then being released, that will form the center of the experience of fog that the ensuing poem will evoke.

The words fog and comes are linked by reversal in more than one aspect of their melodies: fog starts with the fricative [f] and ends with the stop [g], while comes starts with the stop [k] and ends with the fricative [z]. However, they are also linked by a pattern of repetition: The change of voiceless [f] to voiced [g] is echoed by the change of voiceless [k] to voiced [m] and [z]. Summing up all these relationships diagrammatically, we could show some of the ways in which the two stressed words of the first line are related as in Fig. 13.4, where the double line links the repetition of the change in voicing, and the dotted lines indicate reversals:

FIG. 13.4. Phonetic comparison of "fog" and "comes," in terms of fricatives versus stops (arrows) and voicing (dotted lines).

With the tightness of the linkings between these two words, I think it is fair to say that the [m] stands out fairly clearly, especially with it being the only sonorant in the first line (more on the sonorant/obstruent later). Moreover, it is part of the first consonant cluster within a word, forming the first line's finale.

Then comes the next nasal, a slightly less salient one. The [n] of on, a word whose vowel is in no way reduced, but one whose stress is clearly less than that of comes. The third nasal, the velar [ŋ] at the end of looking, is located, for the first time, not in the lexical part of a word but instead in a suffix, a semantically de-emphasized neighborhood. The preceding vowel, though having far less stress than the [U] of look, is probably most naturally pronounced as the unreduced high front vowel [I]. However, when we reach the and of line 4, the most normal pronunciation of its nucleus would be the reduced vowel [ə], or better, a syllabic nasal, [n̩], not the unreduced [æ] of cat. Thus clearly, as typically pronounced, this syllable has the least prominence of the first four to contain nasals.

Significantly, if it is correct to link nasality and activity, this lowest ebb of activity comes just before the place where **we** are—city. Immediately thereafter, as activity begins to pick up, we see that three out of five syllables in line 5 contain nasals, and then that all four of the last line's four words do. Notice that the last line's verb, the prototypical indication of motion, even *starts* with a nasal (which, to top it off, even follows the [n] of then). There are no other sequences of nasals in the poem, nor any other nasal-initial words. Since sounds at the beginning of their syllables are more prominent than are ones at the ends of syllables, this means that nasality attains its highest salience just as the poem awakes from its stasis and bursts into motion.

I have suggested that crossing structures can be one way of "saying" interpenetration, in the symbolic alphabet of art. But there are other ways, one of which being the use of alternating structures. Our poem manifests many kinds of alternation, one salient example being the number of nouns or pronouns per line: $_1$fog/$_2$cat,$_2$feet/$_3$it/$_4$harbor,$_4$city/$_5$haunches. Notice that this pattern starts with two singular nouns and a plural (all monosyllables—note that the first and last start with the poem's only [f]'s). Then, after the pronoun it, the only one in the poem, which marks the center of the alternation, there is a repeat of the sequence of two singulars and a plural, this time all bisyllables, with the first and last starting with the poem's only occurrences of [h]. Again, the locus of this alternating pattern is the first two sections of the poem. Like the locus of the crossings that we have tracked, we see that the locus of alternation in noun number is just that of the fog-cat itself. I think that above and beyond the brute fact of alternation, it is significant that it is nouns that are fluctuating in number, and the fact that the two numbers involved are 1 and 2. Are we perhaps justified in seeing this as a suggestion of the splitting and fusion of the two concepts of fog and cat? This may be stretching a point—I don't insist on it. As I have said, it is not always easy to be sure as to whether some identifiable aspect of a formal structure contributes to the interpretation of a poem or not.

I note in passing that the first five lines of the poem are set off as a unit from the sixth line by two more facts of distribution: lines 1 and 5 are the only lines in the poem which end in the suffix {–z}, and haunches is the only other word in the poem besides fog to contain the vowel [c:]. We will see further examples of the way Sandburg has sectioned off the first five lines, to form a poetic subunit.

To return to alternating patterns, there is another alternation, even more salient, which has as its scope the entire poem—the alternation in the number of words in a line. The odd lines each have three words, and the even lines each have four. This alternation, and the previously cited one involving the number of nouns per line, impose a different sectioning on the poem, a sectioning that groups the six lines into three "couplets"—lines 1 + 2, lines 3 + 4, and lines 5 + 6. Yet another alternation, a phonetic one, which has exactly the same scope as that of the number of words per line, concerns the length of the last vowel in each line. The odd-numbered lines have short vowels (comes[/\], looking[I], haunches[e]), while the even-numbered ones have phonetically long vowels (feet[i:], city[i:], on[a:]). Thus there are two distinct alternations which section the poem into three pairs of consecutive lines.

The previously mentioned ABC sectioning agrees with this "coupleting" in one respect: in establishing a boundary after the first two lines. But then, the coupleting "interferes" with the sectioning off of B—lines 3–5. The alternations break off the first two lines of B, drawing a boundary right after city. Significantly, we have already seen that there are good reasons for thinking that the function of this longest line in the poem is to raise our waiting, our powerlessness, to the limit. Thus it can be maintained that on a deeper level, there is no interference here—the two sectionings are in no sense in competition. Rather, like polyrhythms in music, they play off on one another; each contributes its own voice to the beauty of the poem.

This having been said, let me go on to one last sectioning, one which further reinforces the strength of the central couplet. In this third sectioning, the first line is linked to the last, the second to the fifth, and by elimination, the third to the fourth. The outer lines are linked, as I have already pointed out, by virtue of the fact that they are the only two monosyllabic lines. Furthermore, they contain the poem's only occurrences of voiced th, the sound [e], in the and then, and more saliently, also the only two occurrences of [m], at the end of the first verb, and at the beginning of the last one.

However, the links between lines 1 and 6 pale beside those between lines 2 and 5. Being the poem's only two five-syllable lines, both of these lines begin with on, and each ends in one of the poem's two plurals (which are both body parts of the cat). And finally, these two plural nouns are modified by the poem's only adjectives, which might, by the way, be said to "rhyme" semantically, in light of the fact that silence may be seen as smallness of sound.

This then leaves us with lines 3 and 4, which I do not see any great phonetic similarities between, except for the already noted link between it sits and city. But they are solidly joined by virtue of their syntax: The five-word participial phrase looking/over harbor and city, the locus of the greatest animacy in the poem, is inserted between the verb sits and the on-phrase which is its object. Interestingly, this participial phrase contains the poem's only ambiguity: The over-phrase can be read as a directional object of a motional look (as in looking over them), or the conjoined noun phrase can be taken to be the direct object of the phrasal verb look over (as in looking them over).

The links between lines 1 and 6 are noticeable, and those between lines 2 and 5 are compelling. This, when added to the syntactic cohesiveness that rules over lines 3 and 4, further increases the necessity of hearing the middle two lines as a couplet, thus once again heightening the strength of the tension at the end of line 4.

Let us look at one last type of alternation. Given the various alternating patterns that we have already seen, all of which "rhyme" at a deep phonetic level, with the A–B–A consonant–vowel–consonant structure of fog and cat, there is reason to take a careful look at the network of consonants that Sandburg establishes in composing the music of this poem. Before I do so, I want to make use of a distinction that phoneticians often draw among the various classes of sounds that can be found in the world's languages. The greatest distinction that appears in the domain of phonetics is that between the most musical, or sonorous, of sounds—the vowels—and the least sonorous ones—the stops (e.g., [p, t, č (the first sound of chew), k, b, d, ǰ (the first sound of jaw), g, and so on]). Stops are given this name because in the course of making them, there is one point at which the vocal tract is completely closed, and no air emerges from the lungs through the mouth or nose. One degree more toward the free-flowing vowels is the next most sonorant (or less obstruent, to use a technical term) class of consonants, the fricatives (e.g., [f, s, θ (the first sound of think), ʃ(the first sound of shift), v, z, ð (the first sound of this), ž(the last sound of rouge), and so on]). These sounds are called fricatives because in producing them, instead of stopping entirely the flow of air from the lungs, the tongue or lower lip is put so close to one part of the upper part of the mouth that a turbulence, or friction, in the airstream is caused. Phoneticians use the term obstruent to designate the class consisting of stops and fricatives together, and sonorant to designate the remaining, more vowely, segments: nasals [m, n, ŋ]; liquids [r, l]; glides [w, y]; and vowels.

Returning to our poem, we see that fog and cat both begin and end not only with consonants, but with the subclass of consonants that I have just defined—that is, with obstruents. Let us, therefore, take a close look at all of the other obstruents of the poem.

The fog comes	ð	**f**	g	**k**	z
on little cat feet.	t	**k**	t	**f**	t
It sits looking	t	**s**	t	**s**	k
over harbor and city	v	**h**	b (d)	s	t
on silent haunches	s	**t**	h	č	z
and then moves on. (d)	ð		v		z

For the first three and the fifth lines of the poem, a clear pattern emerges: Each line has just five obstruent (for this purpose, I am treating [h] as an obstruent, though many languages treat it as a glide, like the semivowels [w] and [y]). Moreover, it is clear, in looking at line 2, that here we have another pattern of alternation to deal with; while the same sound, [t], appears in the odd positions in the set of five obstruents, in positions 2 and 4, we find different sounds: [k] and [f]. Thus line 2's obstruents are a clear instance of an abstract alternation schema which we can designate as ABABA. Line 3 presents us with a slightly different variant of the same basic schema: What the odd positions here share is the fact that they are all stops, while the even ones share the property of containing fricatives—here, the <u>same</u> fricative, [s]. The fifth line has fricatives appearing in its odd-numbered positions, with its two stops showing up in its even positions.

So far, so good. Now what of line 1? In order to be able to perceive the same kind of ABABA pattern that has come to light for lines 2, 3, and 5, we will have to introduce one more phonetic distinction—that of *voicing*. Phoneticians classify the two sounds [f] and [v] as both belonging to the same class, the *labiodentals*, since both are made with the lower teeth touching the upper lip, producing a characteristic friction at that point. However, since the two sounds are clearly different, they observe that during the production of [v], the vocal cords, the two bands of muscle in the throat just behind the Adam's apple, continue to vibrate, while this is not the case for [f]. They call all such consonants as [v] *voiced*, with consonants without this characteristic buzz of the vocal cords being called *voiceless*. In English, all obstruents (except [h], a reason for *not* thinking that this sound is an obstruent) come in voiced/voiceless pairs: [b/p, v/f, d/t, z/s, ǰ/č, ž/ʃ, g/k, etc.]. Now when we turn to line 1, to try to find out what the odd positions have that the even ones do not, we can see that it is precisely the feature of voicing.

I have saved until last lines 4 and 6, which raise several problems. First of all, line 4 has six segments that should normally count as obstruents (I will include [h] in this list, as I would like it to be included in the pattern of line 5): <u>**over harbor and city**</u>. The only way that I can see to make this line conform to the generalization that there are just five obstruents in each line is to say that the [d] of and does not count, since it is swallowed up in the [s] which immediately follows it. This does no violence to the phonetic facts; it is very difficult to articulate line 4 so that both a [d] and an [s] are audible. However, even if we take this tack, thus preserving on the phonetic level, at least, the generalization that there are only five obstructs per line, what can we say about the further generalization to the effect that the obstruents manifest an ABABA alternation? What [h] and [s] have in common is that they are both fricatives and voiceless, two properties which no other segments in the line have. While the [v] of over is a fricative, it is a voiced one; and while the [t] of city is voiceless, it is not a fricative. But it is clear that this conjunctive characterization of the even-numbered obstruents of line 4, though it is technically accurate, is a more complex one than was necessary for any of the other lines. Thus line 4, even though it may be seen in such a light as to remain within the ABABA framework of alternating obstruents, only makes it by a whisker, a fact which is highly congruent with the intensity of the poetic experience that this line evokes, as I have called attention to earlier. Line 4, then, is good example of the kind of paradox that poetry delights in: something that is simultaneously the same and different.

It is time to conclude our discussion of the alternation among the obstruents within a line. Line 6 has four obstruents, but I would like to suggest again, as was the case in line 4, that the [d] of and can fuse with the following sound, the [ð] of then, so that we can say that line 6 manifests only three obstruent positions, in the A-slots of our abstract ABABA schema. All of line 6's obstruents are voiced, as are the three odd-numbered ones of line 1, which suggests the return to the beginning that is independently conveyed by the return to monosyllabicity, the return of the [ð] and [m], and the return of a motion verb. However, as we have seen in many ways, just as it is the first five lines that are the locus of the alternation in noun number and also of the chiastic linkings between lines, it is also in these first five lines that we find the full ABABA obstruent alternation. All that remains by the time we come to line 6, when the cat-fog goes, is the wisp of an echo. I think that it is even likely that the dropping out of the B-slots in the ABABA pattern in line 6 is one last way of "saying," in this language of poetry that we have been exploring, that the fog/cat has left. For note that what occupied the B-slots in lines 1 and 2 were the pairs of sounds [f]-[k] and [k]-[f], respectively—the initial and most salient sounds of the parts of the fog/cat. The alternation in order helps the fusion of the two parts along.

There is one final family of patterns which are woven into the fabric of the poem, as they are into the fabric of its central word, fog. This is a feature of the poem which we could refer to as its threeness, or, as long as I am making up words, let me suggest instead a new verb. I will say that Sandburg threes this poem, that this threeing is a primary source of poetic coherence. I have already mentioned many examples of sets of three elements in the discussion; let us have a brief review.

THREEINGS

Syntax: three sections, each consisting of three basic parts—a subject referring to the fog, a monosyllabic verb in the present tense, and an on-phrase (the central section has an adverbial looking-phrase inserted in it)

Experience: arrival of fog—state of being fogged in—departure of fog.

Phonology: three segments of fog, corresponding in their length relationships to the subjective durations of the three parts of the fog experience. Furthermore, each line manifests three obstruents of the same type, with all lines except the last having two more obstruents interspersed between the first two and the last two of the set of three.

Words per line: The odd lines have three apiece, with the even ones having four, which then gives three couplets.

Onion-skinning: First and last lines are linked by virtue of being monosyllabic; second and fifth are linked because of having only plurals, only body parts, only adjectives, and so on. And the third and fourth lines are joined by the syntax: the adverbial gerundive phrase looking/over harbor and city, the peak of the fog/cat's animacy, interrupts the clause that begins on line 2 and ends on line 5. So the poem consists of a set of **three** nested pairs of lines, as shown in Fig. 13.5.

To conclude our preliminary look at the way Sandburg's whole poem is a masterful expansion, or a kind of holographic echoing, on many levels, of the single three-sound word which serves as its title, let us look at the poem one last time with its three alternative sectionings and its chiastic crossings indicated, as in Fig. 13.6.

I have tried to show how the acoustic structure of the word fog, with a basic ABA melody laid down by its sequence of obstruent–vowel–obstruent, harmonizes both with the basic motion–stillness–motion perception of an experience of

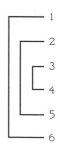

FIG. 13.5. Phonetic and syntactic linkages or parallels between the lines of "Fog."

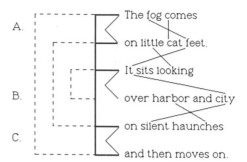

FIG. 13.6. The full structure of "Fog," including bi- and mono-syllabic pairs, phonetic and syntactic linkages, and stanzas.

being fogged in that is given by the three-part sectioning ABC on the level of syntax, and also with the durational structure of two lines–three lines–one line mirroring the durational relatonships among the three phonetic elements of the word <u>fog</u>. In addition, alternation flowers in many ways throughout the poem, as we have seen, with a suggested interpretation that it can be one way of letting fog and cat fuse.

I am afraid, though, that I have probably lost most of you, unless you, like Jack DeWitt and I, just can't help ripping poems apart to try to see where the magic in them comes from. For I have gone into a lot of detail, more than many people will perhaps want to concede might be tolerable, let alone necessary. After all, I hear them saying in my mind, isn't this a rather minor poem? Why all this fuss about it?

To try to answer these possibly only straw people in this imaginary dialogue, let me remind them that I find this poem still extremely beautiful—I think more so than when I started working on it about 6 years ago. The more ways I see in which this poem's 22 words become interconnected, the more radiant it becomes for me, and the better I think my chances are at explaining the incredible memorability of this work of art. It can't be just the admittedly masterful metaphoric linking of fog–cat, for that wouldn't explain why people don't confuse line 2 in their minds with such rotten lines as my <u>on small cat feet</u> or <u>on little cat paws</u>, which would preserve the image/metaphor, but lose on the music. I think that this poem gets its power from the way the aptness of the image **interlocks** with the multiple musical coherences that are generated by the acoustic-articulatory-perceptual event unleashed by a pronunciation of the word fog. This interlocking is made to shine even more brightly in the unguessed depths of our inner selves by the numinosity, the heart-in-the-mouth gripping-ness, of our vulnerability, which we feel when we encounter, all alone, the Vastness. Sandburg "says" this encounter for us, in the universal language of poetry, through the fusion of catfog, fogcat, cfaotg, . . . We have no way to spell such experiences in English, except by a wonder such as the jewel network of these 22 words.

But there is one more person, at the back of the room, after all the others have given up on their questions, the person who asks the most impolite question of all. "So what?" Or maybe, in a slightly different way of voicing the same doubt: "How do we know that all of these patterns are significant? Because if they're not, who cares about how many you can find?"

I know who this haggler is, of course—among others, it is Myself, who was trained as a scientific linguist, and who has only been following this winding path into the depths of Poetry for the past dozen years or so. And Myself wants to know how to clothe all of the intricacies that we have begun to explore with the comforting mantle of certainty, which was partly what got Myself into the speedy world of science in the first place. So for Myself, and for many of you who will read the foregoing observations with probably quite parallel uneasinesses, let me try to give not not an answer, but a description of what I think it is that one must do if one wants to find one for themselves.

To start off with, you must be fascinated by some poem, or poems. These poems, which you love, you then memorize. You carry around copies of them, and look at them at odd moments. You say them out loud, to yourself, and maybe to friends. And you wait, and wait, and wait: until you see something structural that makes sense to **you**. That is, something that in some possibly indescribable way deepens the experience of the poem for you. That makes you want to say, "So *that's* why . . ." or maybe just "Ahhh!".

And this experience you repeat, with as many poems, of as many different kinds, from as many different times and places, in as many different languages, as you can find. And if your journey is anything like mine has been, you will find that **this experience of insight** begins to happen more easily, more rapidly. For me, an example of the kind of insight that I am talking about is the three-way link of the subjective timing of the parts of the experience of fog, the number of lines allotted to each, and the relative durations of the three phonetic segments contained in the word fog. I am not insisting that you accept this particular linking as being the basis of a significant insight for you; I am only giving it to you as an example of one that does work for me. One for which, as the German expression has it, *ich würde die Hand ins Feuer legen*: I would put my hand in the fire for the "correctness" of that three-way correlation.

As you continue along this path, collecting such meaningful structures **for you**, you are pursuing a sort of apprenticeship. You are becoming a hearer of the great universal language of Poetry; the poets, of course, are the speakers. Learning to understand some of the "words" in this language feels to me like learning an art form. (I have taken some beginning steps at learning to "speak" guitar, and painting, and also even poetry, a bit—I have come to write some poems that I like better than the ones that I could write 10 years ago.)

The "answer" then, to Myself's insistent questioning, is not one that can be given intellectually. It is one that must be lived. It is as it is with many things in life, like learning how to bake bread, or how to windsurf—you must put *yourself* into them.

And when you have pursued such an apprenticeship for a time, you will, as a beginning speaker of Poetry, come to "know" some of the words of that vast language. I put *know* in quotes, because the more I follow this curious and fascinating path, the more clearly I perceive how much more complex, and more beautiful, and radiant, is the phenomenon of Poetry than was anything that I could have even begun to imagine before following the path these first few faltering steps. And thus instead of becoming steadily more impressed with the size of the terrain that I have "covered" in my wanderings, I rather seem to sense ever more fully how much more immense is the landscape in which my small garden resides.

So in the end, my answer to Myself can only be: Apprentice yourself. Find poems that you love, grope your way along the path toward the kinds of patternings that you would be willing to put your hand in the fire for, and a funny kind of "knowledge" will be born in you. Your groping will lead you to a willingness to say with something like certainty, "Yes, this pattern is important. I have seen it many times. I recognize it here again." What will make this knowledge funny will be your increasing understanding of the bottomlessness of your own ignorance.

I have probably gone on too long in these ruminations, but that is because they have been with me for so long now, as have been the questions that inspired them in the minds of many puzzled people who have heard me talk about the things that I have been finding. I would like to close them now, with a quote from the English biologist T. H. Huxley, who says so masterfully and pithily what I have spent pages fumbling with: "Sit down before Fact like a little child, and be prepared to give up every preconceived notion, follow humbly wherever and to whatever abysses Nature leads, or you shall learn nothing" (Ferguson, 1982, pp. 15–16).

$$\omega$$

I offer this poem, and the preliminary look at the kind of richnesses of musical texture that reward the hopelessly addicted ripper-to-pieces of poems, as a kind of meditation for all of us who gather here in this volume to celebrate the teaching and thinking of our friend Jim Jenkins, who has delved into many similar depths of cognitive and developmental structure in his work. I am glad to see workers in the broad field of cognition, where Jim has pioneered, turning, from many and varied starting points, to the study of metaphor, which surely plays a fundamental role in the process that Mallarmé refers to as "writing with words." But I want to invite cognitive scientists to remember that mere metaphor, metaphor not even linked as fragmentarily to verbal music as I have tried here to sketch a beginning for, will never lift us to see the profoundest truths of the song of human creativity, which I think is what we are all really longing to understand. If seeing the beauties of this song is what our goal really is, the magic of "writing with words" cannot be something we come to last, as an afterthought, but must instead become a foundation stone for a new, fuller, and deeper understanding of the mysteries of mind.

ACKNOWLEDGMENTS

I would like to thank Richard Boyum, Rosália Dutra, and John Sinclair for a lot of support, for some tough questions, and for a lot of insights. And a special kind of thanks to an audience of teachers in Khartoum, whose enthusiasm for some of the structures I report on in this chapter woke me up: I saw freshly how miraculous they are.

REFERENCES

Ferguson, M. (1982) A new perspective on reality. In K. Wilber (Ed.), *The holographic paradigm and other paradoxes: Exploring the leading edge of science,* Boulder, CO: Shambhala.
Jakobson, R., & Rudy, S. (1981). Yeats' Sorrow of Love" through the years, *Poetics Today.*
Wolfe, D. M. (1965). A *study of poetry.* Cincinnati, OH: McCormick–Mathers.

V THE DEVELOPMENT OF KNOWLEDGE AND PROBLEM-SOLVING SKILLS

14

Children's Theories vs. Scientific Theories: Differences in Reasoning or Differences in Knowledge?

William F. Brewer
Ala Samarapungavan
Center for the Study of Reading,
University of Illinois at Urbana-Champaign

INTRODUCTION

In recent years, in the areas of science education, cognitive psychology, developmental psychology, and cognitive science, a number of researchers have taken the position that in the course of their everyday interactions with the natural world, children construct theories that are in many ways similar to those constructed by scientists (Carey, 1985; Driver & Easley, 1978; McCloskey & Kargon, 1988). However, other researchers have argued that children's theories are very different from scientific theories (diSessa, 1988; Inhelder & Piaget, 1958; Schollum & Osborne, 1985; Solomon, 1983a, 1983b).

In this chapter we argue that children's theories embody the essential characteristics of scientific theories. Our argument takes the following form. First, we give some recent evidence about children's theories in the domain of observational astronomy that shows that children can develop very impressive theories of the natural world. Next we re-evaluate the characterization of children's theories by those investigators who have argued that these theories are very different from scientific theories. We suggest that a knowledge-based approach to child development allows a reinterpretation of earlier findings, and we review a range of recent data that support this reinterpretation. We note that in these discussions many researchers have contrasted theories constructed by the individual child with positivist accounts of cultural achievements, such as Newtonian physics. We suggest that this is not an appropriate comparison and point out the importance of distinguishing between the child as theory constructor and science as a historical institution. Then we shift the argument to the characterization of scientific theories and suggest that the idealized description of scientific theories used in these debates is not supported by recent work in the philosophy and history of science. Next we examine the claim that children's reasoning processes are different from those of adult scientists and that it is these differences that produce the differences in children's theories and scientific theories. We argue that recent historical and experimental work on the reasoning processes of scientists do not support the idealized picture of scientific reasoning given in these discussions. In addition we examine the nature of the reasoning processes in young children and argue that these processes are very similar to those of adults. Overall, we conclude that the child can be thought of as a novice scientist, who adopts a rational approach to dealing with the physical world, but lacks the knowledge of the physical world and experimental methodology accumulated by the institution of science. Finally, we use the framework developed in this chapter to suggest a range of issues that are open for experimental investigation.

CHILDREN'S THEORIES ARE NOT LIKE SCIENTIFIC THEORIES—EXTREME FORM

We will describe an extreme form of the position that children's theories are fundamentally different from scientists' theories. The basic claims of this position can be found in Table 14.1. The first part of the table describes ways in which children's theories are said to differ from scientists' theories; the second part describes ways in which children's thought processes are said to differ from those of scientists.

The perceptive reader will note that we have set up a straw person here, since there may be no single individual who has held the complete view outlined in this table. However, various aspects of this position have been proposed by diSessa (1988), Piaget (1930), Solomon (1983a, 1983b), and Schollum and Osborne (1985). For example, diSessa (1988) states "intuitive physics is a fragmented collection of ideas, loosely connected and reinforcing, having none of the commitment of systematicity that one attributes to theories" (p. 50). The title of one of Solomon's papers (1983a) is "Messy, contradictory and obstinately persistent: A study of children's out-of-school ideas about energy," and in another paper (1983b) she maintains that child conceptions are "inconsistent and context bound" (p. 128) while scientific laws are universal and decontextualized. Piaget (1930) argued that children younger than 12 cannot understand action and reaction phenomena in physics because they lack the logical operations of inversion and reciprocity. Piaget (1980, p. 268) also argued that young children are essentially precausal in their thinking and show no concern for mechanisms that mediate cause and effect. Schollum and Osborne (1985) contrast children with scientists and state that children "are limited in the extent to which they can reason in the abstract . . . tend to view things from a self-centered or human-centered point of view . . . they tend to endow inanimate objects with the

TABLE 14.1
Extreme View: Children's Theories are not Like Scientific Theories

Characteristics of theories

Scientific theories	Children's theories
abstract	concrete
global	fragmentary
internally consistent	inconsistent
universal	context-bound
explanatory	nonexplanatory
extrapersonal	personal
objective	subjective
precise	diffuse
axiomatic	qualitative
empirically supported	empirically false

Characteristics of reasoning processes

Scientists	Children
logical	illogical
consistent	inconsistent
objective	subjective
flexible	rigid
open minded	dogmatic

characteristics of humans . . . they will accept more than one explanation for a specific event, and are not too concerned if some of these explanations are self-contradictory" (pp. 55–56).

EXAMPLES OF CHILDREN'S THEORIES: ASTRONOMY

In this section we will give some examples of impressive theory construction in the domain of observational astronomy. These data are taken from the University of Illinois Astronomy Project (Brewer, Herdrich, & Vosniadou, 1990; Vosniadou & Brewer, 1990, in press) The results of these studies of children's knowledge of observational astronomy show that children do attempt to come up with conceptions of the world around them that satisfy both their empirical observations of the world and the information that is received from adults, even where the adult information appears to contradict their own experientially based beliefs.

Before discussing these findings we will give a brief description of the general methodology used in these studies. Children were interviewed individually, using an astronomy questionnaire that was designed to test various aspects of children's knowledge of observational astronomy. An attempt was made to determine the child's knowledge about objects such as the earth, sun, moon, and stars and to gauge their ability to explain astronomical phenomena such as the day/night cycle, seasons, and eclipses. The set of questions designed to test a particular concept was given in three forms. Initially the child was asked to give only a verbal response. Later in the interview the child was asked to clarify answers to these questions by constructing clay models. Finally, the child was asked to illustrate his or her answers by selecting appropriate models from a set provided by the experimenter. In this way it is possible for the experimenter to determine the consistency of the child's conceptions.

The questions given to the children were of three kinds. The first kind were "factual" questions. These questions were intended to test the child's knowledge of theoretically important facts about the solar system such as the relative size and distance of objects and their location. The second kind of questions were "explanatory" questions. These questions tested the child's understanding of phenomena such as the day/night cycle. The final category of questions were "generative" questions. These questions tested the child's ability to use their concepts to generate answers to questions for which they do not have prestored answers.

We cannot present the quantitative data from these studies here, but we will present some illustrative examples from individual protocols that indicate the general nature of the findings. For example, in attempting to assimilate information that the earth is "round" to their experiences of the ground's apparent flatness, young children often construct interesting models of the earth that are very different from the models of the adults around them:

Hollow Hemisphere Model

(Mathew, first grade; Vosniadou & Brewer, 1990)

Experimenter: If you walked and walked for many days in a straight line where would you end up?

Child: If we walked for a very long time we might end up at the end of the earth.

Experimenter: Would you ever reach the end of the earth?

Child: I don't think so.

Experimenter: Say, we just kept walking and walking and we had plenty of food with us?

Child: Probably.

Experimenter: Could you fall off the edge of the earth?

Child: No. Because if we were outside of the earth we could probably fall off, but if we were inside the earth we couldn't fall off.

Experimenter: You'd be walking inside the earth?

Child: Yeah, I'd be walking on the countries.

Experimenter: Would you ever reach the edge of the earth?

Child: If I had a rocket I could.

Experimenter: Is there an edge to the earth?
Child: Yes.
Experimenter: So could you reach it if you walked long enough?
Child: Well, if I walked and walked, let's say there is a space port down here, and I just walked for days and days and days, I could get to the space port and I'd probably get trained like for a rocket and I could probably reach that edge with a rocket if I blasted off.
Experimenter: Could you walk to the edge of the earth?
Child: No.
Experimenter: How come you can't walk to it but you can take a spaceship to it?
Child: Like if you went up in space and then you were going to come back down you could reach the edge.
Experimenter: But if you were walking on earth could you reach the edge?
Child: No because you can't walk up in space.
Experimenter: So there is an edge to the earth?
Child: Yes.
Experimenter: Can we walk over to the edge and just stand there and look?
Child: Well we can walk to a dead end.

As is evident from this protocol, it took the experimenter a while to understand the model that Mathew was trying to communicate. This child apparently believed that the earth is a huge, hollow hemisphere and that people live inside the sphere, on the bottom. Thus, if one walked along the bottom long enough one would eventually run into the shell or wall of the hemisphere or Mathew's "dead end." The edge of the earth was the upper rim of the hollow hemisphere so that one could not walk up to it, although one could go past it in a spaceship. Models such as those of Mathew were initially so unexpected that many of the verbal responses only made sense when the verbal interview technique was later augmented by having the children construct clay models of the earth's shape.

A different solution to the problem of integrating cultural information about the earth's roundness with the direct experience of its "flatness" can be seen in the following protocol:

Disk Model

(Jamie, third grade; Vosniadou & Brewer, 1990)

Experimenter: If you walked for many days in a straight line where would you end up?
Child: Probably in another planet.
Experimenter: Could you ever reach the end of the earth?
Child: Yes, if you walked long enough.

Experimenter:	Could you fall off at that end?
Child:	Yes, probably . . .
Experimenter:	Now, I want to go back for just a moment and ask a couple of questions . . . What did you say the earth's shape was?
Child:	Round.
Experimenter:	And we said this is a house on earth (shows picture of a house on flat ground) and it looks . . .
Child:	Flat.
Experimenter:	Now, how can that be?
Child:	Maybe it's just flat.
Experimenter:	Maybe it's just flat?
Child:	The earth.
Experimenter:	Let's just take some of this (clay). Why don't you make the shape of the earth with this?
Child:	You mean what I think it is?
Experimenter:	Yes whatever you think it is. (child makes a disk with the clay)
Experimenter:	Now, can people live here? (on top surface of model)
Child:	Yes.
Experimenter:	Can they live under here? (bottom of disk)
Child:	No.

We take these protocols to be examples of generative theory construction by young children. Examination of the full set of data presented in Vosniadou and Brewer (1990) shows that this type of theory construction is characteristic of young children's (age 6 to 9) attempts to understand the concept of the earth's shape.

RE-EVALUATION OF THE CHARACTERIZATION
OF CHILDREN'S THEORIES

Now, having shown that young children can develop impressive theories of the natural world we will attempt to reanalyze the characterization of children's theories by those investigators who have argued that children's theories are very different from scientific theories.

Children's Theories are Concrete

One aspect of the extreme view is the claim that children's theories are more concrete than scientific theories. This is a manifestation of a more general position in child development that children are "perceptually bound" compared with adults (Bruner, Oliver, & Greenfield, 1966; Quine, 1977; Smiley & Brown, 1979). In a recent paper, Brown (1989) analyzes this hypothesis and suggests that young children give the appearance of being perceptually bound because they lack underlying abstract knowledge about a domain and thus are forced to use surface (physical) similarity to respond to questions about the natural world. Palermo (1989) makes a similar argument with respect to children's comprehension of metaphor. He suggests that children's tendency to interpret metaphor literally stems from their lack of knowledge about the relevant properties to be transferred. However, when children know the relevant properties of the objects involved in the metaphor it appears that they can comprehend the nonliteral or figurative meaning of metaphors. Gelman and Markman (1986) have demonstrated that when children's knowledge of categories is tested in tasks that require inductive inferences, they used underlying rather than surface information in their inferences. For example, 4-year-old children were shown a picture of a bird (a flamingo) and told that it feeds mashed-up food to its young. They were also shown pictures of a bat and told that it feeds milk to its young. They were then presented with the picture of a second animal that resembled the bat much more than it resembled the flamingo. The children were told that the new animal was a bird and were asked how it fed its young. The children made an inference based on the underlying category and not the surface characteristics and predicted that it would feed its young mashed-up food. This type of finding provides strong evidence against the view that children are concrete thinkers operating on surface information. Welman and Gelman (1988) show that children as young as 3 can successfully distinguish between external physical phenomena and internal mental entities and states. They argue that this ability of young children to understand the "nonobvious" and distinguish between appearance and reality calls for a re-examination of assertions that children are fundamentally concrete and perceptually bound in their thinking. Overall, it appears that recent work in child development does not support the view that children's theories are perceptually bound or concrete.

Children's Theories are Inconsistent

Discussions of apparent inconsistencies and contradictions in children's theories often fail to take into account the fact that what appears self-contradictory or inconsistent to the expert in terms of the expert's knowledge structure or framework may not be inconsistent or reflect contradictions within the child's conceptual framework. An example of this can be seen in Wiser's (1988) research on children's conceptions of heat and temperature phenomena. Wiser showed that because students have an alternative conception of heat that does not take volume into account, they appear to give confused or contradictory responses to problems from the expert point of view. Thus, while students correctly predict that (when heated on identical burners) a big vessel of water will take longer to boil than a small one, they also make the wrong prediction that it would not take more heat to boil the water in the big vessel because they think of heat as temperature, a quality measured in degrees and do not take volume into account in the way that current physics does. Wiser concludes that children's conceptions of the domain are not impoverished precursors to the expert view nor do they constitute, "a 'confused concept,' in which those features, although irreconcilable, are lumped together." Wiser argues that "this view is forced by the approach taken in the studies, which are designed and interpreted from the expert's point of view" (p. 31).

A similar argument can be made about the recognition of empirical anomalies. Observations or empirical findings that are presented to children as disconfirming evidence for their conceptualizations of a domain may be interpreted by children in ways that make the observations perfectly consistent with their initial ontological commitments in the domain. Thus, in the domain of astronomy our own research (Vosniadou & Brewer, 1990; Samarapungavan & Vosniadou, 1989) shows that children are often able to incorporate information from a Copernican framework into their initial geocentric "flat earth" view. Many children develop the conception that the earth is a hollow sphere with a sky dome for a cover. This allows them to incorporate the information that the earth is a sphere without violating their empirical observation that the earth is flat. It also permits them to explain how people could live on the bottom of the earth and not fall off.

The following is an extract from a protocol that looks inconsistent from the adult point of view but is actually consistent from the child's hollow earth perspective:

Hollow Sphere Model

(Indrilla, second grade; Samarapungavan & Vosniadou, 1989)

Experimenter:	What is the shape of the earth?
Child:	Spherical.
Experimenter:	Where do people live on earth?
Child:	They live inside the earth on the land.
Experimenter:	Can people live on the bottom of the earth?
Child:	Yes.
Experimenter:	Why don't they fall?
Child:	Because they are on the flat land.
Experimenter:	Is there an end or an edge to the earth?
Child:	No.
Experimenter:	If you dug a hole through the earth what would you see on the other side?
Child:	A planet.

Experimenter: From these models pick the one that is the same shape as the earth.
Child: (picks up the hollow hemisphere rather than square, pancake, or spherical shapes) This is part of it only the other half is air.
Experimenter: Where do people live on earth? Show me in your model.
Child: (points to the inside bottom of the hollow sphere) We live all over inside on the bottom on the flat parts.
Experimenter: Could a person reach the end or the edge of the earth?
Child: No, you would go round and come back to where you started. (child traces circle on inside bottom of her hollow earth model with her finger)
Experimenter: Does the earth have an end or an edge? Show me on your model.
Child: (indicates top rim of hollow earth) That's the end.
Experimenter: Could a person fall off there?
Child: No, you can't go there except in rockets and then you don't fall. Because you are in the rocket.

As is evident from the protocol, the child's assertion that people don't fall because they are on the flat land seems to contradict her earlier statement that the earth is spherical in shape, but turns out to be entirely consistent in the light of her articulated model.

Overall, this research suggests that claims about the inconsistency of children's theories must be examined carefully.

Children's Theories are Context-bound

Researchers such as Solomon (1983b) have proposed that children's theories are context-bound. However, Vosniadou and Brewer (1990) argue that the construction of "assimilatory models" such as the disk and the hollow earth models just described is evidence that children do try to integrate contradictory information from different contexts into coherent conceptions. In the domain of astronomy, children who were context-bound would be expected to respond to questions about the local, perceived earth as flat, but respond to questions about the earth as seen from space as if it were spherical. The context-bound approach (or "dual earth" model) is occasionally found among 6–9-year-old children, but the data presented in Vosniadou and Brewer (1990) show that the assimilatory models are much more common. Thus, the data from children's models of the earth's shape argue against the hypothesis that children's understanding of natural phenomena is usually context bound.

Children's Theories are Fragmentary

Vosniadou and Brewer (1990) use the evidence of assimilatory models of the earth's shape to argue against the position that children's theories of the world are fragmentary. Vosniadou and Brewer conclude that the high frequency of assimilatory models in young children's views about the earth shows that children are apparently not content with a set of fragmentary information about the shape of the earth but attempt to integrate the information they have into a more global theory.

Children's Theories Lack Explanatory Power

It seems to us that assimilatory models such as the hollow earth models described earlier possess considerable explanatory power. These models appear to be creative solutions by young children to allow them to give an explanation for the inconsistency of the perceived flat earth and the adults' statements that the earth is round.

Additional evidence for the explanatory force of these child models can be seen in a protocol on the day/night cycle obtained from one of the children described earlier who apparently believes that the earth is a hollow hemisphere with a sky dome for a cover:

Day/Night Cycle

(Indrilla, second grade; Samarapungavan & Vosniadou, 1989)

Experimenter:	Does the earth move?
Child:	Yes.
Experimenter:	Show me how it moves.
Child:	It spins around. (shows axis rotation of hollow hemisphere)
Experimenter:	Does the sun move?
Child:	It moves from the outer space into the sky and to space again.
Experimenter:	Does the moon move?
Child:	Yes.
Experimenter:	Show me how it moves.
Child:	Just like the sun. And the stars too. They go where the moon is.
Experimenter:	(gives child her selected models for earth, sun, and moon) Now, with your models of the earth, sun, and moon, show me how it changes from day to night for this little boy here on earth.
Child:	See here is the sky half of the earth. (child cups her hands to form a dome over the hollow hemisphere) During the day the sun comes down from far in outer space to the sky part and we

get light on earth. And then slowly the sun moves back up into the outer space part and the moon and stars come down from outer space into the sky part . . . So it will be night for the boy. (child indicates that outer space is a region above the sky dome that covers the earth)

As can be seen from this section of the protocol, Indrilla has evidently been taught that the earth rotates on its axis, and has integrated this information into her model of the earth. However, the axis rotation of the earth clearly has no potential for explaining the day/night cycle, given her beliefs about the shape of the earth. Instead, she explains the day/night cycle in terms of the linear movement of the sun, moon, and stars from "outer space" down to the sky and back.

It seems to us that protocols such as these demonstrate that children use their models as explanatory frameworks to generate answers to novel questions. For example, in a later segment of Indrilla's protocol, she was asked what would happen if the sun, moon, or earth stopped moving:

Planetary Motion

Experimenter: Remember you showed me how the earth moves . . . What would happen if the earth stopped moving?
Child: Nothing. It just wouldn't spin around.
Experimenter: What about the sun, does it move?
Child: Yes.
Experimenter: What would happen if the sun stopped moving?
Child: You mean now when it was in the sky?
Experimenter: Yes now.
Child: It would be day all the time and the moon couldn't come down because the sun was in the sky. Or maybe it could still come but it would be very bright for us. It would be hard to sleep and we would be pretty tired.
Experimenter: What about if the moon stopped moving?
Child: The moon? Well if it stops in outer space . . . like now it is in space . . . So if is stops now, then when the sun went back into outer space it would be dark here and we would not have the moon at night. But I suppose the sun would come to sky again so it would be all right.

Once again it appears that the child's theory is used as an explanatory framework to answer new questions, just as scientific theories are used to give explanations of new phenomena.

THE CHILD VS. THE INSTITUTION OF SCIENCE

One important point that must be kept in mind in discussing children's theories and scientific theories is the distinction between the scientist and the cultural institution of science. Science is one of the major cultural institutions in modern society (Merton, 1973). One role of the institution of science is to record and transmit to the current generation of scientists the canon of established scientific knowledge. Over several thousand years this has given rise to a body of scientific knowledge of enormous scope.

The child's situation forms a strong contrast to science as a cultural institution. The child's initial science is constructed by a single individual who does not have access to the shared knowledge and regulatory mechanisms of institutional science. Thus, the child, before formal or informal instruction, tries to understand aspects of the everyday world such as: Where does the sun go at night? Why does a tub of hot water become cold? Where does wood go when it burns? Why do metal boats float? When you roll a ball on a flat surface why does it stop rolling? Why does ice turn into water?

Many of the apparent differences between children's theories and the corresponding scientists' theories result from a comparison of the work of a single individual with the products of a cultural institution. Clearly, the individual child does not yet share the enormous body of knowledge that is part of the institution of science.

Children's Theories are Fragmentary

As the institutional knowledge about a domain accumulates over time, the theories in the domain appear more general and less fragmentary. Thus, the current theory of continental drift incorporates earlier fragments of information about the regions of volcanic activity, about the occurrence of geological forms, and about the distribution of species on different continental land masses.

The description of children's theories as fragmentary could thus derive from the contrast between the child and the institution. The child's observations comprise only a very small component of the data amassed by the institution of science. Thus, in comparison with the institutionalized scientific theories, the child's theories must appear fragmentary.

Children's Theories are Inconsistent

The enormous degree of internal consistency in well-established scientific theories is also an accomplishment of generations of scientists examining these theories and attempting to eliminate potential inconsistencies. At least part of the description of children's theories as inconsistent can be attributed to the child working in an oral tradition, compared with the public written knowledge of the institution of science. All working scientists should feel sympathy for the child. We have all had the experience of constructing a set of ideas and then finding them inconsistent when: we write them down; read over a first draft of our work; have colleagues read a later draft; or occasionally have it pointed out in a published reply to a published work. The journals and written texts of the scientific culture thus often help to overcome inconsistency due to human memory limitations and other forms of cognitive slips.

Children's Theories are Context-bound

The description of children's theories as context-bound may also reflect the contrast between the individual child and the institution of science. As scientific theories develop over time, the earlier scientific theories sometimes look context-bound. Thus, the pre-Newtonian theories of the tides, of terrestrial motion, and of celestial motion seem "context-bound," compared with Newton's theory. Therefore, if one compares children's theories with the "universal" theories that have developed in some areas of natural science, the child's theories will appear context-bound.

Children's Theories Are Empirically False

The assertion that children's theories are empirically false when contrasted with scientific theories may also arise from a failure to make the distinction between the science of the individual and institutional science. Young children tend to believe that matter is continuous (Novick & Nussbaum, 1978) while the atomic theory of institutionalized science treats it as particulate. It seems clear that the child's view of the world accounts for a vast range of observable data and so, in that sense, is empirically confirmed. On the other hand, the institution of science has developed an alternate theory that is empirically confirmed by an even wider range of data.

It seems that the empirical limitations of children's theories may relate to the child's ignorance of the accumulated knowledge of institutional science and thus do not show that the child lacks an appreciation of the importance of empirical confirmation. Therefore, we prefer to align ourselves with those researchers (e.g., Driver & Easley, 1978) who think of the child's theories as "alternative frameworks" instead of "misconceptions."

Thus far, we have focused on the institutional role of science as the vehicle for the organized accumulation of knowledge. However, there are other important aspects of science that we have not yet considered, such as the existence of scientific norms, scientific methodology, and the underlying disciplinary matrix. We will now turn to a brief discussion of these aspects of science.

THE INSTITUTION OF SCIENCE

Institutional Norms

Sociologists of science (Merton, 1942/1973; Ziman, 1984) have argued that the institution of science incorporates a set of norms. Among those mentioned have been: (a) communalism—science is to be public knowledge; (b) universalism—scientific claims are to be treated in terms of their intrinsic merit; (c) disinterestedness—science is done for its own sake; (d) organized skepticism—scientific knowledge must continually be subjected to skeptical analysis.

These are complex issues and it is difficult to know how to treat them. There is considerable controversy about the existence of these norms (cf. Mulkay, 1979), and little or nothing is known about children's adoption of these norms. However, if such norms do exist and are unique to the institution of science, then by the logic we have been using, one would have to assume that children would not necessarily use these norms in the process of theory development. For some of these norms (e.g., communality, universalism) it is not clear that there would be any major consequences for children's theories. However, not sharing other norms (e.g., organized skepticism) might have important consequences for children's theories. Thus, children's theories not subjected to institutional skepticism might show less internal consistency or less agreement with data.

Scientific Method

Another area where there may be a strong contrast between the child and the institution of science is on the issue of scientific method. As with many other aspects of the study of science, recent work in the history and philosophy of science has revised earlier positivist conceptions about this topic. In particular, historical studies suggest that discussions of "the" scientific method are hard to support since there are examples of good science being produced by individuals who violate most of the rules given in prescriptive texts.

Nevertheless, it does seem that over time the institution of science has developed a number of general methodological techniques, such as the use of controls, the advantages of precise measurement, the importance of replicability, and so on. Clearly, this is an area in which young children will differ from scientists who have been trained in the institution of science. However, this probably does not have too much impact on the issue of theory construction since most aspects of "the scientific method" relate to procedures for carrying out experiments, not to theory construction.

Exemplars and the Disciplinary Matrix

In *The structure of scientific revolutions* (1962) Thomas Kuhn introduced a variety of important ideas under the term "paradigm." He argued that scientists in a mature science have been exposed to a number of exemplars of good theories.

He also argued that at a deeper level, as part of the disciplinary matrix, the scientists will have accepted certain patterns of explanation.

These aspects of the institution of science pose important questions for the issue of children's theories. As can be seen from the protocols given earlier, young children in technological cultures produce mechanistic explanatory accounts of the phenomena of observational astronomy. However, we do not know if the mechanistic explanatory mode of theory construction is a characteristic of the human species or if young children in developed nations are exposed to enough scientific exemplars and examples of scientific patterns of explanation so that they construct theories in this framework. Would children raised in a culture not so dramatically influenced by the institution of science also give mechanistic, explanatory accounts of the same phenomena?

CONTEMPORARY VIEWS OF THE NATURE OF SCIENTIFIC THEORIES

In this section of the chapter we shift away from the analysis of the nature of children's theories and examine the nature of scientists' theories. Some of the characteristics of scientific theories assumed by proponents of the extreme view may set a standard for children's theories that, in fact, are not reached by scientific theories. It would appear that many critics of children's science have a view of science that is strongly colored by the logical positivist analysis of science (Ayer, 1946; Feigl & Brodbeck, 1953).

Scientific Theories are Objective

Starting with the work of Toulmin (1953), Hanson (1958), and Kuhn (1962), there has been a major shift in the way that scientific theories are viewed by philosophers of science (see Suppe, 1977, for a review). There is now general agreement that scientific theories are not completely "objective," but are strongly influenced by the prevailing background beliefs of the period (Suppe, 1977; Laudan et al., 1986). For example, the cultural belief that the circle was a special form led to the development of Ptolemaic astronomy and made it very difficult for astronomers to propose a theory based on the ellipse (cf. Kuhn, 1962). Initially Newton's theory was rejected by many eminent scientists of his time because some fundamental assumptions of the theory conflicted with the basic ontological beliefs of the period. Laudan (1977) notes that:

> What troubled many of Newton's contemporaries (including Locke, Berkeley, Huygens and Leibniz) were several conceptual ambiguities and confusions about its foundational assumptions. What was absolute space and why was it needed to do physics? How could bodies conceivably act on one another at-a-distance? . . . How, Liebniz would ask, could Newton's theory be reconciled with an intelligent deity who designed the world? (p. 46)

Thus, finding that children's theories are influenced by their background beliefs about the world would not seem to distinguish their theories from scientific theories.

Scientific Theories are Axiomatic

The position that scientific theories must be axiomatic derives from the idealization of logical positivism and reflects its emphasis on mathematical physics as the canonical scientific domain. There is general agreement that the attempt to capture all scientific theories in terms of axiomatic systems was a failure (Suppe, 1977). Recent philosophers of science have examined a wider range of scientific theories and it is clear that many very powerful theories (e.g., Darwinian theory, continental drift) have a more qualitative flavor. Thus, the observation that children's theories are not axiomatic theories does not seem to distinguish them from scientific theories.

SCIENTIFIC REASONING BY CHILDREN AND SCIENTISTS: A RE-EVALUATION

In this section of the chapter we shift from a focus on the products of scientific reasoning to a focus on the the reasoning process itself. The line of attack is similar to that used earlier. We argue that the traditional view of the scientist as logical, consistent, objective, flexible, and open minded was strongly influenced by the general positivist view of science and is not supported by recent studies of scientists (cf. Laudan, 1984, Chapter 1). On the other hand, we argue that many of the developmental studies of children have underplayed the child's capacities in scientific reasoning.

The Scientist is Logical, the Child is Illogical

One of the first things to notice about the view that the scientist operates by the laws of formal logic is that the importance of this claim is undercut by the current view in the philosophy of science that formal logic plays little role in scientific work (e.g., Toulmin, 1967, 1972). For example, Popper (1959, 1963) pointed out the importance, on logical grounds, of a single disconfirming piece of evidence in proving a theory to be false. However, most current philosophers of science believe that scientists allow a variety of more pragmatic factors to override this logical point and rarely operate by strict logical disconfirmation (cf. Chalmers, 1982). Thus, in general, recent work in the philosophy and history of science does not support the view of the scientist as the paradigm case of a user of formal logic.

There have been few empirical investigations of the reasoning processes of working scientists. However, Kern, Mirels, and Hinshaw (1983) investigated the ability of working scientists to evaluate rules of propositional logic and found error rates as high as 92% for some items. Kern et al. point out that their population consisted of successful scientists and concluded that their data brought into question "the pivotal role of formal logic in philosophical analyses of scientific inference" (p. 131). In a recent monograph reviewing this issue, Faust (1984) concludes that "scientists, along with all other individuals, evidence cognitive limitations that lead to frequent judgment error and that set surprisingly harsh restrictions on the capacity to manage complex information and to make decisions" (p. 3).

Much of the work on children's reasoning in science derives from the work of Jean Piaget. Piaget (1930) proposed that scientific reasoning is based on certain logical capacities (formal operations) and that young children could not carry out these forms of reasoning. This led some of Piaget's followers in the area of science education (e.g., Herron, 1978; Lawson & Renner, 1974) to argue that since young children were lacking the fundamental needed skills for science, there was no reason to teach abstract science concepts to elementary-school children!

In retrospect, it would appear that the hypothesized crucial role of formal operations in science was another reflection of the logical positivist view of science. In addition to this general change in our view of the role of formal logic in science, there have been a number of recent studies suggesting that young children are capable of generating scientific theories to account for aspects of the observed world (e.g., Carey, 1985; Driver & Easley, 1978). Overall, it appears that the reasoning processes of scientists have been idealized and that children's reasoning processes have been undervalued, but that a reanalysis of these positions shows a strong degree of convergence on the position that both the child and the scientist are rational theory constructors, but that formal logic plays little role in this process.

The Scientist is Consistent, the Child is Inconsistent

Work on the history of science shows that many major figures in science have demonstrated inconsistency in developing their theories. For example, Laudan (1977) has shown how Faraday's initial model of electrical integration was designed to eliminate the idea of action at a distance, but in fact required a chain of short-range actions at a distance. This was noted by contemporary scientists such as Hare, who also criticized the theory for proposing contiguous particles that were not contiguous. Such criticisms from within the institution of science led Faraday to revise his conceptions and subsequently to develop the notion of the field. Thus, the consistent theory that he is credited with was the result of an interaction between an inconsistent individual scientist and the regulatory mechanisms operating within the institution of science. Similarly, Lavoisier appears to have held both his new oxygen theory and the earlier phlogiston theory (Thagard, 1990). It was only through a series of investigations over a period of years that the inconsistency was eliminated.

In the earlier sections of this chapter we discussed several characteristics of children that might lead one to overemphasize the degree to which they show inconsistency in their reasoning. Children often have very different theories of the world from those of the adults studying them, and it is very easy for adult researchers to describe apparently inconsistent reasoning on the part of a child because they have failed to see the internal consistency of the child's responses from within the child's world view.

Another important issue is that of memory. Because children's theories are developed by an individual working in an oral tradition, the child faces a severe problem with memory load that the adult scientist can avoid through the use of written materials. In attempting to build theories of the natural world it is often necessary to integrate many different observations. A child whose reasoning processes are quite consistent may thus appear inconsistent because the child has not recalled some fact which is incompatible with a theory the child is developing. The crucial test here to distinguish memory limitations from inconsistency in reasoning is to bring the inconsistent facts to the child's attention. If the problem is due to inconsistent reasoning then the child should not show any signs that there is any difficulty. However, if the problem is due to memory then the child should show that he or she is aware of the inconsistency and perhaps try to resolve the problem. The possibility of inconsistency arising from memory limitation has been noted by a number of investigators (e.g., Cherniak, 1983; Johnson, 1978; Piaget, 1952).

The Scientist is Objective, the Child is Subjective

The view that scientists are objective is one of the aspects of the logical positivist account of science (Ayer, 1946; Feigl & Brodbeck, 1953) that has come under strong attack. Philosophers of science (Kuhn, 1962; Laudan, 1977; Toulmin, 1961) have pointed out that an individual scientist's theorizing is typically carried out within a framework of unrecognized background assumptions. Sociologists of science from the "strong programme" (Bloore, 1976; Mulkay, 1979) have actually attempted to argue that all scientific knowledge is a subjective sociological product. While this is clearly much too extreme a position, the researchers from the strong program have shown that cultural and ideological beliefs do have a strong impact on scientists' practice of science.

None of this scholarly work showing that scientists are often not objective should come as a surprise to working scientists. To give a trivial example, when reading a review of literature on a topic you are not familiar with, you typically want to know what the reviewer's position is in order to evaluate the evidence. Or, on the other hand, if you read a literature review for an area you are familiar with it is usually rather easy to tell what the author's position is by the way the research is reviewed. Clearly, there is a strong subjective component in the thinking of scientists.

Scientists are Flexible, Children are Rigid

Kuhn's (1962) analysis of scientific change in terms of shifting paradigms provided considerable historical evidence that scientists are often not very flexible in shifting their views. In fact, Kuhn (1962 p. 90) suggested that fundamental change in a discipline will often be brought about by individuals trained outside the discipline, or by very junior members of the discipline because it is very hard for the mature scientist in a discipline to show the necessary flexibility required to propose fundamental change.

Scientists are Open Minded, Children are Dogmatic

Several investigators of children's behavior (Chaiklin, 1985; D. Kuhn, Amsel, & O'Loughlin, 1988) have argued that children are being unscientific or dogmatic when they attempt to reject empirical anomalies by saying that the observations provided are inaccurate. However, the children's objections seem to have their counterparts in Duhem's (1954) observation that empirical anomalies may arise from problems in data-gathering and measurement procedures and thus it may often be reasonable to ignore them.

In one of his early papers, Kuhn (1963) made the point that the historical record showed that scientists are often dogmatic. Kuhn argued that dogmatism was a desirable trait for scientists practicing "normal science," since it led to single-minded devotion to the unfolding of the potential of the current paradigm.

Laudan (1977) has pointed out that it is cognitively rational for a scientist to continue to hold a theory in the face of empirical disconfirmation when there is no good alternative theory. Karmiloff–Smith and Inhelder (1975) have provided evidence showing that children operate in a similar fashion. These researchers asked children to carry out a block-balancing task. After some experience with the task most children developed a theory that the blocks would balance at their geometric center. This theory was only partly successful since some of the blocks did not have an even distribution of weight. Children holding this theory rejected some blocks and said they could not be balanced. It was only after much longer experience with a variety of blocks that the children took the failures into account. They noticed patterns in the failures that suggested ways to revise their initial theory so that all the relevant dimensions were included.

Thus, in looking more closely at the characteristics of working scientists and of children reasoning about the natural world, many of the apparent differences between them are dramatically reduced.

The Scientist as Professional

There is one important way in which scientists do differ from children. Scientists are members of a profession and earn their living by developing theories and carrying out experiments to examine those theories. Presumably, for the child the development of theories is a side-effect of trying to make sense of the world and the child's major efforts are directed at more serious matters, such as how to talk their parents into letting them watch certain TV programs or learning to tie their shoes. Note again, this major difference between the child and the scientist reflects an institutional difference between the two.

IMPLICATIONS FOR RESEARCH

Children's Theories

In this chapter we have deliberately taken a strong form of the view that children's theories are essentially the same as scientific theories once one has made allowances for the fact that the child is not a member of the institution of science and does not have the domain knowledge that a professional scientist does. While it seems to us that we have shown that this is a plausible position, it also seems to us that this is a topic in need of much additional research. If one removes the advantage the scientist receives from the institution of science, are children's theories really more fragmentary and inconsistent than scientists' theories?

Domain Generality.   Much of our evidence for the position that children produce coherent explanatory theories has derived from work on children's knowledge of observational astronomy. The researchers who have argued the other side of this issue (e.g., diSessa, 1988) have typically used evidence from other domains, such as mechanics. Clearly, we need research across a wide range of domains in order to establish the generality of the positions across domains.

Children's Thinking.   Throughout this chapter we have taken a knowledge-based view and rejected those aspects of the Piagetian position that hypothesize that the child's thought processes are qualitatively different from those of adult scientists. It seems to us that we have been successful in showing how powerful the knowledge-based position is, but we think this is still an important issue. Once one has made allowance for the enormous differences in knowledge between the child and the scientist, are there any fundamental differences in their reasoning processes?

Theory Evaluation.   An important issue in contemporary philosophy of science is how scientists choose among competing theories. For example, Kuhn (1977) has suggested that the core criteria used in theory evaluation are accuracy, consistency, breadth, simplicity, and fruitfulness. We think it is important to find out if children share these values and one of us has initiated a research project directed at this problem (Samarapungavan, 1990).

Institutional Norms. In our discussion of the institution of science we pointed out that many sociologists of science have argued that there is a set of institutional norms (e.g., universalism, disinterestedness) shared by members of the scientific community. We think it would be important to know if children share these norms.

Recapitulation. The arguments presented in this chapter lead to some interesting predictions about the issue of children's theories recapitulating the historical development of scientific theories. Our position that the child can carry out scientific theory construction but lacks the cumulative cultural knowledge of science predicts that specific child theories of the natural world would recapitulate historical theories, in those cases where the child has available roughly the same data as the early scientists and where there has not been an enormous accumulation of theoretical development. Thus, one might expect recapitulation for the theories held by the pre-Socratics. However, one would not expect the recapitulation of Ptolemaic epicycles since the child would not typically be aware of the retrograde motion of the planets nor would one expect the child to recapitulate highly developed theories such as Newtonian mechanics.

Disciplinary Matrix. In our discussion of the underlying assumptions held by scientists, we noted the possibility that children in developed nations absorb aspects of the scientific world view from their general culture at a very early age. In order to explore this issue we need cross-cultural research that examines children's theories in societies that have not adopted the scientific view of the world.

CONCLUSIONS

In this chapter we have explored the issue of the child as scientist. We show that children can develop very impressive theories of the natural world. We have adopted a knowledge-based approach and have used this approach to re-evaluate earlier characterizations of children's theories as concrete, fragmentary, inconsistent, and context-bound. We argue that in constructing models of the world children show reasoning processes very much like those of adult scientists. However, because the child does not have access to the institutional advantages that a professional scientist enjoys the theories produced by the child are likely to differ in a number of respects from those that are produced by the institution of science. We conclude that the child is best thought of as a novice scientist, who adopts a rational approach to theory construction but lacks the knowledge of the physical world and experimental methodology accumulated by the institution of science.

ACKNOWLEDGMENT

Preparation of this chapter was supported in part by the Office of Educational Research and Improvement under cooperative agreement G0087C1001. We would like to thank Jack Easley, Dedre Gentner, Robert Hoffman, Phil Johnson–Laird, Doug Medin, and Stella Vosniadou for important comments on earlier drafts of this chapter. Their comments were of much help, but they certainly should not be held responsible for our basic position. Indeed, most of them thought our views were a bit extreme.
This chapter is dedicated to Jim Jenkins. The senior author was first exposed to modern philosophy of science in two extraordinarily stimulating years as a postdoctoral fellow at the Center for Human Learning, so this work can trace its roots directly back to the period when Jim showed us what cognitive psychology would come to be.

REFERENCES

Ayer, A. J. (1946). *Language, truth and logic.* London: Gollanez.
Bloore, D. (1976). *Knowledge and social imagery.* London: Routledge & Kegan Paul.
Brewer, W. F., Herdrich, D. J., & Vosniadou, S. (1990). *Universal and culture-specific aspects of children's cosmological models: Samoan and American data.* Manuscript submitted for publication.
Brown, A. (1989). Analogical learning and transfer: What develops? In S. Vosniadou & A. Ortony (Eds.), *Similarity and analogical reasoning* (pp. 369–412). Cambridge, England: Cambridge University Press.
Bruner, J. S., Oliver, R. R., & Greenfield, P. M. (1966). *Studies in cognitive growth.* New York: Wiley.
Carey, S. (1985). *Conceptual change in childhood.* Cambridge, MA: MIT Press.
Chaiklin, S. (1985, April). *The stability of conceptions in novice physical science reasoning.* Paper presented at the annual meeting of the American Educational Research Association.
Chalmers, A. F. (1982). *What is this thing called science?* (2nd ed.). Milton Keynes, England: Open University Press.
Cherniak, C. (1983). Rationality and the structure of human memory. *Synthese, 57,* 163–186.
diSessa, A. A. (1988). Knowledge in pieces. In G. Forman & P. B. Pufall (Eds.), *Constructivism in the computer age* (pp. 49–70). Hillsdale, NJ: Lawrence Erlbaum Associates.
Driver, R., & Easley, J. (1978). Pupils and paradigms: A review of literature related to concept development in adolescent science students. *Studies in Science Education, 5,* 61–84.
Duhem, P. (1954). *The aim and structure of physical theory* (P. Weiner, Trans.). Princeton, NJ: Princeton University Press.

Faust, D. (1984). *The limits of scientific reasoning*. Minneapolis: University of Minnesota Press.

Feigl, H., & Brodbeck, M. (Eds.). (1953). *Readings in the philosophy of science*. New York: Appleton–Century–Crofts.

Gelman, S. A., & Markman, E. M. (1986). Categories and induction in young children. *Cognition, 23*, 183–208.

Hanson, N. R. (1958). *Patterns of discovery*. Cambridge, England: Cambridge University Press.

Herron, J. D. (1978). Role of learning and development: Critique of Novak's comparison of Ausubel and Piaget. *Science Education, 62*, 593–605.

Inhelder, B., & Piaget, J. (1958). *The growth of logical thinking from childhood to adolescence*. New York: Basic Books.

Johnson, G. A. (1978). Child thought and contradictions: Understanding Reyb and To. *Philosophy of the Social Sciences, 8*, 261–264.

Karmiloff–Smith, A., & Inhelder, B. (1975). "If you want to get ahead, get a theory." *Cognition, 3*, 195–212.

Kern, L. H., Mirels, H. L., & Hinshaw, V. G. (1983). Scientists' understanding of propositional logic: An experimental investigation. *Social Studies of Science, 13*, 131–146.

Kuhn, D., Amsel, E., & O'Loughlin, M. (1988). *The development of scientific thinking skills*. Orlando, FL: Academic Press.

Kuhn, T. S. (1962). *The structure of scientific revolutions*. Chicago: University of Chicago Press.

Kuhn, T. S. (1963). The function of dogma in scientific research. In A. C. Crombie (Ed.), *Scientific change* (pp. 347–369). New York: Basic Books.

Kuhn, T. S. (1977). Objectivity, value judgment and theory choice. In T. S. Kuhn (Ed.), *The essential tension* (pp. 320–339). Chicago: University of Chicago Press.

Laudan, L. (1977). *Progress and its problems*. Berkeley: University of California Press.

Laudan, L. (1984). *Science and values*. Berkeley: University of California Press.

Laudan, L., Donovan, A., Laudan, R., Barker, P., Brown, H., Leplin, J., Thagard, P., & Wyskstra, S. (1986). Scientific change: Philosophical models and historical research. *Synthese, 69*, 141–223.

Lawson, A. E., & Renner, J. W. (1974). A quantitative analysis of Piagetian tasks and its implications for curriculum. *Science Education, 58*, 454–459.

McCloskey, M., & Kargon, R. (1988). The meaning and use of historical models in the study of intuitive physics. In S. Strauss (Ed.), *Ontogeny, phylogeny, and historical development* (pp. 49–67). Norwood, NJ: Ablex.

Merton, R. K. (1942). The normative structure of science. (Reprinted in R. K. Merton, 1973, *The sociology of science*, pp. 267–278. Chicago: University of Chicago Press.)

Merton, R. K. (1973). *The sociology of science*. Chicago: University of Chicago Press.

Mulkay, M. (1979). *Science and the sociology of knowledge*. London: George Allen & Unwin.

Novick, S., & Nussbaum, J. (1978). Junior high school pupils' understanding of the particulate nature of matter: An interview study. *Science Education, 63*, 273–282.

Palermo, D. S. (1989). Knowledge and the child's developing theory of the world. *Advances in Child Development and Behavior, 21*, 269–295.

Piaget, J. (1930). *The child's conception of physical causality*. New York: Harcourt Brace.

Piaget, J. (1952). *Judgment and reasoning in the child*. New York: Basic Books.

Piaget, J. (1980). *Experiments in contradiction*. Chicago: University of Chicago Press.

Popper, K. R. (1959). *The logic of scientific discovery*. London: Hutchinson.

Popper, K. R. (1963). *Conjectures and refutations*. New York: Basic Books.

Quine, W. V. O. (1977). Natural kinds. In S. P. Schwartz (Ed.), *Naming, necessity, and natural kinds* (pp. 155–175). Ithaca, NY: Cornell University Press.

Samarapungavan, A. (1990). *Children's meta-judgments in theory choice tasks: An investigation of scientific rationality in children*. Unpublished doctoral dissertation, University of Illinois at Urbana-Champaign.

Samarapungavan, A., & Vosniadou, S. (1989). *What children from India know about the earth, sun, moon, and stars: A cross-cultural study*. Unpublished manuscript.

Schollum, B., & Osborne, R. (1985). Relating the new to the familiar. In R. Osborne & P. Freyberg (Eds.), *Learning in science* (pp. 51–65). Auckland, New Zealand: Heinemann.

Smiley, S. S., & Brown, A. L. (1979). Conceptual preference for thematic and taxonomic relations: A nonmonotonic age trend from preschool to old age. *Journal of Experimental Child Psychology, 28*, 249–257.

Solomon, J. (1983a). Messy, contradictory and obstinately persistent: A study of children's out-of-school ideas about energy. *School Science Review*, 225–229.

Solomon, J. (1983b). Thinking in two worlds of knowledge. In H. Helm & J. D. Novak (Eds.), *Misconceptions in science and mathematics*. Proceedings of the International Seminar, Cornell University, Ithaca, NY.

Suppe, F. (1977). *The structure of scientific theories* (2nd ed.). Urbana: University of Illinois Press.

Thagard, P. (1990). The conceptual structure of the chemical revolution. *Philosophy of Science, 57*, 183–209.

Toulmin, S. (1953). *The philosophy of science: An introduction*. London: Hutchinson.

Toulmin, S. (1961). *Foresight and understanding*. New York: Harper & Row.

Toulmin, S. (1967). The evolutionary development of natural science. *American Scientist, 55*, 456–471.

Toulmin, S. (1972). *Human understanding*. Princeton, NJ: Princeton University Press.

Vosniadou, S., & Brewer, W. F. (1990). *The concept of the earth's shape: A study of conceptual change in childhood*. Manuscript submitted for publication.

Vosniadou, S., & Brewer, W. F. (in press). A cross-cultural investigation of children's acquisition of knowledge in observational astronomy: Greek and American data. In H. Mandl, E. DeCorte, S. N. Bennett, & H. F. Friedrich (Eds.), *Learning and instruction: European research in an international context*, Vol. 3. Oxford: Pergamon Press.

Welman, H. M., & Gelman, S. A. (1988). Children's understanding of the nonobvious. In R. J. Sternberg (Ed.), *Advances in the psychology of human intelligence* (Vol. 4, pp. 99–135). Hillsdale, NJ: Lawrence Erlbaum Associates.

Wiser, M. (1988). The differentiation of heat and temperature: History of science and novice-expert shift. In S. Strauss (Ed.), *Ontogeny, phylogeny, and historical development* (pp. 28–48). Norwood, NJ: Ablex.

Ziman, J. (1984). *An introduction to science studies*. Cambridge, England: Cambridge University Press.

15 Cognitive Physics and Event Perception: Two Approaches to the Assessment of People's Knowledge of Physics

John B. Pittenger
University of Arkansas at Little Rock

The laws of physics determine, to a great degree, the behavior of objects in the environment and people's interactions with objects. Thus, a person must in some sense "know" those laws. Only then can they accurately predict the behavior of objects and the consequences of their interactions with those objects.

While psychologists have long had an interest in understanding people's knowledge of physical laws (e.g., Piaget), research in this area has seen especially rapid growth in the last 10 to 20 years. Researchers in cognition have found the area attractive for a variety of reasons. In everyday life, people have vast experience with physical systems and are in constant interaction with them. However, the laws, as characterized in natural science physics, present quite complex learning tasks. Perceptionists, especially those studying motion and events, are concerned with knowledge of physics, since the patterns of motion characteristic of many events are determined by those laws. Applied psychologists also have good reasons to study people's knowledge of physics. Effective science education is both very important in modern society and notoriously difficult to achieve. Thus, there is interest in understanding the beliefs students develop outside of formal coursework, the effect of formal instruction in changing these beliefs, and how well the results of such instruction transfer to life outside the classroom.

Research on peoples' knowledge of physics has been conducted within a variety of theoretical frameworks. However, most of the work is guided by one of two general approaches. Some researchers use the concepts and methods of *cognitive psychology* and refer to their work as "cognitive physics" (or "naïve physics" if the topic is restricted to knowledge developed without formal instruction). Research that takes the *event perception* approach uses the theoretical constructs and the methods of perceptual psychology.

The discussion of the cognitive and event perception approaches will be presented in three parts. First, the general characteristics of each approach will be described, including the phenomena studied, the goals of the research, and the methods used. In the second section, the results found to date concerning people's knowledge of elementary Newtonian mechanics will be summarized. This branch of physics was chosen because considerable work has been done on it from both perspectives. The summary will be selective, focusing on themes I see running through the literature. In the third and concluding section, I discuss the major unsolved problems in the area and suggest directions that research might take toward their solution.

CHARACTERIZATION OF COGNITIVE PHYSICS AND EVENT PERCEPTION: GOALS, PHENOMENA STUDIED, AND METHODS

Cognitive Physics

Goals.   Research in cognitive physics is motivated by a variety of goals. First, there is a concern for people's beliefs about physical systems: What "laws" or "rules" are believed? What predictions are made on the basis of these ideas? How often are the laws and the predictions made from them correct? For example, researchers ask how moving objects are influenced by gravity and about the path an object dropped from an airplane would take as it falls toward the ground (McCloskey, 1983b).

At a deeper level, there is analysis of conceptualization and reasoning. This includes study of the concepts used to understand physical systems and of the way these conceptual entities interact in determining the behavior of physical systems. Thus, there are studies of what people mean by the idea of "velocity" (Trowbridge & McDermott, 1980), of conceptions of equilibrium (Roncato & Rumiati, 1986) and of how thermostats serve to regulate the temperature in buildings (Kempton, 1986).

Finally, there is study of the patterns of reasoning used by people to analyze a system, develop ideas of the principles of its operation and use these principles to make predictions of the system's behavior (Gentner & Gentner, 1983; Larkin, 1983).

Phenomena Studied.   In principle, any aspect of physics could be studied. In actual practice, the physics of moving bodies, heat, simple electric circuits, and buoyancy have received the most attention. These aspects of physics are widely covered in elementary physics courses; this selection of phenomena to study thus seems in large part due to the fact that many researchers are motivated by such pedagogical concerns as the effectiveness in formal instruction in changing erroneous beliefs. In addition, many phenomena in everyday life involve these physical principles. Thus, it would seem reasonable to suppose that people would have developed beliefs about these aspects of physical systems.

Note that cognitive physics is concerned with physical systems involving change: bombs falling, electrical circuits in operation, objects being placed in a tube of water, and so on. In perceptual terms, these are *events*. Moreover, the events are *fast* rather than slow. Thus, one could see the motion of the bomb, the bulb lighting up in the circuit and the ball bobbing in the tub. Slow events, such as erosion or evolution of a solar system, are rarely studied.

The systems studied are typically simple in the sense of having a simple analysis in natural science physics. Again, I suspect this is (in part) due to pedagogical concerns. It is important to study naïve beliefs so as to understand how they influence the learning of the natural science concepts used in the classroom.

Additionally, it is reasonable to study systems for which a full natural science analysis is both available and simple enough to be stated in a convenient form. From the cognitive point of view, studies of naïve notions about what occurred before the "Big Bang," motion of water molecules in surf at the beach, or the biomechanics of a person lifting a heavy box would not make much sense.

Notice, though, that "textbook" events often constitute simplifications of the corresponding real world events. Frictionless surfaces, massless pullies, point masses, and lack of air resistance are common in physics texts. Idealizations, however, are rare in the world and, therefore, rare in people's experiences.

Methods. A variety of research methods are used in cognitive physics. When prediction of system behavior is at issue, it is often convenient to provide participants with a verbal or pictorial description of the system and then ask them to indicate what will happen next, either verbally or with drawings of their own. Thus, participants could choose which of several bulbs will burn brightest when the circuit is turned on, decide whether a wooden or an iron ball will hit the ground first if dropped from a tower, draw the path taken by the dropped bomb or draw a line indicating the surface of water in a tilted container. The standard for judging the accuracy of such predictions are, of course, the predictions made by natural science physics.

A novel technique was used by Freyd, Pantzer, and Cheng (1988) to test whether or not the dynamics underlying a system influence the perception and memory of static pictures of that system. For example, observers were shown two pictures of a plant and asked to remember its position. The first picture showed the plant resting on a table and the second showed it at the same position but without the supporting table. When shown pictures with the plant below, above, or at its original position, observers tended to recognize the picture falsely, showing it below its original position. That is, they acted as if their memories were distorted in the direction of what would have occurred if the table had been removed: The force produced by gravitational acceleration would have caused the plant to fall.

Analysis of underlying conceptualization and of reasoning processes is considerably more difficult. Extensive questionnaires or interviews are needed to develop a clear picture of the participants' ideas. In some cases, conceptualizations can be inferred from the predictions made by participants. For example, suppose a participant says that a rocket ship moving through space will make a 90-degree turn if a thrust is applied perpendicular to the rocket's present course. You can then safely infer that inertia is not being considered. In analyses of concepts and reasoning, as in prediction studies, natural science physics is the basis for evaluation of error. That is, one asks if participants have the same concepts as physicists and do they use them as physicists do in thinking about the system.

Such techniques do not often involve presentation of actual physical systems to participants. Thus, no actual operation of the systems is visible, nor can participants actually interact with the system. Since cognitive physics researchers are concerned with people's *thoughts* about the systems, this approach seems quite reasonable. We shall see, however, that, according to the event perception approach, such methods are not appropriate.

Event Perception

Events, as conceived of by perception researchers, are temporally extended phenomena involving some sort of change in an object or objects. Thus, motion of a car, bending of a tree, a person walking, a flower blooming, or water boiling are all events.

Phenomena Studied. The range of events that could be studied from an event perception perspective is, in principle, very wide. We can hear a glass break or bounce when it hits the floor, smell food become cooked, feel newly poured concrete become hard, and taste the coffee in the pot become stale as the day progresses. Most event perception research has, however, been concerned with visual perception (this is reflected in the examples used in the majority of chapters in Warren & Shaw, 1985a). One can, of course, take research in other senses and recast it into the event perception framework. An excellent example of this work is Jenkins's (1985) paper showing how studies of a wide variety of auditory phenomena can be reconceptualized as research in event perception.

As in cognitive physics, most studies of event perception have involved fast events, ones in which motion is seen. There are claims that change, though not motion, can be perceived in slow events (Shaw & Pittenger, 1979), and there are some empirical studies of the perception of slow events (Pittenger, Shaw, & Mark, 1979). However, such work is rare.

Goals.   There are at least four general goals motivating event perception studies: (1) Discovery of the aspects of events that can be perceived, (2) Specification of information in the environment which supports perception of events, (3) Understanding of the processes by which information is detected and used, (4) Analysis of how perception of events serves to guide the observer's action in the environment.

In perceiving an event, the observer can typically identify both the event itself and the object engaged in the event. Thus, we see that it is a *ball* that is *bouncing,* a *human face* that is *growing,* or a *tree* that is *bending* in the wind. Both sorts of identities are perceived at what might be called multiple levels. Thus, when a worn-out tennis ball is bounced, we see motion, bouncing and, in particular, a rapidly damped bounce. The object is seen as a solid object, a ball, and, in particular, a soft ball.

Objects have properties, such as mass and viscosity. Since these properties influence, in very specific ways, the patterns of change which occur during the event, they are potentially perceivable. Also forces (e.g. gravitational, frictional, etc.) are at play in events, influence the patterns of change occurring as events unfolds and, therefore, might also be perceived. The argument that kinematics (motion patterns) specify dynamics (masses, etc.) is given in detail by Runeson and Frykholm (1981, 1983).

Notice that these aspects of objects and events are just those that, in the physical world, link particular objects to particular events. That is, the specific pattern of change associated with a given event is determined by the specific properties of the participating objects and the forces involved. Conversely, an object is (in part) the particular object it is because of what it does, (i.e., the events in which it can participate).

As an example, consider a ball of clay. Because of the way its constituent molecules interact, it can be molded but will not bounce. Conversely, a ball supposedly made of clay but which could not be molded but does bounce, is not a ball of clay. Next consider a hammer. The mass of its head (among other factors) allows the hammer to drive a nail. On the other hand, an object of very low mass (say one made of styrofoam) even if shaped and colored like a hammer, could not drive a nail and is thereby not a hammer.

The second major goal of the research is to specify the information used by observers to perceive events. That is, what factors in motions of objects, changes in shape, and so on, are both characteristic of particular events and are actually detected and used by observers in the process of perception? Again, the laws of physics matter very much. The bounce of a ball depends on its elasticity, the speed with which it is thrown, the value of gravitational acceleration, and so on. Thus, the visible aspects of the event (such as motion) that must provide the informational basis for perception of events are themselves determined by physical laws.

Some researchers favoring a "direct" theory of perception postulate invariance as the central explanatory concept for event perception. They hold that for any event there is some specific pattern of change (called a transformational invariant), which occurs as any object participates in the event. As the event proceeds, some aspects of the objects will change but others (called structural invariants) will not change. These invariants are held to provide information to observers for the perception of event and object identity. Warren and Shaw (1986b) discuss this approach to event perception. In addition, they discuss the role of physical law in specification of information for event perception.

Little work has been done on the third goal, specification of the processes by which observers use information in perceiving events. In large part this is because of the theoretical approaches taken by the investigators. Most people in the field have been influenced by James Gibson or Gunnar Johansson. Neither Gibson nor Johansson has made much use of the cognitive approach to the perception of distance, shape, and motion perception. This lack of study of process by perceptionists stands in sharp contrast to the attention that cognitive physics researchers pay to processing.

Analyses of the role of event perception in the guidance of action, the fourth goal, also involve knowledge of physics. In many situations accurate knowledge of physics is central to effective control of our motor acts. Consider, for example, a person who first observes another person bounce a ball on the floor and then attempts to throw the ball by himself or herself so that it rises to some specified height after a single bounce. To control the force of the throw, one must know the elasticity of the ball with respect to the floor. How is one to know the value of elasticity? Warren, Kim, and Husney (1987) have shown that visible aspects of a ball's bounce specify the elasticity of a ball. Thus, if one knows (yet again, "in some sense") the relevant physics, one can perceive elasticity and use it to control the throw.

Methods.   Most studies of event perception present participants with displays representing the events. It is rare for the actual event itself to occur in the presence of the observer. The information available in such displays is often less than that available in the real event. For example, in Johansson's (1973) studies of biological motion, videotapes were made of people wearing reflective tape on their wrists, elbows, and so on. In the displays presented to observers, moving white dots, but not the actor's body contours, could be seen.

Mathematical simulations of events are frequently used to simplify displays by removing the effect of some physical variables. Todd and Warren (1982), for example, studied perception of collisions of objects varying in mass and elasticity. Dots on a CRT were moved in accordance with equations that allowed simulation of motion involving zero friction (not easy to do with real objects) and permitted convenient variation of simulated masses and elasticity.

As in cognitive physics, the task set for observers in event perception studies depends on the goals being pursued. Some studies, typically ones in which there is reduced information such as in Johansson's studies of biological motion, ask for identification of the event and the object. Such studies test whether or not available information is sufficient to support perception of event and object identity.

Perception of dynamic factors has been tested in a variety of ways. Observers can, of course, be asked to make numerical estimates of them (e.g., Todd & Warren, 1982). Alternatively, observers can be asked to perform some action that could be guided by perception of a dynamic factor. Recall that Warren, Kim, and Husney (1987) has observers watch a ball being bounced by another person, and then asked them to bounce the ball themselves, attempting to make it reach a target height. Since observers were quite accurate at this task, we can suppose they were able to perceive elasticity as they watched the ball being bounced by the experimenter.

Several tasks can be used when observers are presented with simulations of events which violate the motions predicted by natural science physics. One can ask participants to rate how much the portrayed event looks like the natural event or can ask for descriptions of the event, looking for statements revealing detection of violation. For example, in studies by Bozzi (1958) and Pittenger (1990), pendulums were made to swing with periods that were either correct or incorrect for their lengths. Observers were asked to judge whether or not the pendulum was swinging at its natural speed. Knowledge of the physical law was assessed by comparing rated naturalness of the motion with the degree of deviation from the correct period. Pittenger also asked participants to describe what they saw. Some made spontaneous correct statements that a pendulum was moving too fast or too slow and thereby provided evidence of their knowledge of the speed–length relationship and demonstrated the salience of violations. Other spontaneous judgments revealed perception of forces, as well as knowledge of the physical law. For example, the statement "The pendulum is slow because of friction in the axle" showed that the observer: (a) Saw the motion was not correct for a free-swinging pendulum, (b) Saw another, but natural, event, and (c) Saw a force which the observer believed would account for the perceived event's deviation from the event of a pendulum swinging freely.

EMPIRICAL FINDINGS

Having discussed the various theoretical and methodological approaches to the study of people's knowledge of physics, I now turn to the empirical findings. In reading this literature I was interested both in seeing if there were broad generalizations to be made about knowledge of physics and whether or not the event perception and cognitive physics approaches showed any systematic differences in their findings.

The following summary of the results of research will largely be confined to studies assessing knowledge of Newtonian mechanics, the aspect physics most thoroughly studied under both approaches. Specifically, I shall discuss results that illustrate three generalizations that may be made on the basis of the available research:

1. The two approaches suggest very different conclusions about the accuracy of people's knowledge of physics. This may be due to the existence of multiple forms of knowledge that are selectively activated by the particular information available and by task demands.
2. People often use heuristics. These are simplified and/or physically incorrect rules that can lead to reasonably accurate predictions in limited situations.
3. People's knowledge of physical systems that involve human interaction tends to be more refined than that of systems which can only be passively observed.

Contrast in Findings Between the Two Approaches

Research on event perception typically finds evidence that people are sensitive to the complex and subtle patterns of change dictated by physical law. In sharp contrast, studies in cognitive physics often conclude that people have seriously erroneous concepts and make flagrantly wrong predictions, even for simple and highly familiar physical systems.[1]

---

[1]*The curse of perception.* Perceptionists may be surprised to learn that some cognitivists find perception often to be a source of error in the development of correct conceptions of, and effective thinking about, physical systems. I have so far found three sorts of danger supposedly presented by perception. First, note that factors such as friction, gravity, and momentum can be taken as "invisible" and thus could be difficult to conceive of accurately. For example, understanding of Newton's First Law might be difficult, in part, because of the fact that moving bodies on the earth do slow down due to "invisible forces." Second, perceptual illusion can lead to incorrect beliefs about motion. McCloskey (1983b) suggests that the "straight down" belief about a ball dropped from by a moving person could arise from the fact that with respect to the frame of reference of person dropping it, the ball does fall straight down. Finally, it has been suggested that people attempting to solve equivalent physics problems presented in different contexts may be so influenced by perceived differences in the specific situations that they find it difficult to realize the situations involve the same underlying physical principles. Ecological perceptionists, myself included, suppose that perception is typically accurate. Claims such as these present a challenge to us, one that should be met. While this is not the place to deal with the issues in detail, I will suggest some approaches that might be taken. First, since we now know that people perceive some forces in certain contexts, it is not self-evidently true that gravity, friction, and so on, are invisible. This is an empirical issue which has not yet, to my knowledge, been studied. Second, with respect to the straight down belief, it seems to me that, from the point of view of the moving observer, the object she drops really does fall straight down. Perhaps the error is cognitive, involving a failure to use the appropriate frame of reference or putting a correct perception to the wrong use.

Findings from Event Perception.   First, consider some selected results found in event perception. Among the best known are Gunnar Johansson's (1973) studies of biological motion perception. Using the point-light technique described earlier, observers shown only dots of light (attached to an actor's joints) can see immediately and with great accuracy that it is a human performing the action. Participants can easily identify the action, be it walking, dancing, or doing push-ups. Cutting and his colleagues (Cutting & Kozlowski, 1977; Cutting, Proffitt, & Kozlowski, 1978) have shown that, with this type of display, both sex and individual identity are recognized at better than chance level. Cutting et al. (1978) have argued that sex identification depends on detection of the center of moment of the moving dots, and they have performed studies demonstrating its role in the perception of point-light displays of other types of motion. Shaw and his colleagues (Mark, Todd, & Shaw, 1981; Pittenger & Shaw, 1975; Pittenger et al., 1979) found that observers presented with extremely small changes in facial shape could see that growth had occurred and could discriminate the pattern of actual growth from other patterns of shape change.

A number of recent studies have documented accurate perception of the masses of objects participating in events and of the forces underlying movement of the objects. For example, Todd and Warren (1982) have shown that patterns of velocities of colliding objects allow one to see which of a pair of objects is more massive. Using the point-light technique, Runeson and Frykholm (1981, 1983) produced films of actors lifting boxes of different weight. Observers could see that the films showed people lifting weights. Beyond that, they could estimate the weights of the boxes being lifted with striking accuracy. When I presented pendulums moving at periods incorrect for their lengths, some observers spontaneously reported "seeing" forces. Pendulums moving too fast for their lengths looked as if they were "pushed" or "driven" while ones moving too slowly were seen as "held back" or operating under "high friction" (Pittenger, 1990). Although period is independent of the mass of the bob, some of my observers saw the slow pendulums as especially heavy and the fast ones as light. Warren, Kim, and Husney (1987) have shown that the elasticity of balls can be estimated both by watching the balls bounce and by listening to bounce sounds. Finally, Warren (1984) demonstrated that observers looking at sets of stairs varying in tread and riser dimensions can accurately pick the dimensions that are the least effortful to be climbed. Since effort in stair climbing involves a complex relationship between stair and body dimensions, this result suggests rather sophisticated knowledge of physics.

Findings from Cognitive Physics.   Results of studies in cognitive physics stand in sharp contrast. Among the best-known results are those of McCloskey and coworkers (Caramazza, McCloskey, & Green, 1981; McCloskey, Caramazza, & Green, 1980). When asked to draw the path a bomb would take when dropped from an airplane, many of the participants (college students) showed the bomb falling straight down, rather than taking a parabolic path. On the other hand, if a bullet is fired through a curved tube, its path after it leaves the tube is thought to continue to be curved. Perhaps even more surprising are beliefs that free fall involves constant velocity motion (Shannon, 1976) and that the surface of a fluid in a tilted container is not horizontal (Howard, 1978). In unpublished studies, I have assessed cognitive knowledge of the law of pendulum motion via interviews and questionnaires. In sharp contrast to the perceptual studies, in which a moving pendulum was visible, I found that many people think that length is irrelevant to period or even that longer pendulums have shorter periods.

Assessments of the reasons for such erroneous predictions disclose errors both in knowledge of physics and in other aspects of cognition. For example, White (1983) had people predict the effect of various forces on the speed and direction of motion of a rocket ship. Participants tended to neglect the effect of momentum and used scalar rather than vector arithmetic in thinking about how forces combine to produce changes in motion.

False conceptions are not always isolated errors. Sometimes people hold organized, internally consistent (but physically incorrect) systems of belief. Moreover, some of these systems are much like those postulated in pre-Newtonian natural science physics. McCloskey (1983a), for example, accounts for many errors as being the result of participants' belief in an impulse theory of motion such as those commonly held in the Middle Ages. Shannon's (1976) results about the perception of velocity in free fall are like beliefs held by Aristotle. Such findings arguments are important since they bear on how we should appropriately conceptualize people's beliefs and the nature of the in-dividual's development from a novice to an expert. Whether or not naïve beliefs are actually equivalent to the ideas of now outdated theories in natural science physics is a matter of some debate. Wiser and Carey (1983) hold that researchers often claim equivalency on the basis of insufficient evidence.

Studies of Children.   The difference in results found in adults studied by the perceptual and cognitive approaches also appears to hold for children. Piaget's well-known cognitive studies showed serious errors in numerous aspects of physics in early childhood. As children grow older, systematic changes in conceptualization result in improved performance. Kaiser, Proffitt, and McClos-key (1985) studied children's predictions of the path a ball would take if rolled off the edge of a table or dumped over the edge from a moving toy train. Kindergartners and preschoolers frequently hold the "straight-down" belief and, depending on particular experimental conditions, showed various degrees of increased accuracy with increasing age. Kaiser and Proffitt (1984) showed children and adults moving collision displays like Todd and Warren's and moving weight lifting displays like Runeson and Frykholm's. Observers of all ages were able to judge weights well, though with adults superior to second and fourth graders and both groups superior to kindergartners.[2] (The chapter by Brewer and Samarapungavan in this volume should be consulted for a more general review of children's knowledge of the world.)

Effects of Formal Instruction.   Finally, it has been shown that error can persist despite formal instruction in natural science physics. Trowbridge and McDermott (1980, 1981) studied the conceptions of velocity and acceleration of students receiving physics instruction at various levels of sophistication. Errors frequently persisted even after several weeks of instruction on the relevant concepts. Clement (1982) showed that many students, including upper-level engineering majors, held the view that continuing motion in a given direction implies a continuing force in that direction (i.e., in accord with Galileo's but not Newton's concepts). Peters (1982) found that velocity, acceleration, and inertia were confused with force by students in a highly selective honors section of a college physics course.

Discussion of the Important Differences in Results.   Overall, there seems to be a strong difference in the general trends in the results of two approaches. What is to be made of these differences?

First, it may turn out that the differences are less severe than I have supposed. Perceptionists are, after all, looking for demonstrations of accurate perception. They generally have good intuitions about what displays will work. Moreover, failures to perceive are rarely reported or analyzed in depth. Cognitivists with pedagogical concerns are trying to isolate false naïve beliefs that reduce the effectiveness of formal instruction. Correct naïve beliefs are not of such urgent concern. In addition, cognitivists often report percentages of participants with correct and with incorrect beliefs and then further investigate and report on errors. Perceptionists often report descriptive statistics, thereby burying errors in the means. (Being guilty of this last myself, perhaps I can cite the problem without undue offense.) Thus, the apparent difference in knowledge shown by the two approaches may, in part, be a methodological artifact. The two groups of researchers are looking at different phenomena and both are meeting with success.

---

[2]*Two menaces to our youth.* With tongue at least partly in cheek, I would draw your attention to the physics being taught to viewers of children's cartoons and to those playing video games. Saturday morning cartoons show Carebears sliding down rainbows and walking on clouds. Roadrunner cartoons show anomalous behavior of catapults and constant velocity free fall. When Wiley E. Coyote runs off the edge of a cliff, he translates first horizontally and then straight down. Often the physics becomes truly cognitive: Wiley moves horizontally until he becomes aware that he is unsupported—only then does he fall straight down. In video games, we see constant velocity-free fall, anomalous changes in velocity as objects collide, and speeding space ships making right angle turns and instantaneous stops. Worse, the player controls these motions, thus learning ways of interacting that could be erroneously applied to actual physical systems.

However, some of the differences are real. A few phenomena have been studied with both techniques and some differences continue to be found. Kaiser and Proffitt's (1984) studies on weight lifting and collisions found poorer performance when subjects viewed sequences of static pictures selected from a moving display than when they viewed the moving displays. Kaiser and Proffitt (1986) showed static and moving CRT displays simulating correct and incorrect trajectories of severed bobs. Physically anomalous paths were better detected in moving displays than in static ones. Finally, recall my cognitive and perceptual studies of pendulum motion. There too, responses to moving displays led to evidence of more accurate knowledge of the underlying physics.

Frustratingly, presentation of moving displays for perceptual judgements does not always lead to high accuracy. For example, in his studies of the water-level principle, Howard (1978) showed movies of a clear pitcher holding a dark fluid being tilted away from the vertical position. Some viewers judged 5-degree deviations of the water level from horizontal as natural. These results are like those he found using static photographs.

While this viewpoint can provide a partial understanding of the difference in results of the two approaches, it does not address a fundamental issue. Are we to suppose that there are two forms of knowledge, one tacit and perceptual and one explicit and cognitive? If so, we are then faced with the problem of accounting for how these two systems of knowledge arise, how "penetrable" each is by the other, and so on. Alternatively, it could be that we have only a single form of knowledge, one which is activated to various degrees in accord with the particular tasks at hand and the currently available sources of information. While these questions are central to the general problem of characterizing knowledge of physics, they are not the sort of questions psychologists have, in other areas, shown much success at resolving.

Conceptions of Error

My second generalization concerns the problem of how to define "correct" and "uncorrect" physical knowledge. Most workers in cognitive physics and event perception use natural science physics as the baseline against which to judge the correctness of laypeople's beliefs. From this perspective, concepts not in accord with natural science are wrong, predictions not in accord with those of physics are errors, and the lack of use of available perceptual information constitutes a failure of the perceptual system. Natural science physics is, after all, one of the great successes of human intellect. Except for micro- and macrophenomena not directly relevant to everyday life, Newtonian mechanics is about as "true" as any complex system of empirically based ideas civilization has devised.

Proffitt and Gilden (1989) have recently suggested that people can make effective use of only a single dimension of information when making judgments about dynamical events. Their proposal predicts that errors in judgment will occur for multidimensional systems when the accurate judgement can only be based on multidimensional quantities. In one test of this theory, Gilden and Proffitt's (1989) observers estimated the relative mass of two objects colliding in two dimensions. Observers were unable to synthesize the angles and speeds of the objects as is needed to estimate the mass ratio in accord with the conservation laws for energy and momentum. They propose a pair of heuristics for these judgments, one based on the angles of the objects' trajectories and one based on postcollision velocities. The relative salience of angles and velocities were found to vary among different patterns of collisions.

I see enough suggestions for the use of what could be called heuristic physical knowledge to give us pause to reconsider what we should mean by "error." By "heuristic" I mean a belief, mental rule, or pattern of perceptual judgment that, while wrong or oversimplified from the point of view of natural science physics, is useful. That is, it allows sufficiently accurate predictions, is sufficient to guide interaction safely with a physical system, to meet everyday purposes in commonly occurring situations, and so on. More simply, it is a way of thinking, reasoning or perceiving that really isn't "right" but does well enough to help us get by.

Analyses of people's use of heuristics will require us to take into account both context and purpose. For example, people may not have a single conception of the paths taken by freely falling objects. It may matter whether a person is in the plane from which an object is dropped or is on the ground observing the object fall. Also, choice of heuristic may depend on whether the person is trying to hit a target with the object, is attempting to catch the falling object or is passively observing the fall while attempting to predict where the object will land. In a heuristics approach "correctness" and "error" become relative concepts.

The notion of heuristic is not new to cognitive or perceptual psychology. It is widely used in analysis of human pattern recognition and decision making. In visual perception, Braunstein (1976) has used the concept in his theory of how depth is extracted from motion patterns. David Lee and his colleagues (Lee, 1976; Lee, Lishman, & Thomson, 1982; Lee & Reddish, 1981) have studied the role of the tau variable in the pattern of light to the eye when observers are making predictions of their impending collision with some object or surface. The variable is strictly accurate only for wholly rigid objects moving at constant velocity along a straight line. However, it has been shown to be used by humans and animals to guide behavior successfully even when motion is not strictly linear or of constant velocity.

Given researchers' commitment to natural science physics, it is not surprising that the notion of heuristics has not been greatly pursued. However, some suggestive results are available. For example, in Todd and Warren's studies of collision, the ratio of the masses is actually specified by the ratio of the changes in the velocities of the two objects before and after collisions. However, people frequently seem to attend to the ratio of the two postcollision velocities. This does lead to correct choice of the greater mass, but only for a range of velocities, masses, and elasticities.

In my perceptual studies of pendulum motion, people seemed to see period as proportional to length rather than the scientifically correct square root of length. This rule is sufficient to guide adjustment of pendulum clocks (which, to the shame of this ecological psychologist, may be the only practical purpose to which this aspect of the pendulum law is commonly put). Participants in my cognitive tasks had great difficulty keeping clear about the difference between period and angular velocity. Also, virtually all were unaware of the near-invariance of period under changes in arc of swing. All of this may be no great surprise if you consider the pendulum with which many of us have had considerable experience; the playground swing. Velocity is what the swinging child cares about, not period.[3]

Going outside of mechanics for a moment, naïve theories of the home thermostat reveal an interesting heuristic. Kempton (1986) found that 25% to 50% of Americans hold some version of the "valve theory" of thermostat operation. That is, they view raising the temperature on the thermostat as "opening a valve," which lets heat flow out at a higher rate. Note that while this is not true from an engineering perspective, actual furnace behavior is partly predicted: For a given outside temperature, the furnace runs more often and for longer periods at a higher setting. Moreover, the valve theory can be more functional in some circumstances than a correct but incomplete theory. If the weather turns colder, the valve theory tells you to turn up the thermostat if you want to keep warm. The feedback theory says to leave it alone. The actual temperature in various rooms will be influenced by heat loss as a function of outside temperature and by patterns of unequal heat delivery among rooms. Thus, action based on the value theory will keep corner rooms and ones with poor heat delivery warmer than will action guided by the feedback theory. The feedback theory, of course, could be used effectively, but only if supplemented by an understanding of patterns of heat loss and delivery.

I do not suggest that everything called an "error" from the natural science perspective will turn out to involve pragmatically effective heuristics. People's beliefs do include many errors which lead to inappropriate behavior. However, it seems valuable to consider the accuracy of people's beliefs about physics from both the heuristic and natural science perspectives.

---

[3] I am here proposing that people's naïve theories can, legitimately, be different from those of natural science, at least as natural science theories are now formulated. Brewer and Samarapungavan (this volume) discuss the relation between children's theories and those of scientists, arguing that they are more similar than generally supposed. My proposal might serve as a supplement to Brewer and Samarapungavan's: Some of the proported differences in the content of the two sorts of theories are real but stem from differences in the goals of the theories and the functional contexts in which they operate.

The Role of Behavior

My final generalization is that people tend to have more accurate knowledge of systems with which they actually interact rather than simply observe. This is no surprise. If you have considerable experience in dealing with a system (and if your accuracy in doing this matters in your life) then you ought to be good at dealing with the system. Still, the notion has not received as much attention as it might. Consider phenomena supporting the claim of high accuracy. First, there is a wide variety of relevant research on the perceptual guidance of behavior. Since this work is discussed elsewhere in this volume let me simply point out that perceptual guidance of one's own behavior often requires that you be able to predict some aspects of a system's future behavior as it will proceed without your intervention and as it will proceed given certain action of your own. This, again in some sense, implies a knowledge of the way the system works.

Second, many everyday examples illustrate the importance of knowledge of physics in guiding behavior. Many people are very proficient at games such as tennis, basketball, and billiards. Elasticity, spin, angles of incidence and reflection, magnitude and timing of the application of forces are all central to effective play. The relevant natural science physics is complex, and in places, not fully worked out. (Jearl Walker's "The Amateur Scientist" column in *Scientific American* often presents the physics underlying sports. For example, see his 1983 essay on billiards.)

Here we start shading into the areas of expert knowledge and perceptual learning. That is, many children are experts at controlling swings, many billiard players are experts at controlling collisions, and violin makers are experts at devising instruments with subtle vibratory properties. While there is a growing body of research into expert knowledge of skills such as chess and medical diagnosis, psychologists have rarely studied the cognitive skills of people sophisticated at controlling physical systems. Researchers outside of psychology, however, are providing suggestive analyses. Hutchins (1981) has shown that three modes of vibration of the back of a violin influence the ultimate sound of instrument. He has observed that, when shaping the back plate, expert violin makers flex it in three ways—just the ways that assess the three important modes of vibration.

Research on event perception also provides some support for the claimed accuracy of knowledge of events with which the observer has had prior experience in controlling. For example, in Runeson and Frykholm's (1981, 1983) studies of perception of weight lifting, note that the subjects of the experiment will have lifted many objects themselves. Warren's (1984) studies of perceived effort used as participants people who have climbed stairs with many variations in riser and tread size. Solomon and Turvey (1988) have shown that observers can perceive the distance reachable by rods which they hold and wield but cannot see. Distance estimates correlated highly with moments of inertia of the hand-rod system, suggesting that the observers' interactions with the rods generate information about the rods' lengths.

Overall, we see knowledge of physics as important in the guidance of actual motor behavior, and such knowledge can apparently influence perception. This fact suggests another question about the possible forms of knowledge. Is there a third form, behavioral, along with cognitive and perceptual, or is knowledge more unified, being engaged to different degrees by the task and information at hand?

A Caution

These three generalizations may be premature. The studies performed to date vary in so many factors that comparisons among them are difficult. These factors include: particular laws studied, information available in displays, tasks set for observers, type of data recorded and statistical analysis made. Thus, while it seems that each generalization has reasonably strong empirical support, they must be taken as tentative proposals.

FUTURE DIRECTIONS FOR RESEARCH

To date, researchers have amassed considerable factual information about people's knowledge of physics, and have developed a number of theoretical formulations to make sense of the facts. However, the empirical research is somewhat patchy. We do not yet have a systematic data base, one with enough breadth in the aspects of physics studied or enough depth on any single aspect of physics, on which to answer the major theoretical questions. In addition, I do not see much agreement on what the major questions are. Lest I be misunderstood, please realize that I do think we have found a significant body of well-documented and theoretically important factual information. Researchers have, in addition, derived important insight from that information. However, the time may be right to become more systematic, applying more thoughtfully our diversity of methods so as to address better articulated fundamental questions. The remainder of this chapter will be devoted to some suggestions, perhaps presumptuous, on how we might proceed.

Problems to be Solved

Understanding the forms that knowledge of physics takes is surely one truly basic goal. Are there really separable behavioral, perceptual, and cognitive forms, or is knowledge somehow unitary? Second, there is the problem of the engagement of knowledge: How do the particular ways a problem is presented (either in everyday life or laboratory situations), the tasks set for the observer, and the perceptual information available influence the knowledge applied to the problem? Third, how does a form of knowledge, once activated, serve to guide behavior, enter into event perception, and influence problem solving?

These three problems are all intimately tied together. For example, the problem of how knowledge is engaged surely depends, in part, on what form the knowledge takes. Also, there are many alternative processing notions used by researchers in the areas of cognition, perception, and behavior control. Which of these will be useful in characterizing people's use of knowledge of physics will depend on the nature of that knowledge.

Looking back on the problems formulated here, it dawns on me that I have reconstructed a list of problems that are currently of urgent concern to those working on basic issues in the development of general theories of psychology. Since these problems have proven recalcitrant, we might be pessimistic about prospects for their solution with respect to knowledge of physics. On the other hand, study of knowledge of physics may well provide us with an attractive opportunity for progress. Resolution of these problems seems more urgent and less avoidable here than elsewhere. If you study how people solve arithmetic problems, it is perhaps easier to ignore the results of event perception. If you study depth perception you can ignore research in problem solving. On the other hand, if you are interested in knowledge of physics, the results found so far seem to cry for a broad, integrative approach.

Suggestions for Research

Switching to the empirical level, I would propose that we reconsider our research strategies. In particular, I see the need to:

1. Become more systematic in how we study a given aspect of physics,
2. Broaden the set of phenomena we study,
3. Take seriously the notion of heuristics and, thereby, reconceive criteria for claiming that error occurs.

First, in collecting our data we should consider a more systematic variation of the tasks set for participants and the information available to them. Thus, when an aspect of physics knowledge is studied, moving displays should be used as well as static ones and the actual physical system in its full complexity should be presented as well as simplified one having precise control over selected variables. Also, observers should make perceptual judgments and act so as to control the system, as well as make cognitive judgments and describe their reasoning processes. This sort of research should help give theorists a much more complete picture of people's knowledge of the system. It should also be of use to educators who are concerned with the impact of naïve physics knowledge on the effectiveness of instruction. It seems reasonable for science educators to build on the knowledge students bring to courses and to confront their false beliefs directly. Basic researchers could help educators by providing a fuller survey of students' knowledge.

My second suggestion follows from a concern about our selection of areas of physical knowledge to study. To a considerable extent, cognitive physics stresses the sort of phenomena analyzed in elementary physics texts. The phenomena are, in a way, everyday sorts of events. Notice, though, that these analyses often entail crucial simplifications, such as point masses, zero friction and so on. Event perception workers have their own biases in selection of phenomena. For example, the existence of mathematical specifications of available information often influences the selection of displays to be presented to observers. Also, when the researcher has a theoretical point to make, it is natural to find a phenomenon whose perceptual properties will allow that point to be illustrated. While these ways of selecting phenomena for study have yielded important results, other selection criteria also have merit. If we wish to assess what people know about physics, we might first think about just what aspects of physics they could reasonably be expected to have learned. That is, some effort should be devoted to analyses of the situations in everyday life where people actually need to make use of knowledge of physics. Ball games and children's swings were mentioned earlier. Other possibilities come easily to mind: Levers are used to pry nails from boards, hammers are used to drive nails, joggers turn and stop without sliding, and so on.

The study of such phenomena would give a broader picture of people's knowledge of physics. It is not self-evident that fair conclusions about the general accuracy of knowledge, sophistication of reasoning processes, and so on will emerge unless we are appropriately systematic in choosing the aspects of physics to study. Cognitive physics may tend to underestimate knowledge and event perception to overestimate it—simply on the basis of what they have chosen to study. I do not say we should abandon the cases now being studied. Rather, we should broaden our bases for selection of phenomena, taking into account what is important to everyday life.

This second suggestion has implications for science education. The notions that students' correct beliefs might be built upon and that errors need to be confronted explicitly were mentioned earlier. I would now add that educators need to know what correct and false beliefs their students have of a broad selection of phenomena, not just of those common in standard textbooks. If we want the knowledge of science that is gained in the classroom to be generalized to everyday life, we should be clear about the phenomena in everyday life to which we want that knowledge to generalize. Along this line, it is interesting to note that journals for professionals in physics education, such as *American Journal of Physics* and *Physics Teacher*, publish many articles giving natural science analyses of everyday events. Teachers, therefore, seem to attach importance to such phenomena. (Also, these analyses provide researchers with tools to use in studies of naïve knowledge of the phenomena.)

Finally, I suggest we include study of heuristics in our assessments of the accuracy of people's beliefs and the adequacy of their reasoning. In dealing with the everyday world, people can be expected to be satisfied with ideas and reasoning strategies that work well enough to meet their needs in the situations they encounter. It is, of course, also important to compare naïve beliefs with the results of natural science physics. Thus, we should not abandon this baseline but rather add to it. By including the heuristic notion, we can help develop a broader and thus a more accurate picture of naïve knowledge. Moreover, there may be educational implications. Beliefs that are heuristically adequate, but wrong from the natural science point of view, might be expected to be especially resistant to change via formal instruction.

CONCLUSIONS

The study of people's knowledge of physics is proving to be a fascinating area. Knowledge of physics is an important area because it both bears on deep theoretical concerns and has strong implication for education. Many interesting phenomena have been studied, with striking errors shown juxtaposed to surprising accuracy and subtlety of knowledge. Since the area is relatively young, goals, methods and theory are in flux, with coherent themes only starting to emerge. The time, therefore, seems ripe for reflection on what we are doing. Workers in cognition, perception, and action can, I think, benefit from more attention to each others' research. In addition, consideration of the ecological validity of the phenomena we study and of how we evaluate the accuracy beliefs may be of value. It appears to me that a growing number of researchers are thinking along these lines. Thus, rather than proposing radical changes I may simply be reporting changes as they are occurring. In any case, for students of people's knowledge of physics the times are most interesting, and promising.

ACKNOWLEDGMENTS

Preparation of this chapter was supported by the Marie Wilson Howells Bequest to the Psychology Department at the University of Arkansas at Little Rock.

The author thanks the editors for comments on an earlier draft of this chapter. While they, of course, are not responsible for the remaining errors, the author does wish to foist off some of the blame on Jim Jenkins.

The author's research interest is in the specification of the visual information available for the perception of events. His graduate training at the University of Minnesota was supervised by James J. Jenkins. The author wishes to thank his mentor for insisting that the old lore be learned, for reminding him that, while theory development is important, one must never let the psychological phenomena become secondary to theory, and for forcing him to understand the statistics he would so rashly compute and report.

REFERENCES

Bozzi, P. (1958). Analisi fenomenologica del moto pendolare armonico. *Rivista di Psicologia, 52*, 281–302.

Braunstein, M. L. (1976). *Depth perception through motion*. New York: Academic Press.

Caramazza, A., McCloskey, M., & Green, B. (1981). Naive beliefs in "sophisticated" subjects: Misconceptions about trajectories of objects. *Cognition, 9*, 117–123.

Clement, J. (1982). Students' preconceptions in introductory mechanics. *American Journal of Physics, 50*, 66–71.

Cutting, J. E., & Kozlowski, L. T. (1977). Recognizing friends by their walk: Gait perception without familiarity cues. *Bulletin of the Psychonomic Society, 9*, 353–356.

Cutting, J. E., Proffitt, D. R., & Kozlowski, L. T. (1978). A biomechanical invariant for gait perception. *Journal of Experimental Psychology: Human Perception and Performance, 4*, 357–372.

Freyd, J. J., Pantzer, T. M., & Cheng, J. L. (1988). Representing statistics as forces in equilibrium. *Journal of Experimental Psychology: General, 117*, 395–407.

Gentner, D., & Gentner, D. R. (1983). Flowing waters or teeming crowds: Mental models of electricity. In D. Gentner & A. Stevens (Eds.), *Mental models* (pp. 99–129). Hillsdale, NJ: Lawrence Erlbaum Associates.

Gilden, D. L., & Proffitt, D. R. (1989). Understanding collision dynamics. *Journal of Experimental Psychology: Human Perception and Performance, 15*, 372–383.

Howard, I. P. (1978). Recognition and knowledge of the water-level principle. *Perception, 7*, 151–160.

Hutchins, C. M. (1981, October). The acoustics of violin plates. *Scientific American, 245*, 171–186.

Jenkins, J. J. (1985). Acoustic information for objects, places, and events. In W. H. Warren, Jr., & R. E. Shaw (Eds.): *Persistence and change: Proceedings of the first international conference on event perception* (pp. 115–138). HIllsdale, NJ: Lawrence Erlbaum Associates.

Johansson, G. (1973). Visual perception of biological motion and a model for its analysis. *Perception and Psychophysics, 14*, 201–211.

Kaiser, M. K., & Proffitt, D. R. (1984). The development of sensitivity to causally relevant dynamic information. *Child Development, 55*, 1614–1624.

Kaiser, M. K., & Proffitt, D. R. (1986, November). *Swingtime: Observers' sensitivity to the dynamics of pendulums*. Paper presented at the Psychonomic Society meeting, New Orleans.

Kaiser, M. K., Proffitt, D. R., & McCloskey, M. (1985). The development of beliefs about falling objects. *Perception and Psychophysics, 38*, 533–539.

Kempton, W. (1986). Two theories of home heat control. *Cognitive Science, 10*, 75–90.

Larkin, J. H. (1983). The role of problem representation in physics. In D. Gentner & A. L. Stevens (Eds.), *Mental models* (pp. 75–98). Hillsdale, NJ: Lawrence Erlbaum Associates.

Lee, D. N. (1976). A theory of visual control of braking based on information about time-to-collision. *Perception, 5*, 437–459.

Lee, D. N., Lishman, J. R., & Thomson, J. A. (1982). Visual regulation of gait in long jumping. *Journal of Experimental Psychology: Human Performance and Perception, 8,* 448–459.

Lee, D. N., & Reddish, P. E. (1981). Plummeting gannets: A paradigm of ecological optics. *Nature,* 293–294.

Mark, L. S., Todd, J. T., & Shaw, R. E. (1981). Perception of growth: A gemometric analysis of how different styles of change are distinguished. *Journal of Experimental Psychology: Human Perception and Performance, 7,* 855–868.

McCloskey, M. (1983a). Naive theories of motion. In D. Gentner & A. L. Stevens (Eds.), *Mental models* (pp. 229–323). Hillsdale, NJ: Lawrence Erlbaum Associates.

McCloskey, M. (1983b). Intuitive physics. *Scientific American, 248*(4), 122–130.

McCloskey, M., Caramazza, A., & Green, B. (1980). Curvilinear motion in the absence of external forces: Naive beliefs about the motion of objects. *Science, 210,* 1139–1141.

Peters, P. C. (1982). Even honors students have conceptual difficulties with physics. *American Journal of Physics, 50,* 501–508.

Pittenger, J. B. (1990). Detection of violations of the law of pendulum motion: Observers' sensitivity to the relation between period and length. *Ecological Psychology, 2,* 55–81.

Pittenger, J. B., & Shaw, R. E. (1975). Aging faces as viscal-elastic events: Implications for a theory of non-rigid shape perception. *Journal of Experimental Psychology: Human Perception and Performance. 1.* 374 382.

Pittenger, J. B., Shaw, R. E., & Mark, L. S. (1979). Perceptual Information for the age level of faces as a higher order invariant of growth. *Journal of Experimental Psychology: Human Perception and Performance, 5,* 478–493.

Proffitt, D. R., & Gilden, D. L. (1989). Understanding natural dynamics. *Journal of Experimental Psychology: Human Perception and Performance, 15,* 384–393.

Roncato, S., & Rumiati, R. (1986). Naive statics: Current misconceptions on equilibrium. *Journal of Experimental Psychology: Learning Memory, and Cognition, 12,* 361–377.

Runeson, S., & Frykholm, G. (1981). Visual perception of lifted weight. *Journal of Experimental Psychology: Human Perception and Performance, 7,* 733–740.

Runeson, S., & Frykholm, G. (1983). Kinematic specification of dynamics as an informational basis for person and action perception: Expectation, gender recognition, and deceptive intention. *Journal of Experimental Psychology: General, 112,* 585–615.

Shannon, B. (1976). Aristotelianism, Newtonianism, and the physics of the layman. *Perception, 5,* 241–243.

Shaw, R., & Pittenger, J. (1979). Perceiving change. In H. Pick, Jr. & E. Saltzman (Eds.), *Modes of perceiving and processing information.* (pp. 187–204). Hillsdale, NJ: Lawrence Erlbaum Associates.

Solomon, H. Y., & Turvey, M. T. (1988). Haptically perceiving the distance reachable with hand-held objects. *Journal of Experimental Psychology: Human Perception and Performance, 14,* 404–427.

Todd, J., & Warren, W. (1982). Visual perception opf relative mass in dynamic events. *Perception, 11,* 325–335.

Trowbridge, D. E., & McDermott, L. C. (1980). Investigation of student understanding of the concept of velocity in one dimension. *American Journal of Physics, 48,* 1020–1028.

Trowbridge, D. E., & McDermott, L. C. (1981). Investigation of student understanding of the concept of acceleration in one dimension. *American Journal of Physics, 49,* 242–253.

Walker, J. (1983, July). The amateur scientist: The physics of the follow, the draw, and the massé (in billiards and pool). *Scientific American, 249,* 124–129.

Warren, W. H. (1984). Perceiving affordances: Visual guidance of stair climbing. *Journal of Experimental Psychology: Human Perception and Performance, 10,* 683–703.

Warren, W. H., Kim, E. E., & Husney, R. (1987). The way the ball bounces: Visual and auditory perception of elasticity and control of the bounce pass. *Perception, 16,* 309–336.

Warren, W. H., & Shaw, R. E. (1985b). Events and encounters as units of analysis for ecological psychology. In W. Warren & R. Shaw (Eds.), Persistence and change. Proceedings of the first International Conference on Event Perception (pp. 1–27). Hillsdale, NJ: Lawrence Erlbaum Associates.

White, B. Y. (1983). Sources of difficulty in understanding Newtonian dynamics. *Cognitive Science*, 7, 41–65.

Wiser, M., & Carey, S. (1983). When heat and temperature were one. In D. Gentner & A. Stevens (Eds.), *Mental models* (pp. 267–297). Hillsdale, NJ: Lawrence Erlbaum Associates.

16

Mathematical Cognition: Accomplishments and Challenges in Research

James G. Greeno
Stanford University and Institute for Research on Learning

INTRODUCTION

This chapter presents an overview of recent research about knowledge and cognitive processes in mathematical problem solving and reasoning. I discuss broad trends that I illustrate with examples; this is not a thorough review of research findings. The chapter has three main sections. First, I discuss research accomplishments that have been achieved in the period from the mid-1970s to the present. The dominant goal of this research has been to understand the knowledge structures that are required for successful performance of school tasks.

Second, I discuss an alternative that many consider preferable to the idea of acquiring knowledge structures as the goal of mathematics education. Rather than focusing on the content of mathematics, instruction could attempt to provide abilities for thinking mathematically and cognitive resources for reasoning in situations other than classrooms. I discuss recent research findings in cognitive anthropology and developmental psychology that support the feasibility of these deeper goals of mathematics education and suggest some features of instruction that could be effective in reaching these goals.

Third, I discuss two general theoretical concepts about knowledge that seem particularly germane to the goals of mathematics education: the situated and the generative character of knowledge. I describe some research related to these concepts, including some recent and current projects in instructional research and development, as illustrations of research directions that could inform educational development in the service of deeper instructional objectives.

THE "KNOWLEDGE STRUCTURE PROGRAM"

Cognitive Models as Instructional Objectives

A program of research that became feasible in the mid-1970s has turned out to be remarkably productive and successful. The idea of formulating objectives of instruction in the form of cognitive models that simulate performance in school tasks was discussed at a conference held in 1974, sponsored by the Office of Naval Research (Klahr, 1976). Hayes (1976) put the idea as follows:

> Cognitive objectives in education [are] intended to replace the more traditional behavioral objectives. To specify a behavior objective for instruction, we state a particular set of behaviors we want the students to be able to perform after instruction, e.g., to solve a specified class of arithmetic problems, or to answer questions about a chapter in a history text. To specify a cognitive objective, we state a set of changes we want the instruction to bring about in the students' cognitive processes, e.g., acquisition of a particular algorithm for division or the assimilation of a body of historical fact to information already in long-term memory. (pp. 235–236)

Examples of this idea of cognitive objectives include processing models of the procedural knowledge needed to solve arithmetic exercises, processing models of the knowledge for setting goals, recognizing patterns, and performing inferences for solving proof exercises in high school geometry, and models of the semantic networks needed to answer text-based questions in psychology (Greeno, 1976a).

Relevant Advances in Cognitive Psychology

The goal of formulating instructional objectives in the form of cognitive models seemed a feasible program at the time because of two important advances in cognitive psychology that had just emerged: the development of models of problem solving and of language understanding. A seminal psychological model of knowledge used in solving novel problems by Newell and Simon (1972) established the feasibility both of using ideas developed in artificial intelligence as a basis for developing hypotheses about human cognition, and of the method of testing those hypotheses by using thinking-aloud protocols obtained while individuals work on problems. Newell and Simon characterized general strategies of problem solving, including means–ends analysis, that can be used to solve problems effectively when an individual without special instruction in a domain is given instructions about the states and operators that can be used to solve a puzzle. Production rules are used to represent knowledge for cognitive activity. In a system of production rules, each rule specifies a pattern of information and a subsequent action, which may be a physical action or a cognitive action, such as a decision or an inference. The action is performed whenever the condition is true in the situation.

A later development, important for modeling knowledge for school tasks, was a model of knowledge for planning, by Sacerdoti (1977), which characterizes knowledge about actions in a domain with their consequences and prerequisites so that a planner can construct sequences of actions to achieve goals.

At about the same time, there were significant advances in artificial intelligence and cognitive psychology regarding the knowledge and cognitive processes that are involved in understanding language. Winograd (1972) developed a system that takes English sentences as input and constructs programs for examining and manipulating objects in a miniature environment. Schank (1972) developed a system that converts English sentences to structures of information about the actions and situations that the sentences describe.

Anderson and Bower (1973), Kintsch (1974), Norman, Rumelhart, and the LNR Research Group (1975), and others, developed psychological models that simulate understanding of language based on the use of schematic knowledge and propositional structures to form representations of meanings of sentences and paragraphs of text. Meanings of specific sentences are represented as semantic networks in which concepts mentioned in the sentences correspond to nodes and links correspond to relations among the concepts. Knowledge in the form of schemata provides generic structures that the understander uses to construct the semantic networks that represent the meanings of specific sentences and situations. The outcome of understanding is a knowledge base that can be used to answer questions, either by retrieving information that was included directly in material that was understood, or by retrieving information that was inferred as part of the process of understanding, or by making inferences based on information that was understood and remembered.

Progress in Research

Several investigators in the mid-1970s began to work on the idea that the concepts and methods of cognitive psychology could be used in understanding what students need to learn to succeed in school instruction. The research effort that I call the "Knowledge Structure Program" takes tasks that are used in instruction and constructs models of the knowledge required to perform the tasks successfully. Students' learning is tested by questions they are asked and by problems they are required to solve. Data used to guide construction of the models may include detailed analyses of successful student performance, often including thinking-aloud protocols. Data may also include characteristic errors of performance or reasoning, with models having explicit features that overcome those difficulties. Some analyses have been based mainly on considerations of the structure of subject-matter concepts and the experience of teachers regarding student difficulties. The strongest work has combined insights into the structure of subject-matter concepts with empirical and theoretical analyses of students' successful performance and their difficulties of understanding and learning.

Significant progress of this kind has been made in several domains of school mathematics. First, cognitive procedures for solving routine problems of calculation have been simulated for elementary arithmetic (Brown & Burton, 1980) and algebra (Sleeman, 1984). This includes detailed hypotheses about the incorrect cognitive procedures of students who make systematic errors as well as the structure of procedures acquired by students who succeed. Data used to test these models are primarily the patterns of correct responses and errors that are obtained in students' test performance. Thus, the model explains the sets of specific responses that students give, rather than just how many items are correct. A contribution to artificial intelligence was made in Burton's (1982) system DE-BUGGY, which diagnoses flawed procedures from patterns of test data.

A contribution to the methodology of cognitive science was made in Van Lehn's dissertation (1983; also see VanLehn, Brown, & Greeno, 1984) where a model of learning was developed and tested by its ability to generate the class of systematic flaws that have been diagnosed in students' performance in subtraction. A model of cognitive structures involved in understanding the place-value concepts underlying the subtraction procedure in terms of part–whole relations was developed and tested in an instructional experiment by Resnick and Omanson (in press).

Ideas about language understanding have been combined with problem-solving hypotheses in models of schematic and procedural knowledge for solving word problems in elementary arithmetic (Briars & Larkin, 1984; Kintsch & Greeno, 1985; Riley & Greeno, 1988). These models have been tested with data on children's performance on different word problems, with the tests based on predictions of the models of which kinds of problems should be more difficult than others (Briars & Larkin, 1984; Riley & Greeno, 1988). Kintsch (1986) tested hypotheses about properties of problem representations, using data obtained by asking children to repeat problems verbally.

Simulations of problem-solving procedures of successful students in high school geometry have also been developed (Greeno, 1978). Data used in developing the model were mainly thinking-aloud protocols obtained from students who were interviewed during the year they took a course in geometry. The data were sufficient to show the need for significant modifications to Newell and Simon's (1972) version of means–ends analysis. The phenomena, involving open-ended search for information relevant to a general goal and processes for adding lines to diagrams, were explained with hypotheses about domain-specific schematic knowledge of general patterns that enables flexible search and planning (Greeno, 1976b; Greeno, Magone, & Chaiklin, 1979). The idea about schematic knowledge for planning provides an explanation for one kind of problem-solving set, and experimental tests of that implication of the idea were successful (Greeno et al., 1979). A promising simulation of learning has been provided in the domain of high school geometry (Anderson, 1983), and a tutoring system based in part on that model has been developed and is being tested in schools (Anderson, Boyle, Farrell, & Reiser, 1984). An idea about understanding a proof in geometry according to part–whole relations that Wertheimer (1945/1959) discussed was put into the form of a computer program that simulates meaningful learning and contrasts it to a more rote version, and the simulation was used successfully to interpret problem-solving protocols of several students (Greeno, 1983).

Models of knowledge required for successful performance are potentially quite important for instruction, especially when they reveal aspects of knowledge that are impicit in performance. Implicit knowledge includes the patterns of information that students need to recognize in understanding word problems, or the constraints of a computational procedure, or the search strategies that are used to organize problem-solving activity. By making some of these usually tacit components of knowledge explicit, students who would otherwise fail to acquire the knowledge that is needed for success might be able to succeed. A system for instruction in word problems using a computer graphics display to construct semantic networks was developed by Shalin and Bee (Greeno, et al., 1986; also see Greeno, 1987), and a system that displays the search path in geometry was developed by Anderson et al. (1984). Empirical evaluations of these systems are currently in progress.

The analyses that have been developed do not include all the topics in the school mathematics curriculum, by any means. However, the feasibility of projects that would develop models of knowledge for the remaining topics seems well established. Remaining to be analyzed are topics such as rational number computation, ratios, percentages, symbolic algebra, and graphing. Cognitive analyses in these and other domains undoubtedly will require significant effort and nontrivial insight. Even so, with a reasonable investment of scientific resources, it would not be surprising if a quite complete set of analyses of the standard precollege mathematics curriculum could be assembled within 5 to 10 years.

A feature of the research on mathematical cognition in the past 15 years or so has been its emphasis on descriptions of cognitive structures and processes. This contrasts to most of the research on human learning and memory that was conducted during several previous decades, where the emphasis was on identifying conditions that would increase or decrease the *amount* of memory for information that is studied. Jenkins (1979, p. 444) noted that a major finding of research in the decade beginning in the late 1960s was that "interaction, contextual sensitivity with respect to all our variables, is the pattern—not the exception." He concluded that "simple laws will not capture the phenomena that we have recorded in so many diverse ways," and recommended two paths of research: "to concentrate on the range of variables involved in particular problems of importance to us for ecological, practical reasons," and "to explore the range of applicability of our generalizations through a 'science by challenge' procedure." The research on mathematical cognition has traveled the first of these paths, although our motivations for conducting that research have been theoretical as well as ecological and practical. Most of the results provide information about the *kinds* of knowledge and memory that individuals acquire and use in their study of mathematics, rather than the *amounts* of knowledge and memory that result from different conditions. Studies involving quantitative comparisons of conditions will probably be needed to test models of learning the cognitive structures that we are not able to construct, and some studies of that kind have been conducted. Nevertheless, the major achievements in this decade of research have been in developing concepts and methods for describing the content and organization of knowledge that is involved in solving problems and understanding principles in domains where the content of knowledge plays a central role.

MORE AMBITIOUS GOALS
FOR MATHEMATICS EDUCATION

Alternative Goals and Assumptions

One consequence of having models of knowledge for tasks that describe knowledge structures specifically is the chance to reflect on whether that knowledge is what we want students to learn. The models that simulate students' performance in routine mathematical tasks emphasize limitations that have been noticed many times: Students can learn to solve the problems that are used in standard instruction without acquiring very deep understanding of the mathematical concepts and principles that the problems are meant to convey, and learning to solve problems in the context of instruction often fails to transfer significantly to other contexts.

Many individuals have wished for a deeper orientation in the teaching of mathematics. Davis (1984) put the point as follows:

> *Mathematics is presented from a wrong point of view:* it is presented as a matter of learning dead "facts" and "techniques," and *not* in terms of its true nature, which involves processes that demand thought and creativity: confronting vague situations and refining them to a sharper conceptualization; building complex knowledge representation structures in your own mind; criticizing these structures, revising them and extending them; analysing problems, employing heuristics, setting sub-goals and conducting searches in unlikely (but shrewdly-chosen) corners of your memory. (p. 347, emphasis in the original)

On this view, the goals of instruction in mathematics should be to strengthen students' abilities to understand and reason productively about the concepts and techniques of mathematics, rather than only knowing the content of the concepts and how to perform the techniques correctly.

This is a lofty goal—in effect, it proposes that students should learn to understand and reason in mathematics as mathematicians understand and reason. Opinions differ as to whether such a goal is feasible. For example, a pessimistic view was laid out by Poincare (1956).

> We know that this feeling, this intuition of mathematical order, that makes us divine hidden harmonies and relations, can not be possessed by every one. Some will not have either this delicate feeling so difficult to define, or a strength of memory and attention beyond the ordinary, and then they will be absolutely incapable of understanding higher mathematics. Such are the majority. Others will have this feeling only in a slight degree, but they will be gifted with an uncommon memory and a great power of attention. They will learn by heart the details one after another; they can understand mathematics and sometimes make applications, but they cannot create. Others, finally, will possess in a less or greater degree the special intuition referred to, and then not only can they understand mathematics even if their memory is nothing extraordinary, but they may become creators and try to invent with more or less success according as this intuition is more or less developed in them. (p. 2043)

Others are more optimistic. Davis (1984) asserted that

> "The trials of the 1950s and 1960s demonstrated that students are well able, cognitively or intellectually, to move ahead far faster in mathematics and to deal with a 'problem-analysis' and a 'heuristic' approach to mathematics" (p. 348).

And in a delightful book, *Thinking Mathematically*, Mason, Burton, and Stacey (1982, p. v) present the following optimistic message for their student readers:

ASSUMPTION 1   *You can* think mathematically
ASSUMPTION 2   Mathematical thinking can be *improved* by practice with reflection
ASSUMPTION 3   Mathematical thinking is *provoked* by contradiction, tension, and surprise
ASSUMPTION 4   Mathematical thinking is *supported* by an atmosphere of questioning, challenging, and reflecting
ASSUMPTION 5   Mathematical thinking helps in *understanding* yourself and the world

Historically, emphasis on rote training of calculation in the curriculum has been justified, in part, by a belief that most students could not achieve understanding of mathematical concepts and principles (Cohen, 1982). On the classical associationistic conception of learning, it is assumed that basic learning is the formation of bonds between ideas or between stimuli and responses, and that simple procedures such as arithmetic calculation are relatively easy to acquire (e.g., Thorndike, 1922). In that theory, conceptual understanding is harder to account for (e.g., Greeno, James, DaPolito, & Polson, 1978, Jenkins, 1979), and perhaps that theoretical difficulty has caused some individuals to expect that conceptual understanding requires exceptional ability by the learner.

Evidence from Developmental Psychology

Recent findings in developmental psychology support a very different picture of cognitive capabilities of young children than that of the classical association theory, and therefore support the feasibility of more ambitious goals for mathematics instruction. In the domain of mathematics, Gelman and Gallistel (1978) found considerable evidence that preschool children implicitly understand principles of order, one-to-one correspondence, and cardinality, rather than having only a mechanical knowledge of counting rules and procedures. A telling piece of evidence is that children can modify their counting procedure correctly when an unusual constraint is imposed. After the child had counted a set of objects, the experimenter selected one of them and said, "Now count them again, but make this the 'one.' " On different trials different objects were selected and different numerals were associated with the selected objects. Most 5-year-olds produced counting performance that complied with the novel constraints as well as the principles of counting. Because these specific counting procedures could not have been learned, the children's generative knowledge must have included implicit understanding of the principles.

Bullock, Gelman, and Baillargeon (1982) showed that preschool children make judgments about causality that reflect significant implicit understanding of principles such as temporal order (causes precede their effects), local action (causes and their effects are proximal), and mechanism (causal systems have components whose interactions collectively produce effects). Children also probably have implicit understanding of causal relations among quantities—for example, throwing something harder makes it travel farther. diSessa (1983) has used a concept of "phenomenological primitives" to analyze explanations given by adults of cause–effect relations between quantities, such as the ordinal relations between pressure, resistance, and rate of flow of a substance through a conduit. It seems likely that children's reasoning also includes primitive structures of this general kind and that these could provide a basis for meaningful learning of more definite and elaborate causal principles.

Carey (1985) and Keil (1989) have studied children's knowledge about living things, and have shown that their understanding grows in ways that reflect a structure of concepts and principles, rather than haphazard accretion of facts and experiences. Carey (1985) argued that between the ages of about 6 and 10, children's understanding of living things undergoes a profound theoretical change. In the early years of this development, children understand issues about activity, body parts, and functions such as eating on the basis of psychological concepts such as intention (e.g., people eat because they get hungry). Later, they understand these matters in terms of biological principles and concepts (e.g., people eat because food is needed to stay alive and grow).

Keil (1989) has provided compelling evidence that children acquire principles with inferential force that go beyond simple classification by features. He showed that principles of biological origin replace features of appearance in determining children's judgments of the category that animals belong to. Children were shown pictures of two animals, a racoon and a skunk, but were told that an animal that used to look like one (the racoon) had been changed by some scientists to look like the other by changing its color, the shape of its tail, and its body size. Older children, though not younger ones, said that the animal was still a racoon, because a change in appearance does not change what an animal is. On the other hand, changes in the functional properties of an artifact lead children to change their judgment of what the object is—for example, when a coffee pot's features are changed to those of a bird feeder.

These studies and others strongly suggest that children's learning should be considered as an active process in which general principles and concepts play a significant role in organizing information and procedures that the child acquires. The fact that most children acquire the procedures of arithmetic more or less correctly but without significant understanding may be the result of a perverse method of instruction, rather than of any significant limitations of the children's ability to grasp the mathematical concepts and principles that make the procedures meaningful.

Reasoning about Quantities Outside of School Settings

Further evidence of children's ability to reason intelligently with mathematical ideas, rather than merely learning rote procedures, has been obtained in studies of performance of young salesmen and saleswomen in street markets in Recife, Brazil. Children who sell produce or lottery tickets compute complex quantities involving novel combinations virtually without errors. In a study of produce sellers, Carraher, Carraher, and Schliemann (1985) asked a 12-year-old salesperson the price of 10 coconuts that cost 35 cents each. The reply was, "Three will be 105; with three more, that will be 210. I need four more. That is—315—I think it is 350" (Carraher et al., 1985, p. 23). Children whose computations in the market had been observed were later given a paper-and-pencil test of problems with the same numbers as problems they had solved correctly in the market; their average score was only 74% for word problems and 37% for numerical operations with no context. Performance of children who sell lottery tickets is even more impressive, because their calculations depend on the number of combinations of numbers that can win, based on numbers chosen by the bettor (Acioly & Schliemann, 1986).

The important characteristic of quantitative reasoning by the street marketeers in Brazil is its situatedness—it is richly connected to the setting in which it occurs. This also characterizes performance of adults who have been observed in tasks that involve reasoning about quantities in practical settings. Scribner (1984) studied performance in the task of preloading orders in a dairy, a poorly paid job that is done in a cold-storage room and does not attract workers who have achieved high levels of academic success. The preloaders are given orders to assemble in an unusual notation, with a number of cases, a "+" or a "–" sign, and a number of units. "$a + b$" means a full cases and b additional units, and "$a-b$" means a full cases less b units. Actions of the preloaders in assembling the orders were observed, and in most cases they chose an action that required minimal effort. This frequently involved use of a partly filled case and a conversion of the problem. For example, to assemble a "1–6" order of a product that has 16 units per case, a literal solution would be to remove 6 units from a full case, but if there was a half-filled case available, preloaders typically used that and added two units to it.

Lave, Murtaugh, and de la Rocha (1984) have studied quantitative reasoning of shoppers and of individuals who were learning to control their diets. Calculation was involved in a significant number of decisions made by individuals shopping for groceries. About one in every six items purchased involved explicit consideration of alternatives. Virtually all of the calculations (98%) were correct, but many of the calculations also were nonstandard. In one example, the price marked on a package of cheese seemed too high, but rather than multiplying its weight by the unit price, the shopper searched for another similar package to confirm that the marked price was in error. The search might have simply been easier for this shopper than multiplication, although the physical effort surely was greater than needed to obtain an approximate numerical answer. Regardless of that, though, the example illustrates a tendency for individuals to use the resources available in a situation to make inferences about quantities in the situation, often in preference to using symbolic computations that are less directly connected with the problem setting.

An especially clear example of generative quantitative reasoning situated in a task setting was observed in de la Rocha's (1986; also see Lave et al., 1984) study of reasoning in the kitchen. A new member of Weight Watchers was asked to work out an allotment of cottage cheese that is three-quarters of the two-thirds cup the program allows. The person filled a measuring cup two-thirds full, dumped the cottage cheese onto a cutting board, spread it into a circle, marked the circle into four quadrants, removed one of the quadrants, and served the rest. De la Rocha also found many examples in which individuals created alternatives to standard measuring procedures that honored equivalences of units. For example, one cook noticed that a specified fraction of a cup of milk filled a drinking glass to a line of flowers, and thereafter filled the glass to that line rather than measuring the amount with a measuring cup.

The individuals observed in these studies had learned varying amounts of mathematics in school that they might have used, but their successful reasoning appeared to have little to do with their school-based knowledge. The man who divided a circle of cottage cheese rather than multiplying ¾ by ⅔ muttered that he had studied calculus in college. More systematically, the shoppers in Murtaugh's (1985; also see Lave et al., 1984) study scored only 59% on a paper-and-pencil test of arithmetic operations involving integer, decimal, and fractional numbers, and the street vendors in Carraher et al.'s study solved only 74% of the problems correctly when they were given paper-and-pencil versions of problems that they had solved correctly in marketing situations.

These studies and others about quantitative reasoning in practical settings emphasize and extend a conclusion of Jenkins (1979). Jenkins noted that few of the kinds of generalizations about memory developed in the laboratory hold up when they are tested transsituationally, and that we therefore must consider memory to be an extremely context-sensitive process. The radical extension of this idea is that a significant part of what we call "memory" involves information that is in the situations we behave in, rather than just in the minds of the behaving individuals. Rather than considering knowledge as something that resides in a person's mind, we may have to adjust our view to something more like a capability of interacting meaningfully with features of situations.

DIRECTIONS FOR RESEARCH AND DEVELOPMENT

The "Knowledge Structure Program" of research has provided analyses of performance in standard instructional tasks. It is now an established research effort, and can be continued productively with strong potential benefits for cognitive theory and educational practice. At the same time, there are opportunities to develop new directions for research and instructional development, related to deeper goals than those that currently dominate mathematics education. There are two general issues for which research findings and methods are in a less developed state than knowledge structures: (1) understanding knowledge as a resource for reasoning, and (2) instructional settings that promote conceptual growth. These issues arise from the two main features of productive knowledge that are seen in the research on everyday cognition and conceptual competence: that it is situated, and that it is generative.

Understanding and Fostering Knowledge Resources for Situated Reasoning

I have discussed research that indicates that individuals, including unschooled children, reason in flexible and strong ways about quantities in practical situations. The relation of school mathematics to this situated reasoning is tenuous, at most. Indeed, in the cases that have been studied it can be argued that the mathematics learned in school plays an insignificant role in the individuals' reasoning and problem solving. The reasoning that has been demonstrated in practical settings occurs at a low level of mathematics. As Resnick (in press) has noted, nearly all of the examples that have been observed are limited to additive compositions of quantities.

A major educational advance would be achieved if we could find ways to teach mathematics beyond the level of addition and subtraction so that it would become a significant factor in individuals' reasoning in everyday situations.[1] This goal is not easy to achieve, and recent theoretical analyses have begun to clarify the causes of the difficulty.

School instruction in mathematics and other subjects is primarily in symbolic domains. If symbolic knowledge transferred easily into physical and social situations, school-based knowledge would be applied naturally and broadly. Researchers have only recently focused on a crucial distinction between symbolic knowledge and knowledge for activity in physical and social situations (e.g., Dreyfus & Dreyfus, 1986; Lave, 1988; Winograd & Flores, 1986).

Heidegger (1962) argued that most of the interactions we have with objects in the world are direct, rather than involving intermediate representations such as images or descriptions. Symbolic representations play a significant role in cognition when something in the world departs from what an individual expects. As an example, the action of opening a door, including reaching to the doorknob, grasping and turning it, and pushing or pulling, is ordinarily done without any significant processing of symbols. However, if the knob doesn't turn or the door is stuck, the individual may well engage in some propositional reasoning (Is it locked? Do I have the key?) or create a mental model to help in inferring where to push or kick the door to get it to open.

Dreyfus and Dreyfus (1986) used Heidegger's idea in interpreting the acquisition of cognitive skills. They argued that rules, descriptions, and explanations play a significant role only in the early stages of acquiring a skill, and that expertise in a domain depends crucially on acquisition of knowledge for responding directly to a very large variety of patterns in complex and flexible ways, most of which is not articulable in verbal or other symbols. While this general idea has been expressed before, notably in Fitts's (1962) theory of skill acquisition, Dreyfus and Dreyfus's emphasis on the limits of symbolic representations to the early stages of skill acquisition puts the idea in an interesting new perspective.

Another recent analysis by Smith (1983) provides a framework for clarifying

---

[1]I am assuming that little everyday reasoning by most persons even includes multiplicative and proportional relations, although the evidence that I have for that involves extrapolations from laboratory studies where proportional reasoning is often problematical. If some level of arithmetic above addition and subtraction is commonly used in everyday reasoning, then my remarks would apply to a somewhat higher level of mathematics instruction.

the problem further. Like Dreyfus and Dreyfus (1986) and Winograd and Flores (1986), Smith developed his analysis in the domain of computer programming, but also like those analyses, it applies to procedures that are learned by students in mathematics instruction. Smith was concerned with the semantics of programming languages, and provided an integration of two previously separate ideas about meaning.

Panel (a) of Fig. 16.1 shows some of the components of Smith's analysis. He distinguished between two fields: a field of symbolic expressions and a domain of objects that the expressions can refer to. In a programming language, the symbolic field is the set of data structures that can be expressed. In mathematics, the symbolic field is the set of expressions that can be written with numerals, operators, variables, and so on. In either case, the denoted domain can be any set of physical or conceptual entities that the symbolic expressions can be about. The relation between symbolic expressions and the things they denote is represented as a mapping from the symbolic field to the denotational domain, Φ_{sd}, in the manner of standard logical semantics. There also is a mapping within the symbolic domain, Ψ_s, which refers to the rules for transforming expressions into other expressions. In a programming language, Ψ_s is the set of transformations that can be made using statements in the language. In mathematics, Ψ_s is the set of transformations that can be performed with the rules that are available. An important result in Smith's analysis is a set of conditions on Ψ_s and Φ_{sd} that make them coherent. It is important that the transformations on symbols do not change the denotations and truth-values of expressions, and Smith showed how

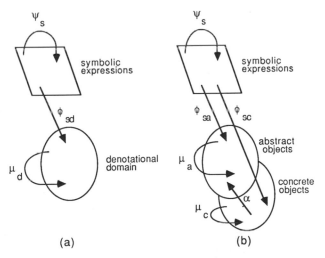

FIG. 16.1.   Components of an analysis of symbols and meanings Panel (a) shows an undifferentiated denotational domain, after Smith (1983). Panel (b) shows the denotational domain distinguishing concrete and abstract objects.

an appropriate set of coherence conditions can be satisfied. (In effect, this generalizes the metamathematical concept of soundness.) The mapping μ_d in Fig. 16.1 refers to transformations that can be performed on the objects in a domain—moving them about, for example.

In panel (b) of Fig. 16.1 the denotational domain is shown as a set of concrete objects and a set of abstract objects, related to the concrete objects by a relation of abstraction, α. This distinction emphasizes that in mathematics, the denotations of expressions are primarily abstract entities—numbers, operations, functions, and so on—that can be understood as abstract structures in physical and social situations. Φ_{sa} is the mapping from expressions to abstract entities, and μ_a is the set of transformations that an individual can perform, such as thinking about relations between numbers or functions. The symbols can also denote properties and relations in concrete situations, with a mapping indicated by Φ_{sc}, and there are operations on the objects in concrete situations, indicated by μ_c.

Fig. 16.2 shows an elementary example, involving objects and sets. "Three blocks, and two more blocks" is an element in the set of English expressions. A child could construct a situation like that shown in the lowest rounded rectangle by placing three blocks on a table, and then placing two more blocks there. This situation would be in the domain of concrete objects, and the operations of counting and placing objects would be in the set of transformations that we call μ_c. The domain of abstract objects includes sets, which are indicated in the remaining rounded rectangle. It is impossible to draw a diagram that has only abstract objects, so there are ovals in the diagram. The ovals, of course, are

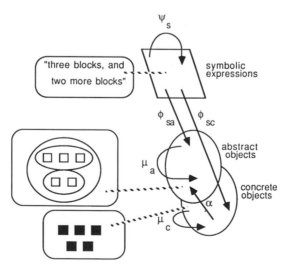

FIG. 16.2. Components of an analysis of symbols and meanings, with illustrative expressions and denotations in elementary arithmetic.

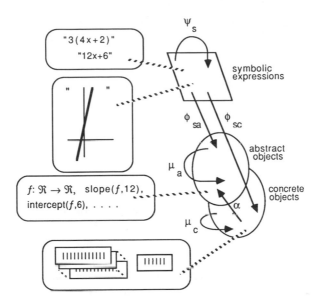

FIG. 16.3. Components of an analysis of symbols and meanings, with illustrative expressions and denotations in algebra.

themselves symbols, rather than abstract entities, but we have to live with the limitations of notational systems in order to draw diagrams. If a child understands the set relations involved in the situation, he or she can perform operations on those objects as well, such as forming the union of sets, and these are examples of the transformations that we call μ_a.

Fig. 16.3 shows another example, involving algebra. Formulas and graphs are symbolic expressions. Students learn operations on the symbolic fields, such as transformations between equivalent expressions. For example, the operation of distributing a coefficient transforms "$3(4x + 2)$" into "$12x + 6$." The denotation of either a formula or a graph can be a relation in a concrete situations, as the lowest rounded rectangle indicates schematically. A situation for "$12x + 6$" might involve shopping from a catalog where each record you purchase costs 12 dollars, and another 6 dollars is charged for handling and shipping. The abstract structures that are denoted include a function that maps the real numbers to the real numbers, with the special properties of being linear, having a slope of twelve and an intercept of 6, and other properties that could be specified.

I can now state a conjecture about why school mathematics learning is related so poorly to reasoning in physical and social situations. School mathematics instruction focuses on symbolic operations, Ψ_s. Students may even believe that the symbolic operations are a self-contained system that is unconnected with any referents in the world. (Children interviewed by Ginsburg [1977], for example, seemed to take that view regarding numerical operations in arithmetic.) Expert mathematicians understand that the symbols refer to the abstract entities of mathematics; that is, they have a conceptual domain containing those entities, they know the mapping Φ_{sa}, and they know what transformations in that domain, μ_a, correspond to transformations of symbols, Ψ_s, because of the denotational mapping Φ_{sa}. In contrast, children may learn the manipulations of symbols, Ψ_s, without connecting them to their denotations either in the domain of abstract entities or concrete objects.

As an example, students in algebra can learn procedures to manipulate symbols to get correct answers for problems, such as "simplify $60t + 50(2 - t)$," giving the answer "$10t + 100$." This uses operations included in Ψ_s, the transformations of symbolic expressions. Abstract entities involved are the functions denoted by "$60t$," "$50(2 - t)$," and "$60t + 50(2 - t)$," and their properties, including that they all are linear in t, the first and third are increasing in t, the third is the sum of the first two, and so on. An important property, not understood by many algebra students, is that "$60t + 50(2 - t)$" and "$10t + 100$" denote the same function, and that all equations that are related by so-called simplifications belong to an equivalence class of expressions that denote the same function. A relation between these expressions and a situation would be involved in the word problem: "Kay drove at a speed of 60 miles per hour for part of a trip, and 50 miles per hour for the rest. The trip took 2 hours in all, and she drove a total of 115 miles. How much time did she travel at each of the two speeds?" Many students apparently learn to translate texts of problems into formulas, a technique that is not very powerful but can get them through courses, without understanding the functional relations in the situations that problems describe or the concepts of variable and function that are denoted by the formulas.

The quantitative reasoning of unschooled domain experts, such as street vendors and many cooks, involves a manipulation of quantities μ_a, in contexts of specific domains of objects, and their lack of success in paper-and-pencil tests indicates that these operations are not well connected with symbolic expressions of arithmetic. The abstract structures that these individuals have are not connected to formal deductive systems of the kind that are known by experts in mathematics. Indeed, there is evidence (L. Resnick, personal communication) that the reasoning of unschooled experts is limited to a subset of numbers that occur frequently in their experience.

The question of how to teach so that operations on symbols are meaningful has been a concern of many educators and cognitive psychologists. Wertheimer (1945/1959) and Dienes (1967) provided examples that have become classical, involving spatial representations coordinated with formulas and proofs in geometry and algebra. The use of manipulative materials in teaching arithmetic, such as bundles of sticks for place-value, has been advocated and studied at least since Brownell's (1935) well-known work, and Bransford (1986) is developing methods of providing concrete contexts for problems that are solved using arithmetic, utilizing the technology of video disks.

The mere use of concrete materials and contexts does not guarantee that children will understand the meanings of symbolic expressions and operations, of course. To understand the meanings of mathematical symbols it is important for students to acquire the appropriate mathematical concepts that the symbols denote. These are abstract structures, such as number, sets, and functions, and they probably are not acquired automatically by experiencing connections between the symbols and specific concrete embodiments. Dienes's (1967) idea of embodying concepts in multiple physical realizations, and Skemp's (1979) discussions of abstraction from a variety of examples, are clearly relevant to this task, but the various illustrations of concepts need to be carefully focused on specific conceptual targets and related systematically to symbolic expressions and operations.

The relations between alternative representations of abstract concepts can be complex (Schoenfeld, in press). Recent findings by Resnick and Omanson (in press) illustrate the complexity. They conducted a systematic study of the effects of an instructional procedure developed by Resnick (1983) for multidigit subtraction. Resnick was concerned with students who made systematic errors in their test performance of a kind analyzed by Brown and Burton (1980). Resnick had preliminary success with a procedure called mapping instruction. This instruction uses blocks to represent numbers, with small cubes for units, $1 \times 1 \times 10$ rods for tens, and $1 \times 10 \times 10$ flat pieces for hundreds. Subtraction is accomplished by representing the larger number with blocks, and taking away blocks corresponding to the smaller number. Borrowing is accomplished by trading a larger block for 10 of the next smaller size, a trade that preserves the total amount in the display. The steps of this procedure are related in a detailed, step-by-step fashion with the paper-and-pencil procedure of subtraction with numerals. Resnick and Omanson's study provided the mapping instruction systematically to a number of children who had shown systematic errors in their performance. Although a few of the children learned to subtract correctly, several did not. There was an intriguing tendency for those children who were remediated successfully to talk about the quantities represented in the problems more than the children whose performance remained flawed. This trend in the data is consistent with the conjecture that understanding involves linking symbolic expressions with abstract conceptual structures, rather than only with concrete objects.

Some recent results by Brown and Kane (1986) are suggestive about the process of acquiring general concepts involving relations between domains. Brown and Kane showed that children can learn in ways that transfer to new problems when: (a) They have a positive set to learn generalizations rather than solutions of specific problems; (b) They perceive the solution tool of a problem as one of many uses of the tool; and (c) The structure of analogous problems is made salient to the children. These conclusions, coupled with the suggestive trend in Resnick and Omanson's data, suggest that instruction that includes discussion as well as presentation of the general properties of quantities and their representations both in written symbols and concrete materials might be especially effective. Exploration of this possibility seems a useful target for research.

Instruction for the Growth of Conceptual Systems

A final direction for research that I will discuss involves ideas and frameworks for developing educational systems that could support the kind of deep conceptual growth that is needed both for students to understand the concepts and principles of mathematics, and to use those concepts as resources for reasoning in the situations of their nonacademic lives.

Kitcher (1984), in a philosophical and historical analysis of mathematical knowledge, developed the idea of a *mathematical practice,* which he used to analyze significant historical changes in mathematics.[2] Components of a mathematical practice include (1) the questions that are understood as meaningful and legitimate, (2) the methods of reasoning that are accepted as supporting conclusions, and (3) a set of metamathematical views that characterize goals and structures of mathematical knowledge, as well as (4) the mathematical language and (5) the statements of findings and conclusions that are accepted as established. Kitcher's discussion suggests that we could try to communicate significant components of mathematical *practice* to schoolchildren, rather than only communicating mathematical concepts and techniques. This idea is consistent with a view that students should learn processes of mathematical thinking, rather than only the content of mathematics. Kitcher's formulation of the components of mathematical practice could be the beginning of a more explicit formulation of the goal of teaching students to think mathematically.

Current instruction focuses on the fourth and fifth components of Kitcher's list, the language of mathematics and the accepted findings and conclusions. The other components of a practice—questions, methods of reasoning, and metamathematical views—are not salient features of instruction as it usually is carried out. To include these goals in mathematics instruction, we would attempt to educate students so they would be able to ask meaningful mathematical ques-

---

[2]Kitcher's idea of a practice shares with Kuhn's (1970) concept of a paradigm the recognition that knowledge in a field involves more than its proved results, but it also recognizes ways in which knowledge remains commensurate even though methods and terms are modified. For example, an important part of Kitcher's accomplishment is to show in considerable detail how changes in practice occur naturally as progress within a field, not as a revolution that restructures the entire framework of inquiry, and how meaningful communication occurs between adherents of different practices as part of the process of modifying and extending knowledge.

tions, construct and evaluate arguments, and understand the goals and structures of mathematical knowledge. All of these goals are attractive, and they have been proposed before (for example, see Brown & Walter, 1983; Kilpatrick, 1987; Schoenfeld, 1985, especially Chapter 5). The question is what we can do now to make these goals more feasible and effective as guides for educational practice.

Each of the goals of education (asking mathematical questions, formulating and evaluating sequences of reasoning, and understanding metamathematical views) involves cognitive capabilities that are poorly understood. We now know how to analyze cognitive capabilities for solving problems and answering questions, and these scientific advances have potential value for developing improved instruction for problem solving and question answering. To move from this successful program of research about knowledge structures to the deeper issues of questioning, reasoning, and metamathematics (in Kitcher's sense), would take cognitive research into territory that is almost entirely uncharted, but would provide important opportunities to extend cognitive theory and methodology, as well as potentially significant resources for meaningful changes in mathematics education.

Directions in Instructional Innovation

In fact, progress toward achieving educational goals will be needed if we are to make progress on the theoretical questions of questioning, reasoning, and metamathematical beliefs. These deeper educational objectives are not achieved frequently in current educational practice, and therefore there are few opportunities to study the very phenomena that we want to understand. We need to create environments in which students learn to ask meaningful questions, compose arguments, and come to understand metamathematical considerations in order to study these phenomena from a cognitive standpoint as well as to provide examples for educational practice. Modifications of the environments in which we conduct education will be required in order to achieve the deeper intellectual goals of communicating mathematical practice. Some interesting innovations have been and are being explored.

We are coming to understand several ways in which learning involves the construction of knowledge, rather than its passive acquisition. Environments that encourage the construction of knowledge include: (1) collaborative settings in which teachers and students work together to construct meanings and ideas; (2) settings in which teachers or tutors function as coaches and models of the activities the students are learning to engage in; and (3) settings in which students engage in exploration of ideas and environments.

A classic case of collaborative learning was described by Fawcett (1938), who developed a course in deductive reasoning that included geometry as well as material from everyday life such as newspaper articles and advertisements. Fawcett and his students discussed definitions of concepts, assumptions that were required for conclusions to follow, the relative advantages of different ways of proving conclusions, and other aspects of reasoning that are ordinarily not explicitly discussed in geometry courses. Lampert (1986) is providing another example of collaborative instruction in her teaching of mathematics in the fifth grade. Lampert and her students engage in conversations about the meanings of mathematical concepts, operations, and notation, and the students play an active role in the process of making sense of mathematics.

Activities of collaborative mathematical work probably offer the best chance of educating students for activities of the practice of mathematics. As Schoenfeld (1987) has put it:

> A significant part of what I attempt to do (in my problem solving courses in particular, but increasingly in all of my mathematics instruction) is to create a microcosm of mathematical culture—an environment in which my students create and discuss mathematics in much the same way that mathematicians do. Having experienced mathematics in this way, students are more likely to develop a more accurate view of what mathematics is and how it is done. (p. 23)

Another way of organizing an instructional environment involves having an instructor model the kind of activity that students are attempting to acquire, and then coach them as they carry out the activity. This is the standard method of instruction in domains that are understood primarily as domains of skill, such as athletics or musical performance, but it has been less standard in school subjects, perhaps because we have understood these as consisting of knowledge, rather than skill. If we shift our goals toward having students learn the practice of mathematics, modeling and coaching will become more appropriate as teaching methods. Modeling and coaching have been demonstrated and evaluated, especially in the context of increasing students' metacognitive skills, for example by Palincsar and Brown (1984) in reading comprehension, by Bereiter and Scardamalia (1982) in written composition, by Schoenfeld (1987) in mathematical problem solving, by Brown, Burton, and deKleer (1982) in electronic troubleshooting, and by Burton and Brown (1982) in strategies of an arithmetic game.

Flexible learning activities can also be encouraged in environments in which students can explore the structure of an environment, generate and test their own hypotheses, and discuss the phenomena that they experience. Exploratory environments for learning can be quite open. For example, LOGO (Papert, 1980) provides an unconstrained programming environment in which students can learn to construct procedures in a wide variety of tasks. Exploratory computational environments also can have relatively definite structure designed to communicate quite specific ideas. Relatively structured microworlds and systems for representing problems have been developed and discussed by many individuals; for example, Bork's (1981) dialogues regarding physical phenomena, diSessa's

(1982) system that represents objects that move according to Newton's laws, Shalin and Bee's (Greeno, 1987) and Schwartz's (1985) systems for representing information about quantities in word problems, and Schwartz, Yerushalmy, and Gordon's (1985) system in which students can explore conjectures in plane geometry.

Cole and his group (Laboratory of Comparative Human Cognition, 1982) have created and are studying an environment that combines aspects of exploration, coaching, and collaboration. Their experiment is in many ways the most adventurous of the various attempts to construct new environments for learning.

POSTSCRIPT

I have been discussing recent advances in theory and research that are relevant to some problems of long standing. The problems of teaching mathematics so that its concepts and principles are understood and can be used by students in their everyday activities have been recognized for decades. These are not the kinds of problems for which we are likely to find "solutions" in the usual sense. Another idea about problems, however, was spelled out in a book about metaphor by Lakoff and Johnson (1980).

An Iranian student, shortly after his arrival in Berkeley, took a seminar on metaphor from one of us. Among the wondrous things that he found in Berkeley was an expression that he heard over and over and understood as a beautifully sane metaphor. The expression was "the solution of my problems"—which he took to be a large volume of liquid, bubbling and smoking, containing all of your problems, either dissolved or in the form of precipitates, with catalysts constantly dissolving some problems (for the time being) and precipitating out others. He was terribly disillusioned to find that the residents of Berkeley had no such chemical metaphor in mind. And well he might be, for the chemical metaphor is both beautiful and insightful. It gives us a view of problems as things that never disappear utterly and that cannot be solved once and for all. All of your problems are always present, only they may be dissolved and in solution, or they may be in solid form. The best you can hope for is to find a catalyst that will make one problem dissolve without making another one precipitate out. And since you do not have complete control over what goes into the solution, you are constantly finding old and new problems precipitating out and present problems dissolving, partly because of your efforts and partly despite anything you do.

The CHEMICAL metaphor gives us a new view of human problems. It is appropriate to the experience of finding that problems which we once thought were "solved" turn up again and again. The CHEMICAL metaphor says that problems are not the kind of things that can be made to disappear forever. To treat them as things that can be "solved" once and for all is pointless. To live by the CHEMICAL metaphor would be to accept it as a fact that no problem ever disappears forever. Rather than direct your energies toward solving your problems once and for all, you would direct your energies toward finding out what catalysts will dissolve your most pressing problems for the longest time without precipitating out worse ones. The reappearance of a problem is viewed as a natural occurrence rather than a failure on your part to find "the right way to solve it." (pp. 143–144)

The problems of teaching so that students understand and can reason with concepts and principles of mathematics surely are the kind to which the chemical metaphor applies. They will not be solved in a simple way, and they probably will not go away completely. It is still reasonable, of course, to work toward improving on the solutions that have already been achieved. Perhaps some reagents can be found that can cause more of these problems to go into solution without causing other problems to reappear more stubbornly.

The research in the Knowledge Structure Program that I have discussed has clarified the solution that we currently have. The models of knowledge structures that have been developed show some of the essential characteristics of knowledge that many students acquire in order to be successful in tasks that are used in instruction. It is likely that instruction in performing those tasks can be improved by providing more explicit instruction in aspects of skill that are ordinarily tacit, partly because of the clearer definitions of the needed structures that cognitive models are providing. Those models also reveal important limitations of instruction that uses those tasks. The models reinforce our realization that students can learn to solve the problems that are used in instruction without achieving significant understanding of mathematical principles and concepts, and without acquiring knowledge that they need to use mathematical knowledge as a significant resource for reasoning in a broad range of nonacademic settings.

The detailed implications of all these ideas for mathematics education are not completely clear yet, but they give considerable promise to the prospects for significant progress during the next period of research and educational development.

ACKNOWLEDGMENT

This is a substantially revised version of a paper presented at a meeting of the American Educational Research Association in April, 1986. An earlier version was published in *The monitoring of school mathematics: Background papers* (Vol. 2), edited by T. A. Romberg and D. M. Stewart, published by the Wisconsin Center for Education Research, School of Education, University of Wisconsin. I am grateful for discussion with Andrea A. diSessa, Marcia Linn, Peter Pirolli, Frederick Reif, and Alan H. Schoenfeld about these matters, including reactions to an earlier draft, and to Robert R. Hoffman for thoughtful and helpful editorial suggestions. Research reported herein was supported by the National Science Foundation through grant No. MDR–8550332.

REFERENCES

Acioly, N. M., & Schliemann, A. D. (1986). *Intuitive mathematics and schooling in understanding in lottery game.* Recife, Brazil: Universidade Federal de Pernambuco.

Anderson, J. R. (1983). Acquisition of cognitive skill. *Psychological Review, 89,* 396–406.

Anderson, J. R., & Bower, G. H. (1973). *Human associative memory.* Washington DC: Winston & Sons.

Anderson, J. R., Boyle, C. F., Farrell, R., & Reiser, B. (1984). Cognitive principles in the design of computer tutors. *Proceedings of the Cognitive Science Society, 2–11.*

Bereiter, C., & Scardamalia, M. (1982). From conversation to composition: The role of instruction in a developmental process. In R. Glaser (Ed.), *Advances in instructional psychology* (Vol. 2, pp. 1–64). Hillsdale NJ: Lawrence Erlbaum Associates.

Bork, A. (1981). *Learning with computers.* Bedford MA: Digital Press

Bransford, J. (1986, April). *The development of conceptual tools.* Paper presented at the meeting of the American Educational Research Association, San Francisco.

Briars, D. J., & Larkin, J. H. (1984). An integrated model of skill in solving elementary word problems. *Cognition and Instruction, 1,* 245–296.

Brown, A. L., & Kane, M. J. (1986). *Analogical transfer in young children: A theoretical conundrum.* Unpublished manuscript, Center for the Study of Reading, University of Illinois

Brown, J. S., & Burton, R. R. (1980). Diagnostic models for procedural bugs in basic mathematical skills. *Cognitive Science, 4,* 379–426.

Brown, J. S., Burton, R. R., & deKleer, J. (1982). Pedagogical, natural language and knowledge engineering techniques in SOPHIE I, II, and III. In D. Sleeman & J. S. Brown (Eds.), *Intelligent tutoring systems.* New York: Acacemic Press, pp. 227–282.

Brown, S. I., & Walter, M. I. (1983). *The art of problem posing.* Philadelphia: Franklin Institute.

Brownell, W. A. (1935). Psychological considerations in the learning and teaching of arithmetic. In *The teaching of arithmetic: Tenth yearbook of the National Council of Teachers of Mathematics.* New York: Columbia University Press, pp. 1–31.

Bullock, M., Gelman, R., & Baillargeon, R. (1982). The development of causal reasoning. In W. J. Friedman (Ed.), *The developmental psychology of time.* New York: Academic Press.

Burton, R. R. (1982). Diagnosing bugs in a simple procedural skill. In D. Sleeman & J. S. Brown (Eds.), *Intelligent tutoring systems.* New York: Academic Press, pp. 157–184.

Burton, R. R., & Brown, J. S. (1982). An investigation of computer coaching for informal learning activities. In D. Sleeman & J. S. Brown (Eds.), *Intelligent tutoring systems.* New York: Academic Press, pp. 79–98.

Carey, S. (1985). *Conceptual change in childhood.* Cambridge, MA: Bradford/MIT Press.

Carraher, T. N., Carraher, D. W., & Schliemann, A. D. (1985). Mathematics in the streets and in schools. *British Journal of Developmental Psychology, 3,* 21–29.

Cohen, P. C. (1982). *A calculating people: The spread of numeracy in early America.* Chicago: University of Chicago Press.

Davis, R. B. (1984). *Learning mathematics: The cognitive science approach to mathematics education.* Norwood, NJ: Ablex.

de la Rocha, O. (1986). *Problems of sense and problems of scale: An ethnographic study of arithmetic in everyday life.* Unpublished doctoral dissertation. University of California, Irvine.

Dienes, Z. P. (1967). *Building up mathematics* (rev. ed.). London: Hutchinson Educational Press.

diSessa, A. A. (1982). Unlearning Aristotelian physics: A study of knowledge-based learning. *Cognitive Science, 6,* 37–75.

diSessa, A. A. (1983). Phenomenology and the evolution of intuition. In D. Gentner & A. Stevens (Eds.), *Mental models.* Hillsdale, NJ: Lawrence Erlbaum Associates, pp. 15–33.

Dreyfus, H. L., & Dreyfus, S. E. (1986). *Mind over machine: The power of human intuition and expertise in the era of the computer.* New York: Free Press.

Fawcett, H. P. (1938). *The nature of proof.* The Thirteenth Yearbook of the National Council of Teachers of Mathematics. New York: Teachers College, Columbia University.

Fitts, P. M. (1962). Factors in complex skill training. In R. Glaser (Ed.), *Training research and education.* Pittsburgh: University of Pittsburgh Press, pp. 177–197.

Gelman, R., & Gallistel, C. R. (1978). *The child's understanding of number.* Cambridge, MA: Harvard University Press.

Ginsburg, H. P. (1977). *Children's arithmetic: The learning process.* New York: Van Nostrand.

Greeno, J. G. (1976a). Cognitive objectives of instruction: Theory of knowledge for solving problems and answering questions. In D. Klahr (Ed.), *Cognition and instruction.* Hillsdale, NJ: Lawrence Erlbaum Associates, pp. 123–160.

Greeno, J. G. (1976b). Indefinite goals in well structured problems. *Psychological Review, 83,* 479–491.

Greeno, J. G. (1978). A study of problem solving. In R. Glaser (Ed.), *Advances in instructional psychology* (Vol. 1). Hillsdale, NJ: Lawrence Erlbaum Associates, pp. 13–75.

Greeno, J. G. (1983). Forms of understanding in mathematical problem solving. In S. G. Paris, G. M. Olson, & H. W. Stevenson (Eds.), *Learning and motivation in the classroom.* Hillsdale, NJ: Lawrence Erlbaum Associates, pp. 83–112.

Greeno, J. G. (1987). Instructional representations based on research about understanding. In A. H. Schoenfeld (Ed.), *Cognitive science and mathematics education* (pp. 61–88). Hillsdale, NJ: Lawrence Erlbaum Associates.

Greeno, J. G., Brown, J. S., Foss, C., Shalin, V., Bee, N. V., Lewis, M. W., & Vitolo, T. M. (1986). *Cognitive principles of problem solving and instruction.* Berkeley: School of Education, University of California, Berkeley.

Greeno, J. G., James, C. T., DaPolito, F., & Polson, P. G. (1978). *Associative learning: A cognitive analysis.* Englewood Cliffs, NJ: Prentice–Hall.

Greeno, J. G., Magone, M. E., & Chaiklin, S. (1979). Theory of constructions and set in problem solving. *Memory and Cognition, 7,* 445–461.

Hayes, J. R. (1976). It's the thought that counts: New approaches to educational theory. In D. Klahr (Ed.), *Cognition and instruction.* Hillsdale, NJ: Lawrence Erlbaum Associates, pp. 235–242.

Heidegger, M. (1962). *Being and time.* New York: Harper & Row.

Jenkins, J. J. (1979). Four points to remember: A tetrahedral model of memory experiments. In L. S. Cermak & F. I. M. Craik (Eds.), *Levels of processing in human memory* (pp. 429–446). Hillsdale, NJ: Lawrence Erlbaum Associates.

Keil, F. (1989). *Concepts, kinds, and cognitive development.* Cambridge, MA: MIT Press/Bradford Books.

Kilpatrick, J. (1987). Problem formulating: Where do good problems come from? In A. H. Schoenfeld (Ed.), *Cognitive science and mathematics education* (pp. 123–146). Hillsdale, NJ: Lawerence Erlbaum Associates.

Kintsch, W. (1974). *The representation of meaning in memory.* Hillsdale, NJ: Lawrence Erlbaum Associates.

Kintsch, W. (1986). Learning from text. *Cognition and Instruction, 3,* 87–108.

Kintsch, W., & Greeno, J. G. (1985). Understanding and solving word arithmetic problems. *Psychological Review, 92,* 109–129.

Kitcher, P. (1984). *The nature of mathematical knowledge.* New York: Oxford University Press.

Klahr, D. (Ed.). (1976). *Cognition and instruction.* Hillsdale, NJ: Lawrence Erlbaum Associates.

Kuhn, T. S. (1970). *The structure of scientific revolutions.* Chicago: University of Chicago Press.

Laboratory of Comparative Human Cognition. (1982). *A model system for the study of learning difficulties.* Center for Human Information Processing, University of California, San Diego.

Lakoff, G., & Johnson, M. (1980). *Metaphors we live by.* Chicago: University of Chicago Press.

Lampert, M. (1986). On learning, doing, and teaching multiplication. *Cognition and Instruction, 4,* 305–342.

Lave, J. (1988). *Cognition in practice.* Cambridge, UK: Cambridge University Press.

Lave, J., Murtaugh, M., & de la Rocha, O. (1984). The dialectics of arithmetic in grocery shopping.

In B. Rogoff & J. Lave (Eds.), *Everyday cognition: Its development in social context*. Cambridge, MA: Harvard University Press, pp. 67–94.

Mason, J., Burton, L. & Stacey, K. (1982). *Thinking mathematically*. London: Addison-Wesley.

Murtaugh, M. (1985). *A hierarchical decision process model of American grocery shopping*. Doctoral dissertation, University of California, Irvine.

Newell, A., & Simon, H. A. (1972). *Human problem solving*. Englewood Cliffs, NJ: Prentice–Hall.

Norman, D. A., Rumelhart, D. E., & the LNR Research Group. (1975). *Explorations in cognition*. San Francisco: W. H. Freeman.

Palincsar, A. S., & Brown, A. L. (1984). Reciprocal teaching of comprehension-fostering and comprehension-monitoring activities. *Cognition and Instruction, 1*, 117–175.

Papert, S. (1980). *Mindstorms: Children, computers and powerful ideas*. New York: Basic Books.

Poincare, H. (1956). Mathematical creation. In J. R. Newman (Ed.), *The world of mathematics* (Vol. 4). New York: Simon & Schuster, pp. 2041–2052.

Resnick, L. B. (1983). A developmental theory of number understanding. In H. P. Ginsburg (Ed.), *The development of mathematical thinking*. New York: Academic Press.

Resnick, L. B. (in press). The development of mathematical intuition. In M. Perlmutter (Ed.), *Minnesota symposium on child psychology* (Vol. 4). Boston: Allyn & Bacon.

Resnick, L. B., & Omanson, S. F. (in press). Learning to understand arithmetic. In R. Glaser (Ed.), *Advances in instructional psychology* (Vol. 3). Hillsdale, NJ: Lawrence Erlbaum Associates.

Riley, M. S., & Greeno, J. G. (1988). Developmental analysis of understanding language about quantities and of solving problems. *Cognition and Instruction, 5*, 49 101.

Sacerdoti, E. D. (1977). *A structure for plans and behavior*. New York: Elsevier–North Holland.

Schank, R. C. (1972). Conceptual dependency: A theory of natural language understanding. *Cognitive Psychology, 3*, 552–631.

Schoenfeld, A. H. (1985). *Mathematical problem solving*. Orlando FL: Academic Press.

Schoenfeld, A. H. (1987). What's all the fuss about metacognition? In A. H. Schoenfeld (Ed.), *Cognitive science and mathematics education* (pp. 189–216). Hillsdale, NJ: Lawrence Erlbaum Associates.

Schoenfeld, A. H. (in press). On having and using geometric knowledge. In J. Hiebert (Ed.), *Conceptual and procedural knowledge: The case of mathematics*. Hillsdale, NJ: Lawrence Erlbaum Associates.

Schwartz, J. L. (1985, April). *The power and the peril of the particular: Thoughts on a role for microcomputers in science and mathematics education*. Paper presented at the meeting of the American Educational Research Association, Chicago.

Schwartz, J. L., Yerushalmy, M., & Gordon, M. (1985). *The geometric supposer: Triangles*. Pleasantville, NY: Sunburst Communications.

Scribner, S. (1984). Studying working intelligence. In B. Rogoff & J. Lave (Eds.), *Everyday cognition: Its development in social context*. Cambridge, MA: Harvard University Press, pp. 9–40.

Skemp, R. R. (1979). *Intelligence, learning, and action*. Chichester, England: Wiley.

Sleeman, D. (1984). An attempt to understand students' understanding of algebra. *Cognitive Science, 8*, 387–412.

Smith, B. C. (1983). *Reflection and semantics in a procedural language* (Report No. MITL/LCS/TR–22). Cambridge: MA: Laboratory for Computer Science, MIT.

Thorndike, E. L. (1922). *The psychology of arithmetic*. New York: Macmillan.

VanLehn, K. (1983). *Felicity conditions for human skill acquisition: Validating an AI-based theory* (Report No. CLS–21). Palo Alto, CA: Xerox Palo Alto Research Center.

VanLehn, K., Brown, J. S., & Greeno, J. G. (1984). Competitive argumentation in computational theories of cognition. In W. Kintsch, J. R. Miller, & P. G. Polson (Eds.), *Method and tactics in cognitive science*. Hillsdale, NJ: Lawrence Erlbaum Associates, pp. 235–262.

Wertheimer, M. (1945/1959). *Productive thinking*. New York: Harper.

Winograd, T. (1972). Understanding natural language. *Cognitive Psychology, 3*, 1–191.

Winograd, T., & Flores, F. (1986). *Understanding computers and cognition: A new foundation for design*. Norwood, NJ: Ablex.

17

Understanding Memory Access

Jeffery Franks, John Bransford, Kevin Brailey, and Scot Purdon
Vanderbilt University

A group of college students is unexpectedly given a journal article to read and instructed to glean as much information from it as possible in 3 minutes. The vast majority of the students begin to read the article's first sentence and continue reading word for word until they run out of time. Only a few individuals use the "skimming" skills that later questioning demonstrated were present for each of them (Bereiter, 1984). All of the students had knowledge that would have allowed them to learn more efficiently. In most cases that knowledge wasn't used.

This example illustrates an all too common situation—a situation where potentially useful knowledge or skills are not accessed and utilized in a problem-solving situation. Our interest in this phenomenon has led to a program of research that examines why people who have acquired relevant information often fail to use it in solving problems. What are the conditions that lead to the activation of various areas of knowledge? We refer to this as the *access* issue. Given that information is accessed, what determines whether that information is used? We refer to this as the *utilization* problem. In the following discussion we examine factors that appear to be important in both access and utilization failures. In addition, we pay special attention to the educational aspects of the issue since both the costs of nongeneralizable instruction and the benefits to be gained in enhancing instruction are obvious.

We begin by discussing the history of the phenomena of memory access and we explain why traditional approaches to memory research fail to reveal many issues and questions involving access. We then discuss new methodologies for studying access and consider some theories that are relevant for understanding the results of these access studies. We conclude by discussing implications for future research.

THE PROBLEM OF "INERT" KNOWLEDGE

We are certainly not the first investigators to examine the processes involved in accessing and utilizing knowledge. Earlier in this century, philosopher Alfred Whitehead referred to failures to access pertinent information as the "inert knowledge problem." He argued that these breakdowns in transfer are often due to the nature of our instructional practices (Whitehead, 1929). According to Whitehead, traditional academic instruction is prone to produce knowledge that is not utilized in real-life situations. Similar views were expressed in the 1940s by Charles Gragg at the Harvard Business School. He believed that a major goal of education should be to prepare students for action, but that ordinary forms of instruction typically fail to achieve this goal. Gragg and his colleagues therefore devised a case-based approach to instruction, an approach designed to overcome the problem of inert knowledge (Gragg, 1940; see also Bransford, Franks, Vye, & Sherwood, 1986). Other figures who have discussed this issue include Dewey (1963), Wertheimer (1959), Polya (1957) and Hanson (1970). Given the importance of the inert knowledge problem, one might expect to see a number of laboratory studies that are designed to explore it. As we shall note, however, many research methodologies fail to reveal the degree to which knowledge remains inert.

Cognitive Psychology and Inert Knowledge

The phenomenon of inert knowledge would seem to inevitably lead an investigator to focus on situations in which people are asked to solve problems without being explicitly prompted to use specific bodies of information. Given the importance of the phenomenon, it is somewhat surprising that nondirected knowledge access has received so little attention from contemporary cognitive psychology. The experimental literature is dominated by results generated through "directed access" paradigms. In this type of experiment, participants are explicitly told both what they should remember along with the context in which the information to be recalled was last encountered. Classic examples of this paradigm include most list-learning experiments from Ebbinghaus (1885) to modern times; research on schema/script abstraction (Bower, Black, & Turner, 1979) and studies of activation and priming (Ratcliff & McKoon, 1981). In all of this research, experimental participants intentionally study acquisition materials and are explicitly informed at the time of the test of the relevance of those materials for the task they are about to perform.

A line of research that varies from this "directed learning and memory" paradigm is the incidental learning paradigm (Hyde & Jenkins, 1969, 1973; Postman, Adams, & Bohm, 1956). In this paradigm, participants are instructed to engage in a wide variety of tasks, ranging from letter checking to pleasantness ratings in learning a set of materials, while remaining uninformed about a subsequent memory test. Results from this paradigm have been used to support both the "levels of processing" approach to memory (Craik & Lockhart, 1972) and counterarguments in favor of transfer appropriate processing (Bransford, Franks, Morris, & Stein, 1979). While the incidental learning paradigm is more closely linked to our approach than is traditional memory research, it still differs from our current work in one crucial regard: Participants continue to remain informed at test about the relevance of a set of acquisition materials for the task they are about to perform. In the next section we discuss research paradigms in which participants are not informed about relationships between acquisition and test. [1]

RESEARCH ON NONDIRECTED ACCESS

What specifically can be gained through the use of a nondirected paradigm? In our view, adding this condition to a traditional directed access experiment allows an investigator to examine two related issues. First, it allows an experimenter to determine if participants will independently notice a connection between present events and past experiences. Second, if noticing in fact takes place, it allows an experimenter to see if participants will spontaneously use this information and hence respond to an experimental situation in the same manner as directed access participants.

In recent years, researchers at a number of different laboratories have begun to use nondirected access paradigms. Examples include Asch (1969), Weisberg, DiCamillo, and Phillips (1978), Gick and Holyoak (1980, 1983), Ross (1984), and Stein, Littlefield, Bransford, and Persampieri (1984). Limited space precludes exploring all of these studies in detail, but we can illustrate the nature of their findings by considering some work conducted in our Vanderbilt labs.

In one of our studies (e.g., Perfetto, Bransford, & Franks, 1983), we asked college students to solve word puzzles such as the following:

1. Uriah Fuller, the famous Israeli superpsychic, can tell you the score of any baseball game before the game starts. What is his secret?
2. A man living in a small town in the United States married 20 different women in the same town. All are still living and he has never divorced one of them. Yet, he has broken no law. Can you explain?

---

[1]Another, recent line of related research is by Daniel Schacter and his colleagues on implicit-versus-explicit systems of memory (see Schacter, 1987, for a review). This work explores the distinction between memory as a directed process aimed at achieving conscious recall (explicit memory) and memory as a nonconscious biasing effect upon performance in an assortment of tasks (implicit memory). Schacter proposes that there are two separate systems of memory with only minimal interaction between them. Our work is concerned with factors, both conscious and nonconscious, that influence noticing in problem solving, a task which primarily involves explicit memory processes. According to Schacter's formulation, our work focuses predominantly on "involuntary" processes in explicit memory.

Participants in our baseline groups simply saw the problems and were asked to solve them. Across several studies, performance in these groups was poor, ranging from 18% to 25% correct. Experimental participants were provided with answers to the problems before trying to solve them. For example, during the *acquisition* phase that began the experiment, participants rated the general truthfulness of statements such as:

1. A minister marries several people each week.
2. Before it starts the score of any game is 0 to 0.

Experimental participants who were then given problems to solve and informed of the relevance of the previous acquisition information performed quite well. In Perfetto et al. (1983), they averaged from 54% to 81% correct.

For our purposes, the most important data involve participants who received the correct answers during acquisition but were *not* explicitly informed that these answers were relevant for problem solving. Initially, it seemed obvious to us that these participants would use the acquisition statements as clues since they were closely related to the subsequent problems. Much to our surprise, the problem-solving performance of participants in this uninformed group (29% correct) was not significantly better than the performance of baseline participants (19% correct). In contrast, the participants in the informed group scored 54% correct. The results from this study suggest that relevant knowledge was available to our uninformed participants but that this knowledge remained inert. Other researchers mentioned earlier have found similar examples of failures to utilize available and potentially valuable knowledge when participants are not explicitly informed about its relevance for a particular task.

Interference from Incorrect Answers

The Perfetto et al. (1983) study also indicates that participants can easily suffer from interference when they consider incorrect answers during their initial attempts at problem solving. In one experiment, participants were given the acquisition clues and asked to attempt only half of the problems on an initial problem-solving trial. Those in the uninformed group were especially likely to generate incorrect answers. Participants were then given a second problem-solving trial involving all of the problems and were informed that their acquisition experiences were pertinent to the problems they were trying to solve. Under these circumstances they suffered from interference. They were less likely to utilize the acquisition information in a correct manner and successfully solve problems that they had previously seen (and tried to solve) than they were to successfully solve problems that they were seeing for the first time. (The results for Olds versus News in the Uninformed condition on Trial 2 are presented in Table 17.1; Olds refer to problems that participants attempted to solve during

TABLE 17.1
Interference in Retrieving Relevant Information

	Trial 1 % Correct problem solving	Trial 2 % Remembered	
		Old	New
Uninformed	18%	43%	63%
Informed	73%	81%	69%

From Perfetto et al., 1983, Study 4.

Trial 1.) Further research (Perfetto, Yearwood, Franks, & Bransford, 1987) has shown that participants who *generate* incorrect answers suffer from more pronounced interference effects than participants who *read* the same incorrect answers.

Facilitating Access

The initial findings of access failures and interference were surprising to us. We thought that participants would spontaneously utilize the acquisition information even under uninformed conditions. Since they did not, we set out to examine the types of acquisition experiences that might aid uninformed participants in accessing and utilizing their knowledge.

In studies reported by Adams et al. (1988), we contrasted two different types of acquisition conditions. One involved a repetition of previous conditions: Uninformed participants rated acquisition statements such as "The score of a game before it begins is 0 to 0" or "A minister may marry several people each week" or "A person walking on water will not fall through" for their plausibility prior to seeing the verbal puzzles.

In the second acquisition condition we changed the structure of the clue statements so that they induced a simple problem-solving process. Thus, participants heard statements such as "It is easy to predict the score of any game before it begins; the score is 0 to 0," "It is common to marry several people each week; if you are a minister," and "A person walking on frozen water will not fall through; if it is frozen." Participants who received the *problem-oriented* acquisition statements were much more likely to use this information during uninformed problem solving than were participants who initially received the simple *factual* statements (see Table 17.2). In follow-up work, we have shown that this effect was problem-specific rather than the result of a general set effect such as "catching on" to the structure of the experimental task (see Adams et al., 1988). These results have been independently replicated by other investigators using similar materials and acquisition conditions (Lockhart, Lamon, & Gick, 1988).

TABLE 17.2
Problem-Oriented Acquisition: Uninformed Participants

	Trial 1 % Correct problem solving	Trial 2 % Remembered	
		Old	New
Factual Acquisition	36%	48%	62%
Problem-Oriented: No Pause	51%	65%	72%
Problem-Oriented: Pause	56%	72%	76%

From Adams et al., 1988, Study 1.

TOWARD A THEORY OF MEMORY ACCESS

Our approach to developing a theory of access has been organized around the concept of "transfer appropriate processing" (Morris, Bransford, & Franks, 1977; Bransford, et al., 1979). This principle states that performance on a task is controlled by an interaction between the acquisition activities of a learner and the specific demands of a test situation (see especially Jenkins, 1979). In this view, no single encoding procedure invariably results in superior performance. Instead, performance is dictated by the extent to which encoding activities at acquisition assist a person in distinguishing between alternative courses of action during a memory test. For example, for some tasks it is more beneficial to engage in "shallow, superficial" processing during acquisition than "deep, semantic" processing (see Morris et al., 1978).

While the principle of transfer appropriate processing has proven to be a beneficial heuristic, in its current form it is too general to serve as a useful predictive model. The general idea of production systems (e.g., Anderson, 1987; Larkin, 1981; Newell & Simon, 1972; Simon, 1980) is consistent with the spirit of transfer-appropriate processing and can provide a language for more precisely articulating the concept. We have begun to use the idea of production systems as a heuristic for guiding our thinking about our access research.

In his 1980 article on problem solving and instruction, Simon argued that the knowledge representation underlying competent performance in any domain is not based on simple facts or verbal propositions but is instead based on productions. Productions involve "condition–action pairs that specify that if a certain state occurs in working memory, then particular mental (and possibly physical) actions should take place" (Anderson, 1987, p. 193). Productions thus provide information about the critical attributes of problem situations that match specific actions with relevant goals. Knowledge-base researchers such as Larkin, (1981), Newell and Simon (1972) and John Anderson (1983, 1987) provide important insights into the need to conditionalize knowledge—to acquire knowledge in the form of condition–action pairs mediated by appropriate goal-oriented hierarchies rather than as isolated facts.

Simon echoes Whitehead (1929) and Gragg (1940) in noting that many forms of instruction do not help students conditionalize their knowledge. For example, he argues that "textbooks are much more explicit in enunciating the laws of mathematics or of nature than in saying anything about when these laws may be useful in solving problems" (p. 92). It is left largely to the student to generate the condition–action pairs required for solving novel problems. One of our favorite examples of the lack of explicit emphasis on conditionalizing one's knowledge comes from a textbook on experimental design. On page 195 of the book is a section entitled "Which Test Do I Use?" It states: "How to choose a statistical test was postponed until now so that various aspects of data analysis could be presented." The text then includes a discussion of the uses of various statistics. The entire discussion totals 13 sentences in length.

Of course, effective learners can and do learn from texts. Simon argues that effective learners are those who generate their own plans by working through examples and sample problems. He also warns that many students do not appreciate the difference between learning isolated facts and heuristics versus generating appropriate condition–action plans. The inability to make this distinction can result in situations such as a student failing an exam in spite of time-consuming preparation.

Inexperienced students often study by working sample problems, a process that supposedly hones problem-solving skills in a specific area. Unfortunately, students often use their knowledge of which chapter they are working on when selecting algorithms and heuristics for problem solving (Bransford, 1979). When deprived of this superficial contextual constraint, students who use this strategy may be unable to solve problems in a test situation. They will quite likely not have learned how to use cues from a problem itself to guide the specific actions that are relevant in constructing a correct solution (see also Nitsch, 1977).

Productions As Applied to the Inert Knowledge Phenomenon

The production-based theory outlined by Simon is helpful for understanding the uninformed access failures revealed by Perfetto et al. (1983). Consider the processing activities of our uninformed participants: They were asked to rate the general truthfulness of a variety of clue statements. Assuming that this activity resulted in the encoding of these sentences in the form of condition–action pairs, one would hypothesize that the resulting productions were not helpful for subsequent problem solving because of the constraints of the original task. Our acquisition task involved the goal of specifying the general truthfulness of statements such as "Before it is played, the score of any game is 0 to 0." Given this goal, an appropriate action is to retrieve general information about games from memory and check to see if they all begin with no score. This type of condition–action pairing is very different from what is needed to solve the superpsychic problem under uninformed conditions. In contrast, for the informed problem–solving condition, the instructions specify the goal of using what had just been learned to solve the problems. Under these circumstances, participants have an opportunity first to reconstruct their initial learning context and then find the relevant answers for each problem that they see.

Productions and Interference

Production-based theory can also account for the interference found during trial 2 of the Perfetto et al. (1983) study that is illustrated in Table 17.2. In a recent refinement of ACT*, a production-based theory of learning, Anderson (1987) suggests that knowledge is successfully transferred from one problem domain to another when there is a high degree of overlap in the production systems of both domains (e.g., when the same knowledge is used in the same way; Anderson, 1987). On the other hand, transfer is inhibited if productions are different, even if the same knowledge is present but is being used for unrelated purposes. This formulation is consistent with the uninformed access failures reported in the Perfetto et al. (1983) studies.

Anderson also suggests that *generating* answers can be a powerful method for creating productions that will be useful in later problem solving. Simply copying an answer, on the other hand, results in the compilation of a production that will make a person "more efficient at copying answers but not at producing them" (Anderson, 1987, p. 203). In the most recent study by Perfetto et al. (1987), we saw that the generation of incorrect answers can be especially likely to cause subsequent interference. Anderson and his colleagues note that a critical factor in avoiding interference is to provide people with immediate feedback so as to prevent the formation of an incorrect or misleading set of productions (Lewis & Anderson, 1985). When this is not done, the results may be very similar to the interference effect we have just described: A powerful but incorrect set of condition–action pairings may become so firmly established that it obstructs access to other, more useful information.

Productions and the Facilitation of Access

An emphasis on production systems can also clarify why Adams et al. (1988) found access to be facilitated under conditions of problem-oriented acquisition. We hypothesize that the problem-oriented acquisition task highlighted features of the problem situation that made the normally uninteresting, taken-for-granted facts used by Adams et al., useful. Thus, the problem-oriented phrasings of the clue statements presumably helped participants generate condition–action pairs that were appropriate for uninformed problem solving. For example, participants who received the problem-oriented acquisition task may have generated productions such as "Given the goal of predicting the score of any game, check to see whether the problem involves the initial score rather than the final score;" or "Given the goal of understanding why it might be commonplace to marry several times per week, check to see if the interpretation of marry can be 'conduct a marriage ceremony' rather than 'get married'." A tendency on the part of participants to form problem-specific productions would account for our findings that, when factual versus problem-oriented statements are manipulated as a within-participants variable, access is facilitated only for those problems whose initial answers appeared in a problem-solving format (see Adams et al., 1988).

NEW METHODS FOR STUDYING THE ACTIVATION AND UTILIZATION OF KNOWLEDGE

Although the studies discussed previously have yielded interesting results, we have been anxious to move beyond the use of verbal puzzle stimuli. Ideally, we want to study processes of access and use for all types of materials: words, pictures, paragraphs, movies, and so forth. It is easy to do this with directed memory paradigms. However, uninformed tests suitable for investigating non-directed access across a wide variety of common learning materials are much less readily available.

Recently, we have used an old experimental task in a new way in order to obtain general information about the degree to which people spontaneously activate and use available information. Our task can best be understood by beginning with a familiar informed task, a task involving recognition memory. Imagine hearing a list of 60 familiar words such as "car," "house," "tree," and so forth. At test, you may hear "car," "cloud," "boat," "tree," and so forth, and be asked to state whether each is "Old" or "New." As is well known, performance is generally excellent on tasks of this type (e.g., Shepard, 1967).

A similar task might involve the presentation of acquisition words such as "car," "house," "tree," and so forth. At test, you may hear "car," "wagon," and so forth, and be asked to state whether each word belongs to category A or to category B. In this situation, feedback about the correct category of each item is provided after each attempt. If all A's turn out to be Old words and all B's turn out to be New words, the task seemingly should prove to be trivially easy for people who have actually experienced the acquisition list—as easy as the prototypical recognition memory task we have just described. For people who have not experienced the acquisition list, the task should be impossible since they do not possess the information necessary to make the correct classification.

We have conducted a series of studies using this A–B classification task with an assortment of different acquisition materials. When designing these studies, it seemed obvious to us that the Old–New dimension would prove to be so powerful that this information would be used even under uninformed conditions. As expected, all our participants reported having noticed that some test words were old. Since these Old words are identical repetitions of the words provided during acquisition, it is not surprising that access occurred even under uninformed conditions. It is also noteworthy that implicit memory effects such as those discussed by Schacter (1987) occur under uninformed conditions. For example, uninformed students are better able to fill in the blanks in word fragments (e.g., s– –t–s–i–s) if relevant words (e.g., "statistics") were experienced during acquisition (Kasserman, 1987).

In order to perform well on our A–B classification task, participants must do more than spontaneously notice that some of the test words were old. They must explicitly notice the perfect correlation between "old–new" and "A–B". We expected this correlation to be obvious to all participants, but the data show otherwise. All of our participants were essentially at chance on the classification task when they were not explicitly told to use Old–New as a basis for classification. Once they became "informed" on the second trial, their performance greatly improved.

We attempted to improve uninformed performance on the A–B task by switching the presentation modality from words to pictures (Brailey, 1987). It seemed plausible to us that elaborate visual information might be more accessible than verbal information and that viewing pictures would result in excellent classification performance under uninformed conditions. Again we were wrong. We were able to replicate the typical finding of superior recognition memory for pictures over words in the informed condition but not with the uninformed classification task (see Table 17.3). We have also attempted to increase participants' elaborations during acquisition by using a variety of "pleasant–unpleasant" rating tasks during the acquisition phase of the experiment (as in Hyde & Jenkins, 1969). We thought that this might facilitate subsequent classification, but it did not.

TABLE 17.3
Access for Words vs. Pictures

	Trial 1: Uninformed % Correct classification	Trial 2: Informed % Correct recognition
Words	54%	77%
Pictures	54%	89%

From Brailey et al., 1987.

Work with More Complex Materials

In order to see if more complex verbal materials might facilitate access, we have presented participants with paragraphs to read and then administered either intentional memory tests or uninformed old–new classification tests (Kasserman & Johnson, 1987; Purdon, 1987). In the Purdon experiment, participants read four acquisition stories, each about a different topic. The tests involved lists of nouns from the acquisition passages. Two different types of presentation orders were used for the tests. For both types of orders, old nouns were interspersed with new nouns. In the *structured* condition, old nouns on the test were blocked so that, within each block, they always came from the same story and appeared in the order in which they occurred in the story. In the *unstructured* condition, the nouns appeared in an order that was random with respect to the four acquisition stories. As illustrated in Table 17.4, the structured presentation had a significant effect on performance in the intentional recognition memory test. However, for the uninformed condition, where classification was once again based on an Old–New distinction, blocking had no effect. Classification performance was, once more, essentially at chance.

In work conducted with Jane Kasserman and Rich Johnson, we presented participants with a multiparagraph acquisition passage and then used Old and New propositions at time of test. Under these conditions there was at last a tendency for participants to catch on during the classification task. In fact, many participants in this experiment noticed the Old–New relationship quite early in the test list and were able to apply it successfully to the remainder of the classification task. Nevertheless, a number of participants did not spontaneously use the story information to perform the classification task. Results are presented in Table 17.5

Overall, our experiments using the A–B classification task have provided us with results that were initially surprising. Except for the Purdon (1987) experiment, participants in all of these studies (the number of participants is in the hundreds) noticed that some words or propositions had just been presented, yet they did not use this information during the Old–New classification unless

TABLE 17.4
Access for Words in Stories

	Uninformed group % Correct classification	Informed Group % Correct recognition
Unstructured	51%	57%
Structured	48%	63%

From Purdon et al., 1987.

TABLE 17.5
Access for Sentences in Stories

	Trial 1: Uninformed % Correct classification	Trial 2: Informed % Correct recognition
Non-Users (n = 12)	57%	88%
Users (n = 18)	77%	94%

From Kasserman & Johnson, 1987.

explicitly told to do so. The uninformed classification task therefore provides information about uses of knowledge (or lack therof) that cannot be discerned from more typical memory measures such as recognition. This series of utilization failures indicates some of the limitations of results obtained from directed-access paradigms. We will return to a discussion of these tasks in the next section, when we discuss the effects on uninformed performance of attempts to help participants conditionalize their knowledge in task-appropriate ways.

FACILITATING UTILIZATION:
THE IMPORTANCE OF CONDITIONAL INFORMATION

In much of our recent work, we have attempted to design acquisition conditions that prompt participants to spontaneously use information under uninformed, A–B classification conditions. In one experiment, Yearwood (1987) created an acquisition list of 60 words that was blocked according to 12 categories with five members per category. At test, category members were either presented as a block (new category members being interspersed with old members within each particular block) or presented randomly. The A–B classification task was, again, Old versus New. Under these conditions, a significant number of participants spontaneously utilized the Old–New dimension for classification (45%).

Why should the use of categorized lists facilitate utilization relative to un-categorized lists? One possibility is suggested by examining the processing activities of participants during acquisition. Given a blocked, categorized acquisition list, uninformed participants notice the category structure. Their experiences as they proceed with the list are consistent with a general production such as "Given the next word, check to see if it belongs to the currently active category or whether it involves a new category." In contrast, when participants receive a single list of unrelated words, they are much less likely to engage in a classification task that involves discovering categorical relationships between test items.

At the time of test, all participants who receive the A–B task are asked to engage in classification behavior. This behavior is congruent with the activities engaged in by participants during the blocked, categorized acquisition list. As an illustration, imagine that, on the test list, participants first hear "couch," a word that was a member of an old category. They guess "A" and are told that they are "correct." Participants then hear a new word, "rock," and realize that it is a new word and does not fit any previously heard category. They therefore call it a "B" and are told "correct." With the blocked acquisition list, participants are more likely to have engaged in the types of processing activities that help them solve the classification test on the uninformed trials. The A–B classification task can be solved by asking oneself whether each word is a member of a previously applied classification. Participants most likely engaged in this type of classification activity during the blocked, categorized acquisition task.

It is useful in this context to compare the results of the Yearwood (1987) study to the one conducted by Purdon (1987). Purdon had participants read four different stories during acquisition. He then presented them with words from the stories during both uninformed and informed tests. Unlike the data obtained by Yearwood, performance on these uninformed tests was no better than chance. One can think of a list divided into four stories as a categorized list analogous to Yearwood's. However, the similarity between the stories and the categorized word lists is imperfect at best. It is highly unlikely that, during acquisition, participants are induced to ask themselves whether each word they hear or read is a member of the theme of their current story or is more consistent with a new theme. During reading comprehension, meaning involves propositional-level information and not semantically isolated words (e.g., Anderson, 1974; Franks, Plybon, & Auble, 1982). In short, in the Purdon experiment there is much less similarity between the acquisition and test activities than there is in the Yearwood experiment. This conclusion is supported by examining the data supplied by Kasserman and Johnson (1987). In this study, paragraph comprehension is followed by uninformed tests involving meaningful sentences rather than individual words. Under these conditions, much better performance is observed on the uninformed classification task.

Successful Classification After Several Months Delay

Consider one last example of an attempt to facilitate participants' access and use of relevant information. In this experiment, participants were exposed to lists of either 60 words or 60 pictures and were then given an uninformed classification task based on the Old–New dimension. As we noted earlier in our discussion of the Brailey, Franks, and Bransford (1987) study, participants who receive this type of acquisition task usually perform at chance rates.

Brailey (1987), however, conducted a variation on this experiment that resulted in nearly everyone performing perfectly on the classification task. The only difference between this experiment and Brailey et al. was the set of prior experiences that participants brought to the study. In his "successful access" study, Brailey used participants who had participated in Yearwood's categorized acquisition experiment 2 months earlier. Brailey did not tell his participants that his experiment was related to Yearwood's and conducted his experiment in a different classroom from Yearwood. His materials were also different in the sense that categorical information was not a feature of the acquisition list. Furthermore, for one of his groups, Brailey used pictorial stimuli rather than words. Nevertheless, nearly all participants used the Old–New information to complete the classification task successfully.

These results are especially noteworthy in light of a recent failure by Spencer and Weisberg (1986) to achieve nondirected access. In the Spencer and Weisberg study, a change in context from experimental subject to class participant was sufficient to prevent analogical transfer in solving Duncker's radiation problem. This transfer failure occurred for uninformed participants when the delay between "story analysis" and "problem solving" was only 6 minutes.

What might participants have acquired during the Yearwood study that helped their performance in the Brailey study? We assume that participants who completed the Yearwood study learned something like the following: "Given that one receives an acquisition list in an experiment at the Vanderbilt lab and is then asked to perform an A–B classification task, check to see if the answer is based on an Old–New dimension." In short, the conditional part of the condition–action pairs developed during the Yearwood experiment provided a clear match to the conditions generated by the Brailey procedure. The clarity of this match was emphasized by virtue of the fact that Yearwood's participants were debriefed. They therefore had an understanding of the purpose of the study.

To use the language of production systems, we propose that, in addition to providing clear conditional information, the resolution provided by the debriefing allowed participants to compile the entire test experience into a group of linked productions which aided in the transfer of learning. If the similarity between the two procedures was accessed (i.e., if the "executive" production postulated here was activated), then the entire set of related productions would as a consequence be activated. In other words, noticing would automatically lead to action since the connection between a complex set of conditions and a series of responses would have been learned and "compiled" into a unit. Receiving a solution to the Yearwood task led to an array of loosely related events being transformed into a rudimentary skill and therefore aided in creating conditions conducive to access and transfer (Anderson, 1983, 1987; Holland, Holyoak, Nisbett, & Thagard, 1986). In contrast, the Spencer and Weisberg study failed to provide participants with a resolution to their acquisition experience and as a result did not assist them in compiling information into a cohesive set of organized productions.

IMPLICATIONS AND FUTURE DIRECTIONS

We have reviewed a series of experiments that were designed to investigate processes involved in accessing and using of knowledge. As we noted earlier, access refers simply to noticing the presence of a relationship between two events; utilization refers to the successful application of knowledge to a problem-solving task. We have shown that access failures are common events, even when relevant information is highly related to subsequent problems to be solved. Furthermore, utilization failures frequently occur in situations where access of the target information is successfully attained. We argued that our findings are consistent with the concept of transfer-appropriate processing (Morris et al., 1977) and that one can use a framework based on production systems to more precisely characterize this concept and its relevance to phenomena such as interference effects, read-versus-generate differences, and problem solving-versus-factual acquisition differences. In every case, our results are consistent with the general patterns that can be predicted from a production systems approach.

For both our verbal puzzle materials and our materials using the A–B classification task, we began our investigations with the firm belief that we would find nondirected access and use of acquisition information. In all cases we were surprised. Being "closet introspectionists," we have regularly used our intuitions to predict the results of our experiments. However, once one knows the design of the current studies, one is in the "informed" condition. Under these circumstances, intuitions about what happens under uninformed conditions no longer apply.

Our work with uninformed access paradigms has prompted us to reconsider arguments such as those of the Wurzburgers (e.g., see Humphrey, 1951) about the importance of "sets" and "determining tendencies." We had always been aware that performance is due in part to task constraints but we had not realized the degree to which these constraints affect how knowledge is activated and utilized. Relatively subtle differences in perceived goals and task conditions can have powerful effects on the degree to which potentially relevant knowledge is accessed and used.

An emphasis on access also illuminates the importance of cues that provide continuity to our understandings and existence. For example, one of us recently telephoned a colleague and said "The spelling manipulation will work." Imagine getting that kind of message from a friend. You would spontaneously attempt to link it with some type of previous experience that made sense of the message. If you failed, you would be perplexed (e.g., see Bransford & Nitsch, 1978). In our case, the message linked well with previous discussions so the recipient of the phone call had no trouble interpreting the message. Clearly, the familiar sound of the caller's voice helped guide the access. People's faces and voices play a very important role in guiding access to previously experienced episodes. Familiar buildings, tasks and so forth undoubtedly play similar roles. These allow us to provide continuity to particular sets of experiences that would otherwise be disrupted unrelated events. It is interesting in this context to note that activities such as "paying attention to the sound of someone's voice" involves the kind of superficial processing that produces less-than-optimal performance in typical memory paradigms (e.g., Craik & Lockhart, 1972). From the perspective of access, however, such "superficial" cues can have powerful effects.

An emphasis on access also has important implications for education. As Simon (1980) notes, people must not only learn *what* is important but also *when* to use particular concepts and procedures. Often, we fail to help students conditionalize the knowledge that they acquire. Simon states:

> In our textbooks and in our teaching, we tend to underemphasize the condition sides of the condition–action pairs. We need to help our participants improve their skills of recognition and to help them acquire techniques for exercising those skills, so that if they have learned what to do, they will not be slow in recognizing when to do it (Simon, 1980, p. 94)

Modern technology, especially videodisc technology, makes it possible to create the kinds of contrast sets (cf. Garner, 1974) that can greatly facilitate the pattern recognition necessary to know when to use one's knowledge (e.g., Bransford et al., 1986). Research on pattern recognition and perceptual learning (e.g., Gibson & Gibson, 1955) is one of the next steps that we are taking in order to understand better how to develop knowledge structures that are accessed and used when needed. By paying more attention to the processes involved in conditionalizing knowledge, we may eventually be better able to "prepare students for action" (Gragg, 1940) and avoid the kinds of experiences that result in knowledge that remains inert (Whitehead, 1929).

ACKNOWLEDGMENTS

We (Jeff and John) express our gratitude to James J. Jenkins, friend and master mentor. It is he more than anyone else who inspired us to attempt to understand the human mind, and it is he who provided the wisdom needed to keep us from entering too many blind alleys. It is an honor to be part of a book that is dedicated to him. Preparation of this chapter was supported in part by U. S. Army Research Institute Grant MDA 903–84–C–0218 to Jeffery J. Franks and John D. Bransford, by Natural Sciences and Engineering Research Council of Canada postgraduate fellowship to Scot E. Purdon, and by a University Graduate Fellowship from Vanderbilt University to Kevin Brailey. We thank Robert Hoffman for his helpful editorial comments.

REFERENCES

Adams, L., Kasserman, J., Yearwood, A., Perfetto, G., Bransford, J., & Franks, J. (1988). The effects of facts versus problem-oriented acquisition. *Memory and Cognition, 16,* 167–175.

Anderson, J. R. (1974). Verbatim and propositional representation of sentences in immediate and long-term memory. *Journal of Verbal Learning and Verbal Behavior, 13,* 149–162.

Anderson, J. R. (1983). *The architecture of cognition.* Cambridge, MA: Harvard University Press.

Anderson, J. R. (1987). Skill acquisition: Compilation of weak-method problem solutions. *Psychological Review, 94,* 192–210.

Asch, S. E. (1969). A reformulation of the problem of associations. *American Psychologist, 24,* 92–102.

Bereiter, C. (1984). How to keep thinking skills from going the way of all frills. *Educational Leadership, 42,* 75–77.

Bower, G. H., Black, J. B., & Turner, T. J. (1979). Scripts in memory for text. *Cognitive Psychology, 11,* 177–220.

Brailey, K. (1987). [Long-term memory and non-directed access]. Unpublished material. Department of Psychology, Vanderbilt University.

Brailey, K., Franks, J. J., & Bransford, J. D. (1987). *Spontaneous use of pictorial versus verbal information.* Unpublished manuscript. Department of Psychology, Vanderbilt University.

Bransford, J. D. (1979). *Human cognition: Learning, understanding, and remembering.* Belmont, CA: Wadsworth.

Bransford, J. D., Franks, J. J., Morris, C. D., & Stein, B. (1979). Some general constraints on learning and memory research. In L. S. Cermak & F. I. M. Craik (Eds.), *Levels of processing and human memory.* Hillsdale, NJ: Lawrence Erlbaum Associates.

Bransford, J. D., Franks, J. J., Vye, N. J., & Sherwood, R. D. (1986). *New approaches to instruction: Because wisdom can't be told.* Paper presented at the Illinois Conference on Similarity and Analogy, Champaign-Urbana, IL.

Bransford, J. D., & Nitsch, K. E. (1978). Coming to understand things we could not previously understand. In J. F. Kavanagh & W. Strange (Eds.), *Speech and language in the laboratory, school and clinic* (pp. 267–307). Cambridge, MA: MIT Press.

Craik F. I. M., & Lockhart R. S. (1972). Levels of processing: A framework for memory research. *Journal of Verbal Learning and Verbal Behavior, 11,* 671–684.

Dewey, J. (1963). How we think. Portions published in R. M. Hutchins & M. J. Adler (Eds.), *Gateway to great books* (Vol. 10). Chicago: Encyclopedia Britannica. (Originally published by Heath, 1933, 1961).

Ebbinghaus, H. (1885/1964). *Memory: A contribution to experimental psychology.* (H. A. Ruger & C. E. Bussenius, trans.) New York: Dover Publications.

Franks, J. J., Plybon, C. J., & Auble, P. M. (1982). Units of episodic memory in perceptual recognition. *Memory and Cognition, 10,* 62–68.

Garner, W. R. (1974). *The processing of information and structure.* Potomac, MD: Erlbaum Associates.

Gibson, J., & Gibson, E. (1955). Perceptual learning: Differentiation or enrichment? *Psychological Review, 62,* 32–51.

Gick, M. L., & Holyoak, K. J. (1980). Analogical problem solving. *Cognitive Psychology, 12,* 306–365.

Gick, M. L., & Holyoak, K. J. (1983). Schema induction and analogical transfer. *Cognitive Psychology, 15,* 1–38.

Gragg, C. I. (1940, October). Wisdon can't be told. *Harvard alumni bulletin,* 78–84.

Hanson, N. R. (1970). A picture theory of theory meaning. In R. G. Colony (Ed.), *The nature and function of scientific theories.* Pittsburgh: University of Pittsburgh Press.

Holland, J. H., Holyoak, K. J., Nisbett, R. E., & Thagard, P. R. (1986). *Induction: Processes of inference, learning, and discovery.* Cambridge, MA: Harvard University Press.

Humphrey, G. (1951). *Thinking: An introduction to its experimental psychology.* New York: Wiley.

Hyde, T. S., & Jenkins, J. J. (1969). Differential effects of incidental tasks on the organization of recall of a list of highly associated words. *Journal of Experimental Psychology, 82,* 472–481.

Hyde, T. S., & Jenkins, J. J. (1973). Recall for words as a function of semantic, graphic, and syntactic orienting tasks. *Journal of Verbal Learning and Verbal Behavior, 12,* 471–480.

Jenkins, J. J. (1979). Four points to remember: A tetrahedral model of memory experiments. In L. S. Cermak & F. I. M. Craik (Eds.), *Levels of processing in human memory.* Hillsdale, NJ: Lawrence Erlbaum Associates.

Kasserman, J. (1987). *An investigation of processes underlying access in word fragment completion.* Unpublished doctoral dissertation.

Kasserman, J., & Johnson, R. (1987). [Non-directed access to words presented in prose]. Unpublished material, Department of Psychology, Vanderbilt University.

Larkin, J. H. (1981). Enriching formal knowledge: A model for learning to solve textbook physics problems. In J. R. Anderson (Ed.), *Cognitive skills and their acquisition.* Hillsdale, NJ: Lawrence Erlbaum Associates.

Lewis, M. W., & Anderson, J. R. (1985). Discrimination of operator schemata in problem solving: Learning from examples. *Cognitive Psychology, 17,* 26–65.

Lockhart, R. S., Lamon, M., & Gick, M. L. (1988). Conceptual transfer in simple insight problems. *Memory and Cognition, 16,* 36–44.

Morris, C. D., Bransford, J. D., & Franks, J. J. (1977). Levels of processing versus transfer appropriate processing. *Journal of Verbal Learning and Verbal Behavior, 16,* 519–533.

Newell, A., & Simon, H. A. (1972). *Human problem solving.* Englewood Cliffs, NJ: Prentice Hall.

Nitsch, K. E. (1977). *Structuring decontextualized forms of knowledge.* Unpublished doctoral dissertation, Vanderbilt University, Nashville.

Perfetto, G. A., Bransford, J. D., & Franks, J. J. (1983). Constraints on access in a problem solving context. *Memory and Cognition, 11,* 24–31.

Perfetto, G. A., Yearwood, A. A., Franks, J. J., & Bransford, J. D. (1987). Effects of generation on memory access. *Bulletin of the Psychonomic Society, 25,* 151–154.

Polya, G. (1957). *How to solve it.* Garden City, New York: Doubleday Anchor.

Postman, L., Adams, P. A., & Bohm, A. M. (1956). Studies in incidental learning: V. Recall for order and associative clustering. *Journal of Experimental Psychology, 51,* 334–342.

Purdon, S. E. (1987). *The search for spontaneous access: Structural similarity and categorical priming.* Unpublished masters thesis, Department of Psychology, Vanderbilt University, Nashville.

Ratcliff, R., & McKoon, G. (1981). Automatic and strategic components of priming in recognition. *Journal of Verbal Learning and Verbal Behavior, 20,* 204–215.

Ross, B. H. (1984). Remindings and their effects in learning a cognitive skill. *Cognitive Psychology, 16,* 371–416.

Schacter, D. L. (1987). Implicit memory: History and current status. *Journal of Experimental Psychology: Learning, memory, and cognition, 13,* 501–518.

Shepard, R. N. (1967). Recognition memory for words, sentences, and pictures. *Journal of Verbal Learning and Verbal Behavior, 6,* 156–163.

Simon, H. A. (1980). Problem solving and education. In D. T. Tuma & R. Reif (Eds.), *Problem solving and education: Issues in teaching and research.* Hillsdale, NJ: Lawrence Erlbaum Associates.

Spencer, R. M., & Weisberg, R. W. (1986). Context-dependent effects on analogical transfer. *Memory and Cognition, 14,* 442–449.

Stein, B. S., Littlefield, J., Bransford, J. D., & Persampieri, M. (1984). Elaboration and knowledge acquisition. *Memory and Cognition, 12,* 522–529.

Weisberg, R., DiCamillo, M., & Phillips, D. (1978). Transferring old associations to new situations: A nonautomatic process. *Journal of Verbal Learning and Verbal Behavior, 17,* 219–228.
Wertheimer, M. (1959). *Productive thinking.* New York: Harper & Row.
Whitehead, A. N. (1929). *The aims of education.* New York: Macmillan.
Yearwood, A. (1987). *Effects of categorical structure on spontaneous access and utilization of information in a classification task.* Unpublished doctoral dissertation, Department of Psychology, Vanderbilt University, Nashville.

VI PEDAGOGY

18 The Aesthetic Basis of Pedagogy

David Premack
École Polytechnique

Pedagogy, the teaching of one individual by another, appears to be a biological novelty, an activity largely confined to humans. Is the proposition sound? Biological generalizations are notoriously subject to exception. If the claim is true, how shall we account for it? What are the psychological mechanisms on which pedagogy depends? Are there implications here for the evolution of human intelligence? According to the standard argument, cultural evolution fueled biological evolution: Early changes in protohuman brain led to more complex forms of social organization. The advancement of human social complexity is then ascribed to language. Though not false, this traditional account is incomplete; human uniqueness does not consist solely of language. For instance, if one added language to an ape, one would not produce a human. Thus one may accept the standard argument: Cultural evolution fueled biological evolution, while at the same time rejecting the standard story of the origin of culture.

This chapter is organized as follows. First, I will compare the social transmission of information in humans and animals. Second, I will show that humans have pedagogy while animals do not, and will identify a condition that makes pedagogy essential for the human though not for the animal. Third, the role of pedagogy in culture will be examined. Fourth, I will present a theory of aesthetics that accounts for the presence of pedagogy in humans and its absence in animals.

THE SOCIAL TRANSMISSION OF INFORMATION IN HUMANS AND ANIMALS

In the social transmission of information, one generation imparts its skill or knowledge to another, sometimes accomplishing in an afternoon what might take biological transmission generations. Although this quick, flexible transformation is best seen in human cultural inheritance, one finds in animals (in what might be called protocultural inheritance) the same social transmission of information. Note that this transmission is not confined to apes and monkeys, but can be found even in the rat. The first solid food a rat eats is likely to be one whose odor it encountered in its mother's milk (Galef, 1981). After weaning, social guidance continues. The rat develops a map of the food sources in its area, so that it can use the food odors it detects on the bodies of its peers as cues for finding particular foods (Galef, 1981).

None of this implacably social transmission of information depends on pedagogy. Simple associative learning will explain all of it. Moreover, more complex cases, such as those seen in monkeys, for instance, the well-known improvisations in food technology in the Japanese macaques, can be accounted for by adding observational learning. The washing of sweet potatoes and winnowing of grain, introduced by the gifted young female, Imo, diffused through the colony, largely on the basis of observational learning (Kawamura, 1959). The fastest diffusion took place among animals that looked at Imo and at one another—her peers—whereas the slowest took place among animals that apparently did not look at Imo or at any other young animal—the old males (Itani, 1958; Kawamura, 1959).

Imo's innovations have a further characteristic. They lie well within the competence of her species in this sense: they were acquired without any assistance. Other members of Imo's group needed only an opportunity to observe Imo, or a member that had already observed her, along with the opportunity to try out what they had observed. That is, they needed only a passive model, not an active or judgmental one who would oversee their learning and correct their errors.

Suppose, however, that an appreciable part of the innovations of gifted individuals did not fall within the competence of the species. That is, suppose that most of the population could not acquire the innovations of its gifted members without assistance. In this case, innovations would not be self-propagating, diffusing through the group, socially transmitted across generations. They would die with the innovator.

Pedagogy is the mechanism that could stay the death of such innovations. It could do so, that is, provided it is more effective than simple learning. If an appreciable proportion of individuals who cannot acquire an innovation without assistance can acquire it with assistance, then pedagogy is the answer. Pedagogy will retain for the species the benefits of the innovator.

IS PEDAGOGY CONFINED TO HUMANS?

In imitation, the novice observes the model, copying his behavior, but the model does not return the observation. He may never know that the novice is there, and, indeed, were the novice not there, the model would behave in the same way. Pedagogy is immediately distinguishable in that observation goes in both directions: novice to model but also model to novice. In addition to observing, the model judges the novice according to internal standards, and intervenes actively to modify the novice's performance should it depart from his standards. Pedagogy thus consists of a combination of observation, judgment, and intervention.

In addition, we may ask about the motivational basis of pedagogy. As we shall see, it is best described as follows: the pedagogue acts so as to reduce the disparity between the acts of the novice that are being observed and the pedagogue's internal standards.

In deciding whether pedagogy is confined to humans we must take into account the parental investment in progeny that is found in many animals. For instance, there is a well-known correlation between the complexity of a bird's food technology and the length of time the parent remains with the fledgling (Brown, 1975). Birds whose diet depends on cracking open mollusks remain longer with the parents than do those that eat simple seeds and insects (Norton–Griffiths 1969).

A more dramatic example of parental investment is the live mice brought to infant kittens by their parents, which the growing kittens then come to stalk with increasing efficiency. This is not confined to domestic cats, of course, but is found in many carnivores (Ewer, 1969; Leyhausen, 1979). Is this not pedagogy?

In the first place, the parental investment of nonprimates is largely confined to one domain (food technology). This should already arouse suspicion, for human pedagogy has no such restriction but applies to every conceivable domain. It is a hallmark of human cognition that is already indicative of the flexibility that often sets the human apart from the animal.

In addition, the animal's investment shows no apparent sensitivity to feedback from the progeny. Consider these rhetorical questions: If a kitten were inept, falling behind the littermates, would the parents give it additional training, bringing it extra mice and delaying the kitten's departure until it caught up with the peers? Or suppose, upon releasing the kittens from the nest, the parents found one to be an inadequate hunter, would they reclaim it for further training? In brief, does a parent judge the quality of an infant's performance and modulate its "training" accordingly?

The lack of such evidence is not the result of a failure to have made the appropriate observations. On the contrary, one can find cases where the animals have been closely observed, the description fine-grained, as in Ewer's account of parental training in the domestic cat (1969). In this acutely described case, the closest approximation to "parental judgment" is this: A mouse that escaped was recaptured by the parent and returned to the kittens. Note this is a reaction to the mouse not to the kittens (and it is not the mouse the cat is "training" but the kittens).

Closer approximations of human pedagogy can be found in nonhuman primates. Both monkey and ape mothers have been observed to remove from the mouths of their infants leaves of plants not eaten by the species. Gorilla and chimpanzee mothers have been observed to hold their infants away from them and to encourage them to walk toward them (Yerkes, 1943). Unlike the previous cases, these examples are not species-specific, do not apply only to food technology, and though exceedingly simple, have something of the flavor of pedagogy. Yet, even if complex, these examples could be ignored because of their sheer infrequency. Wrangham and Nishida, two distinguished fieldworkers, report only two instances of removal of leaves from infants' mouths after approximately 150 hours of field observation (personal communication, 1986). Human pedagogy could be ignored, too, were it equally infrequent.

A more frequently observed example consists of "toilet training" in the monkey. When an infant voids while being carried by its mother, she is likely to pull the infant away until it stops. The infant screams when first torn from its comfortable perch, though in time the two animals improve their reading of each other's signals, so that the infant is anticipated and released before it voids. Is this pedagogy? No, because no matter how subtle the communication may become in this dyad, the mother's response is little more than a simple reaction to an aversive stimulus.

The macaque weans her infant in much the same manner. At first she simply pulls the infant from her breast, and denies it further access, though if the infant persists, she may strike it (Barnett, 1968). Punishment is apparently the prime mechanism animals use in modifying one another, and the macaques's manner of weaning her infant is a good example. Punishment, from the recipient's perspective, is a painful stimulus received just when it is doing what it most wants to do, whereas from the sender's perspective it is a natural reaction to an aversive condition. One individual's painful stimulus is another individual's cathartic response.

One can find appreciably more complex cases which, nonetheless, remain responses to aversive stimuli. For example, when the Hamadryas baboon bites the nape of the female's neck if she wanders too far afield (Kummer, 1971), the male's reaction is again largely an innate response to a negative state of affairs. When the chimpanzee mother intervenes to terminate the excessively rough play that caused her infant to shriek (Goodall 1988), she provides another example of basically the same kind. Finding the infant's shrieking aversive, she acts to terminate it. The infant may benefit from its mother's intervention, but protection is not pedagogy. One can help or protect another without training it in any way.

The issue is not whether animals modify one another. They do. When in a dominance fight, one animal has been defeated, its behavior has been undeniably modified. But not all modification is pedagogy. In pedagogy, one individual has a mental representation of properly executed behavior, compares the actual behavior of the other one with the representation, and trains the other one to bring its behavior into conformity with the representation. One does not *know* that the individual has mental representations and engages in planned action. Mental representations (and planning) cannot, of course, be observed. However, the complexity of the observed training warrants the assumption.

Complex Examples from the Laboratory

A most complex case of pedagogic-like behavior in animals occurred in my laboratory, not as the product of an experiment, but as a spontaneous action. Captive animals, when properly maintained, often show forms of behavior that are more complex than can be seen in the field. Though complex, these cases are rare. In more than 20 years of observation, I have seen only three or four such cases. Here is the first of two examples.

Among captive chimpanzees, one of the prerogatives claimed by the dominant animal is that of being accompanied when changing locations. While submissive animals change locations alone, dominant animals demand company. By stationing themselves in front of the submissive animal, they lead the latter to abandon its current enterprise—foraging, grooming, or resting. The two then move off together to a new location chosen by the dominant.

Before moving, the submissive animal connects itself to the dominant in either of two ways: grasping the other one around the waist from behind, or lining up alongside and putting an arm around the other's shoulder.

Sadie and Jessie were among the four juvenile animals that had lived in a group in the lab for more than 3 years, but they were not a natural pair. They did not choose one another's company, had never before been placed in the compound (a walled half-acre field) by themselves, and had no history of walking together.

When first placed together, Jessie ran off whenever Sadie approached. Sadie's first job was thus to calm an extremely skittish Jessie. She accomplished her purpose by patience and steadfast calm. Over and over, Sadie approached Jessie, slowly, peaceably, until finally Jessie did not run off. Now Sadie stood before Jessie and actually patted her shoulders and head. Her next step was to position herself alongside Jessie. Then Sadie took Jessie's arm, lifted it up and, ducking her head, dropped Jessie's arm around her shoulder. Why didn't Sadie simplify matters by placing her own arm around Jessie? I have no idea, though in fact that is not the normal arrangement. In this social exchange, the submissive animal makes the connection, placing its arm around the dominant one, and it was this canonical form that Sadie taught Jessie.

Once Sadie had placed Jessie's arm where it belonged, the two animals set off. All would have been well, except that Jessie was too short for Sadie. Her arm slipped from Sadie's shoulder, down along Sadie's back until finally both her arms and full weight lay across Sadie's back and Sadie stopped. Whereupon Jessie ran off. Sadie did not hotly pursue her, but reinstated the whole cycle, beginning with the slow, patient approach. At the end of about two hours, Jessie was perfectly trained. Not only was all skittishness gone, she carried out perfectly the services of the submissive animal. When Sadie approached, Jessie abandoned her current enterprise, lined up beside Sadie, placed an arm around Sadie and the two set off together. The problem caused by Jessie's relative stature had not been solved, of course, and after a short distance, Jessie slumped across Sadie. The two stopped. But now rather than running off, Jessie righted herself and the two set off again.

I have described this case in full to show that on occasion one can find in the chimpanzee training that has the cognitive complexity of the human case. Sadie's behavior has everything we could wish for in order to argue that the trainer has in mind a representation of a desired state of affairs consisting of the behavior of the other one, and carries out a highly deliberate set of planned acts to bring about the representation. Sadie's acts are not simple reactions to an aversive stimulus. On the contrary, she successfully inhibited the disposition to strike or attack the originally uncooperative Jessie, substituting calm and even a few pats for the inhibited aggression. And putting Jessie's body into the desired position, a beautiful act of passive guidance, also differs from chasing a fleeing female or pulling a voiding infant from one's body. Lifting the other one's arm and placing it around her own shoulder probably has no base frequency. That is, it probably does not occur in any setting except this one; it is an act designed for the occasion.

In every respect save one, Sadie's training of Jessie was a perfect example of pedagogy. What was the exception? The training was carried out for the trainer's benefit. Can we prove this? In principle, quite easily. The distinction could be drawn in this manner: Allow Sadie to train two animals, Jessie and a female twin, Leslie. In the case of Leslie, allow Sadie not only the opportunity to train but also to benefit from training, whereas in the case of Jessie allow the training but not the benefits. Does Sadie train both of them or rather concentrate her efforts on Leslie, ignoring Jessie evermore? If in the long run Sadie trains only Leslie, we can be reasonably confident that the point of the training was to benefit the trainer.

By contrast, a pedagogue, tested in the same way, would not differentiate between the two sisters, but would seek to bring the performance of both into conformity with his or her standards. This, as we noted earlier, is the goal of pedagogy. Suppose the goal of the training were to change, becoming that of benefitting the trainer. The main consequence of such a change would be to limit the occasions on which pedagogy occurred. No longer keeping an eye on the young, surveying their performance in the light of standards, the pedagogue would train only those whose improved performance was of benefit. For instance, one would not train the young to climb trees—thereby producing a well-formed act—but train only those who would bring back fruit.

In the case of Kohler's star pupil, Sultan, we find another animal whose pedagogic-like behavior would probably also fail on motivational grounds, though in a slightly different way. Kohler (1925) reported that Sultan watched his less-gifted peers struggle with problems that he had already solved, and often went to their aid, apparently to assist them. For example, on one occasion, Sultan stacked the boxes they had failed to stack, reached the banana, brought it down and then departed, leaving the banana behind. Although this may look like pedagogy, one could probably show that it is not in a straightforward way. Allow Sultan to observe the failure of his peers to solve the problem, but then remove the peers before allowing Sultan to enter. Does Sultan nevertheless enter, stack the boxes and leave the banana behind? If he does, then Sultan's behavior does not qualify as pedagogy. More likely, Sultan has observed a state of affairs that he finds nonoptimal, and is therefore disposed to modify it. But modifying the condition of the inanimate world is not pedagogy. Note that changing the inanimate world can have only an indirect affect on the future. By contrast, pedagogy, in improving the competence of the next generation has a direct effect. In training the young, the pedagogue effectively arranges for a world that will be brought into an optimal state even though he is no longer present to make the change.

WHAT IS THE NEED FOR PEDAGOGY?

Although forms of behavior resembling pedagogy are to be seen in animals, they fall short of the human form on several grounds. Those that qualify in even some respects are extremely infrequent, whereas those that have the desired complexity are not only infrequent but motivationally incorrect, clearly done solely for the trainer's benefit.

Is pedagogy more effective than unassisted learning? Will it enable individuals to learn skills and acquire knowledge that they do not learn otherwise? Though the answer is emphatically "yes," I will delay discussion of that question for a later section. Let us return now to the question of the need for pedagogy, and how such a need could have arisen.

A need for pedagogy could have been brought about by a sufficient increase in the variability of intelligence within a species. When individual differences in intelligence reached a sufficient magnitude, then innovations by the gifted members might lie beyond the range of the less gifted; the latter could acquire such innovations only with assistance.

Human intelligence is indeed more variable than that of animals. However, it differs from that of animals not only in having greater within-species variability—it is also more divisible into separate or specialized components. This modularity is only hinted at in animals. One does not find the chimpanzee that is strong on verbal factors but weak on quantitative ones; high on social skills but low on spatial. Or any such profiles that one may find in animals are certain to be less pronounced than they are in humans. Among humans, one finds individuals who are capable of significant innovation in one component but incapable, without assistance, of acquiring even existing knowledge in another component. This is not a condition one is likely to find in an animal.

Is the variability and modularity of human intelligence sufficient to make pedagogy a necessity? Presently it is. Scientists provide examples of this kind of innovation everyday. So, for that matter, do homemakers. A close look at the kitchens of the world would reveal new ways of preparing food that only expert cooks could acquire on an observational basis. Most of the population would require pedagogy. So much for the present.

But when did this condition first arise? When did the divisibility of human intelligence into specialized components attain a magnitude that would make pedagogy beneficial, not to the pedagogue, of course, but to her kin (who would be the principal beneficiary in any case)? Though I leave the definitive answer to appropriate scholars, prehistorians and others, one can speculate about these matters from the already known variability in tools. For instance, the transition from the protractedly unchanging tool kit of *homo erectus* to the subsequent rapid growth, suggests the kind of change we are looking for (Jelinek, 1977). The transition may mark both the change in intelligence that would make pedagogy advantageous, as well as the emergence of pedagogy itself.

In summary, whenever an appreciable proportion of a group cannot acquire the innovations of its gifted members by the usual combination of imitation and learning, a need for pedagogy arises. It is not necessary, of course, that the innovator do all the teaching. At most, he or she need teach only one other individual, or not even one, for the population may include others who, though incapable of producing the innovation themselves, understand it, and could teach it to others.

THE ROLE OF PEDAGOGY IN CULTURE

Advantages of Pedagogy

Earlier we asked whether pedagogy is more effective than unassisted learning, and answered emphatically "Yes," for these reasons.

1. The pedagogue provides superior feedback. He or she knows what the ideal product should look like and judges the novice accordingly. By contrast, the novice, being ignorant of what the ideal looks like, may settle for a decidedly inferior product, a tool that "works" but with suboptimal efficiency. In this connection, I'm reminded of the cooking of two generous young anthropologists who guided me through the Kalahari, sharing their food with me. Though both had had ample opportunity to observe their colleagues cooking in the field, and thus to learn the basics of this discipline, certain details had

escaped them. They neither preheated their cooking utensils nor lubricated them. Steak was placed in a cold pan and eggs cracked into one that was neither heated nor greased. Somehow, the wayward products that emerged from their campfire never led them to question their procedures. In fact, not until the peculiarity of their cooking was pointed out to them did they recognize the inadequacy of the food they had been eating for months or perhaps years. Yet when pedagogy exposed them to preheating and lubrication, they immediately adopted these practices. Which is to say, often the first contribution of the pedagogue is to teach the novice how things are supposed to be.

2. The pedagogue may encourage the novice. He or she may know, as the novice does not, that a period of intermediate achievement, a plateau, intervenes at a certain stage, but that one has only to persevere in order to achieve final excellence. One may also encourage the novice, simply by subdividing the task, astutely assigning the novice subgoals that one can reach and that will therefore encourage continued effort.

3. At a more advanced level, the pedagogue can explain the purpose of an act or an artifact to the novice, so that the novice need no longer learn by a kind of blind mimicry. In understanding the causal intent of the device, the novice can modify his construction in the light of that intent. Indeed, the novice may even attempt to innovate, to depart somewhat from the pedagogue's model, the better to suit his individual purposes.

4. When language is added to pedagogy, the novice can be given the benefit of explicit definitions. Now, the pedagogue can go beyond ostensive definitions, for example, in the case of the kinship system, beyond pointing to cousins or aunts, and provide the novice with formal definitions of these classes.

5. One may teach the novice that one is better at some things than others, that it may be a waste of time to make any investment at all in certain skills. It would be better to devote efforts to skills where one appears to have some talent; he could then trade his products with those of other individuals whose skills complement his own. Although these are judgments that lie well beyond a novice, they could be readily made by a pedagogue.

6. Finally, although the novice in some cases may not learn at all without pedagogy, in other cases the advantage may reduce to one of efficiency, a reduction in error. Even this advantage should not be underestimated, however, for while in the laboratory the cost of error is often small, in the real world it can be substantial. Sometimes the novice is not given a second trial.

Origins of Culture

Cultural evolution is said to have fueled biological evolution (e.g., Mayr, 1982; Maynard–Smith, 1972; Tinbergen, 1964). On this analysis, behavior, once a neglected part of evolutionary theory, has emerged as a major source of natural selection. Conjectures concerning protohumans (e.g., Isaac, 1978; Washburn, 1963) are compatible with this view. At a time when protohuman brain was little larger than that of contemporary ape, protohuman behavior already differed from that of ape. Upright posture, stone tools, home base, and possibly food sharing, distinguished protohumans. Individuals who lived in semipermanent shelters (as opposed to nests constructed each night), made stone tools (rather than stripped twigs), and shared food (rather than scrounged from one another) are likely to have formed social organizations whose complexity would put a premium on intelligence and therefore lead to selection of mutations making for larger brain.

There is no doubt that the ability to communicate through language could greatly increase social complexity, thus applying pressure for the evolution of intelligent forms. However, pedagogy could have a comparable effect. Any procedure that increased the diffusion of innovations of gifted individuals, as pedagogy would, will increase the complexity of the group in which the innovations occurred. Moreover, this is not an effect that depends on language. Even the passive guidance that Sadie used in training Jessie shows how effectively training can proceed without language. In addition, simply being competent in language would not itself assure that the competence would be used for pedagogical purposes. A species that lacked all pedagogical disposition would no more use language to teach its young than it would use nonverbal means.

Anthropologists commonly point out that one cannot acquire a certain level of tool making without assistance, and stress that language would therefore be needed before a group could attain to this level (e.g., Harris, 1975; Jelinek, 1977; Leroi–Gourhan, 1964). The confounding of language with pedagogy is a common error; what the anthropologists mean to say is that since the skill could not be acquired without assistance, what would be needed for the skill to diffuse through the group is pedagogy. Pedagogy, as we have seen, does not require language.

The Anthropology of Pedagogy

Do all human groups engage in pedagogy, as the present account would require? Data on pedagogy are surprisingly hard to find. Pedagogy is not an official anthropological category: No catalog lists the pedagogical practices of different groups. One finds ethnographies that contain pertinent sections, for example, material on socialization, as well as the occasional monograph devoted to child education. But the questions for which one wants answers—for example, Who are the pedagogues: parents, older children, and so on? How much pedagogy is verbal? How much reliance is there on passive guidance? Is the pedagogy used in teaching social practice the same as that used in teaching technology or are there systematic differences? Do cultures differ in the domains to which they apply pedagogy? These questions are left unanswered by the information presently available. The anthropology of pedagogy is largely nonexistent; the proper study of pedagogy has yet to begin.

The !Kung San or Kalahari Bushmen may be an exception to this pessimistic conclusion. The infants and children of this group have been extensively observed (e.g., Draper, 1976; Konner, 1976), and some of this observation has even led to the impression that pedagogy is not to be found among the Bushmen.

It is said that the foraging technology of the !Kung is simple, and that the children are not taught it. When parents forage, young children are not taken along; they are left behind in camp in the presence of other adults and older children. However, not all !Kung technology is simple. Collecting melons may be simple but making jewelry, poisoning arrows, butchering, and so forth, is not. Bushman technology is of variable complexity. For instance, the !Kung make their jewelry from pieces of ostrich egg shell (each of which is pierced and rounded to a more or less uniform shape) before being strung in one of several characteristic fashions. How do children learn this skill, or that of making and poisoning arrows, or butchering the several large ruminants that the group eats?

How shall one determine whether or not a group is pedagogical? Perhaps one can simply watch for a time, and if no pedagogy appears, conclude that there isn't any. But how long must one watch before drawing this conclusion? How many pedagogical interventions does an average parent make in a day? Without some basis for estimating these rates, watching without a specified target may be uninformative. One does better to observe children as they actually acquire the technologies and social practices of their culture.

Furthermore, we know that there is a domain in which the !Kung infant is subjected to intensive training. The domain is one in which we do not train our children, for we do not believe that the ability to sit, stand, or walk requires training. Bushmen believe otherwise, however, and train their infants intensively in these early motor skills (Konner, 1976).

The connection between Bushman belief about child development and their practice of pedagogy is informative, for it suggests how pedagogy is likely to operate in all human groups. Most human dispositions, no matter how strong their innate component, are not reflexes; they are affected by cognitive factors, by the beliefs an individual holds. Thus, groups that hold different theories about child development may be expected to direct their pedagogy at different targets. Although we do not teach our children to walk, we do teach them how to eat. Bushmen are likely to do the opposite: teach their children how to walk, but not how to eat.

The human need for pedagogy is sometimes demeaned on the grounds that important competencies such as that of language can be acquired without instruction. We do not teach our children grammar—we do not, it is said, even correct their grammatical errors (e.g., Brown & Hanlon, 1970). Incidentally, this claim cannot be entirely correct, for the literature provides amusing counterexamples, for instance, a case in which a child, though repeatedly corrected for grammatical error, retains his or her grammatical error, while changing virtually everything else (Cazden, 1965, 1968). Of course, if grammatical correction really never occurred, one could hardly discover that it does not work. But this case is intriguing from the present point of view for a different reason: Even where pedagogy does not work, some parents still apply it.

Not every human activity is subject to pedagogy in every culture, nor does every human competence require pedagogy. Language is distinctive because it does not require pedagogy, though language is not alone in this regard. Attributing causal relations to inanimate objects, as well as attributing states of mind to the other one ("theory of mind," Premack & Woodruff, 1978) are evidently also natural competencies; they, too, develop without instruction.

On the other hand, much of what humans learn is not derived from natural competence. At stake here are not only the technologies and social practices that characterize every culture. There are also the theories that every human group entertains. These theories, detailing how the world began and how it works, are all transmitted by instruction, the cosmologies that trace the world's origins to, for example, a benevolent snake, no less than the scientific theories that replaced them. Although the predilection to hold such theories is not taught, the theories themselves are.

Pedagogical targets will vary among cultures, influenced not only by actual need but also by the theories cultures hold as to how competencies are acquired. Although the acquisition of some human competencies obviously requires more instruction than others, to recognize a need for pedagogy is hardly to endorse a *tabula rasa* view of human knowledge.

AESTHETICS: THE MOTIVATIONAL BASIS
OF PEDAGOGY

Although the pedagogue may appear to judge the novice on grounds of efficiency, in most cases such a judgment would require a complex computation of which the pedagogue is incapable. The efficiency of an act or product is likely to be highly correlated with its appearance, but the judgment itself, which is typically quick and unstudied, is based on appearance alone.

In describing pedagogical judgment, I have referred to "internal standards," suggesting that these standards motivate and direct the pedagogue, that all discrepancies in the novice's behavior are computed relative to them. One needs an account of these standards, their origins, and their content.

One also needs an account of these standards to explain why the chimpanzee does not engage in pedagogy. The extreme simplicity of examples from the field (e.g., the removal of leaves from the infant's mouth) may suggest that the animal is cognitively incapable of pedagogy. But this is repudiated by examples from captive animals. Though cognitively capable of training the other one in elaborate ways, on those rare occasions when the chimpanzee engages in such training, it does so for its own benefit. The "internal standards" driving the human do not appear to drive the chimpanzee.

In the theory I will present here, aesthetics is ultimately granted broad social consequences. It emerges as an integral part of pedagogy, and therefore affects what one individual does to another. Nevertheless, we first encounter aesthetics not in social but in individual behavior—in the human investment in self-betterment, in the practice of one activity or another in which humans recurrently engage.

Practice

One can expect to see little pedagogy—little correction of the other one—in a species whose individual members do not correct themselves. Pedagogy starts at home, with self-correction. In speaking of self-correction, self-betterment, or the like, I have in mind what we mean when speaking of practice, as in the practice of musical instruments, sports, cooking, speech, any of indefinitely many activities in which humans pursue excellence. Practice should not be confused with learning. Members of all species learn or eliminate errors, obtaining the pellet more efficiently, but that is not what is meant by practice. There is no pellet in "practice," no consequence extrinsic to the act itself.

Practice is so rare in the nonhuman that when I first saw what appeared to be a case, I ceased to do any counting or recording, and simply watched. Here was the same Jessie of the earlier example, once again in the compound, evidently practicing somersaults. Most of her attempts were successful, achieving a proper form and carrying the animal straight ahead. But occasionally she failed, twisting off to the side as children do when they first learn to somersault.

The failures were interesting. They appeared to lead Jessie to "try" again, where by try I mean that, following a bad somersault, Jessie appeared to produce the next somersault more quickly and with greater vigor than following a good one. I could have begun the defense of this impression, had I been less fascinated, simply by counting the number of times the chimpanzee quit (did not somersault for, say, 5 seconds) following good and bad acts respectively. If the conditional probabilities were appropriate, they could have defended the idea that animals do "practice," that is, engage in acts that have no extrinsic consequences, actively discriminate good form from bad, and try to produce one while avoiding the other. By themselves they could not have proved the claim— additional data would be needed—but they could have begun the proof.

Practice presupposes three factors: (1) The behavior is done without extrinsic consequences; (2) One can distinguish good from bad on some criterion; (3)

Individuals act to maximize the good and minimize the bad. How one carries out (3) may vary over individuals and/or occasions. Following a bad act, one may respond more vigorously and after a shorter latency (as appeared to be the case with Jessie); on another occasion, respond with less vigor and after a longer interval, taking time to "think things over" and responding with special care or delicacy. What is essential is that there be systematic differences in the behavior following good and bad acts.

We see little practice in nonhuman animals. The somersault case, because it appears to realize all three factors, is rare. Chimpanzee stone throwing is more typical. Though chimpanzees are robust, if inaccurate, stone throwers (accurate enough, however, to endanger visitors on the observation platform) they never practice stone throwing. They throw only when someone is there.

Play, though common in vertebrates, does not qualify as practice because, while the first factor obviously applies, it is not clear that either the second or third does. That is, there is no serious evidence that animals, when playing, reject bad forms, even to the extent of being more likely to quit after a good act than a bad one, thus providing differential conditional probabilities of the kind described here. Perhaps birdsong is more nearly an example of practice, though here too it is not clear whether either the second or third factor applies. Moreover, the mere elimination of wrong notes, as may occur in the development of birdsong, does not automatically qualify as practice. Indeed, the elimination of errant forms is neither a necessary nor sufficient conditon for practice. On the one hand, an individual may try repeatedly to perfect a form of movement, fail completely and nonetheless be said to practice. On the other, if errant forms that do not conform with a template are eliminated automatically, this does not constitute practice. Finally, one must be dubious that the improvement in an activity results from practice when, as is apparently the case with birds, only one activity is subject to "practice." Humans show no such restriction, one behavior being as likely a target of practice as another.

A more provocative example is afforded by placing mice in a square wheel. When placed in a square wheel, mice of some varieties run more than normal (Kavanau, 1966). Though Kavanau gives these data a simple interpretation, one could interpret them more liberally. One could say that the mice run until their increasing mastery of the square corner enables them to restore a more or less normal form of running. The same procedure might have a comparable effect on other species. Stones placed in a bird's mouth, weights tied to a horse's leg, a clothes pin attached to a pike's fin—these impediments could heighten responding, leading the animal to respond until it had more or less restored the species-specific form of the act.

The investment induced by the impediment would simulate human practice; but it would depart from true practice in two essential respects: First, human practice does not depend on impediments. A human might, in the course of practicing, place a stone in his or her mouth, but only to sharpen the challenge;

the act of practicing does not depend on the stone or any other impediment (moreover, no bird would put a stone in its own mouth). Second, the acts that humans practice do not have species-specific forms. Stereotypical form and rate of responding are a characteristic of the rat and of other nonprimates. Not only do rats lick at a fixed rate (cf. Schaeffer & Premack, 1961, for evidence of fixed lick rate in neonatal rats licking for the first time), they also eat, groom, copulate, run, executing all recurrent behaviors at a fixed rate (e.g., Premack & Collier, 1962). But this is not a characteristic of primate behavior, human or nonhuman. Hitting a ball, diving, driving a car, carving a stick, whistling, riding a horse, playing the piano, shooting an arrow—none of these acts or the untold others that humans practice has species-specific forms. Humans do not practice to achieve or reinstate a species-specific form; they practice to achieve a "best possible" form. It is the sense of this ideal, rather than an external impediment, that goads the human.

Practice is a response to an aesthetic constraint under which all humans operate. Although naturally of variable magnitude, the constraint is present in some degree in all humans. To understand this constraint we require a theory of aesthetics. Here is an outline of the form that such a theory should take.

A Theory of Aesthetics

Aesthetic judgment does not apply only to the few special domains—music, visual art, literature—to which it has been confined by tradition. Aesthetics applies first and foremost to one's own species. This will affect the judgments one makes about one's self and others, assuring that aesthetic factors play a role in mate selection (and even perhaps child care, handsome children being likely to receive better care than less handsome ones).

We require two assumptions to account for human aesthetic behavior: First, the three levels on which humans characterize humans—appearance, behavior, and character—are all subject to aesthetic judgment. Second, the three levels are interconnected. In the rest of this section, I will explicate these assumptions, starting with the first one.

Every culture provides a characterization of positive and negative value on the three levels, thus a characterization of good/bad appearance, good/bad behavior, and good/bad character. Consider first the matter of appearance. The hope to find universal features—for instance, a universally beautiful face—has been largely frustrated. A bone passed through the lip, enhancing the face in one culture, makes it ugly in another. Often these differences have been taken to mean that aesthetics has no universal components and is strictly learned. However, this judgment is comparable to concluding that since people talk different languages, language has no innate or universal components. Both language and aesthetics are obviously affected by learning, but both have unlearned components.

What is invariant in the aesthetic judgment of appearance can be compared with what is invariant in language. From the features that can be used to describe human appearance each culture may select a different subset (even as each language "selects" a different subset of phones). If these subsets differ widely, and there is no apparent reason why they should not, then what is regarded as good/bad appearance may vary widely over cultures (as widely as languages vary over cultures). What will not vary is the selection of *some* features with which to characterize good/bad appearance. That is, beautiful/ugly appearance will be a universal contrast, one found in every culture.

In turning from appearance to behavior, one is surprised by both the simplicity and possible universality of the system that is used to distinguish good from bad. In the judgment of behavior no less than in that of appearance, one can be certain of cultural elaborations; nevertheless, these differences may be elaborations on a common core. According to a recent theory (Premack, 1990), human infants use a simple system in coding the valence of the action of self-propelled objects. Infants code the action of an object as positive if it preserves or increases the liberty of a second object; as negative if it reduces the liberty of a second object. Cultures may specialize even at this level, denying liberty in different ways—for example, by forcing action, forcing inaction, forcing changes in pace, speedups or slowdowns. Yet this need not obscure the unitary code that may underlie the judgment of behavior.

As appearance and behavior are the external components of aesthetic theory, so character or personality is the internal component. Personality and character differ in that the latter has a moral component. Character, as a folk theoretical notion, concerns not only the quality of what an individual does, whether it is good or evil, but, more importantly, the moral quality of what an individual is. In folk theory, character is the essence of an individual, the innermost determinant of his actions. Although this feature has occasionally been ascribed to animals (we find societies in which pigs and cows have been executed for capital offenses); by and large the feature is confined to humans. Cows as a rule no more have character than do robots. What is inconceivable is a person to whom character is not ascribed. Naturally the notion has undergone extensive cultural elaboration. For instance, whether human character is thought to be good or evil, mutable or immutable, subject to free will or determined, caused by devils or genes, and so on, are cultural decisions. As such, they confuse the issue, for they obscure from view what may be invariant or species-specific in the human perception of humans. What appears to be species-specific is the characterization of human character as good or bad on the basis of some features, and the ascription of this property to all humans.

The reality of these levels of description may be enhanced for some readers by pointing to the recent neuroscience that establishes detectors revelant to at least two of the three levels. For instance, cells in macaque monkey and human cortex are sensitive to faces in general, specific faces, parts of faces, and so on (Perrett,

Mistlin, & Chitty, 1987). In the judgment of appearance, the face is a principal target.

More recent work by Perrett and his associates (Perrett, Harries, Chitty, & Mistlin, 1989) has established cells in macaque monkey temporal cortex sensitive to hand movement and other body movements. These movements are of a kind that could easily serve as cues for reading goal orientation or intention. Though work of this kind is of quite recent origin, there are already grounds for anticipating the discovery of a more comprehensive detector system for coding human and animal movement.

Are there detectors for character or personality? More to the point, what are the features they would detect? The answers to these questions depend in large measure on the decision one makes about the level of this system. Is the analysis of personality or character based on perceptual cues or is the system entirely conceptual? If perceptual or perceptual in part, there must be detectors; cells sensitive to whatever physical events or features provide the basis for the detection of character or personality.

Our theories of character or personality are based on two bodies of information, one dealing with the short-term mental states, the other with the long-term dispositional states that humans ascribe to others. Short-term states are the propositional attitudes—for example, intention, want, and belief—that children not only ascribe as early as the fourth year, but ascribe with remarkable skill (Wimmer & Perner, 1983, etc.). Long-term states are the personality traits—kind/cruel, aggressive/gentle, truthful/deceitful, and so on—that children ascribe, too, but not until somewhat later.

Humans characterize one another in terms of these short- and long-term states as readily as they do in terms of appearance and behavior. When an individual says of John that he has red hair, or that he bats left-handed, one makes claims no more real or natural than those when saying John wants to date Mary (short-term state) or John is a kind person. None of these levels of description—appearance, behavior, character—has special privileges; none takes priority over the other. Humans find them equally natural.

Are humans the only species that uses all three levels of characterization? In the chimpanzee, one finds evidence for the ascription of short-term states (e.g., Premack, 1988a; Premack & Woodruff, 1978) but none for long-term states (Premack 1988b). Even though research is at a tender stage, one may doubt that the chimpanzee has a personality theory. Only a minority of chimpanzees pass tests for the attribution of short-term states, and while those that do pass may have a theory of mind, the theory is profoundly weaker than the human one. For example, the animal fails the "false belief" test (which some see as a litmus test for theory of mind; Premack, 1988b), has yet to be shown to assign states of mind different from its own, does not distinguish *know* from *guess* (Premack & Woodruff, 1978) and so on. That so weak a theory of short-term mental states would be accompanied by a theory of long-term dispositional states, a personality theory, seems highly doubtful.

If chimpanzees, unlike humans, characterize the other one on only two levels (or perhaps two and a third), this will pose a problem for neuroscience. Detectors for the third level of description will be present, or present in well-developed form, only in humans. This is the same problem, of course, that is faced in the case of language. With the evidence restricted to a clinical rather than experimental form, the brain map for language does not begin to equal that for vision.

In summary, according to the first assumption humans perceive one another on three levels: appearance, behavior, and character. Every culture, using some set of features, characterizes positive and negative values on each of these levels. Cortical cells that detect features relevant to two of the three levels have already been found. Though chimpanzees may be said to have a theory of mind, the theory is weaker than the human one, and there is no evidence for personality theory. Only humans perceive one another in terms of the three levels.

The second assumption claims that humans see the three levels as interconnected. If shown a picture of a conspecific, the human does not see only the picture; he or she projects the behavior (and character) that would go with such a picture. One has definite anticipations of how a person of a certain appearance will act. Aesthetics is therefore in part a theory of the comportment or general demeanor that "goes with" a certain appearance. These anticipations constitute a species-specific theory, which is the proper substance of aesthetics.

We find suggestions of this theory (i.e., of the prediction of character or general demeanor from physical appearance) in both the laboratory and everyday life. The most striking laboratory evidence is the judgments people make, without hesitation, on the basis of the face alone. When shown a group of human faces, and asked to decide who is good and who is bad, they do not decline (pointing out the unreasonableness of the request). On the contrary, despite the lack of information, they willingly judge which face is that of a good person and which that of a criminal, who is the teacher, who the robber, and so on (Fiske & Taylor, 1984; Goldstein, Chance, & Gilbert, 1984; Hamilton, 1981; Schneider, Hastorf, & Ellsworth, 1979; Secord, 1953).

Why are people willing to make these judgments? Could they be responding to actual correlations? Do the criminals in any given culture look different from the law-abiding citizens? At what age do children make these judgments? Even if one should find evidence for a relation between criminality and appearance, this would not eliminate the possibility that people believe in the association of appearance and character. Beliefs of this kind could foster the relation, contributing to any actual correlation that may exist. The extreme willingness of people to make these judgments is difficult to understand unless one assumes that they connect the several levels of description, and believe that appearance (in this case, the face alone) predicts character or behavior.

Evidence of a more suggestive sort can also be discerned in everyday life especially on those occasions when the theory (of interconnected levels) suffers mild disconfirmation. For example, we are led to make such remarks as "she was beautiful until she opened her mouth;" physical beauty leading to the anticipation of intelligence, we comment when the anticipation is not met.

What is the nature of the assumed interconnection among the three levels? Do humans believe that it is causal, and if causal symmetrical or asymmetrical, or do they assume that the relation is merely associative and in no way causal? For instance, do they believe that an individual is intelligent or generous because he or she is beautiful, beautiful because he or she is intelligent or generous? The unease that these questions may induce already suggests that the assumed connection between levels is not causal, but is merely associative.

On the other hand, folklore treats the relation as causal. Pinocchio is probably the best-known example. With each lie his nose grew longer, a clear case of bad conduct causing bad appearance (appearance again located in the face). In the *Picture of Dorian Gray*, one finds a similar relation. Degenerate behavior caused his once-splendid picture to fall into increasing ruin. In both cases, bad behavior adversely affected appearance. Positive cases are more difficult to find, cases where exemplary conduct improved appearance. Should we take seriously the suggestions from folklore? Are there circumstances under which humans assume not only an associative relation among the levels but also a causal one?

WILL AESTHETIC THEORY EXPLAIN HUMAN–ANIMAL DIFFERENCES?

Will it account for the fact that humans engage in pedagogy while animals do not? One may decide that it will not on the grounds that animals, too, have aesthetic theories. After all, mate selection, which can be affected by aesthetic factors, is found in animals. And one can find other preferences as well, not only for mates but also for shelters or nesting places, food some or all of which may be derived from aesthetic factors. The key questions is: Do animals have aesthetic theories, and are they based on mechanisms comparable with human ones?

To answer this question we need cases where the mechanism underlying animal preferences has been identified. Fortunately, we have such a case in the Japanese quail. Bateson (1982) reports that in this species both sexes prefer to mate with their first cousins. This is an interesting outcome because it not only concerns mate selection—a kind of preference likely to involve aesthetic factors—but already shows that mate selection in the quail cannot be derived from an aesthetic theory comparable with the human one.

First cousins could not possibly have physical or behavioral features in common. Instead, what they could share is a certain degree of similarity with ego, the target bird. That is, first cousins could share the well-known "intermediate degree of familiarity," which is widely thought to be a general stimulus condition for attraction, not only for the act of mating and not only for birds (Berlyne, 1960).

Neither highly familiar nor unfamiliar stimuli are a source of attraction, the former producing boredom, the latter fright or avoidance. For instance, whereas rats show no interest in exploring familiar stimuli, if faced with highly unfamiliar ones, they freeze and/or defecate, showing general signs of fear (Berlyne, 1960; Premack & Collier, 1962). It is only stimuli of intermediate familiarity that induce rats to leave the home base and explore. The quail's predilection for the first cousin may have a similar basis. Repelled by strangers (too unfamiliar), and bored by siblings (too familiar), the bird may find the first cousin just right, a perfect (intermediate) degree of unfamiliarity.

But if this is the mechanism for mate selection in the quail, it could not possibly lead to either self-betterment or to pedagogy. Both these behaviors require that the individual compare one's own (or the other one's) present condition with an ideal, and act vigorously to eliminate any disparity he or she finds between them. Attraction for stimuli of intermediate unfamiliarity could not have this effect. The quail data underscore the impropriety of leaping from the demonstration of comparable *behavior* (e.g., mate selection) to the conclusion of common *mechanisms*. Animal mechanisms need not even be a precursor of human ones; certainly those of the quail are not.

Chimpanzee mechanisms are more likely to be precursors of human ones. But here there is a question of the development of the mechanism. Even if the chimpanzee's mechanisms resemble those of the human, the animal's competence is slight, relative to that of the human. In the chimpanzee, one finds a little of everything, some capacity for analogies (Gillan, Premack, & Woodruff, 1981; Premack, 1988b), a touch of "theory of mind" (Premack, 1988a; Premack & Woodruff, 1978), causal inference (Premack, 1976). For instance, the chimpanzee can be trained to do analogies, not only to complete incomplete ones (Gillan et al., 1981), but also to construct them from scratch. However, there is essentially no spontaneous construction of analogies. Further, there is no evidence that the animal can partition the world into elements, which it then arranges into analogies. That is, the animal's analogies are not built from elements that the animal produced itself but from elements given it by humans.

The near-absence in the chimpanzee of either practice or pedagogy is compatible with the overall evidence. Not all human competencies can be found in the chimpanzee (e.g. language), and those that can be found are profoundly weaker than the human counterpart. The chimpanzee's aesthetic competence is evidently commensurate with its other faculties, too weak a device to give rise to more than a suggestion of either practice (self-betterment) or its social counterpart, pedagogy.

SUMMARY

One can distinguish three grades of socially transmitted information, depending on the degree of intention in the system. A system is make up of at least one novice and one model, and in the lowest grade of transmission information is exchanged without intention by either party. For instance, a rat often eats as its first solid food one whose odor it encountered in its mother's milk. The information exchanged here was not exchanged intentionally; the neonate did not seek the information nor did the mother seek to impart it.

In the intermediate grade, the novice behaves intentionally, though the model remains unintentional. This is traditional imitation or observational learning. For instance, a monkey, ape, or child observes a model, acquiring a new technology, but the model behaves in the same way whether the novice is present or not.

In the highest grade, both novice and model act intentionally. Not only does the novice seek information but also the model seeks to impart it. The novice observes the model, as in imitation, but now the model returns the observation, in fact, not only observing the novice but also judging and correcting when he or she fails to conform with a standard. This is pedagogy, the most efficient form of social information exchange.

Though one finds precursors of pedagogy in animals, the full-fledged activity is found only in humans. The absence of pedagogy in the chimpanzee cannot be explained on cognitive grounds; it requires a motivational explanation, one we provided in the form of a theory of aesthetics. The theory consists of two assumptions. First, all three levels on which humans describe humans—appearance, behavior, character—are subject to aesthetic judgment. Every culture characterizes a positive and negative value on each level. Second, humans believe that the three levels are interconnected, associatively at least and in some cases even perhaps causally.

Though animals show preferences of an aesthetic kind, either these preferences are based on mechanisms too weak to give rise to pedagogy, or on mechanisms different from the human ones, mechanisms that will not give rise to either practice or its social counterpart, pedagogy. The former is apparently the case with the chimpanzee, the latter with the Japanese quail.

Because differences in intelligence among animals are relatively small, innovations of gifted individuals can be transmitted by ordinary learning and imitation, that is, by a combination of the first and second grades of social transmission of information. But this is not true among humans. Given the greater variability and modularity of human intelligence, most humans cannot acquire the innovations of gifted members by the ordinary combination of learning and imitation. They require assistance. This is one of the advantages of pedagogy for the human species.

ACKNOWLEDGMENT

Based upon the Kenneth Craik Lecture, Cambridge University, May, 1987. Supported in part by a grant from the McDonnell Foundation. My thanks also to École Polytechnique, Centre de Recherche en Epistemologie Appliquée, Paris, with which I was associated during the period in which I revised this chapter. Finally, it is a pleasure to express my debt to Ann James Premack, with whom I have discussed the present ideas and many others over the course of a long period.

REFERENCES

Barnett, S. A. (1968). The "instinct to teach." *Nature, 220,* 747–749.
Bateson, P. P. G. (1982). Preferences for cousins in Japanese quail. *Nature, 295,* 236–237.
Berlyne, D. (1960). *Conflict, arousal and curiosity.* New York: McGraw–Hill.
Brown, J. L. (1975). *The evolution of behavior.* New York: Norton.
Brown, R., & Hanlon, C. (1970). Derivational complexity and order of acquisition in child speech. In J. R. Hayes (Ed.), *Cognition and the development of language* (pp. 155–207). New York: Wiley.
Cazden, C. B. (1965). *Environmental assistance to the child's acquisition of grammar.* Unpublished doctoral dissertation, Harvard University, Cambridge, MA.
Cazden, C. B. (1968). The acquisition of noun and verb inflections. *Child Development, 39,* 433–448.
Draper, P. (1976). Social and economic constraints on child life among the !Kung. In R. Lee & I. Devore (Eds.), *Kalahari Hunter-gatherers* (pp. 199–217). Cambridge, MA.: Harvard University Press.
Ewer, R. F. (1969). The "instinct to teach." *Nature, 222,* 698.
Fiske, S. T., & Taylor, S. E. (1984). *Social cognition.* Reading, MA: Addison–Wesley.
Galef, B. J., Jr. (1981). The ecology of weaning. In D. J. Gubernick & P. H. Klopfer (Eds.), *Parental care in mammals.* New York: Plenum Press.
Gillan, D., Premack, D., & Woodruff, G. (1981). Reasoning in animals: I. Analogical reasoning in the chimpanzee. *Journal of Experimental Psychology: Animal Behavior, 7,* 1–17.
Goldstein, A. G., Chance, J. E., & Gilbert, B. (1984). Facial stereotypes of good guys and bad guys: A replication and extension. *Bulletin of the Psychonomic Society, 22,* 549–552.
Goodall, J. (1988). *The chimpanzees of Gombi Stream.* Cambridge, MA: Harvard University Press.
Hamilton, D. L. (1981). *Cognitive processes in stereotyping and intergroup behavior.* Hillsdale, NJ: Lawrence Erlbaum Associates.
Harris, M. (1975). *Culture, people and nature.* New York: Crowell.
Isaac, G. L. (1978). The food-sharing behavior of proto-human hominids. *Scientific American, 238*(4), 90–108.
Itani, J. (1958). On the acquisition and propagation of a new food habit in the natural group of the Japanese Monkey at Takasakiyama. *Primates, 1,* 84–98.
Jelinek, A. J. (1977). The lower paleolithic: Current evidence and interpretations. *Annual Review of Anthropology, 6,* 11–32.
Kawamura, S. (1959). The process of sub-culture propagation among Japanese Macaques. *Primates, 2,* 43–60.
Kavanau, J. L. (1966). Wheel-running preferences of mice. *Zeitschrift für Tierpsychologie, 23,* 858–866.

Köhler, W. (1925). *The mentality of apes*. London: Routledge–Kegan.
Konner, M. J. (1976). Maternal care, infant behavior and development among the !Kung. In R. Lee & I. DeVore (Eds.), *Kalahari Hunter-gatherers* (pp. 218–245). Cambridge, MA: Harvard University Press.
Kummer, H. (1971). *Primate societies*. Chicago: Aldine.
Leroi–Gourhan, A. (1964). *Le geste et la parole: Technique et language*. Paris: Albin Michel.
Leyhausen, P. (1979). *Cat behavior: The predator and social behavior of domestic and wild cats*. London: Garland.
Maynard–Smith, J. (1972). *On evolution*. Edinburgh University Press.
Mayr, E. (1982). *The growth of biological thought: diversity, evolution and inheritance*. Cambridge, MA: Harvard University Press.
Norton–Griffiths, M. N. (1969). Organization, control, and development of parental feeding in the oystercatcher. *Behavior, 34,* 55–114.
Perrett, D. I., Harries, M. H., Chitty, A. J., & Mistlin, A. J. (1989). Three stages in the classification of body movements by visual neurones. In H. B. Barlow, C. Blakemore & M. Weston–Smith (Eds.), *Images and understanding*. Cambridge, England: Cambridge University Press.
Perrett, D. I., Mistlin, A. J., & Chitty, A. J. (1987). Visual cells responsive to faces. *Trends in Neuroscience, 10,* 358–364.
Premack, D. (1976). *Intelligence in ape and man*. Hillsdale, NJ: Lawrence Erlbaum Associates.
Premack, D. (1988a). Minds with and without language. In L. Weiskranz (Ed.), *Though without language* (pp. 24–50). Oxford, England: Oxford University Press.
Premack, D. (1988b). "Does the chimpanzee have a theory of mind?" revisited. In W. Byrne & A. Whiten (Eds.), *Machiavellian intelligence: Social expertise and the evolution of intellect in monkeys, apes and humans* (pp. 286–322). Oxford, England: Oxford University Press.
Premack, D. (1990). The infant's theory of self-propelled objects. *Cognition, 36,* 1–16.
Premack, D., & Collier, G. (1962). Analysis of non-reinforcement varibles affecting response probability. *Psychological Monographs, 75* (Whole No. 524).
Premack, D., & Woodruff, G. (1978). Does the chimpanzee have a theory of mind? *Behavioral and Brain Sciences, 4,* 515–526.
Schaeffer, R. W., & Premack, D. (1961). Licking rates in infant albino rats. *Science, 134,* 1980–1981.
Schneider, D. J., Hastorf, A. H., & Ellsworth, P. C. (1979). *Person perception*. Reading, MA: Addison–Wesley.
Secord, P. F. (1953). Facial features and inference processes in interpersonal perception. In R. Tagiuri & L. Petrullo (Eds.), *Person perception and interpersonal behavior*. Stanford, CA: Stanford University Press.
Tinbergen, N. (1964). Behavior and natural selection. In J. A. Moore (Ed.), *Ideas in modern biology*. New York: Natural History Press.
Washburn, S. L. (1963). Behavior and human evolution. In S. L. Washburn (Ed.), *Classification and human evolution* (pp. 190–203). Chicago: Aldine.
Wimmer, H., & Perner, J. (1983). Beliefs about beliefs: Representation and constraining function of wrong beliefs in young children's understanding of deception. *Cognition, 13,* 103–128.
Yerkes, R. M. (1943). *Chimpanzees: A laboratory colony*. New Haven, CT: Yale University Press.

19

Pragmatic Skills and the Acquisition of Linguistic Competence

Judith A. Becker
University of South Florida

One of the major current controversies in developmental psycholinguistics concerns the manner in which adult input influences children's acquisition of language. Most researchers in this area focus on parents' responses to grammaticality, and there is little evidence about parental teaching of pragmatic language skills.

Pragmatics involves the appropriate use of language in social contexts. Pragmatic skills include saying *please* and *thank you* appropriately, using routines such as *trick or treat* at the right time and place, and taking turns in a conversation. A relatively new domain in the area of linguistic competence, the study of pragmatics emphasizes the functions of language for its users. It necessitates the consideration of the influence of context (e.g., participants, prior discourse, physical setting, task) on language use. Among the seminal works on pragmatic language development are Bates's *Language and Context: The Acquisition of Pragmatics* (1976), in which she lays out the domain of pragmatics and presents some cross-sectional and longitudinal data on the acquisition of a variety of pragmatic skills; and Shatz and Gelman's (1973) research monograph demonstrating that 4-year-olds vary their speech as a function of the age of their listeners.

It is important to understand the origins of pragmatic skills because they have implications not just for communicative competence but for social competence as well. In accordance with the claims of several theorists (Bowerman, 1981; Shatz, 1982), anecdotal evidence (e.g., Bates, 1976; Garvey, 1984; Heath, 1983; Miller, 1982) suggests that parents play a more active role in teaching preschoolers pragmatic skills than in teaching syntactic, semantic, or phonological skills. Only five studies (Eisenberg, 1982; Gleason, Perlmann, & Greif, 1984; Gleason & Weintraub, 1976; Greif & Gleason, 1980; Pellegrini, Brody, & Stoneman, 1987) have systematically assessed parental teaching of pragmatics, but each is limited in a number of respects. Specifically, researchers sampled relatively few conversational settings (e.g., dinner table, laboratory, doorways on Halloween), only a few pragmatic behaviors were described (almost exclusively phrases such as *please, thank you,* and *hello*), and only a few general teaching techniques (primarily prompting and modeling) were noted.

This chapter describes some of my recent work in which I have attempted to look more carefully at parents' teaching of pragmatic skills. First, I present the methods used for collecting these descriptive data. Then I present results bearing on the pragmatic behaviors parents taught their preschoolers and their tendency to use indirect teaching techniques. Finally, I discuss possible explanations for the use and effectiveness of these techniques, and some of the implications of such teaching for language acquisition in general.

A STUDY OF PRAGMATIC TEACHING

To develop more comprehensive taxonomies of the pragmatic behaviors parents teach and their techniques for teaching these skills, I began by collecting a relatively large set of observational data from five families. All five were white, middle-class, and intact at the beginning of the study. Each family had a preschooler. The preschoolers, three girls and two boys, averaged 3½ years of age when the study began. Three of the families also had a year-old infant.

Over the course of a year, parents audiotaped interactions that involved at least one parent and the preschooler. Such interactions included meals, bedtime, house cleaning, and craft making. Parents were asked to record "typical" interactions whenever it was convenient and as often as they wished. Otherwise, they were "blind" to the purposes of the study.

The families provided an average of 13 usable tapes over the course of a year. Tapes averaged around 30 minutes each. Thus, the data set involved approximately 33 hours of audiotaped interactions. The taped interactions were transcribed and pragmatic teaching episodes were identified. These included comments about any pragmatic aspect of the child's speech, but excluded pragmatic comments concerning games, songs, spelling, or other nonconversational language as well as pragmatic comments concerning the taperecorder.

There were 296 pragmatic teaching episodes in the transcripts, with an average of 59 episodes per family. Many of these episodes consisted of sequences of several teaching utterances. There were 505 total teaching utterances in the data set.

Pragmatic Behaviors that Parents Taught

Each of the 296 episodes was coded as involving one of 15 different kinds of pragmatic behaviors (with 97% agreement between two coders). These behaviors fell into four categories: behaviors involving what to say, how to say it, when to say it, and discourse rules. The five families were observed to teach pragmatic behaviors from each of the four categories, as can be seen in Table 19.1.

Although there were differences among the families in terms of which specific behaviors they taught and how frequently they taught them, there were also similarities. All five of the families attempted to teach their preschoolers the appropriate use of *please,* the use of a level of volume that was neither too high nor too low for the situation, when to talk, and how to respond verbally when spoken to. Parents in four of the families taught their children about routines (e.g., saying grace at mealtime, using *trick or treat* and *Merry Christmas* appropriately) and speaking clearly (i.e., not mumbling).

It is important to note that these data represent a far wider range of behaviors than previously described in the literature. The data show not only that parents were concerned with teaching their children pragmatic phrases and routines, but that they were also concerned about the skills involved in carrying on an effective and coherent discourse.

Techniques Parents Used for Teaching

The techniques parents used for teaching pragmatic skills were also identified (with a 95% level of intercoder agreement). Across the 505 teaching utterances, parents used 13 different techniques to teach their children pragmatic behaviors,

TABLE 19.1
Proportion of Different Pragmatic Behaviors Parents Taught in 296 Episodes

	Proportion
What to say	
1. *please*	.07
2. *thank you*	.03
3. Polite requests (e.g., *May I X?*)	.02
4. *goodbye*	.02
5. Routines (e.g., *trick or treat, Merry Christmas*)	.07
6. Address terms (e.g., *Sir*)	.12
7. Slang/swearing/taboo words	.10
8. Appropriate subject matter	.01
9. Apologies	.04
How to Say it	
10. Volume (not too loud or soft for the situation)	.17
11. Tone of voice (e.g., not whining)	.03
12. Clarity (e.g., not mumbling)	.12
When to Say it	
13. Knowing when to talk	.10
14. Responding when spoken to	.07
Discourse	
15. Maintaining the logic of the conversation	.02

far more than previously reported in the literature. Table 19.2 lists the techniques used by the families.

Again, there was variability among the families in their tendency to use certain techniques, and again there were similarities. In all five families, parents were far more likely to draw attention to their children's pragmatic errors or omissions than to praise them for appropriate pragmatic usage, even though the children often demonstrated correct usage. Critical comments comprised the vast majority of the parents' teaching techniques, an average of 74%.

Indirectness

Not only were parents typically negative, their criticisms of errors and omissions were also often indirect (see techniques 3b and 4b in Table 19.2). That is, for all of the families, most of the criticisms did *not* state explicitly what the child had done wrong or what he or she had to do to correct the error or omission.

TABLE 19.2
Proportion of Different Teaching Techniques Used by Parents in 505 Utterances

	Proportion
1. Reinforcement	.05
(e.g., *I like it when I can understand you*)	
2. Modeling (providing the required response for the child)	.01
(e.g., Dad: *Hi [child's name].* Mom: *Hi.*)	
3. Comment on omission	
a. direct	.04
(e.g., *Say "please"*)	
b. indirect	.20
(e.g., *What do you say?*)	
4. Comment on error	
a. direct	.08
(e.g., *Don't interrupt*)	
b. indirect	.41
(e.g., *Daddy's talking*)	
5. Posing hypothetical situation for didactic purposes	.01
(e.g., *What would you have said if that ape would have said "hi"?*)	
6. Retroactive evaluation of child's pragmatic behavior	.01
(e.g., *It wasn't very nice to call her that*)	
7. Anticipatory suggestion prior to child's error	.02
(e.g., *Don't forget to say night-night*)	
8. Answer to child's prompt or question about pragmatics	.08
(e.g., *No, we don't say "Merry Christmas" on Halloween, we say "trick or treat"*)	
9. Teaching sibling pragmatic skills in the presence of the preschooler	.07
10. Parents demonstrate skill instruction	.002
(e.g., Mom: *Go get my milk.* Dad: *What do you say?*)	
11. Evaluate another person's pragmatic behavior	.002
(e.g., Mom: *Please.* Dad: *Right, [child's name]?*)	

Parental indirectness took a variety of forms. Some of the comments were so indirect that they provided the child with essentially no information about the required pragmatic behavior or the conditions of its use. Saying *what?, huh?, excuse me?*, the child's name (often in a stern or questioning tone), *oh oh*, or *hey* only indicated that something was wrong. Other indirect comments drew attention to the error or omission—for example, parents repeated the child's error (sometimes with a question or laugh), repeated the child's utterances with the tag *what?*, told the child to *cut it out*, said *what's the magic word?* or *what do you say?*, repeated their own prior utterances, or said that the child was being *bad* or *not nice*.

Another type of indirect comment provided some information about the applicable pragmatic rule or the conditions under which one should follow the pragmatic rule. For example, parents asked rhetorical questions (e.g., *Are you ordering me to do it? Where did you hear that word?, Do you know what quiet is?, When are you ever going to learn to X?*), they provided the correct response themselves when their children failed to, or they referred to situational conditions relevant to the required pragmatic behavior (e.g., *I can't hear you, I asked you a question, Mommy's still sleeping, You're talking like a baby*).

Such indirectness is curious in that one might assume indirectness to be an ineffective way to respond to children's errors and omissions. That is, because parents' comments prompt children to correct their errors, provide omitted responses, and remember the rules in the future, one might suppose that explicitness would maximize the chances of children's understanding and responding to the comments.

In fact, the children seldom expressed confusion about what their parents wanted them to do, and the children generally corrected their pragmatic errors and omissions. They did so following the majority of their parents' uses of indirect techniques. There are at least two reasons why indirect teaching techniques might be helpful. First, learning to be indirect and to mask or mitigate ones intentions is itself an important pragmatic skill (Becker, 1982). For example, in making requests one often avoids directly demanding an object in order to show deference to the listener and thus increase the chances of compliance. That is, one might say *Got an extra pen?*, rather than *Give me a pen* or *I need a pen*. Parents' indirect teaching techniques almost certainly function as models from which children learn indirectness.

A second reason why indirectness may actually be effective is that indirectness places a significant cognitive load on children because it forces them to generate the correct response themselves. Self-generated rules and behaviors would presumably be well remembered.

The frequency of indirect comments and their contexts of use may help children to disambiguate their meaning. The children's ability to respond correctly to indirect utterances suggests that pragmatic teaching episodes become routinized by the time children are three to four years old. Functionally, such parental comments may not be so indirect, even though on their surface they appear to be. It is quite possible that parents use indirect teaching techniques for pragmatic behaviors at which children are relatively competent, but use more direct techniques when children are less adept, or in contexts in which they are less certain that the children will provide the required response. That is, there may be a developmental transition from direct to more indirect techniques for teaching particular pragmatic skills. I am currently exploring this possibility (see Becker, 1990).

Sometimes the indirect techniques were not successful. That is, the children persisted in their errors, failed to provide omitted responses, or changed their language but not in the way their parents intended. Nonetheless, there was only one instance in which a child was clearly puzzled by an indirect comment, and only six occasions in which children made the wrong pragmatic correction. It is difficult to explain the children's failure to correct their language appropriately in all instances. Perhaps the children did not know how to do so, did not hear their parents' comments, were deliberately ignoring their parents, or did not understand what their parents intended them to do (for further discussion of the functions and effectiveness of indirect teaching techniques, see Becker, 1988).

CONCLUSIONS, IMPLICATIONS, AND FUTURE DIRECTIONS

This type of examination of parental responses to children's pragmatic errors and omissions contributes to our understanding of the connection between parental input and children's language acquisition. Researchers need not focus solely on parents' responses to their children's ungrammaticality.

This exploratory study demonstrates that parents teach their preschoolers a wide range of pragmatic skills and do so by means of a wide variety of techniques. Parents were typically critical of pragmatic errors and omissions, and usually made their comments indirectly. Children seldom expressed confusion about their parents' indirect comments, and many of the children's misunderstandings can be seen in terms of their expectations about pragmatic teaching episodes.

It is likely that pragmatic "rules," being far more flexible and contextually sensitive than syntactic rules, require more tuition. In light of this, as well as the relevance of pragmatic skills to both communicative and social competence, parents' emphasis on pragmatic skills and their means for teaching them are quite functional and adaptive.

Insofar as pragmatic socialization is a relatively new area of study, many questions remain to be answered. Researchers might look at the specific manner in which pragmatic skills are modeled and feedback is provided. In addition, they should consider the relevance of various pragmatic skills from the parents' perspective (see Becker & Hall, 1989). This information might help us understand family differences in teaching styles and why parents react to imperfect performances in the ways they do. Similarly, pragmatic teaching should be related to other aspects of socialization. Finally, the connection between pragmatic competence and parental teaching could be further explored. That is, one might investigate the ways that children's level of pragmatic competence affects the behaviors that parents teach and the techniques they use. Researchers might also focus on the effectiveness of parental teaching and how it contributes to the development of pragmatic competence. It is clear that the study of the acquisition of pragmatic skills is a rich and wide-open area, involving research that can make a useful contribution to applied developmental psycholinguistics.

ACKNOWLEDGMENTS

This research was supported by grants from the Southern Regional Education Board and University of South Florida College of Social and Behavioral Science's Faculty Research Enhancement Program. I gratefully note the loan of transcripts collected by Dr. Stan Kuczaj and Dr. Christine Todd that were used in developing the coding systems, Karen Place and the many research assistants who worked on the project, and the five families who participated. I also thank Jim Jenkins for the example he sets for all of us as a scholar, teacher, and human being.

REFERENCES

Bates, E. (1976). *Language and context: The acquisition of pragmatics*. New York: Academic Press.

Becker, J. A. (1982). Children's strategic use of requests to mark and manipulate social status. In S. Kuczaj (Ed.), *Language development: Language, thought, and culture* (Vol. 2, pp. 1–35) Hillsdale, NJ: Lawrence Erlbaum Associates.

Becker, J. A. (1988). The success of parents' indirect techniques for teaching their preschoolers pragmatic skills. *First Language, 8,* 173–181.

Becker, J. A. (1990). Processes in the acquisition of pragmatic competence. In G. Conti-Ramsden & C. Snow (Eds.), *Children's language* (Vol. 7, pp. 7–24). Hillsdale, NJ: Lawrence Erlbaum Associates.

Becker, J. A., & Hall, M. S. (1989). Adult beliefs about pragmatic development. *Journal of Applied Developmental Psychology, 10,* 1–17.

Bowerman, M. (1981). Language development. In H. C. Triandis & A. Heron (Eds.), *Handbook of cross-cultural psychology: Developmental psychology* (Vol. 4, pp. 93–185). Boston: Allyn & Bacon.

Eisenberg, A. (1982). Understanding components of a situation: Spontaneous use of politeness routines by Mexicano two-year-olds. *Papers and Reports on Child Language Development, 21,* 46–54.

Garvey, C. (1984). *Children's talk*. Cambridge, MA: Harvard University Press.

Gleason, J., Perlmann, R., & Greif, E. (1984). What's the magic word: Learning language through politeness routines. *Discourse Processes, 7,* 493–502.

Gleason, J., & Weintraub, S. (1976). The acquisition of routines in child speech. *Language in Society, 5,* 129–136.

Greif, E., & Gleason, J. (1980). Hi, thanks and goodbye: More routine information. *Language in Society, 9,* 159–166.

Heath, S. (1983). *Ways with words: Language, life, and work in communities and classrooms.* Cambridge, England: Cambridge University Press.

Miller, P. (1982). *Amy, Wendy, and Beth: Learning language in South Baltimore.* Austin: University of Texas Press.

Pellegrini, A., Brody, G., & Stoneman, Z. (1987). Children's conversational competence with their parents. *Discourse Processes, 10,* 93–106.

Shatz, M. (1982). Communication. In J. Flavell & E. Markman (Eds.), *Cognitive development.* P. Mussen (Gen. Ed.), *Carmichael's manual of child psychology* (4th ed, pp. 841–889). New York: Wiley.

Shatz, M., & Gelman, R. (1973). The development of communication skills: Modifications in the speech of young children as a function of the listener. *Monographs of the Society for Research in Child Development, 5* (38, Serial No. 152).

20 Educating for Applications: Possibilities and Paradoxes

James J. Jenkins
University of South Florida

This chapter is an attempt to convey a message about educational policies and procedures and to acknowledge that professors and students are all in this together. I begin with stories about my own training and early career and then move on to the experiences of my students in applied settings. In the course of these personal experiences, three aspects of graduate education became apparent. First, I discuss the staple educational contents that we all agree ought to be required; second, I raise the issues on which we academics disagree among ourselves and, finally, I draw attention to those aspects of research style in which academics differ from their colleagues in nonacademic fields, which will be referred to as the "real world." There are many routes through graduate school to the doctoral degree. My message is that the students and their mentors should consider at least these three sets of issues in plotting each student's course.

ONE WAY TO ENTER APPLIED PSYCHOLOGY

Applications of psychology are near and dear to my heart. I began my professional career as an industrial psychologist, as a student of Donald G. Paterson, the "dean" of applied psychology. It was my dream as a young, socially responsible liberal to become an industrial psychologist working with a labor union. There, I reasoned, I could apply sophisticated psychological skills in a good cause. (In the late 1930s and early 1940s there was a strong movement in industry for labor to have a share in management. This trend peaked during World War II, just before I went to graduate school. My thought was that the unions would profit from adding psychologically skilled personnel to their side of the endeavor.) I learned that the Industrial Relations Center at the University of Minnesota had been actively assisting with union–management collaboration to bolster some industries that were in difficulty, so I went to Minnesota, to study applied psychology.

Paterson, who was a driving force in industrial, vocational and occupational psychology, provided his students with an abrupt introduction to the world of applied psychology. The first month that I was in graduate school, Pat found me in the hall and said, "Meet me out behind the building at 4 o'clock." I said, "Yes sir, Mr. Paterson" (graduate students were more respectful in those days). So at 4 o'clock I went out behind the building; we got in his car and drove to one of the big knitting mills in downtown Minneapolis. We went inside and met the man in charge of personnel. Paterson said, "Mr. X here has a problem with the turnover of power sewing-machine operators. I want you to help him solve that problem." That was my introduction to applied psychology. One found a real problem, tried to find some tools that could be applied to the problem, and worked on it to see if a solution could be found. In this particular instance, we did not completely solve the problem, but we did dispel several misconceptions that the personnel man had started with, and we improved the turnover situation somewhat (see Jenkins, 1948; Paterson & Jenkins, 1948).

One Way to Enter Experimental Psychology

I left traditional industrial psychology because it seemed to me that the field consisted entirely of sets of methods or tools. There was no theory except measurement theory and no set of enduring substantial principles. As a young instructor, I lost interest in such applications and cast about to find "real" structure, "real" theory, and "Truth." I allied myself with Wallace A. Russell, a Hullian psychologist who seemed to know the Truth. (Do graduate students these days even know about Hullian psychology? It seems to be relegated to the history course.) Russell had just received a PhD from Iowa and bore the stamp of Kenneth Spence. He had a remarkable skill. He could analyze any problem in terms of the variables of Hull's learning theory and by this technique seemed to be able to devise experiments for any situation. In contrast, those of us trained as applied psychologists took each problem as it came, tried to see what kinds of tools might be available, thought about the problem, struggled with it, turned it over, and finally decided what we could measure and how we were going to proceed.

My theoretical colleague, Russell, regarded our trial-and-error methods as barbarous and old-fashioned. Under his guidance and tutelage, I gradually became an experimentalist and set out to find the Truth. Now, after working in experimental psychology for more than 30 years, I have decided it is very much like industrial psychology. Experimentalists have an abundance of methods and techniques, but the rock-solid Truth I was looking for still eludes us. We still must figure out how to use the methods, and to do that we get in and think about the problem, struggle with it, turn it over and over, and so on. It all sounds very familiar.

It appears that I have come full cycle and I am right back where I started. But as a result of my history I no longer believe there is a single best approach or a single technique by which one can find Truth. That being the case, it is difficult to prescribe the "right kind" of training for graduate students who are now being trained as experimentalists.

HOW SHOULD WE PREPARE OUR STUDENTS?

It is especially important to rethink our training mission at the present time. Our experimental students no longer exclusively look for jobs in academia. Indeed, the number of academic experimental jobs fails to be equal to the number of new experimental PhDs by an appreciable margin, and increasing numbers of our experimental students go to work in applied settings. In my experience I have seen my own and colleagues' students employed at Control Data Corporation, Minneapolis Honeywell, Pillsbury, General Mills, 3M, IBM, Bell Labs, GTE, the Air Force, the Naval Training Center at Orlando, Fla., the Veterans Administration hospitals, Tampa Electric Company, the Cadbury Candy Company, and even Schenleys Distillery and Gallo wines.

This brings me to the real question addressed here. What should we be doing, as educators of experimental psychologists, with respect to training the students we are sending out into the world? How should we be preparing them for these nontraditional positions?

This concern is not entirely new. Throughout the decade of the 1930s one finds reports in the *American Journal of Psychology* concerning the need to train psychologists for nonacademic positions. For example, in the report of the forty-first annual meeting of the American Psychological Association, Paterson stated that "The supply of both PhDs and MAs so greatly exceeds the [academic] demand as to constitute a serious problem" (Paterson, 1934). One major difference from today, of course is that in the 1930s about 30 PhDs in psychology were graduated each year. The APA was alarmed to have a few left-over persons! Now, of course, we graduate more than 3,000 PhDs in psychology every year. Many of these are going to positions for which they have explicitly prepared, but many are going to positions that are entirely new to them, and in roles that they probably never considered when they first undertook graduate training.

For present purposes, let me divide training experiences into three categories. First, there are the courses and experiences that we all agree are useful. Second, there are training experiences that we academics disagree about, some advisers preferring one alternative and some preferring the other. And, finally, there are the aspects of training where academics are likely to take one position (implicitly or explicitly) while the "outside world" takes another.

TRAINING EXPERIENCES ON WHICH WE ALL (MOSTLY) AGREE

Statistics.   The first set of topics, the ones we all agree that everybody should know, is a list that always starts with statistics. Almost universally we agree that all students ought to take at least a year of statistics, and experimental students should take more. We argue that students need such training and that statistical skills are always marketable. If nothing else, psychologists can conduct analyses of variance, perform correlational analyses, and make complicated computer programs run. If, for example, our students can run statistical programs on mainframe computers and work stations, there is a job for them somewhere out in the world because most people do not know how to do that.

Psychometrics.   The second topic on which most of us would agree is measurement techniques. American psychologists since Thorndike have insisted on the value of quantification of psychological variables and Thorndike's dictum still dominates much of psychology. "Whatever exists at all exists in some amount. To know it thoroughly involves knowing its quantity as well as its quality" (Thorndike, 1918, p. 16). It is a good idea to know how to measure things. Measurement problems, all the way from elements of psychophysics to evaluating programs of therapy, are fundamental problems with which very few people, except psychologists, know how to cope. This is one of the things that we academicians know how to do, and we usually ask our students to learn how to do it too.

Content.   The third thing that we agree on is that students should have lots of content. We do not agree on the particular kind of content, but we do agree there should be a great deal of it. The more one knows about sensation and perception, the more one knows about human factors, the more one knows about learning and conditioning, the more one knows about abnormality, the more one knows about anything, the better. My first PhD advisee went to General Motors personnel research division. When he came back to visit, I asked him, "What did you need to know that we didn't teach you here in the courses on statistics, psychometrics, personnel methods, and so on?" He said, "Why didn't you give me more courses in social psychology?" His question foreshadowed the decision of most industrial psychology programs to broaden their preparation in this direction. It also confirmed my belief that we academics do not always know in advance what will be useful.

Experience.   Finally everyone seems to agree that students need real-life experience. If students have had experience doing something technical in the nonacademic world, they (and their subsequent employers) usually report that it was a good thing. When I have asked various former graduate students, "What was useful?" they all agree that real-life experience was important. In many firms, if a résumé has no indication of nonacademic experience, it is discarded in the very first screening. Interestingly, however, the experience can be of almost any kind. One student went so far as to say, "Even experience as a statistician for the Tampa Bay Buccaneers would have been useful" (if one can imagine that!). At any rate, we all agree on this need for real experience, although we may not agree on how the student is to get it.

CONFLICTING STRATEGIES IN TRAINING

Our views about training generate paradoxes. One of the paradoxes is already implicit in the preceeding recommendations. At one and the same time, we want students to be *generalists* and *specialists*, but it is difficult to see how we can train them to be both.

Breadth vs. Depth

Obviously, in one sense, students need to be generalists because no one knows where they are going, and because, wherever they are going, their situation is going to change rapidly. Technology is changing with blinding speed. All of the scholars who write about the future say that people must be flexible and adaptable. It now appears that students will need to retrain themselves several times during their working careers. Consequently, there is a justifiable emphasis on having broad perspectives. It is almost as if liberal arts were coming back into style—in graduate school. Overall, the message is that if students have true breadth, they will be better off, because they will be more adaptable and, perhaps, more resourceful, original, and creative.

A young psychologist I know went to the University of Miami to take their 2-year course leading to the M.D. The school takes PhDs in the sciences and makes them medical doctors in 2 years. Between June and October, for example, they finish their first year of medical school. The students work at an incredible rate under great pressure. My friend competed quite successfully with biochemists, physicists, and organic chemists, in short, with all kinds of PhDs in the program who had their degrees in very difficult areas that appear to be more related to medicine than psychology is. Her professors say that one of the reasons that she did so well is that she came with a breadth of knowledge. She seems to be more widely educated than the rest of the PhD students, and she can make use of the knowledge in ways that the others apparently cannot.

Clearly, on the one hand, we ought to educate for breadth. But, on the other hand, we also know that to make any progress on a specific problem, the investigator must understand that problem at a deep and realistic level. That means that the students (and perhaps the adviser) must really immerse themselves in that problem. It is not unusual to spend 2 or 3 years trying to penetrate and understand a problem. Obviously, this is in direct opposition to the requirement for breadth.

As an adviser, if I am supposed to tell students how to spend their time in graduate school, I must make some sort of compromise between these conflicting demands. At the same time I should say, "Get out of here, take some courses in engineering, economics and business; spread yourself over the whole field." and also say, "If you are serious about working on the cognitive consequences of middle ear infections, you need to concentrate on pediatrics and audiology for the next 2 years." How can the students meet both demands? Obviously they cannot follow both instructions because there is only a finite amount of time. That is one of the fundamental paradoxes.

I do not see any immediate way to solve this problem. We do not have a strong enough theory about general human behavior to permit us to enter any applied area and say, "These are the variables that count in this area and this is what you can do with them." Typically, when we concern ourselves with an area the first question is, "Well, what are the variables?" If we do not understand enough of the problem to even pick out the variables, we surely do not understand enough to bring some powerful psychological theory to bear. Since we do not have powerful theories to call on, we must go in and muck around just like we used to do. I wish it were different but that is the way it seems to be.

Consider another example. A few years ago I decided to do some work in pediatric cardiology as part of a project that Paul Johnson was conducting at the University of Minnesota. Pediatric cardiology is a good field to work in for two reasons. One reason is that the problems are well-defined. There is a relatively fixed number of defects (and their combinations) that are found in the infant's abnormal heart. The other reason is that there are good criteria for evaluating a diagnosis. Sooner or later in almost all cases the physician is going to see the heart and will know whether the diagnosis was correct. Yet it is very important that a diagnosis be made. Surgeons do not like to operate if they do not know what they are going to find in the infant's chest. If the surgeon opens the chest and finds that the diagnosis was wrong, he backs out: he does not improvise. Surgery on infants is a very serious undertaking. Unfortunately, with some of the rarer aspects of pediatric cardiology, the error rates in diagnosis are as high as 40%.

I was interested in the question of how it is that physicians learn to use heart sounds as part of the evidence for diagnosis. What is it that skilled physicians hear? How can other physicians be trained to hear the same things? Some physician friends confess that they do not hear much of anything significant. They listen, and sometimes go through the motions, but they do not get any useful information for diagnosis. On the other hand, there are some physicians of almost legendary skill who make accurate critical decisions on the basis of the heart sounds. There is good evidence that there is a lot of useful diagnostic information in heart sounds, and I wanted to study what it was and how physicians learn to hear it.

At the time I was getting introduced to this problem, I was setting off on a long trip and thought I might use some of my vacation time to read up on the problems. The cardiologist gave me a couple of books on heart sounds, but I rapidly discovered that I could not read them! I believe that I am a smart person; I know that I can read and comprehend along with the best of them. But I could not read those books.

The first thing I learned was that a vast amount of background knowledge must be immediately available to permit effective reading. Sitting down with a dictionary will not do. That is, if I encountered a phrase, like "the soft murmur of mitral stenosis," I could not avail myself of the needed "chunk" of information fast enough to continue reading. The reader cannot say, "Let me see, what is that supposed to mean? Oh yes, murmurs come in six grades of loudness and "soft" is either a 1 or a 2. Murmurs come in different auditory types, such as "machinery murmurs" or "sea gull murmurs" and nothing was mentioned here so it is probably the common type that sounds sort of like a scratch. The mitral valve is called that because it is remotely shaped like a bishop's hat; it is the valve over on the left side . . . the patient's left, that is. Stenosis means . . . " By that time the sentence is hopelessly lost.

Because I could not integrate knowledge fast enough, I could never find out what an entire sentence was about, so I had to do something different. I bought and assembled a model of the heart. I got some popular books about the heart and read those. Next I got an elementary textbook on the heart and read that. I talked to people about the heart, rehearsing my newfound knowledge. Then I took a class on pediatric cardiology in the medical school for 3 months. And, *finally*, I could read those two books on heart sounds.

This whole affair illustrates what I mean when I say, if students are going to venture into an area, they sometimes must steep themselves in that area. They cannot do reasonable work until they develop a considerable amount of specialized knowledge. I was in a position where I could devote a year to acquiring special knowledge. Can we ask graduate students to do that in the middle of graduate school? How will they get their classes taken, their papers written, their examinations passed? There are real problems in training that we have to face, and I think generalization versus specialization is a critical one.

Gaining Experience

Another related problem is that everybody wants to have applied experience, and all of us agree that is a good thing. So students are sent out to get applied experience. They do pretty well on the job . . . but never come back! Of course, we can console ourselves that the student has a job. But there are two things wrong with accepting that state of affairs. In the first place, that kind of outcome is a bad mark for the department! A department whose PhDs never finish, is not going to have a graduate program for long. In the second place, the students may be setting themselves up for being exploited for the rest of their lives. They may work at a lower rate of pay and be denied opportunities for advanced positions because they never completed their degree. We must somehow come to grips with that.

Minneapolis Honeywell is a good instance of both sides of this issue. Honeywell employs many graduate students as research assistants. The difficulty, however, is that some students just stay there and never finish their degrees. On the other hand, Honeywell (like IBM, Bell labs, and others) also offers predoctoral internships. In my judgment, the internships are superior because they are for a fixed period of time. On an internship, students are supposed to go to the parent company, work for a fixed period of time, collect their pay and experience, and return to school to finish their degrees. All in all, that is a much better system.

Of course, the problem is not unique to experimental students; we have the same problem at South Florida with industrial/organizational students. Students go out on a job (say, at Tampa Electric), get involved with their work and find out they like what they are doing. Pretty soon, they are not students anymore: They are employees. On the other hand, the students who go on internships do their job, come back and get their degrees, and then get a *better* job at Tampa Electric. Students need some applied experience, but they also need a terminus, a time to stop that experience, to get around the perennial student or the nondegree student problem.

Incidentally, the same warning applies to another topic everybody agrees on, and that is computer experience. We say, "Students must have computer skills; the more the better!" So we send students over to electrical engineering or the computer science department, and they take courses over there. Then the problem is to keep them from being hired as programmers. In some ways this is parallel to the problem of being a research assistant in industry. Students can earn more money programming for other people than they can make as graduate students in psychology. It is very easy to get lured down that path. Sometimes I feel that there ought to be a ceiling on how much we let our students learn about computers. My former students who are in industry frequently comment that one should know enough to talk to computer specialists and to tell programmers what to do. (They are disinclined, however, to let people know how much more they know about programming to avoid being involved in programming jobs. No psychologist I know enjoys writing code for its own sake.) Perhaps at some point we should say, "That is enough; no more courses in computer science. Wait until after you get your degree. Then if you want more training, take more courses."

Applying Techniques

The third paradox is that on the one hand we urge people to take a lot of research methods and statistics courses; on the other hand, all of us professors know a secret about that. Nobody ever really learned to do psychometrics, statistics, or research methods by taking courses. In my experience, even when a year of graduate statistics is required, the first time students do research they walk in and say, "What do I do with these results?" Students do not learn to apply statistics by taking courses in statistics and they do not learn to apply psychometrics by taking courses in psychometrics. Our conflict is that we want to teach students all this material that is good for them to know, but we know they do not really learn it when they just take courses.

We must do something better than coursework if we are going to get around this kind of paradox. We must realize that one of the main difficulties is that the information in a course is not organized around problems. This is not unique to our discipline, it is paralleled by the case in medicine. Medical students learn about the disease entities in courses. Then they go into the clinic and find a patient who has not been labeled with a disease entity, he or she just has a set of symptoms, that is, they present a problem. But the students did not learn how to deal with that kind of information; their knowledge is organized in the reverse structure. Learning how to work from the symptoms to the diagnosis is what clinical practice is all about. In a sense, medical students must take the information that they have already learned and turn it inside-out. The same thing is true about statistics, psychometrics, program evaluation, or any other methodology. Learning about it in a nice, organized, clean way is necessary but not sufficient. When we encounter a real problem, it does not come labeled with a classification. It does not say, "I'm a biscrial r problem", or "I need a mixed mode analysis of variance." So, again, we have the same kind of paradox; what we teach is not what we do in practice.

CONFLICTS IN ACADEMIC AND NONACADEMIC VALUES

Finally, there are some direct conflicts involved in training. These tend to be found in areas where academics, by training, tradition, or by self-selection, hold particular values and points of view that are in active conflict with the way the rest of the community works. Let me just mention some of these.

Perfection. Academics tend to believe that there is a best answer to a problem. But people who work out in the world say, "I do not need the 'best' answer. I just want *an* answer, one that will solve the current problem." That is a very different attitude. In research and development activities in the real world there is usually not enough time to seek perfection. And, ordinarily, one does not *need* to be perfect. What one needs is a *satisfactory* answer.

Following One's Nose.   The second conflict is that academics have an inclination to search for interesting findings. They may be studying one problem, but they are willing to switch to a new problem. As B. F. Skinner said, "When you run into something interesting, drop everything else and study it" (Skinner, 1956).

This capitalizes on *serendipity,* and we find this praiseworthy (look at almost any introductory psychology text). But the world of application by and large is not organized to facilitate or encourage serendipity. It is a problem-solving world and the problems must be taken care of. If the researcher says, "Gee, we found this interesting thing while working on that problem," the odds are that nobody will care. (There are, of course, noteworthy exceptions, such as the Bell research labs and a few other basic research units supported by industry, but they are a very small proportion of the industry-supported research.)

Do it Later.   The third conflict is with respect to time. In academia we have very lax standards about time. Ask anyone who ever edited a book and tried to get the academic authors to submit chapters by a given date. In the typical case, almost none of the chapters will be in by the deadline. Unfortunately, that is a clue to the general pattern of how academics work. "Oh, I'll do it in a year . . . or two." Most of us will let our students miss a completion date for a class, a paper, or a project without penalty. We assign an Incomplete, and assume that the assignment will be done "sooner or later." This attitude sometimes has painful consequences. For example, one year I gave an invited address at APA. A friend asked, "Can I publish your address in a book I am editing?" I said, "Sure, that's fine." I liked the paper a lot and thought the publication was timely. But *6 years later* the book had still not been published because many of the promised contributions had not been completed! At that point the editor asked if I would like to revise my chapter because he thought that the book was about ready to go to press! My timely paper was no longer timely, so I withdrew it. Even so, I am not sure that the promised book ever reached publication.

The business world does not share the academic attitude about time. Managers and colleagues out there believe in Monday morning at 8:45. They believe that time commitments are supposed to mean something. If an answer is due, they like it to be on schedule.

I or We.   Another conflict that arises has to do with individual versus group performance. In academia we emphasize the individual in many ways. If a person is evaluated for tenure, the promotion committees look for single-author publications. They count how many times the candidate is first author, second author, and so on. My personal opinion is that our attitude in such matters is both unfair and counterproductive, but the fact is that the academic community functions that way. In the nonacademic research world, my strong impression is that people are usually more concerned with getting good answers from a *team.*

They want a solution to a particular problem and they ask a team to furnish it. They do not emphasize which person in the team came up with the idea.

This conflict in values shows up in a variety of ways. Academics do not like to "brainstorm." In the nonacademic research world they think brainstorming is valuable and productive. Academics do not do much teamwork. In the nonacademic world, teamwork is the name of the game, because usually no single person commands all facets of the problem. In the case of this conflict, I think academics would do well to change their position, but I do not see any signs that such a revolution in attitude is brewing.

Let Me Say.   Related to the collaboration problem is a communication problem. The need for "bottom to top" communication is radically different in the academic and nonacademic settings. In many cases, academia has communication problems because academics believe that professors know answers and the students do not. So communication is organized to be top–down. Professors are supposed to tell students "how it is." Students are supposed to respond with the right answers, that is, answers that the professor already knows. This is a strange game to play; asking questions to which we already know the answers! If students do not like to play that game, we coerce them by not giving them the grades or the degrees that they want.

In the nonacademic world, my students tell me, the important thing is that they be effective communicators. One former student who works at a large corporation said, "I spend a third of my time getting ready to make presentations, making presentations, or following-up presentations." One student who had just gone to a different corporation said, "In the last month I have worked with 25 people outside my department." These were nonpsychologists, in various areas to whom he was supposed to offer valuable help. His task was to understand their needs and be able to communicate useful information to them. Another of my former students said, "The most valuable thing I learned in graduate school was how to use an overhead projector. If you don't use an overhead projector in my company, you're out of business. That is regarded as unprofessional." Still another student said, "The most valuable thing I ever did was to present papers at meetings of the Acoustical Society." (In those meetings, speakers have only 12 minutes to present a complex topic and report their research on it. Then there are 5 minutes of questions. The important people in the field come to the meetings and actually attend the paper sessions. They listen to what one has to say and they get up and comment on what has been presented.)

Such training does transfer. One of our former students said, "For the first presentation I had to do on the job, I outlined a 50-minute talk for the big brass." It was a problem the student knew very well. He said, "I began my presentation, but after a minute or two, the president got up and said, 'I'm not interested in hearing this!' and started to walk out. I immediately said, What do you want to hear? The president said, 'Well, I wanted to hear about so-and-so.' So

I said, 'I'm just coming to that!' And I dumped my talk and went directly to his topic."

Another former student said, "I prepare three presentations. I prepare a 40-minute presentation, a 15-minute presentation, and a 10-minute presentation. And frequently when I go in, I'm given five minutes." Our graduates must be skilled communicators. The people listening to them do not want to take notes. And they do not have the responsibility of repeating something back on an examination. Their responsibility is to get on with some problem. The researcher's responsibility is to communicate. I am afraid that often we do not treat our graduate students as if that is what they must learn. There is an important conflict between the top–down and the peer society approach to graduate school.

All Together Now.   The same comments apply to the skills of organization and planning. If the professors are doing all the organizing and planning, how can the students learn to do it? Once they are out in industry, they must be able to plan. Do they know how long it takes to get something done? Do they know what they can expect from team members? One student wrote a very interesting letter in which he said, "One of the most valuable things I did in graduate school was to arrange meetings and plan for colloquia. This involved all steps: rooms, facilities, refreshments, travel arrangements, announcements, entertaining and making schedules for speakers and all the rest. Then, of course, I also had to conduct the meetings and discussion. It's a thing I never would have thought of. But I'm called on to do that over and over again. I know how to do it because I did a lot of it in graduate school." *I* didn't think of these activities as being a part of his training; *he* thinks they were an important part of his training. We must be careful that the relatively autocratic structure of graduate school does not get in the way of graduate students learning the things they need to learn.

RECOMMENDATIONS FOR EDUCATING

Now, let me make some recommendations. The first thing that I must say is that we are not doing too badly. Most of our former students who are out in industrial settings are surviving. And, surprising as it may be to us, most of them like it. Indeed, one of our students who won tenure at a major university gave up academia after a year's leave doing applied psychology. He did not return to academia because he enjoys applied work so much. He finds it much more stimulating than being at a university. (That is rather shattering for us, isn't it?)

The other thing that is suggested by my remarks on conflicts, is that I think we need to make graduate school as nonauthoritarian as it can be, in the sense that we need people to learn skills in managing their own time. There should be strong requirements on them, but a lot of freedom about how they achieve their goals so that they can learn their own management skills and their own time skills. They must learn about organization, and about communicating effectively. We must put the burden on the student, but a different kind of burden. We should not say, "You will do the following step by step." but rather, "You will achieve the following end and you have 3 months in which to do this. You can do it any way you want, but at the end of 3 months you must be finished." Some faculty do that, but many do not. We must believe at some point that we are dealing with emerging professionals and we must give them the kinds of responsibilities that a professional ought to have.

To facilitate many aspects of training, I think that the ideal graduate department will have a whole set of research projects under way. Students should be able to apprentice themselves to a project and try it out, see what it is like to work in one style of doing research with one mentor. Then they can sample another field and work with somebody else on another project. In getting to know the individuals who know how to move research along, students will see a diversity of methods, and a diversity of organizational structures within which research is done. I think that is an important aspect of training. Of course, very few schools can afford to support such a variety of research programs. One of the reasons that we must keep grant research going is so that there are *programs* of research running. That should be a really important part of our graduate training because it gives graduate students an opportunity to affiliate themselves with real programs, working on real problems. It gives them diversity and, if it is handled right, it gives them increasing amounts of responsibility. The students can find programs they like; they can affiliate themselves with somebody with whom they want to study; they can begin proposing studies; and, finally, they can develop entirely new studies on the program. I think that is the very best kind of training we can do.

We should also recognize that we may not need to go it alone. We can get a lot of help from other departments. There are many assets at our universities. For example, one of our graduate students took the senior design course in engineering. He wound up as the head of a team building an experimental boat. First he apologized to me, saying that he had not learned very much psychology doing this. When we talked about it, however, he concluded, "Well, I did learn a lot of other things. I learned how to manage a research group. I learned how to make assignments. I learned how to keep to a time schedule. I learned how the dynamics of the group worked. I learned that you can't just tell people to do things and expect that they will happen automatically. But I also learned that I can trust people. I don't know any hydrodynamics and stuff like that so I had to trust to other's training and skill." All I could say was, "This is what good training is really like."

Well, what can we say about graduate training overall? I think we have both real promise and real problems. We all agree on some things that graduate students ought to learn. We recognize some paradoxes, like the generality–specificity problem, with which that we must struggle. (It would probably help to let our students know explicitly that such problems exist.) Finally, we have to deal with the conflict between the values that we academics have and the values of the outside world. Here, I think, academia needs to be flexible.

Although we are currently doing a pretty good job, I would urge a greater emphasis on application of the research techniques our students are learning about, attention to the need for lively (and time-limited) internships, emphasis on cooperative endeavors in which teamwork and communication are stressed, and participation in ongoing programs of research both in psychology and in related fields. I see vigorous expansion of activities for our students in the high-tech world around us; I think we can learn to prepare them even better for these new opportunities.

REFERENCES

Jenkins, J. J. (1948). *Turnover of power sewing machine operators.* Unpublished master's paper, University of Minnesota.

Paterson, D. G. (1934). The forty-first annual meeting of the American Psychological Association. *American Journal of Psychology, 46,* 150–151.

Paterson, D. G., & Jenkins, J. J. (1948). Communication between management and workers. *Journal of Applied Psychology, 32,* 71–80.

Skinner, B. F. (1956). A case history in scientific method. *American Psychologist, 11,* 221–233.

Thorndike, E. L. (1918). The nature, purposes, and general methods of measurement of educational products. *Seventeenth Yearbook of the National Society for the Study of Education.* Chicago: National Society for the Study of Education.

VII PERCEPTION AND MOTOR SKILLS

21 Light and Mind: Understanding the Structure of Film

Robert N. Kraft
Otterbein College

When photographers and filmmakers depict the world around us, they manipulate many aspects of visual form: lighting, camera angle, perspective, framing, balance, cutting, pacing, sequencing, zooming, tracking, and panning (Andrew, 1976; Coynik, 1974; Eisenstein, 1949; Giannetti, 1987; McLuhan, 1964; Monaco, 1981; Zettl, 1973). These forms are unique to visual expression and can be defined independently of the visual content (Huston & Wright, 1983). Moreover, every choice of angle or lighting or sequencing may influence our perception and understanding of the visual events (Arnheim, 1974; Penn, 1971; Shoemaker, 1964; Tannenbaum & Fosdick, 1960).

It is important in the investigation of complex visual events to consider the psychological influence of visual *form* as well as visual content. The focus of this chapter is on visual form. In general, I will explore the psychological reality of visual cinematic principles, splicing aesthetic insight with experimental work on pictures and film. I will describe some powerful effects of visual form, discuss empirical validation of these effects, and propose some applications of the findings to computer graphics and video technology.

THE ESTABLISHING SHOT: REFLECTIONS ON THE SILVER SCREEN

As a psychologist, why study film? What are the worldly influences that drive research in this area? For one thing, film is perhaps the most universally understood narrative art form. Of the 5 billion people on this planet, more than 2 billion cannot read. There are no comparable deficiencies in the understanding of film. Most cultures have strong film traditions, and even in those without such traditions, people have little trouble comprehending existing films.

Indeed, film is replacing the novel as the primary narrative art form. There is less experimentation in the novel form each year, and fewer innovative novels are being published (McLaughlin, 1974). Moreover, film has changed the way contemporary popular novels are written, with shots and scenes blocked out as in a screenplay (Monaco, 1981). And then there is the recent literary creation—the novelization. In the past, films were based almost exclusively on books, but now we see this process in reverse.

Film easily arouses a broad spectrum of strong emotions. Some films have started riots (e.g., *The Warriors,* Paramount, 1979), produced mass attitude change (e.g., *The Battle of Algiers,* Rizzoli Film, 1967), and influenced the buying behavior of millions of Americans (e.g., *Star Wars,* Twentieth Century–Fox, 1977; and *E.T.,* Universal City Studios, 1982). There is even *experimental* evidence for the emotional power of film. Baggett (1979) conducted a series of experiments on *The Red Balloon,* an eloquent French parable by Albert Lamorisse about a lonely boy who befriends a surprisingly volitional balloon. Baggett presented two different versions of *The Red Balloon* to her subjects: a text version and a movie version. Prior to the presentation, the experimenter painstakingly equated the narrative information in the two versions. During the experiment, some participants actually cried while viewing the film, and many cheered enthusiastically at the happy ending. (Such emotional outbursts, although gratifying, are almost unheard of in the sterile confines of the psychology lab.) No one cried during presentation of the text version of *The Red Balloon,* and no one cheered.

MEDIUM SHOT: RESEARCH ON CINEMATIC FORM AND ITS RELATION TO MEANING

There is a rich and detailed collection of writings in the aesthetics literature describing the influence of cinematic form on the meaning of the visual message. Film directors, cinematographers, photographers, artists, and philosophers have described in varying detail the psychological effects of various manipulations of cinematic form (e.g., Andrew, 1976; Coynik, 1974; Eisenstein, 1949; Mascelli, 1965; Metz, 1974). Table 21.1 presents a partial listing of hypothetical compositional strategies gleaned from the writings of contemporary film theorists. The strategies are in the general form: Technique A → Effect X; that is, Technique A generally produces the Effect of X. To change these descriptive principles into *prescriptive* principles, simply reverse the two: Effect X → Technique A. That is, to achieve Effect X, use Technique A. For characters to appear superior, strong, dignified, and powerful, filmmakers (i.e., experts) should use a low camera angle, vertical lines, and placement at the top of the frame.

Psychological research has, in the main, validated those compositional

TABLE 21.1
Some Principles of Film Composition

Technique	Connotative Meaning of the Technique
Lighting	
Above	Spirituality
Below	Generally unfavorable
45-degree	Generally favorable
Front	Blandness
Back	Mystery
Camera angle	
Low	Superiority
Eye-level	Parity
High	Insignificance
Tilt	Imbalance
Perspective	
Normal	Neutrality
Telephoto	Intimacy
Wide-angle	Loneliness
Selective focus	Forced attention
In-depth	Active viewer
Lines and forms	
Vertical	Strength and dignity
Horizontal	Restfulness and peace
Diagonal	Action and power
Curved	Grace and beauty
Intersecting	Tension and conflict
Triangular	Firmness
Rectangular	Solidity
Circular	Unity
Cross-shaped	Forcefulness
Position in frame	
Center	Neutrality
Top	Power
Bottom	Subservience
Edges	Insignificance
Off screen	Mystery
Balance	
Imbalance	Uneasiness
Balance	Security

principles that have been selected for empirical examination. I have demonstrated the dramatic effects of *camera angle* on viewers' comprehension and
recall of brief visual narratives (Kraft, 1987a), in accordance with cinematic
folklore (e.g., Coynik, 1974; Giannetti, 1987). Changes in camera angle strongly influenced viewers' judgments of physical and personal characteristics of
depicted characters. Moreover, camera angle affected viewers' long-term memory for the characters and for the *gist* of the narratives themselves.

Consider one experiment in some detail. Six four-slide stories were constructed of six different real-world narrative events. The stories depicted a simple
interaction between two characters. For instance, in one story, two men are
playing a one-on-one game of basketball. In another, a man and a woman are
involved in a minor car accident. The first two slides in each story set up the
activity, the third slide showed the first character, and the fourth slide showed the
second character. While constructing the stories, the character shots—the third
and fourth slides—were shot at three different vertical camera angles: high angle,
eye level, and low angle. Each of the characters was depicted in a full-body
medium shot; the camera was placed approximately 7 feet (2.1 meters) away
from each of the adult actors. The vertical angle for low- and high-angle shots
was approximately 40 degrees off eye level, as shown in Fig. 21.1.

Each story was arranged into three different versions, depending on the angles
of the third and fourth slides. That is, a particular version was defined according

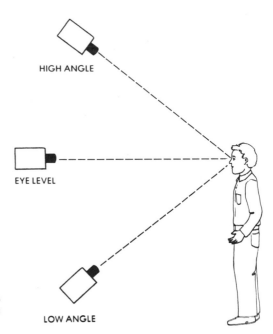

FIG. 21.1   Three vertical camera
angles used in Kraft (1987a): high
angle, eye level, and low angle.

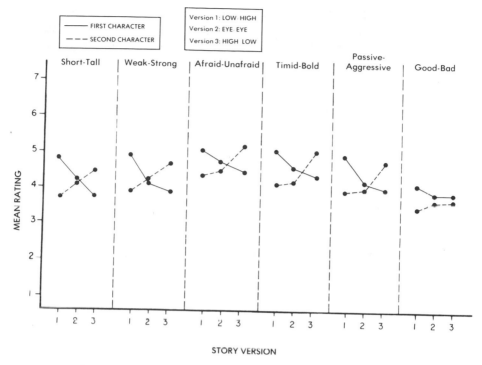

FIG. 21.2.   Ratings of the first and second characters for each of the three versions of the pictorial events (Kraft, 1987a).

to the camera angles of the first and second characters in each story. *Version 1* presented a low-angle shot of the first character and a high-angle shot of the second character (character 1 dominant). *Version 2* presented both characters in eye-level shots (neutral). *Version 3* presented a high-angle shot of the first character and a low-angle shot of the second (character 2 dominant). Thus, there were three versions of the six stories. Narratively speaking, each story had an exposition and a complication, and the participants provided a resolution in their written recall of the stories.

Participants performed three separate tasks with the stories. (1) After each story, participants evaluated the characters along six rating scales: Short–Tall, Weak–Strong, Afraid–Unafraid, Timid–Bold, Passive–Aggressive, and Good–Bad. (2) After all the stories were presented, participants described the depicted events in writing. (3) After recall, participants performed a recognition test for both the content and the form of the original slides.

Figure 21.2 presents the results from the six rating scales for the first and second characters in each of the three versions of the six stories. Five of the six scales yielded statistically significant interactions. That is, for the first five scales, the relationship between the two characters in each story reversed itself from Version 1 to Version 3. Camera angle alone strongly defined the relative roles of the two characters in each story.

Figure 21.3 summarizes the same results for each of the three camera angles. In general, as one changes from a high-angle shot to an eye-level shot to a low-angle shot, the characters in those shots appear taller, stronger, less afraid, bolder, and more aggressive.

When freely recalling the stories, participants spontaneously used such adjectives as "large," "angry," "stern," and "strong" to describe characters who were originally presented in a low-angle shot and "small," "afraid," "timid," and "weak" to describe characters who were originally depicted from a high angle. Eye-level shots evoked significantly fewer adjectives overall. In addition, camera angle influenced the participants' representation of the *gist* of the stories. The relative success of each of the depicted characters in each situation changed as a function of camera angle. For instance, in the story entitled "The Smoker," a woman tells a man to put out his cigarette. When the woman was depicted from a low angle and the man from a high angle, participants recalled that the woman was successful in achieving her goal. When the woman was depicted from a high

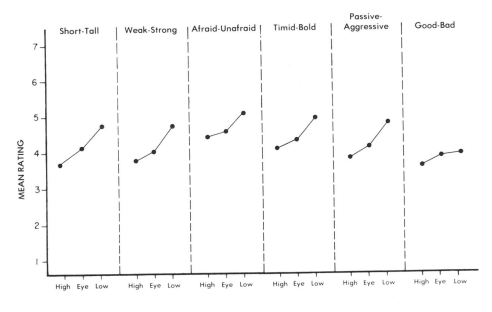

FIG. 21.3.   Connotative meaning as a function of three vertical camera angles: (1) High, (2) Eye-level, and (3) Low (Kraft, 1987a).

angle and the man from a low angle, participants recalled that the *man* successfully repelled the woman's suggestion.

Finally, participants performed a recognition task for content and for angle. Participants correctly rejected unfamiliar content with 99% accuracy; however, they rejected unfamiliar angles with only 68% accuracy. The mean d' score was 4.50 for content discrimination and 2.09 for angle discrimination. Participants easily discriminated "old" and "new" characters and objects, but had more difficulty discriminating "old" and "new" camera angles.

In general, camera angle has significant, predictable effects on judgments made about the physical and personal characteristics of characters in picture stories, on the recall of these characteristics, and on the recall of the gist of the stories themselves. Yet, specific recognition memory for the actual camera angles is comparatively poor. Viewers use the information available to them in order to comprehend discontinuous visual events, and though camera angle can be an important influence in the creation of film memories, angle itself is not an important feature of the recalled events.

Another important aspect of visual form concerns the *lines* that compose a visual display (Cox, 1917; Giannetti, 1987; Hevner, 1935, Poffenberger & Barrows, 1924). Hypothetical aesthetic principles have been proposed that describe the psychological influence of specific linear compositions (Baker, 1961; Chandler, 1934; Coynik, 1974; Hollingworth, 1913; Nelson, 1977; Valentine, 1913). Ongoing research has begun to verify these aesthetic intuitions (Kraft, Smith, & Garrett, 1990).

We constructed object displays with four different background compositions: horizontal lines, vertical lines, diagonal lines, and intersecting lines, as shown in Fig. 21.4. The object displays were presented to participants in the form of photographic slides. Participants evaluated the slides along six rating scales, recalled the depicted objects, and engaged in a recognition task for both objects and compositional form. Fig. 21.5 shows the influence that background composition had on the participants' evaluations of the displays.

Based on the data from the rating scales, each type of compositional line can be described in terms of its predominant characteristics. Horizontal lines engender connotations of passivity, weakness, relaxation, and peacefulness, and are judged to be reclining and static. Vertical lines are primarily judged to be upright and strong. Diagonal displays are regarded as active, strong, upright, and dynamic. Intersecting displays are regarded as highly active, strong, upright, and dynamic, and are regarded as most distinctively unpeaceful and tense.

Generally speaking, the compositional lines in a visual display strongly influence the connotations of that display. Recall and recognition results showed that although participants remembered the specific objects rather well, the actual background information was not always accessible. As with the research on camera angle, forms had their influence and then faded.

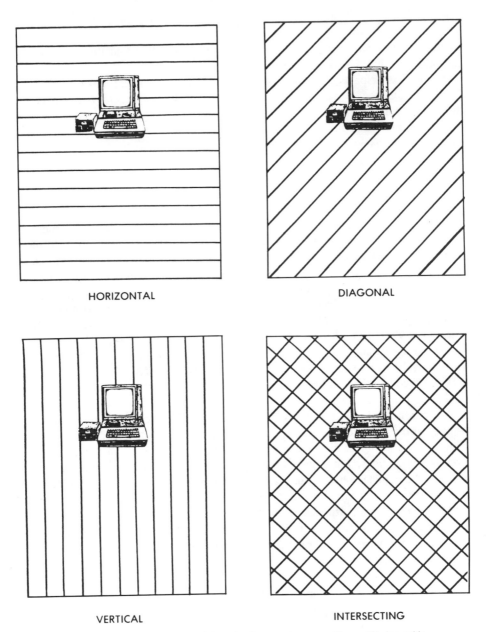

HORIZONTAL

DIAGONAL

VERTICAL

INTERSECTING

FIG. 21.4. An example of four background compositions differing with respect to compositional lines. Stimuli were presented to the participants as photographic slides.

ZOOM IN: NATURE VS. CONVENTION

What is the source of the psychological effects of cinematic techniques? Consider camera angle. The influence of camera angle may not result from learned aesthetic conventions, as some theorists have proposed (Giannetti, 1987; Monaco, 1981), but rather may be derived from the natural visual relationships between viewers and the depicted characters. For example, a low-angle shot

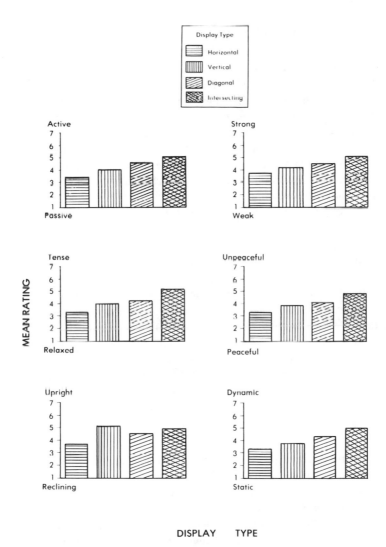

FIG. 21.5. Evaluation of the object displays as a function of horizontal, vertical, diagonal, and intersecting compositional lines.

forces us to look up at the actors, placing them in a position of visual authority and dominance. An eye-level shot places us face to face with the actors, producing visual parity. A high angle allows us to look down on the actors, providing a higher vantage point and placing us in a position of visual dominance. Thus, there is different information available in shots taken from different angles, and this information is directly available to the viewer.

The major arguments of this hypothesis are as follows:

1. Pictures of the same subject matter taken at different vertical camera angles provide different information to the viewer.

2. The critical informational difference between pictures varying only with respect to vertical camera angle involves the things the pictures *afford* the viewer (Gibson, 1979). That is, by changing vertical camera angle, one changes the actual consequences of the pictured scene. Gibson (1979) asserts that a representative pictorial display "puts the viewer into the scene" (p. 283). Thus, a low-angle shot of a given character puts the viewer into the scene on the floor, looking up at that character. And, being on the floor, looking up at a character affords different things than being over the character looking down, as in a high-angle shot. The meaning of one shot is different from the meaning of the other because the affordance structure is different.

3. Of paramount importance in the viewers' comprehension and retention of representational pictorial materials are the real-life consequences of the pictured scenes. Mandler and her colleagues (Mandler & Johnson, 1976; Mandler & Ritchey, 1977) have found that those features of a pictured scene that would most profoundly affect viewers' interactions with the actual scenes (e.g., presence or absence of large objects and spatial relationships among objects) are the most memorable features of the pictures. More specifically, Kraft and Jenkins (1979) demonstrated that memory for left–right orientation of a photographed scene containing a prominent object depends on whether or not orientation is important to the *function* of that object in the natural environment. Thus, any *compositional* manipulations, such as manipulations of camera angle, which alter the real-life consequences of a pictured scene, should affect the viewers' comprehension and recall of these scenes.

Changes in camera angle alter the structure of the visual information, which in turn influences our perception of the depicted scene. The *perceptual* changes that arise may then lead to corresponding changes in *connotative meaning* and *memory* for the original material.

The effects of such features as compositional lines may be accounted for by an extension of the direct perception framework. According to Gibson (1971), a picture makes available to the viewer the same kind of information that is found in the ambient optical array of an ordinary environment. In particular, the lines in a line drawing may specify certain invariants of surface layout such as corners, edges, fissures, and the skyline (Gibson, 1979). Repeated lines may specify meaningful features of the natural environment: rows of horizontal lines, as shown in Fig. 21.4, may specify the surface of a lake or flat ground; a series of vertical lines may specify columns supporting a building, and so on.

A single line may specify the edge of a human body. Thus, in a simple visual composition, a vertical line may suggest uprightness and strength because it specifies the most distinctive characteristic of a standing person; a horizontal line may suggest peace and restfulness because it has abstract information in common with a reclining person; a diagonal line may suggest action and power because it captures the distinctive shape of a person running; intersecting lines may suggest two people in conflict, as in Figure 21.6. The perceptual changes that arise may then lead to corresponding changes in connotative meaning and memory for the original material.

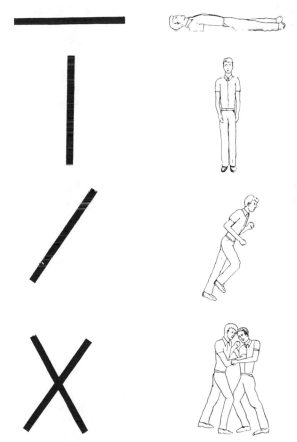

FIG. 21.6.   Actions associated with each type of compositional line.

LONG SHOT: CONSTRUCTING THE VISUAL EVENTS

The elemental operational unit of film construction is the shot, which is a single, continuous film recording from the time the camera starts to the time it stops. Individual shots are then joined together into scenes, scenes into sequences, sequences into episodes, and so on, to create the film narrative. The most common form of structuring and combining different shots is cutting—the direct joining together of individual shots. Cuts can occur within a single scene or between scenes. The focus in this section is on cutting *within* a scene. First, I will discuss the effects of cuts themselves and then I will explore the rules that are used to cut together the various shots within a scene.

Group Shot: Cutting, Segmentation, and Viewer Interest

There are two hypothetical psychological effects of cutting itself (Carroll & Bever, 1976; Kraft, 1986; Penn, 1971). First, cutting may serve as cinematic "punctuation," signaling the viewer to segment the ongoing stream of filmed activities, much as syntactic cues serve to segment language. Second, cutting may enhance viewers' interest, enlivening the film. The most prosaic example of this second effect can be seen on television news; the director cuts back and forth between different camera shots of the newscaster, presumably to enliven a visually lackluster presentation. (Home movies are typically so boring, except to those personally involved, because there often is no cutting, just one long scene.)

Thus, cutting may serve a "syntactic" function by segmenting the flow of filmed activities, and a "rhetorical" function by influencing the connotative and affective characteristics of film sequences. Not coincidentally, these two psychological functions mirror the two cinematic strategies for cutting within a scene: "cutting to continuity" and "classical cutting." Cutting to continuity involves abbreviating an extended sequence of actions while maintaining the fluidity of the actions, depicting the highlights while cutting out unnecessary information. For example, it may take 10 seconds for a man to climb a flight of stairs in real time, but on film, the action may be depicted coherently in less than 2 seconds. The filmmaker may present the man starting up the stairs in one shot, show a close-up of the man's feet in the next shot, and then follow that with a shot of the same man entering a room at the top of the stairs.

Classical cutting refers to cutting for dramatic intensity and emotional emphasis rather than simply for reasons of continuity. For instance, in the stair-climbing example, the filmmaker could intensify the action by rapidly intercutting close-ups of the man's feet pushing against the steps, his hand gripping the bannister, and sweat forming on his brow. These close-ups do not advance the action, they create a dramatic effect (Sobchack & Sobchack, 1987). *High Noon* (United Artists, 1952) is one of the most effective illustrations of how dramatic tension can be achieved through the technique of classical cutting; throughout the movie, the main action is intercut with close-ups of such things as ticking clocks and worried faces.

Generally, psychological research has not supported the notion that cuts act as visual punctuation. Rather, segmentation of film scenes into discrete units appears to be based on the events themselves, independent of the formal structuring within the scenes. However, cutting *has* been demonstrated to have a powerful role in the affective qualities of film (Kraft, 1986). Cutting can enliven and enhance film stories. Films with cutting are preferred over uncut sequences and are judged to be more interesting, more active, more potent, stronger, and quicker than films without cutting. As with camera angle, although cutting profoundly influenced viewers' preferences and the films' connotations, cuts themselves are not well remembered.

The source of cutting effects is not clear. Cutting quickly from one shot to the next may directly influence physiological responses—increased heart rate and general arousal—or it may simply approximate the active visual search patterns of an aroused human being.

Medium Shot: Connecting the Various Shots

In film, sequences of action are not presented as they appear in the world, but rather are structured in accordance with the principles of editing. Many frames are omitted, yet viewers are able to comprehend and remember the depicted events. What makes these shots cohere? For the past 80 years, filmmakers have been developing rules for combining individual shots within a scene. Table 21.2 presents a categorized set of these cinematic rules, gleaned from the psychological literature (Carroll, 1980; Hochberg & Brooks, 1978) as well as the asethetics literature on film (Coynik, 1974; Giannetti, 1987; Mascelli, 1965; Zettl, 1973).

Perceptually based rules are those that prevent unintended apparent movement and brief misidentification of the depicted subjects (Hochberg & Brooks, 1978). For instance, a reverse-angle shot of two boxers in a ring may momentarily confuse the viewer into misidentifying one boxer for the other. Continuity-based rules tell the filmmaker how to conform with viewers' narrative expectations. These expectations involve space, sequencing, causality, identity, viewpoint, and focus. Reverse-angle shots can disrupt both perceptual operations and spatial expectations, with the perceptual disruption being quite brief—less than 1 second (Hochberg & Brooks, 1978), and the disruption of spatial expectations more enduring (Frith & Robson, 1975; Kraft & Jenkins, 1977).

As the filmmaker cuts from one shot to the next within a scene, it is essential to maintain a coherent sense of space. In order to do so, it is important to follow the rule of directional continuity: A line is drawn along the main axis of action in a scene and all camera shots are kept on the same side of that line. The camera may move along a 180-degree semicircle as long as it does not cross the principal axis of action, as shown in Fig. 21.7. When continuity is violated and an activity

TABLE 21.2
Prescriptive Grammatical Rules for Structuring Cinematic Shots Within a Scene.

I.   Perceptually based rules
    A.   Change should occur along more than one dimension between adjacent shots in a scene.
         (Ca, Co, G, HB, M)
    B.   Reverse-angle shots should be avoided.
         (Co, G, HB, M)
II. Continuity-based Rules
    A.   Directional continuity: Reverse-angle shots should be avoided. (Co, G, HB, M)
    B.   Temporal continuity: Actions should be presented smoothly; gaps must be explained by cover shots. (Co, Z)
    C.   Causal continuity: Ordering of shots in a scene should conform with the causal structure of the depicted actions. (Ca)
    D.   Subject continuity: When cutting on the same subject, there should be sufficient commonality between shots to permit identification of that subject. (Co, Z)
    E.   Viewpoint continuity: A subjective camera should not see itself. (Ca, M, Z)
    F.   Vector Continuity:
         1.   Index vector continuity: When one shot depicts pointing to a given location, it should be followed by a shot of that location. (Ca, Z)
         2.   Motion vector continuity: Subject movement and camera movement should be maintained across shots. (Z).
         3.   Graphic vector continuity: Stationary features that guide eye movements should match up between successive shots. (M, Z)

The letters following each rule indicate the sources for that rule. Ca = Carroll (1980); Co = Coynik (1974); G = Giannetti (1987); HB = Hochberg & Brooks (1978); M = Mascelli (1965); Z = Zettl (1973).

is filmed on both sides of the action axis, the subjects appear to flip-flop between successive shots, and the viewer may be unable to extract a coherent flow of action.

Psychological experimentation has validated the assertion that violations of directional continuity do indeed result in more fragmentary or less coherent sequences. Frith and Robson (1975) filmed two brief stories about a boy and his dog. The two films were identical in content but different in structure. One film followed the rule of directional continuity, preserving the consistent flow of movement, and the second film did not. After viewing one of the two films, children between the ages of 7 and 13 reconstructed the sequence of shots by arranging a set of drawings that represented the shots in the film. Those children who saw the film with continuity preserved were able to comprehend and reconstruct the simple events that had been presented. When continuity was violated, by having the camera cross the axis of action on some of the shots, children were less able to reconstruct the stories.

My research program has shown the same pattern of results with adults (Kraft,

1987b; Kraft, Cantor, & Gottdiener, 1988). After viewing simple visual stories where directional continuity was violated, adult subjects could not even recognize, let alone reconstruct, the proper flow of events. The rule of continuity seems to exert a powerful influence on comprehension and recall of visual events. In the following section, I draw a functional distinction between those cinematic principles that preserve the coherence of visual narratives and those that shape connotative meaning.

RE-ESTABLISHING SHOT: RULES AND STRATEGIES OF FILM

One can distinguish those cinematic principles that are rhetorical strategies for a persuasive presentation from those that are grammatical rules for a coherent presentation (Kraft, 1987b). Table 21.1 presents a partial set of rhetorical strategies, which suggest how a film should be shot in order to produce an effective message. Failure to employ an appropriate strategy does not result in an incoherent sequence, but rather a less effective one. These strategies contribute to a *rhetoric* of film. And, just as rhetorical forms of sentences carry meaning, so do rhetorical forms of filmed sequences (Corbett, 1971). Cinematic strategies

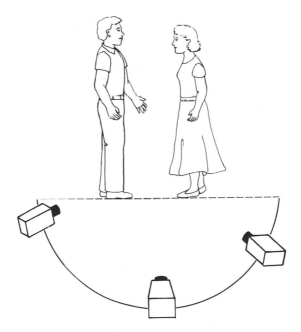

FIG. 21.7. Preserving directional continuity among individual shots in a scene.

shape the connotations of the depicted material, thereby influencing the effectiveness of the visual message.

Table 21.2 presents a set of cinematic rules. These rules constitute a technical *grammar,* prescribing how to meet film viewers' perceptual and cognitive expectations. Violations of the rules may result in an incoherent sequence, what Carroll (1980) refers to as "unfilmic." Just as grammatical rules of English must usually be followed to produce comprehensible sentences, the grammatical rules of film must ordinarily be followed to produce comprehensible visual sequences. These rules are derived from our experience with the natural visual world. The natural environment educates our attention, and this education applies to the viewing of filmed events. For instance, when observing an activity in the real world, we do not dart about like a dragonfly, we maintain our position on one side of the activity; hence, the cinematic rule of directional continuity.

Cinematic rules set limitations on the restructuring of real-world events. Investigation of these rules may lead to an understanding of how viewers comprehend and represent the discontinuous depiction of visual events. The distinction between grammatical rules and rhetorical strategies may be pertinent not only to the psychology of visual events but to cinematic theory as well. Some film theorists have applied the linguistic metaphor to the analysis of film (Carroll, 1980; Eisenstein, 1949; Metz, 1974; Spottiswoode, 1967), whereas others have argued strongly *against* grammatical analysis of film on the grounds that such an approach is overly limiting and didactic (Kael, 1966; Monaco, 1981; Perkins, 1972). One of the sources of contention in this continuing debate on the grammar of film may simply be the failure to distinguish between the optional strategies (rhetoric) of filmmaking and the less optional rules (grammar).

FLASH FORWARD: APPLICATIONS

The applications of psychologically effective formal cinematographic techniques are numerous. Formal features of composition and editing can be used to enrich computer graphics and video displays, creating more evocative and compelling images. In general, the appropriate manipulation of formal display features can enhance learning and maintain viewer interest.

Medium Shot: Education and Research

Conceivably, young children could be taught a variety of specific spatial and mathematical operations. Split screens could be used to emphasize comparison; reverse motion could teach Piagetian notions of conservation and reversibility of operations; revolving tracking shots could train students how to assume different perspectives on the same form (Hayes, 1978). In fact, Salomon (1974) has demonstrated that young children can learn to internalize specific cinematic manipulations, translating them into precise cognitive operations. For example, by showing children how the camera can zoom in on details of a scene, Salomon has enhanced the observational powers of some children, making them better able to scan visual displays and note details.

Slow motion can be used to magnify and analyze very quick movements—in dance and athletics. But also, *fast* motion can be used as a temporal long shot, revealing patterns in movement and behavior that may be too slow to be readily perceived in real time. For example, Eibl–Eibesfeldt (1970) describes the filming of a newspaper vendor going about his everyday business. Viewed at normal speed, the film reveals no interesting regularities. In fast motion, however, the film presents the vendor working a precisely defined territory as if tied to a leash (Newtson, 1976). Fast motion can be especially valuable to ethologists who need to detect patterns and regularities in the behavior of animals living in their natural habitat. The ebb and flow and velocity of pedestrians, shoppers, and automobile traffic have been studied in a similar fashion.

Close-up: Simulation and Photographic Perspective. There is a growing need to design veridical and pedagogically effective visual simulations for training those skills that depend strongly on visual guidance (Haber, 1986; Kraft, Patterson, & Mitchell, 1986). In visual simulations, from driver education to the training of airline pilots, an appropriate representation of visual layout is critical. One variable that strongly influences our perception of layout is the formal feature of photographic perspective. Photographic perspective refers to the overall spatial relationship among objects within a depicted scene and is a direct function of the focal length of the lens used to photograph the scene. Our research has shown that as focal length of the lens decreases, angle of view widens and the perceived distance of the objects in the scene systematically increases (Kraft et al., 1986; Kraft & Green, 1989). In fact, shorter, wider-angle lenses engender more veridical judgments of distance than do the longer, more "normal" lenses. The issue then becomes one of deciding between a visual format that produces the standard attenuation of distance perception that accompanies pictorial displays or one that leads to distance perception as it occurs in the natural environment.

Medium Shot: Advertising

The power of cinematic form is naturally applied to advertising. Television time is extremely costly, so advertisers must convey a wealth of information in very little time. To do so, advertisers must be capable of visual persuasion as well as verbal, using formal techniques that have predictable psychological effects. For example, when advertising a small, economy car, instead of explicitly stating that the car, although economical, is also exciting and powerful, the advertiser can convey this message by filming the car from a low-camera angle, presenting diagonal lines in the composition, and using quick cuts from one shot to another.

Between the late 1960s and early 1970s, commercial messages on television shortened from an average of 60 seconds to an average of 30 seconds. Today, the 10-second commercial is becoming prevalent. In fact, a prominent advertising researcher predicts that moving from a 30-second commercial to a 10-second, to a 5-second, and perhaps a 1-second presentation may be only a matter of time (Ohlsten, 1978). Clearly for a 5-second or a 1-second commercial to be effective, psychologically valid principles must be made known and used. A word from the sponsor may become just that—a word.

Close-up: Videodisk Applications.   Videodisk technology is especially appropriate for effective manipulations of formal features. For instance, a persuasive appeal could be filmed from a number of different perspectives, placed on a laser videodisk, and then restructured at will to determine the most persuasive combination of formal features to relate the message. Or, in situations where the same message is presented repeatedly, considerable variation could be introduced in the formal structuring of the displays without changing the overall appeal. More specifically, teachers of visual communication could have a powerful and relatively inexpensive tool for presenting the principles of visual design and narration by filming stories from many different perspectives and manipulating these different perspectives via optical videodisk technology.

FADE-OUT

Developing a psychology of film is not as easy as it may seem. Years ago, the noted semiologist Christian Metz observed quite accurately that "film is difficult to explain because it is easy to understand" (Metz, 1974). Despite that monition, film psychologists are attempting to uncover and explain the ways we are influenced—sometimes subtly, sometimes profoundly—by cinematic techniques. Nascent psychological experimentation reveals the ways that manipulations of cinematic form can significantly shape our perception, comprehension, and recall of complex visual events.

ACKNOWLEDGMENTS

I would like to thank Robert Hoffman, whose thoughtful suggestions and skillful editing strengthened and clarified this chapter. I would also like to thank Louis Giannetti for his book, *Understanding Movies,* which has provided me with a detailed map for psychological exploration of the cinema. Finally, I would like to express warm and special thanks to James Jenkins for encouraging me to pursue this area of research even before it was an area of research.

REFERENCES

Andrew, J. D. (1976). *The major film theories*. New York: Oxford University Press.
Arnheim, R. (1974). *Art and visual perception*. Berkeley: University of California Press.
Baker, S. (1961). *Visual persuasion*. New York: McGraw-Hill.
Baggett, P. (1979). Structurally equivalent stories in movies and text and the effect of the medium on recall. *Journal of Verbal Learning and Verbal Behavior, 18*, 333–356.
Carroll, J. M. (1980). *Toward a structural psychology of cinema*. The Hague: Mouton.
Carroll, J. M., & Bever, T. G. (1976). Segmentation in cinema perception. *Science, 191*, 1053–1055.
Chandler, A. R. (1934). *Beauty and human nature*. New York: Appleton–Century.
Corbett, E. P. J. (1971). *Classical rhetoric for the modern student*. New York: Oxford University Press.
Cox, K. (1917). *Concerning painting*. New York: Scribner's.
Coynik, D. (1974). *Movie making*. Chicago: Loyola University Press.
Eibl–Eibesfeldt, I. (1970). *Ethology: The biology of behavior*. New York: Holt, Rinehart, & Winston.
Eisenstein, S. (1949) *Film form*. New York: Harcourt, Brace.
Frith, U., & Robson, J. E. (1975). Perceiving the language of film. *Perception, 4*, 97–103.
Giannetti, L. D. (1987). *Understanding movies*. Englewood Cliffs, NJ: Prentice–Hall.
Gibson, J. J. (1971). The information available in pictures. *Leonardo, 4*, 27–35.
Gibson, J. J. (1979). *The ecological approach to visual perception*. Boston: Houghton Mifflin.
Haber, R. N. (1986). Flight simulation. *Scientific American, 255*(1), 96–103.
Hayes, J. J. (1978). *Facilitative effects of audio-visual formal properties on cognitive operations*. Unpublished manuscript.
Hevner, K. (1935). Experimental studies of the affective value of colors and lines. *Journal of Applied Psychology, 19*, 385–398.
Hochberg, J., & Brooks, V. (1978) The perception of motion pictures. In E. C. Carterette & M. P. Friedman (Eds.), *Handbook of Perception: Vol. 10. Perceptual Ecology* (pp. 259–304). New York: Academic Press.
Hollingworth, H. L. (1913). *Advertising and selling*. New York: Appleton.
Huston, A. C., & Wright, J. C. (1983). Children's processing of television: The informative functions of formal features. In J. Bryant & D. R. Anderson (Eds.), *Children's understanding of television: Research on attention and comprehension* (pp. 35–68). New York: Academic Press.
Kael, P. (1965). *I lost it at the movies*. Boston: Little, Brown.
Kraft, R. N. (1986). The role of cutting in the evaluation and retention of film. *Journal of Experimental Psychology: Learning, Memory, and Cognition, 12*(1), 155–163.
Kraft, R. N. (1987a). The influence of camera angle on comprehension and retention of pictorial events. *Memory & Cognition, 15*, 291–307.
Kraft, R. N. (1987b). Rules and strategies of visual narratives. *Perceptual and Motor Skills, 64*, 3–14.
Kraft, R. N., Cantor, P., & Gottdiener, C. (1988, April). *Comprehension and recall of visual narratives*. Paper presented at the meeting of the Midwestern Psychological Association, Chicago.
Kraft, R. N., & Green, J. S. (1989). Distance perception as a function of photographic area of view. *Perception & Psychophysics, 45*, 459–466.
Kraft, R. N., & Jenkins, J. J. (1977). Memory for lateral orientation of slides in picture stories. *Memory & Cognition, 5*(4), 397–403.
Kraft, R. N., & Jenkins, J. J. (1979, May). *Memory for orientation of familiar objects and events*. Paper presented at the Midwestern Psychological Association, Chicago.
Kraft, R. N., Patterson, J. F., & Mitchell, N. B. (1986). Distance perception in photographic displays of natural settings. *Perceptual and Motor Skills, 62*, 179–186.

Kraft, R. N., Smith, S., & Garrett, S. (1990). *Apprehending pictures: The psychological reality of compositional principles*. Manuscript submitted for publication.

Mandler, J. M., & Johnson, N. S. (1976). Some of the thousand words a picture is worth. *Journal of Experimental Psychology: Human Learning and Memory, 2,* 529–540.

Mandler, J. M., & Ritchey, G. H. (1977). Long-term memory for pictures. *Journal of Experimental Psychology: Human Learning and Memory, 3*(4), 386–396.

Mascelli, J. (1965). *The five C's of cinematography*. Hollywood, CA: Cine/Graphic Publications.

McLaughlin, R. J. (1974, January). *Contemporary Latin American Fiction*. [General Literary Studies 402, College Course]. Grinnell College, Grinnell, Iowa.

McLuhan, H. M. (1964). *Understanding media: The extensions of man*. New York: McGraw-Hill.

Metz, C. (1974). *Film language: A semiotics of the cinema*. New York: Oxford University Press.

Monaco, J. (1981). *How to read a film*. New York: Oxford University Press.

Nelson, R. P. (1977). *The design of advertising*. Dubuque, IA: Wm. C. Brown.

Newtson, D. (1976). Foundations of attribution: The perception of ongoing behavior. In J. H. Harvey, W. J. Ickes, & R. F. Kidd (Eds.), *New directions in attribution research* (pp. 223–247). Hillsdale, NJ: Lawrence Erlbaum Associates.

Ohlsten, J. (1978). *How do consumers view commercials?* Paper presented at the Broadcast Promotion Association Conference, St. Paul, MN.

Penn, R. (1971). Effects of motion and cutting rate in motion pictures. *Audio-Visual Communication Review, 19,* 29–50.

Perkins, V. F. (1972). *Film as film*. Middlesex, England: Penguin.

Poffenberger, A. T., & Barrows, B. E. (1924). The feeling value of lines. *Journal of Applied Psychology, 8,* 187–205.

Salomon, G. (1974). Internalization of filmic schematic operations in interaction with learners' aptitudes. *Journal of Educational Psychology, 66*(4), 499–511.

Shoemaker, D. H. (1964). An analysis of the effects of three vertical camera angles and three lighting ratios on the connotative judgments of photographs of three human models (Doctoral dissertation, Indiana University, 1964). *Dissertation Abstracts International, 25,* 5650.

Sobchack, T., & Sobchack, V. C. (1987). *An introduction to film*. Boston: Little, Brown.

Spottiswoode, R. (1967). *A grammar of the film*. Berkeley: University of California Press.

Tannenbaum, P. H., & Fosdick, J. A. (1960). The effect of lighting angle on the judgment of photographed subjects. *Audio-Visual Communication Review, 8,* 253–262.

Valentine, C. W. (1913). *The experimental psychology of beauty*. London: T. C. & E. C. Jack.

Zettl, H. (1973). *Sight sound motion: Applied media aesthetics*. Belmont, CA: Wadsworth.

22 Ecological Units of Analysis and Baseball's "Illusions"

Claudia Carello and M. T. Turvey*
Center for the Ecological Study of Perception and Action, University of Connecticut, and Haskins Laboratories

> For the contextualist no analysis is "the complete analysis" . . . There is no one analysis, no final set of units, no one set of relations, no claim to reducibility, in short, no single and unified account of anything. What makes an analysis good or bad for us is its appropriateness for our research and science and its utility in our pursuit of understanding and application. (Jenkins, 1977, p 416)

Superficially it might seem that the contextualist's relativity would be anathema to realism. One physicist has claimed, for example, that because different contexts permit inconsistent views of reality, it is less "damaging" to science to consider all such views as useful fictions than to consider them legitimate views of reality (Walter, 1983). If one's interest is in understanding the link between perception and action, however, then such a position is problematic—certainly fictions cannot guide action effectively (Carello & Turvey, 1984). But can one assert that actions are guided by actual states of affairs and still allow that the actual state of affairs is X in one context and not X in a different context? In other words, can a realist be comfortable with contextualism?

The answer is, in fact, easily affirmative. The position that there is no privileged level of analysis or set of units or vocabulary of description is maintained by some philosophers (e.g., Ben–Zeev, 1985; Lewis, 1929), physicists (e.g., Prigogine & Stengers, 1984; Rosen, 1978), and psychologists (e.g., Carello, 1989; Carello & Turvey, 1984; Gibson, 1966, 1979; Kugler & Turvey, 1987; Michaels & Carello, 1981; Shaw, Turvey, & Mace, 1982), all in defense of realism:

---

*Correspondence may be addressed to either author at CESPA, Box U-20, 406 Babbidge Rd., University of Connecticut, Storrs, CT 06269-1020.

> If a given notion changes relative to changes in the problem of interest, does this relativity preclude a consideration of that notion as objective and real? We have argued elsewhere that it does not and, indeed, that the concept of an absolute reality that would be appropriate for all grains of analysis is untenable. . . . Appropriateness is the key idea here—the level of description of reality must be commensurate with the level of inquiry, that is, with the type of systemic interactions that are of interest. (Carello & Turvey, 1984, p. 249)

The appropriateness sought by realists is not a mere convenience, like the usefulness of "useful fictions" (Walter, 1983). Analyses will only be appropriate if they are principled. This means that one must be especially careful in identifying the level of inquiry at which a phenomenon should be defined.

In this chapter, we would like to illustrate this point with examples of attempts to use a putatively definitive set of descriptors—classical variables from Newtonian physics—to attack problems of perception for which they are ill suited. We will show how a different set of descriptors—higher-order variables from ecological physics—leads to a different understanding of the problems, one that is more consistent with the behavior of perceivers. The Newtonian analysis was provided in a physicist's examination of a number of situations in the game of baseball (Brancazio, 1984). Before providing an ecological reformulation of those analyses, some relevant issues and concepts must be introduced.

THE PROBLEM OF DESCRIPTION

Periodically in the popular press, dating to the last century, there appears an article purporting to illustrate how some of our better known baseball truisms are not, in fact, true. To the contrary, it is argued, some of the lore flies in the face of basic laws of physics (e.g., Adair, 1990). Often, it is suggested that visual illusions are responsible for observers' reports that the physically impossible has occurred—for example, that a pitch rose as it neared home plate or that it broke suddenly to the left (e.g., "Baseball's Curve," 1941; "Camera," 1943; "Visual Proof," 1943). Perceptual psychologists are, of course, quite familiar with examples of so-called illusions, instances in which experience is said to be at odds with what's "really there." But these usually involve two-dimensional displays or constrained conditions of observation in the laboratory. The possibility that illusions have invaded natural circumstances involving skilled activity echoes the issue of useful fictions: Can baseball players—who are often called on to snare sinking line drives, to hook-slide, or hit behind the runner—survive on illusions?

Given the precise perception–action coordination demanded by the game, we are unconvinced that players' activities are guided by information about conditions that do not actually exist. We think it more likely that the discovery of an illusion means that the scientist, not the observer, is in error—it is the scientist who has failed to find the relevant description (observables, coordinate system, etc.) on which perception is based (Michaels, Carello, & Shapiro, 1985; Turvey, Shaw, Reed, & Mace, 1981). The problem confronting anyone who would try to understand perception and action is discovering *what the relevant observables are*. An observable chosen simply because it's convenient or familiar or quantifiable will not suffice (Bingham, Schmidt, & Rosenblum, 1989). Properties that are useful to baseball players (or any actors/perceivers) may not be found in Newtonian physics; they may not depend on attending to classical physical variables. Rather, they may only be revealed in what has been termed *ecological physics* (Gibson, 1961, 1966), a brand of physics being developed by perceptual psychologists who seek to describe surfaces and events (and the light, sound, and so on structured by them) in ways that are directly relevant to what animals and humans do. Let us turn to the sorts of observables that have been discovered that might be of relevance to the skills displayed on a baseball diamond.

ECOLOGICAL PHYSICS AND THE NATIONAL PASTIME

Much of what baseball players do involves knowing whether or not they will contact something, how soon it will happen, and how violent it will be. They try to avoid some contacts (e.g., being tagged out or hit by a pitch) but seek others (e.g., catching or hitting the ball, sliding into second base). Analyses in ecological optics reveal an optical variable that is specific to (lawfully related to) the control of such collisions and noncollisions. The premise of ecological optics—roughly, the study of large-scale spatiotemporal properties of the light structured by one's surroundings and one's actions—is that the substances and surfaces of our textured environment reflect light in a way that is peculiar to those substances and surfaces. As an example, the polished ash of a Louisville Slugger reflects light differently from the cleat-marked dirt of the batter's box. This creates a uniquely structured arrangement of light available at every point of (unoccluded) observation.

Should the point of observation move, a flowing array—called an optic flow field—will be produced (Gibson, 1966, 1979; Koenderink, 1986). This flow is especially important to guiding activity because its structure or form will be specific to the movement that produced it. As illustrated in Fig. 22.1, for example, running toward first base generates a global flow of the array—a sort of "panoramic streaming"—that means that the point of observation (the baseball player) is moving. The optical structure specific to his locomotion is, to a first approximation, characterizable mathematically as a smooth velocity vector field flowing outward from a point—the point to which the player is heading. In contrast, a thrown or batted baseball traveling toward a fielder generates a *local* disturbance (a pattern of accretion and deletion of optical structure) in an

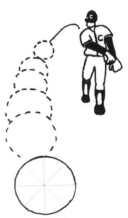

FIG 22.1.   A point of observation moving forward rectilinearly in a transparent medium filled with multiply reflected light generates a particular kind of optical flow pattern.

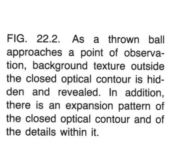

FIG. 22.2.   As a thrown ball approaches a point of observation, background texture outside the closed optical contour is hidden and revealed. In addition, there is an expansion pattern of the closed optical contour and of the details within it.

otherwise static array; this style of optical change, illustrated in Fig. 22.2, specifies movement of the object rather than the perceiver (Gibson, 1966, 1979).

Let's say that a baseball is heading toward you. Its movement generates an expanding optical solid angle whose apex is at the point of observation and whose rate of expansion depends on the velocity of the ball. The upper part of Fig. 22.3 shows three positions of a baseball on its way to the batter; the lower part of the figure shows the three corresponding optical solid angles. It can be seen that the optical solid angle expands as the ball gets closer to the point of observation. As it turns out, the inverse of the relative rate of this expansion is specific to how soon the ball will hit you. For this reason, it is called the time-to-contact variable, or τ (Lee, 1980). Fig. 22.4 illustrates the components of the mathematical representation of τ: $[(\Delta\text{Area}/\Delta\text{time}) \times (1/\text{Area})]^{-1}$.

The ball can approach the point of observation from a variety of directions. Simple horizontal and vertical trajectories are shown in Figs. 22.5 and 22.6, respectively. Let us say that for a ball fired home at close range (by an overzealous fielder of a suicide squeeze), its height off the ground does not change so that the ball only has to cover the horizontal distance to the catcher's eye. τ_x specifies how soon contact will occur. The $\tau_y \times \tau_x$ graph inset for Fig. 22.5 shows that for this situation, τ_y already equals zero. The depicted value for τ_x corresponds to the current position of the ball. τ_x will get smaller as the ball

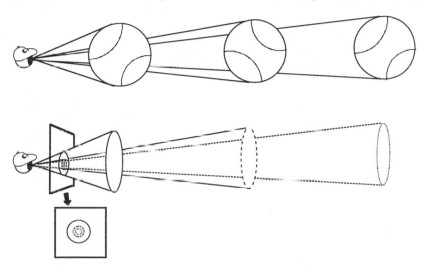

FIG. 22.3.   A ball approaching a point of observation along the line of sight (top) can be described mathematically as generating an optical solid angle with its base at the ball and its apex at the point of observation (bottom). The inset gives an indication of the rate of expansion.

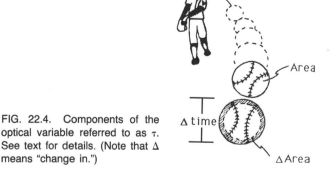

FIG. 22.4.   Components of the optical variable referred to as τ. See text for details. (Note that Δ means "change in.")

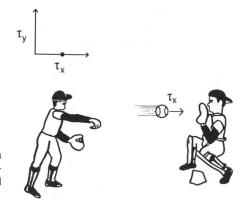

FIG. 22.5. τ_x specifies when a horizontally thrown ball will contact the catcher's eye (adapted from Turvey & Carello, 1986).

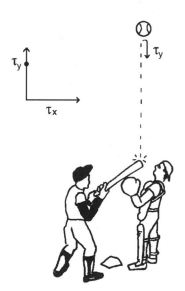

FIG. 22.6. τ_y specifies when the falling ball will contact the catcher's eye (adapted from Turvey & Carello, 1986).

continues along its path until it, too, equals zero. For a checked swing pop up right over the catcher's head, in contrast, the ball only has to cover the vertical distance to the catcher's eye. τ_y specifies when the falling ball will reach the point of observation. The $\tau_y \times \tau_x$ graph inset for Fig. 22.6 shows that for the circumstance described, τ_x equals zero and the value for τ_y corresponds to the current position of the ball. τ_y will get smaller as the ball falls until it, too, equals zero.

On most occasions, the ball does not travel "on a line" but, rather, traces out an arc covering both horizontal and vertical distances. An outfielder needs to know where to go to catch the ball. Such a situation is illustrated in Fig. 22.7 where the $\tau_y \times \tau_x$ graph inset shows that the ratio of τ_y and τ_x is important: If $\tau_y/\tau_x = 1$, then the ball will hit the observer at eye level; if $\tau_y/\tau_x < 1$, then the ball will fall in front of the observer; if $\tau_y/\tau_x > 1$, then the ball will fall behind the observer (Todd, 1981). The optical structure captured by these values specifies those circumstances for which the outfielder should stay put, charge in, or retreat. The particular velocity does not matter—*velocity does not have to be perceived* in order for the outfielder to perceive time and place of contact.

The foregoing optical analysis was verified through an experiment that simulated projectile trajectories with multiple computer displays, randomly varying the starting distance and angle of release of the projectiles (Todd, 1981). On a given trial, a participant had to judge whether the projectile, a square composed of 24 dots, would land in front of or exactly at the point of observation. Even though the displays terminated before the object reached its crest, performance was quite accurate, approaching 100% in some cases. Including the crest did not improve performance appreciably but using an isolated point as the projectile was detrimental. Todd (1981) showed that these facts implicate the τ_y/τ_x ratio as the relevant information. Of course, the outfielder's goal is to catch the ball, not intercept it at eye level. It has been shown recently that the sort of analysis that we have described generalizes: Time to contact between two objects (e.g., a ball and a glove) located anywhere in the field of view is available in optical variables (Bootsma, 1988; von Hofsten & Lee, 1985).

Time to contact is also exploited by baseball batters. It has obvious usefulness if it allows batters to avoid swinging at the ball too early or too late. But the control appears to be even more precise than that. Analysis of films of professional baseball players has revealed that the typical batter synchronizes his step with the time elapsing before the ball is at the strike zone (which we know to be specified by τ_y/τ_x); the faster the pitch, the quicker the step (Hubbard & Seng,

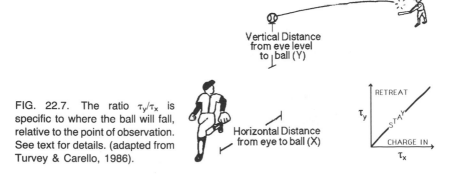

Vertical Distance
from eye level
to ball (Y)

FIG. 22.7. The ratio τ_y/τ_x is specific to where the ball will fall, relative to the point of observation. See text for details. (adapted from Turvey & Carello, 1986).

Horizontal Distance
from eye to ball (X)

RETREAT
STAY
CHARGE IN
τ_y
τ_x

1954). This has an interesting effect on the swing; since it starts right after the finish of the step, swing duration stays constant. No matter how fast the pitch is, the swing occurs an invariant amount of time before the hit. This lack of variation could be interpreted as contributing to better bat control.[1]

It is apparent that rich optical structure is available to guide activity in a variety of circumstances. No doubt, this is what permits the development of skilled activity. In order to get into position consistently to catch or hit a baseball, there must be reliable information about where the ball is heading. It is hard to conceive how one could become skilled if the information were unreliable or wrong. But what if an observer perceives something that is physically impossible? Isn't the information wrong and the perception an illusion? While more traditional psychologists would, no doubt, embrace that interpretation, ecological psychologists would counter that the illusion interpretation itself is an error, due to an inappropriate selection of the unit or level of analysis at which to define the problem. The assumption that classical physics adequately describes the variables that are relevant to perception and the control of activity leads to the appearance of error on the part of perceivers (Kugler & Shaw, 1990). But, to reiterate an earlier point, when the descriptors are ecologically motivated, the appropriateness and reliability of perception will be revealed.

An empirical illustration is provided by perceivers' evaluations of relative mass in collision events. Observers were presented with computer simulations of two objects colliding head on and were asked to judge which of the objects was heavier. They performed significantly above chance for various combinations of relative mass of the two objects and elasticity of the collision. But the patterning of their judgments revealed that they were not responding in accordance with the most generalizable information, embodied in the law of conservation of momentum. Instead of paying attention to the velocities of each object both before and after the collision, observers (92.5% of the time) seemed to use simply the relative speeds after collision (Todd & Warren, 1982). Although using the former would allow them to be right all of the time, the latter is reliable as long as the initial velocities are relatively equal and the collision is relatively elastic (i.e., not fully damped). This simple information was not used in all contexts, however. When the collision events began with one of the objects at rest, observers seemed to rely more on the direction of motion after collision. Again, performance was significantly above chance. In total, these results suggest that observers are reasonably good at evaluating the relative masses of objects participating

---

[1]Don't let the magnitude of major league batting averages undercut the argument for the specificity of time-to-contact information. While even the very best hitters are fortunate to manage as much as a .350 average, this refers to only safe hits, not all contacts. Wade Boggs, a noted contact hitter, swung at 1191 pitches during 1989, but missed only 58 (Will, 1990). Moreover, the game is designed—through equipment, rules, ball park dimensions—to put a ceiling on batting success. In contrast, fielding averages are upwards of .900 and don't reflect the routine accomplishments, such as getting to a base hit after the first bounce.

in collision events. The information that they use is not perfectly general—it breaks down at extremes—but perceptual performance is consistent and predictable. Given that "perceivers operate in the restricted context of a terrestrial environment," the lack of generality may be appropriate (Todd & Warren, 1982, p. 325). The point is that behavior must be evaluated with reference to those observables that are prgamatically well suited to the tasks humans and animals ordinarily perform in the situations that they ordinarily encounter at this scale of nature (Gibson, 1979; Michaels & Carello, 1981; Shaw et al., 1982; Turvey & Shaw, 1978). The variables of classical physics are less likely to be appropriate to problems of perception and action because they often describe events and situations indifferent to what animals and people need to know about them. Let's see how this attitude makes a difference in our understanding of three baseball situations that others have labeled illusory.

THE BOUNCE OFF ARTIFICIAL TURF

Countless baseball announcers have been heard to congratulate shortstops for taking advantage of the boost that their throws receive if they bounce on their way to nipping the runner at first base. The Newtonian analysis of the motion of the ball, however, reveals that a ball bouncing off a stationary surface must lose energy from impact. While some rotation energy is transferred to the energy of forward motion if the ball is thrown with top spin, an infielder cannot make the ball spin so fast that its rotation speed is greater than its forward speed (Brancazio, 1984). Why, then, does the ball appear to gain speed after bouncing off artificial turf but not natural grass? Brancazio suggests that the observer "has the illusion that it gains speed on the bounce" because the ball "does not slow down as much as he expected it to" after years of experience seeing balls bounce off softer natural surfaces which absorb more of the ball's energy.

Brancazio, a physicist, has analyzed this situation as if a Newtonian variable—velocity—should be what ballplayers perceive. But our earlier time-to-contact examples have already shown that velocity as such need not be perceived in order for one to perform speed-related activities. If τ, not velocity, is related to the control of activity, one might argue that perceptual systems ought to perform poorly on tasks—for example, judging absolute velocity (as opposed to relative velocities)—that they were not designed to do. Indeed, it has been shown experimentally that perceivers do not mean the same thing that physicists do by "velocity" (Runeson, 1977). For perceivers, velocity is not an absolute concept; it is inseparable from the notion of an event (for example, a bouncing ball), including how that event starts and stops. Perceivers who were presented with computer displays in which a depicted object went abruptly from a standstill to some constant velocity always reported that such events showed acceleration. Under Newtonian analysis, the objects were moving with constant velocity. The abruptness of a start is important to evaluating a natural, not a Newtonian, event. If the bounce off artifical turf can be considered an abrupt start, then observers should see the ball accelerate. Now, the fact that people use "velocity" in a different way from physicists does not make the perceptual use an illusion; it is not wrong or inferior, just different. And noticing the abruptness of the bounce allows the first baseman to get in the proper position for the catch.

RISING FASTBALLS AND BREAKING CURVES

Pitchers earn their keep by throwing the ball in such a way that batters miss it when they swing. Some can rely on speed alone: Just throw so fast that the batter can't get the bat around in time. Others throw the ball in such a way that the swing initiated by the batter is misdirected relative to where the pitch winds up. Pitches that break down or in, or hop over the plate have made millionaires of their practitioners. The best among them are said to make the pitch "bite" about 10 feet from home plate, leaving the batter shaking his head at how far off his swing was. The question of whether or not a pitcher can throw a ball in such a way to make it curve or flutter or hop has surfaced in baseball circles periodically for more than 100 years. The question in the beginning, asked in the pages of *Life, Look,* and *The New Yorker,* as well as the *American Journal of Physics,* was whether or not the pitcher could spin the ball fast enough, relative to its weight, to deflect it from a straight path. More recently, the corollary has come into prominence in popular science periodicals such as *Science 82* and *Discover:* If the ball curved, could it be made to break suddenly near the end of its flight? Then as now the logic was that if physics doesn't allow thrown balls to assume curved trajectories or trajectories with abrupt changes, then perceiving a curve ball or a breaking pitch or a rising fastball is simply an optical illusion.

Over the years, increasingly sophisticated methods have been used in support of one view or another, usually with the goal to "settle the great curve ball debate once and for all" (Schrier, 1982, p. 5). A number of techniques were used to trace the path of the ball but they were not considered conclusive; stakes ("Baseball's Curve," 1941), mesh screens (Verwiebe, 1942), or high-speed photography ("Visual Proof," 1943) still required a person to judge the shape of the path, so the possibility of illusion was not ruled out. In theory, the ball could curve off a straight path if it could be made to spin fast enough (Brown, 1913). It was not until the controversy was addressed in the aerodynamics laboratory of Igor Sikorsky (cited in Drury, 1953), however, that the amount of spin that a pitcher provided could be measured, along with how that interacted with the airflow generated by the speed of the ball. It was found that the ball does, indeed, curve. It does so uniformly, however, so that the pitch could not break sharply near the plate.

Again, the physicist tells tales of the unexpected: "The illusion is very strong because after looking at countless pitches and throws an experienced player gets so used to the gravity-induced curvature of the ball's trajectory that it begins to look straight to him" (Brancazio, 1984, p. 45). A ball with backspin, therefore, would appear to rise relative to the standard. But aerodynamic analyses of pitched baseballs indicate that none of the pitches (thrown by college hurlers, at least) follows the path of a projectile upon which no forces other than gravity act. Fastballs, sliders, curves, side-arm curves, knuckleballs, and change-ups all deviated up or down or left or right (Selin, 1959). It is not clear, therefore, how batters would get used to a trajectory that they never see. If, instead, one of those other trajectories is the standard, why would it become so? Would it lose the ability to fool batters?

Another variation of the illusion theme is the observation that, because of the batter's perspective on the ball's arc, the ball drops more during the second half of its flight (perhaps 1.5 feet) than in the first (only a few inches). That difference is seen as a break to someone (the batter) who looks at the pitch straight on, but as a perfect circle to someone (the physicist) who looks at the pitch from the side. "It's all a matter of perspective" (Watts, cited in Allman, 1982). Once again, however, this description would be true of any pitch the batter sees and would not distinguish one that "breaks" from one that does not.[2]

The illusion argument is too slippery for us. We share the skepticism expressed by baseball people over the years:

I am not positive whether a ball curves or not but there is a pitch in baseball much different from the fastball that "separates the men from the boys." If this pitch does not curve, it would be well to notify a lot of baseball players who were forced to quit the game they loved because of this certain pitch, and may now be reached at numerous gas stations, river docks, and mental institutions. (Eddie Sawyer, manager of the Phillies, 1948–1952 and 1958–1960).

Isn't it strange that the optical illusion only occurs when someone tries to throw a curve ball, and never when a fast or straight ball is attempted? (Luke Sewell, a catcher with the Indians, Senators, and White Sox, 1921–1939; manager of the St. Louis Browns, 1941–1945, and Cincinnati Reds, 1946–1952)

Is the magazine author crediting pitchers with the power of turning on optical illusions at will? (Earle Mack, son of Connie Mack; the latter managed the Philadelphia Athletics for more than 50 years) [All cited in Drury, 1953]

---

[2]Such overgenerality is true of Bootsma's (1988) analysis as well. He suggests that the perceived break might arise if the relative rate of dilation could not be detected, owing to the small size or great distance of the ball from the batter. Under such conditions, time to contact between the ball and the point of observation would appear to decline nonlinearly. But since the size of the ball and the distance of the pitcher do not differ for different pitches, this would not distinguish breaking balls from other pitches.

Whatever pitchers do when they throw distinct pitches must be generating distinct optical patterns. For both the break and the hop we can return to the time-to-contact variable to appreciate why pitches look the way they do.

Recall the analysis in which τ_y/τ_x specifies when and where a baseball will land relative to an observer. Obviously, both τ_y and τ_x will be getting smaller as the ball approaches the batter. We would expect to find τ_y changing more slowly than τ_x, due to the backspin, with the ratio thereby specifying landing increasingly further behind the plate. The suddenness would come about if, for example, the optical structure captured by τ_y/τ_x shifted from a structure satisfying the relation $\tau_y/\tau_x \leq 1$ to a structure satsifying the relation $\tau_y/\tau_x > 1$. In other words, continuous physical changes, such as the curving trajectory of a pitched ball, can have nonlinear optical and, thereby, perceptual consequences—such as a sudden hop or break near home plate—if the physical changes happen to bracket perceptual category boundaries. Such an optical analysis again suggests that baseball players are, in fact, detecting the available information.

THE CLOTHESLINE PEG FROM THIRD TO FIRST

A third baseman who has snared a shot behind the bag at third rifles his throw to first, just beating the runner. Often, the throw is described admiringly as a clothesline, as if it had a flat trajectory. This situation is somewhat different from our previous examples because the trajectory does not look absolutely flat to observers—there is no illusion, just metaphor. The third baseman certainly knows that the throw is not flat since he's the one who launched it on the appropriate trajectory. But this raises an issue of the sort we have been discussing. A tangent to the start of the trajectory would intersect the plane of the first baseman some 16 feet above his head. Brancazio (1984) claims that the third baseman is "unconsciously aiming" at that 16-foot point. Again he has offered a Newtonian variable—an imaginary geometric point—as the relevant observable for an act. But tangents to other throws under different circumstances will not intersect that point. Do third basemen have to know (unconsciously) at which point to aim for every game situation—whether the throw comes from behind the bag or after cutting in front of the shortstop or charging toward home plate, whether the throw has to be as hard as possible or can be an easy flip? Given the infinite number of situations in which third basemen find themselves, knowledge of such geometrical specifics is unlikely. Besides, the real goal is to get the ball to first base, not to the point. The third baseman must see that distance in terms of a force—a directed magnitude—and the skeletomuscular organization necessary to produce it. For this problem, the ecological psychologist would inquire whether there is structure in the light that could specify the requisite force (Carello, 1987).

This is a tall order, but one that is being filled in analyses of the regulation of gait in long jumping and puddle hopping. (Though they are not quite our sport of interest, the style of analysis is instructive). At the end of the run-up, long jumpers adjust their strides in order to hit the takeoff board. The task of the long jumper can be thought of as one of gauging the amount of time the final strides take, especially the time he or she is off the ground. The "flight time" of a stride is determined by the vertical impulse generated when the foot is in contact with the ground (Lee, Lishman, & Thomson, 1982). These observations suggest that the optically specified time remaining before contact with the board enters into a relation with the jumper's weight to determine the appropriate vertical impulse. A similar relation was found in an experimental simulation of fell running, a cross-country event involving running over irregular terrain (Warren, Lee, & Young, 1986).

The requisite ecological analyses of accuracy skills such as getting a projectile to a target are just beginning. The strategy is to put the dynamics of the task at the forefront of the analysis: What is involved in the act of throwing? Accuracy is not simply a visual skill—information is made available by the haptic perceptual system. For example, people can heft a variety of objects and tell, simply on the basis of how they feel, which could be thrown the farthest (Bingham et al., 1989). They also have a good appreciation of how far a given object can be thrown (Carello, 1987). Interestingly, not all targets can be hit with the same degree of accuracy. A blindfolded individual asked to roll a cylinder along the floor comfortably over repeated trials achieved a consistent distance. When this "comfort mode" distance was subsequently used as a visible target, it was hit with more accuracy and less variability than closer or farther distances (Sim, Sullivan, Carello, & Shaw, 1988). What these studies suggest is that the intrinsic dynamics of action systems is not irrelevant to the kind of information required to constrain the act of throwing. Linking an appropriate optical variable to the dynamics is left as a promissory note but it will certainly be beyond the kind of geometric abstraction offered by Brancazio.

CONCLUSIONS

The illusion label seems to come about when scientists implicitly assume that the units of analysis of physical motion are the units of analysis of perception. While velocity and aerodynamic drag are appropriate to descriptions of the physical motions of a baseball, such variables are inadequate to capture either the richness of the activity-relevant properties of a moving baseball or the information that allows players to perceive those properties. The supposed slippage between what's there and what people perceive disappears when the physical measurement is not indifferent to the natural contraints on perceptual devices—what they were designed to do. "Why do ballplayers see what they see?" is an ecological question, while "why does a baseball do what it does?" is a Newtonian question. Using the right question to guide the search for observables is the aim of ecological physics, not just for baseball but for all skilled action.

ACKNOWLEDGMENT

This manuscript was prepared while the authors were supported by National Science Foundation Grants BNS–8720144 and BNS–8811510.

REFERENCES

Adair, K. R. (1990). *The physics of baseball*. New York: Harper & Row.
Allman, W. F. (1982). Pitching rainbows. *Science, 82(3)*, 32–37.
Baseball's curve balls: Are they optical illusions? (1941, Sept. 15). *Life*, 83–89.
Ben–Zeev, A. (1985). The Kantian revolution in perception. *Journal for the Theory of Social Behavior, 14*, 69–84.
Bingham, G. P., Schmidt, R. C., & Rosenblum, L. D. (1989). Hefting for a maximum distance throw: A smart perceptual mechanism. *Journal of Experimental Psychology: Human Perception and Performance, 15*, 507–528.
Bootsma, R. J. (1988). *The timing of rapid interceptive actions*. Amsterdam: Free University Press.
Brancazio, P. J. (1984, July). Sir Isaac and the rising fastball. *Discover*, 44–45.
Brown, S. L. (1913). The curving of a baseball. *Popular Science Monthly, 83*, 199–203.
Camera and science settle an old rhubarb about baseball's curve ball. (1943). *Life, 35*, 104–107.
Carello, C. (1987). New metrics for distance perception. *Perceiving-Acting Workshop Review, 2(1)*, 15–17. (Technical Report of the Center for the Ecological Study of Perception and Action, University of Connecticut.)
Carello, C. (1989, May). *Realism and ecological units of analysis*. Paper presented at the Person, Society, and Environment Conference, Appenberg, Switzerland.
Carello, C., & Turvey, M. T. (1984). On vagueness and fictions as cornerstones of a theory of perceiving and acting: A comment on Walter. *Cognition and Brain Theory, 7*, 247–261.
Drury, J. F. (1953). The hell it don't curve! *American Mercury, 76*, 101–106.
Gibson, J. J. (1966). *The senses considered as perceptual systems*. Boston: Houghton Mifflin.
Gibson, J. J. (1961). Ecological optics. *Vision Research, 1*, 253–262.
Gibson, J. J. (1979). *The ecological approach to visual perception*. Boston: Houghton Mifflin.
Hubbard, A. W., & Seng, C. N. (1954). Visual movements of batters. *Research Quarterly, 25*, 42–57.
Jenkins, J. J. (1977). Remember that old theory of memory? Well, forget it! In R. E. Shaw & J. B. Bransford (Eds.), *Perceiving, acting and knowing* (pp. 413–429). Hillsdale, NJ: Lawrence Erlbaum Associates.
Koenderink, J. J. (1986). Optic flow. *Vision Research, 26*, 161–180.
Kugler, P. N., & Shaw, R. E. (1990). Symmetry and symmetry-breaking in thermodynamic and epistemic engines: A coupling of first and second laws. In H. Haken & M. Stadler (Eds.), *Synergetics of cognition* (pp. 296–341). Berlin: Springer-Verlag.
Kugler, P. N., & Turvey, M. T. (1987). *Information, natural law, and the self-assembly of rhythmic movement*. Hillsdale, NJ: Lawrence Erlbaum Associates.
Lee, D. N. (1980). Visuo-motor coordination in space-time. In G. E. Stelmach & J. Requin (Eds.), *Tutorials in motor behavior*. Amsterdam: North Holland.

Lee, D. N., Lishman, J. R., & Thomson, J. A. (1982). Regulation of gait in long jumping. *Journal of Experimental Psychology: Human Perception and Performance, 8,* 448–459.

Lewis, C. I. (1929). *Mind and the world order.* New York: Dover.

Michaels, C. F., & Carello, C. (1981). *Direct perception.* Englewood Cliffs, NJ: Prentice–Hall.

Michaels, C. F., Carello, C., Shapiro, B. (1985). Work group on visual perception. In W. H. Warren & R. E. Shaw (Eds.), *Persistence and change: Proceedings of the first international conference on event perception.* Hillsdale, NJ: Lawrence Erlbaum Associates.

Prigogine, I., & Stengers, I. (1984). *Order out of chaos.* New York: Bantam Books.

Rosen, R. (1978). *Fundamentals of measurement and representation of natural systems.* New York: North-Holland.

Runeson, S. (1977). *On visual perception of dynamic events.* Unpublished doctoral dissertation, University of Uppsala, Sweden.

Schrier, E. W. (1982). Take me out to the warehouse. *Science, 82, 3,* 5.

Selin, C. (1959). An analysis of the aerodynamics of pitched baseballs. *Research Quarterly, 30,* 232–240.

Shaw, R. E., Turvey, M. T., & Mace, W. M. (1982). Ecological psychology: The consequences of a commitment to realism. In W. Weimer & D. Pomerantz (Eds.), *Cognition and the Symbolic Processes, II.* Hillsdale, NJ: Lawrence Erlbaum Associates.

Sim, M., Sullivan, J., Carello, C., & Shaw, R. E. (1988). A comfort mode analysis of a simple accuracy skill. *Perceiving-Acting Workshop Review, 3(2),* 35–38. (Technical Report of the Center for the Ecological Study of Perception and Action, University of Connecticut.)

Todd, J. T. (1981). Visual information about moving objects. *Journal of Experimental Psychology: Human Perception and Performance, 7,* 795–810.

Todd, J. T., & Warren, W. H. (1982). Visual perception of relative mass in dynamic events. *Perception, 11,* 325–335.

Turvey, M. T., & Carello, C. (1986). The ecological approach to perceiving-acting: A pictorial essay. *Acta Psychologica, 63,* 133–155.

Turvey, M. T., & Shaw, R. E. (1978). The primacy of perceiving: An ecological reformulation of perception for understanding memory. In L-G. Nilsson (Ed.), *Perspectives on memory research.* Hillsdale, NJ: Lawrence Erlbaum Associates.

Turvey, M. T., Shaw, R. E., Reed, E. S., & Mace, W. M. (1981). Ecological laws of perceiving and acting: In reply to Fodor and Pylyshyn. *Cognition, 9,* 237–304.

Verwiebe, F. L. (1942). Does a baseball curve? *American Journal of Physics, 10,* 119–120.

Visual proof that a baseball curves. (1943). *Look, 13,* 74–77.

von Hofsten, C., & Lee, D. N. (1985). Dialogue on perception and action. In W. H. Warren & R. E. Shaw (Eds.), *Persistence and change: Proceedings of the first international conference on event perception* (pp. 231–242). Hillsdale, NJ: Lawrence Erlbaum Associates.

Walter, D. O. (1983). Creative vagueness in non-realist symbol systems. *Cognition and Brain Theory, 6,* 227–236.

Warren, W. H., Lee, D. N., & Young, D. S. (1986). Visual control of step length during running over irregular terrain. *Journal of Experimental Psychology: Human Perception and Performance, 12,* 259–266.

Will, G. F. (1990). *Men at work: The craft of baseball.* New York: MacMillan.

23 The Role of Attractors in the Self-organization of Intentional Systems

Peter N. Kugler
Center for Brain Research and Informational Sciences, Radford University

Robert E. Shaw
University of Connecticut

Kim J. Vicente
University of Illinois

Jeffrey Kinsella–Shaw
University of Connecticut, and Haskins Laboratories

INTRODUCTION

In general, physics seeks to understand how things change. Mechanics, a branch of physics, seeks specifically to understand inanimate motions. Biomechanics, a branch of kinesiology, seeks to understand animate motions, or movements. Our aim as psychologists is to understand how goals and/or intentions influence animate motions—a problem for ecological mechanics, or, more generally, for *intentional dynamics* (Shaw, Kugler, & Kinsella–Shaw, 1990; Kugler & Shaw, 1990). Traditionally, this problem has been located in the field of philosophy, later, in the collective discipline of cybernetics and control theory, and still more recently, in the fields of artificial intelligence and robotics. Motivational and cognitive psychology have each perennially addressed certain aspects of the problem without appreciably reducing its problematical core. In spite of the generous efforts of all of these disciplines, the role of intention in guiding self-motivated systems still remains shrouded in mystery and haunted by the recursive presence of unexorcised ghosts.

The purpose of this chapter is to consider some of the physical and modeling prerequisites for an informational basis for intentional dynamics. In all likelihood, the content of the problem of intentional dynamics will not be exhausted by known physical laws and their initializing conditions. However, by building upon the basis provided by classical mechanics, we hope to suggest a lawful approach to intentional behavior that follows from, and is consistent with, the constraints put forth by physical theory. In this way, an account of intentional behavior would be viewed as a natural extension of, but not logically reducible to, theories describing the motion of inanimate objects.

The chapter begins by comparing and contrasting the influence of equilibrium points, or attractors, in physically isolated and open systems. Equilibrium points, or attractors, are singularity points. The set of attractors in a system, however, can become nonstationary as competitions develop locally among individual attractors. The first section focuses on the identification of the mechanism driving the nonstationarity of the attractor set. This mechanism provides a generic construct for modeling self-organization within the context of both inanimate and animate systems. In the following section, a biological example of self-organization is presented to show how the mechanism of self-organization can be instantiated in an animate context. Particular attention is paid to the role of attractors in organizing an informational field for the biological system, thereby providing an *information*-based organizing mechanism for behavior—as opposed to the *force*-based mechanism exemplified by inanimate systems. A discussion of some of the theoretical issues associated with goal-directed behavior is undertaken next to provide the necesssary context for the ensuing section on the self-organization of intentional systems. In that section, the generic properties of self-organization are integrated with the problems posed by goal-directed behavior, thereby suggesting how an information-based, ecological approach to intentional dynamics can be pursued.

GENERIC CONDITIONS THAT CREATE
AND ANNIHILATE EQUILIBRIUM POINTS

Whether it be in the domain of classical mechanics, biomechanics, or ecological mechanics, the behavior of a system under observation can be plotted as a *trajectory* in a *state space*. The state of the system is defined by a set of numbers. Knowledge of these numbers and the input functions will, along with equations describing its dynamics, provide the future state and output of the system. State-space is therefore the set of all states reachable by the system, together with the paths for doing so, or alternatively, time series defined over phase planes. In this context, the state of a system is defined as the minimum set of variables that uniquely describes the behavior of the system for any time. An obvious question that arises in trying to understand how a system changes in time is: What state(s) is it changing to? More specifically, in what areas of the state space do various trajectories come to rest, as time tends toward infinity? These resting states are referred to as *equilibrium points*. In some systems, equilibrium behavior can be characterized, not as a point, but as a cycle or as an area of the state space. An example would be a self-sustained, dissipative pendulum that is oriented by a time-dependent equilibrium region in phase space (i.e., a limit cycle or a chaotic regime).

In a mathematical system, the area of the state space toward which the system converges as time tends towards infinity (whether it be a limit point, limit cycle, quasiperiodic, or chaotic) is generically called an *attractor*. In a physical system, an attractor is a region of state space where the resultant force vector converges to zero. A physical system can have one or more attractors, and it is the number and layout of these attractors which influence the behavior of the system. In the case of inanimate particles, each attractor exerts a *force* (by means of *a potential difference*) on the system, and the trajectory that the system follows is determined by the net sum of the forces exerted by the various attractors. In this sense, the temporal flow of events in a dynamic system can be said to be *organized* by its attractors.

Competing Attractors

The familiar context of a magnetic field can help to illustrate the influence of attractors on the behavior of a system. Consider the magnetic field produced by two positively charged magnets that are in fixed locations along a flat surface. A negatively charged particle placed on the top surface will be oriented by the positively charged magnets; that is, the magnets define attractors for a negatively charged particle. The particle's motion is also influenced by the contact friction coupling the particle to the flat surface. This friction defines a force threshold below which there is no motion of the particle. Fig. 23.1 provides three qualitatively different cases of such an arrangement.

The threshold on each of the cross-section graphs represents the minimum amount of force required to move the negatively charged particle (i.e., the amount of force required to overcome friction). For each of the three cases, a horizontal cross-section of the magnetic field is presented. The cross-sections only reveal the part of the magnetic field that is above the frictional threshold. This part defines the force contribution that scales to the motion of the particle in the field.

Fig. 23.1a illustrates the case where the peak values of the force field surrounding both of the magnets are too weak to have any effect on the particle. So, from the perspective of the negatively charged particle, there is no substantial force field. Fig. 23.1b describes what happens when two stronger magnets are placed in the same two locations. Now, the force field exceeds the threshold in certain regions. Thus, if the negatively charged particle is placed close enough to either magnet, it will experience an attractive force that will move it toward that magnet. In this situation, each magnet serves as an attractor, or equilibrium point, for the negatively charged particle. However, if the particle is placed somewhere near the midpoint between the two attractors, it will remain there since the force fields in this location are not strong enough to move the

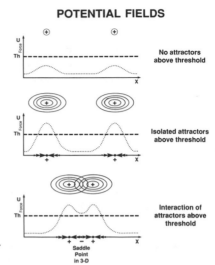

POTENTIAL FIELDS

FIG. 23.1.   Topological characteristics of magnetic gradient fields.

particle. In the configuration shown in Fig. 23.1b, then, there are two independent attractors in different areas of the field. There is no interaction
between the two, and therefore no competition. Depending on where the particle
is, it either experiences the attractive force of one of the attractors, or it
experiences no significant force at all.

Finally, in Fig. 23.1c, the two strong magnets used in the previous case are
brought closer together. This results in a qualitatively different type of situation,
since the force fields of the two magnets interact in the region between them. As
in the previous case, there are still two attractors, but now there is also a
competition between the attractors. If placed in certain regions, the negatively
charged particle will feel the force of *both* attractors. As we shall see later on,
this will result in nonlinear behavior. Basically, a very slight shift in the initial
location of the particle in the region of the "valley" in the force field may make it
move toward one attractor rather than the other.

The point of this example is to show how the configuration of attractors has a
critical influence on the behavior exhibited by dynamic system. A change in the
attractor layout will result in a qualitative shift to a different behavior mode. In
the example given, three different modes (no motion, linear motion to a single
attractor, and nonlinear motion resulting from a competition between attractors)
were illustrated corresponding to three different attractor layouts (subthreshold
force fields, independent force fields, and interacting force fields). The limitation of this example, however, is that the location of the attractors was fixed
beforehand by the placement of the magnets. Thus, there is no self-organization
taking place.

The remainder of this section will be concerned with the question of how
attractors can be *spontaneously* created and annihilated, thereby resulting in

self-organizing behavior. It is axiomatic to the argument we pursue that only self-organizing systems are capable of intentional dynamics (i.e., goal-directed behavior). For reasons to be discussed, only systems that are open to energy, matter, and information flows can exhibit this type of behavior.

Maximum Entropy vs. Self-organization

In an isolated system (i.e., one that is closed to the flow of energy and matter), the temporal flow of events is organized by an attractor defined by the state of *maximum entropy*.[1] The attractive influence of this equilibrium point on an isolated system's dynamic is stated formally in the Second Law of Thermodynamics: *In an isolated system, the organizational state evolves over time to a state of maximum entropy, at which time no further change will occur.* The 19th-century German physicist Rudolf Clausius observed that *the entropy of the universe will tend to a maximum value* (Atkins, 1984). This implies that the intrinsic evolutionary tendency of the universe is towards states of increasing disorder, ultimately converging onto a state of equilibrium where disorder is maximum. Once at equilibrium, all future possibilities of change in order are eliminated.

Unlike most physical systems, self-organizing systems evolve *away* from the state of maximum disorder (i.e., *decreases in* entropy). How is it possible to reconcile this with the Second Law of Thermodynamics? Does the existence of intentional systems contradict this basic law of physics? This is a question that has puzzled scientists for many years. However, recent work on self-organization suggests that movement away from maximum entropy can be achieved through the emergence of new equilibrium points that compete for control of the system's dynamic. In effect, there may be one or more attractors that, in addition to the point of maximum entropy, are simultaneously affecting the behavior of the system. If a new equilibrium point is strong enough, it can locally seize control of the dynamic from the global influence of maximum entropy and evolve the system toward states of greater order, in defiance of the Second Law.

The science of self-organization studies the dynamics of systems that intrinsically and autonomously create and annihilate equilibrium points. The following provides a historical introduction to the role of maximum entropy in orienting a system's behavior, as well as describing how this role changes when the system is open to external flows of energy and matter. It is upon this fact that the possibility of explaining intentional systems rests.

---

[1]Entropy is a measure of disorder, randomness, or uniformity. Any of these terms can be used interchangeably to denote the same concept. Thus, the point of maximum entropy can be described as a state of: maximum disorder; complete randomness; or maximum uniformity. A *decrease* in entropy, therefore, is equivalent to an *increase* in the structure, organization, or order, in a system.

Irreversible Processes, Disorder, and Isolated Systems

The Second Law is one of the laws defining observations at the macroscopic scale of nature. The law identifies why a drop of ink tends to spread out in a glass of water instead of remaining as a localized spot. This same law also predicts that heat will always flow from hot regions to cooler regions. Because the Second Law makes predictions about evolutionary sequences in time, processes which fall under its reign are referred to as *irreversible processes*. Once the event unfolds in time, the reverse process becomes impossible. The system remains at the equilibrium point of maximum entropy. Thus, the ink will not spontaneously form a small drop again and a hot spot will not spontaneously appear in a cool region. But to have goals spontaneously arise as attractors for a living system demands such self-organizing tendencies.

Once at equilibrium, all possibility of change disappears and all that remains are stationary processes that preserve the order of the system constant in time. These are referred to as *reversible* transformation processes. Reversible processes do not increase or decrease the entropy of a system. Once a system's process enters into a reversible mode, no change in order can develop as long as the system remains isolated. If, however, the system becomes *open* to the exchange of energy and matter with other systems, then it is possible that local regions within the total system can achieve a decrease of entropy over time (i.e., an increase in complexity, organization, or order). In these regions, nonstationary, irreversible processes can develop that selectively organize or mix the macroscopic properties of matter (e.g., temperature, pressure, chemical concentration) into states of increased order. The increase in order of local regions is made possible through the siphoning of entropy to neighboring areas, thereby resulting in an overall system whose total entropy increases with time in agreement with the Second Law.

It is in these regions of nonstationary processes that open systems capable of intentional dynamics must have evolved. Let us consider the principles of the "new physics" that have allowed us to understand these processes.

Irreversible Processes, Order, and Open Systems

Classical thermodynamics was associated with the forgetting of initial conditions and the destruction of structure. We now know that, within the framework of thermodynamics, there is another set of phenomena in which, structure may spontaneously appear (Prigogine, 1980). Some of the most influential early investigations into the relationship between irreversible processes and the emergence of structure were made by Prigogine and his colleagues, starting in the mid-1940s, and extending for more than three decades (e.g., Prigogine, Nicolis, & Babloyantz, 1972; Nicolis & Prigogine, 1977; Prigogine & Stengers, 1984). These investigations involved models of chemical systems in which competitions developed between the flows that couple various components of reaction mechanisms. At the time, it was believed that the temporal evolution of a system's states was along a linear *relaxation trajectory*, that is, a trajectory that inevitably moves the system through states of increasing disorder toward a final state of maximum disorder (entropy). This trajectory follows the strictly destructive path prescribed by the Second Law in an isolated system. It was further assumed that the consequences of the Second Law were the same for *both* isolated and open systems.

In contrast to these traditional assumptions, Prigogine and his colleagues found that when their chemical systems were displaced *far from equilibrium* by pumping energy into the system, the linear relaxation dynamic broke down and was replaced by a nonlinear dynamic that drove the system locally further away from equilibrium. In this far-from-equilibrium region, a new thermodynamic path (branch) formed, yielding constructive effects as a *by-product* of the Second Law's dissipative processes.[2] The system exhibited a natural tendency to self-organize. In recognition of the central role played by dissipative processes in self-organization, Prigogine termed these open systems *dissipative structures*. In 1977, Prigogine was awarded the Nobel Prize in chemistry for his work relating dissipative processes to self-organization in open systems.

But can these principles alone explain systems that exhibit intentional dynamics? What other modeling principles are needed? To begin this inquiry, let us first consider the structure of the reaction mechanism in a purely physical context, and then extend it to a biological context.

Nonlinearity, Multiple Equilibrium Points, and Instability

To form a consistent theory of reaction mechanisms that applies to both isolated and open systems, it is necessary to depart from the traditional strategy of modeling the evolutionary dynamics in terms of a thermodynamic state space containing only a *single* equilibrium point defined by the state of maximum entropy (minimum order). As time tends toward infinity, the system continuously converges on the state of maximum entropy (under given boundary conditions) in accordance with demands from Second Law processes. To accommodate the new findings of open systems, however, it is necessary to redefine the thermodynamic constraints in a manner that allows for the emergence of *multiple* equilibrium points in certain regions of state space. The new equilibrium points are added to state space by introducing nonlinear force terms (e.g., quadratic or higher order) into the original state equation. According to the

---

[2]A dissipative process involves a loss of energy from macro to micro degrees of freedom. The prototypical example is friction. Thus, a block sliding on a table will slow down (lose energy from the macro mode), and at the same time dissipate energy in the form of heat (micro mode). According to the Second Law, as time tends toward infinity, the energy in an isolated system will dissipate from macro modes to micro modes, resulting in an increase in entropy.

new equation, the state of maximum entropy identifies an equilibrium point in state space that operates when the system is open to external interactions.

As the system is displaced further from the local state of maximum entropy through the addition of energy, additional equilibrium points (some stable and some unstable) begin to influence the behavior of the system. At first, the equilibrium point at the state of maximum entropy exerts the most dominant influence on the system's dynamic. As the system is displaced further from this equilibrium region, however, a separatrix is crossed where the forces exerted by the new equilibrium point exceed those of the old equilibrium point and act in the opposite direction. At the separatrix region there is a competition between the two neighboring equilibrium points. In this region, both equilibrium points are attempting to gain control of the system. Beyond the separatrix, the new equilibrium point seizes control of the system. The influence of the new equilibrium point displaces the system further away from the state of maximum disorder (thermodynamic equilibrium). As the system evolves away from the separatrix it moves toward a state of greater order: The system *self-organizes*.

A self-organizing mechanism is composed of a coupling between two processes that generate opposing tendencies, thereby resulting in the creation and/or annihilation of equilibrium points. For example, the competition can be between the tendencies of a *dissipative process* and the tendencies of an *escapement process*. If the system is dominated by the dissipative process, then the local maximum entropy attractor will have the most significance in orienting the behavior of the system. If, however, the escapement process dominates, then the behavior of the system can be driven locally away from the state of maximum entropy under the influence of a new equilibrium point.

Later we shall use the concepts of escapement and dissipation to describe systems with attractors that may qualify as goals. Let us pause to consolidate the concepts needed to address the question of how systems may exhibit intentional dynamics without violating the physically lawful accounts of open systems.

A Simple Example and Summary

The patterns of behavior associated with self-organization can be made more concrete through a simple example. Take the case of a falling leaf (Kugler & Turvey, 1987, p. 123), illustrated in Fig. 23.2. Most leaves dropped from sufficient height above the ground, exhibit behavior in three qualitatively different modes of dynamical organization. The first of these is the translational mode, during which the leaf falls straight down. As it accelerates, however, the falling leaf absorbs more and more kinetic energy. Due to the large amount of energy being pumped into the leaf, a critical point emerges where this dynamical system is no longer stable in the translational mode. At this point, the leaf's behavior self-organizes into a new dynamical mode characterized by a side-to-side vibra-

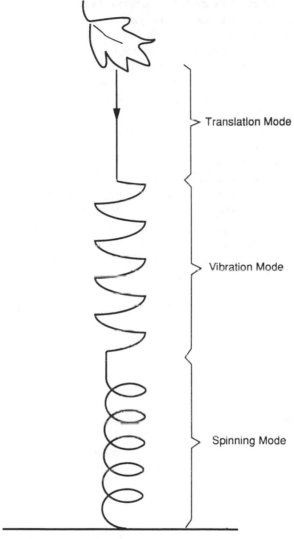

FIG. 23.2. Dynamic modes (translation, vibration, and spinning) of a falling leaf.

tion. This mode consumes the excess energy pumped into the system, permitting its behavior to stabilize. However, as the leaf continues to fall, even more energy accrues, causing the leaf's behavior again to become unstable. Consequently, its behavior must self-organize into an even higher mode. In this third mode, the leaf begins to spin about itself. The example illustrates how increasing the amount of energy flowing into a system causes it to self-organize recursively into successively more complex modes of behavior in order to maintain dynamical stability. From this simple example, the fundamental process by which an open system self-organizes can be abstracted.

Motion in an isolated system is governed solely by the First Law, which states that the total energy in the system (i.e., the sum of potential and kinetic energy) remains constant in a given measurement frame. As a result, the system's dynamic are reversible and conservative. However, as the system is opened slightly to energy flows, the Second Law comes into play. Here the equilibrium point of maximum entropy plays the role of an attractor, irreversibly drawing the system to it. During this irreversible mode of behavior, the dissipative term dominates the system's dynamic. As more energy is added, however, the escapement term begins to dominate and sets up a reversal of forces by creating a competing attractor. This force reversal causes the system to become temporarily unstable and to lurch suddenly further from equilibrium.

As the leaf example shows, the process of self-organization can proceed in a recursive manner. As the system is displaced further from the new attractor a third equilibrium point can emerge and begin competing for control of the system. The identification and application of these critical relationships between nonlinearity, open systems, and self-organization is currently a prominent topic on the scientific agenda in the physical, biological and social sciences (see, for instance, Carreri, 1984; Casti, 1989; Davies, 1989; Haken, 1988; Nicolis & Prigogine, 1989; Yates, 1987).

So far, we have discussed the role of attractors in organizing the behavior of inanimate physical systems. Our aim in this chapter is to characterize their role in the self-organization of intentional systems. Note that the application of attractor dynamics to intentional systems is meant as more than a casual analogy; rather we take it as a working hypothesis about the nature of the mechanism for understanding goal-directed behavior in biological systems. In the next section, we provide an example of self-organization of an ensemble of biological subsystems (insects) that are mutually linked through a low-energy, pheromone field coupling. The model illustrates an open sysem that is as informationally driven as it is energy-driven. It is a system that is not only thermodynamic but *epistemic* as well. That is, its thermodynamically driven activities are informationally controlled toward an evolutionarily selected goal—the self-assembly of a large-scale nest for millions of insects. To achieve this *naturally selected primitive intention*, the system begins in a state of low order and then, guided by the principles of self-organization, subsequently evolves recursively into states of successively greater order as new equilibrium points emerge and compete with existing equilibrium points. Thus the main point of the next section is to show how nonlinear thermodynamics is not restricted to causal inanimate systems but can be generalized to intentional animate systems.

SELF-ORGANIZATION IN SOCIAL INSECTS

The insects of interest are African termites, who periodically cooperate to build nests that stand more than 15 feet in height, weigh more than 10 tons, and persist more than 300 years. This feat is made even more remarkable by the fact that the termites work independently of each other. The insects' flight patterns are controlled locally by pheromone (molecular) distributions that arise from materials excreted by the insects and strewn by them around the building site, at first randomly, and then in increasingly more regular ways. The pheromone-laden excreted building material dictates the patterning of the collective insect activity which, in turn, determines the novel architectural structures that ultimately arise from this dynamically improvised plan (for details obtained from naturalistic observation, see Grasse, 1959, and Bruinsma 1977; for a thermodynamic treatment, see Deneubourge, 1977; for an informational approach, see Kugler & Turvey, 1987).

Attractor Dynamics

The nest construction process involves the coordination of more than 5 million insects, and results in the recursive evolution of a set of macroscopic building *modes:*

> *random depositing→pillar construction→arch construction→*
> *dome construction→random depositing→ . . . and so on.*

Each mode is characterized by a qualitatively different pattern of behavior. The pattern is specified by the unique number and layout of attractors in the pheromone field that is specific to each mode. Thus, a change in the qualitative structure of the pheromone field results in a change in mode.

The qualitative structure of the diffusion field can be classified by the layout of the attractors, which in this case are the local regions in the pheromone field where the gradient vanishes to zero. Because of the field dynamics they impose, this ensemble of attractors comprises a global *organizing mechanism* for local trajectories. As with the magnetic field example presented earlier, the flow pattern is globally organized by the layout of attractors in the state space. If the layout remains constant, the pattern in the field defining the flows is also stable. If an attractor is created or annihilated, however, the pattern defining the flow will become unstable (will change topologically). Instability in the flow field is therefore a function of the creation and/or annihilation of one or more attractors.

In the following section, the various changes that take place in the field governing the insects' behavior as a function of changes in the layout of attractors in that space will be described.

Nest Construction

Each spring, termites develop a sensitivity to a pheromone secretion in their waste. Once this waste has been deposited, atmospheric diffusion of the pheromone creates a gradient field that can "orient" nearby insects. The recent deposit lies at the center of the diffusion field; technically it can be referred to as an equilibrium point where the gradient goes to zero. Each deposit temporarily defines the spatial location of an equilibrium point relative to the global structure of the pheromone field.

The diffusion field spreads out in accordance with Fick's law[3], which relates the rate of flow to the gradient of the field. As time passes, the amount of pheromone at the equilibrium point decreases (a dissipative process), scaling the field gradient accordingly. Eventually the concentration of pheromone at the equilibrium point approaches that of all points in the gradient field, at which time the system is at equilibrium. At equilibrium there are no gradients ($grad = 0$ for the entire field) and, therefore, no local equilibrium points. This means that at equilibrium the global dynamic is identical to the local dynamic. If only a few insects participate in nest building, the depositing is so infrequent that the pheromone field of recent deposits dies out and goes to equilibrium before another insect can be influenced by the deposit.

Perceptual Couplings and Thresholds.   The behavior of insects during nest construction is organized by an evolution of relatively stationary attractors in the pheromone field. A change in the attractor layout induces an instability in the pheromone flow pattern. Following the reaction mechanism described in the previous section, this instability then drives the system to a state of greater order, as instability begets self-organization.

The insects relate to the pheromone field through a perceptual coupling that circularly maps kinematic descriptions of the pheromone field into the insect's nervous system, and back into the world of kinetics through the insects' actuators. The perceptual coupling links the insects to the pheromone field only in regions of the building site where the pheromone concentration exceeds a critical activation threshold for their perceptual system. (The analogy to be drawn here is to the sliding friction that has to be overcome if a particle is to move toward a magnetic pole.) Once insects enter an activation region they follow paths mapping the *streamlines*[4] of the pheromone field. The insects' journey up the gradient terminates ultimately at the region of maximum concentration—the equilibrium point. On arriving at the equilibrium point, the insects deposit their waste. With the loss of their waste material the insects lose their pheromone affinity and cease to be oriented by the pheromone field. The pheromone affinity returns with the buildup of new waste material in the insect.

---

[3]Fick's law states that the rate of transport is linearly proportional to density.

[4]A streamline is a line of flow which is everywhere orthogonal to the isopotential contours of a field. In the case of a gradient field, the streamline defines a path of steepest gradient.

The role of perceptual thresholds in the insect system is similar in some respects to the role of the force threshold in the magnetic field example that was illustrated earlier in Fig. 23.1. Just as the force field may be too weak to move a particle (Fig. 23.1a), the pheromone concentration may be too weak for the insect to detect. Similar to the case in Fig. 23.1b, if the pheromone concentrations are far apart, then they will not interact with each other in regions above threshold. Finally, as we shall see, the case of two attractors that are close enough that their interaction is above threshold will, just as in Fig. 23.1c, result in a competition that leads to nonlinear behavior. Next, we describe the four modes exhibited during the next-building process.

Random Deposits: A Reversible Equilibrium Mode. In the first phase of nest building, the motion of insects is only weakly coupled to the motion of pheromone molecules since only very small localized regions contain enough pheromone to exceed an insect's perceptual limit. The result is a random depositing mode of nest building. The motion of the insects is essentially independent of the motion of the pheromone molecules. In the absence of regions of high concentrations of pheromone, the depositing pattern is dominated by random reversible fluctuations. The gradient dynamic on the pheromone field plays no role in the organization of insect motion. Thus, the motion of the insects is at equilibrium with respect to the pheromone field when the pheromone gradient is uniform. In the equilibrium mode, the motion of each insect is independent of every other insect; no preferred deposit sites orient insect flight patterns (i.e., no local equilibrium points organize the field dynamic). Random depositing persists as long as a small number of insects participate in nest building.

This mode corresponds to the type of behavior governed by the attractor defined by the Second Law, as discussed in the previous section. There is no change in the order of the system, since the pheromone field remains uniform. The maximum entropy equilibrium point is the only attractor in the field.

Pillar Construction: A Linear Near-equilibrium Mode. As more insects participate, the likelihood of an insect's passing an active site increases. Beyond a critical number of participating insects, the equilibrium condition of the flight pattern breaks down, and some preferred deposit sites begin to emerge on the surface of the work space (see Fig. 23.3). Increases in the rate of depositing on preferred sites increase the size of the gradient field that attracts the insects, which, in turn, increases the rate of depositing, and so on. As the size of a deposit site grows, long-range coordination patterns begin to develop among the flight patterns of insects, as more and more insects begin to orient their motion to the pheromone field. The result is an autocatalytic reaction resulting in rapid amplification of material deposits at points of highest pheromone concentration (equilibrium points). As the autocatalytic reaction continues, a pillar begins to be shaped out of the waste deposit (see Fig. 23.4). The pillar is constructed at the location of the equilibrium point, with only the top of the pillar remaining active.

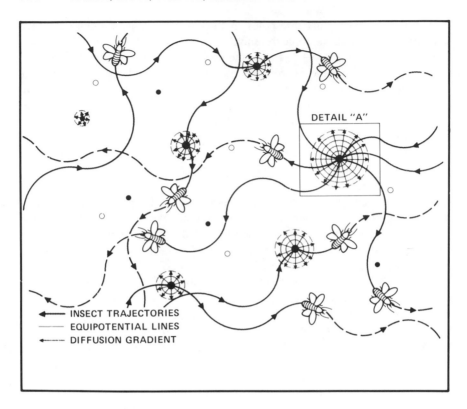

FIG. 23.3. Development of preferred sites. The development of a preferred site marks a sudden transition in the correlational state of the insect
population. As the size and number of preferred sites increases correlations
begin to develop among the insects' external coordinates of motion. The
insect behavior is no longer at equilibrium (independent of one another), it
evolves into nonequilibrium states exhibiting increased correlation (adapted
from Kugler & Turvey, 1987).

During pillar construction, active deposit sites contain only one equilibrium
point. While multiple active deposit sites can exist in the workspace, none
contains multiple equilibrium points. In this construction phase, all pheromone
gradients above the insect's perceptual threshold contain only one equilibrium
point. In these localized regions pheromone flows relates *linearly* to driving
forces generated by the chemical potential.

Arch Construction: A Nonlinear Far-from-equilibrium Mode.   As the size of
the active gradient regions enlarge, however, competitions begin to develop
between gradients generated by neighboring equilibrium points (pillar sites).
This competition occurs when the active portions of the two gradient fields begin

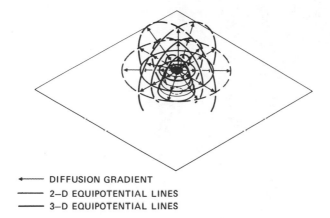

◄──── DIFFUSION GRADIENT
───── 2–D EQUIPOTENTIAL LINES
───── 3–D EQUIPOTENTIAL LINES

FIG. 23.4.   Building a pillar (adapted from Kugler & Turvey, 1987).

to overlap (recall case c in the magnetic field example). *Saddlepoints* organize the interface boundary separating the two gradient fields. The saddlepoint is a fixed point property that defines a common solution that relates the two local gradient fields. The saddlepoint thus forms a set of field constraints that are used by the insects in the construction of an arch (see Fig. 23.5).

The saddlepoint displaces the system further from equilibrium by extending the characteristic size of the correlations among insect motions. Near equilibrium the correlations are restricted to local regions near pillars. In contrast, in far-from-equilibrium conditions the characteristic length for correlations include larger (more global) regions containing multiple pillars. In this region, the linear relaxation dynamic that is organized by a single equilibrium point is replaced by a nonlinear dynamic that is organized by competitions among multiple equilibrium points. The competition is greatest at the saddlepoint where the forces change directions. At the saddlepoint region the linear force-flow dynamic of pillar construction is replaced by a nonlinear force-flow dynamic that results in the construction of arches (see Figs. 23.6 and 23.7).

The saddlepoint breaks the symmetry of the location of deposits by introducing an inward bias in the direction of the competing equilibrium points. The addition of this bias adds a curvature to the pillar that results in the construction of an arch. The saddlepoint defines a common (invariant) solution that simultaneously satisfies the local gradient field constraints of both pillar basins. Thus, the saddlepoint is a higher-order attractor defining a symmetry that is invariant over the two competing gradient basins. The construction of the arch emerges out of the more global symmetry of the saddlepoint. The saddlepoint symmetry defines a set of constraints that insects can use to coordinate their motions relative to two pillars.

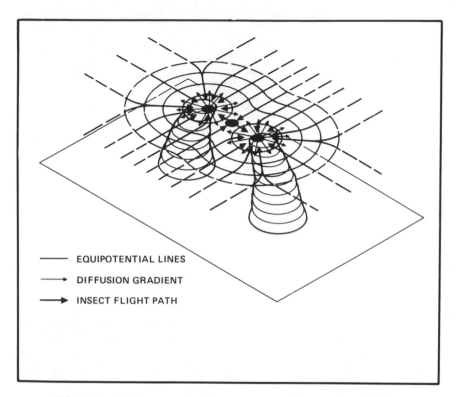

──────── EQUIPOTENTIAL LINES

┈┈┈┈┈► DIFFUSION GRADIENT

━━━━━► INSECT FLIGHT PATH

FIG. 23.5. Building an arch. The emergence of the saddlepoint further displaces the system from equilibrium. The organizing influence of the saddlepoint extends the insect correlations to a region defined over the two pillars (adapted from Kugler & Turvey, 1987).

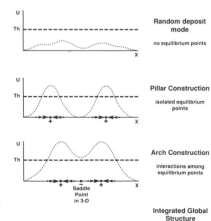

FIG. 23.6. Comparison of the potential fields for the random flight mode, pillar-building mode, and arch-building mode. Compare with Fig. 23.1

402

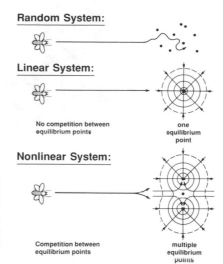

FIG. 23.7. The equilibrium regions partitioned by the perceptual threshold for the random flight (no equilibrium points), pillar construction (isolated equilibrium points), and arch construction (multiply interacting equilibrium points).

Dome Construction: A Return to the Equilibrium Mode. The completion of the arch is associated with the coalescing of the two pillar equilibrium points with the saddlepoint, resulting in the annihilation of the saddlepoint and the emergence of a single equilibrium point at the top of the arch (see Fig. 23.8). Gradient flows emanating from the new equilibrium point interact with neighboring gradient flows, resulting in the emergence of an intricate pattern of new saddlepoints. These saddlepoints organize a new gradient layout that, in turn, provide new constraints which coordinate the construction of a dome (see Figs. 23.9 and 23.10).

Upon completion of the dome, the far-from-equilibrium condition is annihilated; this results in a return to the equilibrium mode. A new construction cycle then begins, starting with the random deposit phase on the surface of the dome. The system begins another cycle through the sequence of construction modes (Fig. 23.11): random deposit→pillar construction→arch construction→dome construction→random deposits, and so on.

There are several aspects of this example we wish to emphasize. First of all, the nest-building cycle of these termites typifies the generic mechanisms of self-organization. Each mode is specified by a unique layout of attractors. The transitions between behavioral modes occur when attractors are either created or annihilated.

Also worth noting is the circular nature of the processes that sustain the construction of the nest. The insect behavior both *contributes to*, and *is oriented by*, the pheromone field. Insects contribute to the pheromone field through their frequent deposits. The structure of this field, in turn, orients the insects' depository activity. In this regard, the nest-building system is exemplary of a *self-reading* and *self-writing* system (see Fig. 23.12). The circular linking of the

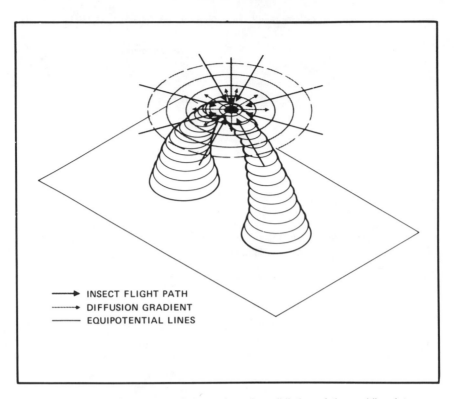

FIG. 23.8.   Completion of the arch and annihilation of the saddlepoint
(adapted from Kugler & Turvey, 1987).

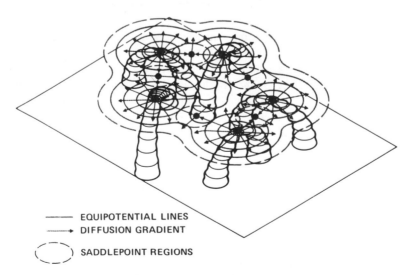

FIG. 23.9.   Emergent saddlepoints are used to build a dome (adapted from
Kugler & Turvey, 1987).

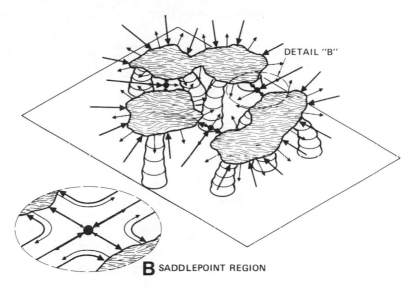

DETAIL "B"

B SADDLEPOINT REGION

FIG. 23.10. Development of a dome (adapted from Kugler & Turvey, 1987).

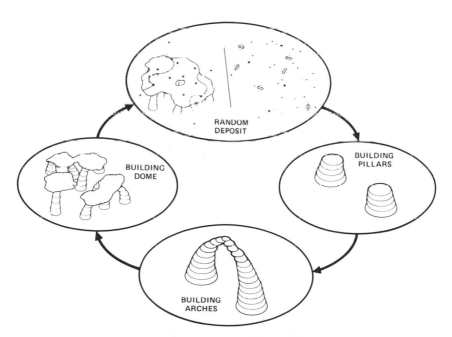

RANDOM DEPOSIT

BUILDING PILLARS

BUILDING ARCHES

BUILDING DOME

FIG. 23.11. Circular ring of building phases. Each phase is dominate by a small set of critical (degenerate) states that organizes the chemical flow fields. These flow portraits provide the controls constraints that orient the insect's motion (adapted from Kugler & Turvey, 1987).

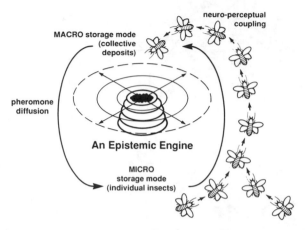

FIG. 23.12.   Self-reading, self-writing, self-organizing information system (adapted from Kugler & Turvey, 1987).

replenishing and dissipation of pheromones through a perceptual coupling forms a new kind of "engine," one that goes beyond mere energetic (i.e., thermodynamical) connections. Because the circular closure of the cycle depends on information flows as well as energy flows, we have a closed thermodynamic-epistemic engine cycle (Fig. 23.13; see Kugler & Shaw, 1990): force field (muscular activity)⟼flow field (pheromone control constraints)⟼force field

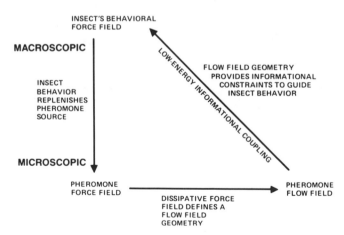

FIG. 23.13.   The individual insects define micro storage modes for the pheromone. The active deposit site on the pillar defines a macro storage mode. The insect's transport of the pheromone to the top of the pillars is an escapement process (micro→macro transport) and the diffusion process that distributes the pheromone from the top of the pillar to a uniform distribution is a dissipative process (macro→micro process).

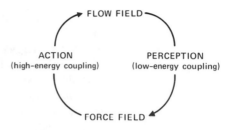

FIG. 23.14. Perception action cycle. A circular causality of self-assembled flows and forces (adapted from Kugler & Turvey, 1987).

(muscular activity)→flow field (pheromone control constraints), and so on. Alternatively, the engine cycle can be described as an action→ perception→action→ . . . cycle (compare the cycle depicted in Fig. 23.14 with the cycles depicted in Figs. 23.12 and 23.13).

Finally, it is important to emphasize that the nest-building system is a thermodynamically open system. As pointed out in the previous section, self-organization is possible only when a system is open to the flow of energy and mass. In any self-organization process, it is the *thermodynamic pump* which plays the critical escapement role, adding a higher grade of energy to the system (local regions of high pheromone concentration). In this case, the part of the pump is played by the insects' depositing of waste in the pheromone field. The construction of the thermodynamic pump is the greatest challenge for any evolutionary system.

Similarly, as an epistemic engine, information is also "pumped" into the system. An understanding of how the informational linkage arises and works in completing this circularly causal system is a strong challenge to any cognitive psychology. Let us consider this informational linkage more closely.

Primacy of Informational Linkages

Like the falling leaf, the insect nest example provides an effective illustration of the properties of self-organization that were discussed in the previous section. However, it also possesses an important property which distinguishes it from both the leaf and magnetic field examples. While inanimate physical and chemical systems are *governed* by a *force* field, the insects are *guided* by an *information* field. The distinction is a critical one, and it will be of prime importance in the discussion of intentional dynamics. Intuitively, physical systems go where they are pushed. The forces acting on the system determine its behavior. The magnetic field example presented earlier is a prime illustration of a force-dominated system. In the insect example, however, the pheromone field is not pushing the insects toward the attractor regions. There are no significant forces from the pheromone field relative to the mass of the insect. Instead, the pheromone field provides the insects with *information* that *specifies* where the building sites are located. The insect can detect this information and then use its own on-board energy supply (i.e., its action system) to travel in the direction of the attractor. Thus, the energy that is propelling the insect is generated internally, whereas in physical systems, the energy guiding the system is a direct result of an external force field acting on the particle in question.

The difference between the two systems can be characterized as follows: *The behavior of inanimate systems is lawfully determined by a force field, whereas the behavior of animate systems is lawfully specified by an information field.* The lawful determination of information was anticipated by J. J. Gibson (1979) in his pursuit of a kinematic field analysis of optical flow couplings (see Reed & Jones, 1982; Kugler, Turvey, Carello, & Shaw, 1985). Gibson's methodology focused on the physical and functional significance of nonforce interactions. By focusing on nonforce field descriptions, a natural transition can be made from the physical theory of self-organization to a theory of self-organizing information systems[5].

What relevance does the analysis of the insect nest example have for the understanding of intentional behavior? Before this question can be answered, some general characteristics of intentional behavior need to be described.

CHALLENGES POSED BY INTENTIONAL SYSTEMS

In this section, several modeling issues associated with goal-directed behavior will be addressed, including different types of teleological mechanisms, the role of the perceiving-acting cycle, and the primacy of perception. This will serve as background for the following section, where we will illustrate how the concepts of self-organization, attractors, and the lawful determination of information can be brought to bear on the problems described here.

An Inventory of Teleological Mechanisms

Teleological determinism is the philosophical view which assumes that goals, as future states, somehow act causally backward in time to guide systems down goal-paths. Many philosophical analyses have rejected the thesis of temporally backward causation because it violates natural law to have an effect precede its cause (Braithwaite, 1953; Russel, 1945; Taylor, 1966; and especially Woodfield, 1976). Such a thesis can be held only if one repudiates the principle of state determinacy.

State-determinacy.   In midcentury, cybernetic approaches attempted a scientific reformulation of the problem of intentional dynamics by identifying *goal*-determinacy in terms of *state*-determinacy (Ashby 1952, 1956; Rosenblueth,

---

[5]For extended discussions on the topic of self-organizing information systems, see Kugler, Kelso & Turvey, 1980, 1982; Kugler 1986, 1988; Kugler & Turvey, 1987, 1988; Kugler & Shaw, 1990.

Wiener, & Bigelow, 1946; and especially Sommerhoff, 1950). It was hoped that this ploy would mechanistically capture the essence of intentional behaviors while, at the same time, avoiding the pitfalls of teleological determinism. There is a danger in mechanistic approaches, however, for they typically attempt to reduce final causes (goal-states) to initial conditions plus efficient causes (laws) (e.g., the setting of set-points by an extrinsic agent rather than by the system itself). Thus such attempts fail because they regress the problem of intention to the problem of determining how and for what purpose the system was designed. This failure has led most scientists to reject out of hand all forms of teleological determinism.

The argument against teleological determinism, however, may be overstated. Perhaps, one might champion a weaker, acausal version of teleological determinism that avoids the scientifically suspect thesis of temporally backward causation. For instance, Weir (1985) offers compelling arguments for the provocative thesis that goal-directed systems are *directed by goals* rather than being merely *self directed toward goals,* as cybernetics would have it. By this change in emphasis, Weir wisely avoids attempting a logical reduction of final causation to efficient causation as others typically do, and takes a different tack than state-determinacy arguments. He argues that goal-directed behavior can be formally distinguished from other behaviors by its characteristic mathematical structure and pattern; or as Aristotle might say, its formal cause. A brief account of Weir's argument follows.

Strong teleology implies temporally backward causation, where an action's cause (its goal) comes later than its effect (its path). This perplexing view abrogates the classical *state-determinacy principle* that requires future states to be caused by past states. Yet, whereas a billiard ball follows a path determined by its *past* events (motion states), we recognize, in some sense, that a hungry predator follows a path determined by an anticipated *future* event (capturing its prey).

Mathematically, state-determinacy implies analyticity. From an infinitely small section of an object's past or future motion path, given by a differential equation, the rest of the path can be analytically projected by integrating the equation. For three centuries, analytical projection in the *temporally forward* direction has provided the best formal description for explanatory laws of motion mechanics. Therefore it is only natural to attempt to use analytical projection in the *temporally backward* direction as a formal description for corollary explanatory laws of action mechanics. Unfortunately, as Weir points out, this strategy encounters serious problems. Let's see why.

Path-determinacy. Corrections introduced into goal-directed actions show up as path bifurcations that are not analytically continuous with either past or future states; and yet action paths are shaped in anticipation of future goal-states. To explain anticipatory control logically requires goal-determinacy. This has convinced many theorists to move from *state*-determinacy to *path*-determinacy in order to accommodate anticipatory goal-constraints (Rosen, 1985).

Path-determinacy is the view that final causation might be expressed lawfully by designing goal-paths, according to a minimum principle, backwards from the system's final condition to its initial condition. How might this be done? This approach grows naturally out of a form of classical mechanics known as *variational mechanics* (Lanczos, 1970). This field was so christened because its mathematical power derives from the calculus of variations—a technique by which laws of mechanics may be rendered in integral form rather than in differential form as is usually the case. In the ordinary calculus one seeks to express state-determinacy by finding the tangent that lies at the minimum (or maximum) to a function (a curve) at a point. Hence, by differentiation, one selects from all points on a curve that point which is the extremum of interest.

By contrast, the calculus of variations provides a method by which one can compare path integrals (i.e., curves) and select from among them that which is minimal. On the assumption that a path is a minimal curve just in case it is the intended goal-path, many theorists (e.g., Maupertuis) were persuaded that where the ordinary calculus of differential equations modeled time-forward causation, this complementary calculus of integral equations provided a way to model backward causation (see, for instance, Mach, 1974/1893, p. 550; Poincare, 1952/1905, p. 128) Since it operated on paths (integrals of curves) while the other operated on points (states of a tangent vector), it seemed to make explicit a principle of path determinacy. It is now accepted that no prescience is implied by this path-determinacy approach, since it reduces, on all occasions, to a formulation in terms of differential equations. Hence path-determinacy provides no theory of goal-determinacy but qualifies only as a variation on the state-determinacy theme, since the two are mathematically equivalent. There is, however, a further alternative formulation which Weir (1985) attempts.

Germ-determinacy.   If forces coordinate action paths with their origins (initial conditions), then what coordinates them with their goals (final conditions)? It does not help merely to say that goals themselves must somehow be responsible for coordinating paths, for the issue is not *whether* but *how* they do so. If postulating backward (efficient) causation is metaphysically bizarre and logically perplexing because it inverts the presumed order of cause and effect, then we must seek another way that goals might constrain actions. For this we need to replace the notion of an analytical function with another mathematical concept— that of a *germ*. To do this moves us from the relatively tame realm of linearly continuous mathematics to the wild regions of nonlinarly discontinuous mathematics.

A goal-path, Weir proposes, is really a bundle of virtual paths that may agree (are defined by the same mapping and show the same analytical continuation) up to a point of discontinuity, called a *bifurcation point;* after which they might bifurcate into a collection of separate paths, with each path representing a different possible realization of the goal. This bundle of virtually separable goal-directed paths is called a germ, and is not a function since, at the bifurcation point, it is *one-to-many* (Auslander & MacKenzie, 1977). Hence the germ is the formal cause of a goal-directed path, that is, a dynamical principle which expresses nondeterministically the distinctive shapes that paths may assume.

Weir proposes that *goal*-determinacy is mathematically identical to *germ*-determinacy, a concept which imputes a special role to perception in constraining goal-directed behaviors. Actors perceive the transformability of current action states, despite thwarts, into future goal-accessible routes precisely because they *perceive* the germ of the generalized action potential specific to a given goal. The germ, as the dynamical principle governing a teleological system, although not a function itself, contains all of the analytical and nonanalytical mappings from past states to goal-states.

In summary, Weir argues that goal-directed behavior is nonanalytical, bifurcatory behavior requiring germ-determinacy rather than state-determinacy or even path-determinacy for its explanation. This implies that a goal is not a designated final state to be reached by a system but a distinctive way of the system reaching a final state over one of several optional paths, given goal variation. Finally, goals play an active role in the control of behavior because their *variation* is perceptually projected directly into corresponding changes in the action control variables, which then shape the actor's path through efficient causes.

For our purposes, we should emphasize the argument that goal-determinacy, when viewed at the global scale of germ-determinacy, promises a bird's-eye view from which to appreciate intentional-dynamics—a view unavailable to the more local scales of path-determinacy and state-determinacy. (Exactly how goals may informationally specify constraints on behavior, which may be followed if the organism intends to do so, has been addressed in detail and, to some degree, made mathematically explicit in Kugler & Turvey, 1987; Shaw & Kinsella–Shaw, 1988, Shaw, Kugler, & Kinsella–Shaw, 1990, Kugler & Shaw, 1990).

This brief summary prepares us to appreciate the full significance of Weir's (1985) solution to the mechanism of teleological determinism. According to him, goal-directed behavior " . . . necessarily involves explaining the behaviour that occurs by reference to some behaviour being perceived to bring about the goal. And if behaviour is brought about because of this perception, then the behavior is goal-directed" (p. 121). But how might a behavior be preceived as bringing about the goal? Does this mean paradoxically that the future somehow controls the present? Perhaps, Weir had something like the following in mind. No paradox analogous to "backward-causation" is encountered if we treat perceptual information as if it flowed temporally backwards relative to the temporally forward flow of action paths. (A defense of the plausibility of this suggestion has been given by Shaw, 1987, and Shaw & Kinsella–Shaw, 1988.)

It is important to distinguish between systems with perceptual abilities that intend as opposed to those that merely have intentions. Both kinds of systems exhibit intentional dynamics, in Weir's sense, but are distinguished by how they do so. We shall term *cognitive* the capacity to intend for the reasons given next. Bear in mind that just as we can take an ecological approach to perception and action, so we can also to cognition, as we attempt to show next.

Intending Systems as Opposed to Systems Merely Having Intentions

In the magnetic field example we saw what it means for an isolated system's behavior to be governed by attractors. But there was no capacity for self-organization. By contrast, in the falling leaf example, we saw how an open system can reorganize into higher-order modes of behavior as more and more energy is pumped into the system *vis-à-vis* an escapement. Our analysis of self-organizing systems was extended once more by the termite nest-building example. Here we saw that higher-order modes of behavior can also emerge from the detection of goal-specific information that controls the energy escapement. Such systems, however, exhibit goal-directed behavior without having the ability to formulate intentions in the cognitive sense, that is, without being able to intend. They are systems that exhibit intentional behavior without *intending* the behavior.

Explicit choices of goals are not made by such systems although ties between attractor influences may be broken by random variation (e.g., perturbation of initial conditions). We might call this *implicit* goal-selection as, for example, when random molecular perturbations temporarily alter the pheromone gradient between two pillar attractors so as to favor one or the other. The termite's goal-path tie gets broken implicitly by environmental (external state) perturbations and not by an explicit (internal state) choice on the part of the insect.

Thus, a system with the ability to make choices must have the capacity for intending and not just for perceiving and moving. We offer, then, the following hypothesis on the nature of intending. Intention is identified with an operator that selects, from among all possible final states (or structures)[6] of a system, a

---

[6]The set of final states need not be points in space-time. Instead, they might consist of a set of observable "tendencies" that are defined along some fitness criteria. For example, a final state might be defined by the system achieving a path that *tends* to improve the performance maximally along the fitness metric. The set of possible final states would then consist of a *collection of tendencies* defined on different fitness criteria defined by a given structural configuration. This exemplifies the distinction between goal-directedness in terms of functions, as opposed to germs, the latter defining a tendency operator for a *distribution* of potential paths, in contrast to the former which identifies a state operator defining a single unique path. The "final state" as a "tendency" is associated with the *structure* of the state equation rather than a unique region of the state space. The intention for the final state would define a constraint that selects a tendency. This class of intentional states is associated with adaptive evolutionary systems.

specific final state (or structure) to be the goal. Goal-selection, we shall argue, is the sensitivity of a self-organizing system to nonlocal constraints that have determine local effects, such as breaking ties between competing attractors. By selecting, implicitly or explicitly, among *possible* final conditions, intentional systems go beyond those physical systems that operate only under the constraints of *actual* final conditions. Final conditions are actualized by the application of natural laws to existing initial conditions. Systems that exhibit intentional behavior satisfy the stipulation offered for the existence of an intentional operator. But to be capable of intending requires something more.

A system *intends* a particular final condition (goal) if from among the possible initial conditions it selects that one which permits attainment of the specified final condition under the existing law domain. Hence intending systems, unlike merely intentional systems, are capable of true choice behavior. Intending is rational when the choice of the initial condition follows consistently from the prioritizing of needs or values. However, the property that is unique to an intending agent is that it can go against the gradients specified by the information field.

Our purpose in this chapter, however, is not to consider the problems of why certain intentions get formulated, but to suggest a law-based explanation for their behavioral efficacy; namely, that intentions identify a higher mode of system organization whereby a new attractor dynamic is defined. From the earlier arguments, this occurs when attractors are created or annihilated in the state space of the self-organizing system by means of energetic and informational couplings equivalent to those found in the nest-building example.

The General Role of the Perceiving–Acting Cycle:
To Conserve Intention

Whenever actions succeed on purpose rather than accidentally, current information must specify what to do next *over and over again* until the goal is reached. This mutual and reciprocal support that information detection processes and action control processes give each other is the job performed by the *perceiving–acting cycle*. Let's examine more closely how it works.

With each step closer to the goal the information must become ever more specific, thereby tightening the reins on how the action path unfolds, until ultimately, at the moment of accomplishment, the path becomes uniquely defined. The elimination of the degrees of freedom for action control options corresponds to a progressive reduction in the number of paths in the germ from which action paths are selected. Our improving prospects for reaching the goal at some future space-time location are noticeable in the here and now. In this way, the successful action of the perceiving–acting cycle is to distill from all possible paths, in the bifurcation set emerging from the germ, that path which best (con)serves the directing intention.

In field-theoretical language, the felicitous perceiving–acting cycle follows a *geodesic,*[7] or streamline, through the ecological field. Thus it defines the optimal goal-path, or near-optimal one if it is less successful in avoiding thwarts, or less accurate in resolving goal-specific information, or less skillful in controlling the action than the ideal. Biological evolution does not require, nor should we expect, perfection. Nature is pragmatic rather than idealistic, demanding only that the goal-path generated by this cycling intention be *tolerably suboptimal* so that life-supporting needs are met and life-threatening situations avoided. Psychological development and health may require more, namely, that information be gathered in the process, or that stress be reduced, affections satisfied, and tastes pleased.

Special Role of Perceiving: To Furnish Anticipatory Information to Intention

Perception provides spatiotemporally "remote sensing," acting as a kind of "early warning" device that informs the system of pending goal variation. In other words, there is information available in the present which lawfully specifies upcoming future events. Evidence that perception can indeed effect projection of future trends is provided by *time-to-contact* research on the perceived imminence of collision with obstacles, as provided by Schiff (1965) and Lee and his colleagues (e.g., Lee, 1976; Lee & Reddish, 1981; Lee, Lishman, & Thomson, 1982) and Shaw and his colleagues' research into the perceptual information for the aging of faces and other objects (see Mark, Shaw, & Pittenger, 1988, for a review). This body of research suggests that perceptual information flows are temporally *antecedent* to the consequent tuning and execution of actions. This relativity of rates accounts for both the apparent temporal backward flow sometimes attributed to goal-specific information and for the temporally forward flow always attributed to the mechanical-energy-producing action paths (Shaw & Alley, 1985).

Other Similar Views

We might ask how this view of goal-determinacy as germ-determinacy compares and contrasts with other contemporary views. On the one hand, it contrasts to Sommerhoff's (1950) view in locating control in the perceiving-acting cycle rather than in some logico/physical state of affairs. This makes perceptual sensitivity to available goal-specific information of foremost importance, with mediating mental states (desires, beliefs, internal representations) taking a contributory but insufficient role in the explanation of goal-directed behaviors.

This approach also puts one in mind of Gibson's (1979) notion of an *intentional rule for the perceptual control of action,* which asserts the conditions

---

[7]A geodesic, or streamline, defines a path which minimizes a metric. Examples are: least work, least time, least distance, least action, least resistance, and so on. The appropriate metric is usually defined as a function of the field's properties.

that any successful goal-directed system must satisfy: *In order to achieve goal x, then act so as to produce the perception y.* Note that, according to this principle, the invariant in goal-directed behavior is the final condition which is defined on the perceptual side. The role of action is to control the approach to the perceptually specified goal. It does so by reinitializing the control laws (e.g., self-produced forces) in a manner appropriate to the goal-specific information. The importance of this fact will be brought out herein. For now, a simple example will serve to illustrate the idea.

Writing one's signature is an effective context for illustrating the primacy of perception. The specific actions one executes in signing one's name depend upon many factors. The exact muscles used, for instance, will be a function of one's current posture and the weight of the writing utensil. Furthermore, if there are external disturbances, motor movements will have to compensate for these if the product is to be legible. In all of these cases, however, what remains invariant is the *product*, not the *process.* That is, what one's signature looks like remains constant, whereas the exact sequence of motor movements used to produce it does not. In this book, whose very title *Behavior: The Control of Perception*, invokes a similar thesis, Powers (1973) argues provocatively for intentional rules of this sort. Unfortunately, he undercuts his own position by adhering strictly to linear feedback (state-determinacy) principles.

Summary

Several concepts relevant to the problems of intentional behavior were introduced in this section, including: germ determinacy as a mechanism for teleological determinism, the relation of the perceiving–acting cycle to intention, and the critical role of perception in providing anticipatory information to support goal-directed behavior. In the following section, these concepts will be integrated with the mechanisms of self-organization discussed earlier. The resulting synthesis represents an ecological approach to intentional dynamics that provides one way for attempting to unravel the mysteries of goal-directed behavior without depending *solely* on internal states (mental acts). The cognitivist who wishes more than this, we refer him or her to our lengthy discussions of why we believe this dual-state (organism–environment) approach is sufficient (Shaw, Kugler, & Kinsella–Shaw, 1990; Shaw & Mingolla, 1982; Shaw, & Kinsella–Shaw, 1988; Shaw & Todd, 1980; Turvey, Shaw, Reed, & Mace, 1981).

THE SELF-ORGANIZATION
OF INTENTIONAL BEHAVIOR

Is it possible to derive a lawful account of intentional behavior in which an information field serves as the guide for goal-directed behavior, just as it did for the insects? The first step toward answering this question is to look at the types of constraints that are operating in intentional systems. The preceding discussion of goal-directed behavior will provide a basis for carrying out this phase of inquiry. The second step is to see if those constraints can be expressed through the generic mechanisms of self-organization. Likewise, the earlier discussion on self-organization provides a background within which to approach this second place.

Constraints on Intentional Behavior

The Perception–action Cycle.   A good way to approach the issue of constraints is through an example. Take a prototypical case of goal-directed behavior: a driver who successfully brings his or her automobile to a controlled stop when approaching the bottom of a hill. The rolling of a car downhill, accelerating due to gravity, is an ordinary physical motion, while the movement of the driver's leg by a controlled change in muscle tonus to the brake pedal and applying the proper amount of pressure is an ordinary biomechanical movement. But the driver's *informed intention* to move one's leg so as to achieve a final outcome is quite extraordinary, for it depends on two things that physics and biology ignore: *the choice of an intended goal-state* (e.g., final velocity of the car) as well as *the detection of information* (e.g., the optical flow field) specifying in what manner he or she is to modulate the relevant actuators, that is, through the biomechanical/mechanical linkage of:

> *leg muscles→brake pedal→hydraulic pressure→tire friction/surface friction.*

Without the intending being logically antecedent to the movement, no temporary biomechanical linkage would be functionally (physiologically) assembled nor sustained throughout the act's required duration; and without the detection of the optical flow which is reciprocally constrained by the act of braking, the intended mode of control could not be monitored and thus the intended outcome would be difficult to achieve.

Consequently, informed intending, after choosing and anticipating the goal-requirements for action, both assembles and sustains the mechanism for the realization of an action and becomes informed in a sustaining way by perception of the conditions required to achieve the stipulated goal. This mechanism is a cycle of;

> *Intending→perceiving→choosing→anticipating→assembling→*
> *(acting→perceiving→intending→sustaining→acting→ . . . etc.)^n→Goal.*

This is the familiar perceiving–acting cycle introduced in the previous section. There, it was pointed out that the role of the perception–action cycle in goal-directed behavior is to *conserve intention*. Thus, the role of *informed intention,* as a constraint on physical motion, is a fact of nature, as undeniable as gravity or a sunset. And since this constraint is not recognized by traditional physics, we might call it an *exceptional constraint* (Kugler & Turvey, 1987; Shaw & Kinsella–Shaw, 1988). Let us explore further the notion of intention as a constraint.

Holonomic and Nonholonomic Constraints. Generically, constraints restrict the physical degrees of freedom of a system. Traditionally, this can occur in two ways. *Holonomic constraints* restrict without requiring material instantiation. Hence they can be expressed functionally as a relationship among coordinates, and, thus, do not materially alter the system. Typically, systems that are governed by holonomic constraints are called *law-governed*, since laws are not materially instantiated. As an example, the trajectory of a projectile moving through the air is constrained holonomically by the laws of physics. By contrast, *nonholonomic constraints* are able to restrict trajectories in state space only because they are physically instantiated—they require some mechanism that materially alters the system. These types of systems are often called *rule-governed* since they require rules that are independent of laws to constrain behavior. An example is a computer program, whose behavior (i.e., output) is nonholonomically constrained by the lines of code that are materially instantiated within the degrees of freedom associated with the electron states that constitute the computer's memory.

In the profound issues separating a law-governed account from a rule-governed account of the intentional behaviors of complex systems, one stands paramount: *Is an intention, or the goal it selects, a holonomic or a nonholonomic constraint?* If intentions are holonomic constraints, then no mechanism is required beyond that which exploits laws relating energy and information in some specific way. In such case, one might argue plausibly that, through evolution or through learning, organisms come to exploit existing laws very effectively in achieving their goals, without necessary recourse to rules of behavior or "internalized" models of goal-paths, and so on. If this is the case, then the insect nest example may be a good model for intentional behavior since the manner in which the nest is constructed is based on lawful specification provided by the pheromone field, not on a "mental model" of the plan for building an arch. On the other hand, if intentions are nonholonomic, then something like cognitively internalized models of the environment and the actors place in it would have to be assumed because rules require such mechanisms in order to be applied.

On the face of it, from a classical external frame perspective, it appears that a goal (or its intention) can constrain in both ways. It acts *holonomically* whenever the organism acts like an inanimate particle by *following* the external potential gradient (e.g., a rock rolling down a hill and hitting a tree). On the other hand, it acts *nonholonomically* whenever the system acts animately *against* an external potential gradient (e.g., a person running down a hill accelerating by gravity but braking and stopping short of the tree).

Abstractly, maintaining the external frame perspective, a system is *holonomically constrained* by a goal over those intervals of the goal-path where the internal potential is inoperative or in a stationary process. These will be those integrable (open) intervals of the goal-path between choice-points. A system is *nonholonomically constrained* when its behavior must be controlled across choice-points. These will be those (closed) intervals that include choice points. Choice-points act as nonintegrable constraints and denote regions in the exterior frame where the goal-path curve becomes nonanalytical (discontinuous). How might this happen?

A system with an active nonstationary interior gradient can be thought of, mathematically, as depositing singular points along its trajectory in the exterior frame where choices may be made (e.g., to brake, change direction, speed up or slow down). These control decisions arise at those points along a trajectory where the system must inject a sustaining "squirt" of interior field potential to keep moving in the same mode toward the same target, or where it can counter the work done on it by an exterior gradient. Structurally, these points in the field are actually equilibrium points (attractors). Psychologically, they are *choice-points* in that there is insufficient information in the field to define uniquely the future path.

Mathematically, the existence of singular points (bifurcation points, equilibrium points, or attractors) represents regions in the external frame where the goal-path geometry becomes *compact*, in the sense of hiding additional (internal) degrees of freedom at singular points along the path. Because these compact singularities determine the point of contact between the two frames, there is no way to integrate the two potentials, and thereby treat them as equations of constraint. Normally, these equations would simply be added to the equations of motion (by elimination) and the resulting system of differential equations solved (integrated) to determine the system's path of motion. Unfortunately, where goal-points crop up this cannot be done.

From the external frame perspective, the problem of modeling intentional systems is exacerbated by the fact that goal constraints must satisfy the final conditions of the involved differential equations as well as their initial conditions. Thus, the value of a goal constraint cannot be found until after the equations of motion for the system are solved (that is, until after the system reaches its goal), yet its value is needed to evaluate the integrating factor before the motion equations can be solved (integrated). Hence a vicious cycle! The integrability problem is compounded when intentions are not stable because this integration process must then be carried out in a piecewise manner between each pair of equilibrium points (choice-points). The final yield will be a goal-path in the external frame that is a mixture of concatenated holonomic and nonholonomic subintervals.

These concatenated regions of holonomic and nonholonomic constraints are exactly those regions within an open system where entropy is high and low, respectively. To cross regions of low order, the behavior of the system need only be dissipation-dominated (controlled by the Second Law) because it is moved by outside forces down the force gradient toward the entropic attractor. By contrast, for the system to cross regions of high order, it must become escapement dominated (perceptually controlled), so that it might move up the information gradient toward the goal. In the dissipation case, work is done on the system by its environment, while in the escapement case, work is done on the environment by the system. Let us define *choice-points as bifurcation points that act temporarily as if they were equilibrium points, or (goal) attractors.*

If we can provide a theory relating the internal frame to the external frame, and vice versa, then there is the possibility that constraints that are nonholonomic in one frame might prove holonomic over both frames. This is equivalent to claiming that there is an invariant of motion, a conservation, that carries the system holonomically over these singular regions without a cognitive mechanism mediating the behavior. What might qualify as such a motion invariant?

Intention as a "Holonomizing" Constraint

To remain consistent with the already existing inventory of symmetries associated with the conservation laws of physics (see Goldstein, 1980), we must formulate the role that intention plays in dynamics as a corresponding symmetry. But if reductionism is unlikely, then this symmetry will not be identified with any existing symmetry, but will implicate a new conservation, and possibly other motion invariants. (As the term is used here, a motion invariant is any dynamical variable whose value does not change as the system moves. For classical systems energy, momentum, and angular momentum are motion invariants.) What might a motion invariant for an intentional system be?

This motion invariant should be the informed and controlling intention itself, formally construed as an operator that selects the goal, seeks anticipatory, goal-relevant information, initiates the action, and sustains it to completion down the goal-path. In other words, intention as a dynamical variable refers to some quantity or to some qualitative condition which remains conserved, if the action is to be successful. (Mathematically, we might think of this as the characteristic function of the operator.) Elsewhere, we have attempted to give a mathematically explicit formulation of this conserved aspect of intentional systems (Shaw, Kugler, & Kinsella–Shaw, 1990). The following is a summary of that effort.

Just as the statement, *A force is identified with the gradient of some potential which is directed toward the local attractor of the field,* applies to inanimate particles to explain how they must get where they are going, so we need a corollary statement in intentional dynamics to express how animate "particles" (possessed of complex interiors) might get to where they intend to go. Provisionally, we might formulate an analogous scientific proposition about informed intentional motion: *An informed intention lays down a goal-gradient of some generalized potential which is directed toward the local attractor[8] of the ecological field* (where *ecological field* = the organism as an internal field plus its environment as an external field.)

A *potential* is a quantity whose organization, and hence its capacity to do work, is a function of spatial coordinates. By contrast, a *generalized* potential is defined by a reciprocal (adjoint) relationship that couples two fields. Unfortunately, the coupling of two fields that are not in the same frame is not standard procedure for classical approaches to dynamics. Classical couplings apply only to potentials that exist in a single (external) frame. The challenge, then, is to develop a holonomic description of intentional behavior that bridges the internal field of the organism and the external field of the environment. We will see that the concepts behind self-organization will play an important role in developing such a description.

Internalization of an Evolving Attractor Set: The Embodiment of Geometry

A cognitive approach to intentional dynamics typically puts all the complexity of the problem into internal states of the organism (Fodor & Pylyshyn, 1981; Ullman, 1980). An ecological approach to the cognitive aspects of the problem tends to distribute the complexity over both internal and external states, what might be called a *dual-state* description (Shaw & Todd, 1980). We can use the insights derived earlier from the analysis of self-organizing information systems, as exemplified by the insect nest example, to explain this latter approach to the problem of intentional dynamics.

While intentional behavior carried out by humans seems to be far removed from the building of a nest by a group of social insects, they share certain abstractly equivalent properties that allow them to be modeled in equivalent ways. For instance, just as the insects go through a set of modes representing qualitatively different types of behavior, so a person exhibits different modes in his or her daily life, such as, sleeping, eating, working, reading, courting (Iberall & McCulloch, 1969) (see Fig. 23.15). Extrapolating from what was learned from the insect example, it is hypothesized that each mode is constrained by a unique number and layout of attractors. That is, just as in all of the other examples of self-organization described in this chapter, the qualitative properties associated with any given mode of intentional behavior will be defined by the attractor set for that mode. To make this idea clear, let us consider some additional facts about field theory.

---

[8]This attractor may sometimes be defined by a variational principle, but it need not be. For example, mini-max solutions can give rise to an attractor that need not be defined by variational principles.

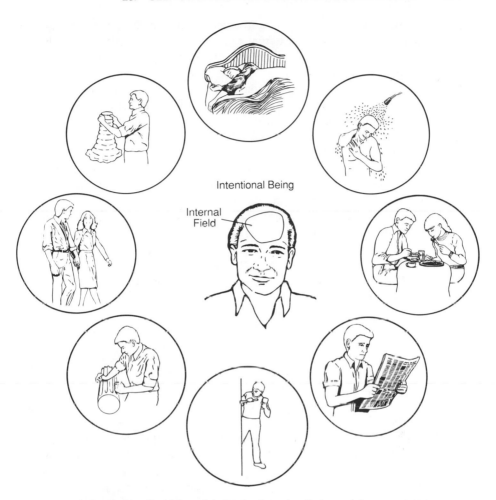

FIG. 20.15.   Examples of behavioral modes that populate an average person's work space.

Classically, an attractor set is used to define a field *external* to a particle in motion. An example is the magnetic field described earlier, where the negatively charged particle is described as moving through an externally defined (relative to the particle) magnetic field. But there is also a nonlinear *internal field* induced locally around the particle that cannot be integrated under the external field through which the particle moves. This is a well-known limitation of the linear superposition principle of classical field theory (see Sachs, 1973). By definition, this internal field must have its own independent attractor dynamics. For instance, a compass will be systematically deflected as it is moved through the earth's magnetic field. The compass, however, will induce a locally confined, internal magnetic field that travels with it which can not be integrated under the external magnetic field. Hence external (state) field descriptions can not be reduced to internal (state) field descriptions, or vice versa. This is the reason a dual-(state) field theory is needed.

Under the external field description, the internal field is a singular anomalous point in whose neighborhood are hidden degrees of freedom not expressible in the classical mathematics of the external field. In other words, charged particles placed in the field (e.g., compasses) will behave differently inside each other's neighborhoods than they do outside. Fields that have hidden degrees of freedom (internal fields) are said to be *compactified*. The relationship between local and global fields is promoted here to express the relationship between an environmental and the organisms acting in that environment. The compacting of an external field by internal field properties expresses exactly the contributory role perceptual/cognitive variables play, along with physical variables, in codetermining the observed behavior of the organism. This, we propose, is what it means to say that an organism, as a perceptually attuned intentional system, is informationally as well as forcefully coupled to its environment.

We propose further that these internal/external field interactions provide an important and literal expression of the facts about the nature of organism–environment interactions—whether they be "behavioral," as viewed from the external field perspective, or "cognitive," as viewed from the internal field perspective. This *dual-field,* or ecological field, perspective expresses all the content of Gibson's (1979) *principle of organism–environment mutuality* upon which the construct of a psychological ecosystem is founded (for details, see Shaw, Kugler, & Kinsella–Shaw, 1990).

It is useful to bear in mind that the field concept is a generic construct; therefore, the set of contents and support the same field relations and field dynamics are legitimately said to be the *same* field. Hence it is just as legitimate to use the field concept in psychology as it is in physics so long as the abstract properties are satisfied. One may think of the field level of abstraction as being as legitimate as the strong simulation claim that two hardware instantiations comprise the same abstract machine so long as the algorithms implemented on them compute the same functions in the same way. If the cognitivist accepts this latter modeling proposition, then consistency demands that he or she must also accept the former. What should be recognized, of course, are the obvious differences that distinguish this ecological approach to cognition and the traditional rule-governed, abstract machine theory (here one might wish to contrast Fodor & Pylyshyn, 1981, 1988, to Turvey, Shaw, Reed, & Mace, 1981, and Carello, Kugler, Turvey, & Shaw, 1984).

Similarly, for both physical and mathematical reasons, it is legitimate to consider the process that takes place in nest building as arising from constraints that are set up by an *internal* field. From a social or ensemble perspective, the insects can be viewed as a single collective system, and the pheromone field can be viewed as a field internal to that system. From this perspective, the self-organization occurs in the internal field, not in the external field. The external degrees of freedom define the movement of the insect society as a whole through an external environment, while the informational (intentional) constraints direct the movement of each insect as a perceptually attuned actor toward its goals.

Taking this step leads to the possibility, illustrated in Fig. 23.16, that an intentional organism is constituted by a similar type of internally self-organizing mechanism. That is, there is an internal field within the organism that is organized by the layout of attractors internal to the organism. These attractors are goal-states which act to constrain the system's internal degrees of freedom. The corresponding field, which is determined by the organism's *effectivities* (i.e., capabilities for action), embodies the internal constraints on action. Thus, a change in the number and layout of goal-states will result in a change in the field, which in turn manifests itself as a qualitative shift in behavior mode. Referring back to Fig. 23.11, each of the modes illustrated there correspond to a unique set of goal-states that organize the field. All of the generic self-organizing properties that were attributed to the insect colony also apply to this internal field of goal-states.

The problem of intentional behavior cannot, however, be relegated solely to

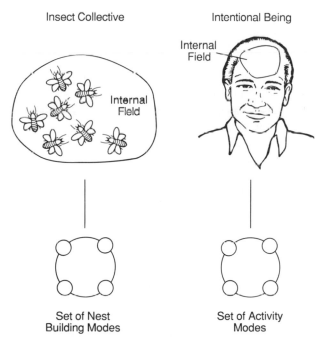

FIG. 23.16. Examples of open systems with cooperative modes defined on internal degrees of freedom.

an internal state description. Previously, we saw that the phenomenon of intentional dynamics is only apparent at a more global scale—the *ecological scale*—because goal-paths are ecological field processes whose support depends on the coupling of *two* fields—the *external field of the environment* and the *internal field of the organism*. Let us look into this notion of an ecological field more closely.

Intentional Systems as Ecological Fields of Nonstationary Attractor Sets

A single field description, whether it be of the environment (external field) or of the organism (internal field), is only one of many possible descriptions. For example, an organism can be described in many different ways as a function of the mode it is in (as illustrated in Figs. 23.11 and 23.15). Similarly, an object in the environment (e.g., an apple) can also be described in several different ways. Some of these are *intrinsic* descriptions (e.g., size, color, weight, density, and elasticity of the apple). Others, however, are *relational* descriptions of the apple (e.g., that it is throwable, edible, etc.). There is an interesting relationship between the various descriptions of the organism and those of the environment.

The possible descriptions of the environment in terms of intrinsic or relational properties form a *set,* where no description is more privileged than another. Intrinsic descriptions are no more "real," in the sense of being more factual, than relational descriptions. In the case of the apple, the fact that it is throwable or edible is a property as legitimate as its color or mass. Similarly, possible descriptions of organisms can be given in terms of intrinsic as well as relational properties. These descriptions also form sets whose members are equally nonprivileged. In the case of an organism, the fact that it can throw or eat apples is as real as its own color or mass. To be scientifically comprehensive, is it not necessary to understand all the useful ways in which the environment or organisms can be described?

Traditionally, the intrinsic properties of most interest to physics have held a privileged status, not only among physicists, but also among philosophers, biologists, and even psychologists. However, by adopting an ecological scale of analysis, the set of relational properties that lives in the *intersection* of the organism and environment sets assumes primary interest. These physical relational properties provide an equally interesting and important object of study, one that Gibson (1979) called *ecological* physics. As mentioned earlier, the decision to approach the problem from a relational perspective is consistent with Gibson's (1979) *principle of organism–environment mutuality.* Moreover, the primary ecological field process, the perceiving–acting cycle, is a dynamical relational construct (Shaw, Kugler, & Kinsella–Shaw, 1990). Consequently, any analysis of intentional behavior must focus its efforts here.

This intersection of organism and environment sets represents what Gibson

(1979) referred to as the *affordances* of the environment. These relational properties are the possibilities for action that the environment makes available to an organism. Affordances are the critical relational properties that permit possible couplings between the internal field of the organism and the external field of the environment. Intentions denote a mismatch between the presence of a goal-state attractor (a possible final condition) and the actual state of the environment (the initial condition). Primitive intentions denote mismatches that need to be removed if the organism is to remain fit. By contrast, derivative intentions denote those that the organism chooses to remove for other reasons.

Effectivities are the attractor processes by which the mismatch between the initial and final conditions is eliminated. Hence effectivities map relational properties into relational properties. Consider: Seeing that a chair across the room affords sitting upon; intending to sit on that chair; locomoting across the room and sitting down. Here we see that intending sets up an attractor dynamics—a mismatch between the current initial condition (i.e., what you are currently doing) and the intended final condition (what you intend to do). We also see that intending assembles and enacts effective means for reaching the intended goal state. Affordances may be viewed as the relevant causal and informational constraints on the intentional behavior; effectivities may be viewed as the informed control processes that accomplish it. More abstractly, effectivities map antecedent affordance descriptions (e.g., affording walking to) into consequent affordance descriptions (e.g., affording sitting upon). Consider next two possible sources of nonstationarity in an ecosystem.

(1) Affordance (goal-state) attractor sets are inherently nonstationary aspects of the external field. As the goal-states (represented by the attractors in the environmental field) are created or annihilated, the intersection set will shift (see Fig. 23.17). In other words, a different set of goal-states (i.e., the layout of attractors specific to an affordance) is specific to a behavior mode. And as the behavior mode changes, different aspects of the environment become relevant to

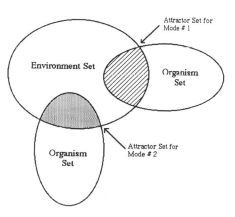

FIG. 23.17. Nonstationary affordance set. The affordance set for an ecosystem is that set of descriptions that is invariant over the state animal and the environment. Since the animal and the environment are both nonstationary, then the common descriptor set (affordances) are also nonstationary.

the organism. For a hungry organism, the objects in the environment will be described in terms of how edible they are, whereas for a sleepy organism, objects in the environment will be described in terms of how well they afford resting.

Note that, in the case of multiple goals, there will be a competition between goal-state (affordance) attractors. Thus, an organism may be both hungry and sleepy, in which case the description of the environment becomes more complex. Each of the goal-states may influence behavior, and as we saw earlier, this can lead to complex nonlinearities. Moreover, as described earlier, all of the generic properties of self-organizing systems are equally important to this account of intentional behavior. Specifically, the organizing of space into fields by attractors, the arising of different modes or qualitative shifts in behavior, the competition between attractors, and the resulting nonlinear behavior all have indispensable roles to play.

(2) Similarly, *effectivity attractor sets are inherently nonstationary aspects of the internal field*. To take a simple example, as a child grows up, the objects in the environment that have the property of being sit-onable will change. While this particular example has a very slow temporal dynamic (the change in the child's ability to sit on various objects evolves over years), there are many other cases where the change is more abrupt. For instance, as her shape and mass change, a pregnant woman will experience noticeable shifts in her effectivities over a period of months (the principle of similitude; see Kugler, Kelso, & Turvey, 1982; Rosen, 1978). An even more drastic example is the effect that fatigue or injury can have. The action capabilities of an athlete can be noticeably transformed over a very short time span if he or she becomes tired or hurt. Changes in effectivities also play an important role when human operators are required to control complex, technological systems (see Kirlik, 1989, for an interesting example).

To summarize: Affordances are potentially nonstationary, relational, external field properties that may act as goal-state attractors. They comprise the goal-relevant constraints on intentional behavior. Effectivities are potentially nonstationary, internal field processes that map the trajectories joining two or more affordance attractors. They comprise the process-relevant constraints on intentional behaviors. Together their coupling forms the ecological field for a given organism at a given time and place. There are *two* ways in which the geometry of this ecological field can change: As intentions change, the set of affordances *relevant* to a particular attractor set (i.e., combination of goals) change. Or, as an organism's effectivities change, the *definition* of what qualifies as an affordance for that organism changes.

A full understanding of intentional dynamics requires an understanding of how the constraints of this field might change but still allow stable goal-directed behaviors. This is the open question that stands as the greatest challenge to ecological psychology.

Intentional Dynamics: An Attractor Field at the Ecological Scale

What type of image of intentional behavior emerges from the marriage of the dynamics of self-organization and ecological psychology? Here are some highlights.

The intending-perceiving-acting cycle must play a key role in this account since it represents the complex energy–information coupling between the organism and the environment. This coupling can be viewed as the intersection between the set of possible descriptions of the organism and those of the environment. Both the affordance set of relational properties and the set of effectivity mappings among these properties reside in this nonstationary intersection. These represent, respectively, the goal constraints and action constraints on intentional behavior.

The basic theoretical strategy has been to apply the concepts of self-organization to the ecological field. This approach reveals the attractor dynamics that lie at the heart of goal-directed behavior. The attractors in this nonstationary field represent the goal-states to be achieved by the organism. These goal-states organize the field in much the same way as in the insect nest example. More specifically, the creation and annihilation of attractors (i.e., goal-states) results in a change in the properties of the field, causing a shift to a new mode indicated by a qualitative change in behavior. Within a mode, nonlinear behavior will result if there is a competition between attractors (i.e., if there are multiple goals to be satisfied).

Perhaps, the most important characteristic of this view of intentional behavior, however, is the nature of the coupling represented by the ecological field. Just as in the insect nest example, this is an information-dominated field, rather than a force-dominated field. This is not to say that there are no forces acting within the field. Clearly there are. Indeed, force fields operate within both the internal field (e.g., biochemical processes) and the external field (e.g., gravitational forces). The interesting point, however, is that the coupling between these two fields is dominated by information transactions rather than forceful interactions.

Intuitively, intentional behavior is active in that the organism determines how it should move. The organism orients itself with its own energy supply and is not passively pushed around by the force fields in the environment. Successful goal-directed behavior is possible whenever goal-specific information, made available by the environment, can be matched by the control of action exercised by the organism. This dual information/control field that couples the organism and environment provides the lawful basis for intentional dynamics.

The primacy of perception implies that the regularity (i.e., holonomy) holds with respect to information, *not with respect to action*. That is, even though there is a lawful relationship in the information field specifying what the organism should do to satisfy an intention, the organism need not obey this information. A property that distinguishes intentional systems from causal systems is that they can go against the gradients specified by the information field. For example, if the organism is tired and there is information available which can lawfully guide the organism to a resting state, the organism can still decide to follow another path. The analogue in the insect example, would be an insect which chose not to follow the gradient to the location where an arch was being constructed, even though the information was available for it to do so. Regardless of the path that is chosen, however, the proposed account of intentional behavior suggests that there will be information available to guide behavior.

In summary, information arises lawfully, but only contingently on the action side, which may be governed by rule of caprice. Perhaps, on the action side the systems must learn how to behave lawfully if its intended goals are to be achieved. Whether these or other lawful (i.e., holonomic) relationships exist which determine goal-directed behavior remains an open question.

CONCLUSION

This chapter has taken a few steps toward providing a better understanding of intentional behavior. One important step was the discussion of germ-determinacy, which may be used to express several central concepts of ecological psychology that have proven difficult to formalize. In this way Gibson's principle of animal (effectivity structure) and environment (affordance structure) mutuality (in the sense of a mathematical *duality*) might ultimately find expression.

Other important steps toward modeling systems with intentional dynamics were suggested by considering the generic mechanisms by which open systems self-organize under energy interactions, on the one hand, and information transactions, on the other. The ecological field, which couples the internal field of the organism and the external field of the environment, was proposed as providing the necessary information to guide intentional behavior lawfully. It was shown how the organization of this nonstationary field (i.e., the organism–environment intersection set) depends on changes in the number and layout of the attractors within it. These attractors are dually specified by the affordance properties of the environment and the effectivity functions of the organism which realize them.

It was further argued that there are unique configurations of goal-state attractors from whose dynamic interplay cycles of qualitative behavioral modes may lawfully emerge. Thus, the principles of self-organization provide a holonomically constrained account of intentional bheavior that reveals how organisms can become and remain *lawfully informed* in the pursuit of their goals. The generalized theory should provide a means to begin to understand how intentions maintain the system on its goal-trajectory even when it must cross regions of nonholonomy where laws at a given level of analysis do not strictly apply or environmental sources of controlling information are obscured or absent.

If successful, a theory grounded on the premises proposed here would take us one step closer to solving the puzzle posed by Gibson (1979) when he asked: How is it that "behavior is regular without being regulated" (p. 225) in a complex, dynamic, and unpredictable environment?

ACKNOWLEDGMENTS

This chapter is respectfully and affectionately dedicated to James J. Jenkins, whose insightful contributions to the field of cognitive psychology and unstinting dedication to his students and colleagues have inspired us all to be better than we might otherwise have been. We would like to thank Gary Riccio, John Lee, and Bob Hoffman for providing comments on earlier drafts. An extended version of this paper appears in Kugler, Shaw, Vicente, and Kinsella–Shaw (1990).

REFERENCES

Ashby, W. R. (1952). *Design for a brain*. London: Chapman & Hall.
Ashby, W. R. (1956). *Introduction to cybernetics*. London: Chapman & Hall.
Atkins, P. W. (1984). *The second law*. New York: W. H. Freeman.
Auslander, L., & MacKenzie, R. (1977). *Introductin to differentiable manifolds*. New York: Dover.
Braithwaite, R. B. (1953). *Scientific explanation*. Cambridge, England: University Press.
Bruinsma, O. H. (1977). An analysis of building behavior of the termite macrotermes subhyalinus. *Proceedings of the VIII Congress*. IUSSI: Wargeningen.
Carello, C., Kugler, P. N., Turvey, M. T., & Shaw, R. E. (1984). Inadequacies of the computer metaphor. In M. Gazzaniga (Ed.), *Handbook of cognitive neuroscience* (pp. 229–248). New York: Plenum Press.
Carreri, G. (1984). *Order and disorder in matter*. Menlo Park, CA: Benjamin Cummings.
Casti, J. L. (1989). *Alternative realities: Mathematical models of nature and man*. New York: Wiley.
Davies, P. (1989). *The new physics*. Cambridge, England: Cambridge University Press.
Deneubourge, J. L. (1977). Application de l'ordre par fluctuation a la descriptions de la construction du nid chez les termites. *Insects Sociaux, Journal International pour l'etude des Arthropodes Sociaux, 24*, 117.
Fodor, J., & Pylshyn, Z. (1981). How direct is visual perception?. *Cognition, 9*, 139–196.
Fodor, J., & Pylyshyn, Z. (1988). Connectionism and cognitive architecture: a critical analysis. *Cognition, 28*, 3–71.
Gibson, J. J. (1979). *The ecological approach to visual perception*. Boston: Houghton–Mifflin.
Goldstein, H. (1980). *Classical mechanics*. Reading MA: Addison–Wesley.
Grasse, P. P. (1959). La reconstruction du nid et le coordination interindividuelles chez Bellicositermes natalensis et cubitermes. La theorie de la stigmergie: essai d'interpretation des termites constructeurs. *Insectes Sociaux, Journal International pour l'etude des Arthropodes Sociaux, 6*, 127.

Haken, H. (1988). *Information and self-organization: A macroscopic approach to complex systems.* New York: Springer–Verlag.

Iberall, A. S., & McCulloch, W. (1969). The organizing principle of complex living systems. *Transactions of the American Society of Mechanical Engineers,* June, pp. 290–294.

Kirlik, A. C. (1989). *The organization of perception and action in complex control skills.* Unpublished doctoral dissertation, Ohio State University, Department of Industrial and Systems Engineering, Columbus.

Kugler, P. N., Kelso, J. A. S., & Turvey, M. T. (1982). On the control and coordination of naturally developing systems. In J. A. S. Kelso & J. E. Clark (Eds.), *The development of movement control and coordination.* New York: Wiley.

Kugler, P. N., & Shaw, R. (1990). Symmetry and symmetry-breaking in thermodynamic and epistemic engines: A coupling of first and second laws. In H. Haken (Ed.), *Synergetics of cognition.* Heidelberg, Germany: Springer–Verlag.

Kugler, P. N., Shaw, R. E., Vicente, K. J., & Kinsella–Shaw, J. M. (1990). Inquiry into intentional systems I: Issues in ecological physics. *Psychological Research, 52.*

Kugler, P. N., & Turvey, M. T. (1987). *Information, natural law, and the self-assembly of rhythmic movements.* Hillsdale, NJ: Lawrence Erlbaum Associates.

Kugler, P. N., Turvey, M. T., Carello, C., & Shaw, R. E. (1985). The physics of controlled collisions: A reverie about locomotion. In W. H. Warren Jr. & R. E. Shaw (Eds.), *Persistence and change: Proceedings of the first International Conference on Event Perception* (pp. 195–230). Hillsdale, NJ: Lawrence Erlbaum Associates.

Lanczos, C. (1970). *The variational principles of mechanics.* New York: Dover.

Lee, D. N. (1976). A theory of visual control of braking based on information about time-to-collision. *Perception, 5,* 437–459.

Lee, D. N., Lishman, J. R., & Thomson, J. A. (1982). Visual regulation of gait in long jumping. *Journal of Experimental Psychology: Human Perception and Performance, 8,* 448–459.

Lee, D. N., & Reddish, P. E. (1981). Plummeting gannets: A paradigm of ecological optics. *Nature, 293*(5830), 293–294.

Mach, E. (1974/1893). *The science of mechanics.* London: Open Court.

Mark, L. S., Shaw, R. E., & Pittenger, J. B. (1988). Natural constraints, scales of analysis, and information for the perception of growing faces. In T. R. Alley (Ed.), *Social and applied aspects of perceiving faces* (pp. 11–50). Hillsdale, NJ: Lawrence Erlbaum Associates.

Nicolis, G., & Prigogine, I. (1977). *Self-organization in non-equilibrium systems.* New York: Wiley.

Nicolis, G., & Prigogine, I. (1989). *Exploring complexity.* San Francisco: W. H. Freeman.

Poincare, H. (1952/1905). *Science and hypothesis.* New York: Dover.

Powers, W. T. (1973). *Behavior: The control of perception.* Chicago: Aldine.

Prigogine, I. (1980). *From being to becoming.* San Francisco: W. H. Freeman.

Prigogine, I., Nicolis, G., & Babloyantz, A. (1972). Thermodynamics of evolution. *Physics Today, 25,* 23–28.

Prigogine, I., & Stengers, I. (1984). *Order out of chaos.* New York: Bantam Books.

Reed, E. S., & Jones, R. (1982). *Reasons for realism: Selected essays of James J. Gibson.* Hillsdale, NJ: Lawrence Erlbaum Associates.

Rosen, R. (1978). *Fundamentals of measurement and representation of natural systems.* New York: Elsevier.

Rosen, R. (1985). *Anticipatory systems: Philosophical, mathematical, and methodological foundations.* New York: Pergamon.

Rosenblueth, A., Wiener, N., & Bigelow, J. (1943). Behavior, purpose and teleology. *Philosophy of Science, 10,* 19–24.

Russell, E. S. (1945). *The directiveness of organic activities.* Cambridge, England: University Press.

Sachs, M. (1973). *The field concept in contemporary sciences.* Springfield, IL: Charles C. Thomas.

Schiff, W. (1965). The perception of impending collision. *Psychological Monographs, 79,* (604).

Shaw, R. E. (1987). Behavior with a purpose. *Contemporary Psychology, 3,* 243–245.

Shaw, R. E. & Alley, T. (1985). How to draw learning curves: Their use and justification. In T. D. Johnston & A. T. Pietrewicz (Eds.), *Issues in the ecological study of learning* (pp. 275–403). Hillsdale, NJ: Lawrence Erlbaum Associates.

Shaw, R. E., & Kinsella–Shaw, J. M. (1988). Ecological mechanics: a physical geometry for intentional constraints. *Human Movement Science, 7,* 155–200.

Shaw, R. E., Kugler, P. N., & Kinsella–Shaw, J. M. (1990). Reciprocities of intentional systems. In R. Warren & A. Wertheim (Eds.), *Control of self-motion.* Hillsdale, NJ: Lawrence Erlbaum Associates.

Shaw, R. E., & Mingolla, E. (1982). Ecologizing world graphs. *Behavioral and Brain Sciences, 5,* 648–650.

Shaw, R. E., & Todd, J. (1980). Abstract machine theory and direct perception. *Behavioral and Brain Sciences, 3,* 400–401.

Sommerhoff, G. (1950). *Analytical biology.* London: Oxford University Press.

Taylor, R. (1966). *Action and purpose.* Englewood Cliffs, NJ: Prentice–Hall.

Thomson, J. A. (1983). Is continuous visual monitoring necessary in visually guided locomotion? *Journal of Experimental Psychology: Human Perception and Performance, 9,* 427–443.

Turvey, M. T., Shaw, R. E., Reed, E. S., & Mace, W. M. (1981). Ecological laws of perceiving and acting: In reply to Fodor and Pylyshyn. *Cognition, 9,* 237–304.

Ullman, S. (1980). Against direct perception. *Behavioral and Brain Sciences, 3,* 373–415.

Warren, W. H. & Shaw, R. E. (1985). (Eds.). *Persistence and change: The proceedings of the first international conference on event perception.* Hillsdale, NJ: Lawrence Erlbaum Associates.

Weir, M. (1985). *Goal-directed behavior.* New York: Gordon & Breach

Woodfield, L. (1976). *Teleology.* Cambridge, England: University Press.

Yates, F. E. (1982). Outline of a physical theory of physiological systems. *Canadian Journal of Physiology and Pharmacology, 60,* 217–48.

Yates, F. E. (1987). (Ed.). *Self-organizing systems: The emergence of order.* New York: Plenum Press.

24 Perception and Representation in the Development of Mobility

Herbert L. Pick, Jr.
University of Minnesota

Karl S. Rosengren
University of Michigan

INTRODUCTION

In recent years the intimate connection between perception and action has been widely recognized by psychologists (e.g. von Hofsten, & Lee, 1983; Turvey & Kugler, 1984). The fact that we perceive in order to act forms the basis of a huge literature on perceptual guidance of action, including analyses of both feedback and feed-forward mechanisms in motor control (e.g., Adams, 1971; Schmidt, 1975). The fact that we act in order to perceive has been particularly acknowledged most recently in the ideas of Eleanor and James Gibson, who have emphasized that perception itself is a dynamic activity and only occurs statically under the constraints of laboratory experiments. Much of the flavor of this intimate relation between perception and action is captured in Reed's (1982) concept of an *action system*. He meant by this term a general class of behavior subserving some biological or practical function for an organism. He exemplified the concept with such activities as consumatory behavior, reproductive behavior, locomotion, manipulation of objects, and communication. One implication of this concept is that motor behavior has an integral organization characterized by responsiveness to certain aspects of perceptual information and directed toward a functional outcome.

The goal of this chapter is to take a functional approach to the understanding of the development of mobility from perceptual guidance of locomotion to orientation with respect to currently nonperceived locations. The chapter will also consider the role of visual experience in the development of these abilities. Mobility will be considered in a very general sense, including such activities as how children move from place to place, how they decide where to go, how they find their way around, know where in the world they are.

433

The plan is to review research on the development of mobility first with respect to locomoting to currently perceived space and then with respect to remote spaces. It is commonly accepted that locomotion to proximal spaces is perceptually guided, while locomotion to remote spaces requires some kind of mental representation of spatial layout. In the present discussion, a thesis will be developed to the effect that some aspects of guidance of locomotion to remove nonperceived locations are also perceptually based. Attention will be focused on several processes: specification of the goal location, choosing the path and mode of locomotion, and negotiating that path. Way-finding and perspective-taking processes will be considered in analyzing locomoting to remote locations. The argument will be made that in some cases keeping track of where one is in relation to remote locations is also based on con-current perceptual guidance.

Functional Approach, Action Systems, and Mobility

The implication of a functional perspective is that guidance of action, that is, motor control, is difficult to understand without knowing the goal-context in which the movement occurs. Consider the flexion of the arm as a part of an act of eating, as part of a defensive act, or as part of a communicative act, such as signing or gesturing. Although formally similar in all those cases, it is quite a different thing when embedded in those different acts. The Russian behavioral physiologists, Nicolai Bernshtein (1948), provided a very nice example of such dissociation in brain-injured soldiers. He described a patient with motor disturbance resulting from a head wound in battle. When asked to raise his hand as high as he could, this soldier was hardly able raise his hand to shoulder height in spite of marked effort. When asked to point to a spot on the wall, a higher, but still limited, height was attained. This limitation was again overcome when the solider was asked to get a hat off a still higher hat rack. Likewise, in animals, John Fentress (1989) has studied the relation of formally similar movements in different action systems involved in various grooming behaviors. The fact that these similar movements are embedded in activities with different goals implies that the perceptual basis of their control is different.

In the human developmental literature related to *mobility*, the distinctiveness of action systems is illustrated in a study by Lockman (1984) of detour behavior with children between 6 and 12 months of age. He examined both reaching detours and locomotor (i.e., crawling) detours in a situation which was formally very similar in the two cases. The infant was shown an interesting object as it was being placed over a barrier in front of her. The barrier was too high for the infant to go over and the object could only be attained by detouring around the end. For the reaching detour, the infant was constrained to reach; for the crawling detour the infant needed to locomote to attain the goal. Although Lockman's infants all could crawl at the time at which they performed the detour behavior by reaching, they were delayed by an average of a full month in attaining the goal by means of a crawling detour. Thus the formally similar problem of circumventing a barrier was found to be developmentally dependent on the action system in which it was embedded.

One appeal of considering a domain of behavior from the perspective of action systems is that it is conducive to relating different behaviors that might be otherwise treated separately. Thus crawling and walking may well be controlled by the *same* perceptual variables. This is an integration of potentially disparate activities (horizontal integration). Another appeal of the concept of action system is that it leads to analysis of extended aspects of the behavior domain in question. Thus a thorough understanding of mobility would seem to involve not only knowing how locomotion is guided to the table across the room but how it is guided to the table in the next room or to the lake behind the hill. This is integration within a particular activity (vertical integration).

In human development, locomotion is a particularly important and interesting action system. The human infant is initially immobile, at least with respect to locomotion. In normal development, the infant proceeds through a transition stage of crawling, and finally attains bipedal locomotion. The importance of locomotion to functioning in the world is attested to by the effort expended when individuals have problems with their mobility. Physical therapists, for example, devote a great deal of time and energy in facilitating the development of locomotor skills in children with physical handicaps, and the profession of "blind mobility specialist" has arisen to serve the particular mobility handicap of visually impaired persons.

The beginning of such a functional analysis has been made in the practical context faced by blind mobility specialists. They are concerned with conveying to their visually impaired clients two types of skills: The first type involve use of the long cane for controlling moment to moment locomotion, such as findings paths and avoiding obstacles. The second type involves techniques for maintaining spatial orientation so that detours can be taken when familiar paths are blocked.

From a more theoretical perspective, Gibson and Schmuckler (1989) described an ecological and experimental approach to the development of mobility. They identified three functions of visual information in the developing child's ability to locomote: guidance to a destination, detection of traversable surfaces, and maintenance of posture during locomotion. They point out that mobility has two functions: getting somewhere in particular and exploring one's environment.

The present discussion will be more concerned with an analysis of how one gets somewhere in particular, rather than with gaining a general acquaintance with the environment, although it is difficult to separate these two functions completely. The activity of going somewhere may be decomposed into a number of components. These would include deciding where to go, determining the location of that place, or selecting an appropriate path, and negotiating that path.

These components could then be broken down further into subcomponents. For example, in the case of negotiating a particular path, a child needs to maintain adequate balance and to avoid obstacles.

DEVELOPMENT OF LOCOMOTION IN NEAR SPACE

Specification of Location

Except for the case of random exploration of an environment, the first process that is implicit in an analysis of mobility is the specification or registration of the target location. How is the location of the place one wants to get to defined? When the goal location or goal itself is visible, localization would seem to pose no particular problem. Yet even in this apparently simple case, it is not always clear how the location is specified. Consider the problem of coordination of multiple egocentric frames of reference. Determining the direction of an object when one is standing with body oriented in one direction, head turned in another direction, and eyes pointed in still a third direction involves, at some level, the interrelation of these different egocentric frames of reference. If one wants to reach for an object under such circumstances the direction of gaze has to be integrated with the orientation of the head and body.[1]

The reference systems in this localization problem are all egocentric. Normally goal locations are also specified in terms of geographical frames of reference or combinations of egocentric and geographical systems. So, for example, we could say that the clock is to my right on the front wall. Just as there are multiple egocentric frames of reference, there are normally multiple reasonable, nonegocentric frames of reference. Thus, we could describe the clock as being on the front wall, the wall facing the street, the north wall, the wall facing the sofa, and so on. In locomoting to a goal, the location needs to be specified with respect to one or more of these geographical and egocentric frames of reference. For any action such as locomotion, the specification at some point must include an egocentric reference system, for the actor's body to be moved appropriately. It is not known how the integration of these egocentric and geographical frames of reference is accomplished.

Several years ago, Acredolo (1976) studied children's preference for frames of reference, and identified a fairly robust developmental trend between the ages of 3 and 7, from use of more proximal to more distal reference systems. She employed a situation in which two environmental and an egocentric frame of

---

[1]The mechanisms for this have been the subject of extensive and elegant research but are still not completely understood (e.g. Paillard, 1980; Paillard & Amblard, 1985). There may be active integration of separate sources of information or there may be some sort of direct sensitivity to relational variables themselves.

reference were pitted aganist each other to determine which children preferred to use. A child was brought into a small room with a door at one end, a table at one side, and a window at the end, opposite the door. The side walls were somewhat distinctive but the room was otherwise relatively barren. The child was led to a position near the corner of the table, blindfolded, and taken on a rambling, and disorienting walk. The walk ended at either the door or the window and the child was asked to return to the place where the walk began, to the place where the blindfold had been put on. The experimental set-up used by Acredolo is shown in Fig. 24.1a. Sometimes during the blindfold walk, the table was quietly moved to the other side of the room. Fig. 24.1a shows the experimental space used by Acredolo. In Fig. 24.1b, the blindfold walk is represented schematically by the dashed line with arrowheads and the table has been moved to the other side of the room.

Acredolo interpreted the results in terms of three possible frames of reference that might be used to define the location of the goal, that is, the place where the walk started: (1) an egocentric frame of reference that specified a body relevant direction, for example, originally going to the *right* side to get to the starting location; (2) an object- or furniture-relevant frame of reference, in this case specified by the table; and (3) a more distal shell or container frame of reference, in this case specified by the walls of the room. Consider a case where the walk

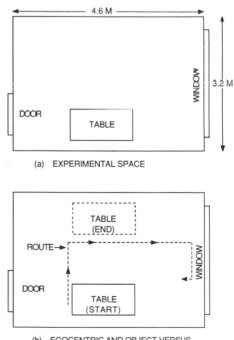

(a)   EXPERIMENTAL SPACE

FIG. 24.1.   Layout and example of one condition of Acredolo's study of children's use of frames of reference. (Adapted from Acredolo. 1976)

(b)   EGOCENTRIC AND OBJECT VERSUS
WALL-DEFINED REFERENCE SYSTEM

ended at the window but the table had not been moved. If the child facing into the room was using an egocentric frame of reference to define the goal location, then going to the right would be the corresponding behavior in spite of the fact that the table and wall would indicate going to the other side of the room. If the walk ended at the window and the table had been moved to the opposite side during the walk as in Fig. 24.1b, both the egocentric and object relevant frames of reference would have biased the child toward moving to the right and away from the original wall.

By having the walk end at the door or window and by moving or not moving the table, it was possible in Acredolo's situation to pit all possible pairs of two reference systems against the third. Acredolo carried this procedure out with 3- to 7-year-old children. The younger children tended to respond mainly in terms of the egocentric frames of reference, the older children in terms of the walls or contained reference system, and the 5-year-olds mainly in terms of the object reference system. This trend from more proximal to more distal frames of reference seems to be quite robust. Many investigators find it; the particular ages at which changes occur is subject to contextual variables such as familiarity with the space or salience of cues, but the general trend holds up (e.g. Acredolo, 1978; Siegel & White, 1975).

A somewhat more complex situation exists when the goal location is in sight but is nondistinctive, what Huttenlocher and Newcombe (1984) refer to as "unspecified." This would be the case when someone is asked to return to a location somewhere in the middle of a large, undifferentiated space, where there is no marking of the correct position (there may be distinctive markings around the edge of the space). Localization of the goal must be accomplished in terms of some kind of reference system. That is, the location of the goal must somehow be specified in terms of landmarks or coordinate dimensions that are somewhat removed from the goal location.

A formal prototype of such a problem has been studied developmentally by Somerville and Bryant (1985), who examined children's ability to use formal coordinate systems. They presented children between the ages of 4 and 6 with problems of the following kind: An X–Y coordinate system on a piece of paper was placed in front of the child. A doll was positioned at some point along the Y-axis facing out into the coordinate space. Another doll was positioned on the X-axis, also facing into the coordinate space. The child's task was to determine where the paths of the two dolls would intersect. Results indicated rather precocious use of coordinate systems by young children when problems were posed in this way.

In order to locomote to a goal location, it is not enough to encode the position of the target. The next stage in achieving the goal is to choose a path that will provide efficient and safe travel to the goal location. There are literally an infinite number of possible routes, but in most situations there are only a limited number of practical routes. In a task as simple as getting to the other side of the room, one often has to choose which side of a table to go around. In such situations, the decision may not be very critical; little would be lost by going one way or the other. However, in some situations taking a particular path might be grossly inefficient or even dangerous.

Choosing a Path

Gibson and Schmuckler (1989) pointed out that one factor entering into the choice of path might be whether the path surface affords support. This factor was explored by Gibson and her colleagues (Gibson et al., 1987), using a paradigm similar to that employed in earlier studies of infants' reaction to the "visual cliff" (Walk & Gibson, 1961). In these recent investigations of choice of path, the visual cliff has been replaced by a set of interchangeable walkways, which varied with regard to the information for traversability they provided.

For example, in an initial study by Gibson et al. (1987), which examined infants with varying degrees of crawling and walking experience, the surfaces included a rigid one (a piece of plywood covered with a richly textured cloth) and a deformable one (a waterbed with a similar surface texture which was gently agitated to reveal its deformability). At the start of each trial the young infant was placed on a starting platform. The child's behavior was then observed as their mother watched and then coaxed the child to come to her across the surface. Infants who had experience walking exhibited much less hesitation, less exploration of the surface, and less evasive activity (e.g., looking away from their mother) before crossing the rigid surface than before crossing the deformable one. While some of the walking infants chose to stand up and walk to the parent across the rigid surface, none attempted to walk across the waterbed surface. In contrast, crawling infants showed little hesitation in crossing the waterbed surface. Infants were also presented with a situation in which they could choose between pairs of surfaces, in which case, choice of surface was observed. The measures for the two situations converged; the walking infants "voted with their feet" for the rigid surface while the crawlers showed no strong preference.

In related experiments, Gibson and her colleagues (Gibson et al., 1989) have investigated other aspects of support surface information. In one of these experiments a cord net was stretched under the plexiglass. All the infants hesitated to cross this net/plexiglass surface but as many eventually walked over this surface as over an opaque, rigid one. In further investigations, the children were presented with a plexiglass surface covered with a textured material. A hole was cut in the textured material to simulate a "hole" in the support surface. The hole was located in such a manner as to just allow passage to either side. Ten of 16 walkers and and 7 of 21 crawlers went around the hole. A majority of the children stopped and peered at the hole. For many of the infants the hole was clearly perceived as something that did not afford support and should be avoided.

Children develop sensitivity to other path properties. Consider the case when a child is faced with going up stairs of different riser heights, a situation presented to infants between 8 and 17 months by Ulrich, Thelen, and Niles (in press). The younger infants in this age range selected the smaller riser heights while the older infants did not differentiate among them. The children's discrimination of riser heights was significantly related to walking and stair-climbing experience but not to other anthopometric measures such as limb-segment length.

Another common path decision occurs in the case when one has to choose between different openings to go through. Palmer (1987) presented 10- to 13-month-old infants with such a choice. A 12-inch opening was paired with another opening which was 2, 4, 6, or 8 inches wide. Infants of this age could reasonably pass through all but the smallest two openings (2 and 4 inches). The infants did not systematically choose the larger opening except when it was paired with the 2- or 4-inch openings. That is, they were differentiating between passable and impassable apertures, but not *among* the apertures that were all wide enough to go through.

Choice of Mode of Locomotion

Choosing a path often implies choice of a mode of locomotion. Humans have a variety of modes of locomotion at their disposal: walking, running, jumping, crawling, and so on. Even young children have at their disposal the possibility of crawling (including creeping and rolling) and walking. Infants displayed such a choice of locomotion in the study by Gibson and her colleagues (Gibson, et al., 1987) described earlier, in which young walkers were presented with a choice of surfaces over which to move across to their mothers. The recently walking children would walk across the rigid surface, but if they chose to cross the waterbed surface they reverted to crawling. A similar result was obtained in Palmer's (1987) aperture study. In one of the conditions of her study, 13-month-old infants were presented with a series of single apertures varying in size and their means of negotiating them was observed. For smaller apertures close to the child's body size (such as 8- and 12-inch openings), the children turned their body in anticipation of going through the opening. Moreover, for these sizes only, the children were more likely to change their mode of locomotion, for example, revert to crawling.

Negotiating the Path

Given that the location of the goal of locomotion is specified and the path and mode of locomotion decided upon, a child is faced with executing the locomotion. How is this accomplished? If walking, one aspect of negotiating the path for the young child involves maintaining balance in the recently acquired bipedal posture. For adults, normal situations pose little problem in maintaining this dynamic posture. However, there are situations such as attempting to stand on a ship rolling in heavy seas, that are problematical even for adults. For young children just beginning to stand and walk, the maintenance of posture during locomotion is very difficult and there is a long-developmental course. For young infants, Goldfield (Goldfield & Michel, 1986) has noted that the beginning of the ability to assume a crawling posture starts with raising the head to a vertical plane and extending the arms at the elbow. This ability develops at around 4 months.

There is evidence for the influence of visual information in the maintenance of posture at very early ages. Research by Butterworth and Ciccetti (1978) has demonstrated a sensitivity to visual information for posture by infants who are just able to sit independently. The use of visual information for maintaining posture and balance while walking goes through an interesting developmental course. Gibson and her colleagues (Stoffregen, Schmuckler, & Gibson, 1987) and Bertenthal and Bia (1989) have found that, for maintaining balance while simply standing, infants at first are equally guided by central and peripheral visual information. Later on, peripheral information controls posture to a greater extent than central. The implication is that central information could be freed up for use in steering, with peripheral vision being used to maintain balance. Stoffregen et al. base this conjecture about the differentiation between central and peripheral vision on the results of experiments on dynamic balance of children from one to five years of age. Their subjects were induced to walk in a version of Lee and Lishman's (1975) "swinging room." The children walked along a three-walled corridor whose walls could be moved independently of the larger environment. Various combinations of optic flow, created by movement of frontal and peripheral arrays, were presented to the children as they walked, and postural compensations (sways, staggers, and falls) were recorded. Peripheral flow, produced by movement of the two side walls, led to more compensatory responses than radial flow stemming from movement of the front wall. However, the youngest children (under 2) were also destabilized by movement of the frontal array. Thus, a differential sensitivity to peripheral and central optical flow seems to be developing with age.

However, other researchers have found that information in the central visual field may also be used by older children for controlling balance while walking. In one case, Williams et al. (1986) measured the balance of 6- and 8-year-olds traversing a balance beam under various visual conditions. These conditions included walking on the beam in total darkness, walking with luminescent tape on arms and legs (body referents), walking with luminescent tape at eye level along the sidewalls of the room parallel to the beam (peripheral referents), walking with a single vertically oriented luminescent strip of tape placed directly in front of the beam (central referent), and walking with various combinations of these conditions. Balance was assessed in terms of the number of times the child stepped off the beam, the amount of time it took to traverse the beam, and a measure of time "in balance." In general, Williams et al. (1986) found that balance while walking along the beam was significantly better when central visual cues were available than when no visual cues were present. When central cues were paired with peripheral, children were able to traverse the beam at a faster rate than under other conditions. These results suggest that for older children, at least, visual information in the central field does play a role in controlling balance while walking.

These findings have been supported and extended to adults by Rosengren (1989), who studied 5-year-olds, 10-year-olds, and adults walking on a treadmill under various visual conditions. The visual conditions included normal vision, eyes closed, peripheral referents (light-emitting diodes on side walls) or central vision (light-emitting diodes on front wall). Balance was assessed by measuring postural oscillations in the anterior–posterior and medial–lateral directions. When participants walked with eyes closed or with only peripheral referents, there were significant, large-amplitude, low-frequency medial–lateral oscillations, which were significantly reduced with the frontal referents (although they were still greater than under normal visual conditions). The results of the studies of Stoffregen et al., which suggested the greater importance of peripheral vision in dynamic balance, differ from those of Williams et al. and Rosengren in emphasis on the importance of central visual information. The discrepancy may be attributable to task differences and difference in balance measures.[2] It may be that central visual information is important in fine-tuning or aiding balance in situations where the individual is confronting difficulties in locomotion, but that peripheral disturbances can produce gross destabilization.

DEVELOPMENT OF LOCOMOTION TO REMOTE PLACES

Choosing a Path, Way Finding

Up to this point, the discussion has focused on locomotion to currently preceived locations. One of the most interesting cases of route determination arises when the goal is not in sight. How does a child know how to get from one place to another location which is currently out of sight? One possibility is that the route is remembered. If a child is led from location A to B on one occasion, he or she may well remember how to go from A to B on a second occasion. A child who is led from A to B might also be able to return from B back to A, if he or she can remember and reverse the route. But if one knows a particular route is it possible

---

[2]Stoffregen et al. generally assessed balance with with relatively gross measures, for example, sways, staggers, falls, which would occur mainly in line with the direction of room movement, which also coincided with the direction of the subjects's facing and were not perpendicular to it. Williams et al. and Rosengren used measures that were more sensitive and would reflect lateral as well as anterior posterior motion.

to take other routes? There is a growing developmental literature on such issues, which can be illustrated with a study of Smith, Haake, and Pick (1985). Children from 16 to 24 months of age were taken with their parent to the outside of a square room within a room. The inner room had a curtained doorway in each wall. Fig. 24.2 shows the experimental room used in this experiment. The parent was left beside the first door and the child was taken on a walk around the inner room, and entered it by one of the doors on a side away from the starting point (see the solid line in Fig. 24.2). When the child got to the center of the inner room, she was asked to go find her parent.

Results indicated that the 16-month-old children practically all returned via the original path, while the 24-month-old children generally went via the shortest route through the door nearest the parent as illustrated in Fig. 24.2. Children 20 months old appeared to be in a transition stage, with some going to the shortest route and some taking the original route.

The results of this experiment are again congruent with a general finding reported in the literature, that young children tend to go from place to place on the basis of repeating (or reversing) routes, while older children will take shortcuts and make detours. Such an ability to take alternative routes is often interpreted in the literature as reflecting a configurational organization of spatial knowledge and indeed a distinction is often made between "route" and "configurational" knowledge (e.g., Siegel & White, 1975). We have tended to think

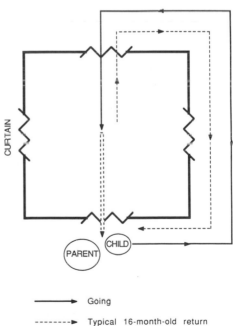

FIG. 24.2. Schematic of room and typical return routes of children.

———————▶ Going

- - - - - - ▶ Typical 16-month-old return

═══════▶ Typical 24-month-old return

of such configurational knowledge in terms of some sort of mental representation of spatial layout. If this interpretation is correct, then the shortcut behavior of the older children indicates some kind of configurational knowledge of the specific space.

There is also more general knowledge of space that we have as thinking adults which is probably important in choosing paths. This includes conceptual knowledge, such as the fact that the shortest distance between two points is a straight line (at least in Euclidean space), or that continued rotation around the same point will bring one back to the starting point. Recent evidence suggests that even young children appreciate such abstract properties of space. For example, Rieser and Heiman (1982) investigated toddlers' understanding that if they turn more than 180 degrees they should continue turning to get back to the starting point. They used a situation illustrated in the Fig. 24.3. A child was taught that if he or she touched a particular window in the cylindrical room then an interesting visual event would occur. On each trial, the child's starting position was 45

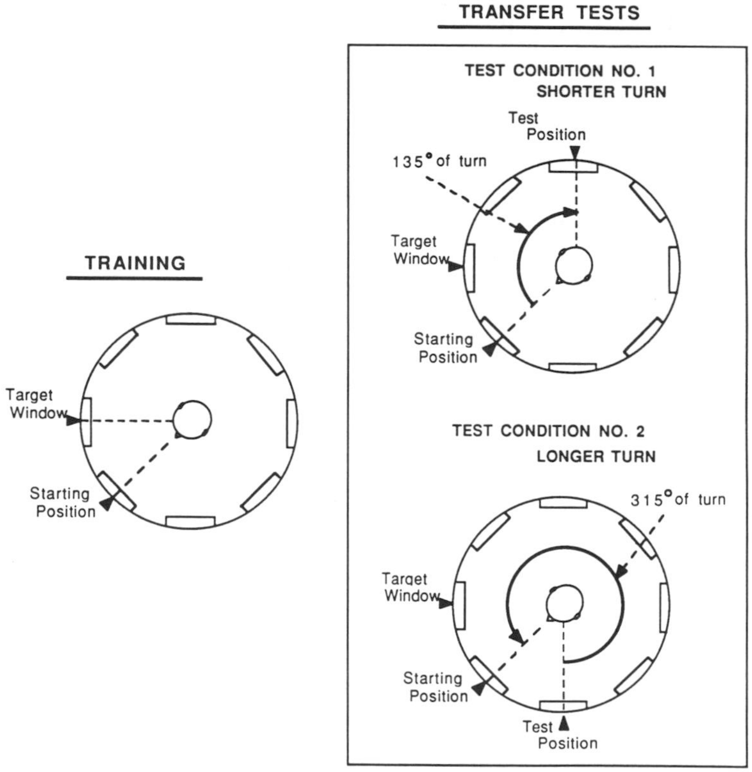

FIG. 24.3. Nature of training and testing used by Rieser and Heiman (1982) for investigating children's appreciation of change of orientation during rotation. (Adapted from Rieser and Heiman, 1982)

degrees counterclockwise from the correct window. After the child had learned to go reliably to the correct window he or she was turned before being permitted to go to the window. (The turning was done in such a way that the child's view of the correct window was occluded.) Sometimes the child was turned 135 degrees and sometimes 315 degrees. In both cases, the 14-month-old children turned in the shortest direction to get to the correct window. Their precision was not great and sometimes they would go to a window too far or one too near, *but their direction of turn was usually appropriate*. Thus these results are congruent with the idea that even young children appreciate the geometrical principle of rotation back to a starting point.

Perspective Taking and Route Finding

If a child's knowledge of space includes such abstract principles and if it includes information about the configuration of specific spaces, more abstract kinds of spatial thinking could be possible. One example of this is the ability to take different perspectives on a spatial layout. There is a long history of the development of such perspective-taking abilities, stemming from Piaget's classical "three-mountain problem" (see also Huttenlocher & Presson, 1979). In the traditional perspective-taking research, children were asked to anticipate how a model would appear if viewed from a different perspective than the current one. In these studies, attention was focused on a model which was embedded in an unchanging external environment. For purposes of spatial orientation (planning routes or way finding) one is often concerned with the problem of determining how the perspective of the wider environment would change with movement. When would children be able to cope with this sort of perspective taking?

Hardwick, McIntyre, and Pick (1976) investigated the development of such abilities in individuals ranging from kindergartners to adults. In a space quite familiar to them, participants were asked to point to each of several target locations *as if* from different station points around the space. On the basis of their pointing judgments, direction lines were plotted on a map of the space from the location of the station points in the direction the subject had pointed toward the targets. The direction lines from the different station points toward particular targets converged in position triangles which could be taken as a representation of the individual's idea of the position of the various targets. The size of the triangles could be taken as a measure of the precision of the subject's knowledge. Kindergartners either didn't understand the task or they pointed in directions that were completely egocentric from their current position. That is, they didn't take a new perspective. While some second graders pointed egocentrically, others knew the egocentric position was incorrect, but they didn't know which direction was the correct one. Fifth graders either knew that the egocentric direction was wrong and pointed in any but that direction, or they were able to figure out in a crude way what the correct direction was. These children could point generally in the correct direction but couldn't fine-tune their pointing to get it precisely correct. Adults were able to point generally correctly or even fine-tune their pointing to gain precision. Thus, there would appear to be a qualitative developmental change in this ability. First, children do not appreciate the nature of the task. Then, children perform egocentrically, or realize that egocentric judgments are incorrect, but do not know how to make the correct response. Finally children understand the general idea of what has to be done to get in the ball park of correct pointing judgments.

Interestingly, the pointing judgments were more difficult when the children and adults were able to view the space as a whole while pointing from the imagined station points than when the view was occluded by a screen. Conflicting perceptual stimulation apparently interfered with this type of judgment. In addition, these perspective judgments were easier for the individuals to make when they were asked to imagine the room had rotated so that they were standing in a different location, than if they were asked to imagine themselves as moving to a new station point. See Huttenlocher and Presson (1979) for an analysis of a similar phenomenon with tabletop model spaces.

Efficient Search Organization

Another type of abstract spatial behavior that might be implied by the presence of general spatial principles and configurational knowledge of specific spaces is what animal behaviorists, (e.g., Menzel, 1978), call "optimal foraging." This refers to a pattern of search behavior, say for food, that optimizes some aspect of the search, such as energy expenditure. Menzel demonstrated that chimps will retrieve, in a relatively spatially efficient manner, a number of food items that they had observed hidden in a random, inefficient order. Will children do this?

Cornell and Heth (1983) have examined the efficiency of search behavior of young children in situations where up to 12 objects within a single room were retrieved. They found that 3- to 5-year-old children retrieve the objects in a more efficient way than the order in which the objects were hidden. Plumert, Marks, Pick and Wegesin (1989) have been studying such behavior in a more complex situation in which the object locations were out of sight of each other on different floors of a house. Six-year-old children who lived in three-story houses participated in the study. Guided by an experimenter, the children went aroumd their own house hiding objects in a random, inefficient order. They then returned to a home position on the second floor and were asked *either* to retrieve the objects themselves *or* to tell another experimenter how to retrieve the objects. The children who retrieved the objects themselves did so in a rather efficient way. The minimum number of floor traversals required to retrieve all the objects and bring them back to the home position was four and the average for these children was about four and a half. In contrast, the directions the children gave to another person would have resulted in relatively inefficient retrieval patterns requiring an average of about eight floor traversals. (Overall memory accuracy for the two conditions was approximately the same.) Apparently, children of this age will display something close to optimal foraging when they are actually retrieving objects themselves, but don't display such efficient strategies in giving directions to someone else.

The spatially efficient behavior might again be evidence for the claim that spatial information is mentally represented in a configurational organization. It is also possible, however, that children of this age are not operating in either case from a mental representation of the spatial positions of the hidden objects. Rather, even in the case of the actual retrieval where they were efficient, the children may be responding to perceptually present stimuli on each floor which cue them to the location of nearby objects. When giving directions to someone else, they may resort to some completely different (and so far unidentified) memory retrieval strategy. It seems intuitively obvious that adults would give more nearly optimal directions in such a case, and we have preliminary evidence that they do so in a similar situation. Also, there is some research (e.g., Linde & Labov, 1975) that suggests that adults describing their apartment take their listeners on imaginary walks through the apartment in a relatively efficient way. It is not known when this strategy would develop in children.

ROLE OF EARLY EXPERIENCE IN THE DEVELOPMENT OF MOBILITY

The general thesis here is that a complete theory of mobility should encompass the entire organization that is relevant to a developing child's ability to get around, from defining where the child wants to go, to determining the routes to be followed, to executing the movements necessary to negotiate those routes. The evidence cited has suggested developmental trends in various parts of this organization. But the discussion so far has been mostly descriptive. Nothing has been suggested about the developmental mechanisms underlying these trends. At this point, we would like to raise the question as to what role early experience plays in some aspects of the development of mobility. Experience can potentially play a role in any of the components of mobility that have been identified. Indeed in the work of Ulrich, Thelen, and Niles (in press) on stair climbing by infants, the single best predictor of skill was amount of experience the infant had in climbing and crawling. In Palmer's (1987) work of infants moving through aperatures, the more experienced walkers moved through the openings with greater speed and fewer steps. However, the following discussion will focus on the role of experience in defining place in locomotion and in the development of ability to determine alternative routes.

Place vs. Response Learning in Infants

In considering experience, and place definition, let us first return to the work of Acredolo (1976) described earlier, in which she identified the reference systems children use to define an initial starting location after taking a blindfolded walk. Acredolo (1978) conducted an experiment with infants that was similar in principle to her initial study with older children. She conditioned infants between 6 and 16 months of age to look at one of two windows on either side of a small room. The conditioning procedure was simple: A Buzzer sounded in the center of the room and was followed a short interval of time later by an experimenter appearing in the target window, saying "peekaboo, nice baby." After a few trials, the baby would begin to anticipate and look at the target window before the experimenter appeared. After reliably responding in such a way, the baby was moved to the other side of the room and turned around, and the buzzer was sounded once again. Acredolo's question was whether the baby would look in a direction based on its own body (e.g. look to the right as it did in training), or look to the same side of the room. A developmental trend similar to that found earlier was reported. The younger infants primarily responded egocentrically, that is they continued looking to the right regardless of the location of the original target window. The older babies responded primarily by looking to the original side. Infants in the middle of the age range were in some sort of transition between these two response modes.

The role of locomotor experience in such spatial problems solving has been investigated by Bertenthal and his colleagues (Bertenthal, Campos, & Barret, 1984). They presented to three groups of 8-month-old infants a problem similar to that used by Acredolo. One group of infants was already crawling. A second group was not yet crawling but had experience locomoting with a walker. The third group, also noncrawlers, had no locomotor experience. The two groups *with* locomotor experience showed less tendency to respond egocentrically in relocating the window after moving across the room than the noncrawlers without walker experience.

In related studies, Acredolo, Adams, and Goodwyn (1984) determined that one probable reason for the nonegocentric behavior of the infants with locomotor experience is that their attention is more focused on the relevant goal while they are moving. Acredolo and her colleagues used a slightly different paradigm with 12-month-old children. First, the children learned which of two lateral positions contained a goal object. Then half of the children were actively moved across the room and the remaining children were moved passively across the room. The responses of these two groups of children were then compared. The children who actively moved responded in terms of a geographical frame of reference, while the children who were passively moved were much more likely to respond egocentrically. In addition, the investigators determine that the active children were more likely than the passive children to keep their attention focused on the goal location during the movement. In a follow-up condition, the view of the goal location was occluded during movement. In this case, responding became more egocentric. By 18 months, egocentric responding had dropped out for both passive and active movers. Occluding the view of the goal during movement did not disturb either passive or active movers. These results are not completely consistent with the results of the study by Bertenthal et al. (1984), which included the children with walker experience. In that study, all the children were passively moved and still the children with *previous* active movement experience responded geographically. Thus, active movement in the particular situation may not be an absolutely necessary condition for geographical responding. Nonetheless, evidence such as this is very compelling in implicating the importance of *experience* with self-produced locomotion in use of nonegocentric reference systems for defining place.

Spatial Orientation in the Blind

A very different kind of variation in early experience is the lack of vision experienced by blind persons. To what extent does this affect their spatial orientation and mobility? In particular, does this deprivation affect ability to take alternate routes to a location, such as making detours or shortcuts? In the literature on the blind there is a frequently observed result that for many perceptual-motor functions, blind persons perform more poorly than blindfolded sighted subjects (Warren, 1977).

With respect to mobility in particular, blind mobility instructors often report that their clients have particular difficulty in staying oriented as they move around. They seem to be at risk in finding their way when a familiar route is blocked. John Rieser and his colleagues reported a study that may shed some light on what underlies that difficulty (Rieser, Guth, & Hill, 1986). They taught a group of blindfolded sighted individuals and a group of blind individuals to walk without vision in a room-sized space from a home base to each of three target locations, A, B, and C marked on the floor. After they had learned to do this to an acceptable level of accuracy, they were tested on their ability to perform certain operations on their spatial knowledge. In particular, they were asked to stand at home base and point to the three locations. As might be expected, because they had been trained to walk accurately to the locations, they were able to point accurately. Walking accurately involves both direction and distance, while pointing only demands responding in terms of direction. They were also asked, while standing at home base, to imagine themselves at each of locations A, B, and C and to point at the other two. For example, imagine yourself at A; now point directly at B and C. Both the blind and sighted individuals performed this *quite slowly* and relatively *inaccurately*. When asked how they accomplished this task, both groups reported a highly intellectualized procedure of reasoning. They described how they moved from home base to the imagined station point and, if they did that, where the target should be from that newly imagined station point.

The individuals were then actually walked (the sighted subjects still blindfolded) from the home base to each of the target locations A, B, and C. Then from each of these station points they were asked to point to the other two. The sighted individuals pointed quickly and accurately, while the blind individuals still pointed hesitantly and relatively inaccurately. In this case, the blind individuals still reported a highly intellectualized cognitive process, while the sighted individuals were unable to provide a very clear introspective report. Thus these reports indicated quick and immediate knowledge by the sighted individuals of where they were and where the other targets were in relation to themselves, but that knowledge was not very accessible to introspection. In short, they seem to have automatically updated their relation to other locations as they moved actively through the space.

What might account for the difference in processing of the sighted and blind individuals after actually moving to the new locations? What is it about the early experience of the sighted individuals that would lead them to update the relative direction of locations as they move about, in contrast to the blind individuals? One possibility is the pervasive exposure to optical flow patterns, which are consequent upon every movement that a person makes from the first head movements of the young infant to the active locomoting movements we all make in everyday life.

As James Gibson (1979) has pointed out, optical flow patterns carry both perspective structure information and invariant structure information. The perspective structure information specifies the spatial relations between the observer and other locations in the environment and how these relations are changing with movement. It is this awareness of, or sensitivity to, the spatial relations between themselves and other locations in the environment that the sighted individuals in Rieser, Guth, and Hill's experiment seem to have. Furthermore it is important to note that perspective structure information specifies the relative change of direction of locations which are *out of sight,* that is locations that are temporarily occluded. Consider, for example, a case where one walks past an open door in such a way that something which is initially visible becomes occluded by the wall of the room. Let us further assume, as the simplest case, that there is some continuously visible object which is located in a position which is symmetrical to the occluded one with respect to the direction of locomotion (such as located on the wall opposite the door). The relative change in position of this object with respect to the walker will also reflect the change in position of the occluded object with respect to the individual. Thus sighted individuals may get used to keeping track of occluded objects on the basis of optical flow information that is present. They may also use that optical flow information to calibrate their own locomotor movements so as to keep track of relative direction when the world is occluded, as when their eyes are closed or they are in the dark.

CONCLUSION

If sighted people, as they grow up, use optical flow information to calibrate their locomotion with respect to occluded objects or an occluded world, such calibration would have to be modified as the person grows and his and her leg length and speed of progression changes. Thus this system might well be susceptible to easy recalibration if the relation between one's walking and the optical flow information could be changed. Rieser, Ashmead, and Pick (1988) have begun a series of studies to investigate this possibility. A treadmill was mounted on a trailer so that the optical flow information can be varied independently of the speed of walking. The optical flow information depends primarily on the speed of the trailer and the speed of walking is primarily dependent on the speed of the treadmill. Consider the case when the trailer is moving rapidly and the treadmill at a normal or slow walking speed. If individuals are exposed to this for a period of time, they may "recalibrate" their normal walking speed to larger changes in relative direction for a given amount of walking. If after such exposure they are given a test of looking at a location, closing their eyes and walking to it, they should undershoot. Conversely, if they are walking at a rate that is faster than the trailer is moving, they should recalibrate their walking so as to overshoot a target when they close their eyes and walk to it. These predictions have been confirmed in an initial experiment.

The implication of this line of reasoning is that early visual experience via information from optical flow patterns increases one's sensitivity to the changing relative direction of things during one's locomotion. Besides helping to explain the difference in spatial cognition of blind and sighted persons, this analysis may have more general implications. Recall the experiments by Acredolo and her colleagues with babies of 18 months of age who responded in terms of the geographical position of the target and not the egocentric position even when the target was occluded during movement. These results could be interpreted from the perceptive that optical flow patterns provide updating information. They, like the sighted adults in Rieser, Guth, and Hill's (1986) experiment, may be updating where the target is in relation to themselves as they move around.

This would be an alternative explanation to the one which suggests that geographical responding is based on defining the position of the target by external frames of reference. It also might be an alternative explanation to the shortcut-taking by the 24-month-olds in the experiment in the room within a room by Smith, Haake, and Pick (1985). The toddlers of this age may simply have been keeping track of the changing direction of their parent as they moved about, rather than constructing some sort of configurational representation of the layout of the space. The updating explanation may also be an alternative way of thinking about how Rieser and Heiman's (1982) toddlers know which way to turn to get to the interesting window in the cylindrical room. That precocious behavior may not have so much to do with abstract geometrical principles as much as keeping track if where relevant locations are when one moves around. If one knows the direction of the interesting location, efficient (shortest turn) behavior will follow automatically. More generally, it may be *sufficient* but not necessary to have representations of spatial layouts in order to make detours and take shortcuts. Perhaps as the spatial situation or problem becomes more complex, individuals rely more on representations of spatial layout or combinations of representation and optical flow information for updating. It would seem that to give efficient optimal foraging directions to someone else when one is removed from the space in question, some kind of configural representation is necessary. This ability, on the basis of the study of Plumert, Marks, Pick, and Wegesin (1989), apparently develops sometime after 6 years of age. Updating skills, which are perceptually based, may contribute to the development of the ability to form mental representations of spatial layout. Just how such updating skills interact with development of layout representations such as we all use when giving directions about remote spaces is next on the research agenda.

ACKNOWLEDGMENTS

Preparation of this chapter has been greatly helped by the support of the Center for Research in Learning, Perception, and Cognition of the University of Minnesota. It was completed while the second author was a postdoctoral fellow at the University of Michigan under Grant No. 5t32HD0710912 from the National Institute of Child Health and Human Development.

With the chapters in this volume, we, along with the many authors represented here, are attempting to express our admiration of Jim Jenkins for his intellectual contributions to cognitive psychology broadly construed. In addition, we are indebted to Jim for the model he provided as director of the Center for Research in Human Learning of the University of Minnesota. Jim was one of the founders of the Center and its first director. In that capacity he displayed for many years both intellectual leadership and unusual administrative skill. But more importantly, he created an atmosphere of stimulation and appreciation of intellectual endeavor among the faculty and student members that helped us all be more productive. He exemplified a rare concern for the enterprise that we all should emulate.

REFERENCES

Acredolo, L. P. (1976). Frames of reference used by children for orientation in unfamiliar spaces. In I. G. T. Moore & R. G. Gollege (Eds.), *Environment knowing*. Stroudsburg, PA: Dowden, Hutchinson, & Ross.

Acredolo, L. P. (1978). Development of spatial orientation in infancy. *Developmental Psychology, 14,* 224–234.

Acredolo, L. P. Adams, A., & Goodwyn, S. W. (1984). The role of self-produced movement and visual tracking in infant spatial orientation. *Journal of Experimental Child Psychology, 38,* 312–327.

Adams, J. A. (1971). A closed-loop theory of motor learning. *Journal of Motor Behavior, 3,* 111–150.

Bernshtein, N. A. (1948). *On the construction of movements.* Moscow: Medgiz.

Bertenthal, B. I., Campos, J. J., & Barret, K. C. (1984). Self-produced locomotion: An organizer of emotional, cognitive, and social development in infancy. In R. Emde & R. Harmon (Eds.), *Continuities and discontinuities in development* (pp. 175–210). New York: Plenum Press.

Bertenthal, B. I., & Bai, D. L. (1989). Infants' sensitivity to optical flow for controlling posture. *Developmental Psychology, 25,* 936–945.

Butterworth, G., & Ciccetti, D. (1978). Visual calibration of posture in normal and motor retarded Down's syndrome infants. *Perception, 7,* 513–525.

Cornell, E., & Heth, C. D. (1983). Spatial cognition: Gathering strategies used by preschool children. *Journal of Experimental Child Psychology, 35,* 93–110.

Fentress, J. (1989). Developmental roots of behavioral order: Systematic approaches to the examination of core developmental issues. In M. R. Gunnar & E. Thelen (Eds.), *Systems and Development: The Minnesota Symposia on Child Psychology* (Vol. 22, pp. 35–76). Hillsdale, NJ: Lawrence Erlbaum Associates.

Gibson, E. J., Riccio, G., Schmuckler, M., Stoffregen, T., Rosenberg, D., & Taorimina, J. (1987). Detection of the traversability of surfaces by crawling and walking infants. *Journal of Experimental Child Psychology: Human Perception and Performance, 13,* 533–544.

Gibson, E. J., & Schmuckler, M. (1989). Going somewhere: An ecological and experimental approach to development of mobility, *Ecological Psychology, 1,* 3–25.

Gibson, J. J. (1958). Visually controlled locomotion and visual orientation in animals. *British Journal of Psychology, 49,* 182–194.

Gibson, J. J. (1979). *The ecological approach to visual perception.* Boston, MA: Houghton-Mifflin.

Goldfield, E. C., & Michel, G. (1986). The ontogeny of infant bimanual reaching during the first year. *Infant Behavior and Development, 9,* 81–89.

Hardwick, H. A., McIntyre, C. W., & Pick, H. L. Jr. (1976). Control and manipulation of cognitive maps. *Society for Research in Child Development Monographs, 41,*(3, Serial No. 166).

Huttenlocher, J. A., & Newcombe, N. (1984). The child's representation of information about location. In C. Sophian (Ed.), *The origins of cognitive skills.* Hillsdale, NJ: Lawrence Erlbaum Associates.

Huttenlocher, J. A., & Presson, C. (1979). The coding and transformation of spatial information. *Cognitive Psychology, 11,* 375–394.

Lee, D. (1974). Visual information during locomotion. In R. B. MacLeod & H. L. Pick, Jr. (Eds.), *Perception: Essays in honor of James J. Gibson.* Ithaca, NY: Cornell University Press.

Lee, D. N., & Lishman, J. R. (1975). Visual proprioceptive control of stance. *Journal of Human Movement Studies, 1,* 87–95.

Linde, C., & Labov, W. (1975). Spatial networks as a site for the study of language and thought. *Language, 51,* 924–939.

Lockman, J. J. (1984). Development of detour abilities in infants. *Child Development, 55,* 482–491.

Menzel, E. W. (1978). Cognitive mapping in chimpanzees. In S. H. Hulse, H. Fowler, & W. K. Honig (Eds.), *Cognitive processes in animal behavior.* Hillsdale, NJ: Lawrence Erlbaum Associates.

Paillard, J. (1980). The mutichanneling of visual cues and the organization of a visually guided response. In G. E. Stelmach & J. Requin (Eds.), *Tutorials in motor behavior,* Amsterdam: North-Holland, pp. 259–279.

Paillard, J., & Amblard, B. (1985). Static versus kinetic visual cues for the processing of spatial relationships. In D. J. Ingle, M. Jeannerod, & D. N. Lee, (Eds.), *Brain mechanisms of spatial vision,* Dordrecht, Netherland: Martinus Nijhoff, pp. 299–330.

Palmer, C. (1987). *Infant locomotion through apertures varying in width.* Paper presented at the International Conference on Event Perception and Action, Trieste, Italy.

Plumert, J., Marks, R., Pick, H. L., Jr., & Wegesin, D. (1989). *The ability of children and adults to organize efficient searches and route directions.* Manuscript submitted for publication.

Reed, E. S. (1982). An outline of a theory of action systems. *Journal of Motor Behavior, 14,* 98–134.

Rieser, J. J., Ashmead, D. H., & Pick, H. L., Jr. (1988). *Perception of walking without vision: Uncoupling proprioceptive and visual flow.* Paper presented at the annual meeting of the Psychonomic Society, Chicago.

Rieser, J. J., Guth, D., & Hill, E. (1986). Sensitivity to perspective structure while walking without vision. *Perception, 15,* 173–188.

Rieser, J. J., & Heiman, M. L. (1982). Spatial self-reference systems and shortest route behavior in toddlers. *Child Development, 53,* 524–533.

Rosengren, K. S. (1989). *The role of vision and proprioception in the development of balance control.* Unpublished doctoral dissertation, University of Minnesota, Minneapolis.

Schmidt, R. A. (1975). A schema theory of discrete motor learning. *Psychological Review, 82,* 225–260.

Siegel, A. W., & White, S. H. (1975). The development of spatial representations of large-scale environments. In H. Reese (Ed.), *Advances in child development and behavior.* (Vol. 10, pp. 9–55). New York: Academic Press.

Smith, R., Haake, R. J., & Pick, H. L., Jr. (1985). *Toddlers' use of visual and auditory information for location in spatial orientation.* Paper presented at a meeting of The American Psychological Association, Los Angeles.

Somerville, S. C., & Bryant, P. E. (1985). Young children's use of spatial coordinates. *Child Development, 56,* 604–613.

Stoffregen, T. A., Schmuckler, M. A., & Gibson, E. J. (1987). Use of central and peripheral optical flow in stance and locomotion in young walkers. *Perception, 16,* 113–119.

Turvey, M. T., & Kugler, P. N. (1984). An ecological approach to perception and action. In H. T. A. Whiting (Ed.), *Human motor actions: Bernstein reassessed.* Amsterdam: North–Holland.

Ulrich, B. D., Thelen, E., & Niles, D. (in press). Perceptual determinants of action: Stair-climbing choices of infants and toddlers. In J. E. Clark & J. Humphrey (Eds.), *Advances in Motor Development Research* (Vol. 3). New York: AMS Press.

von Hofsten, C., & Lee, D. N. (1983). Dialogue on perception and action. *Human Movement Science, 1,* 125–138

Walk, R. D., & Gibson, E. J. (1961). A comparative study of visual depth perception. *Psychological Monographs, 75.*

Warren, D. H. (1977). *Blindness and early childhood development.* New York: American Foundation for the Blind.

Williams, H. G., McClenaghan, B., Ward, D., Carter, W., Brown, C., Byde, R., Johnson, D., & Lasalle, D. (1986). Sensory-motor control and balance: A behavioral perspective. In H. T. A. Whiting & M. G. Wade (Eds.), *Themes of motor development.* Dordecht, Netherlands: Martinus Nijhoff.

VIII APPLICATIONS OF COGNITIVE PSYCHOLOGY

25 An Eventful Approach to Studying Mental Retardation

Penelope H. Brooks
James Van Haneghan
Vanderbilt University

Retardation has been defined many ways. There have been formal definitions for the purpose of classification and informal ones that serve for routine communication. Basically, however, mental retardation involves difficulties in efficiently gaining and using knowledge from the environment. There is a mismatch between the organism that must learn to exist in the environment and the structure of the environment. The nature of the match between individuals who are retarded and the demands of the environment may vary. The match may be relatively close or very distant. Individuals with a close match are designated as "mildly" retarded and those with distant matches are labeled "severely" to "profoundly" retarded; there is a "moderate" category in between. Most mild retardation is attributed to polygenic factors or environmental insufficiency (or both) while profound mental retardation often has an identifiable organic base. These distinctions in degree of retardation and in origins of retardation are important because they allow us to place bets on change strategies—where and how the social context and socializing agents can enhance as well as impede cognitive development.

In this chapter we will try to characterize the nature of the environment in light of recent theoretical and empirical notions and juxtapose that characterization with the relevant cognitive skills that are known to be problematic for retarded children. The emphasis in this chapter is on theoretical formulations that focus on the concept of "events." We chose this emphasis because it appropriately describes the information that is important to the individual.

Events as a theoretical concept currently has two lineages in psychology. To ecological perception theorists, events specify invariant information in the environment. For cognitive psychology, what is interesting about events is their cognitive representation. Both theoretical approaches have limitations for characterizing mental retardation. From ecological perception's view, the condition of mental retardation would render one less able to detect relations between one'e self and the environment. From a cognitive theorist's viewpoint it would make one's event representations less accurate or less easily acquired.

In our examination of the literature, we found that there is very little research on how retarded children differ from nonretarded children in their ability to benefit from the dynamic information available to them. Some of the previous cognitive and behavioral research in the domain of retardation has *indirect* implications for event-oriented approaches although it was designed to address other issues.

There are three such generic approaches. One research approach has explored the information-processing deficits of retarded adults. For example, Sperber and McCauley (1984) reported that retarded adults are slower in encoding stimuli at a variety of levels. Spitz and Borys (1984) suggested that retarded individuals have working memory limitations. Nettlebeck (1985) found that retarded adults are about twice as slow as normal adults in making simple stimulus discriminations, suggesting that retarded individuals show a basic processing deficiency which is likely to manifest itself at all levels of information processing. The presence of general information processing deficits implies difficulties in the processing of information related to events.

Another line of research examining retarded individuals has considered their use of strategies to aid their recall and recognition. As Bray and Turner (1986) and Turnure (1985) point out, strategy use by mentally retarded individuals varies as a function of age, instructions, and task content. In general, the results of this line of research indicate that retarded individuals are less likely than normal individuals to use strategies, and that they sometimes use strategies inappropriately (Bray & Turner, 1986). Belmont and Butterfield (1977) and others point out that strategies can be taught successfully to mentally retarded children, although the generalizability and transfer of those strategies to other contexts have been weak. Thus, retarded individuals are not necessarily nonstrategic, but apparently are less sensitive to when and how to apply strategies. Again, strategies are applied to information and information originates from events in the environment. Failure to use strategies assures that information remains unselected and untransformed.

A third line of research on mental retardation is concerned with training mentally retarded individuals using behavior modification techniques. Much of this research has involved investigating different schedules of reinforcement and finding better ways to teach retarded individuals to carry out particular tasks or behaviors. These latter studies have implications for event-based research in that they have engaged in extensive task analysis and have revealed some strategies for teaching segments of activities to retarded people (e.g., Haring, Kennedy, Adams, & Pitts-Conway, 1987).

Each of these three lines of research has its strengths and weaknesses. Aside from research on behavior modification, there is little research that examines retarded individuals' everyday cognition. Behavior modification researchers, however, have little concern about the supraordinate issues that describe every-day behavior, for example, such questions as whether retarded individuals perceive and comprehend events in a similar way to normal individuals. These huge gaps in research on everyday cognition, especially the large proportion that involves events, led us to try to apply some of the perceptual learning/ecological perception concepts and the cognitive event-related concepts to the study of mental retardation.

Before we can begin our explorations, one important parameter must be discussed and included—that of development change.

THE ROLE OF DEVELOPMENT IN MENTAL RETARDATION

One of the foremost controversies in mental retardation is a disagreement as to whether mental retardation is a delay in the development of normal abilities, a lag in an otherwise normal progressive of development, or whether it is a qualitatively different course destination (see Detterman, 1987; Ellis & Cavalier, 1982; Weiss, Weisz, & Bromfield, 1986; Weisz, Yeates, & Zigler, 1982). Because of this controversy, developmental perspectives always provide interest-ing, if not revealing insights, into both theory and intervention regarding mental retardation.

One resolution to the controversy is the conclusion that both sides are correct, but that their respective explanations apply to different kinds of retardation. These kinds have been variously labeled as organically based versus psy-chosocially based, severe-profound versus mild. For people with retardation of organic origins (usually severe retardation), the normal developmental ex-pectations would not be met. For persons with psychosocial retardation (mild mental retardation), however, skills, abilities and behavior should appear in a normal developmental sequence albeit at a slower rate.

Another resolution of the controversy has been proposed by Detterman (1987), who describes human intelligence as a set of independent abilities organized in a complex system. These abilities differ in their importance or centrality in the system. Mental retardation is a deficit in abilities with high centrality. At a molar level of analysis, development would occur along its usual path but slower. The developmental delay would occur because of deficits in abilities that are central to development. Regardless of the resolution of the controversy, for many retarded individuals, the description of their problem involves developmental concepts. For that reason, much of the developmental research and theory is relevant to the task of describing the phenomenon of retardation.

The intersect between event-oriented and developmental approaches to describing cognitions, perception, and behavior holds some promise as an explanation of retarded intellectual performance and as a guide for intervention approaches. Included in each section is a brief summary of the mental retardation research conducted within the domain of that approach and some suggested research directions that would be beneficial in providing explanations for retarded cognition and learning.

ECOLOGICAL PERCEPTION/PERCEPTUAL LEARNING APPROACHES

Ecological perception theory's emphasis on adaptation to the environment (Gibson, 1979) and its inquiries into the perceived affordances of events (Shaw & Hazelett, 1986) make it an excellent candidate for an underlying explanatory system for mental retardation. Its emphasis on mechanisms associated with adaptation and, therefore, everyday survival opens a continuum of physical and social phenomena to individual difference issues.

According to this theory, the perceptual system is sensitive to invariants that are relevant to the organism in its current functioning mode. Just as opossums and humans might perceive different things, what is perceived by an infant may not be the same as what is perceived by an adolescent. For retarded children, the environment may afford different actions from nonretarded children because their developmental levels are different or because their nervous systems are different. A retarded child of 36 months may detect the affordances that are perceived by a 12-month-old normally developing child, for example, objects that afford grasping, throwing, or transporting food from plate to mouth.

Perceptual Research on People with Mental Retardation

Recent research on children with Down syndrome (DS) has begun to explore in more detail these developmental as well as retarded–nonretarded differences. Cichetti and Sroufe (1978) compared nonretarded and infants with DS in their reponses to looming objects and visual cliffs. In response to the looming stimulus, infants with DS apparently detected impending collision as early as 4 months (the earliest age examined by the investigators) but their emotional reaction was not as intense as that of normal babies. The retarded infants acted is if they perceived only part of the meaning of the looming object—that it was on a collision course—but not that they should be upset about it.

A similar conclusion was reached by Cichetti and Sroufe from subjecting the children to the visual cliff experience. Unlike their normal counterparts, few infants with DS cried, froze, or exhibited heart rate acceleration. Novice crawlers crossed the deep side; veteran crawlers (the same children, 1 month later) largely refused to cross the deep side. Furthermore, degree of negative reaction was associated with higher functioning. These results suggest that learning to detect depth develops from locomotion experience; but fearing depth is another process, apparently related to cognitive-developmental age or muscle tone.

Using a different method and different population of subjects, Reiser, Guth, and Weatherford (1987) also asked whether retardation involves problems in detecting and using spatial information. They led retarded and nonretarded adults through unfamiliar space with and without blindfolds and then asked them to point to their starting point when the participants were not blindfolded. The authors reasoned that when visual-environmental cues were absent, both groups used well-ingrained associations between proprioceptive information and movements in space. When visual-environmental information was available, only the nonretarded participants used it to determine their starting point. In other words, the retarded adults did not use the information about the relations between their location, the walls, and the target. There are several alternative explanations for their failure. Were they unable to consider simultaneously all the information available to make inferences from spatial relations present? Were they able to consider the information, but unable to make the inferences? Or, did they simply fail to direct their attention to the information available?

Rieser et al.'s findings suggest that perceptual learning processes in retarded individuals are rather uneven. Retarded adults seem to have an ability to perceive basic spatial-proprioceptive relations, a finding reported elsewhere (Anwar, 1983), but are deficient in more complex (but also rather basic) abilities to coordinate visual-spatial perspectives.

Still another form of the question about retardation and spatial abilities was examined by Fox and Oross (1988) in a series of studies on stereoscopic vision and perception of biological motion in *mildly* retarded adults. Using random element stereograms, they found that a heterogeneous group of retarded adults appeared deficient in their use of stereoscopic cues. In one experiment, they found that decreases in the density of the stereogram that had no effect on normal adults' abilities to discriminate a stereoscopically created object led to deterioration in the performance of mildly retarded adults. In another experiment, they asked retarded adults to identify objects in stereograms. They found in this study that the retarded individuals had trouble discriminating the shapes, performing at much poorer levels than normal participants who perfectly identified the objects. On the other hand, Fox and Oross's experiment examining biological motion, found that the retarded adults were 100% accurate in identifying biological motion.

The results reported here suggest that retarded individuals show some delays in perceptual learning deficits in processing speed, but also some similarities to nonretarded individuals. The research on very young children indicates that some events necessary for survival (e.g., impending collision) are highly canalized since very delayed children display sensitivity to the distinctive features of the phenomena. Other perceptual learning opportunities are less canalized, such as coordinating environmental information with instructions to locate a starting point.

How Mental Retardation Can Influence Ecological Theory

Just as ecological theory can identify learning and training needs, for mentally retarded individuals, the phenomenon of mental retardation highlights direction for development of ecological theory. First, it is difficult to assess whether a retarded individual is perceiving affordances unless one knows that affordances need to be perceived. Thus there is a need for taxonomy or organizational scheme for what affordances and affordance structures are important for what skills in what stage/level of development. There is a significant amount of activity on the identification of affordances and their invariant structures. American Sign Language (Poizner, Klima, Bellugi, & Livingston, 1986), swimmers' kicks (McCabe, 1986), and gender identification (Runeson & Frykholm, 1986) are just three of the recent diverse phenomena that have been successfully subjected to the search for invariant structure. The reverse process is that of taking the relevant environment as a starting point and looking for important invariant structures in it relative to the activity of the organism. This would require observers' looking at what babies or adolescents do and inferring the presence of affordance structure for those activities. Then, retardation could be described in terms of affordance perceived (or not).

Another type of formulation is also needed—that of a levels-of-affordance designation. This formulation would identify linear, hierarchical, or other relationships between affordances. It would designate some as perceptual precursors to others; some as general affordances, for example, surface gradients, while others are specific, for example, hardness of a tennis court. It would address the question of whether detection of some invariants is a prerequisite or building block for others. For example, how are affordances that specify something as "lift-able," "mouth-able," "grasp-able," and as capable of containment combined to specify an object as affording drinking. If there are some affordances that are common to several contexts within an ecological niche, are they not prepotent for other affordances? This formulation of relationships between affordances would include basic change or motion as well as complicated, purposeful changes, depending to a large degree on experience.

Development is also critical in that what one perceives in a given situation may be determined by one's cognitive capabilities. For example, what adults perceive as cleaning may appear to be some interesting sensorimotor activities to an 18-month-old. The presence of developmental differences in perceived affordances raises the question of when and how children discover particular affordances. The discovery of some affordances almost seems to be a necessary consequence of acting in the environment. For example, affordances that specify surface support (e.g., the visual cliff) become specified when children begin to crawl and walk. Others may be discovered in the course of goal-directed activities, modeling of others' activity, through the shaping and guidance of others, or even accidentally, while intending to carry out another act.

The wide diversity of contexts in which perceptual learning takes place makes it difficult to decide a necessary order of acquisition without considering factors which influence and shape the opportunities to experience objects and events in particular ways. These include biological constraints, social-cultural constraints and other proximal or distal factors that determine interest and motivation (E. Gibson, 1969). The modulation of action and perception by each other (e.g., see Shaw & Hazelett, 1986) point out the importance that the physical and social environment have in the kinds of affordances children will discover. If we consider for the moment the Vygotskian notion that the actions and events to which infants and young children are exposed are controlled by parents and other socializing agents (e.g., Wertsch, 1979), one would expect individual differences in the kinds of affordances perceived. Socializing agents may help shape "anticipatory schemata" (Neisser, 1976), which bias how children act on an object and therby shape the affordances they discover. On a more global level, socioeconomic and cultural conditions also may influence the kinds of affordances perceived as well as the kinds of anticipatory schemata that children bring to events.

In addition, a complication which needs to be considered in some forms of retardation is the presence of brain damage or differences in brain chemistry (Baumeister & MacLean, 1979). The effects of brain damage could relate to a number of components of perceptual learning, ranging from mechanisms influencing attention and arousal to problems in the physiology of the perceptual system that make the discovery of some affordances difficult or impossible. Given mental retardation with a "social-cultural" basis, one might expect that affordances more basic to survival to be relatively intact, whereas the discovery of affordances that are part of the adaptation to social and cultural aspects of the environment may be a source of individual differences. On the other hand, retarded individuals who are biologically "different" may have difficulty in picking up even some basic affordances.

COGNITIVE APPROACHES TO EVENTS

Not only are events an important unit of analysis in perception research, they are also important units of analysis for other cognitive research. Information-processing researchers, as well as ecologically oriented researchers, use events as a unit of analysis (e.g., Jenkins, Wald, & Pittenger, 1986). While ecologically oriented researchers have been interested in how information in the environment provides a dynamic context for directly perceiving events, cognitive scientists have been interested in how events are presented by the organism (e.g., Schank, 1982). Thus, while the ecological researcher asks about the invariant information specified in the event, the cognitive scientist might ask about how the organism represents and stores information about an event. In our discussion of the cognition of events, we will not only discuss learning and memory observed events but also events in which an individual is an actual participant or has planned the sequence of actions. We discuss these two aspects together because they are organized in a similar fashion. In addition, because mental retardation is the result of less than optimal development of the arresting of development at a particular level, our discussion will have a developmental emphasis.

Information-processing Approaches

Perhaps the most explicit theory of how people remember and learn about events in Schank's (1982) theory of dynamic memory. Schank's theory suggests that the development of event understanding is a process of abstraction and coordination. That is, it involves the abstraction of repeatable aspects of events at various levels. Initially, these representations are quite specific to particular situations and highly personalized; as a child develops they begin to construct more socialized representations of events at a variety of levels of generality. The major mechanism by which this occurs is a comparison process between previous experiences and expectations that remind one of the present situation. Reminding at various levels is crucial to development in that what-an-event-reminds-one-of varies in generality across development. Initially it occurs at a more specific level between events that occur in relatively similar environments and have relatively similar goals. With development, reminding can be based on quite abstract relations between events. For example, one might be reminded of a play or story because the motivations of the protagonist are the same as a character in another story, even though the plots involve very different settings and goals. Thus to explain development, one has to explore both the construction of event representations at various levels and the mapping of representations onto other representations.

Several types of event representations are discussed in Schank's theory. One type of representation mentioned is a plan. Plans are hierarchically organized action-sequences directed toward a series of goals and subgoals (Miller, Galanter, & Pribram, 1960). Traditionally, planning has been viewed as strictly a top–down, decontextualized process in which an individual devises a plan a priori. More recent cognitive science research (e.g., Hayes–Roth & Hayes–Roth, 1979) has shown that planning is often opportunistic in nature, and that it is a complex function of how an individual's plan interacts with what the environment affords. Plans which are carried out routinely are what Schank and Abelson (1977) originally labeled "scripts." Scripts are routinely carried-out action sequences that vary in their performance only in the variability of a few parameters. The overworked example of a trip to McDonald's is the classic example of a script. There are certain actions at McDonald's that one carries out to obtain food. Those actions are successful at McDonald's or almost any fast food location. Scripts vary in their causal structure and the degree of empirical necessity surrounding the action sequence (Schank & Abelson, 1977). For example, in a script for making cookies, one could not bake the cookies without first making a batter. A third kind of representation is in terms of scenes (J. Mandler, 1985; Schank, 1982). Scenes can be viewed as parts of scripts. For example, in a script for going to a restaurant, there would be an ordering scene, a paying scene, and eating scene and so on. In more recent theorizing, Schank (1982) has abandoned the notion of a script as an entity stored in memory because of its failure to account for memory confusions among similar episodes (e.g., going to the doctor versus going to the dentist) and its inefficiency as a structure for episodic memory. That is, one could have hundreds of scripts for very similar activities, which would lead to hundreds of representations of the same information which would be an extremely inefficient storage mechanism. Consequently, a different kind of representation—Memory Organization Packets (MOPS)—has been hypothesized by Schank (1982), "Memory Organization Packets (MOPs)." MOPs are like scripts in that they are formed through the abstraction of similarities of many episodes, but are different from scripts in that they can record the similarities at a variety of levels of generality. MOPs may represent the organization of particular kinds of scenes (e.g., what one does when someone pays for something), or may index very abstract similarities concerning events (e.g., at all restaurants one pays, orders, and eats). Scripts in this conceptualization of event representation are not present in memory, but are constructed in the process of trying to understand or recollect an event. Scripts emerge from the combinations of MOPs at various levels of generality brought into play to understand an event.

Lichtenstein and Brewer (1980) have looked at event sequences, emphasizing their hierarchical structure. They discussed what they label "plan schema." Plan schemata refer to the underlying organization of events according to goals and subgoals. For instance, they used the example of writing a letter to illustrate the organization of events around goals. Actions are organized in their enablement of other actions that lead to a goal. For example, in order to sign a letter, one must obtain a pen and take the cap off the top. They found that the higher-order goals tend to be remembered better than the specific details of the actions carried out, and that details were remembered better in a temporal position consistent with the underlying goal hierarchy than in a position inconsistent with that hierarchy. Thus, events are encoded simultaneously on a number of levels, but we are typically only conscious of the information related to our goals.

Developmental Approaches to Events

As many researchers point out (e.g., Gibson & Spelke, 1983; Huttenlocher & Smyth–Burke, 1987) there is no doubt that infants under 1 year have some ability to grasp events. For instance, habituation studies have shown that by 5 months, children are sensitive to the velocity and direction of motion (see Huttenlocher & Smyth–Burke, 1987, for a review). They react with surprise to anomalous events (e.g., Baillargeon, Spelke, & Wasserman, 1985), suggesting they have some recognition of crucial elements of events. J. Mandler (1983) notes that many games played by infants less than 1 year old of age with their parents involve violations of expectations which are greeted with curiosity and often delight. However, the events that infants understand or represent depend to a large extent on their abilities to perceive and act on the world. Children can only learn what their world affords them. Children are quite precocial in their perceptual development, but the experience of many events awaits the time in which the infant gains control over his or her world. This does not mean that children are not able to represent events, only that their event understandings will be limited in scope; the experiences of young infants are limited by their lack of physical mobility (see Bertenthal & Campos, 1987, for a similar argument).

Children's opportunities to experience events, to be an agent of action, greatly increase as they become mobile. As Schank (1982) notes, failed expectancies require us to build new understandings of events. To some extent, failed expectancies may be fewer for the premobile infant whose world is predictable. The proportion of events in which they are the agent of action versus the recipient of action changes as they begin to crawl and to walk. The reproduction of simple interesting events by children during the second half of the second year of life (i.e., secondary circular reactions, Piaget, 1959) show that the child is not only able to show recognition of an event, but is also able to control its appearance. They begin to gain some sense that events occur, over time, in order. At the end of the first year of life there is little doubt that infants have perceptual and procedurally based event understandings.

During the second year of life, researchers have typically noted how these early event representations become differentiated and used in various domains of representation (e.g., play, language, deferred imitation, notions of agency). Thus, early event representations are purported to feed into the development of more context-independent representational abilities, resulting by 24 months in the genesis of symbolic thought. Brownell (1986) reports that a number of a rapid changes in the ability to construct and reconstruct multi-unit events or behavioral sequences and to abstract particular items from events occurs around 20 to 24 months. Children become able to imitate sequences of behaviors (Bauer & Mandler, 1987), combine words into sentences, engage in multischeme play (Bretherton, 1984) and differentiate passive and active roles of actions in events (Watson & Jackowitz, 1984; Wolf, 1982) among other things; the child labels these abilities to handle relations between behavior units "combinatorial abilities." Whether these differences are the result of a gradual differentiation of skills over the second year of life or represent the result of a rapid change in information-processing capacity is an open question. However, as Brownwell (1986) notes, there is a general belief among many researchers that changes in overall processing capacity at around 24 months play a major role in these developments.

Research during the preschool period has shown that preschoolers know a great deal about events. Work by Nelson and her colleagues (see Nelson, 1986) has shown that preschool children, like adults, can produce verbal scripts that represent the temporal order of events (Nelson & Gruendel, 1981). Additionally, preschoolers, like adults, tend to remember sequences as actions that have more of a degree of empirical necessity (e.g., you can't make cookies without dough) than those that do not. Work by Bullock (1985) has shown that preschoolers use principles of causal reasoning from events similar to those of adults.

One important point about the development of scripts in young children is that while Schank and Abelson argue that scripts derive from plans that take on a degree of automaticity, Fivush and Slackman (1986) argue that they do not necessarily develop out of plans. That is, the child does not necessarily understand the goal of the action sequence, at least they do not understand it in the same way as an adult. One way of solving this apparent problem is simply to note that children have many experiences with such events and the help of adults and other individuals who frame the events. Thus, they have many opportunities to remember them. However, this explanation does not explain why children seem to respect, and to some extent understand, the necessity of the temporal order of events (French, 1986). Perhaps ecological perceptual theory could help resolve this conflict. That is, the discovery of affordances and perceptual invariants may provide the glue to hold a sequence of actions together. Thus, perceptual learning processes rather than "planning" may explain some aspects of early script development.

Later developments during school age involve the elaboration of more details of scripts and on measuring understanding of what are the necessary and interchangeable elements of scripts. As children get older, there are many more MOPs and these MOPs can represent events at many levels of abstraction. Thus both the breadth and depth of remembering increase.

So far we have talked about developments in the observation and memory for action sequences. We would like to move on to discuss the *generation* of action sequences, the development of planning. Planning involves generation of one or more symbolic representations, prior to behaving, which are used to help determine how one will behave in a situation. Developmentally, plans vary in both complexity and the degree to which they are made up of old plans. The processes involved in planning also change; new criteria for evaluating plans evolve and children become more opportunistic in their planning (Meyer & Rebok, 1985) in that they become better able to adjust their plans to circumstances (Rogoff, Gauvain, & Gardner, 1987). De Lisi (1987) described different kinds of plans that evolve with development. Early plans tend to be much like Nelson's scripts. As children develop they become better able to generate plans, to use planning in a deliberate fashion, to generate plans for more abstract goals, and are better able to evaluate their plans.

Research on Persons with Mental Retardation

In terms of mental retardation, these developments present a rich, descriptive backdrop to look for the emergence of differences in event understanding. Research on the development of event understanding mentally retarded individuals is plagued with the mental age issue: Is their development consistent with developmental levels as measured by mental age? Are their plan schemata, scripts, and other more general representations of events consistent with their mental age, or do retarded children show deficits above and beyond what one would expect based on mental age? If they do show deficits, what are the sources of these differences? There have been many researchers who have argued for mental processing limitations among mentally retarded individuals (e.g., Spitz & Borys, 1984). These limitations in processing would seem to limit the ability of these children to abstract information from events, just as purportedly the processing limitations of children prior to 24 months of age limit their abilities to combine acts into sequences in imitation and symbolic play. At the same time, speculations involving the socialized aspects of event understanding attribute mental age lags to socialization differences in situations that would otherwise yield equivalent development to mental age peers. We will discuss examples of research and theory that relate "events" and mental retardation, keeping in mind the questions already raised. First, we will discuss research with children looking at lexical development, symbolic play, and children's comprehension of event-sequences. Then we will discuss a study examining event-knowledge in mildly retarded adults.

Lexical Development.   Nelson's (1985, 1986) emphasis on event knowledge as important to lexical development, may prove useful for the understanding of retarded children's deficits in this area. Often, retarded individuals lag in lexical development, even behind children of a similar mental age. For example, Cardoso–Martins, Mervis, and Mervis (1985) in a longitudinal study of Down's syndrome and normal children, report a lag in the early vocabulary of DS children beyond what one would expect, based on their level of sensorimotor development or their mental age (as defined by the Bayley scales and later on the Stanford–Binet).

Nelson (1985) in her theory of conceptual development, sees children's representation of events as the source of early concepts. She suggests there gradually emerging overlapping phases of development. During the first year of life the infant builds up event representations from actions and interactions in the world. Nelson suggests that these early generalized event representations (which she suggests are analogous to Schank and Abelson's [1977] notion of a script) are global, conceptually unanalyzed perceptual representations of frequently observed or engaged in events. During the first half of the second year of life, what Nelson labels the *prelexical phase*, children's use of words reflects events, and words are used primarily to label events. Nelson notes the example of a child who uses the word "car" only when standing in the window watching automobiles pass by her house. As children gain more experience labeling events and seeing the same thing in more than one event context they begin to recognize that words refer to things as well as contexts, and they begin to differentiate the word from its context. During this phase, there is an increased analysis of event representations in order to grasp when words do or do not fit into contexts; one also finds the rapid rise in vocabulary found by many researchers (Nelson, 1985). At the same time that object concepts are developing, relational concepts tend to be more context-bound. The use of words outside of context helps in the creation of novel combinations of words. Children in this phase start out with concepts based on the ability to substitute particular objects in certain contexts, and move to the comparison and contrasting of contexts such that concepts of things can be abstracted and used in different contexts. Finally, toward middle childhood, children develop a separate lexical system that examines relations purely at a linguistic level. Even in this later stage, however, events still play a role in conceptual development in that new understanding can originate in the context of events.

An important element of Nelson's model, particularly in early stages, is the socialization of various scripts by parents. As mentioned earlier, much of mental retardation is associated with social-cultural factors. Current event-oriented theories have not clearly explicated the role of social factors in the development of event knowledge. Parents and other socializing agents control the events children have access to, the manner of access, and the emotional tone.

If socializing agents do not frame events for children, or fail to frame those events within the child's zone of proximal development, one would expect delays in the development of basic scripts or schemata for understanding the world. Likewise, if socializing agents do not provide regular, predictable behavioral routines for a child to carry out, then one would expect that a child would have more difficulty picking regularities out of the social world and also show developmental delays. Thus, an analysis of the regularity and organization in the caretaker and child's world might suggest reasons why we might find delays or differences in the development of event understanding. Because the largest chunk of mental retardation has been attributed to social-cultural circumstances, an analysis of the social mediation of early events could provide some clues about later difficulties in development.

Symbolic Play.   Symbolic play research is another area where events are the important unit of analysis (Bretherton, 1984). Motti, Cichetti and Sroufe (1983) and Hill and McCune–Nicolish (1981) report delays in DS children's symbolic play abilities consistent with other levels of development. Riguet, Taylor, Benaroya, and Klien (1981) report similar findings, although they report a qualitative difference: DS children made fewer alternative uses of a given prop during play periods than normal children, thus suggesting that they may have difficulty separating symbol from context. However, more research and theory are needed to understand the significance of such findings. We know much about the normative development of symbolic play, but we know very little at present concerning the meaning of individual differences in symbolic play activity.

Retarded Children's Grasp of Action Sequences.   Our work has centered on retarded children's grasp of sequences of actions. Brooks and McCarrell (1975) examined the ability of retarded adolescents, nonretarded adolescents, and 5-year-old children to segment event sequences. The children watched a video tape of someone engaged in an activity (e.g., wrapping a package) and pushed a button when the actor finished one thing and began another. Since these component actions did not have names, the subjects had to rely on visual cues to detect completion (e.g., separation of hands from object). All subjects, including the retarded adolescents, were able to identify when one subtask ended and another began. These results suggest that it is not retarded individuals' insensitivity to these types of visual cues that makes it difficult for them to grasp sequences of activity. However, when the sequence was stopped in the middle, the retarded adolescents were significantly less able to identify actions that came next. This suggests that they didn't use the information from the previous segment to select (from four pictures) the picture that portrayed the next segment.

Van Haneghan, in some preliminary work, examined whether preschool children at risk for mental retardation were able to imitate simple common action sequences. He asked children to view videotapes of another child fixing a snack and a child giving a doll a bath. In addition, similar to Lichtenstein and Brewer's work, in one sequence the children viewed, the location of a particular action was moved from its goal-directed function. For example, the child obtained the towel, washcloth, and soap from a shelf prior to starting the bath rather than obtaining them as they were needed (e.g., getting the washcloth just before it was used.) The idea was to determine whether Litchtenstein and Brewer's finding that recall tends toward a functional rather than a temporal order would hold with these children. Examination of recall for the sequences indicated that even though there was no difference in the number of task behaviors recalled, there was a marginally significant advantage in the number of actions recalled in the modeled order when functional and temporal ordering coincided.

Everyday Cognition in adults.   Very little research has looked at retarded adults understanding of events, although teaching retarded adults behavioral sequences (e.g., dressing themselves, going to the grocery store) is probably the central focus of intervention with them. These interventions have been studied largely in terms of how learning theory principles, such as modeling and shaping, apply (e.g., see Haring et al., 1987; Kayser, Billingsley, & Neal, 1986). Theoretically relevant contributions, however, would ask what retarded people do when confronted with a routine but demanding task. This type of task provides a picture of everyday cognition at work. Grocery shopping was the subject of the one study we found with everyday cognition as its topic. Levine and Langness (1985) analyzed various elements of retarded adults' plans and actions in shopping. The retarded individuals varied widely in their skill in grocery shopping, although some common themes emerged. First, many of the retarded adults plans tended to be either weak or rather rigid. For example, some set up grocery lists they followed so strictly that the lists led them back and forth across the store to find different items. Others simply had no list, buying food every night, or buying the same items every time they went to the store. A second theme that emerged was that a major motivational factor in the retarded adults' shopping activity was looking normal and feeling comfortable in the situation. For example, some went to the same cashier each time they went to the store, or brought large amounts of cash to avoid not having enough money. For the most part, despite what might be seen as performance deficits, the retarded adults were able to carry out this event sequence. Indeed some of the strategies that the retarded individuals used were not unlike those used by nonretarded individuals. For example, one might not want to make the mental effort to estimate the cost of items in the store, and consequently, bring a large amount of cash. Thus, retarded individuals do learn to carry out behavioral sequences, albeit in a less then optimal way sometimes.

This example shows the complexity involved in a sequence of behaviors. First, sequences are undertaken which have several layers of goals which direct them. For example, acquisition of food is the primary goal of grocery shopping, but other goals are present in the situation, which alter how this goal is attained. For some individuals spending as little money as possible to obtain groceries is an important goal, whereas for other individuals spending as little time and effort in the grocery store as possible takes precedence. Understanding the goal structure surrounding an event sequence might clarify retarded individuals' behavior in the grocery shopping context. A retarded individual may view surviving the trip to the grocery store without embarrassment as more important than selecting reasonably priced, nutritious foods.

Mentally retarded individuals' plans and scripts present a dilemma, because they appear to be so much less efficient than individuals' of normal intelligence. Nevertheless, their rudimentary plans, at least in the grocery shopping context are successful; they are able to obtain groceries. Take the individual who rigidly buys everything in the exact order on his or her list. That individual probably takes twice as long to shop as other individuals. This is only a problem, however, if there are time constraints, or if that individual is extremely fatigued at the end of the grocery trip. Yet, even though such a plan might be successful, most individuals of normal intelligence would replace that plan with a more efficient one. Thus, one important question for mental retardation research is explaining why such plans are not replaced. Part of the reason, as has been suggested, is that mentally retarded individuals tend to be failure-avoidant. That is, their failures are so frequent, they tend to stick with anything that works. But their motivational differences may not explain all their failures. It appears that mentally retarded individuals do not sometimes use all the information available to them in the environment. For example, in the Levine and Langness (1986) study, the individual running across the store did not coordinate the visual information in the physical environment with the list information to make shopping easier. In the Reiser et al. (1987) study, mentally retarded individuals did not make use of visual information available in a route to help make a spatial location judgment. Perhaps, then, processing limitations and motivational factors interact to lead to fixation at a particular level, or perhaps less planning.

SUMMARY AND CONCLUSIONS

The rich theoretical networks focusing on the concept of "events" as the major unit of perception and representation provide a promising framework for understanding mental retardation. Ecological perception could be a limitless source of hypotheses about individual differences in ability and opportunity to detect affordances. Cognitive-developmental theories furnish a moderately well-developed account of the development of representations of events. Mentally retarded people's failure to learn and adapt may be attributable to their failure in the detection of affordances or in the construction of representations of events. These descriptions of cognitive-developmental deficiencies are not mutually exclusive. Obviously, if affordances of events are not detected, the events will not be represented. On the other hand, does detection entail representation? Obviously not, if higher-order representational activity, for example, planning, is considered. Further, our work and that of others (e.g., Turnure, 1985) illustrate the complexities of assessing event knowledge in these children. Retarded individuals are a rather heterogeneous group of people who have somewhat different motivations in approaching tasks. For example, there were some children in Van Haneghan's study who looked to the experimenter to get feedback on their performance. There was also one child whose primary interest was to get back to the classroom as quickly as possible. Thus, it was unclear whether that child's poor performance was a function of a lack of competence or superficial attempts at the task that would allow him or her to be done with it more quickly. Van Hanegan's results also suggest why such children might be variable at encoding events. It may not be due to their ability or inability to do so, but their styles of interacting with the world. For some children, the events seemed to go by too fast for them to encode them completely. For others, their own actions prevented them from attending to information, either because they were actively engaged in repetitive behavior or because they were perpetually in motion. Thus, motivation and behavioral style, as well as processing deficiencies, influence event learning by controlling the attention children give to sequences of actions.

Hence, if a mentally retarded adult had trouble understanding a television program, it could be because he or she couldn't detect different events portrayed (e.g., facial expressions) or had inadequate representations of the events (e.g., could he or she recognize and understand the meaning of footprints) or had no script into which that event fell. Similarly, if the person couldn't learn to wash one's clothes, it could be because he or she couldn't detect the necessary affordances in the washing sequence, for example, clothes into large hole in machine, quarters into slots, and so on, or couldn't remember what to do next. Or perhaps he or she couldn't plan the task so that he or she had everything needed before approaching the washer. Perhaps the person didn't care whether his or her clothes were clean or would rather be watching television or couldn't maintain attention long enough to watch someone do a whole sequence. The possibilities are constrained only by our limited number of perceptual-cognitive theories about events.

Mentally retarded individuals are people who vary significantly in their ability to adapt—for many different reasons. Their adaptation, to the degree it is successful, depends on meaning they make from the events that engage them. In our view, the conceptualization of events is the most promising approach to understanding everyday cognition and, hence, adaptation in mentally retarded people.

ACKNOWLEDGMENT

Preparation of this chapter was supported in part by National Institute of Child Health and Human Development Grants HD–07226 and HD–15052.

REFERENCES

Anwar, F. (1983). Vision and kinaesthesis in motor movements. In J. Hogg & P. Mittler (Eds.), *Advances in mental handicap research* (Vol. 2). New York: Academic Press.

Baillargeon, R., Spelke, E. S., & Wasermann, S. (1985). Object permanence in five-month-old infants. *Cognition, 20,* 191–208.

Bauer, P., & Mandler, J. (1987, April). *Factors affecting very young children's recall of events.* Paper presented at the biennial meeting of the Society of Research in Child Development, Balitmore.

Baumeister, A. A., & MacLean, W. E., Jr. (1979). Brain damage and mental retardation. In N. R. Ellis (Ed.), *Handbook of mental deficiency research* (2nd ed., pp. 197–230). New York: McGraw–Hill.

Belmont, J. M., & Butterfield, E. C. (1977). The instructional approach to developmental cognitive research. In R. V. Kail & J. W. Hagen (Eds.), *Perspectives on the development of memory and cognition* (pp. 437–481). Hillsdale, NJ: Lawrence Erlbaum Associates.

Bertenthal, B. I., & Campos, J. J. (1987). New directions in the study of early experience. *Child Development, 58,* 560–567.

Bray, N. W., & Turner, L. A. (1986). The rehersal deficit hypothesis. In N. R. Ellis & N. W. Bray (Eds.), *International review of research in mental retardation* (Vol. 14, pp. 47–71). New York: Academic Press.

Bretherton, I. (1984). Representing the social world in symbolic play: Reality and fantasy. In I. Bretherton (Ed.), *Symbolic play: The development of social understanding* (pp. 3–41). New York: Academic Press.

Brooks, P. H., & McCarrell, N. (1975, September). *Mental retardation: Comprehension gone awry.* Presentation at John F. Kennedy Center colloquium, Peabody College, Nashville.

Brownell, C. A. (1986). Convergent developments: Cognitive developmental correlates of growth in infant/toddler peer skills. *Child Development, 57,* 275–286.

Bullock, M. (1985). Causal reasoning and developmental change over the preschool years. *Human Development, 28,* 169–191.

Cardoso–Martins, C., Mervis, C. B., & Mervis, C. A. (1985). Early vocabulary aquisition by children with Down's syndrome. *American Journal of Mental Deficiency, 90,* 177–184.

Cichetti, D., & Sroufe, L. A. (1978). An organizational view of affect: Illustration from the study of Down's syndrome infants. In M. Lewis & L. Rosenblum (Eds.), *The development of affect* (pp. 309–350). New York: Plenum Press.

De Lisi, R. (1987). A cognitive developmental model of planning. In S. L. Friedman, E. K. Scholnick, & R. R. Cocking (Eds.), *Blueprints for thinking* (pp. 79–109). New York: Cambridge University Press.

Detterman, D. (1987). Theoretical notions of intelligence in mental retardation. *American Journal Mental Deficiency, 92,* 2–11.

Ellis, N. R., & Cavalier, A. R. (1982). Research perspectives in mental retardation. In E. Zigler & D. Balla (Eds.), *Mental Retardation: The developmental difference controversy,* (pp. 121–152). Hillsdale, NJ: Lawrence Erlbaum Associates.

Fivush, R., & Slackman, E. A. (1986). The acquisition and development of scripts. In K. Nelson (Ed.), *Event knowledge: Structure and function in development* (pp. 71–96). Hillsdale, NJ: Lawrence Erlbaum Associates.

Fox, R., & Oross, S. (1988). Deficits in stereoscopic depth perception by mildly mentally retarded adults. *American Journal Mental Retardation, 93,* 232–244.

French, L. A. (1986). The language of events. In K. Nelson (Ed.), *Event knowledge: Structure and function in development* (pp. 119–136). Hillsdale, NJ: Lawrence Erlbaum Associates.

Gibson, E. J. (1969). *Principles of perceptual learning and development.* New York: Appleton–Century–Crofts.

Gibson, E. J., & Spelke, E. (1983). The development of perception In P. H. Mussen (Ed.), *Handbook of child psychology* (pp. 2–76). New York: Wiley.

Gibson, J. J. (1979). *The ecological approach to visual perception.* Boston: Houghton Mifflin.

Haring, J. G., Kennedy, C. H., Adams, M. J., & Pitts–Conway, V. (1987). Teaching generalization of purchasing skills across community settings to autistic youth using videotape modeling. *Journal of Applied Behavior Analysis, 20,* 89–96.

Hayes–Roth, B., & Hayes–Roth, F. (1979). A cognitive model of planning. *Cognitive Science, 3,* 275–310.

Hill, P. M., & McCune–Nicolich, L. (1981). Pretend play and patterns of cognition in Down's syndrome children. *Child Development, 52,* 611–617.

Huttenlocher, J., & Smyth–Burke, T. (1987). Event encoding in infancy. In P. Salapatak & L. Cohen (Eds.), *Handbook of infant perception* (Vol. 2, pp. 209–229). New York: Academic Press.

Jenkins, J. J., Wald, J., & Pittenger, J. B. (1986). Apprehending pictorial events. In V. McCabe & G. J. Balzano (Eds.), *Event cognition: An ecological perspective* (pp. 117–133). Hillsdale, NJ: Lawrence Erlbaum Associates.

Kayser, J. D., Billingsley, F. F., & Neal, R. S. (1986). A comparison of in-context and traditional instructional approaches: Total task, single trial versus backward chaining, multiple trials. *Journal of the Association for Persons with Severe Handicaps, 11*, 28–38.

Levine, H. G., & Langness, L. L. (1985). Everyday cognition among mildly retarded adults: An ethnographic approach. *American Journal of Mental Deficiency, 90*, 18–26.

Lichtenstein, E. H., & Brewer, W. F. (1980). Memory for goal directed events. *Cognitive Psychology, 12*, 412–445.

Mandler, J. M. (1983). Representation. In P. H. Mussen (Ed.), *Handbook of child psychology*. New York: Wiley.

Mandler, J. M. (1985). *Stories, scripts, and scenes: Aspects of schema theory*. Hillsdale, NJ: Lawrence Erlbaum Associates.

McCabe, V. (1986). Event cognition and the conditions of existence. In V. McCabe & G. J. Balzano (Eds.), *Event cognition: An ecological perspective* (pp. 3–24). Hillsdale, NJ: Lawrence Erlbaum Associates.

Meyer, J. S., & Rebok, G. (1985). Planning in action across the life span. In T. M. Schlecter & M. P. Toglia (Eds.), *New directions in cognitive science*. Norwood, NJ: Ablex.

Miller, G. A., Galanter, E., & Pribram, K. (1960). *Plans and the structure of behavior*. New York: Holt, Rinehart, & Winston.

Motti, F., & Cichetti, D., & Sroufe, L. A. (1983). From infant affect expression to symbolic play: The coherence of development in Down syndrome children. *Child Development, 54*, 1168–1175.

Neisser, U. (1976). *Cognition and reality*. San Francisco: Freeman.

Nelson, K. (1985). *Making sense: The acquisition of shared meaning*. New York: Academic Press.

Nelson, K. (1986). *Event knowledge: Structure and function in development*. Hillsdale, NJ: Lawrence Erlbaum Associates.

Nelson, K., & Gruendel, J. (1981). Generalized event representations: Basic building blocks of cognitive development. In M. E. Lamb & A. L. Brown (Eds.), *Advances in developmental psychology* (Vol. 1, pp. 131–158). Hillsdale, NJ: Lawrence Erlbaum Associates.

Nettlebeck, T. (1985). Inspection time and mental retardation. In N. R. Ellis & N. L. Bray (Eds.), *International review of research in mental retardation* (Vol. 13, pp. 109–139). New York: Academic Press.

Piaget, J. (1959). *Construction of reality in the child*. New York: Basic.

Poizner, H., Klima, E. S., Bellugi, U., & Livingston, R. G. (1986). Motion analysis of grammatical processes in a visual-gestalt language. In V. McCabe, & G. J. Balzano (Eds.), *Event cognition: An ecological perspective* (pp. 155–174). Hillsdale, NJ: Lawrence Erlbaum Associates.

Rieser, J. J., Guth, D. D., & Weatherford, D. L. (1987). Mentally retarded and nonretarded adults' sensitivity to spatial structure. *American Journal of Mental Deficiency, 91*, 379–391.

Riguet, C., Taylor, N., Benaroya, S., & Klein, L. (1981). Symbolic play in autistic, Down's and normal children of equivalent mental age. *Journal of Autism and Developmental Disorders, 11*, 439–448.

Rogoff, B., Gauvain, M., & Gardner, W. (1987). Children's adjustment of plans to circumstances. In S. L. Friedman, E. K. Scholnick, & R. R. Cocking (Eds.), *Blueprints for thinking* (pp. 303–320). New York: Cambridge University Press.

Runeson, S., & Frykholm, G. (1986). Kinematic specification of gender and gender expression. In V. McCabe & G. J. Balzano (Eds.), *Event cognition: An ecological perspective* (pp. 259–274). Hillsdale, NJ: Lawrence Erlbaum Associates.

Schank, R. C. (1982). *Dynamic memory: A theory of learning in learning in computers and people*. New York: Cambridge University Press.

Schank, R. C., & Abelson, R. (1977). *Scripts, plans, goals, and understanding*. Hillsdale, NJ: Lawrence Erlbaum Associates.

Shaw, R. E., & Hazelett, W. M. (1986). Schema in cognition. In V. McCabe & G. J. Balzano (Eds.), *Event cognition: An ecological perspective* (pp. 45–58). Hillsdale, NJ: Lawrence Erlbaum Associates.

Sperber, R., & McCauley, C. (1984). Semantic processing efficiency in the mentally retarded. In P. H. Brooks, R. Sperber, & C. McCauley (Eds.), *Learning and cognition in the mentally retarded* (pp. 141–164). Hillsdale, NJ: Lawrence Erlbaum Associates.

Spitz, H. H., & Borys, S. V. (1984). Depth of search: How far can the retarded search through an internally represented problem space. In P. H. Brooks, R. Sperber, & C. McCauley (Eds.), *Learning and cognition in the mentally retarded* (pp. 333–358). Hillsdale, NJ: Lawrence Erlbaum Associates.

Turnure, J. E. (1985). Communication and cues in the functional cognition of the mentally retarded. In N. R. Ellis & N. W. Bray (Eds.), *International review of research in mental retardation* (Vol. 13, pp. 43–76). New York: Academic Press.

Watson, M. W., & Jackowitz, E. R. (1984). Agents and recipient objects in the development of early symbolic play. *Child Development, 55*, 1091–1097.

Weiss, B., Weisz, J. R., & Bromfield, R. (1986). Performance of retarded and nonretarded persons on information processing tasks: Further tests of the similar structure hypothesis. *Psychological Bulletin, 100*, 157–175.

Weisz, J. R., Yeates, K. O., & Zigler, E. (1982). Piagetian evidence and the developmental difference controversy. In E. Zigler & D. Balla (Eds.), *Mental retardation: The developmental difference controversy* (pp. 213–276). Hillsdale, NJ: Lawrence Erlbaum Associates.

Wertsch, J. (1979). From social interaction to higher psychological processes: A clarification and application of Vygotsky's theory. *Human Development, 22*, 1–22.

Wolf, D. (1982). Understanding others: A longitudinal case study of the concept of independent agency. In G. Forman (Ed.), *Action and thought: From sensori-motor schemas to symbolic operations*. New York: Academic Press.

26 An Ecological Framework for Ergonomic Research and Design

Leonard S. Mark, Marvin J. Dainoff, Robert Moritz, David Vogele
Center for Ergonomic Research
Miami University, Ohio

The project reported in this chapter began as an applied investigation of the postural requirements for sitting at video display terminals (VDTs). Our work has been driven by three fundamental propositions about the application of psychology to human factors/ergonomics. These propositions not only address some recent concerns that have been raised about the application of psychological research to the human factors/ergonomics enterprise (e.g., Meister, 1985; Rouse & Boff, 1987), but they may well lead to a more viable framework for ergonomic research. In short, they point to the efficacy of James Gibson's (1979) ecological framework for examining how perception guides action for addressing the needs of designers who want to optimize the *fit* between the users (specifically their action capabilities) and the environment.

However, before looking at the application of the ecological framework to the field of ergonomics, we will examine the importance of identifying appropriate postural objectives for people who work at computer terminals and the implications of ergonomic intervention for their health, well-being, and productivity. At the outset of our work there had been three different postural recommendations for these computer operators. In our view, the supposed "conflict" among these postural prescriptions results from the lack of a comprehensive framework for analyzing the act of sitting for prolonged periods.

The second part of the chapter outlines just such a comprehensive perspective on ergonomic research, beginning with our three propositions about the goals of the ergonomic enterprise. These objectives have encouraged us to re-examine the act of sitting, from the ecological perspective of James Gibson. Investigators of the coupling of perception and action, ergonomic researchers and designers share a common concern with the fit between people's actions and properties of the environment that are required to support these actions. Thus, developments in the ecological study of perceiving and acting bear on the interaction between ergonomic research and the design process. In the third section, we examine our research program which has exploited Gibson's seminal insights and has begun to elucidate postural requirements for sitting. Finally, we suggest that the principles of ecological psychology constitute a framework for ergonomic research and the design enterprise. In sum, seated posture: (a) entails rich and interesting research problems that integrate applied and basic science, in general, and psychology, in particular, and (b) is of considerable practical importance.

ERGONOMIC INTERVENTION IN THE WORKPLACE

Since the mid-1970s, computers have been the focal point for a drastic technological transformation of the workplace and the VDT has become a common part of the office environment. Associated with this change were a series of health problems, including eye strain, musculoskeletal disorders, and psychosocial stress.[1] From the outset, field studies of VDT operators have consistently found complaint levels of eyestrain and musculoskeletal disorders to be high on both an absolute (50%–90% incidence) and a relative scale in comparison with non-VDT operators doing comparable tasks (e.g., Smith, 1984).[2] Presumably, the causes were related to some physical aspect of the changed workplace which resulted from the introduction of the VDT. The geometry of the VDT workplace entailed new visual and postural demands on the operator, which, in turn, required new design considerations, that were largely neglected in the initial VDT installations. At the same time, psychosocial changes in work structure might have been sufficiently stressful to generate the same kinds of symptoms (Smith, 1984).

That ergonomic interventions can lead to substantial improvements in daily productivity has been substantiated in a series of laboratory studies (Dainoff, 1982) and field studies (Ong, 1984; Springer, 1982). Greico (1986) and Hettinger (1985) have further documented the physical and physiological complaints associated with VDT work for prolonged periods and delineated the connection between postural fixity and musculoskeletal disease. The recent findings of a 15-year field study (Spilling, Eitrheim, & Aaras, 1986; Westgaard & Aaras, 1985) have demonstrated a substantial reduction in health complaints and sick

---

[1]The concern, however, has not disappeared, but rather shifted to the area of extra low-frequency (ELF) electrical and magnetic fields. The area currently one of considerable controversy; however, at this writing no definitive health effects have been demonstrated. See Scallet (1987) for a recent review.

[2]We are concentrating here on posture. Visual concerns will be introduced only to the extent that they have an influence on posture, and vice versa. There are a whole class of issues related to vision and work in general, and the VDT in particular, which will not be dealt with here; such concern related to display characteristics, imaging, contrast enhancement, and visual deficits.

time with the introduction of adjustable ergonomic furniture. They reported that the introduction of this furniture resulted in significant savings to the company in the form of reduced employee turnover and sick leave; these savings resulted in a return of 851% on the original monetary investment in workplace redesign.

Our point is that ergonomic intervention can make a substantial difference both to workers, by decreasing the incidence of musculoskeletal and other complaints, and to employers, by increasing worker productivity and reducing the costs associated with health disorders. We contend that improving workstation design represents a worthwhile goal, which will enhance the quality of life. However, while manufacturers have rushed to produce adjustable chairs and workstations to meet these demands, little consideration has been given either to the working postures that must be facilitated or how the furniture should be used. There is considerable disagreement on specific details of the ergonomic goals, in particular the postural objectives that ergonomic furniture should support. People cannot take advantage of chairs in which backrest angle, seatpan angle, and seatpan height can be adjusted, unless appropriate postural objectives can be specified. We now turn to examine the controversy about seated posture that has emerged from the results of traditional (nonecological) biomechanical analyses and ergonomic research.

Postural Recommendations: The Cubist Approach and Its Challengers

In the various guidelines, standards, and recommendations that are the primary means of communication between the ergonomic and the design communities, seated posture has usually been conceptualized as "cubist" in nature (Fig. 26.1). That is, prescribed working postures can be abstractly represented by three cubes at right angles to one other: a head/trunk cube with its long axis normal to the floor, a high cube parallel to the floor, and a lower leg cube again normal to the floor. What results is the standard upright or 90-degree posture. Anthropometric differences are reflected by variation in cubic dimensions. The designer must be able to take these variations into account within the context of an upright posture.

The cubist conception was strongly challenged by Grandjean, Hunting, and Pidermann (1983). From their research findings, they argued that chairs for VDT workers ought to allow the individual to lean backward 15 degrees or more (Fig. 26.2a). Not only was this posture preferred by operators (compared with the upright posture), but it had the physiological advantage of reducing stress on the lower back. At the same time Grandjean et al. realized that the work surface would likewise need to be adjustable, since the operator's arms would now be elevated above the usual working height associated with an upright posture. Grandjean's proposal emphasizes the obvious but often neglected premise that chair design should not be considered independently of work surface design.

An alternative challenge to the cubist prescription was put forth by Mandal

FIG. 26.1.   A depiction of the 90-degree upright "cubist" seated working posture.

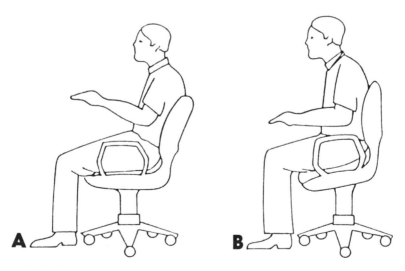

FIG. 26.2.   A depiction of two alternatives to the upright or "cubist" seated working posture. A: The backward tilt posture proposed by Grandjean; B: The forward tilt posture proposed by Mandal.

480

(1986). He argued that strain on the lower back might best be relieved by a seatpan that was tilted forward (Fig. 26.2b). His rationale for this unusual configuration was based on differences in spinal load between upright sitting and standing. For a person standing erect, the side view of the spine resembles an elongated "S" with a concavity in the lumbar region called a lordosis. When the individual moves to a 90-degree sitting posture, the pelvis, which is tilted forward in standing posture, rotates backward, and, as a consequence, the lumbar lordosis increased strain on spinal disks and muscles. By tilting the seatpan forward, the pelvis can rotate forward, thereby restoring the lordosis. Mandal's findings showed not only that people were quite willing to work in this posture, but that individuals with lower back pain reported alleviation of that pain with the forward tilt posture.

Thus, we see the standard "cubist" conception of office seating as being challenged by two seemingly contradictory approaches. Each appears to be reasonably well supported by biomechanical analyses as well as user acceptance. How does the designer decide which, if any, of these perspectives, to adopt?

We contend that to pose the question in terms of conflict between competing design solutions is likely to generate spurious debate because each prescription was formulated from a static biomechanical view of sitting that neglects both the dynamic nature of the act as it flows over time (Branton, 1976) as well as the task being performed (Dainoff & Mark, 1987); sitting is a dynamic activity in which extensive postural changes are required to remain "seated" for long periods of time (cf. also Mark, Vogele, Dainoff, Cone, & Lassen, 1985).

Research on seated posture has proceeded in the absence of a coherent framework within which physical attributes of people and their environment can be explicitly related to the behavioral acts required of those people. An integrated conception of seated posture is needed in which each person's behavioral, physiological, anatomical (postural), and biomechanical capabilities are examined with reference to properties of the work environment that are required to support those capabilities. At this point we turn to examine our three propositions about the field of ergonomics, which have led us to appreciate the efficacy of James Gibson's ecological framework for the ergonomic enterprise.

THE GOALS OF ERGONOMICS

What should be the goals of an applied psychology? In our view, the *sine qua non* of a truly applied psychology should be to provide useful information in aid of some *design* process. Design, here, is used in its broadest sense: People design environments for work, play, and living; they design tools, equipment, and furnishings to be used within those environments; and they design procedures and processes to be used by those inhabiting such environments. By this definition, virtually everyone participates in some kind of design activity—if only in the layout of one's own schedule of weekend errands or in the arrangement of one's apartment.

Within this context, the task of the applied psychologist is to provide information to the designer, such that the resulting design product is not only efficient (in that a given amount of work is accomplished with a relatively low expenditure of human energy and resources), but it enhances human values—health, safety, and quality of working life. Our first proposition, then, is a statement of mission: *Proposition 1: To be useful, applied psychology must be able to contribute to the design process.* Unfortunately, this ideal is but a promissory note. The actual problem of technology transfer—of extracting useful information from the precisely controlled but often unrealistic paradigms of the experimental researcher, in a form accessible to the "real world" with which the working designer must cope—has always been regarded as problematical. Indeed, the ongoing debate in the *Bulletin of the Human Factors Society*, spawned by Meister's (1985) criticisms of human factors research, highlights the mismatch between the needs of the designer and the existing research (Rouse & Boff, 1987). We contend that this disparity is at least partly the result of the human factors/ergonomic community's failure to address what we regard as the focus of ergonomics, namely the *fit* between people's goal-directed actions and their environment (Dainoff & Dainoff, 1986). This leads to our second proposition, a statement about how ergonomic research might contribute to the design process:

Proposition 2: To be of use to the design process, ergonomic research has to provide information about human action capabilities and the environmental properties required to support the performance of specific actions. The designer's task, broadly defined, is to build objects, environments, and systems, whose structures take into account the (physical and functional) capabilities and needs of prospective users. To meet the designer's objective, the task of the ergonomist must be directed toward the description (i.e., measurement) of the person–environment fit.

Our third proposition, which pertains to the requirements of any theoretical framework for guiding the course of ergonomic research: *Proposition 3: In order for any applied science to provide the requisite information for realizing the designers' objective, the theoretical framework must be directed toward the description (i.e., measurement) of the fit between people (specifically, their action capabilities) and their environment.* To generate such a description requires a theory of the *relationship* between people's action capabilities and those environmental properties needed to support those capabilities.

The traditional cognitive approach to human factors focuses on people's perceptual-cognitive-motor capabilities. Each process is studied independently not only from other psychological processes, but from the environment to which they are directed. Difficulties arise when investigators attempt to relate those psychological processes to particular situations. Traditional psychological theories lack a theory of context. Hence, the applicability of principles of cognitive functioning to various situations is often unclear. It is to this point that, we believe, recent criticisms of the human factors/ergonomic research are rooted. It is our view that the ecological approach of James Gibson (1979) provides the appropriate theoretical framework for not only understanding basic action capability/environmental property relationship, but also for providing a pragmatically useful language that will allow these relationships to be directly translated into design implications.

TOWARD AN ECOLOGICAL FRAMEWORK
FOR ERGONOMIC RESEARCH

The problem confronting the field of ergonomics is, in essence, the same problem to which James Gibson's ecological framework for understanding the coupling of perception and action is directed. Ecological psychologists have recognized that the performance of commonplace actions, such as reaching, grasping, climbing, or sitting, depends critically on the actor's ability to perceive properties of the world relevant to the desired mode of action (Warren, 1984). To catch a baseball, for example, a fielder has to know about the flight of the ball in order to determine whether it is necessary to move forwards or backwards, left or right, how fast those movements must be executed, and where to place the glove in order to intercept the trajectory of the ball. Similarly, a person looking for something to sit on (say, for reading a book) has to determine whether a surface can support her body weight as well as whether the height, size, and contour of the surface will permit him or her to reach and maintain a stable, comfortable seated posture. As an information-gathering act, perception keeps a person apprised of the arrangement of surfaces (or layout) of the environment, one's own movement, and, most importantly, their relationship to the environment.

The ability to perform these actions varies as a consequence of each person's body size, proportions, and biomechanical capabilities. The maximum height of a surface that can be climbed on bipedally, for example, is a function of the size of relevant dimensions of the actor's body (e.g., leg length) and biomechanical potentials (e.g., joint mobility). For each person, there is a maximum stair riser height beyond which a switch from a bipedal to a quadrupedal climbing mode is required. Thus, an action has to be designed to fit the existing layout of the environment. To function in the world, actors have to perceive those environmental properties, such as riser height, that are needed to support their action capabilities.

Constraints on Action

Of course, there are constraints on the possible kinds of actions that an individual can perform. Ecological psychologists have identified two types of constraints: *geometrical* and *kinetic* (Mark & Vogele, 1987). Geometrical constraints emerge from the relationship of the actor's body size to the size or scale of those aspects of the environment that are involved in performing the action. For instance, the actor's leg length establishes a limit on the maximum height of surfaces that can be sat upon as well as an important restriction on the optimal height (requiring minimum expenditure of energy) of surfaces for that person to sit on. The actions permitted by the environment are also determined by kinetic variables, such as mass, force, friction, and elasticity. These variables constrain the metabolic exchange of energy between the actor and environment. In the case of sitting, the material properties of the surface must be able to support the actor's mass, and the actor must have sufficient joint mobility to make the movements needed to sit on the particular surface.

While the geometrical and kinetic constraints establish boundaries on the actor's capabilities, the *task* itself determines which of the many possible actions is actually performed. In the case of sitting, the task (reading, eating, data entry, editing) constrains the postures that the chair must facilitate. Together, the geometrical, kinetic, and task constraints determine both the possible and the optimal physiological, postural, and biomechanical states for performing a task.

Affordances and Effectivities

Since the performance of coordinated, goal-directed actions requires that individuals tailor their actions to the environmental layout, actors need information about whether that layout meets their specific needs for performing an action. In the case of vision, Gibson proposed that this information does not have to be inferred or computed mentally, but is available in the optical field surrounding each person. Actors need only detect certain optical relationships to determine whether relevant properties of their environment will satisfy their specific action requirements (Gibson, 1979; Mark, 1987; Warren, 1984; Waren & Whang, 1987). Gibson introduced the concept of an *affordance* to refer to the properties of an object/environment/system taken with reference to an individual's action capabilities and goals. In order to determine whether a given arrangement of surfaces affords sitting on, each person has to perceive properties of surfaces relative to the geometrical, kinetic, and task constraints on their action.

Whereas affordances entail a perspective on the environment relative to the actor's capabilities, a complementary perspective on the person–environment fit views an individual's action capabilities with reference to the environment. The concept of an *effectivity* (Turvey & Shaw, 1978) refers to those goal-directed actions that a person can perform within a particular environment. Taken together, geometrical, kinetic, and task constraints constitute a description of a person's effectivities, which have to be considered in the design of affordances for a given action. Geometrical and kinetic constraints are intrinsic to physical properties of the actor and can be directly measured/calculated with respect to an external frame of reference (i.e., height, weight). Task constraints are more functional and "psychological." They include all of the intentional, goal-directed considerations that encourage the person to perform one action rather than another.

For our purposes it is important to distinguish two aspects of a person's effectivities (E. Gibson, 1988). The first is a *performatory* aspect, which refers to actions performed on the environment (e.g., climbing a flight of stairs, grasping an apple, or kicking a football). To take a simple, though nontrivial example in the domain of seating, a seat surface of a given height above the ground is, from the affordance persective, an object which may afford "sitting upon" in an upright postural orientation, that is with the legs straight and the feet flat on the ground. The qualifying "may" in this statement refers to the need to consider simultaneously a relevant effectivity, namely that unless the individual's lower leg length (more properly, popliteal height) is equal to the seat height, the upright posture, in its strict definition, cannot obtain.

A second important aspect of effectivities concerns people's capacities for *exploring* the environment in order to pick up on information about what is afforded. James and Eleanor Gibson have frequently pointed out that the information specifying the affordances of a given environment is usually not specified at a glance, that is, in a static snapshot of the world (E. Gibson, 1988; J. Gibson, 1979). Often the requisite visual information for guiding action is revealed only in the optical disturbances resulting from the actor's movements through the environment. Prior to performing an act on the environment, the individual has to explore the affordances of the environment.

Exploration, then, is prerequisite to the perception of the affordances of the environment. In talking about a person's effectivities, we are dealing with an intentional, goal-directed individual, someone who has a particular need state and intent to act. The performance of a goal-directed activity requires the exploration of the affordances of the environment to ascertain which environmental properties will support the realization of the goal-directed activity.

The affordance of a given environment can change with the needs and state of the actor. The latter point is especially important to consider in the context of sitting for prolonged periods, where fatigue increases over time. As a result, postures that were comfortable earlier in the day may no longer permit the individual to work in comfort later on.

Our third proposition emphasized the need for a theoretical framework focusing on the fit between actor and environment. In this regard, affordances and effectivities are complementary components of that fit. A perceiver is really a designer of actions that are tailored to the existing layout of the environment. A designer, on the other hand, is faced with the complementary problem of building objects (i.e., designing affordances) that will fit or support the user's action capabilities (effectivities). In service of the design enterprise, the goal of ergonomic research must be to inform designers about the human user's action capabilities, together with the environmental properties required to optimally support those capabilities. Another goal, no less important, is to understand how users *explore* the affordances of the designed object or system in order to facilitate the requisite exploratory behavior.

The challenge, then, is to describe the fit between the user's capabilities and those properties of the environment required to support an activity. Gibson's ecological framework (for the confluence of perceiving and acting) has focused our efforts on delineating those affordances and effectivities associated with the act of sitting for prolonged periods.

However, before looking at these efforts, it is important to lay some groundwork. Our goal is to examine the mutuality of affordances and effectivities in the regulation of posture. We begin with a surface that provides the minimal affordance for sitting. Next, we examine the problems facing a sitter in maintaining a stable, seated posture under those affordances. Finally, we progressively add affordances (design a series of chairs) to approach optimal support for the act of sitting.

Building (Designing) Affordances for Sitting

Imagine that you are sitting (balancing) on the edge of a high, solid, flat surface, such as a physician's examining table. This situation embodies the minimal affordance for sitting: Most of your weight is supported by a pair of inverted pyramids, the pelvic structures known as ischial tuberosities. The resulting posture is fairly unstable. As your body moves, you attempt to locate that limited region around the base of support in which the posture is stable (i.e., uncontrolled movements are minimized) and beyond which the seated posture can only be sustained by making active postural adjustments. The boundary of this region is signaled by the perception of increased pressure toward the edges of the buttocks (Riccio & Stoffregen, 1988). In this situation most people would place their arms and hands on the support surface, using them as braces to increase the base of support. If the critical boundary of this region is violated, the posture can still be maintained by some muscular activity. For a person without arms, most of the motor activity needed to maintain the seated posture would be produced by muscles of the lower back and abdomen; at the very least, it would be tiring to maintain the requisite degree of control for more than a brief period of time. Even for people who can use arms to maintain stability of this seated posture, the posture can be quite uncomfortable to maintain because of the discomfort that accompanies the pressure on the pelvic structures. What can be done, then, to build up the affordances for sitting?

One possibility is to increase the area of the support surface (i.e., seatpan), thereby permitting the actor to increase the base of support to include the upper legs (thighs). To be sure, this is a significant advance because the posture becomes far more stable and quite a bit easier to maintain. Under these conditions, people tend to lean their upper body slightly forward in order to move their center of gravity toward the middle of this larger base of support. This forward-leaning tendency (not to be confused with Mandal's forward tilt) often results in a rounded back with a highly undesirable kyphosis (the reverse of lordosis) of the spine. Over time, the effects of blood pooling in the lower legs as well as constriction of blood flow in the thighs (ischemia), due to pressure on the thighs, result in fatigue and discomfort. To relieve the discomfort, people begin to squirm about. (Over a period of months, these conditions can lead to significant health hazards.) Although it would be difficult to offer a precise description of the optimal posture under this set of affordances, the fatigue which builds in the legs, thighs, pelvis, and back over time effectively changes what would be the optimal posture. Thus, as a result of changes in the actor's effectivities (resulting from fatigue), the affordances of the support surface (for the actor) change over time.

So far, this exercise has revealed the existence of an important tradeoff between (the presence or absence of) affordances and the amount of postural regulation needed to maintain a stable posture. The absence of appropriate affordances places significant demands on the actor's (motor) resources in order to maintain a stable posture. As the affordance structure of the environment is built up, those demands on the actor diminish, since the affordances provide support for more efficient actions for maintaining a stable posture. Moreover, the postures afforded expand the tasks that can be performed.

Although we can still build new affordances, any seated posture, even with the support of the best chair, can, over time, take a serious toll on the actor. Branton's (1976) study of riders on the English rail system provides an important illustration. In monitoring the posture of people sitting on hard, upright seats, Branton observed that the seat seemed to "eject" the person at roughly 25-minute intervals. Throughout that period, people slid out of their chairs until the posture was sufficiently unstable that people had to right themselves. Similarly, Mark et al. (1985) have shown that even under "optimal" working conditions people who sit for prolonged periods will assume more than one posture. For this reason, we believe that *there is no single optimal posture*, an idea that we will return to later.

Let us continue designing affordances for seated posture. Having enlarged the seatpan, we might now add a backrest to our seat, perhaps one with a lumbar support that will promote spinal lordosis, which we noted earlier is highly desirable. Initially, we will assume that the backrest is perpendicular to the seatpan and the ground plane, much like the cubist model of seated posture described earlier. Although the backrest adds to the stability of the resultant posture (i.e., minimizes uncontrolled movements), at best, it provides only a slight reduction of the pressure on the supporting thighs and pelvis.

At this point we can make a significant addition to the affordances of the seat by making the seatpan and backrest angles adjustable. The seat now affords leaning backward, as Grandjean recommends. Stability has increased even further, since this posture cradles the torso in a bucket-like structure. While this posture has important benefits as noted earlier, as with any posture, fatigue of the supporting body parts still develops, though perhaps more slowly. Indeed, any of the three postural prescriptions (upright, backward lean, even Mandal's forward tilt) discussed earlier are initially stable; time, however, is the enemy of postural stability in sitting because certain body parts have to bear a substantial load, which eventually produces fatigue, discomfort, or worse.

How, then, do we reconcile the debate among alternate postural recommendations? Remember that postural control entails three sources of constraints. Our discussion of seated posture to this point has addressed only two: the actor and the environment. For us, the crucial insight to the problem of specifying appropriate seated posture came when we realized that virtually all prescriptions of seated posture, to date, have neglected task contraints (i.e., goal of sitting). Similarly, the affordances which we are trying to specify are clearly task-dependent.

To appreciate why this is the case, imagine that we provide a seat with an adjustable seatpan and backrest. This chair affords any of the stable postures we have identified to this point and more. The posture that an actor should assume depends on what the actor wants to do. Working at a VDT constrains the number of possible seated postures by requiring certain head and finger orientations with respect to the keyboard and monitor. However, there are important task differences even within the general category "VDT work." In data entry tasks, for example, the operator must typically execute very rapid keying movements while focusing visually on paper copy. These combined visual-motor demands tightly constrain the positions of head and fingers.

The Mandal forward-tilting chair would seem to provide an effective solution, given this particular set of constraints. A stable support surface is provided which maximizes the precise finger–key and eye–screen–copy relationships needed for efficient work; at the same time it minimizes the load on the lumbar spine. However, there is a physiological cost associated with a forward tilt, namely increased pressure and blood pooling in the lower legs. While this condition is tolerable for short periods, movement eventually becomes necessary, thereby leading to a decrease in stability.

On the other hand, consider an editing task, such as an operator having to search for errors in a manuscript. Now, most of the visual attention is devoted to the screen with a marked reduction in keying requirements. The Mandal posture might still be appropriate here. However, since type size on typical VDT monitors tends to be roughly 50% larger than print on paper, the operator could tolerate a greater viewing distance than was true for the case of data entry. Therefore, the Grandjean backward-leaning posture would also be appropriate and would have the additional benefit of allowing postural change when the operator shifts from one task to another. Our point is that each of these postures may well approximate the optimal working posture for a particular task. For a person working at a VDT, the optimal posture is changing over time. The actor has to accommodate his or her posture to those changes and, if necessary, change tasks (though we recognize this is not always possible).

The Degree-of-freedom Problem

In concluding this exercise, let us take stock of the chair, whose affordances we have just constructed. This chair has two adjustable dimensions: seatpan angle and backrest angle. In practice, we would also have to allow seatpan height and backrest height to be adjustable in order to accommodate people of different sizes and proportions. Thus, our state-of-the-art ergonomic chair now has 4 degrees of freedom. (Ergonomic chairs currently available have as many as 10 degrees of freedom.) Such chairs are highly complicated tools that can be difficult to use effectively because of the number of independent adjustments that have to be made. Therefore, such chairs are useful only insofar as people can learn to take advantage of those adjustable dimensions. Not only is there the mechanical problem of simply learning how to work the controls, but the user has to determine what posture to adjust the chair to. Most state-of-the-art ergonomic chairs come with instruction manuals that address the first problem, but ignore the latter. As ergonomists, it behooves us to suggest a strategy for facilitating the use of these chairs. This goal is particularly important in view of the compelling evidence from the field that most users simply do not take advantage of the adjustability available in state-of-the-art ergonomic chairs (e.g., Oman, 1988).

Our approach to this strategy is to view seated posture as an example of the classic "degrees of freedom" problem (Bernstein, 1967), in which the user must control (adjust) a number of independent chair dimensions.[3] We have, in the previous discussion, argued that degrees of freedom have to be added in order to improve the flexibility of the system in coping with a variable environment. However, each independent degree of freedom has a (cognitive) cost associated with the processing required for its control. At some point, the cognitive overload will be such that the user will simply ignore the adjustment (cf. Oman, 1988). The solution is to find some way of constraining or linking degrees of freedom. We have considered two approaches: physical linkages between adjustable surfaces and cognitive constraints through training.

Consider the chair we designed in the previous exercise. Each of the four dimensions—seatpan angle, backrest angle, backrest height, and seatpan

---

[3]The degrees of freedom (df) of any system is given in terms of the number of elements in the system (N), the dimensionality of the system (D) and the number of equations of constraint (C): df = ND – C. Take a chair with an adjustable seatpan angle, seatpan height, backrest angle, and backrest height. There are four adjustable elements in this system ($N = 4$), each requiring one coordinate (piece of information) to establish its value. Unfortunately, there are no equations of constraint linking the value of one or more elements to one another. Thus, there are 4 degrees of freedom.

height—are not only independent, but they require an *act* of adjustment by the user (operations of push button or lever) to be moved from one orientation to another. Once in position, they remain *fixed* in orientation.

How could this 4-degrees-of-freedom system be physically constrained. One approach utilized by some chair manufacturers is to, in effect, write an equation of constraint between two of these dimensions—seatpan angle and backrest angle—such that the latter is linked to the former in some ratio: typically 2 : 1 or 3 : 1. The result is that 4 degrees of freedom have been reduced to 3.

A second approach, which usually is associated with the first, is to unlock the adjustment mechanisms, thereby, allowing the seat surfaces to move or "float" with movements of the body. In this *dynamic* mode of adjustment control, the user's control of his or her posture "automatically" constrains the orientation of seatpan and backrest (possibly within the additional constraint of the mechanical linkage that has been described).[4]

There are problems associated with each of these approaches. The current physical linkage ratios between seatpan and backrest angles on commercially available chairs appear to be based on informal design rules of thumb, rather than on scientific principles. In fact, unpublished data from our laboratory suggest that users prefer seatpan–backrest angle ratios that are rather different from the 1 : 2, 1 : 3 range typically provided. In effect, the designers' equation of constraint between seatpan and backrest does not appear to match the users' equation of constraint between trunk and thigh. Similarly, in providing a dynamic adjustment, the designer assumes that the physical characteristics of the chairs motion capability (stiffness, spring constant) will simultaneously afford ease of movement from origin to destination *and* support once destination is attained. As will be seen later, our own research leads us to question this assumption.

A very different strategy for addressing the degrees of freedom problem focuses on the development of *short training programs* for prospective users. As has been stated, *cognitive* constraints are established when users are familiar not only with how the mechanical adjustments are carried out, but, more importantly, why they should be used, and in what combination. (For example, to move into the forward tilt posture, the seatpan and backrest should be moved forward and the seat height should be raised.) Ideally, such training should provide a series of suggested comfort zones/attractors (e.g., forward tilt for data entry; backward tilt for editing), as well as instruct/encourage exploration of the work space so that user can discover his or her individual attractors. This approach, in which training becomes an integral part of the design process, is

---

[4]The situation is actually more complicated. Within the dynamic mode of adjustability, there are actually—at present-two possibilities. The seatpan and backrest can either move independently, or they can be linked by some mechanism such that for every degree of rotation of seatpan, the backrest moves some (typically greater) amount. Presently, a ratio of one to three seems to be standard. The Discovery chair model used in this study had independent linkage, and discussion will be limited to this case.

congruent with a broader perspective on system design in which training becomes an integral part of the design process (Boies, Gould, Levy, Richards, & Schoonard, 1985).

Summary of Our Ecological Perspective on Ergonomics

To recapitulate, our theoretical perspective has led us to specify certain characteristics that must be taken into account in thinking about seated work posture. These include: task demands, postural orientations that will minimize energy expenditure, changes in position that are needed to alleviate fatigue, and, overlaying much of these factors, anthropometric differences among individuals. Designers must build sets of affordances that complement these characteristics, thereby accommodating the user's action capabilities. In the case of chair design, these *affordances* would entail a chair in which the range of adjustability of seatpan angle (forward and back), seatpan height, backrest angle, and backrest height are sufficient to allow a large variety of individuals (i.e., 5th percentile female through 95th percentile male) to attain comfortable alternative postures, such as Mandal's forward lean or Grandjean's backward lean. This ergonomic chair must afford task-specific/task-dependent postures, while, at the same time, facilitating movement as the sitter shifts from one task to another or has to make minor postural adjustments. In light of these design objectives, an ergonomic research program that focuses on the relation between affordances and the users' action capabilities should be of direct benefit to the design community.

Each of these factors has had a direct impact on the experimental design and methods which we have developed to investigate the problem of seated posture at a VDT workstation: (a) The postural requirements of different tasks (e.g., data entry vs. editing) become an integral part of the experimental design. (b) Tasks must be performed for significant periods of time (at least 3 hours, usually several days) in order to examine movements and transitions from one stable posture to another. (c) An ergonomic chair that affords alternation between forward- and backward-leaning postures as well as height adjustability must be used. (d) All participants must be instructed not only in the workings of the chair mechanism, but also in the physiological rationale for forward and backward postures and the tasks for which they might be used most effectively. Our own research has been designed within this perspective and it is to these efforts that we now turn.

ECOLOGICAL RESEARCH ON SEATED POSTURE WHILE WORKING AT A VDT

Our investigation of seated posture has utilized certain theoretical formalisms that have been borrowed from dynamic systems theory (Abraham & Shaw, 1982). These formalisms have provided an analytical framework for our own work as well as recent studies of coordinated movement (Kugler & Turvey, 1987) and postural regulation (Riccio & Stoffregen, 1988). In view of their increasing impact on ecological investigations of motor control, we will briefly identify the concepts of a configuration space and an attractor as they bear on seating research.

Given a chair with adjustable seatpan and backrest surfaces, and assuming height to be constant, we can, to a first approximation, describe specific postural configurations in terms of a particular combination of seatpan and backrest angles. A three-dimensional plot of seatpan against backrest angle on the X and Y axes and dwell time per configuration on the Z axis defines a *configuration space*. At any given point in time, we can define a region within the configuration space where posture is stable, as evidenced by high levels of dwell time. This region represents an optimal zone or *attractor* in which there is a (temporary) state of biomechanical balance and the energy expended in maintaining posture is minimized (Kugler & Turvey, 1987). If posture is perturbed away from the attractor (say, by some external disturbance), an active movement or set of movements can be generated to return the actor to the attractor.

Since any fixed posture will generate fatigue, all (postural) attractors are necessarily temporary. Nevertheless, we belive that there are a limited number of attractors in the configuration space for seated posture, each of which is specific to the task constraints, properties of the environment (e.g., affordances of the seat) and action capabilities of the individual.

Study 1: Task Affordances of Forward- and Backward-leaning Postures

Our first step was to examine the proposal that different optimal postures afford performance of different tasks. Explicit in this proposal is the assumption that the operator is trained to coordinate the adjustments of 3 degrees of freedom in the chair—seatpan angle, backrest angle, and seat height—so as to achieve optimal posture. In this study the chair was kept in the fixed mode of operation. Ten trained clerical workers worked 3 hours per day for 5 days, alternating between data entry and editing tasks at 30-minute intervals. The first day (Day 0) was devoted to training and practice on the tasks. On each of the subsequent 4 days (Days 1–4), operators alternated between tasks for a total of 3 hours without breaks. An incentive pay system was employed which emphasized speed but penalized errors. Ratings of subjective discomfort were obtained by having operators complete a questionnaire both before and after each 30-minute period. All sessions were videotaped.

The entry task required operators to type in alphanumeric characters from a page of paper copy in response to prompts from the screen. Since the operators were skilled typists (at least 50 words per minute), the task involved high-speed keying with visual attention focused on the relatively small characters (height =

0.32 cm) of the printed copy. Under these conditions, the forward leaning posture should be most effective at relatively short viewing distances; this brings the fingers into close proximity to the keyboard, keeping the wrist flat, the forearm at a right angle to the upper arms, and rotates the lumbar spine in lordosis.

The editing tasks used the same copy format as the entry task, but, in this case, all files were displayed in pairs on the screen. Operators were required to compare similar fields and to make a same/different judgment by pressing one of two keys after scanning each screen display. For this task, the keying demands were minimal while the operators' visual attention was on the larger characters on the screen (height = 0.67 cm). Under these conditions, operators might tolerate a longer viewing distance, and more awkward orientation of fingers with respect to keyboard in favor of the direct support of the back afforded by backward tilt.

A videotaped instructional sequence suggested to operators that the forward tilt posture was most effective for an entry task, while a backward tilt was most effective for editing. They were shown (and practiced) how to get the chair into these positions, including raising the seatpan when going into forward tilt and lowering it in rearward tilt. However, the training program also emphasized that these were "theoretical" suggestions and that they were free to assume whatever postures felt most comfortable.

By digitizing significant landmarks from the videotaped records of each session, we were able to establish chair and body orientations throughout the sessions. The results of these analyses indicated that, throughout 12 hours of repetitive work, operators preferred to use the forward tilt orientation for entry and the backward tilt for editing. Table 26.1 shows the means and standard deviations, averaged across all sessions. Since typical nonadjustable office chairs have a fixed backward tilt of roughly 3 degrees, the amount of forward tilt

TABLE 26.1
Mean Values (in degrees) of Seatpan and Backrest
Angle and Seatpan Height (in centimeters)

Task	Seatpan angle
Entry	−3.65 (4.29)
Edit	4.57 (2.60)
	Backrest angle to vertical
Entry	0.24 (2.66)
Edit	7.76 (3.16)
	Seatpan height
Entry	49.98 (2.79)
Edit	47.12 (2.08)

Standard deviations are indicated in parentheses.
Data from Dainoff & Mark (1987).

observed in this study is almost 7 degrees from the typical seatpan orientation. Furthermore, as instructed, operators also adjusted the seatpan height to a higher level in the entry task than in editing.

Analysis of the discomfort questionnaires presented an interesting pattern of results. As expected, the operators expressed higher levels of discomfort as each daily session progressed. More importantly, for both the entry and editing tasks, the average discomfort level progressively *decreased* as the week progressed. This finding is consistent with operators' comments that the chair felt more comfortable as they became more familiar with its operations. There was no difference in complaints between entry and edit conditions. These results are especially significant in view of the fact that subjective fatigue usually increases across days (e.g., Alluisi & Morgan, 1982).

The results of this study provide at least initial support for the proposed link between task demands and postural orientations. The operators were willing to follow our instructions and adjust the chair to a position that is optimal for the task at hand. Moreover, the lack of a difference in discomfort scores between the two conditions argued against the view taken by some critics, who hold that forward tilt puts excessive pressure on the lower legs (Bendix, Winkel, & Jessen, 1985).

Of course, it is tempting to attribute the results of this study to demand characteristics. That is, the operators were doing what we told them to do simply because they were following instructions, and not because the recommended postures were actually more effective. We do not find this objection compelling. Operators were working at a (rather generous) incentive pay rate. To argue a strict demand characteristic explanation, one would have to suggest that our operators were willing to tolerate 12 hours of work under uncomfortable conditions simply because we told them to—this despite the fact that we clearly gave them permission to adopt other postures. While we might have run a control condition, in which operators were given no instructions, the experience of those in the furniture industry indicates that it is not necessary to conduct a controlled experiment to discover that people will not adjust ergonomic furniture if they are not taught how and why (see, for example, Oman, 1988). The outcome of a later study, however, provides even stronger evidence against the demand characteristic argument.

With respect to our ecological model of seated posture, then, the outcome of this study highlights the importance of task constraints on seated posture. Analyses of seated posture have to consider the task employed; the failure of past researchers (and standards writers) to pay attention to this constraint is a serious omission. Furthermore, operators' comfort ratings indicate that switching between tasks and consequently assuming different postures over time may well have significant benefits to workers who are required to sit for long periods. Still, training is clearly required in order for people to exploit the affordances of these ergonomic chairs.

Study 2: The Dynamic Mode of Chair Operation

During the previous experiment, chair adjustment was limited to the *fixed* mode. That is, in order to change any of the three adjustments from one position to another, the operator had to depress a push button and hold it while moving to the desired orientation. The push button was then released and the surface remained rigid until the control was again activated. For any major postural change (e.g., moving from forward to backward tilt or vice versa), the operator is required to manipulate 3 degrees of freedom. However, in the chair's *dynamic* mode, the degrees of freedom are reduced. Both seatpan and backrest float so that their angular position changes automatically as the body shifts. Thus, the only fixed adjustment which is required is that of seatpan height. Accordingly, we designed a replication of the previous study in which the chair was placed into the dynamic mode of operation.

Six operators worked at the same entry and editing task 3 hours per day for 4 days. For practical reasons, the operating schedule was slightly modified in that operators worked each day for two 90-minute sessions (rather than four, 30-minute sessions), and the training period was held earlier on the first day rather than on a separate day. The training instructions were modified to reflect the absence of fixed controls for seatpan and backrest angles.

Another change from the previous study concerned the height of the keyboard support surface. In the previous study, keyboard as well as monitor support surfaces were independently adjustable. While these additional degrees of freedom had been explained to operators, they were not emphasized   in terms of physiological rationale—to the same degree as were the seat controls. In Study 1 these surfaces were initially set to a standard height (30 in.) by the experimenter and rarely if ever changed by the operators. In the current study, the adjustable keyboard surface was initially set to a height such that, for each operator, the seatpan (angle) would be at its maximum forward tilt when the forearms were parallel to the floor and the feet flat on the floor. For any seatpan inclination less than maximum forward, the operator's feet would be off the floor. In order to maintain foot contact, an adjustable footrest was provided, along with instructions for its use. Operators were not informed about the seatpan height control, but were expected to use the footrest to compensate.

Finally, in Study 2, we were able to achieve a much finer grain of analysis through the use of potentiometers attached to each of the three control surfaces, seatpan angle, height, and backrest angle. Thus, each operator's orientation in three dimensions could be continuously tracked throughout the session. To depict the postural configurations assumed in this study of seated posture in the dynamic mode, we have constructed configuration spaces for the Entry and Editing tasks, which are depicted in Fig. 26.3.

The collective outcomes of the two tasks are striking. Backrest angles ranged from −3 to +30 degrees, while the seatpan angle ranged from −5 to +7 degrees.

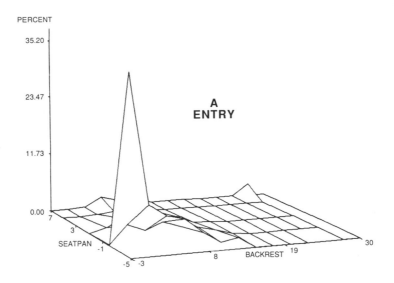

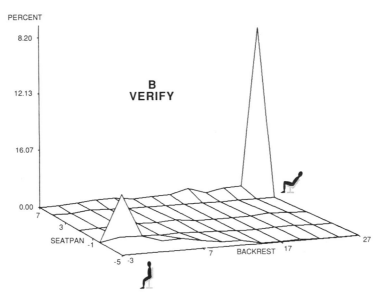

FIG. 26.3.   Configuration space describing the results of Study 2. Abscissa
indicates degrees of backrest angle from the vertical. Negative values are
forward of vertical. Ordinate indicates degrees of seatpan angle from the
horizontal. Negative values represent forward tilt. Z axis represents mean
time per position as assessed by potentiometer readings. A: Entry task; B:
Editing task.

The Z axis depicts the *amount of time* operators worked at each orientation. The resulting configuration spaces reveal that under this particular set of dynamic affordances, operators tended to avoid most of the range of adjustability provided by the chair, and remain only at the most extreme positions, that is, extreme forward tilt for the Entry task and extreme backward tilt for the Editing task. Operators' comments support this assessment. They reported feeling unstable at any posture other than the extremes, in which case the chair is resting against its limit stops.

Study 2 represents our first attempt to describe research results in terms of configuration space analysis. Within that framework, it seems quite reasonable to argue that we have defined two distinct attractors, each of which reflects specific postural constraints (affordances) inherent in the combination of task demands and instructions. Operators virtually abandoned the remainder of the available postural configuration space. This result is not surprising in view of their reported feelings of instability in the dynamic mode. These subjective comments were in clear contrast to the almost universally favorable attitudes toward the same chair in fixed mode during Study 1. Thus, although the outcomes of both studies were superficially similar (forward tilt used in entry task, backward tilt used in editing task), there were definite indications that postural configurations might differ between fixed and dynamic modes of adjustability. Since Studies 1 and 2 were not strictly comparable because work surface height was adjustable only in Study 1, the next logical step was a factorial experiment in which fixed and dynamic modes of adjustability were examined under identical conditions.

Study 3: The Search for Stability

The third study followed the same basic procedures described previously. However, in this case, a four-way, within-operators design was employed. The two independent variables were Task (Edit/Entry) and Mode of Adjustability (Fixed/Dynamic). Twelve operators, whose typing speed was at least 20 words per minute, worked for 180-minute sessions on 2 separate days, alternating between 90-minute sessions of Entry and Editing. The Entry task, in this case, was simply manuscript typing using a standard word-processing package; the Editing task involved a search of that same manuscript for flagged spelling errors. A training session, similar to those in earlier studies, was held on the day preceding the start of the study.

While several dependent measures were employed, the only ones that have been analyzed at this writing were the measurements of chair position obtained from potentiometers mounted to the chair. Table 26.2 contains the mean values of seatpan angle from horizonatal, backrest angle from vertical, and seatpan height weighted by time in position.

The data for the Fixed condition showed a similar pattern to that obtained in

TABLE 26.2
Mean Values of Seatpan and Backrest Angle and Seatpan Height.
Weighted by Time in Position at Each of 4 Experimental Conditions

| | Task (T) | | |
Mode (M)	Entry	Edit	Significant Effects
	Seatpan angle		
Fixed	−3.67 (3.31)	7.90 (0.46)	T, M, T*M
Dynamic	2.92 (3.69)	7.95 (0.21)	
	Backrest angle to vertical		
Fixed	1.94 (4.90)	16.62 (5.41)	T
Dynamic	2.42 (3.75)	15.14 (4.34)	
	Seatpan height		
Fixed	52.75 (0.96)	46.18 (1.20)	T
Dynamic	51.74 (1.43)	47.03 (1.17)	

Standard deviations are indicated in parentheses. Also indicated as
statistically main effects and interaction terms ($p < .05$).
Results from Moritz (1988).

Study 1. A forward tilt (seatpan angle = −3.68 degrees; backrest angle = 1.94
degrees) was used as the average posture for the copy-intensive entry task,
whereas backwards tilt (seatpan angle = 7.90 degrees; backrest angle = 16.62
degrees) was the average posture for the screen-intensive Editing task. However,
the postural configurations observed under the Dynamic condition were quite
different from those observed in either of the previous studies. In the Entry task,
operators *rejected* our advice and assumed a posture that on average (seatpan
angle = 2.92 degrees; backrest angle = 2.42 degrees) was very close to the
90-degree cubist position. (Since our instructions did not even mention this
posture as a desired alternative, this result provides an indication that operators
were not simply responding to task demands.) It was only in the Editing task that
the average posture conformed with the backward tilt observed in previous
studies and recommended in the training session (seatpan angle = 7.96 degrees;
backrest angle = 15.14 degrees). In both Studies 1 and 3, operators set the height
of the seatpan higher for entry than for editing, though the absolute difference
was less in Study 3 (0.51 vs. 1.43 cm).

As a whole, then, the primary inconsistency among the three studies seems to
be in the dynamic mode-Entry task combination. Operators reported feeling
particularly unstable in this condition, using terms such as "rocking horse" and
"seasick." Accordingly, a more sophisticated analysis was attempted. By plotting seatpan angle against backrest angle, as we did in Study 2, we attempted to
define a configuration space analogous to that of Riccio and Stoffregen (1988)

discussed earlier. Figures 26.4 and 26.5 describe this postural configuration space, and what follows is a description of how those spaces were constructed. Initially, we defined four configuration spaces—one per experimental condition—for each operator at each value of seatpan height. For each configuration space, we know both the amount of time spent at each seatpan-by-backrest orientation as well as the number of times the operator moved into that orientation. To obtain a metric for stability, we simply divided time per position by frequency. This stability metric now constitutes the Z-axis of the configuration space.

There still remains the problem that different operators spent different amounts of time at different heights. What we needed was a principled method of integrating seatpan height into the space, without computing separate spaces for each height. In ergonomic design it is generally assumed (e.g., Kroemer & Price, 1982) that the height of an adjustable seatpan is determined by the operator's popliteal height, the distance between the ground and the back of the knee while sitting upright. However, in field studies, Sauter and Arndt (1986) have found that seatpan heights tended to be adjusted higher than popliteal heights—presumably, in order to bring the fingers in closer register with the

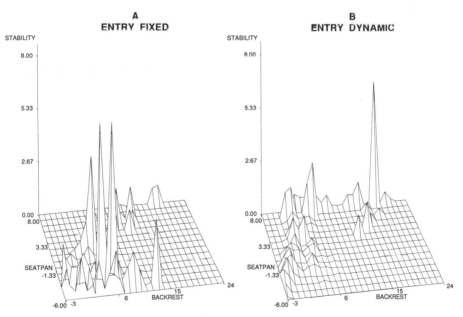

FIG. 26.4. Configuration space describing the results of Study 3. Abscissa indicates degrees of backrest angle from the vertical. Negative values are forward of vertical. Ordinate indicates degrees of seatpan angle from the horizontal. Negative values represent forward tilt. Z axis represents mean normalized stability measures (time in position/frequency) while performing the Entry task. A: Fixed mode of adjustability; popliteal ratios 1.13–1.16. B: Dynamic mode of adjustability; popliteal ratios 1.11–1.15 (Moritz, 1988).

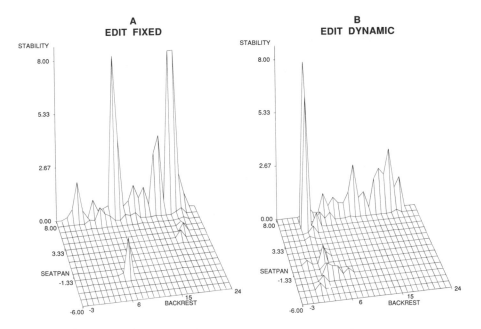

FIG. 26.5.   Configuration space describing the results of Study 3. Abscissa indicates degrees of backrest angle from the vertical. Negative values are forward of vertical. Ordinate indicates degrees of seatpan angle from the horizontal. Negative values represent forward tilt. Z axis represents mean normalized stability measures (time in position/frequency) while performing the Editing task. A: Fixed mode of adjustability; popliteal ratios 1.00–1.02. B: Dynamic mode of adjustability; popliteal ratios 1.00–1.05 (Moritz, 1988).

keyboard. Accordingly, it seemed reasonable to approach our analysis problem by employing a metric–popliteal ratio—in which seatpan height is expressed as a proportion of each operator's popliteal height.

Figs. 26.4 and 26.5 depict such configuration spaces, one for each experimental condition. Both figures depict average normalized stability measures for operators within a narrow band of popliteal ratios (seatpan height/popliteal height). Fig. 26.4a, for example, depicts popliteal ratios from 1.13 to 1.16. That is, the operators represented by the configuration space in Fig. 26.4a set their seatpan heights from 13% to 16% higher than their popliteal heights. This figure accounts for 83.5% of all data in the Entry Fixed condition. Likewise, Fig. 26.4b, which accounts for 77.25% of all data in the Entry Dynamic condition, represents a band of popliteal ratios from 1.11 to 1.15.[5]

---

[5]Two additional configuration plots were created for each of the two entry conditions; however, these accounted for relatively few data, and were not markedly different than those depicted. The four additional plots represented popliteal ratios which were *lower* than those in Figs. 26.4a and 26.4b. That is, the highest popliteal ratios represented the majority of the operators in both Entry conditions.

It is instructive to compare Figs. 26.4a and 26.4b. Fig. 26.4a, representing Entry Fixed condition, illustrates a few highly stable peaks in the region of forward tilt (lower left quadrant of the space). In terms of the configuration space, we believe these peaks represent postural attractors. The Entry Dynamic condition, however, is much less stable. The region of forward tilt is almost totally empty. Instead, there is a "ridge" of postures with lower stability in the region corresponding to upright posture (seatpan angles from 0–8 degrees; backrest angles from 0 6 degrees). A high stability peak appears at 17 degrees of backward tilt, with a ridge of low stability postures at 8 degrees of seatpan angle extending backward. Given the subjective impressions of those using the Dynamic mode, it is at least plausible that the relatively large number of regions of low stability in Fig. 26.4b represent attempts to explore the configuration space in an attempt to locate a region of stability (i.e., attractor).

The comparison between fixed and dynamic modes of adjustability in the Editing condition is seen in Figs. 26.5a and 26.5b. These depict, respectively, configuration spaces representing 100% of the operators in each condition. In both cases, all operators adjusted their seatpan heights at or very slightly above their popliteal heights. (Popliteal ratios were 1.00–1.02 for Editing Fixed and 1.00 1.05 for Editing Dynamic.)

Although virtually all operators performing the Editing task with the seatpan at the maximum rearward tilt, there were still clear differences between modes of adjustability. Fig. 26.5a, which depicts the Edit Fixed condition, shows a very stable posture at the most extreme backward tilting configuration at about 20 degrees backrest angle. (For scaling purposes, the Z-axis values were truncated at a maximum of 8; the obtained stability value at the upper rear corner of the space in Fig. 26.5a was actually 16.) A second major attractor seems to occur at backrest angle of about 8 degrees. Interestingly, this is almost exactly the configuration preferred by Grandjean et al.'s (1983) operators. In the case of the dynamic mode, the observed configurations are somewhat less stable, and the most stable peak is very close to the 90-degree, cubist posture.

Summary

To summarize our research efforts, when the chair is in fixed mode, operators will consistently use forward tilt for entry tasks and backwards tilt for editing tasks (Study 3 vs. Study 1). The results are markedly different, however, when the chair is in dynamic mode (cf. Studies 2 and 3). For the data entry task, when the work surface and seat height are fixed and relatively high, the operators use forward tilt almost exclusively (Study 2). When the operators can adjust the heights of the seat and work surface, they avoid forward tilt and seem to search for a stable location. For the Editing task, the configurations are similar in both studies, though less extreme in Study 3. With a fixed high seatpan and work surface, backward tilt is now used almost exclusively. When these surfaces are adjustable, the operator avoids extreme rearward tilt, thus moving closer to the upright cubist posture.

These observations must be regarded as tentative because Studies 2 and 3 involve slightly different tasks and different operators, in addition to important differences in height adjustability. Nevertheless, there are some clear directions for further research as well as direct implications for ergonomic design and its implementation.

IMPLICATIONS FOR ERGONOMIC RESEARCH AND DESIGN OF CHAIRS

Our conceptual framework for ergonomic research has been rooted in James Gibson's ecological approach toward understanding the confluence of perception and action. While we have focused on an individual seated at a VDT, we have emphasized that any activity of practical interest to the ergonomist can be conceptualized in terms of an individual's perception of the ecological possibilities (affordances) which guide his or her actions. A key component of this perception–action coupling involves a search for *postural stability*. Performance of any action (e.g., walking, running, bending, sitting, or stretching) must preserve postural stability. Ultimately, we need to understand the way in which people learn to do so.

Our research on seated posture at VDTs was grounded on the premise that relying on a single stable posture as a basis for design decisions is clearly insufficient. That is, over time any posture becomes less stable as a result of physiological changes (e.g., ischemia, blood pooling) that occur when body weight is supported by the same body structures for prolonged periods. This suggests the following prescriptive design principle: *A chair–workstation environment must simultaneously afford both movement and stability*. Therefore, it is better to construct an environment that allows for several clearly defined attractors among which the operator can alternate (e.g., Fig. 26.4a), than an environment in which points of stability are harder to find (e.g., Fig. 26.4b).

The problem facing a VDT operator is one of searching for comfortable working postures over time. As such, some degree of stability allows for efficient use of energy resources, thereby minimizing fatigue and, by implication, increasing work performance. Our theoretical analyses and research have indicated that postural stability is closely linked to: (1) *characteristics of the chair and workstation* (physical layout of surfaces, controls for adjustability, linkages between adjustable surfaces, mode of adjustability), (2) *action capabilities of the operator* (anthropometric and kinetic characteristics, knowledge structures for effective operation of controls) and (3) *task demands* (rapid keyboard entry of small printed characters, visual scanning of larger displayed characters). In order to study the effects of these factors on postural stability, we have constructed diagrams of the postural configuration space (Figs. 26.4 and 26.5) across task and mode of chair operation. We believe that these topological analyses provide a sensitive tool for detecting changes in the affordance structure of the workplace environment. We have already seen how the interaction among task, height of work surface, and mode of adjustability affects the distribution of stable working postures, also known as attractors. Changes in the configuration space reflect changes in the person, environmental and task constraints on postural stability. Mapping out changes in the configuration space should provide usable information for the designer. It is important to note that the concept of a configuration space is general; that is, it could, in principle, be constructed for any activity of interest.

Prospects for Further Work

This kind of analysis can be used to answer some very specific questions posed by the design community. For example, we noted earlier that a standard approach in furniture industry is to link the seatpan and backrest adjustability angles in a ratio of 1:2 or 1:3 for dynamic mode chairs. Our own study can address this issue empirically through individualized configuration plots where seatpan and backrest are free to move independently. Preliminary examination of our data suggests that this linkage would probably have to be nonlinear and adjustable. The issue to be addressed would compare the relative costs and benefits of: (a) providing the nonlinear/adjustable linkage, (b) retaining the less-optimal linear linkages, (c) dropping the linkage altogether in favor of independent adjustability. The latter alternative, of course, adds the additional degrees of freedom which users will have to master. Using experimental chair mechanisms, each of these alternatives could be assessed in terms of configuration space plots, thereby providing immediate guidance to the designer.

Of particular importance in an applied context is the question of *fatigue*. If an attractor represents a kind of minimum of energy expenditure, it seems clear that, in a complex musculoskeletal system, the location of the attractor will shift as muscles fatigue differentially. It is crucial to select a sufficiently large time scale so as to measure these shifts. In the future attempts will have to be made to document, through some combination of physiological measurements, changes in energy utilization in coordination with changes in the configuration space.

The issue of *training* is of great importance in the applied world. While we have repeatedly stressed the relevance of training in our own research, our interest in training has been as a strictly pragmatic approach to addressing the degrees of freedom problem (i.e., learning to use a chair with numerous independent adjustments). A recent paper by E. J. Gibson (1988), which reassesses and reintegrates the concept of exploratory behavior, suggests a mechanism for conceptualizing the role of training within the ecological perspective. In brief, training is an efficient means of helping the user to explore the configuration space in order to find the affordances of postural stability. For example, in urging the user to at least try the forward-leaning posture, a new set of affordances becomes available. Our future research will depend on this notion of exploration of configuration spaces.

In sum, the ecological approach can have an impact on ergonomic research and design far beyond the issues of seating in particular and posture in general. In effect, we have been dealing with a particular case of a general problem; the problem of: (a) designing the affordances of a complex system with independently adjustable components; and (b) teaching the user of that system the most efficient way to manipulate/coordinate those components. It is this general problem in human factors and ergonomics which provides a challenge for ecological analyses.

ACKNOWLEDGMENTS

The authors acknowledge the contributions of John Pittenger and Gary Riccio to the theoretical and methodological development of this work and Robert Hoffman for his thoughtful criticisms and analysis of an earlier draft of this manuscript. Research described in this article was supported by grants from Fixtures Furniture, Inc., and the Ohio Board of Regents to M. Dainoff and L. Mark.

REFERENCES

Abraham, R. H., & Shaw, C. D. (1982). *Dynamics—The geometry of behavior: Pt. 1. Periodic Behavior*. Santa Cruz, CA: Aerial Press.

Alluisi, E. A., & Morgan, B. (1982). Temporal factors in human performance and productivity. In E. A. Alluisi & E. A. Fleishman (Eds.), *Human performance and productivity: Stress and performance effectiveness*. Hillsdale, NJ: Lawrence Erlbaum Associates, pp. 165–247.

Bendix, T., Winkel, J., & Jessen, F. (1985). Comparison of office chairs with fixed forwards or backwards inclining, or tiltable seats. *European Journal of Applied Physiology, 54*, 378–385.

Bernstein, N. A. (1967). *The coordination and regulation of movements*. Oxford: Pergammon Press.

Boies, S., Gould, J., Levy, S., Richards, S., & Schoonard, J. (1985). *The 1984 Olympic Message System—A case study in system design*. (IBM Research Report RC 11138 (-50065)). Yorktown Heights, NY: IBM Corp.

Branton, P. (1976). Behavior, body mechanism and discomfort. In E. Grandjean (Ed.), *Sitting posture*. London: Taylor & Francis.

Dainoff, M. J. (1982). Occupational stress factors in VDT operation: A review of empirical literature. *Behaviour and Information Technology, 1*, 141–176.

Dainoff, M. J., & Dainoff, M. H. (1986). *People and productivity: A manager's guide to ergonomics in the electronic office*. Toronto: Holt, Rinehart, and Winston.

Dainoff, M. J., & Mark, L. S. (1987). Task and the adjustment of ergonomic furniture. In B. Knave & P. -G. Wideback (Eds.), *Work with display units*. Amsterdam: North–Holland.

Gibson, E. J. (1988). Exploratory behavior. In M. R. Rosenzweig & L. W. Porter (Eds.), *Annual review of psychology, 39*, 1–41.

Gibson, J. J. (1979). *The ecological approach to visual perception.* Boston: Houghton Mifflin.

Grandjean, E., Hunting, W., & Pidermann, M. (1983). VDT workstation design: Preferred settings and their effects. *Human Factors, 25,* 161–175.

Greico, A. (1986). Sitting posture: An old problem and a new one. *Ergonomics, 29,* 345–362.

Hettinger, T. (1985). Statistics on diseases in the Federal Republic of Germany with particular reference to diseases of the skeletal system. *Ergonomics, 28,* 17–20.

Kroemer, K. H. E., & Price, D. L. (1982). Ergonomics in the office: Comfortable workstations allow maximum productivity. *Industrial Engineering, 14.7,* 24–32.

Kugler, P. N., & Turvey, M. T. (1987). *Information, natural law, and the self-assembly of rhythmic movement.* Hillsdale, NJ: Lawrence Erlbaum Associates.

Mandal, A. C. (1986). The influence of furniture height on back pain. In B. Knave & P. -G. Wideback (Eds.), *Work with display units.* Amsterdam: North–Holland.

Mark, L. S. (1987). Eyeheight-scaled information about affordances: A study of sitting and stair climbing. *Journal of Experimental Psychology: Human Perception and Performance, 10,* 683–703.

Mark, L. S., & Vogele, D. (1987). A biodynamic basis for perceiving categories of action: A study of sitting and stair climbing. *Journal of Motor Behavior, 19,* 367–384.

Mark, L. S., Vogele, D. C., Dainoff, M. J., Cone, S., & Lassen, K. (1985). Measuring movement at ergonomic workstations. In R. E. Eberts & C. G. Eberts (Eds.), *Trends in ergonomics/Human factors II.* Amsterdam. North–Holland.

Meister, D. (1985). The two worlds of human factors. In R. E. Eberts & C. G. Eberts (Eds.), *Trends in ergonomics/Human factors II.* Amsterdam: North–Holland.

Moritz, R. R. (1988). *Stability of seated work posture.* Unpublished M. A. thesis, Miami University, Oxford, OH.

Oman, P. W. (1988). College survey: Arc VDT operator complaints real? *The Office, 108*(2), August.

Ong, C. N. (1984). VDT work place design and physical fatigue. A case study in Singapore. In E. Grandjean (Ed.), *Ergonomics and health in modern offices.* London: Taylor & Francis.

Riccio, G., & Stoffregen, T. (1988). Affordances as constraints on the control of stance. *Human Movement Science.*

Rouse, W. B., & Boff, K. R. (1987). *System design: Behavioral perspectives on designers, tools, and organizations.* Amsterdam: North–Holland.

Sauter, L. S., & Arndt, R. (1986). Ergonomics in the automated office: Gaps in knowledge and practice. In G. Salvendy (Ed.), *Human and computer interaction.* Amsterdam: Elsevier.

Scallet, E. A. (1987). *VDT health and safety.* Lawrence, KA: Ergosyst Associates.

Smith, M. (1984). Health issues in VDT work. In J. Bennett, D. Case, J. Sandelin, & M. Smith (Eds.), *Visual display terminals.* Englewood Cliffs, NJ: Prentice–Hall.

Spilling, S., Eitrheim, J., & Aaras, A. (1986). Cost–benefit analysis of work environment investment at STK's telephone plant at Kongsvinger. In N. Corlett, J. Wilson, & I. Manenica (Eds.), *The ergonomics of working postures.* London: Taylor & Francis.

Springer, T. J. (1982, June). Redesigning the office. *Computerworld* OA, pp. 33–38.

Turvey, M. T., & Shaw, R. E. (1978). The primacy of perceiving; An ecological reformulation of perception for understanding memory. In L. G. Nilsson (Ed.), *Perspectives on memory research* (pp. 167–222). Hillsdale, NJ: Lawrence Erlbaum Associates.

Warren, W. H. (1984). Perceiving affordances: Visual guidance in stair climbing. *Journal of Experimental Psychology: Human Perception and Performance, 10,* 683–703.

Warren, W. H., & Whang, S. (1987). Visual guidance of walking through apertures: Body-scaled information for affordances. *Journal of Experimental Psychology: Human Perception and Performance, 13,* 371–383.

Westgaard, R. H., & Aaras, A. (1985). The effect of improved workplace design on the development of work-related musculo-skeletal illnesses. *Applied Ergonomics, 16,* 91–97.

27

Methodological Problems in Applied Cognition and Perception Research: Theoretical Implications

Rik Warren
Armstrong Aerospace Medical Research Laboratory
Wright–Patterson Air Force Base, Ohio

OVERVIEW AND TRIBUTE TO JIM JENKINS

A fitting tribute to a great teacher should contain a lesson and not be a mere listing of the teacher's virtues and accomplishments. The lesson I wish to convey—that the realities of applied psychology reveal nontrivial shortfalls of theory and method in academic psychology—emerges from my experience, which contrasts applied psychology to academic psychology. I have found that the research environment, not just the research question, imposes powerful constraints on the conduct of research. These constraints go beyond issues of money, equipment, and time, and thus reveal fundamental problems with both theory and methodology.

There are many routes to becoming an applied psychologist. Here I discuss the route I took, what I expected to find before embarking, and what I've actually found so far. My journey has taken a rather indirect route that has benefited by the wisdom of James Jerome Jenkins. Thus this chapter is intended as a tribute to Jim.

Since much of this chapter is a personal history, it is useful to set the context and antecedents. I had intended to pursue an ivory tower career, but although I did not know it at the time, the roots of my training were deeply embedded in a bedrock of applied psychology in general and aviation psychology in particular. Indeed, one of the key lessons of this chapter is that theoretical psychology has greatly benefited from applied aviation psychology. However, the lesson is often either unappreciated, quickly forgotten, or never learned. One reason for this may be that psychologists are generally unfamiliar with the historical forces behind their field.

APPLIED PSYCHOLOGY BENEFITS THEORY

The benefits of applied research to advances in basic theory are manifold. Many of these advances came from psychology's involvement with World Wars I and II, since the demands of war resulted in many psychologists' redirecting their research away from pure to applied problems. Further, the challenges of war provided both a motivation and criteria for success that is often missing in abstract programs. See Koonce (1984) for an eye-opening history of aviation psychology and for general historical and analytical references.

Aviation problems attracted talented people and made lasting impressions on them. Koonce identifies no fewer than 11 of the first 77 presidents of the American Psychological Association as directly involved with aviation psychology and another 2 on the periphery. We may easily examine the fruits of a large body of research since, under the leadership of J. C. Flanagan (1947), the psychological research from World War II was assembled in a 19-volume "encyclopedia" (Army Air Forces, 1947), whose volume editors/authors include many prominent psychologists, for example, Miller (1947) and Thorndike (1947).

One of these theorists, J. J. Gibson (another "James Jerome"!), who had earned a reputation as an academic researcher, began studying the applied problem of how people land airplanes. The result of that encounter with the "real" world led Gibson to abandon traditional perceptual theory and begin the development of his ecological approach to perception (Gibson, 1947, 1979; Lombardo, 1987). I do not review the approach here. The point is that the study of applied problems can reveal deficiencies with basic theory. Gibson explicitly developed his theory of perception so that it would be relevant to real-world issues. However, his concern was with theoretical issues and not with the solution of applied problems or with research methods. The strong interest in theory was, in turn, passed on to his students.

MY EARLY VIEWS OF APPLIED PSYCHOLOGY

Graduate School View

As a student of Gibson, I received a "pure" academic training in experimental psychology, albeit with a strong emphasis on the ecological approach to perception. Although Gibson's ecologically inspired theory was embraced in an academic sense by most of his students, the lesson of respect for applied problems was not always learned. There was a belief among some students—but definitely not Gibson—that applied research was beneath intellectual dignity at best and, very likely, "dirty." In this context I believed myself very open-minded and used to say with a tone of magnaminity: "If anyone ever finds a use for my work, I will not be offended."

Of course, I had not done much "basic" research let alone any applied work whatsoever. My concept of applied psychology was partly self-generated and partly absorbed by osmosis from a rarefied, ivory tower atmosphere. That atmosphere contained—and unfortunately, still contains—high concentrations of antipractical attitudes. My noncritically accepted conception assumed that applied psychology was essentially only studies of product preferences. Is breakfast cereal *A* preferred over breakfast cereal *B*? Note that this (mis)conception of applied psychology assumes there to be no differences in research methodology between academic and applied research.

We students were proud of our powerful and elegant research methods (cf. Jenkins's concept of "methodolatry," Jenkins, 1986) which we learned from impressive textbooks. I assumed that out classmates who would "sell out" to study cereal preferences would "only" be giving up the hallowed pursuit of truth and theory. I grudgingly acknowledged that they would have earned their spurs as researchers and would faithfully apply our common statistical and design skills to mundane and, therefore, dead-end problems.

The Impact of Jenkins

It was with these attitudes that I started a postdoctoral fellowship at the University of Minnesota. Jenkins was director of the Center for Research in Human Learning and the atmosphere he created there was unsurpassed in both intellectual excitement and deep concern for people. The Center was a congenial place to grow, to deepen insights about previous knowledge, to learn new ideas, and to broaden a narrow mind.

We had no industrial psychologists at Cornell; Jim had been trained as one. We had no courses in psychometrics at Cornell; Jim taught me that a thorough grounding in the area of psychological tests and measurements would be most helpful to an experimental psychologist. However, with all the emphasis on research methods in the training of experimental psychologists, it is surprising how little attention is given to psychometric methods.

Here, then, is a basic difference in methodology between some applied and experimental psychologists. What is the basis for this difference? I speculate that, generally speaking, experimental psychologists are not interested in individual differences, but rather in differences due to experimental manipulations. Experimental research often favors repeated measures on the same people who are carefully chosen to be similar in general characteristics. "Observer" or "Subject" sections of experimental journal articles or reports emphasize the homogeneity of the people—same source, same age, same vision, same handedness, and so on. Applied researchers, on the other hand, are often faced with the task of assessing the characteristics of a possibly very heterogeneous population, either for selection or training purposes. But applied cognition or perception does not end with assessment. Successful application often means custom tailoring a machine environment to a person and vice versa, and that means individual differences are not nuisances but stock in trade.

I thus learned in an abstract sense that there was a respectable research world outside of academia full of significant problems but still had not experienced it at first hand. Ohio State University would provide a transition by exposing me to practical and methodological problems within an academic setting.

From Theoretical to Methodological Problems

Dean Owen's Aviation Psychology Laboratory at Ohio State University was dedicated to theoretical research using a flight simulator, which had blatant applied potential. Practical concerns were unavoidable, and because of them, we made several theoretically interesting discoveries (Owen & Warren, 1987; Warren & Owen, 1982). Aviation perception is a complex skill, scenes are generally rich, compared with typical academic research, and as a result, there are wide individual differences in detection ability. A small sample of observers could, by chance, easily misrepresent both central tendencies and variabilities. So the injection of real-world relevance required a methodological difference from many psychophysical studies, namely, the use of a large number of observers. The experiments were otherwise standard in the sense that observers were tested for a total time of one-half to at most 4 hours each; there were many trials per observer, trials were short (often 10 seconds or less), and the task was a yes/no judgment plus a confidence rating. One consequent of the combination of many observers and many trials per observer was that statistical F ratios greater than 100 and even 1,000 were common.

The research was aimed at identifying, describing, and assessing the perceptual effectiveness of various sources of information for self-motion. The displays were as complex as the computer resources permitted since we were after both main effects (relative strengths) of naturally co-occurring cues and their interactions. It thus came as a surprise that it was impossible to independently cross certain types of cues in a classical factorial design. The problem was that many factors that are interesting in aviation are not independent, but rather are functionally related. For example, the detection of loss of altitude is affected by descent rate, forward speed, and glide path angle. However,

$$\text{path angle} = \text{arctan}(\text{sinkrate} / \text{forward speed})$$

so that assigning values to any two automatically determines the third. That is, there are only 2 degrees of freedom for determining these three factors of interest. The problem then is how to determine the importance of these factors for a person or other flying animal. This is the problem of multicolinearity in a particularly insidious form. Warren and Owen (1982) found the problem so prevalent in naturally occurring scenarios that they suggested that a new methodology was needed for aviation research. Here the pursuit of applied issues led to methodological problems, which in turn have broad theoretical implications.

On to Human Factors

The Human Engineering Division of the Armstrong Aerospace Medical Research Laboratory (AAMRL) at Wright–Patterson Air Force Base is only a short drive from the Aviation Psychology Laboratory at Ohio State University. A natural interaction with Grant McMillan's flight simulation program grew and grew until I found myself a civil servant in an applied psychology setting.

The impact of the research at the AAMRL Human Engineering Division on my thinking has been so great that a brief overview of some of its programs is useful. The discussion is selective and emphasizes research methodology.

HUMAN ENGINEERING: NEW PROBLEMS AND METHODS

The Human Engineering Division is a major force in the application of experimental psychology to solving human factors problems in complex machine systems. From its founding by Paul Fitts in 1945, the division has conducted numerous in-house studies, awarded millions of dollars for contract research by both academia and industry, sponsored many meetings and workshops, and has enabled academics to benefit by learning about complex problems and by interacting with their counterparts in government laboratories and industry through various visiting scientist programs.

The Division actively engages in the creation, systematization, and transfer of knowledge.

Creation of Knowledge

The research programs in the Division are many and diverse. The following are only a sampling which illustrate methodological issues.

Mental Workload Assessment.   It has been said that the modern fighter plane is the most complex machine designed to be operated by a single person (Eugene Adams, McDonnell Douglas Aircraft Co., personal communication, 1984). The sea of information surrounding a fighter pilot can be overwhelming. The flood of information and the speed and number of responses required can greatly exceed the cognitive capacities of a pilot as well as the capacities of cognitive theory. Thus, the problem of mental workload makes new demands of cognitive science and serves to aid its growth and keep it from becoming an interesting but irrelevant ivory tower exercise. Even the basic problem of defining and measuring workload challenges both modern theories and methods (Wilson & O'Donnell, 1988).

Workload Alleviation. Even more difficult than the problem of workload assessment is the problem of workload prediction. The goal is pilot workload alleviation and success depends on creative application of perceptual and cognitive principles. Determining what those principles are and how they are to be applied is, in general, a major task for psychologists and engineers (McNeese, Warren, & Woodson, 1985). In order to accomplish this task systematically, the Human Systems Division (the parent organization of the AAMRL Human Engineering Division) established the Crew Centered Cockpit Design Program (CCCD). This advanced development project draws on the talent of Human Engineering Division personnel and is dedicated to developing methods to ensure that the fruits of human factors research directly benefit pilots (Arretz, 1984).

A fundamental methodological problem that has emerged from the activities of the CCCD program is that of the procedure for determining success. For example, how is workload alleviation to be quantified? Standard methodology indicates the use of control and experimental groups and manipulation of initial levels of workload and techniques for alleviation. Assuming that good workload metrics and manipulation techniques exist, it would seem to be the case that any competent experimental psychologist should be able to design a well-controlled and sensitive experiment. Such a design, however, would soon be seen to be impractical. The realities of complex human performance in complex systems often mean that experimental trials are inordinately time consuming and expensive. This is due to the need for real vehicles, or more usually, for high-fidelity simulations, together with large technical staffs for operation.

The "validation" problem with few trials is further exacerbated by the small number of available and sufficiently expert human subjects. A tiny subject pool carries with it two problems which arise from the need to conduct preliminary studies. If experimentally naive subject matter experts must be used, the pool may quickly dry up. Even if fully naive expert subjects are not required, then the pool may still become polluted by differing degrees of subject familiarity with the experiment. The problem of decimating and desiccating the subject pool may be finessed by using alternative subjects for preliminary studies. But this is also not a trouble-free solution. The use of less-than-qualified subjects may be useful for fine-tuning a study but if preliminary results are used to guide the selection of experimental values, those values may be inappropriate for assessing the abilities of experts. For example, the level of wind gusts that college students can control in a flight simulator is much less than that of experienced pilots. How then, does an experimenter choose levels of wind gusts without risking floor or ceiling performance effects?

The triple constraints of a small subject pool, high expense, and limited time means that traditional research methodologies cannot be employed. But do not make the mistake of thinking that the "fault" is the applied researcher's. Our task as scientists is to study the world as it is, not as it would be convenient for us to be. The situation is similar to the old story about the person who loses keys in a dark alley but looks for them near a lamp post "because the light is better" there. Methodologies developed for academic laboratories are simply not adequate for studying complex cognitive functioning under real-world conditions. This state of affairs, however, can lead to advances in research methodology, which in turn can lead to advances in basic knowledge.

Vision and Visual Processes.   Another area of practical concern but also significant for basic sensory processes is that of vision through aircraft windscreens. Modern windscreens such as that of the F-16 are curved and made of multiple layers of plastic laminates. These advanced products are not optically perfect and vision through them is subject to geometrical distortion, multiple imaging, halation (glare or white-out due to intense sunlight scattering and refraction by surface scratches), and birefringencing (oil slick-type rainbowing due to polarization effects; Merkel & Task, 1989). These effects can be far from subtle, and can be high intensity, suprathreshold, long lasting, and cover a very large field of view (e.g., Kama, Genco, Barbato, & Hausmann, 1983). In contrast, much current visual research is concerned with low-intensity, near-threshold, brief duration, and small visual extent displays. Hence, the problems of sensory processes involved in flight are not merely practical but serve to challenge the existing science base (Cannon, 1984, 1985; Warren, Genco, & Connon, 1984). Who knows how perception and control are affected during gross dynamic nonlinear distortions? Thus, the AAMRL windscreen program is an acid test for sensory psychology.

Perception and Control in High-speed Flight.   The last area to be described is my own: the perception and control of low-altitude flight (PACLAF; see Warren, 1988b, for an overview of the problems and studies). High-speed, low-altitude flight is rich perceptually, and demanding in terms of attention and control activity. Thus the area challenges both basic and applied science and promises great payoffs for each. However, systematic research on low-altitude flight is difficult because such flight is so unforgiving of mistakes. Fortunately flight simulators provide safety and computer graphics provide opportunities to vary scene content systematically.

At AAMRL, I expected to use essentially the same methodology I used at Ohio State. Although Ohio State had a flyable flight simulator, observers generally did not "fly" during an experiment. Instead, we showed dynamically changing scenes and observers merely watched and answered yes/no questions, made magnitide estimates, gave confidence ratings, and had their reaction time recorded. At no time did an observer's action affect the appearance of the current scene. Data analyses involved computing the indexes and statistics familiar in the perception journals.

But the essence of flight and flight simulation is *active control*. What the operator sees is a joint function of the scenario selected by the experimenter and what the operator *does*. It can further be a joint function of "forcing functions" such as a wind gust disturbance. These differences lead to differences in the data collected and data treatments. Even the selection and use of observers/operators differs.

The selection differs because the tasks to be performed require much skill. Learning to control an airplace cannot be done in a 1-hour session. Hence, participants either have to have certain skills before an experiment (e.g., be experienced pilots), or undergo a long period of training to achieve a degree of proficiency. For example, we might train a person 1 hour a day, 3 days a week, for 4 weeks *before* experimental testing. This is a rare procedure in academia. One consequence of the selection and training constraints is the problem of the small number of persons for design and statistics. Another consequence is the related problem of a tiny subject pool. These problems were discussed in the section on the CCCD program. A third consequence is that often the observers/ operators are not naive. After a full month of training, the experimental manipulation can become quite transparent.

The data collected during an active control experiment are very different than during a passive judgment study. The time duration of an active control trial may be several minutes long while that of a passive judgment trial might be just a few seconds. The data from a passive trial are often just a few numbers such as a magnitude estimate, a confidence rating, and a reaction time. The raw data from *one* active trial can easily be several thousand numbers. These numbers are the *time histories* of what the observer/operator did and the effects of the control actions. For example, in an altitude holding task, we record as functions of time, observer pitch commands, altitude error, and vertical gust. If these three "channels" are sampled at 40 Hz and a trial is 120 seconds with data collected on the last 102.4 seconds, each of the three time histories would contain 4,096 numbers. Further, if each number requires four computer memory bytes, than one trial yields 48 kilobytes of data. Clearly, record and bookkeeping procedures are very different for passive and active studies.

Data analysis of active control time histories is relatively new to most psychologists. Fortunately, control engineers have a rich and mature body of techniques and concepts for studying active control. These engineering concepts and techniques were, for example, used by Flach, Riccio, McMillan, and Warren (1986) and Levison and Warren (1984).

Although borrowing techniques from systems and control theory has proven useful, these procedures do carry certain assumptions and constraints with them. For example, tasks are often chosen to be amenable to linear mathematical analyses and goals are set by the experimenter, not the human operator. But as psychologists, we know that humans are characteristically nonlinear in their operations. Thus finding good, even great, linear approximations or models for human performance is useful, but can never be deeply satisfying. Even more unsatisfying is a psychological theory built on data collected from people who had their goals and tasks dictated to them and even their action choices constrained. What then is our basis for understanding people free to use their own cognitive powers for negotiating their environment?

The methodology required for such natural activity is so different that I believe we need a new "active psychophysics" to supplement the traditional "passive psychophysics" (Warren, 1988a; Warren & McMillan, 1984). Although this enterprise draws heavily from control engineering, it is only beginning in its own right.

Systematization of Knowledge

In order to better achieve its mission, the AAMRL Human Engineering Division has expended considerable effort to collect, organize, and digest the scattered academic literature to produce coherent compendia of psychological theory and research that have direct use in, and have served to guide, applied research (Boff, Kaufman, & Thomas, 1986; Boff & Lincoln, 1988; McMillan et al., 1989; Warren & Wertheim, 1990). The act of producing these handbooks and compendia, as well as the final products, has helped to define the fields of applied cognitive psychology and perception. These efforts have pointed out the valuable in academic research and have also pointed out deficiencies.

Transfer of Knowledge—CSERIAC

These handbooks, source books, and compendia cannot contain all available theory and data and once they are issued, the appearance of new material can make their contents "stale." To be really useful, not only must ideas and data be fresh but also be easily available. Although computerized literature searching has helped, easy access, however, is not the hallmark of much of the applied and some of the basic literature. To meet this problem, the Crew Systems Ergonomics Information Analysis Center (CSERIAC) was established in 1988 (Boff, Polzella, & Morton, 1990; Henessy & McCauley, 1986). CSERIAC is a national resource dedicated to the active support of research and the intelligent transfer of technology between developers and potential users. In addition to its search and retrieval functions, it can perform evaluations and this greatly increases its value to both the basic and applied communities.

FINAL COMMENTS

The functions of knowledge systematization and especially knowledge transfer are extremely important in the applied world. It often happens that workers attempting to systematize or needing to transfer knowledge find that the knowledge just doesn't exist. How this is dealt with depends on the particular situation. Options include ignoring, dropping, or postponing the original problem. Since this is not always possible, and if time is critical (*"I need the answer yesterday!"*); there is often little alternative but to "guesstimate." The ability to guesstimate well is a valuable skill and perhaps we should systematically train and foster it. Rather than be horrified, maybe we should acknowledge guesstimation as a legitimate and worthy method.

If time is not critical, or an accurate data-based answer is critical, the preferred option to filling gaps in knowledge is, of course, to experiment. But experience with complex systems shows that such experimentation is not necessarily easy nor even doable using standard methods.

Finally, there is another sense to applied methodology. So far, I have used the terms *applied psychology* and *applied research* synonymously, but a distinction might be useful. Applying psychology and discovering new knowledge are not the same nor do they use the same methods. If performance principles and data exist, or if they can be produced by new research, there is no guarantee that a successful application will be made. Traditional experimental skills are not the only skills a person needs to apply psychology successfully. I have come to appreciate the subject matter mastery, ingenuity, creativity, and intelligence that are required to apply successfully cognitive and perceptual theory and principles to the betterment of our lives. The study of these methods of application is overdue.

ACKNOWLEDGMENT

I am grateful to the support provided by the Harry G. Armstrong Aerospace Medical Research Laboratory, Human Systems Division, AFSC, United States Air Force. Although the writing of this chapter was a part of my official duties, the opinions are my own and do not represent an official United States Air Force position.

REFERENCES

Army Air Forces. (1947). *The aviation psychology program in the Army Air Forces* (Research Reports Nos. 1–19). Washington, DC: U. S. Government Printing Office.

Arretz, A. J. (1984). Cockpit automation technology. *Proceedings of the Human Factors Society 28th annual meeting, 1984,* pp. 487–491.

Boff, K. R., Kaufman, L., & Thomas, J. P. (Eds.). (1986). *Handbook of perception and human performance* (Vols. 1, 2). New York: Wiley.

Boff, K. R., & Lincoln, J. E. (Eds.). (1988). *Engineering data compendium: Human perception and performance* (Vols. 1–3). Wright–Patterson Air Force Base, OH: Armstrong Aerospace Medical Research Laboratory.

Boff, K. R., Polzella, D. J., & Morton, K. (1990). Crew Systems Ergonomics Information Analysis Center: A gateway for technology transfer. In the proceedings of the 15th Annual Meeting on *Technology Transfer in a Global Economy.* Dayton, OH.

Cannon, M. W. (1984). A study of stimulus range effects in free modulus magnitude estimation of contrast. *Vision Research, 24,* 1049–1055.

Cannon, M. W. (1985). Perceived contrast in the fovea and periphery. *Journal of the Optical Society of America, A–2,* 1760–1768.

Flach, J. M., Riccio, G. E., McMillan, G. R., & Warren, R. (1986). Psychophysical methods for equating performance between alternative motion simulators. *Ergonomics, 29,* 1424–1438.

Flanagan, J. C. (Ed.). (1947). *The aviation psychology program in the Army Air Forces* (Army Air Forces Aviation Psychology Program Research Report No. 1). Washington, DC: U. S. Government Printing Office.

Gibson, J. J. (Ed.). (1947). *Motion picture testing and research* (Army Air Forces Aviation Psychology Research Program Report No. 7). Washington, DC: U. S. Government Printing Office. (NTIS No. AD–561 783)

Gibson, J. J. (1979). *The ecological approach to visual perception.* Hillsdale, NJ: Lawrence Erlbaum Associates.

Henessy, R. T., & McCauley, M. E. (1986). *Proposal and justification to establish a Department of Defense Crew Systems Ergonomics Information Analysis Center* (AAMRL–TR–86–022). Wright–Patterson Air Force Base, OH: Armstrong Aerospace Medical Research Laboratory.

Jenkins, J. J. (1986). Beyond methodolatry: An interview. In B. J. Baars, *The cognitive revolution in psychology* (pp. 237–284). New York: Guilford Press.

Kama, W. N., Genco, L. V., Barbato, M. A. H., & Hausmann, M. D. (1983). *The effect of haze on an operator's visual field and his target detection performance* (AFAMRL–TR–83–066). Wright–Patterson Air Force Base, OH: Air Force Aerospace Medical Research Laboratory.

Koonce, J. M. (1984). A brief history of aviation psychology. *Human Factors, 26,* 499–508.

Levison, W. H., & Warren, R. (1984). Use of linear perspective scene cues in a simulated height regulation task. *Proceedings of the 20th annual conference on Manual Control.* Moffett Field: NASA Ames Research Center.

Lombardo, T. J. (1987). *The reciprocity of perceiver and environment: The evolution of James J. Gibson's ecological psychology.* Hillsdale, NJ: Lawrence Erlbaum Associates.

McMillan, G. R., Beevis, D., Salas, E., Strub, M. H., Sutton, R., & van Breda, L. (Eds.). (1989). *Application of human performance models to system design.* New York: Plenum Press.

McNeese, M. D., Warren, R., & Woodson, B. K. (1985). Cockpit automation technology: A further look. *Proceedings of the 29th annual meeting of the Human Factors Society,* 884–888.

Merkel, H. S., & Task, H. L. (1989). *An illustrated guide of optical characteristics of aircraft transparencies* (AAMRL–TR–89–015). Wright–Patterson Air Force Base, OH: Armstrong Aerospace Medical Research Laboratory.

Miller, N. E. (1947). *Psychological research on pilot training* (Army Air Forces Aviation Psychology Program Research Report No. 8). Washington, DC: U. S. Government Printing Office.

Owen, D. H., & Warren, R. (1987). Perception and control of self-motion: Implications for visual simulation of vehicular locomotion. In L. S. Mark, J. S. Warm, & R. L. Huston (Eds.), *Ergonomics and human factors: Recent research.* New York: Springer–Verlag.

Thorndike, R. L. (1947). *Research problems and techniques* (Army Air Forces Aviation Psychology Program Research Report No. 3). Washington, DC: U. S. Government Printing Office.

Warren, R. (1988a). Active psychophysics: Theory and practice. In H. K. Ross (Ed.), *Fechner Day '88: Proceedings of the Fourth annual meeting of the International Society for Psychophysics* (pp. 47–52). Stirling, Scotland: University of Stirling.

Warren, R. (1988b). Visual perception in high-speed low-altitude flight. *Aviation, Space, and Environmental Medicine, 59*(11, Suppl.), A116–124.

Warren, R., Genco, L. V., & Connon, T. R. (1984). *Horizontal diplopia thresholds for head-up displays* (AFAMRL–TR–84–018). Wright–Patterson Air Force Base, OH: Air Force Aerospace Medical Research Laboratory.

Warren, R., & McMillan, G. R. (1984). Altitude control using action-demanding interactive displays: Toward an active psychophysics. *Proceedings of the 1984 IMAGE III Conference* (pp. 37–51). Williams Air Force Base, AZ: Air Force Human Resources Laboratory.

Warren, R., & Owen, D. H. (1982). Functional optical invariants: A new methodology for aviation research. *Aviation, Space, and Environmental Medicine, 53,* 977–983.

Warren, R., & Wertheim, A. H. (Eds.). (1990). *Perception & control of self-motion.* Hillsdale, NJ: Lawrence Erlbaum Associates.

Wilson, G. F., & O'Donnell, R. D. (1988). *Measurement of operator workload with the neuro-psychological workload test battery.* In P. A. Hancock & N. Meshkati (Eds.), *Human mental workload.* Amsterdam: North–Holland.

AUTHOR INDEX

Note: Italicized page numbers refer to bibliography pages.

A

Aaras, A., 478, *505*
Abelson, R., 465, 467, 469, *476*
Abelson, R. P., 167, 168, *180*
Abraham, R. H., 491, *504*
Abramson, A. S., 67, *75*
Acioly, N. M., 263, *277*
Acredolo, L. P., 436, 437, 438, 448, 451, *452, 453*
Adair, K. R., 372, *384*
Adams, A., 448, *453*
Adams, E., 511
Adams, J. A., 433, *453*
Adams, L., 285, 288, 289, *297*
Adams, M. J., 88, 458, *92, 474*
Adams, P. A., 282, *298*
Adler, M. J., *297*
Ahroon, W. A., *57*
Alford, J. A., 143, *148*
Alley, T. R., 414, *430, 431*
Allman, W. F., 381, *384*
Allport, A., *57*
Alluisi, E. A., 494, *504*
Amblard, B., 436, *453*
Ambler, S., 60, *74*
Amiel-Tison, C., *56*
Amsel, E., 227, *231*
Anderson, D. R., *369*
Anderson, J. M., *75*

Anderson, J. R., 257, 259, 286, 288, 293, 294, *277, 297, 298*
Andrasik, F., 166, *180*
Andrew, J. D., 351, 352, *369*
Antos, S. J., 177, *183*
Anwar, F., 461, *473*
Archer, D., 170, *183*
Army Air Forces, 508, *516*
Arndt, R., 499, *505*
Arnheim, R., 351, *369*
Arnold, M. D., *181, 183, 184*
Arretz, A. J., 512, *516*
Asch, S. E., 176, 283, *180, 297*
Ashby, W. R., 408, *429*
Ashmead, D. H., 451, *454*
Aslin, R. N., 49, *54*
Atkins, P. W., 391, *429*
Atkinson, R. C., 9, *14, 15*
Auble, P., 119, 128, 134, *138*
Auble, P. M., 293, *297*
Aurelius, G., 52, *55*
Auslander, L., 411, *429*
Averbach, E., 10, *14*
Averill, J. R., 166, 173, *180*
Ayer, A. J., 223, 226, *230*

B

Baars, B. J., xiv, 153, *161, 517*
Bablovantz, A., 392, *430*

519

SUBJECT INDEX